BLUE GUIDE

FLORENCE

Alta Macadam

with illustrations from the
Alinari Archive

Somerset Books • London

Tenth edition 2011

Published by Blue Guides Limited, a Somerset Books Company
Winchester House, Deane Gate Avenue, Taunton, Somerset TA1 2UH
www.blueguides.com
'Blue Guide' is a registered trademark.

ISBN 978-1-905131-52-5

A CIP catalogue record of this book is available from the British Library.

Distributed in the United States of America by
W.W. Norton & Company, Inc.
500 Fifth Avenue, New York, NY 10110.

The editor and publisher have made reasonable efforts to ensure the accuracy of all the
information in *Blue Guide Florence*; however, they can accept no responsibility for any loss,
injury or inconvenience sustained by any traveller as a result of information or advice
contained in the guide.

Statement of editorial independence: Blue Guides, their authors and editors, are prohibited
from accepting payment from any restaurant, hotel, gallery or other establishment for its
inclusion in this guide, or on www.blueguides.com, or for a more favourable mention than
would otherwise have been made.

All other acknowledgements, photo credits and copyright information
are given on p. 400, which forms part of this copyright page.

Your views on this book would be much appreciated. We welcome not only specific
comments, suggestions or corrections, but any more general views you may have: how this
book enhanced your visit, how it could have been more helpful. Blue Guides authors and
editorial and production team work hard to bring you what we hope are the best-researched
and best-presented cultural, historical and academic guide books in the English language.
Please write to us by email (editorial@blueguides.com), via the comments page on our website
(www.blueguides.com) or at the address given above. We will be happy to acknowledge
useful contributions in the next edition, and to offer a free copy of one of our titles.

CONTENTS

About the author

ALTA MACADAM is the author of over 40 Blue Guides to Italy, including the last eight editions of *Blue Guide Florence*. She lives in the hills above Florence with her husband, the painter Francesco Colacicchi. In the 1970s she worked for the Photo Library of Alinari and in the following two decades for Harvard University's Villa I Tatti. She is also author of *Florence: where to find Giotto, Brunelleschi, Masaccio, Donatello, the Della Robbia, Beato Angelico, Botticelli, Domenico Ghirlandaio and Michelangelo* (2001, Scala) and of *Americans in Florence: a complete guide to the city and the places associated with Americans past and present* (2003, Giunti). She is at present external consultant for New York University at the photo archive of Villa La Pietra in Florence, and as author of the Blue Guides to Rome, Venice, Concise Rome, Tuscany, Umbria and Central Italy she travels extensively every year to revise new editions of the books.

The contributors

CHARLES FREEMAN (C.F.) is a freelance academic historian with widespread interests in the history of the Mediterranean. His *Egypt, Greece and Rome* (Oxford University Press, 2004) is a standard introduction to the Classical world and his knowledge of the sites is contained in his *Sites of Antiquity: 50 Sites that Explain the Classical World* (Blue Guides, 2009). His latest book, *Holy Bones, Holy Dust*, a study of the medieval cult of relics, was published by Yale University Press in 2011. He is a fellow of the Royal Society of Arts.

NIGEL MCGILCHRIST (N.McG.) is an art historian based near Orvieto. He has worked for the Italian Ministry of Arts and for six years was director of the Anglo-Italian Institute in Rome. He has taught at the University of Rome, for the University of Massachusetts, and was for seven years Dean of European Studies for a consortium of American universities. He lectures widely in art and archaeology at museums and institutions in Europe and the United States. He has contributed to many recent Blue Guides and is the author of *Blue Guide Greece the Aegean Islands*.

HISTORICAL SKETCH

by Charles Freeman

There will always be mystery at the heart of the history of Florence. How could a city that prided itself on its republican principles come to be ruled by one of the most famous hereditary dynasties Europe has ever known? How did a commercially-minded city also become the centre of revolutionary new approaches to art and ideas? Great wealth is often the enemy of good taste, but the patrons of Florence—its guilds, the Church or its great families—commissioned brilliantly-executed works of art which are still regarded as masterpieces today. Less visible, but just as fascinating, are the intellectual and literary achievements of the Florentines. Dante's *Divine Comedy*, his journey to the next world, represents the peak of medieval Christendom; Petrarch introduces the new age of humanism, taken up in the city by a host of penetrating scholars, historians and political thinkers who defined an ideology of republican greatness which harked back to Athens and Rome. All this in a city which was continually ravaged by internal faction, devastated by floods and plagues, and at war with its neighbours.

The difficulty for the historian lies in exposing the complexity of the city's history, teasing out the nuances of political control as exercised by its most successful family, the Medici, noting how works of art, remarkable in their quality, gained much of their resonance from the places they were displayed, sensing how even the most revolutionary work drew on ancient levels of meaning, both Christian and pagan. In the opulently decorated Sala dei Gigli (Hall of Lilies) in the Palazzo Vecchio (*see p. 47*), St Zenobius, a 4th-century bishop of the city, is portrayed alongside six heroes of the Roman Republic, while Dante and Petrarch are shown on the connecting doors. Heroes from three distinct periods of history interact in a triumphant expression of republicanism just at a time when the city appeared dominated by the wealth and influence of one family, the Medici. The essence of the Florence of the 15th century is concealed under so many layers of meaning that it often seems irrecoverable.

It was Jacob Burckhardt who defined this outburst of energy as the Renaissance, and its intellectual driving force as humanism (*The Civilization of the Renaissance in Italy*, first German edition, 1860). He assumed a stagnant Middle Ages which was swept away by the vigour of a Renaissance—but this dramatic cultural break proved difficult for later historians to locate. Even the most enterprising and innovative 'Renaissance' societies remained rooted in medieval faith, while other 'Renaissances' appeared from earlier centuries (the 12th century in France, for instance) and in other parts of Europe outside Italy, such as Flanders and Paris. Burckhardt's Italian Renaissance of the 14th–16th centuries risked being stifled under a blanket of scholarly caveats.

Yet to enter Florence's Piazza Santissima Annunziata and be confronted by Brunelleschi's Spedale degli Innocenti (*see p. 170*), or to mount the stairway of the monastery of San Marco and emerge face to face with Fra' Angelico's *Annunciation*, soon dissolves scholarly inhibitions. Donatello's *David* (now in the Bargello, *see p. 89*) is a biblical subject undressed as a pagan Classical hero, with a sensuality and frivolity which is alien to both. Across the river in the Brancacci Chapel of Santa Maria del Carmine, Masaccio's Adam and Eve howl with a desolation no medieval *Last Judgement* achieves (*see p. 276*). All these works were created at the same period, the first half of the 15th century, and were revolutionary in their own terms. They demand an explanation. That explanation lies partly in the city's origins—or at least in how Florence defined those origins.

The Roman city

Florence was founded as a Roman colony, *Florentia*, 'the place of flowers', by Julius Caesar in 59 BC. A colony was a defensive settlement of Roman citizens, often made up of ex-soldiers, which was planted on a strategically important route. In *Florentia*'s case this was at the crossing of the Arno by the Via Cassia, one of the roads which radiated northwards from Rome. In the long centuries of Roman peace, *Florentia* grew prosperous from road and river traffic, and became the administrative capital of Tuscia. Like other cities of Italy, Florence adopted Christianity in the 4th century and its earliest patron saint was Reparata, a martyr from Palestine.

The emergence of the *Comune*

Florence suffered from the collapse of the Roman Empire and the tortuous wars between the invading forces of Byzantines, Goths and Lombards that pulled Italy into the Dark Ages. The city became part of the kingdom of Lombardy, which was finally overthrown by the Frankish king Charlemagne. Charlemagne was created Holy Roman Emperor by Pope Leo III in 800. As heirs to the Lombards, and in Charlemagne's eyes to the Roman Empire itself, Charlemagne and his successors claimed sovereignty over northern Italy, and so Florence was technically under imperial control. With the emperors based far north of the Alps, however, it was the papacy that exercised more immediate influence over the Italian cities, and for centuries rivalry between popes and emperors formed the backdrop to Italian politics. The most important development, however, was the slow revival of Mediterranean trade, of which the Italian cities took every advantage. The expansion of Florence was at first hindered by her remoteness from the seas and isolation from the major land routes which ran north along the coast, but from the 11th century there was a growing Mediterranean demand for cloth. The waters of the Arno, which narrowed at Florence, were ideal for washing and fulling wool, and the countryside had a surplus of labour. Florence's weakness was a lack of good local supply, but this stimulated the rise of enterprising merchant companies who would travel as far as Flanders and England in search of the raw material, and then sell the finished cloth throughout the Mediterranean. In order to cover the time lapse between buying raw materials and selling them as finished goods, credit arrangements were needed, and thus the Florentines developed a banking network. The city's gold currency, the florin, first minted in 1252, became the most stable and widespread currency in Europe. By 1300, Florentine family firms such as those of the Bardi and

Peruzzi were the richest of the continent, and the road north from Rome now ran through Florence. The demand for labour was so powerful that the city's population tripled to about 120,000 between 1200 and 1300.

Florence's political history was much less happy. A formidable early ruler, Matilda, Countess of Tuscia, gave the city its independence in 1115, and this allowed a communal government to become established—in whose survival the emperors acquiesced. The city was to be ruled by a council of a hundred men. Yet there were heavy pressures on the early commune. Florence was repeatedly caught up in the rivalries between popes and emperors, while the neighbouring coastal cities of Pisa and Lucca, as well as Siena to the south, resisted its growth. Warfare was a continual strain on resources, although Florence gradually extended its territory into the countryside, absorbing its smaller towns and citadels as it did so. Most of its leading families, some of noble origins, some more humble, had migrated from the countryside to take advantage of the growing economic opportunities in the city, but competition between them was fierce. 13th-century Florence was dominated by the rivalry between the Guelphs and the Ghibellines. In origin the Ghibellines were supporters of the Holy Roman Emperor, anti-papal, and drawn from the nobility. The Guelphs were more from the merchant classes, and supported the pope against the emperor. These distinctions became blurred as the factions became more self-serving; even when the Guelphs finally triumphed, they soon split into Black and White Guelph factions, with the two sides largely reflecting family rivalries.

Forms of government

This turmoil encouraged the search for political stability. One device, used in other cities in the same period, was the appointment of a *podestà*, a chief magistrate, from outside the city for a period of a year. The first, from Lombardy, arrived in 1207. By the middle of the century, however, another political force, *il popolo*, the people of the city, was asserting itself. *Il popolo* was a shifting concept. It might genuinely be the people of the city meeting in open session, but it could also be a small oligarchy of families, claiming to be the representatives of the people. In 1250 a determined, and genuinely popular, rising of the *popolo* in Florence drove out the *podestà*, banned the nobles from government and established a *capitano del popolo* to defend its interests. He was set up in a fortress-like structure in the centre of the city, which still remains as the Bargello (so called after the title of the city's chief of police in the 16th century). The new regime (known as the *primo popolo*) lasted only until it was discredited by a dramatic defeat of Florence at Montaperti by Siena in 1260. The city was spared destruction, but the richer families regained control. A more successful reassertion of the *popolo* took place in the 1280s, when a new city government was installed (the *secondo popolo*). This was made up of six (later eight) priors, each representing a district of the city and chosen by lot for two months' service. In order to impose better order on the streets a *gonfaloniere di giustizia* was appointed, with a militia of 1,000. These nine officials were collectively known as the Signoria (literally 'magistracy'), and were housed in the imposing Palazzo della Signoria (now Palazzo Vecchio), begun in the 1290s in a space left vacant by the expulsion of a defeated family. The Palazzo's tower came to symbolise the dominance of the republican government over the nobility, many of whom were now excluded from politics under the so-called Ordinances of Justice of 1293 (ordinances which it was the specific duty of the *gonfaloniere* to enforce).

An important requirement of the new constitution was that the priors had to be members of one of the leading guilds, thus tying the government of the city to its commercial interests. The guilds were fundamental to the economic and social structure of the city, and they were graded according to their importance. Among the leading guilds the Lana represented all the activities involved in the manufacture of wool, the Calimala the importers of cloth (to be reworked or redyed in the city), the Cambio the bankers, and the guild of Por Santa Maria the silk weavers. Notaries and lawyers had their own guild as did doctors and apothecaries. These major guilds were supplemented by a host of minor ones, including shoemakers, bakers and builders, 72 in all by 1301, though only the 21 major guilds could provide priors. (Exactly which guilds could supply priors shifted with time depending on whether conservative or popular groups held power.) The guilds looked after the needs of their own members, carried out charitable works and took responsibility for major buildings in the city.

The fourteenth century

Florence was no more settled in the 14th century than it had been in the 13th. Just to list the disasters is to emphasise the extraordinary resilience of the Florentine people. The century started with a great fire (1304). In 1333 a massive flood swept away all the city's bridges (it is the replacement of the Ponte Vecchio, constructed in 1345, which survives today). Then the Bardi and Peruzzi family banks, which had lent heavily to the English king Edward III, were driven into bankruptcy when the king defaulted on the debt, and this failure rippled through Florence's economy. Just two years later, in 1348, the Black Death swept through the city, killing perhaps half its inhabitants. Wars with Siena, Pisa, Lucca and, between 1375–78, with the papacy, added to the strain on the city, while in 1378 the discontent of the wool workers (the Ciompi) led to a major uprising in which the government was temporarily overthrown by the rioters. The reaction led to the renewed dominance of the greater guilds in government, and the century ended more successfully when an invasion by the Duke of Milan, Gian Galeazzo Visconti, which appeared to be on the brink of success, collapsed in 1402 with his death from plague. In 1406 Florence finally gained control of Pisa, and with the city its own outlet to the sea.

The disasters of the century also mask the extraordinary shift in economic power. The loss of half the city's population in the 14th century meant, in fact, that wealth was consolidated among the survivors. A similar contraction in the rest of Europe led to an increase in demand for luxury goods, which the sophisticated Florentine merchants were able to meet. Soon the skills of many cloth workers were being diverted into the making of silk, the city's most successful new industry of the 15th century. A mass of commodities, from slaves to spices, were picked up on the trade routes and sold alongside these staples. The shock of the Bardi and Peruzzi bankruptcies led to more efficient methods of managing credit, and the merchant families of Florence remained the most resourceful of all players on the international stage. In Venice easy access to the sea and the confident architecture of the city emphasise its openness to the outside world. In Florence the narrow streets and the heavy fortress-palaces give the impression of defensiveness, and it is difficult for the visitor today to appreciate the extent of the city's international reach and its ruthless exploitation of new markets, whether in Spain and Portugal, Antwerp and Bruges, Rhodes and Jerusalem and—after the fall of Constantinople in 1453—the triumphant Ottoman Empire. A typical Florentine firm may have had 25 overseas branches across the Mediterranean and northern Europe.

In the 14th century something in the mood of the city changed. In his *Divine Comedy*, written after his expulsion from the city in 1302, when the Black Guelphs ousted the White, Florence's greatest poet Dante Alighieri takes a journey through Hell and then ascends through Purgatory to Heaven, where, accompanied by his beloved Beatrice, he comes to realise that only through the acceptance of God's love and divine order can peace be found on a troubled earth. This is a medieval world view. In the 1350s, after the Black Death, another Florentine, Giovanni Boccaccio, sets the tales of his *Decameron* among a group of survivors who are determined to enjoy life on earth. Socially confident, the women virtuous but at ease with their male companions, they approach the world with no illusions, and would certainly not assume any divine solution to its troubles. They live in a city which is shifting from the functional in its building—as shown in the walls, administrative buildings and churches of the 13th century—to display. The greatest painter of the day, Giotto, provided the frescoes of the chapels of the Bardi and Peruzzi in Santa Croce (in the 1330s, before their bankruptcy) and then went on to design the graceful campanile of the cathedral. The Signoria commissioned the elegant Loggia della Signoria in 1376 as a reception area for visiting dignitaries and the public swearing-in of officials. One of the strangest buildings of the city was also put in hand. The city needed a grain market backed by a permanent store of grain for emergencies. The store was to be built on the site of an oratory to St Michael, on one of whose pillars there was a miracle-working image of the Virgin. The shrine (surmounted by an awesome tabernacle of 1355 by Andrea Orcagna), store and market are combined in the massive Orsanmichele (*see p. 98*), whose exterior was covered with statues provided by the guilds in the early 15th century.

The rise of humanism

The readiness to spend the city's wealth on its glorification was now given impetus by an intellectual revolution. The catalyst was Francesco Petrarch (1304–74). Petrarch came from a Florentine family which had been exiled at the same time as Dante, and almost all his life was spent outside Florence. He had a passion for ancient texts, and through them he rediscovered Latin as spoken and written by major Classical authors such as Cicero and Virgil. The texts he and other scholars accumulated dealt with law, oratory, history and moral philosophy, and their study gave birth to the movement known as humanism. In Florence, humanism was given focus by the city's official representative on formal occasions, its chancellor Coluccio Salutati (chancellor 1375–

1406). A scholar in his own right, Salutati wove the republican language of ancient Rome, its sense of moral purpose and suspicion of tyranny, into an ideology of Florentine republicanism. He also invited a Greek scholar, Manuel Chrysoloras, to the city to teach Greek. Soon Florence was a centre of scholarship, with Greek texts being read for the first time in the west for a thousand years, and many being translated into Ciceronian Latin. Coluccio's successor as chancellor, Leonardo Bruni (1370–1444), was another fine scholar who rewrote the history of the city to make it appear as if it was one long story of resistance to tyranny. His *Laudatio* (1403), a panegyric of Florence, in which he compares the city to ancient Rome, struck a chord with his fellow citizens. and he was honoured by a fine Renaissance tomb in Santa Croce (*see p. 199*), where he lies with his *History of the Florentine People* on his chest. To be able to speak and write Latin was now essential for any man of status, and the ancient virtues of sobriety and civic responsibility were absorbed with the studied texts.

By the early 15th century, therefore, a combination of wealth, intense civic pride and commitment to the glorification of Florence through patronage made the city the intellectual and artistic capital of Italy. Patronage flowed through many channels: the city itself, its guilds, the Church and wealthy individuals. It was set within an atmosphere of intense competition, of which the contest for the Baptistery doors, sponsored by the guild of the Calimala, is the most celebrated (*see p. 91*). Such competition between patrons for artists and between artists for patronage helped liberate architecture, painting, sculpture and a host of minor crafts from conventional themes. The Classical world, revived and brought into the core of Florentine republican ideology, must have provided its own inspiration as a pinnacle of excellence which, alone among its rivals, the city might meet. Florence not only absorbed the achievements of the Classical past; it transformed them into something radically new.

The dominance of the Medici

The family which best symbolises the achievement of Renaissance Florence is the Medici. This is partly because they retained their influence so successfully over most of the 15th century—a consummate achievement for any family in faction-torn Florence. Then, in the 16th century, they transformed themselves into a dynasty which was to rule Florence for 200 years. Yet their position was never so dominant or assured as outsiders believed it to be. What is remarkable about Florence in the 15th century is the range of families who prospered. This was the great age of palace-building. In 1470, 35 palaces are recorded as under construction, and more were to follow. The forbidding exteriors concealed large open courtyards (an innovation for domestic buildings) and public audience rooms for the display of the family. Politics was now turned inwards. The Signoria and the committees which supported it remained as the public face of the city, while control over them was manipulated behind palace façades.

Giovanni di Bicci de' Medici (1360–1429), the founder of his family's pre-eminence in the city, was a merchant and banker rather than a politician. It was his conservative investment policies (including the purchase of property inside Florence and farmland outside it) and his shrewd building up of contacts which led to a steady accumulation of wealth. In 1410 one of his contacts, Baldassare Cossa, became Antipope (if only temporarily) as John XXIII and the Medici took over the papal finances. Returns of over 30 percent a year were possible, and Rome now provided half the Medici income. Even when Cossa was deposed and failed to repay a large loan, Giovanni did not desert him and this added to the Medici reputation for loyalty and trustworthiness. (In fact, Giovanni paid for Cossa's fine tomb in the Baptistery, *see p. 65*.) Within Florence itself, Giovanni was cautious. He did hold office, as *gonfaloniere*, in 1421 and served on other committees. He put in hand the rebuilding of the family church of San Lorenzo but was never a great patron of the arts. On major political issues he carefully sided himself with the lesser guilds, supporting, for instance, the *catasto*, a tax system which demanded more from the rich who had to declare all their assets. He died popular and respected.

Giovanni was from the last generation of wealthy Florentines not to know Latin. His son, Cosimo (1389–1464), was already 40 when his father died, and educated in the new humanism. He was also a man of exceptional political shrewdness. He revealed little of his personality or his thoughts, but he understood the city's deep distrust of any form of tyranny. When Brunelleschi offered to build him a vast new palace, he opted for a more modest, though still substantial, building. One of his protégés, Marsilio Ficino, was given the task of providing the first Latin translations of the Greek philosopher Plato, and this led to a revival of Platonism in the intellectual circles of the city.

As a politician Cosimo worked carefully behind the scenes. What appeared to be a disaster, his exile at the hands of the Albizi family in 1433, became a triumph when he re-entered the city to general rejoicing in 1434. Occasionally, as in 1458, when he was threatened with unrest, he risked calling an assembly of the *popolo* to consolidate his control over the constitution, but he preferred the steady winning over of his rivals through his wealth or patronage. He would use his allies to restrain or exile enemies and so presented to the outside world the image of a settled and well-governed state. A major diplomatic coup was the holding of the Council of Florence, an important meeting of the Eastern and Western Churches under the auspices of Pope Eugenius IV, in the city, in 1439 (*see p. 187*). Cosimo had himself elected *gonfaloniere* so that he could personally welcome the pope, the Eastern emperor, and other dignitaries on behalf of the city. Hardly had the Council's business finished than Florence achieved a major victory over the Milanese at Anghiari in 1440, which further boosted Cosimo's position. Many were tempted to compare him with Octavian, later the Roman emperor Augustus—even to the extent of spreading a myth that Florence had been founded by Octavian rather than Julius Caesar. The titles given to Cosimo—*princeps*, 'first citizen', and, after his death, *pater patriae*, 'father of the fatherland'—had, in fact, been used of Augustus fourteen hundred years earlier.

Cosimo died in his bed in 1464, still without any formal title, but undoubtedly the leading citizen of the city. Despite massive spending, the fortunes of the family were intact, and in 1466 were boosted through being awarded, by the papacy, the lucrative monopoly on the alum mines in papal territory (alum was a mineral salt used to fix dyes into cloth). Cosimo's son, Piero il Gottoso (the Gouty), maintained Medici control of Florence, and when he died in 1469 his twenty-year-old son Lorenzo was in place to carry on the Medici name and fortunes. In fact, Lorenzo was immediately approached by a delegation of citizens asking him 'to take charge' of the city.

Despite his youth, Lorenzo was already skilled in the exercise of power. He had visited Milan, Venice and Rome on official business and his wife, Clarice Orsini, came from one of the most ancient and aristocratic families of Rome. He was energetic, intelligent and had a charisma which transcended an ugly face. He was deeply schooled in humanist values. He had been taught Greek by Marsilio Ficino himself, and was attracted like his grandfather to the philosophy of Plato. In fact, he felt at home with intellectuals. One of his circle, the poet Agnolo Poliziano (1454–94), was such an erudite Classicist that many of his emendations to corrupt Greek manuscripts are still accepted as correct by scholars today. Another intimate, Pico della Mirandola (1463–94), was one of the first Christians to master Hebrew in depth. This role of cultural patron went hand in hand with a solid grip of the government of Florence. Political business was often referred to Lorenzo directly.

While Lorenzo appeared to be successfully fulfilling the ambiguous role of *princeps* in a city which detested tyranny, not all his fellow citizens were ready to acquiesce in his influence. In 1478, he was lucky to escape with his life when a plot to assassinate him (the Pazzi Conspiracy) almost succeeded (*see p. 203*). However, the backlash was easy to exploit. Lorenzo issued a medal to commemorate his survival and basked in the period of comparative stability which followed. Lorenzo played his own part in keeping the peace. He intervened to thwart the ambitions of Naples against Florence and engineered an alliance with Florence's old enemy, Milan, which he was able to use against the papacy, Venice and Naples if they threatened him. He turned around his relationship with the papacy so successfully that in 1489 he was able to persuade Pope Innocent VII to make his son Giovanni a cardinal at the tender age of thirteen.

Behind the façade, however, things were not so secure. The Medici fortune was being eroded by economic uncertainty and unwise investments. Lorenzo was not a good businessman, and his manager, Sassetti, despite the glorious frescoes in his family chapel in Santa Trínita (*see p. 214*), was less astute than he might have been and all but bankrupted the firm. When Lorenzo died, aged only 43, in 1492, his son Piero no longer had the capital to secure goodwill with largesse as Lorenzo had done. A much weaker character than his predecessors, Piero also alienated the Signoria through his arrogant behaviour, losing all remaining support when he surrendered some of Florence's possessions to the French king Charles VIII, who had invaded Italy in 1494. An outraged populace drove out the Medici and their palace was sacked. Donatello's *David*, which had been commissioned by Cosimo as a mark of the family's commitment, real or imagined, to republicanism (David symbolising the plucky resistance of humble Florence to the surrounding tyrannical Goliaths), was repositioned in the Piazza della Signoria.

Troubled times and the emergence of the Duchy, 1494–1570

Charles VIII's invasion introduced a period of intense instability in Italy. The Dominican friar Girolamo Savonarola (*see p. 34*), whose influence had been growing in Lorenzo's reign, played on his support among the poorer classes of the city to proclaim a popular republic which was also a city of God. An elected Grand Council of a thousand members was to be set up to act as a restraint on the Signoria, but the new government turned against the spirit of Renaissance humanism and instituted a reign of puritanism. The backlash eventually led to the burning of Savonarola for heresy. Italy, meanwhile, was in turmoil. There were fresh French invasions in 1499 and 1515, and the Spanish invaded southern Italy in 1512. Then the powerful Habsburg monarch Charles V, elected Holy Roman Emperor in 1519, made his own entrance, and in 1527 his undisciplined troops sacked Rome. While the Medici pope Clement VII cowered in his stronghold, Florence erupted in yet another pro-republican revolt. Pope Clement elected to come to terms with Charles, whose status as emperor in Italy he endorsed. A deal was then done by which Charles would help restore the Medici to Florence, and the imperial troops surrounded the city. After an appalling ten-month siege in which half the city's population may have died of hunger or disease, Florence capitulated. An illegitimate great-grandson of Lorenzo the Magnificent, Alessandro de' Medici, was imposed on the city with the title of Duke (1531), and his position was further secured by his marriage to Charles V's own illegitimate daughter, Margaret.

The city was now under imperial control, but when Alessandro was murdered in 1537, in a sordid conspiracy which even members of his own family supported, the city attempted to reassert its independence by asking a distant cousin of Alessandro, Cosimo de' Medici (who traced his lineage back to Cosimo il Vecchio's brother, Lorenzo), to be head of government. Cosimo had no support outside the city, but fought off his rivals and consolidated himself so successfully that eventually both pope and then emperor accepted him as Duke of Florence. In theory this was not an overthrow of the republic, but Cosimo tightened his grip. An important symbolic move was made in 1540 when he transferred his headquarters from the Medici palace to the Palazzo della Signoria (Palazzo Vecchio) itself. Further success came after Cosimo's only military adventure ended with the conquest of Florence's old rival Siena in 1557. The increasing splendour of Cosimo's position was marked by the adoption of the Palazzo Pitti for ceremonial occasions and the creation of a fine set of administrative offices, the Uffizi, which soon became a gallery for the family's art collection. In 1570 the pope created Cosimo Grand Duke of Tuscany, and this was the title the Medici were to hold, as a hereditary dynasty, until 1737.

The Medici dukes and the decline of Florence

Florence's economy after 1600 went into decline as economic vitality passed to northern Europe, and Mediterranean trade was superseded by the new routes across the Atlantic. While the city was still producing 30,000 pieces of cloth in the 1570s, by 1610 that figure stood at only 10,000 and was only half as many by 1650. This decline was typical of Italy as a whole, and marked a shift towards agriculture as the core of the economy and the strengthening of ancient feudal custom. In Florence the grand dukes, few of whom were outstanding personalities, presided over a provincial kingdom where court life was more important than entrepreneurship, and where it was land rather than a vault full of gold florins which now gave status. As with many such states (Venice provides a comparable example), inner decay was masked by extravagant display. The dukes searched for their brides on the European stage—Austria, France and Italy—and each was welcomed to Florence with pageants and feasting.

The story of the Medici grand dukes could, in fact, be told through the embellishment of the Palazzo Pitti and the care, nurture and display of their fabulous collection of art (see pp. 231–57). The palace was extended and extensively remodelled over three centuries by the Medici dukes, the dukes of Lorraine, Napoleon and Vittorio Emanuele II, the first king of a united Italy, whose royal palace it briefly became. The Medici collection, enhanced by Raphaels and Titians from Urbino brought in by the marriage of Ferdinando II (grand duke 1621–70), was displayed here and in the Uffizi, where the Tribuna became the home to the family's Classical sculpture (the Venus de' Medici was the highlight of many a Grand Tour). After so much care had been lavished on collection and display, it seems fitting that the sister of the last grand duke, Anna Maria Luisa, heiress of her childless brother and thus of all his property and art, would bequeath it on her death in 1743 to the House of Lorraine, which was to rule the city, on condition that it remained in Florence 'for the ornament of the state, the utility of the public and in order to attract the attention of foreigners'.

However, to pass on too quickly is also to miss some important developments. Cosimo's son and successor, Francesco, (grand duke 1574–87) deserves to be remembered for championing Tuscan as the purest form of Italian. However, it was also in his reign—and with his acquiescence—that Spain became the dominant influence in Tuscany as in much of the rest of Italy. The independence of Florence, so vigorously asserted by Cosimo I, was lost. Francesco's brother, Ferdinando I (grand duke (1587–1609) was an effective ruler at a time when the city was still prosperous. The strength of his position is emphasised by Giambologna's equestrian statue of him in the Piazza Santissima Annunziata (1608), the first self-glorifying statue any ruler of Florence dared to erect in his own lifetime. Ferdinando's short-lived son Cosimo II (grand duke 1609 –21) can be remembered for his patronage of Galileo: he appointed the great scientist Philosopher and Mathematician to the Court for life after Galileo shrewdly named the moons of Jupiter which he had discovered, 'the Medicean stars'. His successor Ferdinando II (grand duke 1621–70) continued the patronage, even if he was unable to prevent Galileo's eventual condemnation by the Vatican. His successor, Cosimo III (grand duke 1670–1723), spent much of his long life in a state of pious gloom (the nakedness of Michelangelo's David was concealed under a tarpaulin), the population of his city shrinking to only 42,000 as grass began to grow on the streets and buildings to fall inwards. With Cosimo's childless son Gian Gastone the dynasty came to an end in 1737. By now an untaxed but influential Church, a feudal system of land ownership, and a stagnant industrial sector combined to make Tuscany a backwater.

Then the duchy had some luck. Gian Gastone had secured a promise that the duchy (which was still under the nominal control of the Holy Roman Emperors) would remain an independent state on his death. The Spanish Bourbons tried to impose their own grand duke, but the European powers assigned Tuscany to the House of Lorraine, cousins of the Austrian Habsburgs. The first Lorraine grand duke, Franz Stephan (later

Holy Roman Emperor Francis I), spent little time in Florence, but through his regents he set in hand desperately needed reforms. The power of the Church and the feudal aristocracy was challenged, trade was liberalised and the state debt reorganised. More was to come. Under his successor, his son Peter Leopold, Tuscany moved to the forefront of the Italian Enlightenment. The ramshackle state administration and bureaucracy was overhauled, the vast landed wealth of the Church redistributed, and an attempt made to create a class of small landholders. An enlightened penal code which outlawed the death penalty and torture was promulgated in 1787. However, the duchy remained miserably poor, and there was no social group of sufficient maturity to sustain the reformed state. By the time Peter Leopold succeeded to the title of Holy Roman Emperor in 1790, and installed his son Ferdinand as Grand Duke Ferdinand III of Tuscany, there was severe unrest in the city.

Then came the whirlwind of the French Revolution, followed by Napoleon's conquests of Italy in the late 1790s. Tuscany briefly became the (independent) Kingdom of Etruria, before Napoleon absorbed it back into his reconstituted Italy, with his sister Elisa as its grand duchess. She prepared the Palazzo Pitti for her brother by building an exquisite Neoclassical bathroom for him—but he never came. Instead, many of Florence's finest works of art were moved to Paris to glorify the Louvre. Fortunately they were restored to the city, together with Ferdinand III, who ruled peaceably until his death in 1824.

One effect of Napoleon's reorganisation of Italy was to stimulate a nationalist reaction. In Florence this is manifested by Canova's monument to the 18th-century poet Vittorio Alfieri in Santa Croce (see p. 198). A personification of Italy mourns the poet—and the spirit of the monument entirely reflects the spirit of the times. It was not that the last Grand Duke of Tuscany, Ferdinand's son Leopold, was inadequate. He conscientiously drained marshes and modernised parts of the city, but he represented a foreign power—Austria—at a time when a vocal minority of Italians were looking towards unification and self-government. Even though Tuscany's prime minister Fossombroni was unsure whether Florence under the House of Savoy would enjoy more autonomy than it did under distant Vienna, Leopold's rule could not last. In 1859, the machinations of Camillo Cavour, the first minister of the Kingdom of Savoy, saw Tuscany swept into the newly unified Italian state. Leopold left Florence without a struggle. Cavour and his king, Vittorio Emanuele, entered the city to some enthusiasm. Florence was even to serve as the capital of the new Italy between 1865 and 1871.

By the second half of the 19th century Florence was being recreated in the European—and above all the British—imagination as the centre of the Renaissance. Art lovers, romantics and self-improvers, all in search of cultural enlightenment, took advantage of the new railway system to reach the city. The process has been cumulative, so that any visit to the city today is defined almost as much by the massed groups being led from one icon to the next as by the city and its treasures themselves. It is perhaps the visitor who breaks out and explores for him or herself who most learns to appreciate what Florence has to offer. Perhaps the finest Renaissance garden in Italy, at the Villa di Castello, lies only a short distance from the city centre (see p. 319).

THE MEDICI FAMILY

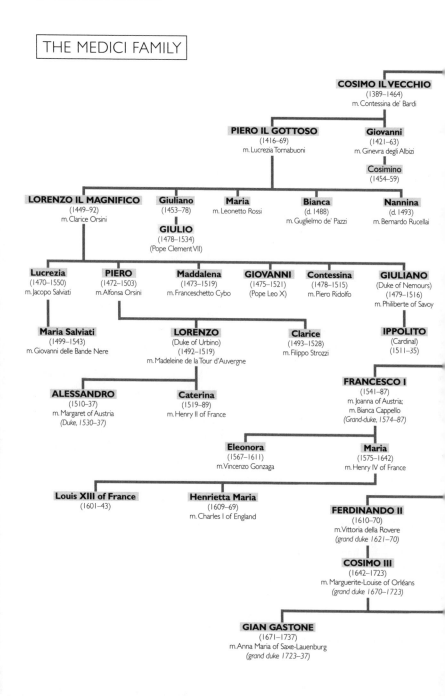

COSIMO IL VECCHIO
(1389–1464)
m. Contessina de' Bardi

PIERO IL GOTTOSO
(1416–69)
m. Lucrezia Tornabuoni

Giovanni
(1421–63)
m. Ginevra degli Albizi

Cosimino
(1454–59)

LORENZO IL MAGNIFICO
(1449–92)
m. Clarice Orsini

Giuliano
(1453–78)

Maria
m. Leonetto Rossi

Bianca
(d. 1488)
m. Guglielmo de' Pazzi

Nannina
(d. 1493)
m. Bernardo Rucellai

GIULIO
(1478–1534)
(Pope Clement VII)

Lucrezia
(1470–1550)
m. Jacopo Salviati

PIERO
(1472–1503)
m. Alfonsa Orsini

Maddalena
(1473–1519)
m. Franceschetto Cybo

GIOVANNI
(1475–1521)
(Pope Leo X)

Contessina
(1478–1515)
m. Piero Ridolfo

GIULIANO
(Duke of Nemours)
(1479–1516)
m. Philiberte of Savoy

Maria Salviati
(1499–1543)
m. Giovanni delle Bande Nere

LORENZO
(Duke of Urbino)
(1492–1519)
m. Madeleine de la Tour d'Auvergne

Clarice
(1493–1528)
m. Filippo Strozzi

IPPOLITO
(Cardinal)
(1511–35)

ALESSANDRO
(1510–37)
m. Margaret of Austria
(Duke, 1530–37)

Caterina
(1519–89)
m. Henry II of France

FRANCESCO I
(1541–87)
m. Joanna of Austria;
m. Bianca Cappello
(Grand-duke, 1574–87)

Eleonora
(1567–1611)
m. Vincenzo Gonzaga

Maria
(1575–1642)
m. Henry IV of France

Louis XIII of France
(1601–43)

Henrietta Maria
(1609–69)
m. Charles I of England

FERDINANDO II
(1610–70)
m. Vittoria della Rovere
(grand duke 1621–70)

COSIMO III
(1642–1723)
m. Marguerite-Louise of Orléans
(grand duke 1670–1723)

GIAN GASTONE
(1671–1737)
m. Anna Maria of Saxe-Lauenburg
(grand duke 1723–37)

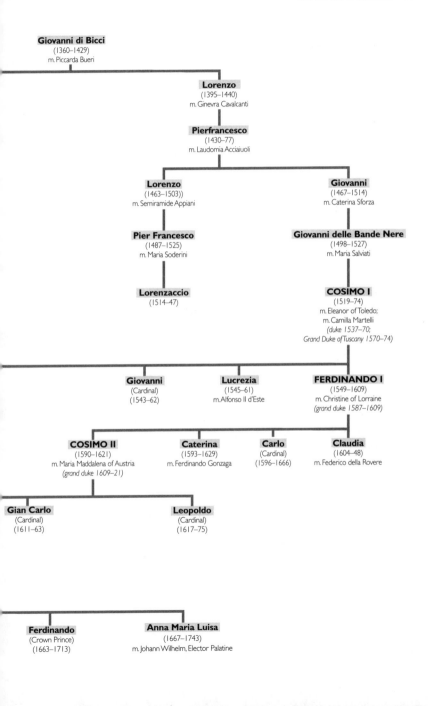

Giovanni di Bicci
(1360–1429)
m. Piccarda Bueri

Lorenzo
(1395–1440)
m. Ginevra Cavalcanti

Pierfrancesco
(1430–77)
m. Laudomia Acciaiuoli

Lorenzo
(1463–1503))
m. Semiramide Appiani

Giovanni
(1467–1514)
m. Caterina Sforza

Pier Francesco
(1487–1525)
m. Maria Soderini

Giovanni delle Bande Nere
(1498–1527)
m. Maria Salviati

Lorenzaccio
(1514–47)

COSIMO I
(1519–74)
m. Eleanor of Toledo;
m. Camilla Martelli
(duke 1537–70;
Grand Duke of Tuscany 1570–74)

Giovanni
(Cardinal)
(1543–62)

Lucrezia
(1545–61)
m. Alfonso II d'Este

FERDINANDO I
(1549–1609)
m. Christine of Lorraine
(grand duke 1587–1609)

COSIMO II
(1590–1621)
m. Maria Maddalena of Austria
(grand duke 1609–21)

Caterina
(1593–1629)
m. Ferdinando Gonzaga

Carlo
(Cardinal)
(1596–1666)

Claudia
(1604–48)
m. Federico della Rovere

Gian Carlo
(Cardinal)
(1611–63)

Leopoldo
(Cardinal)
(1617–75)

Ferdinando
(Crown Prince)
(1663–1713)

Anna Maria Luisa
(1667–1743)
m. Johann Wilhelm, Elector Palatine

Heads of the Medici family, de facto leaders in Florence

Cosimo il Vecchio (*Pater Patriae*)	1434–64
Piero di Cosimo (*il Gottoso*; the Gouty)	1464–69
Lorenzo (*il Magnifico*; the Magnificent)	1469–92
Piero di Lorenzo (*il Fatuo*; the Unlucky)	1492–94

[Republic 1494–1512]

Giovanni (later Pope Leo X)	1512–13
Giuliano, Duke of Nemours	1513
Lorenzo, Duke of Urbino	1513–19
Giulio (later Pope Clement VII)	1519–23
Ippolito	1523–27

[Republic 1527–30]

Alessandro	1531–32

Dukes of Florence

Alessandro	1532–37
Cosimo	1537–70

Grand Dukes of Tuscany

Cosimo I	1570–74
Francesco	1574–87
Ferdinando I	1587–1609
Cosimo II	1609–21
Ferdinando II	1621–70
Cosimo III	1670–1723
Gian Gastone	1723–37

Lorraine Grand Dukes

Francis (Franz Stephan of Lorraine)	1737–65
Peter Leopold (later Holy Roman Emperor Leopold II)	1765–90
Ferdinand III	1791–99

[Napoleonic interlude 1799–1814]

Ferdinand III	1814–24
Leopold II	1824–59

TWENTIETH-CENTURY FLORENCE

Between the two world wars, Florence continued to be regarded as a meeting place for intellectuals, writers and artists. Amongst the important foreigners in residence at this time was the historian of the Italian Renaissance Bernard Berenson, who made Villa I Tatti a gathering place for some of the most renowned scholars of Italian art.

The German Occupation in 1943 and subsequent liberation of the city by the Allies in August 1944 was a time of hardship. With the exception of Ponte Vecchio, all the bridges over the Arno were blown up by the retreating German army, and Ponte Vecchio itself was made impassable by destroying the medieval buildings close to it on both sides of the river. More destruction would have taken place and more lives would have been lost without the heroic deeds of Dr Gerhard Wolf, the German Consul, later made a freeman by grateful Florentines. A committee, presided over by Berenson, was formed so that by 1957 Florence's most beautiful bridge, Ponte Santa Trínita, had been perfectly reconstructed. The waterfront around Ponte Vecchio was also rebuilt in the least invasive way possible. Giorgio La Pira is remembered as an outstanding mayor in the 1950s: he felt that Florence had a mission to promote peace, and his profound Christianity meant that he took special pains to give help to the underprivileged.

The terrible Arno flood of 1966, treated as an international disaster, damaged many works of art and hundreds of thousands of books and archives, as well as destroying hundreds of artisans' workshops, many of which never recovered. There is still great concern that if the Arno basin were again to be affected by exceptionally heavy rainfall, the river would once more overflow its banks. Uncontrolled building both upstream and downstream since the 1960s has increased the risk of another catastrophe and a flood prevention programme is still under discussion.

After 1966 the art of restoration and conservation received fresh impetus and Florence, together with the Istituto Centrale in Rome, soon became Italy's most important restoration centre. After emergency work had been carried out, other restoration projects were undertaken on numerous fresco cycles in churches and on sculpture in the open, most of which has been brought under cover for conservation reasons (including Ghiberti's bronze panels from the Baptistery doors, all the statues in the exterior niches of Orsanmichele, and Donatello's *Judith* outside Palazzo Vecchio). The meticulous restoration of individual paintings continues apace, and amongst the most spectacular results in the last few years have been the cleaning of Raphael's *Madonna del Cardellino* from the Uffizi and of Fra' Angelico's *Tabernacolo dei Linaioli* from the Museo di San Marco.

The lovely hills dotted with villas and country churches which surround the city have been largely preserved from new buildings, partly thanks to the efforts of the conservation committees instituted by the Florentines themselves in the 1970s and 1980s. But the post-war years saw urban sprawl on the plain to the northwest as well as the expansion of Florence's airport, which is uncomfortably close to the city. The Palazzo di Giustizia, built to house the law courts, was completed a few years ago but has remained empty as it is apparently proving difficult to furnish and maintain. Much bigger than any other building in the vicinity of the city it has irreparably altered the skyline of Florence and its townscape.

The historic centre of the city was first closed to traffic (except for residents) in 1988 (and the area was extended to the Oltrarno in the following decade) but pollution levels are still high and the traffic still chaotic. A tramline was inaugurated in 2010 to serve Scandicci, one of the most populated suburbs of the city, and two more are planned. But one of the most radical decisions by any administrator in recent years was the present mayor's order in 2009 to close Piazza del Duomo to motor traffic, which has brought pleasant relief to those on foot, and has restored a welcome air of peace in the heart of the city. More such closures, including Piazza Pitti, are planned.

Great progress has been made in the last decades in the rearrangement or reopening of the city's museums. A general restoration programme has been underway on the three floors of the huge Palazzo Pitti, and more and more suites of rooms used by the grand dukes, and later by the royal house of Savoy, have been opened to the public, and the museums renovated. The superb ceilings frescoed by Pietro da Cortona in the main reception rooms of the Galleria Palatina have been restored, as well as numerous paintings. There has been important work on the exhibition spaces in other museums too, including the Museo dell'Opera del Duomo and the Casa Buonarroti, and both Palazzo Davanzati and the Museo Stefano Bardini have been reopened after years of closure. Palazzo Vecchio now has an excellent programme for young visitors and has opened up some of its 'secret' corners, as well as its ramparts. In 2010 Florence's museum dedicated to the history of science was reopened and renamed the Museo Galileo, using all the latest multi-media supports to guide visitors around its fascinating collection. The paintings on the first floor of the Galleria dell'Accademia were rearranged in 2011.

In 1993, a Mafia car bomb exploded in Via Lambertesca killing five people and causing much structural damage to Florence's most famous art gallery, the Uffizi (some 90 paintings had to be restored). Here work has been underway for several decades to expand the exhibition space down to the *piano nobile* but progress has been slow.

The lovely garden of Villa La Pietra has been carefully restored and can now be visited by appointment, together with the interior of this interesting villa which belonged to Harold Acton. In the very centre of Florence the park of Villa Bardini, which has wonderful views of the city, has become accessible on a daily basis. There are also plans to improve the Cascine park. Since 2006, when it came under excellent new management, Palazzo Strozzi has been Florence's most important exhibition venue.

Although Florence's population decreased in the 1990s, since 2006 it has begun to register more births (and the present population of the municipality is just over 370,000). There has been a notable influx of immigrants in the last few years. There are now over 30 American college and university programmes in Florence, and it is also home to the prestigious European University Institute, founded in 1972. The city somehow manages to deal with its over 6.5 million visitors a year—but when it gets very crowded it is well worth taking a walk out to the lovely hills in its immediate environs.

THE FLORENTINE RENAISSANCE

by Nigel McGilchrist

The origins of Florentine Art

'A painting is a window looking onto the world', wrote Alberti in 1436. We take this so completely for granted today that it is easy to forget that the idea of a picture coherently and realistically describing the world around us was born in Florence in the early 1400s. Or rather, it was re-born in Florence for the first time since the end of the Roman Empire. Florence, as her name so happily implies, embodies the very flowering of a new European art. Within her walls were born the individuals and the ideas which were to shape the nature of our modern visual sensibility. Certainly Florence could not have achieved what she did without the roots and the tree of Italian art as a whole: but Florence remains the flower of that tree, in particular in the 1400s when her pre-eminence was uncontested anywhere in Italy, or even in Europe. The fact that so many figures of genius who have become household names well beyond the shores of Italy and of Europe—Giotto, Dante, Petrarch, Donatello, Masaccio, Botticelli, Leonardo da Vinci, Michelangelo, Galileo, Machiavelli—should all have come from or worked in this small and hitherto insignificant town in the space of little more than 300 years—is not only statistically extraordinary, but it requires some kind of explanation. So also does the fact that, after Michelangelo's death in 1564, Florence produced no artists of comparable stature ever again, and indeed she all but vanishes from the pages of art history books.

In this way Florence appears like a blazing comet in the artistic firmament in the 14th and 15th centuries, and just as dramatically disappears at the end of the 16th century. For the visitor this means that the city, in marked contrast to Rome, presents itself as an architectural and artistic unity, a complete expression of one particular period and spirit. This spirit we commonly call the Renaissance. It was a conscious re-birth or 're-naissance' of the principles of ancient Roman and Greek thinking, and the art of the city cannot be understood except by reference to that ever-present emulation of, and desire to exceed, the achievements of antiquity. We think of the Florentine Renaissance as principally an artistic revolution: revolution it certainly was, but it was as much about science—about optics, geometry and anatomy in particular—as it was about art. It just happens that in Florence, that scientific thinking was linked to visual expression. Hence the unforgettable physical beauty of this tiny city and its disproportionate wealth of monuments and pictures.

Florentine art begins, as so often, with money. Ancient Roman Florence was perhaps only a quarter of the size of Pompeii, and would have remained comparably insignificant had it not begun in the 12th century to play an important role in the continent's wool trade. Wool was always needed for clothing and was a big industry in medieval Europe. The raw material was produced in Northern Europe, but was processed, dyed and carded in a number of centres in the Mediterranean, of which Florence became one of the foremost. This was a lucrative business, and it made a small group of Florentine families immensely rich. That wealth, however, might never have had the determining influence it was to have on European art, had not some of those families begun, in the 13th century, to use their wealth for banking and for making substantial loans, both locally and internationally. The gold florin, named after the city, was minted from 1252 onwards and became an internationally recognised coinage. The wealthy banking families of Florence became steadily wealthier. But there was one moral issue that gnawed at their sophisticated, Christian consciences. Banking was based on usury, and usury was a sin—a deadly sin, furthermore, that might jeopardise the comfort of their souls after death. One way of atoning for this was to underwrite fine buildings for the Church, and to commission sculptures, murals and altarpieces to the greater glory of God. It is, of course, difficult to know exactly how much early Florentine art is a product of this desire to atone for the sin of usury; but its influence as an idea was undoubtedly far-reaching, and the great families who patronised the artists of Florence in the 1300s and 1400s soon realised as well that their artistic—and highly visible—commissions could also be fruitful vehicles for propaganda and personal glorification. The fertile soil for an artistic revolution was thus created, and in that soil, around the year 1400, a remarkable group of free-thinking and curious minds found an ideal environment for intellectual and artistic growth.

What happened in the miracle of the Florentine Quattrocento (15th century) did not appear from nowhere, and we need first to look for its roots in the previous hundred and fifty years.

The Duecento and Trecento

A remarkably durable tradition has seen a figure by the name of Cenni di Peppi (c. 1240–1302) or 'Cimabue' (about whom we know little that is certain) as the first exponent of a style in painting that we can begin to call distinctively Florentine. We can see what this refers to by looking at a great work, probably by this master, in the cloisters of the Florentine church of Santa Croce. This unexpectedly moving (although much damaged) processional Crucifix (see p. 204) is created in a tradition which descended from Byzantine religious painting. But if we look at it carefully we see that, although it is rhythmically stylised and rigorously icon-like in appearance, it nonetheless reveals an attention to modelling and a quality of pathos and drama which is essentially alien to the spirit of Byzantine art. And if we imagine the huge cross-shaped panel held high above a surging procession in the streets of the town, we can begin to see the purpose of that pathos. We have our first intimation also of how important and recurrent the processional element is going to be in the greatest Florentine art.

This new and sculptural tendency in the creations of Cimabue was deeply felt and understood by his greatest pupil, Giotto (c. 1267–1337). The anecdotal version of the relationship between this master and pupil of genius is delightfully told by Giorgio Vasari, who in 1550 published his famous *Lives of the most excellent Painters, Sculptors and Architects*—one of the first modern pieces of art-historical writing. Giotto took that hint of drama and human pathos which he found in Cimabue and fashioned it into his own inimitable visual language. In almost the first room of the Uffizi Gallery you have the opportunity to compare these two painters side by side in the two strikingly similar paintings of the Madonna enthroned (the *Maestà; see p. 113*): the *Santa Trinita Madonna*, generally attributed to Cimabue, and the *Ognissanti Madonna*, attributed to Giotto. Several things distinguish Giotto's work from his master's: the pared-down simplicity of Giotto's version; the coherence and unity of its design; the awakening humanity of the faces; and the new, weighty solidity of the figures. It was these characteristics that opened the way to generations of later Italian and European painting. Masaccio was to learn these lessons, and Piero della Francesca and Michelangelo, too, amongst the many artists who came to study and to draw in front of the works of Giotto.

Widely admired, appreciated for his humanity, and written about by Dante and Boccaccio, Giotto was one of the greatest men of his age. Though his masterpiece, the Scrovegni Chapel, is in Padua, his works can be found elsewhere in Florence—principally in the (rather damaged) murals of the Bardi and Peruzzi chapels in Santa Croce. He also left behind influential works not just of painting but of architecture, such as the design of the graceful bell-tower of the Florence Duomo, considered by many one of the city's most beautiful buildings.

Was Giotto then really the founding spirit of the Italian Renaissance? The answer is complicated by the fact that perhaps a whole generation of potential artists who immediately followed him was virtually eliminated by repeated outbreaks of the plague in the middle of the 14th century. Florence suffered terribly, both economically and demographically, and, in concomitance, the momentum of Giotto's artistic revolution seems to falter. The 14th century, or Trecento, may have been a period of lost potential, but nonetheless it was one of productivity of a high technical quality. In its pantheon of lesser known artists, two families of painters stand out: the di Cione (Andrea, always called 'Orcagna', and his brothers Nardo and Jacopo), and the Gaddi (Taddeo, the father, and Agnolo, the son). Outside the Uffizi Gallery, the works of these accomplished artists are to be found in the two magnificent and spacious churches of the preaching orders which mark the western and eastern extremities of medieval Florence: Santa Maria Novella of the Dominicans and Santa Croce of the Franciscans.

To the eyes of the uninitiated, the religious works and altarpieces of the 14th century can appear to have an unwelcome sameness to them. This impression is not helped by museums which exhibit these beautiful, but often damaged, works side by side, spreadeagled and pinned uncomfortably to the walls under a harsh and uncompromising light, like patients in a hospital ward. We owe it to the works themselves to undo this damage, and in our mind's eye to set them once again on the quiet altars in dark churches for which they were originally created, with the light of candles or oil-lamps in front of them, giving a tender and deep illumination to their gold backgrounds and jewel-like colours. Nor should we ever forget that many people in the 14th century might have seen no more than three or four paintings in a whole lifetime: they would therefore have given them the time and the concentration that we no longer have, and would have appreciated above all else the technical refinement of their execution.

It must also be remembered that much of the city's creative energy in the 1300s was concentrated solely on its greatest project: the cathedral of Santa Maria del Fiore. The vastness and the grandeur of this project were an expression of the wealth and optimism of Florence at this period. But it risked overshooting in its optimism, and would in fact have done so had it not been saved by the scientific brilliance of the following generation. In designing one of the largest churches in existence, the architects had left themselves with a seemingly insoluble problem: the octagonal drum on which the final dome was to be placed was just over 43m in diameter—a distance too great to construct the wooden jig, or 'centring' as it is called, which was necessary for the construction of any solid dome. To Florence's humiliation in the eyes of her neighbours, work on the Duomo stopped, and the building had no dome. It needed a new generation and a radically new and different way of thinking to solve this problem. That solution was to be typical of the mentality and the genius of the Quattrocento.

The Quattrocento

One of the things that had most astonished contemporaries about Giotto's pictorial art was its uncanny ability (as it seemed to them) to give a convincing sense both of human emotion and of spatial reality. What they were observing was not only a change in artistic practice; it was a fundamental change in human thinking. Whereas Byzantine and medieval religious art aimed always to take the gaze of human devotion up and away from the sordid parenthesis of earthly life to an unchanging and golden eternity where emotion and descriptive reality had no place, suddenly, with Giotto, the direction was being reversed and the scenes of spiritual life were being brought down to the world of human reality, put into an earthly setting, given physical depth and weight, and imbued with human feeling. In other words, instead of striving to raise human devotion to the level of the sacred, the sacred was brought down to the level of the human. Many had sensed the beginning of this change in Giotto, but none was to absorb its lesson so completely and so deeply as a young 20-year-old painter, working 100 years after Giotto, by the name of Tommaso di Mone, known as Masaccio (1401–28).

Florentine art—and the achievements of Donatello, Piero della Francesca and Michelangelo, all of whom studied his work in these places—cannot be understood without visiting the church of Santa Maria Novella to see Masaccio's fresco of the *Trinity*, or the Brancacci Chapel in the church of Santa Maria del Carmine, where Masaccio worked, after 1423, on a cycle of frescoes depicting the life of St Peter and other biblical scenes. All the lessons learnt from Giotto are there: the sheer reduction to the essential elements, the narrative urgency, the concentrated sculptural forms, and the calibrated ratio of figure to space. But there is much else that is new: a concern for convincing anatomy and physical presence (see *St Peter Baptising*), for the accurate evocation of three-dimensional space and the grouping of figures in it (see *The Tribute Money*), and a completely new and unflinching sense of human drama (see the electrifying *Expulsion of Adam and Eve from Paradise; p. 276*). These paintings are among the most groundbreaking works in the history of Western art, and no visit to Florence should overlook them. Though Masaccio's works in the Brancacci Chapel are alongside the work of other painters—Masolino, 18 years his elder, and Filippino Lippi, who carried on Masaccio's work after his untimely death at the age of 27—Masaccio's style is so irreducibly different and individual, that it is not hard for even the first-time visitor to distinguish those elements painted by him. Indeed it is very instructive to attempt to do so.

In an altogether gentler and less dramatic way, the Dominican friar Fra' Angelico (1387–1455) had also learnt much from Giotto's example. His works can be found in many locations in the city, but the greatest concentration is in the ex-convent of San Marco, which today functions partly as a museum dedicated to the painter. Here one gets a full sense of the jewel-like brilliance of his works—as if they were illuminated manuscripts enlarged upon panels or walls. Everywhere we look, we find a simplicity and clarity of form learnt from Giotto; but it is Fra' Angelico's delight in clear colour— the characteristic coral pinks and pale blues—that is unforgettable and which, together with the often intricate work in gold on the surface of many of his paintings, imparts a radiance which is far from the spirit of Masaccio's more austere world.

Fra' Angelico loved colour; for Masaccio, it was an afterthought. Fra' Angelico enjoyed extraneous detail; Masaccio rigorously banished it. There is a linear grace and instinctive draughtsmanship in Fra' Angelico; in Masaccio all line is subordinated instead to a powerful sense of volume and sculptural weight. The two painters are completely different. There were, in the end, only a few in Florence who followed Fra' Angelico's instincts—most notably Benozzo Gozzoli (c. 1421–97), whose exquisite and tapestry-like pageant of the *Procession of the Magi to Bethlehem* decorates the walls of a tiny chapel in Palazzo Medici-Riccardi; and, greatest of all, Sandro Botticelli. The mainstream of Florentine painting, however, felt the irresistible influence of Masaccio right down to the time of Michelangelo who, as a young man, must have sat and sketched in the Brancacci Chapel, and never forgot the lessons he learnt there.

Masaccio shows how sculpture and sculptural instincts are never far from the surface in Florentine painting. His contemporary and friend Donatello (1386–1466) was one of the greatest and most versatile sculptors of all time, and it is impossible to say which of the two artists influenced the other more deeply. The sheer scope of Donatello's visual language is astonishing: sometimes solemn, as in the *St George* from Orsanmichele; sometimes riotous, as in the dancing putti and the dissolved architectural divisions of his cantoria for the Duomo, now in the Museo dell'Opera del Duomo; sometimes sensual and elegiac, as in the bronze *David* of the Bargello, one of the first wholly nude pieces to be sculpted in Europe since Antiquity; sometime terrifying, as in the haggard *Mary Magdalene* in the Museo dell'Opera del Duomo; but always profoundly idiosyncratic, technically faultless, and pushing the very limits of conventional taste in his treatment of subject matter.

We know that Masaccio the painter, Donatello the sculptor, Brunelleschi the engineer, and Leon Battista Alberti the theorist were all close friends; all of them in turn were acquainted with Lorenzo Ghiberti, Luca della Robbia, Paolo Uccello, Piero della Francesca, and so forth. But the complexity of human relationships is such that their closeness to one another gave rise at the same time to a cross-fertilisation of ideas and skills, and also to a powerful competitiveness. These two together were an irresistible force, increasing the critical mass and driving forward the achievements of Florentine art. As in Periclean Athens or late 19th-century Paris, the sheer density of contact—friendly and competitive—within a group of artists, coupled with the possibility of unstinting financial support, gave rise to a ferment of activity that was to change European art for ever.

The city itself contributed to the momentum of invention by instituting public competitions for designs for new doors for the Baptistery (1401 and 1425) and for the completion of the cathedral's cupola (1418). Lorenzo Ghiberti (1378–1455), a stranger perhaps to modesty but an artist and metalworker of incomparable technical prowess, won both the competitions for the Baptistery doors. When we compare his far bolder second series of 1425 (created for the east door) with the first series begun in 1403 (on the north entrance), we can see how clearly he has absorbed the influence of Donatello in the intervening years. And it was Donatello, in turn, who had accompanied the person whom Ghiberti had most notably defeated in the 1401 competition, Filippo Brunelleschi (1377–1446), on a journey to Rome immediately after the competition results had been announced. That journey was to teach both artists an immense amount, as they came in contact with the wealth of buildings and sculpture still visible in Rome. It was Brunelleschi's meticulous study of the Pantheon and its dome that would help him understand how to solve the problem of the construction of a dome for Florence's cathedral. His solution had many brilliant aspects; but most importantly it involved throwing away the received idea of a single, vertical 'centring' for the dome, and using instead a one-level, horizontal centring, which rose *pari passu* with the dome's construction, and was dismantled and reconstructed, therefore, with each successive completed ring. The lateral thinking involved, the willingness to return to first principles, to learn from Antiquity, and to embrace new solutions was typical of Florentine ingeniousness and originality: it was to make Brunelleschi the hero of his city.

No painter or sculptor or architect in Florence in the mid-15th century could remain wholly unaffected by these developments, nor by the profound impression left by Brunelleschi's practical demonstration on the steps of the Duomo in 1425 of the principles of perfect pictorial perspective. Brunelleschi produced an instrument consisting of a polished mirror and a painted panel, with a metal bar holding the two at a pre-determined distance from each other. The viewer squinted through a pin-hole in the back of the panel, on which was painted a mirror-image perspective depiction (on a scale of 1:75) of the view of the piazza and the Baptistery. The viewer either saw this depiction reflected in the mirror or, if the mirror was lifted, he would see the piazza itself. If the two scenes were identical and indistinguishable, then Brunelleschi had proved his point: that there is one, and only one, coherent and exact way to represent 3D space in two dimensions. The experiment proved a complex point of optics and geometry, but more perhaps than anything else, it showed how deeply underpinned by science were the developments of the Florentine Renaissance. In some, the influence of such developments became almost obsessive, as in Paolo Uccello's desire to master perspective illusion at all costs in his whimsical, idiosyncratic paintings (*The Battle of San Romano* in the Uffizi and the *Flood* in the cloister of Santa Maria Novella);

or in Andrea del Castagno's emulation of Masaccio's sculptural qualities in the severe and sinewy figures of his brooding *Last Supper*, painted in the refectory of Sant'Apollonia. But perhaps no one assimilated all the lessons together so intelligently nor harmonised them so completely as one painter, born in rural Tuscany but who worked in Florence and who expresses almost better than any the quintessence of Florentine painting—the thoughtful and taciturn Piero della Francesca (c. 1420–92). In him we find the gravity and clarity of Giotto, the limpid colour of Fra' Angelico, the sculptural weight of Masaccio, and the clear logical design of Brunelleschi—all transfigured by a bright Florentine light which once seen can never be forgotten. There is no sentiment in Piero's works, only a profound thoughtfulness.

One of the only artists who remains largely untouched by this Florentine severity was Sandro Filipepi, known as Botticelli (1445–1510), who seems—almost thankfully—to be travelling in a different flight-corridor from all the others. To stand in the Botticelli room in the Uffizi Gallery between his two huge paintings, the *Birth of Venus* and the *Primavera*, is one of the happiest experiences that great painting can offer. Nowhere in Florence does painting so closely resemble music. The pictures can be appreciated simply for their consummate beauty and decorative splendour: but that should not blind us to the fact that they are also complex philosophical expositions. The *Primavera*, for example, is an effortless disquisition on the relationships between different kinds of love, and of the passage of love through the human sphere as it evolves from the earthly passion of a coming spring on the right-hand side of the picture, and is transmuted into a sublime and platonic love, above the clouds which are gently stirred by Hermes's caduceus in the top left of the picture. Commissioned for one of the young, rising stars of the Medici family, these paintings give us an intimation of the rarefied and subtle ideas that circulated in the philosophical *soirées* of Florence's aristocracy.

Botticelli's dalliance with that sophisticated world was always fragile, however. In the autumn of his very productive life, he fell—if we are to believe what Vasari tells us—under the spell of the terrifying preaching of Girolamo Savonarola. In thrall to Savonarola's fundamentalist rejection of the vanity of Florentine society, legend has it that Botticelli consigned many of his paintings and drawings to the flames. True or not, it is certainly the case that Florence was deeply shaken by the Savonarola episode (*see p. 34*). But in the aftermath of this cultural earthquake a new generation of artists, in every way as great as the one before, was waiting to emerge.

The Cinquecento

The image of David, the young boy who slew the giant Goliath, had always been dear to the Florentine imagination as a symbol of the tiny and virtuous republic of Florence in its struggle against the monolithic forces at its borders—the Papal States of Rome, and the Duchy of Milan. For this reason, sculptures of David recur frequently throughout early Florentine art. In January of 1504, a committee was convened to decide where the latest and greatest *David* yet should be placed in the city. On the committee sat Leonardo da Vinci, Botticelli, Perugino, Andrea della Robbia and Filippino Lippi—amongst a total of 30 distinguished artists. The *David* in question had been sculpted by Michelangelo Buonarroti from a huge block of marble that had been taking up space in the cathedral workshops ever since an earlier project on it had been abandoned.

Michelangelo (1475–1564) was only 26 at the time he received the commission for *David*, and 29 when he completed it. The *David* he had sculpted was triumphantly nude, brooding and vast, when compared with Donatello's winsome version of almost a century earlier: he stands in a pose sacred to the aesthetic of ancient Greek and Roman statuary—neither walking, nor standing. His magnificent profile conceals a new and more troubled spirit—one in which a restlessness and grandeur have replaced the human ease and human scale of the art of the early Renaissance. Alongside a surviving preparatory sketch for this *David*, we find a few curious words written by the artist: these have often (perhaps fancifully) been interpreted as implying that Michelangelo saw the *David* as his bid to slay his own personal Goliath, namely Leonardo da Vinci (1452–1519), who, over 20 years his elder, was then the prince of artists in Florence. True or not, this hypothesis evokes an important fact: that these two giant spirits, so different from one another and yet so similar in many ways, dominate the psychic landscape of early 16th-century Florence in a way that leaves little space for the other artists of the age.

Leonardo was agnostic; Michelangelo, a devout believer. Leonardo appears to have been gregarious, humorous, good-looking, if not a little vain; Michelangelo was combative, short, sinewy, unnaturally serious and solitary, and gave little thought to outward appearance. The physical and material fascinated Leonardo; the invisible and abstract fascinated Michelangelo. Leonardo's curiosity knew no limits as he turned his brilliant mind to every aspect of the world around him: Michelangelo returned again and again with increasing intensity to the same few artistic passions. Yet both had a prodigious capacity for work; both had a profoundly introverted and thoughtful nature; both were perfectionists with a persistent tendency to leave projects unfinished. The very fact that we are here making these comments about their personalities is another indication of the changing status of the artist in the Renaissance: the artist is no longer the anonymous artisan, but a complex figure whose passions and idiosyncrasies are inextricable from his creations. With the coming of the Renaissance, psychology and art are no longer separable.

Leonardo is today a strangely invisible presence in the city: in part because his greatest paintings are elsewhere, and in part because so much of his achievement was in his writings. On his death he left few more than a dozen pictures which we can safely say are his. Of these, not all are finished, many have been cut down, and most would now be unrecognisable to Leonardo because of changes which have occurred in the oil medium with which he so relentlessly experimented in his search for perfection. But to look closely at the surface of any one of his paintings is to witness something miraculous. The transparency, subtlety and perceptible depth of the paint surface can be compared only with the very finest Flemish masters. It is all peculiarly un-Florentine. None of this could have been possible without the new medium of oil which Leonardo tried unstintingly to master. And in this he could not have been further from the technique of Michelangelo.

Michelangelo was first and foremost a sculptor and architect, and this is apparent even in his paintings, where there are vigorous and confident hatching strokes, as he uses his brush like a chisel. He never enjoyed painting; he found it a torment, and complained that he had been dragged to Rome with a 'halter about my neck' to paint the Sistine Chapel for the pope. It is instructive to look at his *Pietà* in the Museo dell'Opera del Duomo, which was intended to mark his own tomb in the cathedral. It is left unfinished like the majority of his sculptures, but was given some semblance of completeness by his pupil, Tiberio Calcagni, after Michelangelo himself had abandoned the piece and smashed part of it in rage at the appearance of a fault line in the marble, at a point when much of the preliminary work had already been done. The vivacity of the claw-chisel strokes with which Michelangelo delicately draws out the form of Christ's torso and of the face pressed against his mother's, as if in a pen and ink drawing, is astonishing, and forms a fascinating comparison with the flat and pedestrian strokes of his pupil's work on the head and the leathery face of Mary Magdalene. Michelangelo's passion for his material made the stone become a sensitive, obedient and living substance, completely at one with his intentions.

To understand Michelangelo's architectural genius, we must turn to the Biblioteca Laurenziana, the library commissioned by Giuliano de' Medici (Pope Clement VII) and built according to Michelangelo's design. The justly famous vestibule which precedes the library reading-room is one of the most extraordinary spaces in the history of Western architecture. The vocabulary of architectural elements it contains is precisely what we might find in a serene and perfectly proportioned interior by Brunelleschi: likewise, the sober white colour and the grey *pietra serena*. But that vocabulary no longer expresses the meanings we expect of it: it has become, with Michelangelo, a highly original, dense and allusive poem. Architecture is often at its greatest when it succeeds in surprising us: and everything in this small space does just that. The proportions confound us; the elements of construction seem iconoclastically to do the opposite of what is expected of them, and, in the midst of it all, the staircase bursts out into the space before us like a flow of lava that cannot even be contained by its railings—more a piece of sculpture than of architecture, made of turbulent oval shapes and strange volutes. But then we enter the library itself, and order, serenity and enlightenment return. The contrast is total. But Michelangelo reserves just one last twist: the block of grey *pietra serena* that forms the pediment over the door at the far end of the reading-room is traversed diagonally by a minute and perfect line of some natural, white, geological impurity. This time Michelangelo has not raged at the defect as he did with the *Pietà*, but has exalted it. It is the master's finest punctuation mark: never had a humble imperfection become such a brilliant protagonist.

After Michelangelo

Michelangelo's death in 1564 left the artistic community of Florence in a stall. His presence had been so monumental, and his pre-eminence in all fields so total, that life after Michelangelo was hard for the Florentines to contemplate. To any artist living at that time, Michelangelo had always been there, always revered and endlessly producing works of genius for as long as could be remembered. How then were they to proceed now that he was gone? What direction to follow? But the story does not just end there: Michelangelo was more directly involved in the crisis which was effectively to end—or at least drastically to shorten—Florence's artistic future. He deliberately turned his back on the one important technical revolution which was to carry painting forward into the next four centuries: the development of oil painting, as against egg-tempera and fresco technique. This inconspicuous but far-reaching technical revolution was to transform both art and the artist, and to give them a new life. It liberated the artist from his studio of assistants, it freed him to paint in front of nature, it gave him new territories of possibility in the description of light and surface, and the creation of mood and colour, and, when combined with the canvas support currently being developed in Venice, it allowed works to travel easily and be seen in places they could never have reached before. The potential of oil as a medium had captivated the far-sighted Leonardo; but he was now gone from Florence for good. Oil paintings from Flanders, too, had come to Florence and caused a sensation. Michelangelo had even seen them. People held their breath to hear what the great master's opinion might be. And it was this:

> …that it was all very well, and could bring tears to the eyes of the devout, but these were mostly women, young girls, clerics, nuns and gentlefolk without much understanding for the true harmony of art.

Michelangelo had spoken, and, to all intents and purposes, oil painting was now dead in the water in Florence. And as Florence stalled, the artists of Venice embraced the new technique, and forged ahead evolving a new kind of painting that was to shape and influence virtually all European art for the next 300 hundred years, and which was to make Florentine painting suddenly look remote and archaic. Titian was a contemporary of Michelangelo: he said himself that he had no desire to emulate Michelangelo's greatness for fear of being judged by those high standards. But history has proven him to be a painter of a far greater influence than Michelangelo, showing the way forward to later generations of artists. Michelangelo, whose greatness is no less unimpeachable, was to become instead the closing chapter in the story of a city that had once led the world.

The story ends, ironically, with the person who first wrote it down. Giorgio Vasari (1511–74) came as a young man to Florence from his native Arezzo. He idolised and was eventually befriended by Michelangelo. He was a not indifferent painter, in technical terms, and an architect of genuine brilliance, designing what is for the visitor one of the most memorable buildings in Florence, the Uffizi, appropriately now the home to the firmament of Florentine painting which Vasari so admired and did so much to promote. Fifteen hundred years earlier, Plutarch had paid eloquent tribute to the city of Athens in a series of *Lives* of the personalities that had made her great. But both Plutarch's and Vasari's *Lives*, brimming as they are with urbanity and insight, are fundamentally autumnal works of profound nostalgia. By their very urge to look back and describe the greatness in words, they close the wide arc of time in which their cities' greatness was incarnate instead in monuments and deeds and wondrous works of art.

PIAZZA DELLA SIGNORIA

Piazza della Signoria (*map 1, 6*) is Florence's most imposing square. It is totally closed to traffic, but always animated by numerous tourists and Florentines, and you can usually find a peaceful corner from which to contemplate this great space and ponder the history of the city. The magnificent stone façade and tall tower of Palazzo Vecchio have dominated the square ever since the first years of the 14th century, when this fortified palace was built as the residence of the city's ruling priors. For more than a century it was the tallest edifice in Florence, and its design was copied for the seat of government in many other Tuscan towns. The history of the piazza has followed that of Palazzo Vecchio. The area at its foot was laid out as Piazza del Popolo in 1307. During the 14th century, houses were demolished in order to expand the piazza, and by 1385, when it was fully paved and heavy traffic was banned, it had nearly reached its present dimensions. The piazza was used for centuries as the place where the *parlamento*, or assembly of Florentine citizens, would gather in moments of crisis. It was also the scene of public ceremonies, and today popular celebrations and concerts are held here and the city's most elegant café, Rivoire, still flourishes.

Sculptures in the piazza

The numerous statues which decorate both the square and the medieval Loggia della Signoria were made by some of Florence's leading sculptors and are a special feature of the townscape. In front of Palazzo Vecchio is a **copy of the statue of *Judith and Holofernes* by Donatello**; the original is inside (*see p. 48*). It was the first of all the statues to be installed in the piazza, after its confiscation from Palazzo Medici following the family's temporary expulsion in 1494. The republican rule that followed this expulsion was to last for 18 years. During that time the most famous of all Florentine statues was commissioned: **Michelangelo's *David***, a replica of which stands outside the palace. This great work was commissioned by the city of Florence in 1501 and set up here in 1504 to symbolise the victory of republicanism over tyranny. When it was unveiled, it was heralded as a masterpiece and at once established Michelangelo as the greatest Florentine artist of his age. The original was moved to the Accademia in 1873 (*see p. 166*).

In 1534 Michelangelo left Florence for Rome never to return, and it was in this same year that the **colossal statue of *Hercules and Cacus*** was sculpted by Baccio Bandinelli, in a disastrous attempt to imitate the *David*. All the defects of this two-figure group were pointed out by Cellini to Cosimo I in the presence of the sculptor, but despite its failure Bandinelli, under the secure patronage of the Medici grand duke and in the absence of Michelangelo, quickly became the most important sculptor in Florence and remained unrivalled for some two decades (his most successful works were carried out for the Opera del Duomo). He also carved one of the bizarre statues between the two colossal figures here (the other is by his pupil Vincenzo de' Rossi).

Beyond a **copy of Donatello's** *Marzocco*, the heraldic lion of Florence (the original is in the Bargello; *see p. 89*), is the **Neptune Fountain** (1560–75). The colossal flaccid figure of Neptune is always known to Florentines as *il Biancone* ('the white giant'). It was carved from a block of marble which, despite the opposition of Cellini, was first offered to Bandinelli and on his death to Ammannati. In the more successful and elegant bronze groups on the basin, Ammannati was assisted by other sculptors, including Giambologna.

The **porphyry disc** with an inscription in the pavement in front of the fountain marks the spot where Savonarola was burnt at the stake on 23rd May 1498.

Girolamo Savonarola (1452–98)

Girolamo Savonarola, a native of Ferrara, became a Dominican friar in Bologna. In 1489 he came to Florence and was appointed prior of San Marco just two years later. He was famous for his eloquence as a preacher, and in his fiery sermons— which he declared were divinely inspired—he denounced luxury and wantonness and was particularly savage in his attacks on Florence's ruling class. It was Cosimo il Vecchio who had claimed that 'you cannot govern a state with paternosters'. Savonarola maintained that there was no other way for a state to be governed. His advocation of theocracy and his fierce puritan streak made him unpalatable to many, but he had a wide following as his congregations show (his sermons had to be held in the Duomo as the only church large enough to hold them).

He was more than a demagogue: he was also a learned theologian, admired by humanists such as Pico della Mirandola and Poliziano. Botticelli was one of the Renaissance artists probably influenced by him, both in the content of his sacred paintings and in his burning of earlier secular works. Michelangelo is said to have commented as an old man that he could still hear the friar's voice ringing in his ears. Although Savonarola had been critical of Lorenzo the Magnificent, it seems Lorenzo called him to his death-bed in order to receive his blessing. But Savonarola remained an enemy of the Medici, and his address to the Great Council in 1496 did much to strengthen republican zeal in the government of the city. Success made him reckless, and his public criticism of the licentious Borgia pope Alexander VI eventually led to his excommunication. He was accused of heresy and sedition, and was hanged and burned, together with two of his fellow friars, in Piazza della Signoria, where, at his instigation only a few years earlier, bonfires had been lit to destroy profane books and works of art. Every year on 23rd May, the anniversary of his death, a ceremony is held here in his memory by those who consider him a martyr. The feelings he arouses among historians today are as divided as were the reactions of his 15th-century contemporaries.

On a line with the statues across the front of Palazzo Vecchio is a beautiful bronze **equestrian monument to Cosimo I** by Giambologna (1595). It was commissioned by the grand duke's son Ferdinando I, and on the base are scenes of Cosimo's coronation and conquest of Siena. The horse's head is particularly fine. Cosimo is also commemorated by the bust (*removed for restoration at the time of writing*) on the façade of Palazzo Uguccioni (no. 7): its unusual design has sometimes been attributed to Michelangelo.

Loggia della Signoria

The Loggia della Signoria is also known as Loggia dei Lanzi after the *lanzichenecchi* (bodyguards) of Cosimo I, who were stationed here. Its three beautiful lofty arches, semicircular in form, break free from Gothic shapes and anticipate the Renaissance. The loggia was intended not only as an ornament to the square but also for use by government officials during public ceremonies (and in the 18th century it came to be used as an open-air museum of sculpture). It was built in 1376–82 by Simone Talenti, son of the architect Francesco, with the help of Benci di Cione, but the design is probably by the more famous architect Orcagna. In the spandrels are seven marble reliefs of Virtues (1384–89) against a blue-enamelled ground, designed by Agnolo Gaddi. It is thought that the head of *Faith* was probably substituted by Donatello, after the original fell to the ground. The columns are decorated with (worn) statuettes and lions' heads, and have composite capitals in *pietra forte*; there are two elaborate corbels on the back wall.

Cellini's magnificent bronze **Perseus**, in which Perseus exhibits the Medusa's severed head, was commissioned by Cosimo I in 1545; it is considered Cellini's masterpiece. It was his last public commission and took him nine years to complete: afterwards, when Bandinelli was favoured by the grand dukes, Cellini retired to write his *Autobiography*, where he provides a graphic description of the difficulties he encountered while casting the *Perseus* (during which time his studio caught fire and he retired to bed with a fever). He saved the situation at the last moment by seizing all his pewter plates and bowls and throwing them into the melting-pot, and he was thus able to found the statue in one piece, an extraordinary technical achievement. It is known that his studio was at no. 59 Via della Pergola (*map 4, 5*), and this was where he died in 1571. The statue's elaborate pedestal (replaced by a copy; the original is in the Bargello; *see p. 87*), using classical motifs, incorporates bronze statuettes and a bas-relief of Perseus rescuing Andromeda.

The three-figure group of the **Rape of the Sabines** was commissioned for this position from Giambologna by Francesco I in 1583. The elaborate serpentine composition is designed to be seen from every angle, and this was one of the works most admired by the Flemish sculptor's contemporaries. Giambologna also carved the statue of **Hercules and the Centaur**, with the help of his pupil Pietro Francavilla. The two other dramatic statues in the centre, even if at first glance difficult to date, were made at very different times: **Ajax with the Body of Patroclus** is a Roman copy of a Greek original of 240 BC, which entered the Medici collections in 1570 (restored in the 17th and 19th centuries), and the amazing four-figure group illustrating the **Rape of Polyxena** is the masterpiece of Pio Fedi (1866). It is also difficult to tell which of the lions at the entrance is the Roman work and which was made in the late 16th century (that on the left). The Roman statues (2nd century AD) along the back wall came from the Villa Medici in Rome.

Palazzo della Mercanzia

Apart from Palazzo Vecchio and the Loggia della Signoria, the most interesting and earliest building in the square is **Palazzo della Mercanzia** on the east side (at no. 10, behind the equestrian monument). This was built in 1359 for the Mercanzia, an institution founded in 1308 to protect the interests of those Florentine merchants who belonged to the most important commercial guilds. It acted as an independent civil court which settled internal disagreements as well as disputes with foreign traders, and it came to regulate much of the economic activity in Florence throughout the 14th century. Its important position was underlined by the presence of its headquarters here, very close to Palazzo della Signoria. Today the worn frieze of the guilds' coats of arms marks the dimensions of the original building, which had three ground-floor arches and five windows on each of the two upper storeys (the top floor is a later addition). It had an impressive façade but was only two bays deep, and the façade is slightly curving since it was expected to adapt to the urban plan for the piazza. Since 2008 it has been occupied by the offices of Gucci, the most famous of the fashion houses founded in Florence.

The most powerful guild in Florence, the Arte di Calimala, which represented the merchants of wholesale imported cloth, set up their headquarters in the late 14th century in the short lane on the opposite side of the piazza, still called simply **Calimaruzza**. Their *stemma*, an eagle holding a bale of cloth in its talons, can be seen on a house here, and also above the elegant shop window of Pineider (one of the best-known old-established leather shops and stationers in Florence). Calimaruzza is one of a number of narrow medieval lanes leading into the square, the most interesting of which is the dark Chiasso dei Baroncelli, with the 14th-century Palazzo Benini-Formichi, just to the right of the Loggia della Signoria.

The other buildings, including the huge neo-Renaissance edifice directly opposite the façade of Palazzo Vecchio (on the ground floor of which is the elegant Caffè Rivoire), mostly date from the 19th century.

PALAZZO VECCHIO

Map 1, 6. Open 9–7, Thur 9–2; T: 055 276 8224. Reduction for those aged 18–25 and over 65, and further reduction for children; family tickets also available. Combined ticket with the Brancacci Chapel valid 3 months. 'Secret' itineraries (percorsi segreti) of areas not normally open to the public (including the battlements and remains of the Roman theatre below its foundations) are shown on special tours, also in English, which are highly recommended. There is also an excellent didactic department for all ages run by an organisation called 'Museo dei Ragazzi' (see p. 50). For information and to book a visit: T: 055 276 8224 or enquire at the ticket office. www.palazzovecchio-familymuseum.it.

There are entrances on Piazza della Signoria and Via della Ninna. Room numbers given in the text refer to the plans. In situ the rooms are only named in Italian.

Detail of Cellini's *Perseus*, with Palazzo Vecchio. Photograph by Vincenzo Balocchi c. 1934.

PALAZZO VECCHIO

Palazzo Vecchio, also known as Palazzo della Signoria, was the medieval Palazzo del Popolo and is still the town hall of Florence. The palace stands on part of the site of the Roman theatre, built in the 1st century AD. The *priori* (the governing magistrates of the medieval city) lived here during their two months' tenure of office. In times of trouble the bell in the tower, called the 'Martinella', summoned citizens to *parlamento* in the square below. It also rang out on 11th August 1944 to announce the liberation of the city by Allied forces (and it still rings on that day every year to commemorate the event). In 1433, Cosimo il Vecchio was imprisoned in the tower before being (temporarily) exiled. The building became known as Palazzo della Signoria during the Republican governments of the 15th century, and alterations were carried out inside by Michelozzo, Giuliano and Benedetto da Maiano and Domenico Ghirlandaio. At the end of the century, after the expulsion of the Medici, the huge Salone dei Cinquecento was built by Cronaca to house the Great Council.

One of the most significant moments in the history of the palace came in 1540 when Cosimo I moved here from Palazzo Medici. Vasari and later Buontalenti were called in to redecorate the building, now called Palazzo Ducale, and to extend it at the back without, however, altering the exterior aspect on Piazza della Signoria. The surviving interior decoration also dates mainly from the time of Vasari, who produced frescoes and paintings honouring his patron. His assistants included Marco da Faenza and the Netherlandish painter Jan van der Straet (known in Italian as Giovanni Stradano).

The building became known as Palazzo Vecchio only after 1549, when the Medici grand dukes took up residence in Palazzo Pitti. The provisional governments of united Italy in 1848 and 1859 met here, and from 1865 to 1871 it housed the Chamber of Deputies and the Foreign Ministry when Florence was capital of the Kingdom of Italy. Since 1872 it has been the seat of the municipal government.

The exterior

Palazzo Vecchio is an imposing fortress-palace built in *pietra forte* on a trapezoidal plan, to a design traditionally attributed to Arnolfo di Cambio (1299–1302). The façade has remained virtually unchanged, with its graceful divided windows and a battlemented gallery. It became the prototype of many other *palazzi comunali* in Tuscany. Until the 15th century it was the tallest edifice in the city; the tower (1310), asymmetrically placed, is 95m high.

The flank of the building on Piazza della Signoria includes the battlemented 14th-century nucleus of the palace, the unfinished exterior of the Salone dei Cinquecento, with a hipped roof and marble window, and the handsome façade added by Buontalenti in Via de' Gondi. The 16th-century additions at the back of the building on Via dei Leoni incorporate medieval houses. On Via della Ninna parts of the 14th-century masonry can be seen, and extensions of various dates (the three large windows high up, with two smaller ones below, belong to the 15th-century Salone dei Cinquecento).

A mechanical clock, which activated a bell, was first installed on the tower in 1353, and was superseded by another in 1502 by the celebrated clockmaker Lorenzo della Volpaia. The first pendulum clock was installed in the mid-17th century by Philipp Treffler of Augsburg, on a design by Galileo's pupil Vincenzo Viviani, and in 1667 this was substituted by yet another clock made by Georg Lederle, also from Augsburg, when for the first time a clockface was provided on the exterior, painted by Jacopo Chiavistelli, which was renewed in 1936 and still adorns the tower today.

Above the main entrance is a frieze dedicated to *Cristo Re* (Christ the King), set up in 1529, with the monogram of Christ flanked by the two symbolic lions of Florence.

GROUND FLOOR

The courtyard (*Cortile*) was reconstructed by Michelozzo in 1453 and the decorations were added in 1565 by Giorgio Vasari as part of the elaborate preparations for the celebration of the marriage between Francesco, son of Cosimo I (*see p. 43*), and Joanna of Austria, youngest daughter of the Holy Roman Emperor Ferdinand I. The columns were covered with stucco and the vaults and walls painted with grotesques and views of Austrian cities, to help make the new grand duchess feel at home.

The fountain designed by Vasari bears a copy of Verrocchio's charming little *Putto Holding a Dolphin* (c. 1470), a bronze made for a fountain at the Medici villa at Careggi. The original is preserved inside the palace (*see p. 44*).

In the adjoining courtyard (with the ticket office and bookshop) can be seen the 15th-century weather-vane with the *Marzocco* lion, which was removed from the top of the tower in 1981 (when it was replaced by a copy), near a fragment of the original terracotta pavement in herring-bone style.

In the large rectangular Sala d'Arme, the only room on this floor which survives from the 14th-century structure, exhibitions are held. The rest of the ground floor is taken up with local government offices. The monumental grand staircase by Vasari ascends in a theatrical double flight to the first floor (there is also a lift).

FIRST FLOOR

(1) Salone dei Cinquecento: This immense hall (53.5m by 22m, and 18m high) was built by Cronaca in 1495 for the meetings of the new legislative body of the Republican government, the *Consiglio Maggiore* (Great Council). But the room was transformed and heightened by Vasari in 1563–65 when the present decoration was carried out in celebration of Cosimo I, who moved into the palace three years after he became duke in 1537. The iconographical scheme was devised by Vasari's friend, the prior of the Spedale degli Innocenti, Vincenzo Borghini, who was an outstanding figure in 16th-century Florence and counsellor to Cosimo on artistic and literary matters. He was later to provide the ceremonial procedure for Cosimo's funeral, as he had for that of Michelangelo.

In the centre of the magnificent ceiling is a tondo with the apotheosis of the duke surrounded by the *stemme* of the guilds. The other panels, by Vasari

and his workshop, including Jan van der Straet (Giovanni Stradano), Jacopo Zucchi and Giovanni Battista Naldini, represent allegories of the cities of Tuscany under Florentine dominion, the foundations and early growth of Florence, and the victories over Siena and Pisa (1554–55 and 1496–1509 respectively). On the walls are huge frescoes by the same artists illustrating three more episodes in the wars with Pisa (entrance wall) and Siena.

The most important sculptures in the room line the two long walls: Michelangelo's *Victory* **(A)** is a strongly knit two-figure group, probably intended for a niche in the tomb of Julius II in Rome. It was presented to Cosimo I by Michelangelo's nephew in 1565 and set up here by Vasari as a celebration of the victory of Cosimo I over Siena. The serpentine form of the principal figure was frequently copied by later Mannerist sculptors.

Giambologna's original plaster model for *Virtue Overcoming Vice* (or *Florence Victorious over Pisa*) **(B)** was commissioned as a pendant to Michelangelo's *Victory* (the marble is in the Bargello).

The other 16th-century statues around the walls **(C)** represent the *Labours of Hercules* and are the best works of Vincenzo de' Rossi, pupil of Bandinelli.

Above the raised dais, or **Udienza (2)**, the narrow triangular section of the ceiling (produced by the irregular plan of the building) was filled in with putti and self-portraits of Vasari's assistants. On the dais are statues of distinguished members of the Medici family: Cosimo I, Giovanni delle Bande Nere, Leo X (seated), Duke Alessandro, Clement VII (crowning the emperor Charles V) and Francesco I. Many of them, dressed as Romans, are by Baccio Bandinelli. On the wall at the other end of the room there are niches with four antique Roman statues.

LEONARDO & MICHELANGELO IN THE SALA DEI CINQUECENTO

Despite the magnificent decorations in this vast hall, they are nothing to what was originally planned for it in the very first years of the 16th century, when two of the greatest painters who ever lived were both in the city: Leonardo da Vinci and Michelangelo. The governors were quick to take advantage of this extraordinary circumstance and commissioned them to decorate the two long walls with huge murals representing two famous Florentine victories: that over Milan at Anghiari in 1440, and that over Pisa at Cascina in 1364. Leonardo experimented, without success, with a new technique of mural painting, and completed only a fragment of the work before leaving Florence for Milan in 1506. Michelangelo only had time to produce the cartoon for the *Battle of Cascina* before being called to Rome by Julius II. But the cartoons of both works and the fragment painted by Leonardo were famous in their day and frequently copied and studied by contemporary painters (a rare copy of a detail of Leonardo's work survives in the Sala di Ester; *see p. 46*). The cartoons were subsequently lost (Michelangelo's huge chalk drawing was some 116m square and was therefore probably also cut up and passed through many hands), and it is not known whether Leonardo's fragment had disappeared by the middle of the 16th century or was destroyed by order of Cosimo I to make way for the new decorations. The idea of its possible survival beneath the plasterwork continues to tantalise art historians to this day.

---

(3) The Studiolo: This tiny study, reached by an inconspicuous door in the entrance wall, is a charming, windowless room created by Vasari and his school in 1570–75, with the help of Vincenzo Borghini, for Cosimo's son Francesco I. Entirely decorated with paintings and bronze statuettes, it celebrates Francesco's interest in the natural sciences and alchemy and is a masterpiece of Florentine Mannerist decoration. It is on a much smaller scale than the Salone dei

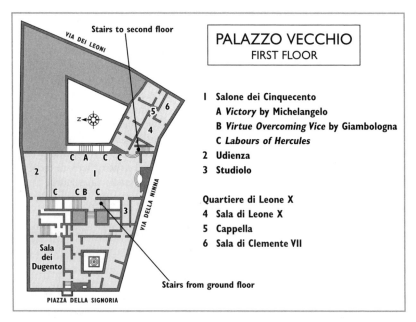

PALAZZO VECCHIO
FIRST FLOOR

1 **Salone dei Cinquecento**
A *Victory* by Michelangelo
B *Virtue Overcoming Vice* by Giambologna
C *Labours of Hercules*
2 **Udienza**
3 **Studiolo**

Quartiere di Leone X
4 **Sala di Leone X**
5 **Cappella**
6 **Sala di Clemente VII**

Cinquecento and hence much easier to appreciate.

The present entrance from the Salone was opened later and unfortunately it can now only be seen from the doorway. The original entrance from the private rooms of the dukes is used in one of the *percorsi segreti* (*see p. 50*), when you are also allowed into the interior.

The lower row of paintings conceals cupboards in which Francesco kept his treasures. On the barrel vault, by Il Poppi, are allegories of the four Elements and portraits by Bronzino of Francesco's parents, Cosimo I and Eleanor of Toledo. The four walls each symbolise one of the four Elements, with paintings and bronzes by the leading artists of the day (including Vincenzo Danti, Santi di Tito, Alessandro Allori, Giambologna and Bartolomeo Ammannati).

Quartiere di Leone X

This well-preserved suite of rooms was decorated in 1555–62 for Cosimo I by Vasari and assistants (including the Netherlandish painter Jan van der Straet), to illustrate the political history of the Medici family. Two rooms and the chapel are open to the public; the others are used by the Mayor of Florence.

(4) Sala di Leone X: The paintings on the walls and ceiling illustrate the life of Cardinal Giovanni de' Medici, son of Lorenzo the Magnificent and later Pope Leo X (the first ever Florentine pope). The pink-and-white terracotta pavement survives, as well as the fireplace designed by Ammannati.

THE MEDICI AT PALAZZO VECCHIO

Cosimo I (duke 1537–70; grand duke 1570–74)

Cosimo became duke in 1537, following the murder of his cousin Alessandro. Even though both pope and Holy Roman Emperor had combined forces to see the Medici reinstated seven years before, Cosimo managed to keep the Tuscan state free from any more outside interference during his long reign, and brought the subject cities of Tuscany firmly under Florentine rule. In 1540 he left the Medici palace and moved into Palazzo della Signoria to assert his position publicly as leader of the government. Various suites of rooms in the palace were frescoed by Vasari, culminating in the 1560s with the decoration of the huge Salone dei Cinquecento, which celebrates the rule of Cosimo through elaborate allegories. He was, all in all, an enlightened despot who commissioned works of art and architecture to embellish Florence as well as to glorify his own name. In 1549 his wife, Eleanor of Toledo, used part of her immense fortune to buy the even grander Palazzo Pitti, which became the official seat of the Medici dynasty.

Francesco I (grand duke 1574–87)

Francesco was an introvert and a chemist and alchemist, little interested in affairs of state. His first marriage, to Joanna of Austria, was loveless and unhappy, and he conducted a long liaison with Bianca Cappello, a beautiful Venetian girl who had fled to Florence with her husband at the age of 15. Medici protection saved her from her family's ireful revenge. Joanna was congenitally deformed and childbirth was an ordeal for her. She died during the course of her eighth pregnancy, of a ruptured uterus, aged only 31 (in 1578). Francesco married Bianca scarcely two months later.

Francesco made much use of the Mannerist architect Bernardo Buontalenti (who earned the sobriquet 'delle Girandole' from the whirling pyrotechnics he created for his patrons' masques), and commissioned a number of works from Giambologna including the famous *Rape of the Sabines* in the Loggia della Signoria. He also built two of the most beautiful small rooms in Florence, the Tribuna in the Uffizi and the Studiolo in Palazzo Vecchio. It was Francesco who invented the idea of making mosaics out of *pietre dure*, so founding a craft which was practised for centuries in Florence. But perhaps his greatest achievement was to assemble all the family pictures and antiquities in the Uffizi, thus introducing the idea of keeping the Medici treasures together in a single place. He died without male heirs and was succeeded by his brother Ferdinando.

(5) Cappella: In this tiny chapel, the wedding between Isabella, daughter of Cosimo I, and Alfonso d'Este was cel- ebrated, and the secret marriage between Francesco I and Bianca Cappello took place. The altarpiece is a copy made in in 1589 of the *Madonna dell'Impannata* by Raphael, now in Palazzo Pitti (*see p. 237*). It is flanked by *Cosimo I as St Damian* and *Cosimo il Vecchio as St Cosmas*, the Medici patron saints, both good works by Vasari.

(6) Sala di Clemente VII: This room, the mayor's office until 2007, was decorated in 1556–62 by Vasari and Jan van der Straet. The scene of the siege of Florence by the imperial troops of Charles V shows a remarkable panorama of the city, seen from the south. Outside the walls are the tents of the imperial army. The only 'action' in progress is the white smoke from the cannon fire from the hill of San Miniato. Florence looks particularly vulnerable and indeed its inhabitants suffered terrible privations during these months (Oct 1529–Aug 1530), when food supplies dwindled and disease broke out. By the time the last republican government was forced to surrender and the Medici were returned to power (paving the way for their dynastic ducal reign), some 30,000 civilians had died out of a total population of around 90,000.

Steep stairs decorated with pretty grotesques lead up to the second floor, past an interesting fresco (c. 1558) by Jan van der Straet of the fireworks in Piazza della Signoria celebrating the festival of St John the Baptist (*see p. 349*).

SECOND FLOOR

Quartiere degli Elementi

This group of rooms is entered to the left at the top of the stairs. The walls and ceilings are decorated with allegories of the Elements and Classical divinities, again intended as a glorification of the Medici, and also by Vasari and assistants. Some of the ceilings are finely carved and some of the pink-and-white terracotta floors survive. There are also some 17th-century cabinets exquisitely decorated with tortoiseshell and *pietre dure*.

(7) Sala degli Elementi: In the deeply recessed ceiling there are good panel paintings illustrating the four Elements.

(8) Terrazzo di Saturno: This lovely terrace, with delicately carved eaves, has a delightful view of Florence.

(9) Sala di Ercole: The ceiling, by Vasari, shows scenes from the life of Hercules. Here are displayed some of the most beautiful cabinets.

(10) Sala delle Grottesche: This small room takes its name from the grotesques on the ceiling.

(11) Terrazzo di Giunone: This was enclosed in the 19th century but was once open on three sides and surrounded by a hanging garden: only one wall still has frescoes and a lovely stucco niche. Here is displayed Verrocchio's charming *Putto with a Dolphin*, the original removed from the courtyard below.

(12) Sala di Giove: The ceiling, by Vasari, shows Jove being suckled by the goat Amalthea.

(13) Sala di Opi: The terracotta floor is particularly beautiful and there is another fine ceiling, carved by Battista di Marco del Tasso.

(14) Sala di Cerere: The ceiling shows Ceres searching for her daughter

Cosimo I in the guise of St Damian (one of the Medici patron saints). Detail of a painting by Vasari, dating from around 1557, in the chapel in the Quartiere di Leone X in Palazzo Vecchio.

Persephone, surrounded by putti with garlands and other mythological figures. **(15) Scrittoio di Calliope:** The charming ceiling painting of Calliope (Muse of epic poetry) is by Vasari, the grotesques by Marco da Faenza and the late 16th-century stained-glass window by Walter of Antwerp (the only one of this date to survive in the palace). In this tiny room, now sadly empty, Cosimo kept his most precious treasures, including miniatures, gems, coins and bronze statuettes (Etruscan, Roman and Renaissance). When he purchased the ancient bronze statue of Minerva (now in the Museo Archeologico; *see p. 177*), he is known to have kept it here for a while also. He would take refuge here from his busy life and enjoy his beautiful treasures in solitude.

On the other side of the stairs there is access to the **balcony (16)** which leads across the end of the Sala dei Cinquecento, providing a splendid view of the huge hall.

Quartiere di Eleonora di Toledo

This suite of rooms was the apartment used by Eleanor of Toledo, the wife of Cosimo I and daughter of the Viceroy of Naples.

(17) Cappella di Eleonora: The chapel was decorated by Bronzino in 1541–43, and is one of his most important and original works. On the vault, divided by festoons, are *St Francis Receiving the Stigmata*, *St Jerome*, *St John the Evangelist on Patmos* and *St Michael the Archangel*. On the walls are episodes from the life of Moses, which may have a symbolic reference to Cosimo I. Bronzino's original altarpiece of the *Lamentation* was sent to France by Cosimo, so the artist was asked to replace it with the present replica. **(18) Camera Verde:** The vault is painted with grotesques by Ridolfo del Ghirlandaio (c. 1540), which include a great variety of delightful birds. The duchess's tiny study preserves its ceiling painted by Francesco Salviati. It used to have an iron chest where Eleanor, known to be an astute businesswoman, would keep her money and accounts. **(19) Sala delle Sabine:** The ceiling painting shows the story of the Sabine Women. **(20) Sala di Ester:** The pretty frieze shows putti intertwined in the letters of Eleanor's name. A painting of 1557 showing the struggle to take possession of the battle standard is probably the best copy that has survived of the lost fragment of the central part of the *Battle of Anghiari* by Leonardo (*see p. 41*). **(21) Sala di Penelope:** The ceiling has a fine frieze by Jan van der Straet. **(22) Sala di Gualdrada:** The frieze at the top of the wall shows charming views of festivals in the *piazze* of Florence. The cabinet in *pietre dure* and mother of pearl has mythological scenes.

A **passageway (23)** connects Eleanor of Toledo's apartment with the older rooms of the palace, and you can see remains of the old 14th-century polychrome ceiling and parts of the ancient tower. Displayed here is a copy of the death mask of Dante. The **Cappella dei Priori (24)**, a chapel with a barrel-vaulted ceiling, was entirely deco-

rated by Ridolfo del Ghirlandaio c. 1510 with frescoes against a gold ground. The grotesques imitate wood intarsia panels. The *Annunciation* shows the church of the Santissima Annunziata in the background (before the addition of the portico).

The Sala d'Udienza and Sala dei Gigli

These are the two most beautiful rooms in the palace, formerly one huge hall. The dividing wall was built in 1472 by Benedetto da Maiano. He and his brother Giuliano designed the magnificent doorway in the centre, crowned with a statue of *Justice* facing the Sala d'Udienza, and with a statue of the *Young St John the Baptist* and putti on the other side. They also made the exquisite intarsia doors, with figures of Dante and Petrarch. Giuliano and assistants designed the splendid gilded and coffered ceilings.

In the **Sala d'Udienza (25)**, above the door from the chapel, designed by Baccio d'Agnolo, is a dedication to Christ (1529). The huge mural paintings of stories from the life of the Roman hero Marcus Furius Camillus were added c. 1545–48 by Francesco Salviati; they are one of the major works by this typically Mannerist painter.

The **Sala dei Gigli (26)** takes its name from the fleurs-de-lys of the French house of Anjou—the golden lilies on a blue ground painted in 1490 on the walls, and the carved lilies on the ceiling. Domenico Ghirlandaio was to have frescoed all four walls, but he only ever carried out one, in 1482. The well-preserved fresco was intended as a celebration of the Florentine Republic: it shows Florence's patron saint Zenobius enthroned between Sts Stephen and Lawrence, in an open loggia behind which there is a glimpse of the Duomo. In the lunette above is a painted relief sculpture of the *Madonna and Child with Two Angels* against a golden 'mosaic' ground. The two lions of Florence hold the flags of the *popolo* and the *comune* (one of them was damaged in the late 16th century when the marble doorway was constructed). In the two other lunettes there are the splendid figures of six heroes of ancient Rome, standing out against the bright blue sky.

Donatello's magnificent bronze *Judith and Holofernes*, removed from the Piazza della Signoria, has been displayed here since its restoration. One of his last and most sophisticated works (c. 1455), it was commissioned by the Medici and used as a fountain in the garden of their palace (the holes for the water can be seen in the cushion). On their expulsion from the city in 1495, it was expropriated by the government and placed under the Loggia della Signoria with an inscription warning against tyrants.

Cancelleria and Sala delle Carte Geografiche

A window of the old palace serves as a doorway into the **Cancelleria (27)**, a pleasant, spacious chamber built in 1511. It may have been here that Niccolò Machiavelli worked during his term as government secretary. He is commemorated with a fine bust (16th century) and a painting by Santi di Tito.

The **Sala delle Carte Geografiche (28)** was decorated in 1563–65 with a fine ceiling and wooden cupboards, on which 57 maps illustrate the then-known world. Of great scientific and historical interest, they were drawn up for Cosimo I by the cosmographer Fra' Egnazio Danti and painted in 1585 for Francesco I by the Olivetan monk Stefano Bonsignori. The huge globe in the centre was also designed by Danti.

Collezione Loeser

Four rooms on the mezzanine floor display the collection left to the city in 1928 by the American connoisseur and collector Charles Loeser, who came to live in Florence in 1907. The masterpiece of the collection is the portrait of Laura Battiferri, whose second husband was Bartolomeo Ammannati. Painted around 1555, this is one of Bronzino's most sophisticated portraits. Laura, like Bronzino himself, was known for her poetry (she is holding a volume of poems by Petrarch). Other works of art include a portrait of Ludovico Martelli attributed to Pontormo, a Crucifix dating from 1290, a *Madonna and Child* by Pietro Lorenzetti, a tondo of the *Madonna and Child with the Young St John* by Alonso Berruguete, and the *Passion of Christ*, a very unusual painting by Piero di Cosimo. The sculptures include a marble angel by Tino di Camaino (from the Bishop Orso monument in the Duomo), two statuettes of angels by Jacopo Sansovino, a head of Cosimo I by Vincenzo de' Rossi, a bronze statuette of *Autumn* by Benvenuto Cellini, a small wax *Hercules and the Hydra* by Giambologna, a bronze horse, and two battle scenes in terracotta attributed to Giovanfrancesco Rustici (inspired by Leonardo's lost fresco of the *Battle of Anghiari*).

Beyond are two rooms which were once part of the medieval palace. In the first there is a detached 14th-century fresco illustrating the expulsion of the Duke of Athens (with an interesting view of Palazzo Vecchio) and a stone bas-relief of *St George and the Dragon* (c. 1260, attributed to Orcagna) removed from the Porta San Giorgio, an old gate in the walls. The room beyond displays a series of small panels by Pontormo of saints, religious scenes and putti, which used to decorate the ceremonial carriage used at the festival of St John (*see p. 349*). The stairs continue down to a vestibule (the coved ceiling of which has painted grotesques) outside the Sala dei Dugento (*closed to the public; see plan on p. 42*), where the Town Council meets. The name is derived from the council of 200 citizens who used to meet here.

Niccolò Machiavelli (1469–1527)

Niccolò Machiavelli is famous as the author of *The Prince*, probably the most celebrated treatise on governance and statecraft ever written. The son of a Tuscan lawyer, he first came to prominence during the republican period of 1494–1512, when his talents were spotted by the ruling magistrate (*gonfaloniere*) Piero Soderini, who took charge of the republic's affairs after the execution of Savonarola. Soderini made Machiavelli secretary of the Council of Ten and used him for diplomatic missions, relying greatly on his reports. He was also influenced by Machiavelli's ideas on how the republic should be administered and defended. Machiavelli proposed doing away with the *condottiere* system, which had shown itself to be costly and ineffective (for *condottieri* too often placed their own interests above those of the states they served) and introducing a Florentine militia. When Pope Julius II called upon the states of Italy to help him drive out the French, Soderini—who, advised by Machiavelli, had always steered a pro-French course—demurred. Enraged, the pope's Holy League sent an army marching on Florence, intent on restoring the Medici, who would institute a regime more amenable to the pope's demands. Soderini resigned and went into exile. Machiavelli was removed from office after serving 15 years as Chancellor of the Republic. The Medici were restored and a few months later Machiavelli was arrested on conspiracy charges. Certainly innocent, he was subsequently released, and retired to the country to write. He completed *The Prince* in 1514, drawing on the turbulent political experiences of his own lifetime to paint a portrait of how strong and lasting government should be achieved. It was published three years after his death. He also produced numerous historical studies, and some plays, the best known of which is *La Mandragola*, which was performed for Pope Leo X (Giovanni de' Medici) in 1519. Though the Medici never restored Machiavelli to public office, Giulio de' Medici (later Pope Clement VII) did commission him to write a history of Florence.

Machiavelli died, leaving a wife and six children in near poverty, in 1527. One of the most famous Florentines of all time, he was called by the English 'old Nick' and associated with the devil (and as such had an influence on Elizabethan drama), but this was because his political ideas were misunderstood (or deliberately distorted), suggesting that he equated the wise government of princes with that of a cruel tyrant. In the popular imagination of the Italians he has always been considered a positive figure and a patriot.

Percorsi Segreti

These fascinating 'secret itineraries' are shown on guided tours (*see p. 36*). One of these starts at the staircase known as the Scala del Duca d'Atene, built in 1342 by Walter de Brienne—known as the Duke of Athens—who held absolute power in the city for one year before his expulsion by popular uprising. In a small room, the original wall of the back of the medieval building can be seen. The secret staircase, partly spiral, built inside the later wall leads up to the first floor into a room which was later part of Cosimo I's private apartment. From here there is access to the **Studiolo** (*see p. 41*) through its original entrance. A small staircase leads up to the **Tesoretto**, the richly decorated tiny private study of Cosimo I, preserved intact from 1562 with stuccoes, vault frescoes, a marble and *pietra serena* floor, and the original cupboards which used to house Cosimo's treasures.

From the balcony above the Salone dei Cinquecento a staircase gives access to its remarkable **roof**, where there is an extraordinary sight of the complicated system of rafters and beams which support both the roof and the paintings of the ceiling.

Another tour takes you up to the splendid 14th-century **battlements**. You can walk all the way around them, high above Michelozzo's courtyard, and look down through the trap doors (provided here in case of attack) at the people in the piazza far below. The views over Florence are breathtaking. The laboratory here has been at work restoring some magnificent tapestries illustrating the story of Joseph, woven in Florence in 1545 for Cosimo I by Flemish masters on designs by Bronzino and others.

Another tour takes in the so-called **Camerina di Bianca Cappello**, a 'secret' room off the Sala delle Carte Geografiche, from which you can look down into the Salone dei Cinquecento.

The excavations beneath the building include the impressive remains of the **Roman theatre**, rebuilt during the reign of Hadrian and which could hold some 10,000 spectators. Remains of some of the radial passageways beneath the cavea survive but nothing of the scena (*for more on the history of the Roman city, see p. 104*).

Museo dei Ragazzi

The so-called 'Children's Museum' (*booking required; see p. 36*) uses parts of the palace not otherwise open to the public to illustrate certain historical periods or to explain architectural principles or scientific theories (such as the rules of perspective) to both children and adults. There is a laboratory where fresco technique is explained and a theatre workshop where representations of the court of Cosimo I and Eleanor of Toledo are held.

THE DUOMO, CAMPANILE & BAPTISTERY

The confined space of Piazza del Duomo (*map 1, 4*) is almost entirely filled with the massive building of the cathedral. The square was recently totally closed to cars, making it possible to appreciate the magnificent coloured marble exterior of the Duomo, the delicately patterned Campanile (bell-tower), and the compact little octagonal Baptistery.

The Duomo is dedicated to the Madonna of Florence, Santa Maria del Fiore, and was begun in 1296 or 1298 by Arnolfo di Cambio (*see p. 53*). It is not known precisely how far building had progressed by the time of his death in the first decade of the 14th century. In 1331, the guild of wool merchants assumed responsibility for the project and Giotto was appointed *capomaestro* (director of works). It was decided to cover the exterior with a magnificent pattern of red, white and green marbles, brought from quarries in Tuscany. Things moved slowly until 1355, when Francesco Talenti took charge of the work, and it seems that he followed Arnolfo's original design of a domed basilica with three polygonal apses at the east end. During the 14th century numerous other architects, including Orcagna, joined Talenti, and the octagonal drum was practically completed by 1417. The construction of the dome had for long been recognised as a major technical problem. A competition was held and Brunelleschi and Ghiberti were appointed jointly to the task in 1418 as project supervisors. Their relationship was sometimes antagonistic, but in 1426 Brunelleschi's dominant role was recognised when his salary was increased beyond that of Ghiberti. The wonderful huge dome was finished up to the base of the lantern by 1436, when Pope Eugenius IV consecrated the cathedral.

EXTERIOR OF THE DUOMO

Building was begun on the south side, where the magnificent decorative pattern of the red, white and green marble can be seen to full advantage. The most elaborate of the doors, all of which are adorned with sculpture, is the **Porta della Mandorla** on the north. It takes its name from the almond-shaped aureole around the *Assumption of the Virgin* by Nanni di Banco (c. 1418–20), a sculptor who was at work for the Opera del Duomo at the same time as Donatello. The lower part, dating from 1391–1405, had an important influence on early Renaissance sculpture. In the lunette is an *Annunciation* in mosaic added by the Ghirlandaio brothers at the end of the century.

The old **façade**, erected to a third of its projected height by 1420, was demolished in 1587–88 (the sculptures are preserved in the Museo dell'Opera del Duomo). It was not until 1887 that a new façade was erected, funded by public subscription and with conspicuous contributions from the foreign community, including Frederick Stibbert and Paolo Demidoff. The overall neo-Gothic design, by Emilio de Fabris, is unambitious, but some of the best-known artists of the day worked on the elaborate decoration, including Giovanni Dupré and Tito Sarrocchi. To celebrate its unveiling, a historical cavalcade processed through the streets in splendid 15th-century costumes and a ball was held at Palazzo Vecchio. The novelist Henry James was among the guests.

The **east end** is magnificent, with three domed tribunes around the base of the octagonal drum which supports the huge dome. Brunelleschi designed the four small exedrae decorated with niches. The rough masonry at the base of the dome still remains uncovered: a competition was held in 1507 for the execution of a balustrade here, and projects were submitted by the leading artists of the day. Baccio d'Agnolo began the construction of a balcony (to a design by Giuliano da Sangallo) on the southeast side, but work came to a halt when Michelangelo (who had himself taken part in the competition) declared that it reminded him of a cricket's cage. The row of stone chains which protrude from the structure were used by Brunelleschi to stabilise his dome.

The **dome** itself, built in 1420–36, is one of the masterpieces of the Florentine Renaissance—though it makes less of an impact from Piazza del Duomo than it does when seen from anywhere else in the city or the surrounding hills. It is the greatest of all Brunelleschi's works. The largest and highest of its time, it broke away entirely from Classical forms and from medieval architecture. This domical vault, with its pointed profile, is an astonishing feat of engineering skill and Brunelleschi had the audacity and bravura to invent a way of constructing it without the need for a wooden supporting frame (which by its very size would in any case have been impossible to supply). On the completion of the dome, Brunelleschi won the competition then held for the crowning lantern. It was begun a few months before the architect's death in 1446, after which work was continued by Michelozzo. Verrocchio placed the bronze ball and cross on the summit in 1471. (*For more on the engineering and construction of the dome, see pp. 58–60 and 71.*)

Arnolfo di Cambio (c. 1245–c. 1302)
Much about the life and work of this sculptor and architect remains a mystery. It is certain that he worked on the Duomo since he is named as its architect in a document of 1300, and the death of 'Magister Arnolfus' is recorded here sometime between 1302 and 1310. Scholars believe that he had a major impact on building activity in the city in the 1290s and they often recognise his hand in some of the most important buildings of that time: Palazzo Vecchio, Santa Croce and the Badia Fiorentina, all of which are attributed to him by Vasari. He was born in Colle Val d'Elsa (between Florence and Siena) and his early life is documented in Pisa and Siena as assistant to Nicola Pisano. He travelled widely in Italy to carry out commissions for the papacy in Rome and the Angevin court in Naples. His sculpture combines elements of classicism (he often made use of ancient Roman spolia) with French Gothic, and it is possible that he visited France. In Rome and Orvieto he designed a number of innovative funerary monuments which include effigies of the deceased. It is thought that he must have made frequent use of working drawings so that his *bottega* could carry out projects in his absence. By the time of his death the new cathedral façade of Florence had been erected as far as the masonry above the portals, but it is uncertain how much of the overall design of the entire building was due to Arnolfo. He carved remarkable huge sculptures for the west front which can be seen today in the Museo dell'Opera del Duomo and include classical reclining figures of the Virgin as well as an enigmatic seated figure of the Virgin with glass eyes.

INTERIOR OF THE DUOMO

Open 10–5, Thur 10–4.40, Sun and holidays 1.30–4.45. Entrance from a door in the main façade; exit by the door beside the Campanile: the entrance and exit gates are electronically monitored so that no more than 800 people are inside the building at any one time. Excavations of Santa Reparata open 10–5 except Sun and holidays. Entrance and ticket office below the nave. The dome can be climbed 8.30–6.20; first Sat of the month 8.30–3; other Sats 8.30–5; closed Sun and holidays. Ticket office in winter near the Porta dei Canonici and in summer near the Porta della Mandorla (marked on the plan on opposite).

Excellent guided tours (also in English) are often provided of areas of the church not otherwise open to the public. For information, artecultura@operaduomo.firenze.it; T: 055 282226. These include the roof terraces (tours usually at 10.30, 12, 3, and also 4.30 in summer) except on Sat afternoon and Sun. Tickets (which include access to the dome) at the entrance to the excavations of Santa Reparata. The clock on the west wall and the north sacristy at the east end can each be visited on guided tours of a minimum of 10 people (advance booking required).

The plain Gothic interior is somewhat sombre after the warm colour of the exterior, whose splendour it cannot match. It is a huge building (if you also take into account the volume of the dome, it is second in Italy only to St Peter's in Rome). In the nave the massive pilasters which support the stone vault have unusual composite capitals, and the great grey stone arches reach the clerestory beneath a balcony supported on carved brackets. Three tribunes with a Gothic coronet of chapels surround the huge dome. The beautiful stained-glass windows date mostly from 1434–45 and are among the most important works of their kind in Italy. The marble pavement, which dates from 1526–1660, adds to the rather gloomy feel of the nave, which is remarkably empty compared to most churches in Italy.

West wall

The *Coronation of the Virgin* **mosaic** is attributed by Vasari to an otherwise unknown artist called Gaddo Gaddi. It seems likely Gaddi also worked on the Baptistery mosaics and that this mosaic (c. 1290) was originally in the old cathedral of Santa Reparata. Ghiberti designed the three **round stained-glass windows**. The 16th-century **frescoes of angel musicians** are by Santi di Tito. The recomposed **tomb of Antonio d'Orso**, Bishop of Florence (d. 1321) by Tino di Camaino, includes a fine statue of the mournful bishop.

The huge **clock** uses the *hora italica* method of counting the hours—the last hour of the day (XXIIII) ends at sunset or Ave Maria (a system used in Italy until the Lorraine grand dukes in the 18th century brought the calendar into line with the rest of Europe). Paolo Uccello decorated it and painted the four heads of prophets in 1443. It is still in working order and its mechanism (which was renewed in the 17th century) is wound by hand every week. Reached by a staircase through the little door on the left, it is shown on guided tours.

Monuments in the nave

(B) Medallion with a portrait of Brunelleschi: This half-length figure was carved by the great architect's adopted son Buggiano (1446). The likeness was probably taken from his death-mask.

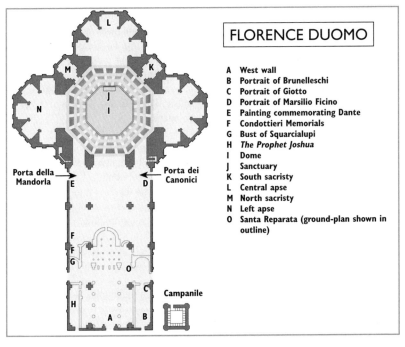

FLORENCE DUOMO

A   West wall
B   Portrait of Brunelleschi
C   Portrait of Giotto
D   Portrait of Marsilio Ficino
E   Painting commemorating Dante
F   Condottieri Memorials
G   Bust of Squarcialupi
H   *The Prophet Joshua*
I   Dome
J   Sanctuary
K   South sacristy
L   Central apse
M   North sacristy
N   Left apse
O   Santa Reparata (ground-plan shown in outline)

Porta della Mandorla

Porta dei Canonici

Campanile

(C) Medallion with a portrait of Giotto: Commissioned by the Opera del Duomo to commemorate Giotto's contribution to the building of the Duomo and Campanile. The idealised portrait (1490) is by Benedetto da Maiano, with an inscription by Poliziano, the scholar-poet and friend of Lorenzo the Magnificent.

(D) Medallion with a portrait of Marsilio Ficino: This half-length figure is by Andrea Ferrucci (1521). Ficino (1433–99) was a famous Neoplatonist philosopher and friend of Cosimo il Vecchio—he claimed that Cosimo had taught him as much as Plato. He went on to become the mentor of Cosimo's grandson Lorenzo the Magnificent. The beautiful stained-glass window with six saints (1394–95) was designed by Agnolo Gaddi.

(E) Painting commemorating Dante: This is one of the few known works of Domenico di Michelino (1465). It shows Dante holding his *Divine Comedy*. On the left Hell is portrayed, in the centre Purgatory, with its conical mound, and on the right Paradise in the guise of Florence. The townscape shows the drum of the dome before it was faced with marble. This was the only memorial to Dante in his native city until 1830, when his cenotaph was erected in Santa Croce.

(F) Condottieri Memorials: These two splendid frescoes of equestrian statues, executed in green tones of *terraverde* to look like bronze funerary monuments, commemorate two famous *condottieri*: Sir John Hawkwood (by Paolo Uccello,

1436; *see box below*) and Niccolò da Tolentino (by Andrea del Castagno, 1456). In 1432 Niccolò da Tolentino led the Florentine army against Siena at the Battle of San Romano: although the outcome was in fact indecisive, the Florentines considered it their victory and a painting of it in three episodes was commissioned from Paolo Uccello by the Medici a few years later (*see p. 115*).

(G) Bust of Antonio Squarcialupi: This portrait bust is by Benedetto da Maiano (1490). Born in 1416, Squarcialupi was cathedral organist from 1432 until his death in 1480. He was also a composer, and although none of his music has survived, his name is famous because of a manuscript he left to the Biblioteca Laurenziana (the 'Squarcialupi Codex') which represents the most important collection of 14th-century Italian secular music. The epigraph is thought to be by Poliziano.

(H) *The Prophet Joshua*: This sculpture (traditionally thought to be a portrait of Poggio Bracciolini, a humanist friend of Cosimo il Vecchio) is attributed to Donatello. It was probably destined for a niche in the Campanile.

Sir John Hawkwood (?1323–94)

This famous English mercenary was born at Sible Hedingham in Essex, England, and almost certainly took part in the battles of Crécy and Poitiers before arriving in Italy in 1361. As was often the case with professional soldiers, he changed allegiances with ease, and served Pisa, Milan and the Kingdom of Naples at various stages of his career, but it is as the captain of the Florentine army from 1380 onwards that he has always been best remembered. He became extremely wealthy and famous in his lifetime and acquired the nickname of Giovanni Acuto ('John the Astute') as he was a very skilled diplomat as well as a cunning and cautious soldier. It is known that there were numerous English soldiers amongst his troops and that he was always also careful to protect the interests of the English king, Richard II. After his death in 1394, he was given a magnificent state funeral by the Florentines, and a procession accompanied his body from Piazza della Signoria to the Baptistery, where he lay in state. Despite a decree around this time that no tombs should ever be erected in the Duomo above the level of the pavement, a splendid wall tomb, to be financed by public subscription, was planned for the hero here. In the end, however, he was honoured by a wall painting, commissioned from Agnolo Gaddi. This was replaced several decades later by the present frescoed equestrian memorial commissioned by the Medici from Paolo Uccello. Although he was one of the most famous painters of his day Uccello had to paint it twice, since the first version was rejected. At the end of his life Hawkwood had intended to return to England and after his death Richard II asked for his body to be returned there, but it seems that this never happened (even though there is a monument to him in the church at Sible Hedingham).

The dome and sanctuary

Above the octagon the great **dome (I)** soars to an incredible height of 91m. The huge fresco of the *Last Judgement* (1572–79) is a very impressive work by Vasari and Federico Zuccari (*see p. 343*). At the very top, seated in a circle, are the *Elders of the Apocalypse* by Vasari, who stand out above the rather pale figure of Christ and the female figure of *Charity* below. All around are scenes of the dammed and the blessed. The very fine 15th-century stained glass in the round windows of the drum is described on p. 59. Against the piers of the octagon stand eight 16th-century statues of Apostles.

The marble **sanctuary (J)** was part of a grandiose project begun in 1547 by Baccio Bandinelli, who had been appointed head of the Opera del Duomo in 1540 by Cosimo I. It included some 300 reliefs (*see example illustrated on p. 69*) but was never finished. Only the wall of the choir remains today. The high altar was installed here in 1973, and a Crucifix by Benedetto da Maiano.

The east end

NB: The east end of the church is usually closed to visitors (although the north sacristy can be visited on guided tours) and some of it is reserved for private worship, so the works of art described below are very difficult to see.

Each of the three apses is divided into five chapels with stained-glass windows designed by Lorenzo Ghiberti. High up on the keystone of the entrance arch of the central apse can be seen the emblem of the *popolo* of Florence: a shield with a red cross on a white field. This records the political involvement in the building of the Duomo, apparently seen at the time as a deliberate attempt to circumscribe the power of the cathedral canons.

(K) South sacristy: Above the entrance is an enamelled terracotta lunette of the *Ascension* by Luca della Robbia.

(L) Central apse: The east chapel (now the Chapel of the Holy Sacrament) was dedicated to St Zenobius in 1432, when Lorenzo Ghiberti was commissioned to cast the bishop-saint's bronze reliquary urn, carved with exquisite bas-reliefs. The two graceful kneeling angels are by Luca della Robbia.

(M) North sacristy: Over the door is a fine relief, again by della Robbia, of the *Resurrection*. This was his earliest important work (1442) in enamelled terracotta. The iconographical composition was copied by later artists. The doors were Luca's only work in bronze (1446–67); he was assisted by Michelozzo and Maso di Bartolomeo. It was in this sacristy that Lorenzo the Magnificent took refuge on the day of the Pazzi Conspiracy (*see p. 203*). The interior has fine intarsia cupboards dating from 1436–45 by a group of artists including Lo Scheggia, Antonio Manetti and (end wall) Giuliano da Maiano (1463–65). The organ, by Matteo da Prato (1432), was installed in 1448 above Luca della Robbia's cantoria (now in the Museo dell'Opera del Duomo).

(N) Left apse: In the pavement is Toscanelli's huge gnomon (1475) related to a perforated bronze plate at the base of the south window in the lantern of the cupola. At midday on the summer solstice a ray of sun passing through this hole lights up the marble disc in the floor of the church 90m below. The solstitial disc, modified in 1755, served to make astronomical observations. Toscanelli, a famous scientist, mathematician and geographer, discussed his calculations concerning perspective with his friend Brunelleschi. In the second chapel from the right, there is a dossal of the *Madonna and Child with Four Saints* and, on the back, the *Annunciation*, with four more saints. This is attributed to the hand of Giotto (probably with the intervention of his *bottega*).

Brunelleschi's tomb and excavations of Santa Reparata

A broad flight of steps **(O)** leads down from the nave to a bookshop (left), where beyond a grille you can see the simple tomb slab of Brunelleschi, which was found here in 1972. The architect of the cupola, here aptly described as 'ingeniosus', was the one Florentine granted the privilege of burial in Santa Maria del Fiore. Although now in a busy spot and often ignored by visitors, it is one of the most moving sights in the Duomo.

To the right of the steps is the ticket office (*for opening times see p. 54 above*) for the excavations of the ancient cathedral of Santa Reparata. This early Christian church, dedicated to the Palestinian saint Reparata (a young girl of noble family executed by order of Decius c. AD 249 because she refused to sacrifice to the gods), is thought to have been founded in the 6th–7th centuries or possibly earlier and was reconstructed several times in the Romanesque period. The first bishop of Florence is believed to have been St Zenobius, who died in 429, and the bishop's seat, formerly at San Lorenzo (*see p. 141*) is thought to have been transferred here in the late 7th century. When the body of the bishop-saint was moved from San Lorenzo to Santa Reparata in the 9th century, an elm tree outside the Baptistery is said to have flowered, signifying the willingness of the saint to move here, and there is still a column of cipollino marble (probably an ancient Roman spoil) on that spot, erected in the 14th century to commemorate the miracle. As can be seen from the plan on p. 55, the cathedral of Santa Reparata was considerably smaller than the present building and by the 13th century, a new and larger cathedral was deemed necessary.

The complicated excavations include Roman edifices on which the early Christian church was built, a fine mosaic pavement from the earliest church (the precise plan of which is not known) and remains of the pre-Romanesque reconstruction and the Romanesque edifice with its five apses. Finds from the excavations include the gilded bronze sword and spurs of a magistrate of the city, Giovanni de' Medici (whose tomb also survives here), Roman sculpture and paving tiles, Romanesque architectural fragments, majolica and unglazed pottery from earth fills and tombs dating from the construction of the present cathedral (1296–1375), and fresco fragments.

Inside the dome

For admission, see above, p. 54; the ticket entrance changes between the north and south side of the Duomo in summer and winter, so the description below has to be reversed in summer.

The vast dome would have been impossible to build without its two concentric shells: the outer, protecting shell is thinner than the inner shell and slightly more tapering in shape. The consecutive rings of radially laid masonry, at first in heavier *pietra forte*, get lighter nearer the top, where bricks are used. The vertical herring-bone pattern of these meant that the masonry could be held in place as it was being laid on its ever-increasingly inclined axis. Lateral arches and hidden structural stone chains or beams embedded in the masonry also helped to secure and stabilise the structure as the inclination became more and more pronounced towards the top. The strong closing ring at the summit acted like a keystone, locking the entire structure into place, and its effect was strengthened by the weight of the lantern above. The method of construction and the marvel of this structure can be examined closely on the ascent of the dome, following the labyrinth of corridors, steps and spiral staircases used by the builders themselves. The climb (463 steps) is one of the most fascinating and moving experiences to be had in all Florence and is not as difficult as you might expect (though not for those who suffer from claustrophobia).

It is clear that the success of Brunelleschi's extraordinary enterprise, which involved erecting a self-supporting structure some 54m above ground level, was due in large part to the smooth-running by the Opera of the bureaucratic administration and the regular flow of finance which ensured its progress. The wardens who supervised the work held only a brief term of office, and each week one of them was named provost. This support structure ensured that Brunelleschi could work with ease, and that he also had a constant supply of bricks and mortar, as well as *pietra serena* from the quarries near Settignano. Much about the organisation of the worksite is now known through archival documents (*see p. 71*).

From the narrow balcony which encircles the octagonal drum, you have a splendid view of the inside of the Duomo and of the late 16th-century frescoes by Vasari and Federico Zuccari which cover the dome vault. When Brunelleschi and Ghiberti were commissioned to construct the dome, the cathedral was already built to this point: from here you can appreciate the huge space (45.5m in diameter) which the architects were required to cover. On the floor far below, Brunelleschi installed a magnificent hoisting device, complete with four gears and driven by two oxen, which supplied the building materials to the workmen at this level and above. The holes in the masonry visible here were where the loading platforms were fixed. The seven beautiful stained-glass windows in the roundels were designed in 1443–45 by Paolo Uccello (*Nativity* and *Resurrection*), Andrea del Castagno (*Deposition*), Donatello (*Coronation of the Virgin*), Ghiberti (*Ascension, Prayer in the Garden* and *Presentation in the Temple*).

After this you proceed to the base of the double dome, the curve of which can be seen clearly. The ascent passes between the two shells by means of short corridors and flights of steps, and small windows frame views of the monuments of the city. Above the second walkway the distinctive herring-bone pattern of the bricks in the masonry, used at intervals in the construction of the dome, is clearly visible, as well as some of the transverse arches and stone beams which acted as chains to strengthen the structure and bond it together during construction (as well as helping to carry the outer shell). Above the third walkway, on the right, a steep flight of narrow steps (one way up) scales the uppermost part of the inner dome and its closing ring which locks in the whole structure (like a cork!). Another short flight of steps continues out onto the lantern, beautifully carved in marble. The mighty marble ribs which decorate the exterior of the dome can be appreciated from here, and the breathtaking view from this point (91m) embraces the entire city.

THE CAMPANILE

The Campanile (*open 8.30–7.30; T: 055 230 2885*), nearly 85m high, was once one of the most admired buildings in Florence: its effect was perhaps diminished when the elaborate façade of the Duomo was constructed beside it (and in the same style) at the end of the 19th century.

The Campanile was begun by Giotto in 1334 when, as the most distinguished Florentine artist, he was appointed city architect, and it seems that he was responsible for the entire design, including the sculptural decoration. However, it is known that Andrea Pisano was also involved in the work, and it was he who carved most of the bas-reliefs. The tower was completed by Francesco Talenti in 1348–59. It is built of the same coloured marbles as the Duomo, in similar patterns, in an extremely well-proportioned design. Between the various storeys are horizontal bands of green, white and pink marble inlay. The bas-reliefs on the lowest storeys illustrating the *Creation of Man* and the *Arts* and *Industries*, and the statues of prophets and sibyls in the niches above are all copies of the originals now displayed at eye-level in the Museo dell'Opera del Duomo (*described on pp. 70–71*). There are two storeys above, each with a pair of beautiful double-arched windows in each side, followed by the highest storey, with large and triple-arched openings, and the cornice.

The ascent of the bell-tower, by 414 steps, is interesting for its succession of views of the Duomo, the Baptistery and the rest of the city. The third and fourth storeys, with their Gothic windows, overlook the Duomo and the Baptistery. The terracotta pots along the roof of the aisle of the Duomo serve to protect the building from the direct fall of rainwater from the gutters. On the Campanile's highest storey, with its beautiful slender windows, the modern bells can be seen hanging above the original ones (the 'Apostolica' bell, displayed on a platform, dates from the beginning of the 15th century).

THE BAPTISTERY

Open 12–6.30, Sun and holidays 8.30–1.30. The matroneum can be visited on guided tours of a minimum of 10 people usually on Mon, Thur and Sat at 3 (but these have to be booked in advance. For information, artecultura@operaduomo.firenze.it; T: 055 282226).

The Baptistery of San Giovanni is one of the oldest and most revered buildings in Florence and has always held a special place in the city's history. Interestingly enough, even today the date of its foundation is uncertain, although it is documented by 897. It is now generally considered to have been built in the 6th or 7th century, or even as early as the late 4th or early 5th century. We know that it was reconsecrated in 1059, when for a period it served as the cathedral of Florence. In Dante's time it was thought to have Roman origins: in later centuries, Florentines, intent on emphasising the city's glorious past, were quick to support this claim.

The Calimala guild of wholesale cloth importers ran the Opera di San Giovanni responsible for the Baptistery and it was they who proclaimed the competition in 1401 to decide which of the greatest artists of the day should provide it with a second set of bronze doors. This was a practice which had been abandoned since Roman times and it is significant that it was this building that was chosen for adornment at the very beginning of the 'Renaissance' (art historians often take this as a convenient date to mark the birth of that great artistic movement). The competition was won by Lorenzo Ghiberti and the two trial panels from the competition, submitted by Ghiberti and Brunelleschi, are, incredibly enough, still preserved and displayed in the Bargello (*see p. 91*).

Exterior of the Baptistery

The Baptistery is an octagonal building on a centralised plan derived from Byzantine models, with an exceptionally large dome. The classical geometric decoration of the exterior was carried out in the 11th–13th centuries using precious coloured marbles, all at the expense of the Arte di Calimala, the most important guild (representing cloth-importers) in the medieval city. The design became a prototype for numerous Tuscan Romanesque religious buildings (including, in Florence, Santa Maria Novella and San Miniato al Monte). Both the rectangular apse (which replaced a semicircular one) and the white pyramidal roof which conceals the cupola are particularly unusual architectural features, probably both dating from the 13th century (although the lantern which crowns the building was made in the 12th century). Low down on the side furthest from the Duomo can be seen an ancient Roman relief, now very worn, but which includes a ship with its rigging and its sails furled, thought to have been related to the cult of Isis.

The Baptistery is famous for its three sets of gilded bronze doors, one at each of its three entrances.

South doors

Now used as an exit, these doors were made by Andrea Pisano in 1336: a few years later he took over from Giotto as architect of the Campanile close by (where he also worked on its sculpted decoration). The doors have 28 panels containing very fine reliefs enclosed in Gothic quatrefoil frames. They illustrate the history of St John the Baptist and the Theological and Cardinal Virtues. They were at first erected at the main entrance facing the Duomo, but in the 15th century were moved to their present position to make way for Lorenzo Ghiberti's new doors (*see below*). The elaborate decorations of the bronze frame were added by Lorenzo's son Vittorio.

North doors

The doors now used as the entrance, by Lorenzo Ghiberti (1403–24), are again divided into 28 panels and the Gothic frames are copied from the earlier Pisano doors. A chronological sequence of scenes from the life of Christ begins on the left-hand door on the third panel from the bottom and runs left to right towards the top. The two lower registers depict the Evangelists and Doctors of the Church. Ghiberti's self-portrait appears in the fifth head from the top of the left door (middle band), wearing an elaborate hat. The exquisite decoration of the frame is also by Ghiberti.

East doors
This is the most celebrated work of Lorenzo Ghiberti, and it took him most of his life to complete it (1425–52). Michelangelo is said to have called it the 'Gate of Paradise'. The ten separate panels contain reliefs of scriptural subjects, the design of which probably owes something to Ghiberti's contact with the humanists. The artist was assisted by Michelozzo, Benozzo Gozzoli and others. The pictorial reliefs, no longer restricted to a Gothic frame, depict each episode with great conciseness. They are exquisitely carved, with scenes in low relief extending far into the background. The use of perspective here is of great importance, and typical of the new Renaissance concept of art. The panels were cast nearby—a plaque at no. 1 Via Bufalini (*map 1, 4*) marks the site of Ghiberti's workshop.

The current doors are copies installed in 1990. The original panels have been restored but were not on view at the time of writing as they were being reinstalled in the original door frame, to be exhibited in the new extension to the Museo dell'Opera del Duomo. The original panels are masterpieces of the early Renaissance. Each describes in continuous narrative various episodes from Old Testament stories. The subjects of the panels, going left to right and starting with the left panel of the pair at the top, are as follows:

The Creation and the Story of Adam and Eve: This beautiful panel shows the *Creation of Adam*, the *Creation of Eve*, the *Fall* (in a wood full of birds), and the *Expulsion from Paradise*. The human figures are extraordinarily elegant, and numerous graceful angels add particular charm to the scenes.

The story of Cain and Abel: Here we see the elderly Adam and Eve sitting in front of their hut with their children Cain and Abel. Below are two distinct scenes, with Abel tending his flock of sheep and Cain tilling the soil with the help of two oxen. At the top of the panel the brothers are depicted sacrificing a lamb and the fruits of the land to the Lord, who shows his preference for Abel's offering. Then Cain, in anger, is shown killing Abel, and

in the last scene the Lord appears to Cain beside a stream asking him where his brother is and Cain replies, 'I know not; am I my brother's keeper?'

Noah's sacrifice and drunkenness: The Ark is shown in the form of a huge pyramid in the upper part of the panel, surrounded by a few animals. Noah and his family form a circle in the centre, and the disaster of the Flood is represented by a drowned body. In the upper right corner the rainbow appears with God approving Noah's sacrifice of a ram. Another scene illustrates the *Drunkenness of Noah*, with his sons covering his shame.

Abraham and the Angels and the Sacrifice of Isaac: In front to the left Abraham kneels before three angels (one of whom is God the Father disguised)

Lorenzo Ghiberti's original bronze Baptistery doors (1425–52), in a late 19th-century photograph.

while his wife Sarah is shown leaving their tent. Above a group of beautiful tall trees is the scene of the *Sacrifice of Isaac* (the subject of the trial reliefs by Brunelleschi and Ghiberti; *see p. 91*). Abraham's two servants, who wait below with the mule, may be a reference to the intimate friendship between the brothers Isaac and Ishmael.

The Story of Jacob and Esau: Set in an elegant arcaded building. Some of the scenes are difficult to interpret, but pride of place is given to an elegant group of four serving women in the left foreground. Isaac is shown with his eldest son Esau (accompanied by two dogs) and Rebecca with her favourite younger son Jacob who, in another scene, disguised by the kid on his shoulders, kneels in front of his blind father to receive his blessing. Rebecca is also shown in her bedchamber and (at the top right) kneeling before God the Father, and Esau leaving for the hunt is carved in low relief.

The Story of Benjamin and Joseph: The scene takes place in front of a circular building where the Egyptians are emptying sacks of grain. At the top of the panel Joseph is seen saved from the well to be sold by his brothers to the Ishmaelites. In the left foreground are Joseph's brothers opening their sacks to find, to their despair, Joseph's silver chalice. On a raised platform in front of a niche, Joseph is embracing his youngest brother Benjamin, and Joseph reveals his identity to his brothers. In the right foreground, a camel is being loaded with sacks while Joseph takes leave of his brothers, on their way back to their father.

Moses Receiving the Tablets of Stone: This panel shows a large crowd beside the Red Sea and their encampment in a group of exquisite trees. Moses is seen on Mount Sinai receiving the Law on the Tablets of Stone from God the Father, who is accompanied by a glory of beautiful angels. Just below Moses his brother Aaron kneels in wonder.

Joshua and the Fall of Jericho: The walls of Jericho at the top of the panel can be seen damaged by cracks and falling masonry as a procession led by trumpeters leaves the city carrying the Ark of the Covenant. In the centre in low relief is the encampment of the Israelites. As Joshua, in a chariot taking up the rear of the procession of the Ark, reaches the Jordan, the river dries up to allow the people to cross it. In the right foreground the crowd are shown carrying huge stones and rocks obeying God's wish that they should be moved to the far bank as memorials of this miraculous event.

Saul with David and Goliath: This panel shows the battle between Saul (in his war chariot) leading the men of Israel against the Philistines. At the bottom of the panel, David cuts off Goliath's head with a sword, after the giant has fallen 'upon his face to the earth' having been killed by a stone from David's sling. In the background can be seen a group of women rejoicing as they come out of the city to meet Saul and David bearing the head of Goliath.

The Meeting of Solomon and the Queen of Sheba: The scene takes place in a splendid vaulted hall filled with a large crowd of people, divided into four groups. Unlike the other nine panels, which include various different episodes in each biblical story, here we see only the symbolic handshake between the two royal figures.

Surrounding the reliefs are 24 fine statuettes of prophets and sibyls and 24 medallions with portraits of Ghiberti himself (the fourth from the top in the middle row on the left) and his principal contemporaries. The splendid bronze door frame is also by Ghiberti.

The two porphyry columns, formerly free-standing between the Baptistery and the Duomo, seem to have been given to Florence by grateful Pisans for help in vanquishing the Saracens in the Balearic Islands in the early 12th century. But the tale is told that they turned out to be (intentionally?) unsound and therefore couldn't be used as architectural elements, proof of the age-old rivalry between the two Tuscan cities. Perhaps instead they were simply bought back from the islands as booty by the Florentines and set up here in civic pride. In any case, it is known that the war carriage which flew the flag of the *Comune* and bore an altar, and which led the Florentines into battle during the Middle Ages, was kept inside the Baptistery and the soldiers' battle cry was 'for San Giovanni'. St John the Baptist is the patron saint of Florence and his likeness was proudly displayed on the gold florin first minted in the early 13th century.

Interior of the Baptistery

The lovely old marble interior has huge granite columns from a Roman building with gilded Corinthian capitals alternating with pilasters flush with the wall, below a cornice and a gallery with divided windows and primitive marble decorations. There are also two marble cipollino columns which must be Roman spolia. The walls are in panels of white marble divided by bands of black, in the dichromatic style of the exterior. As the floor shows, the centre of the building used to be occupied by a huge octagonal font. Dante mentions this (*Inferno*, Canto XIX) in a passage in which he recalls saving a boy from drowning in it, and it is at this point in the poem that he makes his famous reference to '*mio bel San Giovanni*', illustrating what a significant place the building held in the great Florentine poet's mind. Indeed, towards the end of the *Paradiso* (Canto XXV), when he speculates on the possibility that his poem might one day be recognised by his detractors in Florence and that on its account he might be allowed to return from exile to his beloved city, he imagines an occasion on which he might be crowned with the poet's laurels here at the font where he had been baptised.

The font was dismantled in 1576 and around the present Gothic font the oldest part of the splendid **mosaic pavement** (begun in 1209) can be seen. Made out of tiny square tesserae, and contemporary with the lovely pavement in San Miniato (*see p. 299*), it includes geometric designs, Oriental motifs and the signs of the Zodiac. The marble decoration in the rectangular apse, which was added in the 13th century, has very unusual, almost eccentric geometric designs. Beside the handsome high altar (13th century; reconstructed) is an elaborate 14th-century paschal candlestick. To the right is the **tomb of the antipope John XXIII**. When Baldassare Cossa was elected pope during the Great Schism in 1410, he helped Giovanni di Bicci de' Medici (father of Cosimo il Vecchio) become a papal banker. But he was expelled from Rome by imperial troops and fled to Florence in 1413 before being deposed by the Council of Constance and imprisoned. Through his Florentine connections, he was finally released in 1419 and returned to Florence, but died in the same year. Giovanni di Bicci was an executor of his will and, since the pope had asked to be buried in the Baptistery, it was he who in 1424 commissioned Donatello and Michelozzo to design the funerary monument. It is one of the earliest Renaissance tombs in the city, and apart from the exquisite carving, it is especially remarkable for the way it is inserted into a narrow space between two huge Roman columns, in no way disturbing the architectural harmony of the building. Michelozzo was later to introduce a beautiful Renaissance structure at the very centre of the Romanesque church of San Miniato, again demonstrating the extreme sensibility of the great Renaissance artists to the artistic masterpieces of previous centuries. It is usually thought that it was Donatello who sculpted the bronze effigy of the pope himself. On the left of the apse are two late Roman sarcophagi adapted as tombs (one showing a wild boar hunt and the other, adapted as the tomb of a bishop in 1230, with scenes of Roman life).

The **mosaics in the vault**, the only mosaic cycle which exists in Florence, are remarkably well preserved (and superbly lit). The earliest (c. 1225) are above the altar; they are signed by the monk 'Iacopo', a contemporary of St Francis, who was influenced by Roman or Venetian mosaicists. The little vault is decorated with an elaborate wheel with the figures of the prophets, which surround the *Agnus Dei*. This is supported by four caryatids kneeling on Corinthian capitals. On either side, enthroned, are the *Virgin* and *St John the Baptist*. On the first arch are half-figures of saints flanking a striking image of the Baptist, and on the intrados of the outer arch a frieze of saints in niches. The outer face is decorated with vine tendrils. Work on the mosaics of the main dome was well advanced by 1271, but probably continued into the 14th century. The graceful decoration around the lantern includes early Christian symbols surrounded by a band of angels. Lower down is a broad band with full-length figures of angels in pairs and the Baptist between seraphim. On the three sections nearest to the altar is the *Last Judgement* with a huge figure of Christ (8m high) in a central tondo. The remaining section of the cupola is divided into four bands: the inner one, beneath the frieze of angels, has scenes from Genesis (beginning over the north entrance door) with the *Creation*; the second band, the *Story of Joseph*; the third band, the *Story of Christ*; and the lowest band, the *Story of St John the Baptist*. All the scenes are divided by mosaic columns of different designs. The marble rectangular frames at the base of the dome contain mosaic saints. It is not known with certainty which Florentine artists were responsible for the design of the mosaics, but most scholars now agree that Cimabue, the greatest artist of the 13th century, was not directly involved. They can be examined in detail from the matroneum, or women's gallery (*open on guided tours by previous appointment; see above*).

MUSEO DELL'OPERA DEL DUOMO

Map 1, 4. Open 9–6.50, Sun and holidays 9–1; T: 055 230 2885. Entrance behind the east end of the Duomo, at Piazza del Duomo 9.
The building has been the seat of the Opera di Santa Maria del Fiore since the beginning of the 15th century. The Opera was founded in 1331 when the guild of wool mer-

chants was appointed to oversee the building and financing of the cathedral, and their successors on the board of works have been responsible for its maintenance ever since.

The museum, first opened in 1891, contains numerous masterpieces of sculpture from the Baptistery, Duomo and Campanile, and illustrates the complicated histories of all these buildings. It includes very fine works by Donatello and Luca della Robbia. There are long-term plans to expand the exhibition space into a former 18th-century theatre next door. Highlights are described below.

Ground floor

Panels from the Baptistery doors
The original gilded bronze panels by Lorenzo Ghiberti (*described on p. 62*), removed from the east doors of the Baptistery, were not on display at the time of writing since they are to be reinstalled in their original door frames. The huge doors will be exhibited in the museum's new extension.

Three-figure statue groups from above the three Baptistery doors
The magnificent *Beheading of St John the Baptist*, with Salome present, is a masterpiece in bronze by Vincenzo Danti (1570). Since its restoration in 2008 the details of the work can really be appreciated (the head of the executioner is particularly remarkable). The bronze statues (1506–09) of *St John the Baptist in Discussion with the Levite and the Pharisee* are the most important work of Giovanfrancesco Rustici (also restored in 2008). The rare iconography records an episode in St John's gospel in which priests and Levites are sent from Jerusalem to interrogate St John about his true identity. Rustici was a pupil of Leonardo da Vinci and it is believed that the master (who is known to have been in Florence staying with the Martelli family in 1508) was responsible for the design of this magnificent three-figure group. Rustici, who was extremely skilled in terracotta as well as in casting bronze, went to France in 1527 to work for Francis I and spent the last decade of his life there. His output was limited and there are very few works in Italy by his hand. The stone group of the *Baptism of Christ* was begun by Andrea Sansovino in 1505 and finished later in the century by Vincenzo Danti (with an angel added by Innocenzo Spinazzi in the 18th century).

Sculptures from the Duomo façade
A large hall displays sculptures from the Duomo's old façade (never completed), designed by Arnolfo di Cambio and demolished in 1587. The facsimile of a drawing by Bernardino Poccetti of the old façade made shortly before its demolition is the most detailed illustration of it to have survived (and there is a scale model suggesting a reconstruction in an adjoining room). Works attributed to Arnolfo's own hand include the enigmatic seated *Madonna and Child* (with striking glass eyes), the *Madonna of the Nativity* (shown lying on her side) and *Pope Boniface VIII*. On the other long wall are the four seated Evangelists, including *St John the Evangelist* (1408), interesting as Donatello's first large-scale statue. The upper part of the body is elongated to compensate

for its raised position. The other three Evangelists, still Gothic in spirit, are by his contemporaries Nanni di Banco, Niccolò di Pietro Lamberti and Bernardo Ciuffagni. They were added to the lower part of the façade in the early 15th century.

Works from inside the Duomo
Another room displays 13th–15th-century paintings, including (displayed on its own) a processional painting of *St Agatha* with an icon of the saint, Byzantine in spirit, dating from c. 1270 by an unknown master named after this work (the painting on the other side of the panel dates from the 14th century). St Agatha was venerated in Florence as a protectress from fires and this icon would have been carried through the streets on her feast day (5th Feb). The very fine marble panels from the choir of the Duomo by Baccio Bandinelli and Giovanni Bandini (1547) representing prophets, apostles and nude male pagan figures, are beautifully carved. Beyond is the Treasury, with 14th-century reliquaries and a very unusual painting by Bernardo Daddi (dated 1335) showing a half-length figure of the Madonna between smaller figures of St Catherine of Alexandria, St Zenobius and donors.

Michelangelo's *Pietà*
This beautiful late work, carved when Michelangelo was almost 80 years old, is displayed on the stair landing. It was intended for Michelangelo's own tomb, which was to have been in the basilica of Santa Maria Maggiore in Rome. According to Vasari, the head of Nicodemus is a self-portrait. Dissatisfied with his work, the sculptor destroyed the arm and left leg of Christ, and his pupil, Tiberio Calcagni, restored the arm and finished the figure of Mary Magdalene. The sculpture was brought to Florence by Grand Duke Cosimo III for the crypt of San Lorenzo. From 1721 it was exhibited in the Duomo.

First floor

The Della Robbia and Donatello *cantorie* and statues from the Campanile
These two famous works were made in the 1430s by Luca della Robbia and Donatello, probably as organ lofts rather than singing galleries (*cantorie*) to go above the two sacristy doors in the Duomo. The one on the left, by Luca della Robbia, was his first important public commission, and is his masterpiece. The original panels are displayed beneath the reconstructed cantoria. The children (some of them drawn from Classical models), dancing, singing or playing musical instruments, are exquisitely carved within a beautiful architectural framework. Donatello's cantoria, opposite, provides a striking contrast, with a frieze of running putti against a background of coloured inlay.

Around the walls are the 16 statues of prophets and sibyls from the four sides of the Campanile. When they were removed they were already very ruinous, and for this reason they are difficult to attribute. The earliest ones, by Nino and Andrea Pisano, date from after 1337; others are attributed to their contemporary Maso di Banco and the early 15th-century sculptor Nanni di Bartolo, but the most important are those by Donatello. *Jeremiah* is one of his most remarkable marble sculptures, with a striking portrait head. *Habakkuk* was one of the sculptor's most admired works and the subject of Vasari's story that Donatello was found one day in his studio looking intensely at Habakkuk and commanding him to talk. It has always been nicknamed 'lo Zuccone' or big-head, and the form of the skull indicates that the sculptor almost certainly used a life model, perhaps a disabled man: it may be that Donatello wished to suggest that wisdom, a gift from God, is in no way connected to one's physical aspect. Donatello also sculpted the *Abraham and Isaac* (a two-figure group) and probably also the head of Jonah (sometimes identified as St John the Baptist).

Donatello's *Mary Magdalene* and the Altar of St John the Baptist

Donatello's famous wooden sculpture stood formerly in the Baptistery and is thought to be a late work (c. 1454). This dramatic statue shows the penitent Magdalene as an old, toothless woman with only her long hair covering her nakedness and her palsied hands seeming to shake as she attempts to join them in prayer.

The magnificent silver-gilt Altar of St John the Baptist (*undergoing restoration at the time of writing*), also from the Baptistery, is a Gothic work by Florentine goldsmiths, begun in 1366 and finished in the 15th century. It includes a statuette of the Baptist by Michelozzo, a relief of the *Birth of the Baptist* by Antonio Pollaiolo (on the left flank) and the *Beheading of the Baptist* by Verrocchio (on the right flank), and a Cross (1457–59).

The 27 needlework panels with scenes from the life of St John the Baptist formerly decorated vestments made for the Baptistery. These are exquisite works by the craftsmen of the Arte di Calimala, made in 1466–87 to a design by Antonio Pollaiolo in a technique known as *or nué*, created by using minute stitches in coloured silk thread over a backing of silk wrapped in beaten gold (these panels are recognised as being the best examples known of this type of needlework). There is also a remarkable early 14th-century Byzantine diptych from Constantinople made of miniature mosaic (a magnifying glass is provided) illustrating the twelve Great Feasts of the Christian year.

Prophet and a pagan nude (1547) from the unfinished choir of the Duomo, by Baccio Bandinelli. Bandinelli was the favoured sculptor of the first Medici grand dukes. These reliefs are among his finest works.

Detail from the cantoria of Luca della Robbia. Its sculpted panels illustrate Psalm 150: 'Praise the Lord! Praise God in his sanctuary; praise him in his mighty firmament! Praise him for his mighty deeds; praise him according to his surpassing greatness! Praise him with trumpet sound; praise him with lute and harp! Praise him with tambourine and dance; praise him with strings and pipe! Praise him with clanging cymbals; praise him with loud clashing cymbals! Let everything that breathes praise the Lord!'

Bas-reliefs from the Campanile

The original bas-reliefs, probably designed by Giotto and removed from the two lower registers of the Campanile, are exhibited in a room on their own (some have been restored and others are awaiting restoration). The overall programme includes a fascinating mixture of biblical subjects, personifications of the arts (with special reference to the occupations represented by the guilds) and ethical and cosmic symbols. The lower row, dating from the early 14th century, are charming works by Andrea Pisano; they illustrate the *Creation of Man* and the *Arts* and *Industries*. The last five reliefs (on the right wall) were made in 1437–39 by Luca della Robbia to fill the frames on the north face of the Campanile: *Grammar*, *Philosophy*, *Orpheus* (representing Poetry or Rhetoric), *Arithmetic* and *Astrology* (with the figure of Pythagoras). The upper row of smaller reliefs, by pupils of Pisano, illustrate the seven planets, the Virtues and the Liberal Arts and the lunette of the *Madonna and Child*, formerly over a door of the Campanile, is by Andrea Pisano, who also carved the exquisite statuettes of the *Redeemer* and *Santa Reparata*. Andrea, as his name suggests, came from Pisa. A goldsmith by training, he was called to Florence at the end of the 14th century to carry out the bronze panels for the south door of the Baptistery. As both sculptor and architect he then collaborated closely with Giotto on the Campanile from 1334 onwards.

The worksite for the construction of the dome
In a corridor, scaffolding and tools reconstruct a building site thought to be similar to that set up by Brunelleschi when working on the dome of the cathedral. The apparatus which may have been used in the construction of the cupola (or in its maintenance), including pulleys, ropes, tackle, hoists and technical instruments, is displayed here, as well as Brunelleschi's original brick moulds.

An analysis since 1994 of the 20,000 or so documents in the archives of the Opera of Santa Maria del Fiore for the period 1417–36 have provided us with a detailed account of the people connected with the construction of the dome (available online; *www.operaduomo.firenze.it/cupola*). The workforce during the 16 years it took to build the dome was usually around 70 or 80, including master builders and manual labourers. Only one fatal accident is reported during the entire operation.

The wooden model of the lantern on display here is thought to have been made by Brunelleschi himself as his (winning) entry in the competition of 1436. It is displayed next to the great architect's death mask, an extraordinarily moving work.

The last rooms have exhibits relating to the architecture of the Duomo from the 16th century onwards: models entered for the competition held in 1507 for a balustrade to cover the brickwork on the upper part of the drum; the large models entered in the competition held in 1587 for a new façade; and the drawings made for the present façade, the first stone of which was finally laid in 1860.

BETWEEN THE DUOMO & THE BADIA FIORENTINA

NB: The best time to visit this part of town is Mon afternoon, since that is the only time the cloister of the Badia Fiorentina is open, and the Museum of the Misericordia can also be visited then.

THE CONFRATERNITY OF THE MISERICORDIA

Ambulances are usually parked in waiting outside the building on the south side of Piazza del Duomo, which houses the Misericordia, a charitable institution which gives free emergency help to those in need (*for more on confraternities, see box opposite*). Members of the Order were to be seen all over the medieval city helping the plague-stricken, and their headquarters were moved to this site in 1576 when Francesco I provided them with a building here, although the present building dates from the time of Leopold I (1782). The members of the confraternity used to wear distinctive black capes with hoods covering all but their eyes so that their anonymity was preserved, and many 19th-century travellers to Florence recorded that they were a familiar sight in the streets. In 2005 the black habits were replaced by the standard uniform for those who work in emergency services. The cape is recorded in Pietro Annigoni's painting (1970) outside the entrance, showing a member of the confraternity carrying a sick person.

The confraternity continues its remarkable work today, with about 1,450 volunteers who run an ambulance service and carry out home visits and social services as well as providing surgeries. They have also recently begun helping those in need in foreign countries afflicted by war. Over 12,000 Florentines are enrolled in the Misericordia. It is run by 72 *capi di guardia*, with representatives both from the clergy and the lay community under a *magistrato* elected on a rotating basis.

The museum

Map 1, 4. Only open on Mon 9–12 & 3–5. Donations welcome.

The main door leads into the busy Sala di Compagnia, which preserves its old-fashioned cupboards and furniture. On the end wall is a seated statue of the *Madonna and Child* by Benedetto da Maiano (left by him to the Bigallo; finished by Battista Lorenzi in 1575). The two kneeling statues of angels are by Giovanni della Robbia.

The museum is on the second floor. In the first room there is a painting of *St John the Baptist* by a certain Giovanni Martini from Udine, recently donated to the confraternity. Also here can be seen one of the baskets in which the sick used to be transported up until 1850, when litters or sedan chairs were introduced. The lovely late 15th-century fresco of the *Madonna and Child with Two Saints* was detached from the tabernacle in Via del Campanile outside. Another room has models of the cloaks and hoods which members of the confraternity used to wear: these were red until 1489 and afterwards black. In the third room is the 16th-century altar from the oratory and a tiny Crucifix attributed to Benedetto da Maiano. The painting of the *Madonna and Child with the Young St John* by Giovanni Antonio di Francesco Sogliani was donated to the Misericordia in 1782 by Grand Duke Peter Leopold. Also here are works by Santi di Tito, including small panels showing the work of the brotherhood. *The Prodigal Son* by Valentin de Boulogne and *Christ among the Doctors* (1617) by Dirck van Baburen both show the influence of Caravaggio.

The meeting room of the *capi di guardia* can also be visited, as well as two other panelled rooms where the *conservatori*, or administrators, and the *magistrati* who control the regulations of the brotherhood all still meet. Ready on the desks are the black and white balls which have always been used in the complicated voting systems.

CONFRATERNITIES

These lay brotherhoods played an important part in the life of the medieval city. They were mostly religious organisations and one of their most important roles was to help those in need: to give alms and medical care to the poor. They were organised along the lines of the guilds (*see p. 98*), and membership was open to all. It has been estimated that only about 18 confraternities had existed in Florence before 1300, but that the number had grown to around 68 by the end of the century. Some of the earliest were *laudesi* companies, who concentrated their pious efforts on singing hymns. One of these, at Santa Maria Novella, founded c. 1245 by the first Dominican saint, Peter Martyr, became wealthy enough to commission a *Maestà* from Duccio for their chapel in 1285 (*see p. 113*). The most famous of the charitable confraternities, the Misericordia, came into being after the terrible plague of 1326. From then on it was particularly active during plague years, when it not only tried to alleviate the sufferings of those who contracted the disease but also attended to their burial. The Compagnia del Bigallo, the successor to a brotherhood probably founded in the 13th century, was also involved in charitable works, in particular in looking after orphans. In 1425 these two confraternities were merged by Giovanni di Bicci de' Medici (they both still have their headquarters beside each other in Piazza del Duomo).

Even Florentine merchants who had fallen into penury, sometimes for political reasons, and who were too proud to beg for charity, were given help through the Compagnia dei Buonomini di San Martino, founded in 1442 by St Antoninus Pierozzi (the prior of San Marco), and which still operates today (*see p. 78*). All these confraternities depended on bequests from the wealthy for their income. In later years, on the feast day of St Bonaventura, the prison in the Bargello was opened to various confraternities and charitable companies, who were allowed to visit the prisoners and bring them food and clothing.

Particularly interesting frescoes and paintings depicting members of these confraternities at work can be seen in this part of town.

The oratory

The pretty little oratory (*entered to the left of the main door*), decorated in the 17th century, contains a very fine marble statue of *St Sebastian* by Benedetto da Maiano which is said to have influenced the early work of Michelangelo. This was left unfinished by Benedetto in his studio to the northeast of the Duomo (on the corner of Via dei Servi and Via del Castellaccio), where he had been at work on many fine sculptures since 1480, and was also bequeathed by the sculptor to the Bigallo. St Sebastian became the brotherhood's patron saint in 1575 and his feast day (20th Jan) is still celebrated here, when the exterior is hung with garlands. The enamelled terracotta altarpiece by Andrea della Robbia was commissioned by Francesco Sassetti for his chapel in the Badia Fiesolana.

THE CONFRATERNITY OF THE BIGALLO

The small Gothic **Loggia del Bigallo** was built for the Misericordia in 1351–58, probably by Alberto Arnoldi, who also carved the reliefs and the lunette of the *Madonna and Child* (1361) above the door into the oratory (facing the Baptistery). The Compagnia del Bigallo moved to this seat in 1425 when it was merged with the Misericordia. Its main purpose was to take care of orphans, and lost and abandoned children were exhibited beneath the loggia for three days before being consigned to foster mothers. The three 14th-century statues in tabernacles high up above the loggia came from the Bigallo's former headquarters near Orsanmichele. Today the Bigallo runs a hospice for the elderly in Via Guelfa.

The **Museo del Bigallo** is the smallest museum in the city and one of the most charming (*map 1, 4; open in winter 10–5.50 except Tues and Wed; in summer 10–6.50 except Tues; the entrance ticket supports the Bigallo's charitable work*). It preserves precious works of art commissioned from Florentine artists by the Misericordia and the Bigallo.

In the oratory the statues of the *Madonna and Child* and two angels by Alberto Arnoldi (1359–64) were placed in a gilded wood tabernacle by Noferi di Antonio Noferi in 1515. Beneath them the predella by Ridolfo del Ghirlandaio includes a scene (on the right) of Tobias burying a corpse, in which the Loggia del Bigallo has been taken as the setting and hooded members of the Misericordia are shown at work. The tondo of the *Madonna and Saints* in a beautiful contemporary frame is by Jacopo del Sellaio. The painted Crucifix is attributed to an unknown mid-13th-century painter, named from this work the Master of the Bigallo.

The tiny sacristy preserves one of Bernardo Daddi's most important early works, an exquisite little portable triptych dated 1333, still in very good condition. The charming *Madonna of Humility*, painted against a lovely brocaded curtain held up by two angels, is by Domenico di Michelino (1359–64).

The Sala dei Capitani has a fresco of the *Madonna of the Misericordia* by an artist in the circle of Bernardo Daddi, which bears the date 1342 but was probably carried out in 1350. At the Madonna's feet is the earliest known view of Florence, with the marble Baptistery prominent in the centre near the incomplete campanile and façade of the

Duomo, and the towers of Palazzo della Signoria, the Badia and the Bargello all present. The fresco fragment of the captains of the Misericordia entrusting lost and abandoned children to foster mothers outside the Loggia dei Bigallo (1386) is by Niccolò di Pietro Gerini and Ambrogio di Baldese. It was detached from the outside of the building in 1777 (the complete fresco is shown in its original position in the small 18th-century watercolour exhibited here). Between the windows is a painting by the school of Orcagna (c. 1360) of St Peter Martyr giving the standard to twelve captains of the Bigallo, recording the tradition of the founding of the confraternity. Dating from around the same time are the twelve charming frescoed scenes (damaged when they were detached from the old meeting hall) which illustrate the life of Tobias, the first patron saint of the Misericordia. There are several old wall cupboards containing statute books, and a relief in *pietra serena* with the Altoviti coat of arms by Desiderio da Settignano. Beyond the fine inlaid doors (1450), which bear the arms of the Misericordia and the Bigallo, stairs lead up to an exhibition about Leonardo da Vinci, with models and diagrams of relative interest—and without any connection to the Bigallo.

THE SASSO DI DANTE & VIA DELLO STUDIO

Palazzo dei Canonici on Piazza del Duomo (no. 15) was built by Gaetano Baccani in 1826. It has heavy columns and two colossal statues of Arnolfo di Cambio and Brunelleschi by Luigi Pampaloni (1830). It replaced the medieval canonry which had a long stone bench on which Dante is supposed to have enjoyed taking the air on hot summer evenings in the company of friends. An old stone slab can still be seen set low down into the façade of the 19th-century building (by no. 13) inscribed '**Sasso di Dante**' ('Dante's Stone'). This perpetuates a legend, particularly popular with 19th-century visitors, that Dante used this very stone as a foot-rest. Samuel Rogers, Ruskin, Wordsworth, Dickens and the Brownings all mention it and hallowed this spot, as did so many other travellers, attracted by its supposed association with the poet. In 1903 Mrs Oliphant put the story into its true perspective: 'The beautiful cathedral, which so many a traveller, thoughtless of dates, has contemplated from the Sasso di Dante, with a dim notion that Dante himself must have sat there many a summer evening watching the glorious walls rise and the great noble fabric come into being, had not, even in the lower altitude given to it by Arnolfo, begun to be when the poet was born.' (*The Makers of Florence*).

Via dello Studio, still with its lovely old paving stones, slopes gently downwards to the Corso. On the corner with Via Canonica is the 13th-century **Palazzo Tedaldini**, with an inscription recording the birthplace of St Antoninus (with his terracotta portrait bust above it, a copy of the one in San Martino; *see p. 79*).

The low building with a cast of the relief of the stonemasons' and carpenters' guild on Orsanmichele, has been used since the mid-19th century as a **workshop of the stonemasons of the Opera di Santa Maria del Fiore**, and they can usually be seen at work here. Over the centuries the stonework of the exterior of the Duomo has had to be constantly renewed in order to preserve it against the elements, a task which continues to this day. The interior is shown on guided tours by previous appointment (*for information, artecultura@operaduomo.firenze.it; T: 055 282226*).

Pegna, on the left hand side, is one of the smartest shops to have survived in Florence, where Florentines come to buy luxury foods or even just household cleaners—a place which is bound to have the best but sometimes obscurest brand of just about everything—and opposite is Zecchi, one of Florence's best shops for artists' materials. It is in an old low building with a damaged fresco and the arms of the Opera di Santa Maria del Fiore and medieval ground-floor arches. The neo-Renaissance doorway, surmounted by a pretty della Robbian lunette, bears the date 1926. **Palazzo Salviati** (now the head office of the Banca Toscana) was built in 1470–80 by the Portinari family. This was the family of Dante's beloved celestial muse, Beatrice. In 1546 the palace was bought and enlarged by Jacopo Salviati, nephew of Maria Salviati, wife of Giovanni delle Bande Nere and mother of Cosimo I. In the banking hall there is a 14th-century fresco of the *Madonna and Child*.

MEDIEVAL TOWERS

By the mid-11th century there were towers on the northern side of Piazza della Signoria. During the following century it became the custom for wealthy Florentines to erect towers next to their houses, for defensive reasons, as refuges in times of trouble, as well as status symbols. It is estimated that there were as many as 150 towers in the medieval city, many of them over 50m high, and some reaching 70m. But in time they came to be seen as a threat to security since their owners only had to throw stones or shoot missiles from their upper storeys to cause serious damage in the street below and spark off a spate of urban warfare. Thus after 1250 the government of the *Primo Popolo* ordered that no tower could be higher than 29m. This decree also ensured that their own tower, built to a magnificent height of 57m, could dominate the townscape (now called the Bargello, it is still one of the highest buildings in Florence). Private towers were often connected to the family residence well above ground level by means of scaffolding supported by beams inserted into holes in the masonry (many of which can still be seen), which is why today some of the doors appear suspended in mid-air. Groups of towers were sometimes connected by overhead walkways around a courtyard in which there might be a well. Later in the 14th century many towers were adapted as houses. Their battlements indicated the owners' allegiance: rectangular merlons signified support for the Guelphs and swallow-tail merlons for the Ghibellines.

ON & AROUND VIA DEL CORSO

Via dello Studio leads into the Corso (*map 1, 4*), on the line of a Roman road. Today this narrow street, lined with shops and some smart new wine bars, is always busy with pedestrians. Opposite the end of Via dello Studio is the 13th-century **Torre dei Donati**, a truncated medieval tower. The Donati were rivals of the Cerchi (*see p. 79*) and headed the *Neri* (Black) faction of the Guelph party, responsible for Dante's exile. A short way along the Corso on the right is the church of **Santa Margherita** (1508), preceded by a portico by Gherardo Silvani (1611). The interior was reconstructed by Zanobi del Rosso in 1769, and contains paintings by Giovanni Camillo Sagrestani (1707). It is kept open all day and often has rather over-loud music. Beyond, the entrance to **Via Sant'Elisabetta** is flanked by two medieval towers. It leads to a little piazza of the same name with the ancient Torre della Pagliazza, built of round pebbles of *alberese* found in the bed of the Arno. One of the very few round towers to have survived, its shape is thought to derive from the curved exedra of the Roman baths once on this site. It was used as a prison in the 13th–14th centuries but was sadly over-restored in 1988 for use as a hotel.

Back in the Corso and on the left, by a pleasant old-fashioned café (Cucciolo) which has an ingenious 'slide' from the back kitchen down which delicious hot doughnuts are rolled, there is an old archway. It leads into a passage which preserves its ancient 'crazy' paving and passes a tabernacle with a 16th-century *Annunciation*. The little church of **Santa Margherita de' Cerchi**, of 12th-century foundation, is where Dante is supposed to have married Gemma Donati. The 14th-century porch bears the arms of the Cerchi, Adimari and Donati, who lived in the parish. In the interior there is a lovely altarpiece of the *Madonna Enthroned with Four Female Saints* by Neri di Bicci.

Dante Alighieri (1265–1321)

Via Dante Alighieri probably runs near the site of the birthplace of the greatest Italian poet, Dante Alighieri, whose famous *Divine Comedy* established Tuscan as the literary vernacular of Italy. As a young man he fought in the Battle of Campaldino (1289) on the winning (Guelph) side against the Ghibellines of Arezzo. In 1295 Dante entered Florentine politics and in 1300 served a two-month term as one of the six priors of the city. At this time the Guelph party split into two factions, the *Bianchi* (Whites) and the *Neri* (the Blacks). Dante was sent to Rome as part of an official delegation to dissuade Pope Boniface VIII from his support of the *Neri* in Florence, but during his absence the *Neri* were able to take control of the city government and there followed a period of vindictive repression of the *Bianchi*. Dante was accused of fraud and corruption and when he failed to return in 1302 to defend himself he was sentenced to death and so went into exile. Although at first he kept in touch with the other exiled *Bianchi*, he soon became disillusioned with politics and was disappointed with his Florentine contemporaries who became dominated by factious rivalry. He never returned to Florence, and died in 1321 in Ravenna. Although Dante married Gemma Donati, his love for Beatrice inspired much of his work: Boccaccio, his biographer, identified her as the daughter of Folco Portinari. We know that Dante and Giotto were good friends.

Casa di Dante

In a group of houses that were carefully restored and partly rebuilt in 13th-century style in 1911 is the Museo Casa di Dante Alighieri (*map 1, 4; open April–Sept every day 10–6, otherwise 10–5; closed Mon; T: 055 219416*). It is an interesting example of Revival architecture by the Florentine architect Giuseppe Castellucci, with attention to every detail, both inside and out. The little piazza here was created at the same time. The museum has interesting reconstructions, models and maps of Florence in Dante's time, well labelled also in English. You can also climb right up to the enclosed loggia at the top, from which there is a view of the summit of the tower of Palazzo Vecchio.

San Martino del Vescovo

The charming little Oratory of San Martino del Vescovo or San Martino dei Buonomini (*map 1, 6; open 10–12 & 3–5 except Sun and holidays and some Fri afternoons; closed for restoration at the time of writing*) stands near the site of the 10th-century parish church of the Alighieri and Donati families. On the exterior there is a 17th-century tabernacle by Cosimo Ulivelli showing *St Martin Distributing Alms*. The chapel was rebuilt in 1479 when it became the seat of the Compagnia dei Buonomini di San Martino, a charitable institution of 'good men' founded in 1442 by St Antoninus Pierozzi (the prior of San Marco) for Florentine citizens (often merchants) who had fallen on hard times (their requests for help would be posted through the marble letterbox, still marked '*per le istanze*'). It was administered by twelve men who each held the office of *proposto* for one month of the year, and the charter stipulated that alms should be distributed as soon as they were collected. When their resources ran out, the *compagnia* would light a candle (*lumicino*) over the doorway to alert the populace to their need for funds (a Florentine expression, '*essere al lumicino*', survives to this day, indicating that someone is in dire straits). The twelve members of the confraternity, with their assistants, still meet in a hall behind the oratory every Friday afternoon to deliberate: they receive written requests for financial help and then decide how to distribute the donations they receive (visitors are kindly asked to make a contribution).

Inside, the lunettes are decorated with charming 15th-century frescoes by the workshop of Domenico Ghirlandaio. They are of great interest for their portrayal of contemporary Florentine life. They illustrate the *Seven Acts of Mercy* being carried out by the Buonomini (identified by their black or red cloaks). These are: distribution of clothing, giving food and drink to the hungry and thirsty, visiting the sick, visiting prisoners (the painting of the grey-haired official in a red cloak shows the influence of Filippino Lippi), giving lodging to travellers and burying the dead. On the altar wall are two scenes from the life of St Martin: *St Martin Dividing his Cloak with the Beggar*, and *Christ Appearing to St Martin in a Dream Wearing his Cloak* (the angels are reminiscent of the hand of Botticelli). On the right wall are two more scenes of the Buonomini at work: compiling an inventory of possessions left to them in a will and providing a poor girl with a dowry.

Also here are two beautiful paintings of the *Madonna*, one of them Byzantine (11th century) and the other very close to the style of Perugino but attributed to his near contemporary, the little-known painter Nicolò Soggi. On the altar is a reliquary bust of St Antoninus attributed to Verrocchio. Two terracotta angels by the school of Verrocchio are kept in the meeting hall. The archives of the company include the registers used in the daily administration of charity from 1469 to the present.

Via de' Cerchi

The splendid 13th-century **Torre della Castagna** (*corner of Piazza S. Martino and Via Dante Alighieri*) is one of the best-preserved medieval towers in the city. From 1282 onwards it was the residence of the priors who represented the interests of the guilds and controlled the government before they moved into Palazzo dei Priori (now Palazzo Vecchio), which was specially built for them in the first decade of the 14th century.

Via Dante Alighieri ends in **Piazza de' Cimatori**, which has a stall selling tripe sandwiches, one of many all over the city specialising in this Florentine 'delicacy'. There are a number of plaques on buildings in this district which were part of a series set up all over Florence in 1907 to record people and places mentioned by Dante in his *Divine Comedy*. The narrow medieval streets here, close to Piazza della Signoria, are well worth exploring. They include **Via de' Cerchi** (*map 1, 4–6*), a local shopping street, which still has its pretty iron lamp brackets. If you follow it to the left it crosses Via de' Cimatori, which has another Cerchi family tower, erected just at the time when Dante first became interested in Florentine politics. The next cross-street is Via Condotta where, on the corner of Vicolo de' Cerchi, can be seen the 13th-century Palazzo Cerchi. The Cerchi were one of the most important and wealthiest families in Florence by the end of the 13th century, allied to the Guelph party. The priors of the city even chose to meet in the Cerchi's residence here before Palazzo dei Priori was erected as the town's seat of government.

THE BADIA FIORENTINA

Map 1, 6. Open all day for prayer. Vespers at 6pm. Visitors are asked to come only on Mon afternoon (3–6), which is the only day the cloister is also open. Main entrance on Via del Proconsolo; if closed, side entrance on Via Dante Alighieri 1. Since 1998 the church has been used by the Monastic Fraternity of Jerusalem, founded in Paris in 1975. Some of the 20 or so monks and nuns are nearly always to be seen in silent prayer and contemplation kneeling on the floor in front of the altar (while others are out on their bicycles serving those in need in the community).

Excellent natural products from numerous monasteries are sold in a pleasant little shop called Monastica in a chapel off the portico, open Tues–Sat 10–12 & 3–6; Mon only 3–6.

The Badia Fiorentina is the church of an ancient Benedictine abbey founded and richly endowed in 978 by Willa, the widow of Uberto, Margrave of Tuscia, in memory of her husband. At this time Tuscia (Tuscany) was a province of the Frankish empire with its capital at Lucca. Willa and Uberto's son, Count Ugo of Brandenburg, also a benefactor of the abbey, was buried in the church when he died in 1001. Since he preferred Florence to Lucca, he is praised by Dante as the '*gran barone*' in his *Paradiso* (Canto

Detail of two angels from Filippino Lippi's *Madonna Appearing to St Bernard* (c. 1485).

XVI, 127) and the poet mentions that he is remembered every year on the feast day of St Thomas the Apostle (a Mass is still said here on 21st Dec to honour his memory).

One of the first hospitals in the city was established in the abbey in 1031, and the church was rebuilt in 1284–1310, probably by Arnolfo di Cambio, but little of its medieval architecture remains today.

Exterior of the Badia

The church has no real façade but there is some old masonry from its medieval east end on Via del Proconsolo, beside its main entrance through a handsome portal by Benedetto da Rovezzano (1495). This incorporates the dolphin motif, the emblem of the Pandolfini family, who were important benefactors of the church over several centuries. The enamelled terracotta *Madonna* in the lunette is by Benedetto Buglioni. Benedetto da Rovezzano designed the Corinthian portico from which there is a good view of the graceful campanile, the bottom portion of which is Romanesque (1307) and the top Gothic (after 1330). It is an important feature in Florence's skyline, and the tolling of the bell at the beginning and end of the working day, also mentioned by Dante (*Paradiso*, Canto XV, 97–98), regulated life in the medieval city.

Interior of the Badia

Nothing remains of the medieval appearance of the church, which was rebuilt on a

Greek cross plan in 1627–31. The splendid carved wood ceiling dates from that time. The religious community here have managed to imbue a very special atmosphere of silence and prayer or contemplation, so that you can feel as if you are intruding on the peace unless you come here on a Monday afternoon.

On the entrance wall, the tomb of Giannozzo Pandolfini, who died in 1456, consists of a plain sarcophagus (without effigy) supported by the family emblem of two dolphins beneath a finely carved lunette. It is attributed to the workshop of Bernardo Rossellino. The painting of the *Madonna Appearing to St Bernard of Clairvaux* is a large panel of great charm by Filippino Lippi (c. 1485), very unusual for its iconography. As well as founding some 68 Cistercian abbeys, St Bernard was also very learned and he is here shown seated at lectern made from the stump of a tree with his books piled up beside him. The Madonna is accompanied by a playful group of angels, while below the devout donor (Piero di Francesco del Pugliese) is shown witnessing the scene. The painting was commissioned as an altarpiece for another church outside the walls, but was removed for safekeeping during the siege of Florence in 1530, and has remained here ever since.

The carved altarpiece of the *Madonna Between Sts Leonard and Lawrence* is a very fine work by Mino da Fiesole (1464–69). This important Renaissance sculptor also carved the two similar funerary monuments in the right and left arms of the nave: that on the right is the tomb of Bernardo Giugni, a Florentine statesman (1396–1466), with a good effigy and statue of *Justice*, and the one on the left commemorates Ugo, Margrave of Tuscia, and dates from 1469–81. Both these exquisite works have reclining effigies and beautifully carved lunettes and the marble details are highlighted against deep red porphyry panels, but each of them has a very original design.

The very fine organ by Onofrio Zeffirini dates from 1558. It is often used for recitals. It is decorated with early 17th-century paintings including two tondi by Francesco Furini. The matching choir loft opposite bears a good painting of the *Assumption and Two Saints* by Vasari (1568). The painting of the *Way to Calvary* by Giovanni Battista Naldini in the chapel nearby dates from the same period. In the other chapel in the left arm of the nave are displayed four damaged frescoes by Nardo di Cione, with scenes from the Passion of Christ (including Judas hanging from a tree after his suicide). These were detached from a wall of the medieval church, and other very interesting fresco fragments of the same date, attributed to Giotto, were discovered in the 1950s, including the head of a shepherd with his sheep (now exhibited in the Galleria dell'Accademia). Off the right arm of the nave there is a large Baroque chapel with 18th-century vault frescoes and quadratura (by Vincenzo Meucci and Pietro Anderlini) and an altarpiece (by Onorio Marinari, 1663) all celebrating the life of the obscure Benedictine saint Maurus. The impressive frescoed decoration of the east end of the church also dates from the 18th century and is the work of Giovanni Domenico Ferretti. Here are preserved fine choir stalls carved in 1501 by Francesco and Marco del Tasso.

The cloister

The peaceful cloister was built in 1432–38 to designs by Bernardo Rossellino. It has been called the Chiostro degli Aranci since the 17th century, when it was used to cultivate orange trees (one of which still flourishes here). From here you can see three of the most important towers of the city: that of the Badia itself, as well as those of the Bargello and Palazzo Vecchio. The interesting and well-preserved fresco cycle illustrates scenes from the life of St Benedict by an unknown master (usually called the Master of the Chiostro degli Aranci), working in the decade after the death of Masaccio. Some scholars have attributed them to Giovanni di Consalvo, a Portuguese artist and follower of Fra' Angelico, since we know that the abbot who commissioned them in 1432 was from Portugal.

North walk: In the first scene (right) St Benedict is shown leaving Rome, where he had moved from Norcia to study, coming out of a gate on horseback (the city is depicted with numerous medieval towers). The young saint is next shown kneeling before his nurse performing a miracle in which he mends a sieve which she has broken (and on the right it is exhibited above the door of a church for an admiring crowd). In the third lunette the saint is shown being robed in his black habit, and as a hermit in a rocky landscape (with a basket and bell being lowered to him in his grotto). The priest on the left, enjoying his Easter lunch, is being chastised by the angel above, who reminds him that at that very time his brother Benedict is suffering the pangs of hunger. The fourth lunette was painted some hundred years later, around 1525, by Bronzino and shows Benedict nude in a bramble bush resisting temptations, and then in prayer, in a fine landscape. The last lunette on this side shows Benedict seated in the interior of his monastery blessing a glass of wine held up to him by one of the monks (the vessel promptly breaks from the pressure of holiness).

West walk: The first lunette shows a monk being dragged out of a monastery by the devil, but saved when Benedict touches him with a stick. The next scene shows Benedict pulling a scythe out of a river full of fish. It had been deliberately thrown there in anger by a peasant while working in the monastery fields (and he is shown kneeling in contrition on the right). The eighth scene shows a monk sent by Benedict (seated on the right) saving another monk from drowning in a river. The rocky landscape includes a garden of orange trees. The next scene is one of the most delightful: it is set in the refectory of a convent with the monks neatly seated at an L-shaped table with the memorable detail of a towel hanging on a rail above them. The story goes that when a brother monk offered Benedict a poisoned piece of bread, a raven flew in and pecked it away before it could do any harm. The next scene shows a large group of monks at work building a monastery: as they try to lift up a huge block of stone, the devil, in the form of a basilisk, stands on it and so makes it too heavy for them. Only through the prayers of Benedict are they able to continue work. The next scene shows a ruined building and a monk buried in the debris: he is extracted and miraculously brought back to life by Benedict on the left. The last two scenes, evidently painted by a less-skilled master, illustrate the story of Benedict with King Totila and his entourage.

In the remaining lunettes of the cloister, six of the fascinating sinopie discovered during the restoration of the cycle (when the scenes were detached) are exhibited.

PALAZZO DELL'ARTE DEI GIUDICI E NOTAI

Map 1, 4. Via del Proconsolo 16r (Alle Murate restaurant). Patrons of the restaurant eat beneath the 14th-century painted vault, which can also be seen by appointment, usually from 5–7 except Mon, T: 055 240618. There is a walkway which allows you to get very close to the ceiling, and an excellent audio guide in English is lent to visitors.

Almost opposite the Badia Fiorentina, on the corner of Via de' Pandolfini, is the tall and narrow Palazzo dell'Arte dei Giudici e Notai (with an open loggia on the top floor). This was the seat of the guild of the judges and notaries. Its head was the 'proconsul': the palace is also known as Palazzo del Proconsolo and the street here, Via del Proconsolo, is named after this official, whose rank took precedence over all the other guild leaders.

The 14th-century painted decorations on the vault and upper walls of the guildhall, mentioned by Vasari but subsequently whitewashed when the palace was in private hands, have been uncovered and carefully cleaned since 2005 by the owner of the restaurant. They are considered one of the most important discoveries in recent years in Florence, since very few depictions of secular subjects have survived from this time. We know that Jacopo di Cione carried out paintings here in 1366, commissioned from the guild, although it does not seem that they are all by his hand.

On the vault a very unusual circular composition shows the stylised walls of Florence with four open gates and eight towers enclosing the arms and symbols of the institutions which made up the government of the medieval city, including the 21 guilds and their patron saints, and the symbols of the four districts of the city. There are fascinating allegorical figures of the Virtues and figures apparently associated with Justice against a blue ground in the rest of the vault. Around the top of the walls, and probably dating from later in the 14th century, are four worn lunettes including one with a group of illustrious Florentines where the profile of Dante has been recognised as the earliest such portrait in existence (the other one is thought to represent Boccaccio). In the basement (also used by the restaurant) you can visit the Roman remains which have recently been uncovered. These include foundations with wooden piles driven into the ground (of uncertain significance; they may have been connected to a fuller's workshop).

THE BARGELLO

The massive crenellated Palazzo del Bargello (*map 1, 6*), with its very high tower, is thought to have been built in the 1290s as the Palazzo del Primo Popolo, and is the oldest seat of government that survives in the city. According to Vasari it was begun to a design by a certain Lapo, the master of Arnolfo di Cambio, and building continued until 1330–50. Constructed in *pietra forte* and well restored in 1857–65, the Bargello preserves its 14th-century appearance to this day.

History of the palace

At first it was the seat of the *Capitano del Popolo*, an office which had been created in 1244. The *capitano* was a non-Florentine, who, during his one-year term of office, held supreme authority in the government of the city. By the end of the 13th century the government was ruled by priors (*priori*), who took up residence in Palazzo Vecchio. From that time up until 1502, the Bargello became the official residence of the *podestà*, the governing magistrate, who was also traditionally a non-Florentine. In the 16th century, the building became known as the Bargello, when the police headquarters were moved here and prisons were installed (in use until 1858–59, when Tuscany joined the Kingdom of Italy). In 1786, when the enlightened grand duke Peter Leopold abolished the death sentence, instruments of torture were burnt in the courtyard. This was only a short time after Cesare Beccaria (1735–94) had made his famous denunciation of capital punishment and torture, and published his far-sighted theories on crime prevention.

The tower still houses the bell called the 'Montanina' (in 1302 it was seized from the castle of Montale near Pistoia after a Florentine victory there). It used to be rung to announce executions, but on 11th August 1944 its loud peals welcomed the arrival of British and American soldiers in Florence and the liberation of the city from German occupation (it made itself heard again in May 1945 at the end of the war).

MUSEO NAZIONALE DEL BARGELLO

Open 8.15–1.50; closed 1st, 3rd and 5th Sun and 2nd and 4th Mon of the month; usually longer opening hours (until 5pm) from Easter–Sept and when exhibitions are in progress; T: 055 238 8606. Entrance in Via del Proconsolo. Rooms 11, 15, 17 and 18 are often kept closed. The museum that is housed in the Bargello is one of the most important in Florence, and all the more appealing for hardly ever being overcrowded. It is perhaps the best place in the city to understand the significance of the Florentine Renaissance, since it has a superb collection of sculpture from that period, including numerous works by Donatello and the della Robbia family. Sixteenth-century Florentine sculptors are also well represented, with masterpieces by Michelangelo, Cellini and Giambologna among others, and it has an exquisite collection of small Mannerist bronzes. The building also houses a notable collection of decorative arts.

The museum came into being in 1859, when the Uffizi's collection of sculpture and applied arts was transferred here, and it was first opened to the public in 1865. In 1888, the important Carrand collection was left to the museum, and later acquisitions included the Ressmann collection of armour and the Franchetti collection of fabrics.

Ground floor

NB: Letters assigned in the text correspond to the plans displayed in each room.

(1) **The Courtyard:** The splendid old Gothic courtyard of the palace survives, adorned with the coats of arms of the former *podestà*. Here are arranged large sculptures from various periods. Under the north portico (on the left as you enter) is an unusual large high relief of the *Coronation of Ferdinand of Aragon*, with six boy musicians, by Benedetto da Maiano. The extraordinary lamp on the wall dates from the 16th century. Under the east portico are six fine statues (including *Juno*) by Ammannati (1556–61) from an allegorical fountain which was intended for the south end of the Salone dei Cinquecento in Palazzo Vecchio. Instead it was first put in the Villa di Pratolino, and then, in 1588, moved to the terrace above the courtyard of Palazzo Pitti (where it was later replaced by the Fontana del Carciofo). The statues were then dispersed in the Boboli Gardens and were only finally reassembled here in the 1970s. Another statue from those gardens (under the south portico) is Giambologna's colossal *Oceanus*, which was the largest work in marble he made. The *Fisherboy* (1877) is by the Neapolitan sculptor Vincenzo Gemito.

The Cannon of St Paul is a wonderful piece of casting by Cosimo Cenni (commissioned in 1638 by Grand Duke Ferdinando II for Livorno castle). The smaller cannon, cast by Cenni in 1620, shows the planet Jupiter with its four

satellites discovered by Galileo just ten years earlier. The colossal statues of the *Madonna and Child* and *Sts Peter and Paul* from the Porta Romana, by Paolo di Giovanni, date from the 14th century.

(2) **The Michelangelo Room:** This fine hall contains 16th-century sculpture by Michelangelo and his Florentine contemporaries. The four superb works by Michelangelo represent different stages in the great sculptor's highly successful career. The **Bacchus Drunk** is his first important sculpture, and clearly shows the influence of Classical works. It was made on his first visit to Rome c. 1497 for Cardinal Raffaele Riario, who provided the sculptor with the ancient block of marble. But once completed the cardinal was unhappy with it, so his associate, the banker Jacopo Galli, agreed to buy it, and he kept it in his garden of antique sculptures for over 50 years. Galli recognised the genius of Michelangelo and it was he who suggested his name to the French cardinal Jean de Bilhères, who was looking for a sculptor for his tomb in St Peter's (and so it was that Michelangelo carried out his wonderful *Pietà* there for the Frenchman). The *Bacchus* was brought to Florence when it was later purchased by the Medici.

The tondo of the **Madonna and Child with the Infant St John** was made for Bartolomeo Pitti c. 1503–05. It is a deeply moving work, and a fine example of the sculptor's *schiacciato* technique.

The **bust of *Brutus*** was made much later (probably in the 1540s). It is the only bust Michelangelo ever sculpted and was left unfinished. It owes much to imperial Roman portrait busts (Michelangelo's pupil Tiberio Calcagni added the toga) but transcends the familiar Classical static pose since the head is turned so dramatically to the left. It was made for Cardinal Niccolò Ridolfi (a grandson of Lorenzo the Magnificent), who became a friend of Michelangelo in the 1530s as leader of the Florentine exiles in Rome. Since it was made just after the murder of Duke Alessandro de' Medici by his cousin Lorenzaccio, it is usually seen as an exaltation of Republicanism—more idealistic than strictly appropriate to the circumstances. Alessandro was certainly a tyrant, but Lorenzaccio was not much more wholesome. His bid to glorify himself as a tyrannicide led merely to the election of his kinsman Cosimo, son of Giovanni delle Bande Nere, as duke, ushering in the second period of hereditary Medici rule.

The small figure called *Apollo*, who is apparently extracting an arrow from his back, is another beautiful work by Michelangelo with a *contrapposto* pose. Also known as *David*, it was commissioned by Baccio Valori, who took control of the government of Florence after the siege by imperial and papal troops in 1530, and was left unfinished in the artist's studio when he left Florence for good in 1534. Cosimo I later acquired it and kept it in his bedroom, and it was then set up in the Boboli Gardens before being displayed amongst the antique sculptures in the Uffizi corridor.

Don't miss the bronze **portrait bust of Michelangelo** displayed against one of the central pillars. This is one of several by Daniele da Volterra, a pupil of Michelangelo who became one of his closest friends towards the end of his life and who was present at his death. It is the best portrait of the great artist, who lived to the exceptional age of 89. Another version, sent by Daniele to Michelangleo's heir Lionardo, is still in the Casa Buonarroti (*see p. 210*).

In the corner of the room towards the courtyard are **works which show Michelangelo's influence on other artists**, such as Giovanfrancesco Rustici and Andrea Sansovino and his pupil Jacopo, whose own *Bacchus* takes its inspiration from Michelangelo's statue close by. The statuettes, models and replicas (in cases against the wall) by followers of Michelangelo include works by Pietro Francavilla, Tribolo, Giambologna, Bartolomeo Ammannati and Vincenzo Danti. The small marble figure of *Leda and the Swan* by Ammannati (c. 1536) is one of the best works inspired by a famous lost painting by Michelangelo commissioned by Alfonso d'Este (which was based on an antique gem owned by the Medici). The marble bust of Cosimo I (against the far wall) is a fine work by Ammannati's master **Baccio Bandinelli**, who became the Medici's favourite sculptor after Michelangelo. He left for Rome in 1534, having overstepped the mark by carving the two colossal nude statues displayed here of Adam and Eve (with a bow in her hair!) for the Duomo, which were thought unsuitable for a church. Out of jealousy, Bandinelli ensured that Ammannati's funerary monument to the warrior Mario Nari, showing him reclining beneath an allegory of Victory, intended for the church of Santissima Annunziata, was never set up there.

Also in this part of the room is displayed an *Allegory of Fiesole* by Tribolo, in the delicate dark stone known as *pietra serena*, which was one of a series of statues (the others now lost) representing allegories of the cities and mountains of Tuscany, made for the garden of the Medici Villa di Castello. The *Dying Adonis* (with the boar which killed him) is by Bandinelli's pupil Vincenzo de' Rossi.

There follow a group of **works by Benvenuto Cellini**, Bandinelli's famous rival and one of the greatest sculptors of the age, with a style all his own, less influenced than his contemporaries by the art of Michelangelo. His works often have echoes of Hellenistic sculpture. The *Narcissus*, carved from a worn block of grey Greek marble with two holes (hence the position of the arms), was damaged in Cellini's studio during a flood of the Arno. The delicate youth is shown turning to look at his reflection in the water. Together with the *Apollo and Hyacinth*, also displayed here, it was given to Francesco I, who sent them to the park of Pratolino. They later found their way to the Boboli Gardens, and the two statues were only re-identified and brought under cover just before the Second World War. The *Apollo* was never finished as the marble was defective (since this had been ordered specially for Cellini by Bandinelli, it seems this was a deliberate plot to discredit him). Cellini's first important work in marble was the statuette of *Ganymede* (a Trojan prince carried to Olympus by an eagle to be cup-bearer to the gods), which consists of an antique Parian marble

torso (which perhaps once represented a Bacchus or an Apollo), to which Cellini added the beautiful head, arms and feet, as well as the eagle and the naturalistic details on the base in Carrara marble. We know that Cosimo I kept this piece in his bedroom, together with the *Bacchus* by Andrea Sansovino (*see above*) and another *Bacchus* by Baccio Bandinelli (now in Palazzo Pitti). The bronze statuette of Ganymede riding the eagle exhibited here is perhaps by Ammannati. The scale models made by Cellini for his famous statue of *Perseus* (*see p. 35*), one in wax and one in bronze, are very precious survivals, and between them is displayed the original marble pedestal for that statue with its small bronze statuettes and the relief of *Perseus Releasing Andromeda* (all replaced *in situ* by copies). In a more formal rhetorical spirit, Cellini cast the colossal bust of Cosimo I—his first work in bronze (1545–48). This is by the door on the end wall, and here his talent as a goldsmith can be seen in the delicate carved details of the armour.

The two-figure group representing *Honour Overcoming Deceit* is Vincenzo Danti's first and best work in marble. It was commissioned in 1561 by Sforza Almeni, chamberlain to Cosimo I, who came from Perugia where Danti was also born. The chamberlain is supposed to have chosen the subject as an allusion to an episode in which Cosimo attacked him in a fit of anger. It is exhibited near another colossal two-figure group representing *Florence Victorious over Pisa* (or *Virtue Overcoming Vice*) which was carved by **Giambologna** with the help of his pupil Pietro Francavilla around 1572. Giambologna demonstrated his incredible technical skills when he produced the bronze *Mercury* exhibited here and which seems almost on the point of flying away. The god balances on the tip of one foot held up by the wind from Zephyr. His most famous statue, it was made in Florence and sent to Rome in 1580 to adorn a fountain in front of the garden façade of the Villa Medici, but the Lorraine grand dukes moved it back to Florence. Numerous replicas have been made over the centuries. The huge bronze *Bacchus* is an early work by the same sculptor.

Giambologna (c. 1529–1608)

Jean de Boulogne was born in Douai in Flanders (now part of France) around 1529 but since he spent most of his life in Italy his name became Italianised to Giambologna. He was perhaps the greatest Mannerist sculptor to work in Florence, exerting a wide influence on his contemporaries. When he first came to Italy in 1556 he went straight to Rome, where he was inevitably influenced by the work of Michelangelo. We know he was settled in Florence by 1558 and he had the good fortune to come under the protection of Bernardo Vecchietti, who helped him start out on a brilliant career. For the last 40 years of his life he was court sculptor to the Medici. He was skilled in all media, from marble to bronze, and produced both colossal works and exquisite small bronzes. He favoured allegorical and mythological subjects. Many of his statues were designed to stand in public squares while others served as garden fountains. He produced two equestrian statues for Florence: those of Cosimo I in Piazza della Signoria and Ferdinando I in Piazza Santissima Annunziata. He had a busy workshop and very skilled pupils, including Pietro Tacca, Pietro Francavilla and Antonio Susini. He is buried in a chapel in the sanctuary of Santissima Annunziata, which he designed himself and which he intended as a memorial to all Flemish artists who died in the city. Although today the Bargello is the best place to study his work, other sculptures by him can be seen all over Florence, including the Loggia della Signoria, the Boboli Gardens and the Villa della Petraia. Perhaps the most original of all his works is the giant *Appennino* in the Villa Demidoff at Pratolino (*see p. 321*).

First floor

The most pleasant approach is by the outside stairs in the courtyard, although the stairs up from the other side of the courtyard are signposted.

(7) **The Loggia:** This provides a charming setting for more **works by Giambologna**. The life-like group of bronze birds was made for the grotto at Villa di Castello, and are masterpieces of casting. The turkey, 'fluffed up' in anger, is particularly fine (turkeys were first introduced from America into Italy in the 16th century). Some of them are the work of Ammannati or his school. Giambologna's nude female statue in marble represents Architecture.

Donatello (c. 1386–1466)

Donatello was the most important sculptor of the Quattrocento and is of fundamental importance to the development of Renaissance art; indeed, he is often considered the greatest sculptor of all time. He was born in Florence around 1386 of humble parentage (his father was a wool-carder who had taken part in the famous Ciompi revolt of 1378, when workers in the woollen industry—the name *ciompi* comes from the clogs they wore—rose up in protest at starvation wages; *see p. 227*), and he probably had little idea how to read and write. Donatello first worked as assistant to Lorenzo Ghiberti, the bronze sculptor, and as a young man visited Rome with his friend Brunelleschi to study antique sculpture. He worked almost exclusively in Florence throughout his long life (he died in his eighties), except for an important period in Padua. He produced superb sculptures in all media, whether bronze, marble or terracotta. Cosimo il Vecchio recognised his exceptional talent and protected him and ordered that he be buried beside him in the Medici vaults below San Lorenzo (the great ruler died just two years before the sculptor). We know that at the time of his death he had 20 assistants employed in his workshop. In this room in the Bargello (*described below*) are some of his most famous works in bronze, marble, terracotta and *pietra serena* (the attribution of some of them is still under discussion; indeed the attribution of many undocumented works to Donatello remains a great art historical issue to this day). Other splendid works by him in Florence can be seen in San Lorenzo, the Museo dell'Opera del Duomo, Palazzo Vecchio, Santa Croce and the Baptistery.

(8) The Donatello Room: This splendid Gothic hall was vaulted by Neri di Fioravante and Benci di Cione in 1345. Council meetings would be held here when the palace was the seat of government. The neo-Gothic painted decorations were carried out in 1857–65. Masterpieces by Donatello and his contemporaries are displayed here.

In the middle of the room is Donatello's genial **Marzocco**, the Florentine heraldic lion, in *pietra serena*. On the end wall is the reconstructed tabernacle from Orsanmichele which contains **St George**, as the young champion of Christendom, made for the guild of armourers c. 1416. By endowing this remarkably well-composed statue with a sense of movement, Donatello's work represents a new departure from traditional Gothic sculpture where the static figure was confined to its niche. The bas-relief of **St George and the Dragon** is an exquisite work in low relief, using an innovative *schiacciato* technique and showing a fresh interest in linear perspective and pictorial space.

Donatello's most famous work is perhaps his bronze **David with the Head of Goliath**. One of the earliest and most beautiful free-standing male statues of the Renaissance, it was probably made for Cosimo il Vecchio between 1439 and 1443 for the courtyard of the Medici palace (it is mentioned in the sources for the first time only in 1469, on the occasion of Lorenzo the Magnificent's wedding). In 1495, a year after Lorenzo the Magnificent's son Piero was expelled from Florence (for ceding a part of Florentine territory to France), it was confiscated by the Signoria and moved to their palace. Donatello's portrayal of David nude follows the story in the Book of Samuel, where he is described as shedding his armour before his famous fight, and, indeed, most statues of David, including Michelangelo's, portray the hero naked. The statue was designed to stand on a column and to be seen from below. Here Donatello invented a new concept in sculpture, where the silhouette produced by the dark bronze is its most important feature. The statue was very well restored for the first time in 2008, when part of the original gilding was revealed.

The other *David*, in marble (on the left between the windows), is an early work by Donatello. It was commissioned by the Opera del Duomo, but placed in Palazzo della Signoria in 1416.

The two statues of *St John the Baptist* (both shown holding crosses) are of uncertain attribution: the one of him as an older man is ascribed to the school of Donatello (Michelozzo?), and the *Young St John* (owned by the Martelli) is attributed to Desiderio da Settignano.

The humorous winged bronze putto known as *Atys-Amorino*, also by Donatello, dates from around 1440, when it was cast using the lost wax technique. The original patina and traces of gilding were exposed during its careful restoration in 2005. We know that by the end of the 15th or early 16th century it was owned by the Doni family. It represents a mythological subject of uncertain significance, thought to be linked with the

cult of Cybele and inspired by Classical works. The laughing boy has a goat's tail, and his breeches, with the belt decorated with poppy seeds, are all in disarray.

At the end of the entrance wall is an exquisite bronze reliquary urn (1428), a classical work by Lorenzo Ghiberti made around 1425. As the inscription states, it contains the relics (brought to Florence a few years earlier) of two Roman martyrs, Protus and his brother Hyacinth, killed during the reign of Valerian, and an Egyptian named Nemesius, martyred in Alexandria at the time of Decius. Above are fine works by Bertoldo di Giovanni, Donatello's pupil, including a battle scene (a relief based on a Roman sarcophagus at Pisa), an unfinished statuette of *Apollo* (or *Orpheus*), and reliefs of the *Pietà*, *Triumph of Bacchus* and the *Crucifixion*.

On the next wall are displayed the **trial reliefs executed in competition by Lorenzo Ghiberti and Brunelleschi** for the east Baptistery doors (*see opposite*). The attribution of the bronze *Bust of a Youth* (with a medallion at his neck) has long been debated by scholars: many detect the hand of Desiderio da Settignano, while others think it is the work of Donatello or Bertoldo. The medallion, which shows Eros in his chariot, reproduces a cameo in the Medici jewellery collection. The bust in coloured terracotta (c. 1430), full of character and traditionally thought to be a portrait of Niccolò da Uzzano, is usually considered to be by Donatello.

One of the fine painted marriage-chests, dating from around 1428, shows the procession of San Giovanni (with a view of the Baptistery). The gilded relief of the *Crucifixion* is now attributed to Donatello, and the profile relief of the *Young St John* is by Desiderio da Settignano.

THE TRIAL RELIEFS FOR THE BAPTISTERY DOORS

These two trial reliefs of the *Sacrifice of Isaac* were executed by Brunelleschi and Ghiberti. Ghiberti was given the commission, in 1403, a decision reached by a narrow majority. It is remarkable that the reliefs have survived from this famous contest—the first of its kind and usually regarded as the point at which Renaissance art was born. The subject chosen presented each contestant with a series of difficulties. These included fitting the narrative into an awkward space (the quatrefoil frames copied from the first set of doors by Andrea Pisano) and the need to depict both the nude figure of Isaac as well as the clothed figures of Abraham and his servants, and also animals and the rural setting of the event. The greater technical skill of Ghiberti is not perceptible; nevertheless his composition

Abraham draws the knife on his son Isaac, as depicted by Brunelleschi (below right) and Ghiberti (above).

conveys more of the drama of the scene, as contrasted with Brunelleschi's

artful assemblage of the component elements. Ghiberti's victory meant that he went on to carve the superb east door of the Baptistery, considered one of the greatest masterpieces of sculpture ever produced in Western art. Brunelleschi was left free to concentrate his energies on the construction of the huge dome of the cathedral, although Ghiberti accompanied him in that task in an official, if less important, role of responsibility.

On the next wall can be seen a bronze head of a sea god attributed to Donatello, and (above, hanging on the wall) the coat of arms of the Martelli (*see p. 222*), almost certainly by Donatello (acquired by the Italian state in 1998; repainted in the 19th century). The exquisite marble relief of the *Madonna and Child with Angels* in a *pietra serena* tabernacle

is a masterpiece by Agostino di Duccio, who was born in Florence but worked mostly in other regions of Italy. Beside it is a beautiful *Madonna* in very low relief by Desiderio da Settignano, from Palazzo Panciatichi. Beyond are more Madonna reliefs by artists close to Donatello, including one attributed to Michelozzo, who was also an architect and worked with Donatello on a number of projects. The bronze effigy of Mariano Sozzino, which for a long time was attributed to the Sienese artist Vecchietta, is now thought to be the work of Francesco di Giorgio Martini. There are also a number of charming glazed enamelled Madonnas by **Luca della Robbia**. Luca invented a special technique of enamelled terracotta sculpture, which was a jealously guarded secret of his workshop for most of the 15th century and was handed down through three generations of his family. His colourful, luminous half-length Madonna reliefs became popular for private devotion. He is recognised as one of the most impor-tant early Renaissance sculptors, also highly skilled in marble, and was clearly influenced by Classical art. The *Madonna and Child in a Rose Garden* is by Luca; the tondo of the *Madonna and Child with Two Angels* is thought to be an early work by his nephew Andrea.

On the last wall, there are two marble reliefs of the *Deliverance and Crucifix-ion of St Peter*, made for an altar in the Duomo and left unfinished in 1439 by Luca della Robbia, who also made the *Madonna of the Apple* (c. 1460), which was owned by the Medici. The *Bust of a Lady*, probably a female saint, is attrib-uted to Luca della Robbia or his nephew Andrea.

The next three rooms are dedicated to the decorative arts and display the Carrand col-lection. This includes pieces from all over Europe, dating from earliest times up until the 17th century, which were assembled by Louis Carrand, a wealthy art collector from Lyon who bequeathed his collection to the museum in 1888.

(9) The Islamic Room: This room (Sala della Torre) has a fine collection of Islamic art including 15th-century armour, 16th- and 17th-century bro-cade, damascened dishes, works in brass and ivory, a case of ceramics (including Persian tiles), and carpets.

(10) The Carrand Room: Amongst the many exquisite works here are the *Money-changer and his Wife* by Marinus van Reymerswaele (1540); Limoges enamels; 11th–12th-century ivories; French and Italian cutlery (15th–16th centuries); European clocks; ecclesiasti-cal ornaments, many of them enamelled, including reliquary caskets, pastoral staves, processional crosses and ewers; 15th–16th-century metalwork from France; a 15th-century Venetian astro-labe in gilt bronze; a painted diptych of the *Annunciation* and the *Presentation in the Temple* (with monochrome figures on the reverse), a 15th-century Flemish work attributed to the Master of the St Catherine Legend, a close follower of Rogier van der Weyden; and Vene-tian and Bohemian glass (16th–17th centuries). At the end of the room, flat cases contain a beautiful collection of jewellery and goldsmiths' work from the Roman period to the 17th century, and tiny Flemish and Italian paintings are displayed together here including a *Madonna and Child* by Dirk Bouts.

(11) The Chapel of Mary Magdalene: This chapel dates from the early 14th century. A sensation was caused in 1840 when the frescoes were discovered on the walls by Richard Henry Wilde, an American writer and lawyer and former member of Congress, and an elderly English painter Seymour Kirkup, who carried out studies here following Vasari's reference to works by Giotto in this chapel. On the altar wall, the scene of *Paradise* includes a portrait of Dante as a young man (shown in profile dressed in maroon, in the group of standing figures to the right), and the whole cycle was immediately attributed to Giotto. As a consequence this little room became one of the sites in the city most visited by Anglo-American travellers. It is now considered much less interesting as the frescoes are usually attributed only to the school of Giotto and dated 1340, and they are in very poor condition. The 15th-century Carrand triptych of the *Madonna and Saints* by Giovanni di Francesco is painted in wonderful bright colours. Beneath it is displayed an exquisite gilded bronze and enamelled frieze (1313) with half-length figures of saints, which was once part of the Baptistery altar. The velvet embroidered cope was made in Florence in 1450 for Nicholas V. The lectern and stalls date from the same time. Two cases display church silver, including two paxes decorated with niello by Maso Finiguerra, goldsmiths' work, chalices, processional crosses and reliquaries.

The former **Sacristy (12)** is usually kept closed.

(4) The Ivories Room: A fine collection of ivories from the Etruscan period onwards, including Persian, Arabic, German and Sicilian ivories, and Carolingian reliefs (9th century). There is also one valve of a diptych which belonged to the Roman consul Basilio (6th century); part of a Byzantine diptych with the empress Ariadne (8th century); an early Christian diptych (5th century) showing Adam in Earthly Paradise and scenes from the life of St Paul in Malta. The case on the entrance wall contains the right side of a very precious Anglo-Saxon coffer, known as the Franks Casket, the rest of which is in the British Museum. Carved out of whalebone, with runic inscriptions, this dates from the 7th or 8th century and was probably made in Northumbria. The chessboard with intarsia ornament and bas-reliefs is a 15th-century Burgundian work. There are also numerous caskets and panels carved in bone from the Embriachi workshop, headed by the Florentine Baldassare, which produced numerous such works in the early 15th century.

There is also a small *Madonna and Child with Saints* attributed to Duccio, which was donated to the museum in 2000. Displayed around the walls are wooden sculptures including an unusual seated female statue (sometimes interpreted as a Madonna Annunciate or a sibyl) by Mariano d'Angelo Romanelli (c. 1390), and early 15th-century gold-ground panel paintings.

(5) The 14th-century Room: Here are displayed the earliest sculpture and paintings in the museum. In the centre is a pedestal with three acolytes by Arnolfo di Cambio. The high relief of the *Madonna and Child* is by Tino di Camaino.

(6) The Majolica Room: Part of the Medici collection of Italian majolica (mostly 15th and 16th century) is shown in this room, including works from the Deruta, Montelupo, Faenza and Urbino potteries, and part of a service which belonged to Guidobaldo II della Rovere, Duke of Urbino. The beautiful garland, on the end wall, with the Bartolini-Salimbeni and Medici emblems, is by Giovanni della Robbia.

Second floor

(13) The Giovanni della Robbia Room: Colourful and elaborate enamelled terracottas are displayed in this room, many of them by Giovanni della Robbia, son of Andrea, who used more colours than either his father or great-uncle Luca. These include a fine tondo of the *Madonna and Child and Young St John*, partly unglazed. The large relief in terracotta (*Noli me Tangere* with St Augustine in the lunette) is by Giovanfrancesco Rustici (c. 1510) and is interesting as the only work known in this medium which makes use of just the two colours yellow and white. Works by Benedetto Buglioni include a polychrome terracotta statue of the *Madonna and Child* and a relief of the *Noli me Tangere*. The four-figure group of the *Lamentation* is an unglazed terracotta work by Andrea della Robbia.

There is a superb collection displayed here of bronze plaquettes and medals arranged by artists and schools from the early 15th to the 18th centuries. These small reliefs were often based on casts taken from gems in the Medici jewellery collection. Most of them were collected by the Medici grand dukes, but some come from the Carrand collection. Italian masters represented include L'Antico (Jacopo Alari Bonacolsi), Caradosso, Cellini, Filarete, Giambologna, Leone Leoni, Moderno, Riccio (Andrea Briosco) and Giovanfrancesco Rustici. There are also examples from France and Germany.

(14) The Andrea della Robbia Room: Arranged in this room are beautiful works in enamelled terracotta by Andrea della Robbia. His charming *Bust of a Boy* is displayed next to a *Portrait of a Lady* (a circular high relief), now usually attributed to Andrea's uncle, Luca. The tabernacles include the *Madonna of the Cushion* (the Christ Child is shown sitting comfortably on a pillow) and *Madonna of the Stonemasons* (1475; their instruments are illustrated in a charming frieze). A collection of seals and coins is also displayed here.

(16) The Verrocchio Room: Here there is a superb display of Renaissance portrait busts and some very fine works by Verrocchio. In the centre is Verrocchio's bronze **David**, made for the Medici in 1469 and then acquired by the Signoria in 1476. Beautifully restored in 2003, it owes much to Donatello's earlier statue of the same subject (*see p. 89*).

To the right of the door are charming marble works by Mino da Fiesole: busts of Cosimo il Vecchio's two sons, Giovanni and Piero il Gottoso (1453; the first dated portrait bust of the Renaissance) on either side of a portrait of Rinaldo della Luna, who was a Florentine aristocrat who worked for the Roman Curia.

The works exhibited along the window wall include a portrait of Pietro Mellini, signed and dated 1474 by Benedetto da Maiano, a remarkable likeness of this rich Florentine merchant as an old man; a 15th-century bust of Giuliano de' Medici, murdered in the Pazzi Conspiracy (*see p. 203*), of unknown attribution. The two busts of a young woman and a boy are excellent works by Desiderio da Settignano, and between them hangs a wooden Crucifix, attributed to Verrocchio.

On the end wall, the works by Antonio Rossellino include a bust of Francesco Sassetti (the general manager of the Medici bank under Lorenzo the Magnificent, and who commissioned the Sassetti Chapel in Santa Trínita), also attributed to Verrocchio; busts of a young boy and the *Young St John the Baptist*; and the portrait bust of Matteo Palmieri, Renaissance statesman and scholar (1468). This was on the façade of his Florentine palace until the 19th century, which accounts for its weathered surface.

On the wall opposite the windows are a bust of a young cavalier, thought to be a portrait of a member of the Medici family, by Antonio Pollaiolo (in dark painted terracotta, c. 1470), and a marble portrait bust also by him. Verrocchio's *Bust of a Lady Holding Flowers*, once attributed to his pupil Leonardo da Vinci, is one of the loveliest of all Renaissance portrait busts. It is particularly interesting as it is the first instance in a 15th-century portrait bust in which the hands are depicted. The *Death of Francesca Tornabuoni-Pitti* is a tomb relief by Verrocchio. The polychrome terracotta relief of the *Resurrection* was discovered in the Villa Medici in Careggi in the 19th century in a number of pieces and it is still very damaged. It is thought to have

been made by Verrocchio in the early 1460s and possibly was once in a chapel in the Medici villa above Rogier van der Weyden's *Mourning over the Dead Christ*, now in the Uffizi (*see p. 120*).

The remarkable marble bust of Battista Sforza, duchess of Urbino, is by Francesco Laurana, a Dalmatian artist who worked at the Court of Urbino.

(17) The Baroque Sculpture and Medals Rooms: These rooms (often kept closed) contain part of a huge collection of Italian medals started by Lorenzo the Magnificent. The first room has works by L'Antico, Pisanello and Matteo de' Pasti.

In the centre of the room is Bernini's charming **bust of Costanza Bonarelli**. This is the famous sculptor's most memorable portrait, and we know that he kept it in his own house. It must have been a constant reminder of the allure of Costanza, who was his mistress. The next room has an allegorical female statue and a marble bust of Virginia Pucci Ridolfi, both by Domenico Poggini; a bas-relief of *Christ in Glory* in a tabernacle by Jacopo Sansovino; a very fine marble *Bust of Christ* by Tullio Lombardo dated 1520 (donated to the museum by the heirs of Carlo de Carlo in 2001), and a bust of Cardinal Paolo Emilio Zacchia Rondanini by Alessandro Algardi. Here the chronological display of medals is continued with works by Francesco di Giorgio Martini, Francesco da Sangallo, Gasparo Mola, Leone Leoni and Massimiliano Soldani Benzi.

(15) The Small Bronzes Room: This superb display of small Renaissance bronzes constitutes the most important

Bust of a Lady Holding Flowers (detail; 1472–80) by Verrocchio, the first portrait bust in which the subject's hands were also shown. Exquisitely carved, it was once attributed to Leonardo da Vinci, Verrocchio's pupil.

collection of its kind in Italy. The fashion of collecting small bronzes was begun by Lorenzo the Magnificent following a Roman tradition. The statuettes, which include animals, bizarre figures and candelabra, were often copies of antique works, or small replicas of Renaissance statues. In the wall cases on the right, there are splendid bronzes by Giambologna including several statuettes: *Venus*, *Architecture* and *Hercules and the Calydonian Boar*; as well as Benvenuto Cellini's relief of a dog. There are works by Danese Cattaneo (including *Fortune*), Tribolo and a fine group of statuettes by Baccio Bandinelli. The splendid chimneypiece is the work of Benedetto da Rovezzano, and the firedogs are by Niccolò Roccatagliata. The wall cases on the opposite wall contain an anatomical figure, a famous work made in wax by Lodovico Cigoli (1598–1600) and fused in bronze by Giovanni Battista Foggini after 1678. Beyond are charming animals by 15th- and 16th-century artists from the Veneto and Padua, including fantastical works by Il Riccio.

The central cases contain copies from works by Giambologna, as well as the *Dwarf Morgante Riding a Monster* by Giambologna himself. Morgante is thought to have been Pietro Barbino, Cosimo I's favourite dwarf, who can also be seen in a statue in the Boboli Gardens. Also here are works by Giovanni Francesco Susini, *Satyr* by Massimiliano

Soldani Benzi, and 16th–18th-century bronzes from the Veneto. Displayed in the case on the entrance wall there is a bronze statuette known as *The Frightened Man* (it may represent a pugilist), a very unusual work attributed by most scholars to Donatello (c. 1435–40). The beautiful small bronze group of *Hercules and Antaeus* is by Antonio Pollaiolo (he also made a painting of this subject, now in the Uffizi). We know this was in the Medici palace in 1492 and it is considered one of the earliest and most important small Renaissance bronzes ever made.

(18) The Armoury: The magnificent display of arms and armour is from the Medici, Carrand and Ressmann collections. It includes saddles decorated with gold, silver and ivory, a shield by Gasparo Mola (17th century), and numerous sporting guns, dress armour and Oriental arms. There is also a fine bust in marble by Francesco da Sangallo, which is an idealised portrait of Giovanni delle Bande Nere (father of Cosimo I). The bronze bust of Ferdinando I is by Pietro Tacca, and he also made the statuette of a horse and the model for an equestrian statue of Louis XIII of France displayed here. There is a case of Japanese swords and daggers, one of which was made in 2006.

ORSANMICHELE, MERCATO NUOVO & PALAZZO DAVANZATI

This chapter takes in some of the medieval buildings in the centre of the city, many of them once guild headquarters. This was also an area of markets, one of which still survives. The straight Via de' Calzaioli, on the line of a Roman road, was the main thoroughfare of medieval Florence. It was widened in the 1840s and is still the busiest pedestrian street in the city. On its west side stands Orsanmichele, with its famous decorations by the Florentine guilds.

THE FLORENTINE GUILDS

In the 13th century there was a proliferation of guilds (*Arti*), instituted to protect the rights and interests of members of the same trade or occupation. Those who belonged to guilds were mostly from the middle classes, often referred to as the *popolo*. The way the guilds were organised in many ways reflected the way that the communal government functioned, so it is perhaps not surprising that the seven *Arti Maggiori*, or major guilds, actually took control of the government of the city at the end of the 13th century. Their regime, known as the *secondo popolo*, lasted for nearly a century. Bankers, professional men and merchants in the most important trades were members of these major guilds, which were the Calimala (the premier guild, named from the street where the wholesale cloth importers had their warehouses), the Giudici e Notai (judges and notaries), the Cambio (bankers), the Lana (woollen cloth merchants and manufacturers), the Por Santa Maria (named after the street which led to the workshops of the silk-cloth industry), the Medici e Speziali (physicians and apothecaries, and dye merchants, the guild to which painters belonged), and the Vaiai e Pellicciai (furriers).

The *Arti Minori* represented shopkeepers and skilled artisans. Guild members were required to maintain a high standard in their work, and carry out specific duties and respect their obligations to other members. In the early 15th century, most of the public works in the city were commissioned by the guilds, and many important buildings were put in their charge (the Duomo itself was the responsibility of the Arte della Lana from 1331 onwards). The guilds competed with each other in spending vast sums of money on buildings and their embellishment in order to add to their prestige.

The guilds survived until 1770, when Peter Leopold abolished them.

ORSANMICHELE

One of the most unusual buildings in the city, this very tall, rectangular edifice (*map*

1, 6; open 10–5 except Mon, museum open Mon only 10–5) bears little resemblance to a church, although it is consecrated as such and is on the site of an oratory called San Michele ad Hortum (meaning 'orchard'), founded in the late 8th or early 9th century. The first two letters of its name are a shortening of Hortum, or Orte. The oratory contained a miraculous image of the Virgin around which a local cult grew up, and when in 1239 the oratory was destroyed, the image was preserved in the loggia which was subsequently erected as a grain market (perhaps by Arnolfo di Cambio) around 1290. This building burnt down in 1304. The present Orsanmichele (1337), also built as a market, is by Francesco Talenti, one of the architects of the Duomo, together with Benci di Cione and Neri di Fioravante. Its arcades were enclosed a few decades later by huge three-light Gothic windows, which in turn were bricked up shortly after they were finished (but their superb tracery can still be seen). The venerated image of the Virgin was replaced by a new devotional painting by Bernardo Daddi which, together with its magnificent tabernacle, is still the glory of the interior. The upper storey, a large, brick-vaulted Gothic hall completed in 1404, was intended as a granary but from the 16th–19th centuries was used as an archive. Today the original statues from the exterior are housed here.

The statues on the exterior

The decoration of the exterior of Orsanmichele was undertaken by the guilds, who commissioned statues of their patron saints from the best artists of the age to fill the canopied niches. The statues are an impressive testimony to the skill of Florentine sculptors over a period of some 200 years. All of them have been replaced by copies, but since the originals can only be seen on Mondays, they are described in full here. The description begins on the side facing Via de' Calzaioli and goes round to the right.

Calimala (wholesale cloth importers): Tabernacle and *St John the Baptist* (1413–16) by Lorenzo Ghiberti (signed on the cloak). This was the first life-size statue of the Renaissance to be cast in bronze, though still very Gothic in spirit.

Tribunale di Mercanzia (beyond the church door): The bronze group of the *Incredulity of St Thomas* (1473–83) is a superb work by Verrocchio, Leonardo da Vinci's master, who (like his pupil) was both sculptor and painter. The subject, with its allusions to evidence and proof, was particularly suited for the merchants' court, where guild matters were adjudicated. The bronze group replaced a statue of *St Louis of Toulouse* by Donatello (now in the Museo dell'Opera di Santa Croce; *see p. 204*), which had been commissioned earlier by the Parte Guelfa to whom the tabernacle formerly belonged. Above is the round *stemma* of the Mercanzia, in enamelled terracotta by Luca della Robbia (1463).

Giudici e Notai (judges and notaries): Tabernacle by Niccolò di Pietro Lamberti (1403–06), with a bronze statue of *St Luke* (1583–1601) by Giambologna (note the pencil holding his place in the book).

Beccai (butchers): St Peter (c. 1425; *see illustration*). The fine della Robbian *stemma* was made in 1858.

Conciapelli (tanners): Tabernacle and *St Philip* (c. 1410–12) by Nanni di Banco.

Maestri di Pietrai e di Legname (stonemasons and carpenters, the guild to which architects and sculptors belonged): Tabernacle and statues of four soldier saints (the *Quattro Santi Coronati*) are the masterpiece of Nanni di Banco (c. 1409–16/17), modelled on antique Roman statues. The relief, by the same artist, illustrates the work of the guild. Above is their *stemma* in inlaid terracotta by Luca della Robbia.

Armaioli (or Corazzai e Spadai; armourers): *St George* by Donatello (c. 1415–17). The original marble statue is in the Bargello, together with the exquisite bas-relief.

Cambio (bankers): Tabernacle and bronze *St Matthew* (1419–22), by Lorenzo Ghiberti.

Lanaioli (wool manufacturers and clothiers; beyond the door): Bronze *St Stephen* by Lorenzo Ghiberti (1427–28).

Maniscalchi (farriers): *St Eligius* (c. 1417–21), and bas-relief of the saint in a smithy by Nanni di Banco.

Linaioli e Rigattieri (linen merchants and used clothes dealers): *St Mark* (1411–13) by Donatello, still showing Gothic influence.

Pellicciai (furriers): *St James the Greater*,

St Peter, patron saint of the guild of butchers. The sculpture is generally attributed to Bernardo Ciuffagni, though some scholars detect the hand of Brunelleschi or Donatello.

with a bas-relief of his beheading attributed to Niccolò di Pietro Lamberti (c. 1422), also with Gothic elements.

Medici e Speziali (merchants of spices, medicines and dyes): Gothic tabernacle attributed to Simone Talenti (1399), with a *Madonna and Child* (the *Madonna della Rosa*) thought to be the work of Pietro di Giovanni Tedesco (c. 1400) or Niccolò di Pietro Lamberti or Simone Ferrucci. Above, *stemma* by Luca della Robbia.

Setaioli e Orafi (silk weavers and goldsmiths): *St John the Evangelist*, bronze statue by Baccio da Montelupo (1515).

The church interior

The church (*open 10–5 except Mon*) is a dark rectangular hall, divided into two aisles by two massive pillars. Two altars are set at one end on a raised platform. The vaults and central and side pilasters are decorated with frescoes of patron saints painted in the late 14th or early 15th century by Tuscan artists. The fine Gothic stained-glass windows include one showing St Jacob among the shepherds designed by Lorenzo Monaco.

The **Gothic tabernacle** over the high altar, by Andrea di Cione, called Orcagna (1352–60), is a masterpiece of the decorative arts, ornamented with marble and coloured red and blue glass, as well as some 120 reliefs and statuettes. At present, sadly, it is difficult to see in its entirety. It was the most costly work of its kind ever made in Florence and Orcagna was helped by a team of sculptors, many of whom apparently learnt their skills while at work on it. Although this is the only important sculptural work by this artist (who probably trained in the *bottega* of Andrea Pisano), he signed it as a painter and 'archimagister' and has indeed been recognised as the only 'universal' artist of the 14th century. Around the base are superb reliefs of the life of the Virgin (including, in front, the *Marriage of the Virgin* and the *Annunciation*), by Orcagna's hand. Behind the altar is an elaborate sculptured relief of the *Transition and Assumption of the Virgin*. A beautiful frame of carved angels encloses the altarpiece itself, a lovely painting of the *Madonna and Child* by Bernardo Daddi (1347), which replaced the original venerated image of the Virgin. (NB: There is a carved Crucifix dating from around the same time by Orcagna in San Carlo dei Lombardi, just across the road on Via Calzaioli; *see p. 326*).

On the other altar is the *Madonna and Child with St Anne*, a statue by Francesco da Sangallo (1522). The fresco in the vault above shows St Anne holding a 'model' of Florence (with the Baptistery prominent).

Museo di Orsanmichele

This museum (*opened by volunteers on Mon 10–5*), on the upper floors of Orsanmichele, is entered from Palazzo dell'Arte della Lana (*see below*) by an overhead walkway built in 1569 to give access to the archives housed here until 1883. Here are displayed the splendid restored marble and bronze statues from the niches outside. The arrangement follows the sequence of the original positions of the statues. The only statue missing is Donatello's *St George*, which is in the Bargello. A steep flight of modern stairs leads up round a pilaster to another Gothic hall with a wooden roof, which houses very damaged late 14th-century stone statuettes of saints and prophets, removed from the exterior of the building. There are splendid views from the windows.

THE HEADQUARTERS OF TWO GUILDS

Opposite the tabernacle of St George on Orsanmichele, in a row of houses dating mostly from the 19th and 20th centuries, is the attractive little **Palazzo dell'Arte dei Beccai** (*Via Orsanmichele 4*), which still retains its appearance from when it was built c. 1415 for the Butchers' Guild (it was their office until 1534). Their *stemma* (a rampant goat) can be seen high up on the façade. It is now the seat of the Accademia delle

Arti del Disegno, the first of all art academies, founded in 1563 by members of the Compagnia di San Luca including Vasari, Bronzino and Ammannati. Cosimo I and Michelangelo were elected the first Academicians.

Opposite the present entrance to Orsanmichele (and connected to it by a flying bridge) is **Palazzo dell'Arte della Lana**, built in 1308 by the Guild of Wool Merchants. Only a small part of the 14th-century building survives, since it was radically restored in 1905. The Arte della Lana represented the most important Florentine industry, responsible for the city's economic growth in the 13th century (it has been estimated that a third of the population was employed in the woollen cloth industry in the 13th and 14th centuries). The *stemma* of the guild, the *Agnus Dei*, features in a number of the stone reliefs on the exterior, several of which date from 1308. On the corner, at the base of the over-restored tower, is the little **oratory of Santa Maria della Tromba** (late 14th century), one of the largest of the many tabernacles in the city, moved here when the church of the same name in the Mercato Vecchio was destroyed. Behind the neo-Gothic grille (difficult to see through the glass) is an early 14th-century painting of the *Madonna Enthroned* by Jacopo del Casentino and, in the lunette, the *Coronation of the Virgin* added by Niccolò di Pietro Gerini later in the same century. On Via Calimala you can see the remains of early frescoes in two lunettes, now rather incongruously in a fashionable clothing shop on the ground floor of Palazzo dell'Arte della Lana. The name 'Calimala' is derived from '*calle maia*', the principal street of the Roman town.

On the corner of Via dell'Arte della Lana and Via Lamberti is the **site of the first headquarters of the Medici bank**, set up in 1397 by Giovanni di Bicci, father of Cosimo il Vecchio. He began his working life in Rome, where in the 1380s he had founded his own bank, and after he moved to Florence he kept branches in both Rome and Venice.

PIAZZA DELLA REPUBBLICA & THE MERCATO NUOVO

The spacious **Piazza della Repubblica** (*map 1, 3*) occupies the site of the Roman forum, which in turn became the commercial centre of the medieval city, known as the Mercato Vecchio. The single granite column, dating from the 15th century, survives to record the old buildings which used to occupy this area, almost all of which were demolished at the end of the 19th century, despite vehement protests. Unlike many other parts of the old city, very little visual documentation exists of its appearance before its destruction (*see illustration opposite*). In 1898, to protect the rest of the historic centre of Florence, an association was founded which included many distinguished foreign residents such as John Temple Leader, Frederick Stibbert and Herbert Horne as well as Violet Paget, the only woman on the committee. Piazza della Repubblica itself, with its sombre colonnades, triumphal arch and undistinguished buildings, is not an architectural success, but it has several large cafés with tables outside, including the Giubbe Rosse, which in the early 1900s was a famous meeting place of writers and artists (including the poet Eugenio Montale and the writer Italo Svevo, widely thought

The Mercato Vecchio, painted by Telemaco Signorini in the 1880s, just before the medieval buildings and market stalls were cleared away and Piazza della Repubblica was laid out.

to have been the inspiration for Joyce's Leopold Bloom). The arcades are brightened up on Thursdays when a flower and plant market is set up.

From the north side of the present square, the small **Jewish ghetto** extended as far as Via de' Pecori. Created in 1571 by Cosimo I, it had a single piazza with a well, two synagogues, and one narrow street with gates at either end, which were locked at night. In 1622, 495 Jews are recorded here, and it is known that they suffered from terrible living conditions. The doors of the ghetto were opened in 1848 and a new synagogue was constructed in 1882 (*see p. 226 for more on the Jewish community in Florence*).

The Mercato Nuovo

The area occupied by the Mercato Nuovo (*map 1, 5; open daily in summer, closed Mon and Sun in winter*) has been the site of a market since the beginning of the 11th century. The market was named to distinguish it from the Mercato Vecchio nearby (*see above*), which dated from even earlier. The loggia was erected by Cosimo I in 1547–51 and in his day it was used principally for the sale of silk and gold. It is still a busy market-place, and usually good value, almost exclusively frequented by tourists, for leather goods, scarves, gloves, bags and souvenirs. In English it was formerly called the Straw Market, since it was famous for the sale of straw and raffia work. To Florentines it is known as *Il Porcellino* ('the piglet'), after the well-loved sculpture of a wild boar, whose snout has been kept polished by generations of admirers, shown seated beside a watering hole, surrounded by plants and small living creatures. The original bronze, made in the 17th century by Pietro Tacca, is now in the Museo Stefano Bardini (*see p. 291*). Coins thrown into the water are collected and given to charity. Hans Christian

Andersen wrote a children's story inspired by the statue (*The Metal Pig*). High up on the building opposite is a tabernacle with a painting of the *Madonna and Child* by Giovanni Colacicchi (1953). Next to it a plaque has recently been set up to record the name of a street vendor (Il Lachera) who died in 1864 and who had become a well-known character in the town (he was also mentioned by Collodi, author of *Pinocchio*).

ROMAN FLORENCE

After Julius Caesar promulgated his agricultural laws in 59 BC a colony was founded on the site of present-day Florence, but it was not until 30 BC that it was actually laid out, close to an easy crossing-place over the Arno, orientated north–south by the cardo maximus (the present Via Roma and Via Calimala) and east–west by the decumanus maximus (the present Via del Corso, Via degli Speziali and Via Strozzi). It was enclosed by walls some 480m long by 420m wide. The subsequent Roman town of *Florentia* flourished under Hadrian and by the late Imperial period it had become the capital of this region of the peninsula, known as Tuscia et Umbria. The present Piazza della Repubblica is on the site of the forum, which had a temple and basilica fronting the piazza (remains of the temple were found in the late 19th century when the Meracato Vecchio was demolished). When the town expanded, public edifices were built outside the walls, including an amphitheatre, the form of which is still clearly visible in the streets of Via Torta and Via dei Bentaccordi (*map 7, 1*) and in the curving façades of the Peruzzi houses nearby. Other remnants of the Roman city are less visible but the site of the baths is recalled by the name of the present Via delle Terme (*map 1, 5*). Important excavations were begun in the 1970s beneath Piazza della Signoria when more Roman baths were found, on a much grander scale and dating from the 2nd century AD, next to a building evidently used for treating and dyeing cloth. A palaeochristian church dating from the 6th century has recently been identified on a subsequent level on that site. Beneath Palazzo Vecchio excavations have unearthed remains of the Roman theatre (*see p. 50*). It is thought that there may have been a circus or stadium on the site of the present Piazza Santa Maria Novella but no archaeological evidence has yet been found. Archaeologists today suggest that Roman Florence was of more importance than previously believed, even though only part of its street plan and a few architectural spolia survive.

Palazzo dell'Arte della Seta and Palazzo di Parte Guelfa

The narrow Via di Capaccio leads past the **Palazzo dell'Arte della Seta** (*map 1, 5*), established as the headquarters of the guild of the silk-cloth industry at the end of the 14th century. Although heavily restored in the 20th century, it still bears its beautiful *stemma* encircled by a wreath supported by delightful cherubs, in the style of Donatello. Next door is the large **Palazzo di Parte Guelfa**, built as the official residence of the captains of the Guelph party in the 13th century. The pretty terrace with a corner loggia (and the Medici coat of arms) was added in the 16th century by Vasari, and the handsome row of four arched windows with tondi above belongs to a fine hall designed by Brunelleschi when it was enlarged in the 15th century as far as Via delle Terme. At the back of the building, in a little piazza, you can see a tall Gothic window and crenellations, beneath which is a row of *stemme*. Vasari also modified the outside stair here. Beside it is the rough stone façade of the old church of Santa Maria Sovraporta (now used as a library), and attached to one side of it is the quaint little Cappella di San Bartolomeo (1345–52), with its gabled front. It is unfortunately kept locked as it preserves interesting frescoes high up in the vault, including a fragment of a townscape. The other buildings in the piazza include Palazzo Giandonati, dating from the 14th century, with two arches on the ground floor, and the 15th-century Palazzo Canacci (no. 3) with grisaille decoration and a fine loggia (heavily restored at the beginning of the 20th century).

The pretty medieval **Via delle Terme** (*map 1, 5*), which retains its lovely old paving stones, takes its name from the Roman baths which were in this area. The back of the medieval portion of Palazzo di Parte Guelfa and a number of medieval tower houses can be seen from here. A series of ancient lanes known as *chiassi* connect this street with Borgo Santi Apostoli towards the river (*see p. 281*). The palace at no. 9 has a Renaissance courtyard and there is a medieval tower at no. 13 (red). At no. 17 an unusually small house survives, just one storey high, above two wide arches. There is a good view of the Column of Justice in the busy Piazza Santa Trínita, where numerous streets converge.

GUELPHS & GHIBELLINES

These two names have persisted down the centuries in the popular imagination, conjuring up the idea of an eternal feud. In modern Italian parlance they are still used to denote political squabbling between two opposing factions. The names derive from two German families who contested the Imperial throne in 12th-century Europe: the Welfen and the Weiblingen. In 13th-century Italy, supporters of the pope were called Guelphs and those who took the side of the Holy Roman Emperor were called Ghibellines. The rivalry between Florentine families apparently came to a head with the murder of Buondelmonte dei Buondelmonti in 1216, which sparked off the civil war which lasted up until the end of the century, although the long and complicated story involving also the Donati and Arrighi seems to be more or less legendary, but made all the more famous through Dante's description in the *Inferno*, and in Canto XVI of the *Paradiso*. In fact it was only in the 1230s, when Emperor Frederick II invaded northern and central Italy, that real hostilities broke out in Florence between the pro-imperial faction and those who supported the pope, and it was nearly always the political and military organisation called the Parte Guelfa who came out on top, since they virtually controlled the government of the city from around 1267 until 1376.

MUSEO DI PALAZZO DAVANZATI

Map 1, 5. Open 8.15–1.50 except the 2nd and 4th Sun and the 1st, 3rd and 5th Mon of the month. The second and third floors are open only at 10, 11 and 12 o'clock for a maximum of 25 people at a time; it is best to book the visit, T: 055 238 8610. There is a lift.

On Via Porta Rossa (so named since at least the beginning of the 13th century, apparently from the red Roman bricks which were reused in a medieval gate here) stands a 16th-century palace built by the Bartolini-Salimbeni (no. 19). The projecting upper storey is supported on stone *sporti* and the family's heraldic emblems decorate the façade. The Porta Rossa hotel has operated here for many years (*see p. 361*) and the interior is still interesting for its Art Nouveau decorations, including colourful stained glass, all of it made for the hotel.

In the 16th century the Bartolini-Salimbeni also acquired the next palace, Palazzo Davanzati, which despite numerous restorations remains a superb surviving example of a medieval nobleman's house, particularly interesting as an illustration of Florentine life in the Middle Ages. The typical 14th-century façade consists of three storeys above large ground-floor arches. The proportions have been altered by the loggia at the top, which was added in the 16th century and probably replaced battlements. The ironwork includes brackets which carry diagonal poles across the windows, used to hang out washing, suspend birdcages, or to hold the banners put out on special occasions. The huge Davanzati coat of arms dates from the 16th century.

History of the palace

Built in the early 14th century by the Davizzi family, the palace became the property of Bernardo Davanzati, a successful merchant and scholar, in 1578. In 1904 it was bought by the antiquarian and art dealer Elia Volpi (1858–1938), who restored it and recreated the interior of a medieval Florentine house, opening it as a museum in 1910. However, Volpi soon fell on hard times and he sold most of the contents to American buyers in two famous sales in 1916 and 1917, fetching the unbelievable sum of one million dollars. He was then able to furnish the palace anew, but was finally forced to sell it and its contents between 1924 and 1927. The antiques that Volpi had acquired found their way into various museums around the world and helped form tastes in interior design in the early 20th century.

The interior: first floor

The interior is of great interest for its architecture and contemporary wall-paintings, which are rare examples of a decorative form typical of 14th-century houses. The 16th–17th-century furniture is a special feature, and not always easy to distinguish from the fine imitation pieces made by Florentine craftsmen in the early 20th century.

The spacious vaulted **entrance hall**, which runs the whole width of the building, was used as a loggia for family ceremonies. In the 15th century it was closed in and used as shops. The courtyard could be entirely cut off from the street in times of trouble. The storerooms here were replenished directly from the alleyways at the back and side of the building. The well served all five floors of the house. The corner pilaster bears carved heads traditionally supposed to be portraits of the Davizzi family.

The old staircase to the first floor survives, with its lower steps in stone and the upper in wood. To the right is the most important room in the house, the **Sala Madornale**, used for family gatherings. It still has its original painted wood ceiling. Four holes in the floor were used for defence against intruders in the entrance hall below. The four lovely Florentine tapestry panels, highlighted with crimson and gold metallic threads, were made in the 16th century. On the window wall is the bust of a boy by Antonio Rossellino. The two small rooms off the Sala Madornale have a display of lace and embroidery as well as an illustration of the craft of spinning and weaving, and a collection of samplers. You can open the drawers to see more of the beautiful collection.

The **Sala dei Pappagalli**, or dining room, with displays of pottery, has painted imitation wall-hangings with a motif of parrots. Above is a frieze showing a terrace with trees and flowering shrubs. The fireplace, which bears the arms of the Davizzi, Ridolfi and Alberti, was probably already here by the end of the 14th century. The **Studiolo** has three early 16th-century paintings of the story of Perseus by the Master of Serumido. The bronze statuette of *Venus* is attributed to Massimiliano Soldani Benzi.

A painted corridor leads into the **Camera dei Pavoni**, the main bedroom. The fine wall paintings bear the coats of arms of families related to the Davizzi between a delightful frieze of birds. In a niche the portable altarpiece has two little doors painted by Neri di Bicci and a stucco relief of the *Madonna and Child* by the workshop of Desiderio da Settignano. The *Madonna in Adoration* beside the bed is by the workshop of Filippino Lippi. Off this room is one of several bathrooms in the house, this one decorated with bright red flowers.

Second floor

The main room is the **upper Sala Madornale**. Around the top of the walls are four exquisite small tapestry panels woven in Brussels in the early 16th century, illustrating the story of David and Bathsheba. On the right wall there is an engaging portrait of Giovanni di Bicci de' Medici (father of Cosimo il Vecchio), attributed to Zanobi Strozzi or a Florentine painter of the late 15th century. The bedroom known as the **Camera della Castellana di Vergy** is named after the charming frieze illustrating a medieval French romance of courtly love. It is the most interesting of all the painted decorations in the palace and includes the Dovizzi and Alberti coats of arms: it was probably painted to celebrate a wedding between the families in 1350. There are two wall niches: one has a 14th-century frescoed Crucifix and the other a very fine painting of the *Madonna del Parto* (Madonna 'of Childbirth') by Rossello di Jacopo Franchi (the Madonna in a stunning pink dress!). The handsome painted *cassone* would have contained the bride's dowry of household linen. The tondo displayed near the 16th-century bed is a *desco da parto*. There was a tradition that these circular 'trays' were presented to a mother after giving birth, to be used for her first meal, and they were painted with appropriate scenes (this one, by Lo Scheggia, shows a typical Florentine street scene, perhaps to remind the mother of life out of doors after her long confinement).

THE FLORENTINE DOWRY

By the 15th century the status of a Florentine family depended also on its ability to provide dowries for its female offspring and it was generally considered that the better the dowry, the better the match. Upon her marriage, a girl's dowry passed directly from her father to her husband and would be used to run the new bride's home. However, it remained legally the wife's property and if a wife outlived her husband, what was left of the dowry would usually came back into her possession—a fact often of the first importance since only male heirs were entitled to the family inheritance. It is interesting to note that marriage in Renaissance Florence was considered simply a contract and so weddings were normally devoid of all religious overtones. An amusing summary of the dowry system is given in Charles FitzRoy's witty 'guide' to the Florence of 1490:

[Dowries cost] a small fortune, as much as 1,400 florins, and sometimes 2,000 for a really good match. When Lorenzo de' Medici married his aristocratic wife she brought a dowry of 6,000 florins with her from Rome. Considering that even the best-paid lawyer is unlikely to earn more than 500 florins per annum, it is no wonder that so many eligible young women end up as nuns (though not all enter wholeheartedly into this vocation and there have been a number of scandals…).

There are all sorts of stipulations attached to the contract. If the dowry is unpaid, the husband is allowed to send his wife back to her family, a humiliating fate. The Medici insisted that Lorenzo could return his wife if she did not bear children.

Most rich Florentines, like good businessmen, start paying money into the Dowry Bank (Monte delle Doti), a communal fund set up to guarantee a dowry on their daughter's marriage. It is treated as a taxable asset. The government uses the money over a fifteen-year period, after which the girl is deemed eligible for marriage. Some people reckon the amount in the Dowry Bank accounts for half the assets in the city.

Charles FitzRoy, from *Renaissance Florence on Five Florins a Day*, 2010

Third floor

The **kitchen** is located on the upper floor, a typical feature of medieval houses since it was the warmest part of the building. The women would spend most of their day here, spinning and weaving around the large fireplace. Some old household utensils are fittingly displayed here. The top bedroom, known as the **Camera delle Impannate** from the old wooden shutters which survive on the windows, has delightful painted animals on the walls and some interesting furniture. Near the fireplace is a rare processional wooden mannequin, made in Siena in the early 16th century. In a niche is a painted terracotta statuette of *St Onophrius* by the circle of Jacopo Sansovino (1505–10).

Map 1, 6. Open Tues–Sat 8.15–6.35. In July and Aug it is often open until 9pm on one or two days a week. Booking service (T: 055 294883, Mon–Fri 8.30–6.30, Sat 9–12) highly recommended to avoid the infamous queue. You pick up your ticket 5 or 10mins before the booked time (and pay an extra booking fee).

Although it costs slightly more, you can also book online at www.b-ticket.com through the website of the Florentine Museums: www.polomusealefiorentino.it (search for 'orari e biglietti' and then 'orari dei musei'). NB: The other unofficial websites which offer tickets for museums in Florence charge more.

The Corridoio Vasariano was open at the time of writing from Feb to mid-April for guided visits by previous appointment only; T: 055 294883, but opening times vary from year to year. The Collezione Contini-Bonacossi (free admission by appointment only; T: 055 238 8809) was open at the time of writing on Thur at 2 and 4.15).

The former church of San Pier Scheraggio is only open for exhibitions.

The massive Palazzo degli Uffizi extends from Piazza della Signoria to the Arno. Houses were demolished to create a long, narrow building plot next to Palazzo Vecchio, and Vasari was commissioned by Cosimo I to erect a building to serve as government offices (*uffici*, hence '*uffizi*'). The unusual U-shaped *palazzo*, with a short façade on the river front, was begun in 1560 and completed, according to Vasari's design, after his death in 1574 by Alfonso Parigi the Elder and Bernardo Buontalenti (who also made provision for an art gallery here for Francesco I). Resting on unstable sandy ground, it is a feat of engineering skill. The use of iron to reinforce the building allowed for the remarkably large number of apertures. A long arcade supports three upper storeys pierced by numerous windows and a loggia in *pietra serena*. The pilaster niches were filled in 1842–56 with statues of illustrious Tuscans by the leading sculptors of the day, including Lorenzo Bartolini, Giovanni Dupré and Pio Fedi. The building now houses the famous Galleria degli Uffizi, the most important collection of paintings in Italy and one of the great art collections of the world.

History of the Uffizi collection

The origins of the collection go back to the Medici grand duke Cosimo I and the galleries were enlarged and the collection augmented by his son Francesco I. The Medici dynasty continued to add works of art in the following centuries: Ferdinando I transferred sculptures here from the Villa Medici in Rome; Ferdinando II, who married Vittoria della Rovere, inherited paintings by Raphael, Titian and Piero della Francesca from Francesco Maria della Rovere of Urbino; and Cardinal Leopoldo began the collection of drawings and self-portraits. The last of the Medici, Anna Maria Luisa, settled her inheritance on the people of Florence through a family pact in 1737 (*see p. 255*). The huge collection was partly broken up during the 19th century, when much of the sculpture went to the Bargello and other material was transferred to the Museo Archeologico. In the 20th century many paintings removed from Florentine churches found a home in the gallery, which was partly redesigned for them in the 1950s by Giovanni Michelucci and Carlo Scarpa, who redesigned a number of important museums in Italy.

Since the state archives were moved from the building in 1989, plans have been underway to expand the gallery in stages. The rooms on the third floor will probably remain more or less as they are, while in 2004 the *piano nobile* was partially opened to display works by Caravaggio and his school and to provide a route to the new exit from the gallery at the back of the building in Piazza dei Castellani (where a huge projecting roof designed by Arata Isozaki—already criticised for its gigantic proportions—is also planned). Alterations are expected to take until at least 2013, when the exhibition space will be more than doubled and about 3,000 paintings will be displayed (instead of the present 1,000). At the same time, it will be possible to house 1,500 visitors simultaneously (over twice the number at present permitted). The description below reflects the status quo at the time of writing.

In 1993, the gallery was damaged by a Mafia car bomb in Via Lambertesca, which killed five people and injured 29. There was severe structural damage to part of the Corridoio Vasariano and the rooms off the West Corridor. About 90 works of art were damaged, but they have been (or are being) restored.

Planning a visit

Except from Epiphany (6th Jan) to mid-Feb, the gallery tends to be extremely crowded with tour groups, but is usually more peaceful in the early morning, over lunchtime and in the late afternoon. Automatic signals provide information about expected waiting time if there is a queue (a maximum of 660 people are allowed into the gallery at once). It is too much to try to see the entire collection in one day; the first rooms (up to Room 15) include the major works of the Florentine Renaissance; the later rooms can be combined in a second visit.

The collection is arranged chronologically by schools. The following description includes only some of the most important paintings and sculptures (the most important artists or works are given in bold). Many of the paintings have superb contemporary frames. The labelling of the works is kept to a minimum, and the lighting is very poor in the earlier rooms. Round red labels indicate the date a work was restored.

THE GALLERY

Ground floor

A series of large rooms, once occupied by law courts and then by the state archives, now house ticket offices (separate one for pre-booked visits), a large specialised bookshop and cloakrooms. Tickets are shown at the foot of the grand staircase, just beyond which there are lifts, officially reserved for the staff, but which can usually be used on request if you are on your own.

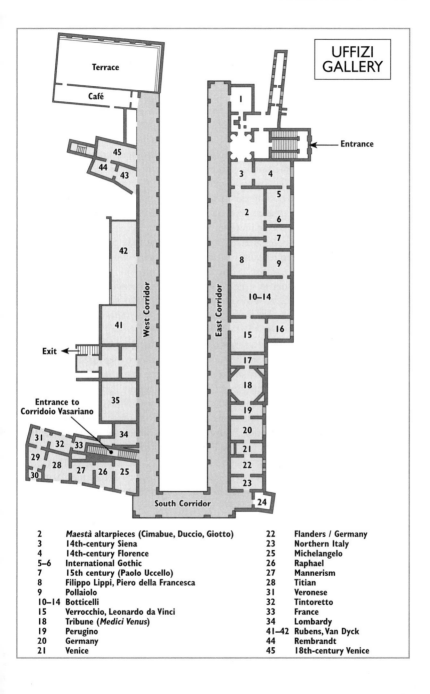

UFFIZI GALLERY

Terrace

Café

45
44
43

Entrance

42

West Corridor

East Corridor

41

Exit

Entrance to
Corridoio Vasariano

35

34

31 32 33
29
28
30 27 26 25

1

3 4
5
2
6
7
8 9

10–14

15 16

17
18
19
20
21
22
23
24

South Corridor

2	*Maestà* altarpieces (Cimabue, Duccio, Giotto)	22	Flanders / Germany
3	14th-century Siena	23	Northern Italy
4	14th-century Florence	25	Michelangelo
5–6	International Gothic	26	Raphael
7	15th century (Paolo Uccello)	27	Mannerism
8	Filippo Lippi, Piero della Francesca	28	Titian
9	Pollaiolo	31	Veronese
10–14	Botticelli	32	Tintoretto
15	Verrocchio, Leonardo da Vinci	33	France
18	Tribune (*Medici Venus*)	34	Lombardy
19	Perugino	41–42	Rubens, Van Dyck
20	Germany	44	Rembrandt
21	Venice	45	18th-century Venice

The staircase, lined with antique busts and statues, leads up past part of the huge theatre built into the building by Buontalenti for Francesco I in 1586–89. Over the central door is a bust of the grand duke attributed to Giambologna. On the left the old entrance now serves as the entrance to the Prints and Drawings Room (*open to scholars with special permission, 9–1*). The collection is one of the finest in the world and is particularly rich in Renaissance and Mannerist works. Exhibitions are held periodically.

Third floor: East Corridor

At the top of the stairs, the landing, which has two ancient Roman sarcophagi, is decorated with ten busts of the Medici from Lorenzo the Magnificent to the last grand duke, including one, in bronze, by Giambologna (Cosimo I) and two by Giovanni Battista Foggini. Also here are two paintings by Jacopo da Empoli showing two famous weddings in the Medici family: that of Maria de' Medici to Henri IV of France, and that of Caterina de' Medici to Henri II of France.

Tickets are checked in the vestibule decorated at the time of the Lorraine grand dukes, which contains antique sculpture including a statue of Augustus and two dogs (these last are well-preserved Greek works).

Beyond is the long, U-shaped gallery's East Corridor, arranged with portraits and antique sculpture (all of them well labelled with diagrams), more or less as it was in the 16th century. At the top of the walls is a series of portraits of famous men, commissioned by the Medici in 1552–89 from the otherwise little known Cristofano dell'Altissimo. They are copies of a series of portraits which had been collected by the historian Paolo Giovio, who died in 1552. At intervals between them are hung portraits of members of the Medici dynasty in the 15th and 16th centuries, beginning at the short north end (right) with a portrait of Giovanni di Bicci de' Medici, founder of the dynasty, by Alessandro Allori. Both series of paintings are continued right round the walls of all three corridors. The grotesques in the vault (1581) are also by Allori.

The superb **collection of antique sculpture** (mostly Hellenistic works dating from around 325–31 BC), collected by Cosimo I and augmented by his sons Francesco and Ferdinando, was first arranged in this corridor (and provided with an inventory) in 1595–97. The statue of *Hercules and a Centaur*, which has been at the end of the corridor since that time, is a Roman copy of a Hellenistic original, but with numerous restorations: the Hercules was restored in 1579 (only the feet are original) and the tail, head and upper part of the torso of the centaur were remade by Giovanni Battista Caccini ten years later. The portrait busts include one known (erroneously) as 'Augustus' and one of Agrippa (the heads are original, but the busts are probably by Caccini), considered the founders of Rome; these were given to Lorenzo the Magnificent in Rome by Pope Sixtus IV and bought back to Florence to decorate Palazzo Medici.

On the window wall, the so-called *Mercury* or *Hermes* was formerly in the Cortile del Belvedere in the Vatican and was moved to Florence in 1536, when it was displayed in the Sala delle Nicchie in Palazzo Pitti. The hat, arms and base are all restorations, and it in fact represents a young man or satyr (and is a replica of a work by the famous Greek sculptor Praxiteles).

The rooms off the East Corridor

Room 1 (*often kept locked*): The **antique Roman sculptures** here clearly influenced Florentine Renaissance sculptors and include a circular altar with reliefs showing the *Sacrifice of Iphigenia* (late 2nd century BC), a basalt torso, a Roman copy of a bronze statue by Polyclitus, and a marble torso, an original Greek work dating from the 2nd century BC.

Room 2: This provides a fitting introduction to the painting galleries illustrating Tuscan painting of the 13th century. Three huge paintings of the *Madonna Enthroned* (known as the *Maestà*) dominate the room. On the right, the **Madonna in Maestà** by **Cimabue** (c. 1285), painted for the church of Santa Trínita, marks a final development of the Byzantine style of painting, where a decorative sense still predominates. On the left is another exquisite version of this subject, the **Rucellai Madonna** by **Duccio di Buoninsegna**, commissioned by the Laudesi confraternity in 1285 for their chapel in Santa Maria Novella. Between the 17th and 18th centuries it was put in the Rucellai Chapel (hence the name) in the same church, and has been housed in the Uffizi since 1948. It was painted on five planks of poplar wood 4.5m high and c. 60–65cm wide. Since the wood was unseasoned, huge cracks formed, but the painting was beautifully restored in 1990 when the splendid blue mantle of the Virgin was discovered beneath a layer of over-painting from the 17th century. The frame, with painted roundels, is original. The painting was traditionally attributed to Cimabue, but is now recognised as the work of the younger Sienese artist Duccio, who is known to have worked in Cimabue's studio.

The **Madonna in Maestà** by **Giotto** was painted some 25 years later for the church of Ognissanti. The figure of the Madonna has acquired a new monumentality, and she is set in a more clearly

The three great paintings of the *Madonna in Maestà* by (left to right) Cimabue, Duccio and Giotto, showing how Florentine painting developed from about 1285 to around 1310.

defined space. This is considered one of the masterpieces of an artist whose work heralded a new era in Western painting. Giotto also painted the polyptych which is displayed here of the *Madonna and Four Saints* for the Badia Fiorentina.

Room 3: This room displays 14th-century Sienese painting, which flourished under the influence of Duccio. His greatest follower was **Simone Martini**, whose charming *Annunciation* (1333) dominates the room. The Gothic elegance of the Madonna and annunciatory angel set against a rich gold ground makes this one of the masterpieces of 14th-century Tuscan painting. It is the only major work by Simone in Florence (painted for the Duomo of Siena, it was moved here by the Tuscan grand duke in 1799). It is signed by Simone and his brother-in-law Lippo Memmi, who may have painted the lateral saints. The neo-Gothic frame was added in 1900. The small *Madonna and Child* exhibited on the same wall, by Andrea Vanni, clearly shows the influence of Simone.

The brothers **Pietro and Ambrogio Lorenzetti**, also important artists of the Sienese school, are represented in a number of fine works: the *Presentation in the Temple* (1342), four scenes from the life of St Nicholas, and a triptych reassembled when the central panel was left to the Uffizi by Bernard Berenson in 1959, are all by Ambrogio, while the panels of a dossal with the story of the Blessed Umiltà and the *Madonna in Glory*, signed and dated 1340, are both by Pietro.

Room 4: Florentine painting of the 14th century. The very fine panel depicting the *Mourning over the Dead Christ* (from the church of San Remigio) is by Giotto's great-grand-child known as Giottino, or Giotto di Stefano. The son of another painter, Stefano, this artist who is documented in Florence only for a couple of years around 1368, seems to have had a very limited output. This is considered his masterpiece and is thought to date from around 1359. It has a very original composition against a plain gold ground with a stylised Cross and twelve figures surrounding Christ. The Madonna and Mary Magdalene are shown with their faces red from weeping, while the two donors, a Benedictine nun and a young girl in a fashionable dress, kneel in front of St Benedict and St Remigius. Giottino's work has affinities with Giotto's most gifted pupils Maso di Banco and Giovanni da Milano. Giovanni is represented here with panels of saints, martyrs and virgins in wonderful colours, from a dismembered polyptych from the high altar of Ognissanti. There are also works by Bernardo Daddi (including a triptych and a tiny portable altar), as well as Orcagna and his brothers, Nardo and Jacopo di Cione, all of whom left numerous works in the city. The elegant *Dossal of Santa Cecilia*, by an unknown master who takes his name from this work, is another beautiful piece.

Rooms 5 and 6: These are in fact one room, and illustrate the International Gothic style. The monk known as **Lorenzo Monaco** is represented by two superb altarpieces: the large *Coronation of the Virgin* (1413) and the *Adoration of the Magi*. His wonderful colouring and graceful, elongated figures make him one of the greatest artists of this period. His focus is often on the depiction of the human figure, leaving the landscape behind (as can be seen in the *Adoration of the Magi*, an abstraction of rocks and unreal buildings seemingly there to add yet more colour to the work). The central angel (kneeling below and playing the organ) in the *Coronation* was carefully painted in 1998 to cover a hole when the altarpiece was restored.

The other important painter of this period was **Gentile da Fabriano**. He was born in the Marche but moved to Florence in 1420 at the invitation of Palla Strozzi, who commissioned the richly decorated *Adoration of the Magi* (on the end wall) in 1423, in which the horses' bridles and the brocaded costumes, as well as the crowns worn by the Kings, are highlighted in gold. This famous work has a charming, fairy-tale quality and numerous delightful details, including the animals and the servant bending down to take off one of the king's spurs, and the two graceful serving ladies behind the Madonna examining one of the Kings' gifts. The predella is also exquisitely painted, with a beautiful scene set in a grove of orange trees showing the Flight into Egypt. Gentile also painted the *Mary Magdalene, St Nicholas of Bari, St John and St George* in 1425 (formerly part of a polyptych), all of them sumptuously dressed and standing on a decorated pavement.

The window in this room affords a good view of the top of Santa Croce and the hill of San Miniato.

Room 7: Early 15th-century paintings representing the early Renaissance. *The Battle of San Romano* (*removed for restoration at the time of writing*) is an amusing exercise in perspective by **Paolo Uc-**

cello. Together with its companions, now in the Louvre and the National Gallery, London, it decorated Lorenzo the Magnificent's bedroom in Palazzo Medici-Riccardi in 1492. It celebrates the battle in which the Florentines were victorious over the Sienese. The most important elements in the painting are the horses and lances.

The *Madonna Enthroned with Sts Francis, John the Baptist, Zenobius and Lucy* by **Domenico Veneziano** is one of the few known works by this artist, who was born in Venice but moved to Florence, where he lived until his death in 1461. It is painted in beautiful soft colours in a Renaissance setting, and is one of the loveliest altarpieces of this familiar subject in Florence (the figure of St Lucy recalls the style of Piero della Francesca, who was Domenico's pupil).

The *Madonna and Child with St Anne* was painted by Masolino, but Masaccio is thought to have added the Madonna and Child to his master's painting, which has, however, been otherwise completely repainted. Also here are two works by Fra' Angelico, including a lovely *Coronation of the Virgin* (the painter's self-portrait is in the third row back, to the left). In the middle of the room is a tiny painting of the *Madonna and Child* (with the Madonna tickling the Child's chin), an undocumented work attributed to Masaccio.

Room 8: This contains paintings by **Filippo Lippi and his son Filippino**. Those by Filippo are the most representative collection of his works in existence, and have been the subject of a restoration programme in recent years, completed in 2010. The gentle *Madonna and Child* with two playful angels (c. 1465) and a particularly beautiful Madonna, is justly one of his most famous works. The Pala del Noviziato was painted for the chapel of the same name built in 1445 in Santa Croce to a design by Michelozzo; his architecture clearly inspired the background of the painting. The Medici red balls on a gold ground in the frieze pay homage to Lippi's patron who commissioned this work, Cosimo il Vecchio. It is one of the first Renaissance panels of this subject: the Madonna enthroned between saints, often called a *Sacra Conversazione*. Restoration has revealed the superb colouring, from the rich lapis lazuli of the Virgin's mantle to the *terraverde* and other bright colours used for the green marble steps and inlaid panels of the pavement, in abstract designs. The light which invades the scene from the left casts delicate shadows. Filippo had his brilliant pupil Pesellino paint the predella for him, but the first two panels were seized by Napoleon and are now in the Louvre (replaced at the same time by the copies still *in situ* here). There are also two paintings by Filippo of the *Adoration of the Child*, one painted for the convent of the Annalena, dated c. 1453 and which includes the penitent saints Jerome and Mary Magdalene in a rocky landscape, with a field of wild flowers in the foreground. The crowded *Coronation of the Virgin*, once on the high altar of Sant'Ambrogio, is also by him, as is the exquisite *Barbadori predella* (the altarpiece itself is now in the Louvre), which has a remarkable sense of space.

Filippino Lippi is represented by a lovely *Adoration of the Child* and two large altarpieces (*Madonna and Saints* painted for the Sala degli Otto in Palazzo Vecchio, and the *Adoration of the Magi*). Another

Madonna and Child with Saints and an *Annunciation* are by Alesso Baldovinetti.

In the centre of the room is the famous **diptych by Piero della Francesca**, with the portraits of Federico da Montefeltro and his duchess, Battista Sforza, in profile against a superb detailed landscape in a transparent light stretching into the far distance. On the reverse are their allegorical triumphs, in a rarefied atmosphere with another wonderful landscape. These exquisite miniature works, profoundly humanist in spirit, were painted in Urbino c. 1465 in celebration of this famous Renaissance prince, always depicted in profile since he lost his right eye in a tournament. The frame dates from the late 19th or early 20th century.

In the corridor outside, on the window wall, is a statue of a girl stepping forward in a billowing dress holding a sash full of fruit, formerly identified as Pomona, the Roman goddess of tree-fruits, now thought to be an allegory of Autumn (the head is a restoration). Five other similar statues are known and it is possible that one of them could have influenced Botticelli when he painted the figure of Flora in his *Primavera*.

Room 9: The altarpiece of *Sts Vincent, James and Eustace* by **Antonio Pollaiolo** is one of his best works. The three saints, full of character, are splendidly dressed in rich velvet robes and stand on a terrace behind which can be glimpsed an open landscape. It was painted for the chapel of the Cardinal of Portugal in the church of San Miniato, where it has been replaced by a copy. Antonio (or his younger brother Piero) is also thought to have painted the charming but damaged *Portrait of a Lady in Profile*. The portrait of Galeazzo Maria Sforza is now usually attributed to Piero. The seven paintings of the Theological and Cardinal Virtues are also by the Pollaiolo brothers except for *Fortitude*, which is an early work by Botticelli. On the window wall are two small panels by Antonio Pollaiolo showing the Labours of Hercules.

Rooms 10–14: These rooms have been converted into one huge space and the rafters of the stage of the old Medici theatre exposed. This is now home to **Botticelli's masterpieces**, which include both religious and mythological subjects. The *Primavera* is one of his most important and most famous pictures. It was painted probably c. 1478 for Lorenzo di Pierfrancesco de' Medici, Lorenzo the Magnificent's younger cousin. An allegory of spring, the season which began the year in 15th-century Florence, it is thought to have been inspired by a work of Poliziano, although its precise significance is still debated. There is a rhythmical contact between the figures, who are placed in a meadow of flowers within a dark orange grove, the Garden of the Hesperides of Classical myth. To the right, Zephyr chases Flora and transforms her into Spring, who is shown bedecked with flowers. In the centre Venus stands with Cupid above her, and beyond the beautiful group of the Three Graces, united in dance, is the figure of Mercury (perhaps an idealised portrait of Lorenzo the Magnificent). The work is richly painted on panels of poplar wood. The varnishes which had been added in various restorations were removed in 1982, and the painting was cleaned to restore its original appearance. The botanical details which were revealed

include a variety of spring flowers, most of which can still be seen today growing in Lorenzo di Pierfrancesco's Villa di Castello (*see p. 319*).

The Birth of Venus is perhaps the most famous of all Botticelli's works. It was probably also painted for Lorenzo di Pierfrancesco and hung in the Medici villa of Castello. The pagan subject is taken from a poem by Poliziano and illustrates Zephyr and Chloris blowing Venus ashore while Hora, her fluttering dress decorated with cornflowers and daisies, hurries to cover her nakedness. The elegant figures are painted with a remarkable lightness of touch in a decorative linear design. The classical nude figure of Venus balances on the edge of a beautiful scallop shell as it floats ashore. A strong wind blows through this harmonious Graeco-Roman world.

The splendid **religious works by Botticelli** in the room include two tondi of the Madonna (the *Madonna of the Magnificat* and the *Madonna of the Pomegranate*), the *Madonna of the Rose Garden* and the *Madonna of the Loggia*. Of the three fine altarpieces painted for Florentine churches, the *Madonna and Saints* from Sant'Ambrogio is the earliest and is particularly lovely, with a beautiful Mary Magdalene. The *Coronation of the Virgin* (from San Marco), which has recently been restored, has a charming circle of angels in the sky and a delightful predella. The late *Annunciation* shows an extraordinary spiritual bond between the two figures. The relatively small *Adoration of the Magi* has an unusual setting but the Holy Family is relegated to the back of the painting and the interest lies above all in the portraits of the Medici courtiers who are depicted as the Kings and their entourage. Giuliano de' Medici (or possibly Lorenzo the Magnificent), lost in thought, is dressed in black and red on the right and Botticelli himself is shown in a self-portrait (dressed in a yellow cloak; *illustrated below*). The proud standing figure by the horse's head on the left may be Lorenzo the Magnificent next to the poets Poliziano and Pico della Mirandola (who were with Lorenzo at his death). The 'Magus' in black who kneels before the Virgin represents Cosimo il Vecchio, and the one dressed in red, his son Piero il Gottoso.

Sandro Botticelli (1446–1510)

Botticelli was one of most important and most original painters of the Italian Renaissance, greatly admired in his lifetime. He fell into oblivion soon after his death, however, and was only 'rediscovered' by the Anglo-American community living in Florence at the end of the 19th and beginning of the 20th centuries. John Ruskin, Walter Pater, Dante Gabriel Rossetti, Herbert Percy Horne and Ezra Pound all wrote about him with great enthusiasm. In 1870, Walter Pater noted that 'the peculiar character of Botticelli is the result of a blending in him of a sympathy for humanity in its uncertain  condition, its attractiveness, its investiture at rarer moments in a character of loveliness and energy, with his consciousness of the shadow upon it of the great things from which it shrinks, and that this conveys into his work somewhat more than painting usually attains of the true complexion of humanity'. In 1881, Dante Gabriel Rossetti wrote a poem entitled 'Spring by Sandro Botticelli':

... the Graces circling near,
Neath bower-linked arch of white arms glorified:
And with those feathered feet which hovering glide
O'er Spring's brief bloom, Hermes the harbinger.

Botticelli's skill as a portrait painter is also shown in his early *Portrait of a Youth in a Red Hat*, a very fine and well restored painting of an unknown sitter who is holding a medal of Cosimo il Vecchio.

The subject of the small, elaborate painting entitled *Calumny* (after 1487) is taken from the ancient Greek writer Lucian's account of a picture by Apelles described in Alberti's treatise on paint-ing. The *Pallas and the Centaur* was probably intended as a moral or political allegory. Pallas, whose clothes are decorated with Lorenzo's emblem, is shown taming the centaur, and it may be that Pallas represents Florence or Lorenzo the Magnificent, and the centaur—half-man and half-beast—represents disorder and barbarism. Another interpretation is that Pallas symbolises Humility or

Prudence, restraining Pride.

The tiny painting of *St Augustine in his Cell* is one of a number of pictures Botticelli painted of this saint. He is shown writing, with discarded sheets of paper littering the floor at his feet.

In the centre of the room are two exquisite small works: *Judith Returning from the Camp of Holofernes* and the *Discovery of the Decapitated Holofernes in his Tent* (c. 1470).

The huge **triptych of the *Adoration of the Shepherds*** (*see box below*) was commissioned between 1464 and 1478 from **Hugo van der Goes** by Tommaso Portinari, when he was in Bruges serving both the Burgundian court and the Medici, as director of their bank there.

THE PORTINARI TRIPTYCH

In 1483 this huge work was shipped from Bruges to Pisa and from there to Florence (the documents mention that 'eight strong men' were required), for the high altar of Portinari family chapel in the hospital of Santa Maria Nuova (Sant'Egidio). The triptych was typical of the form often used by Flemish artists, and here the wings are painted with saints and members of the Portinari family (all kneeling and shown smaller; the two boys on the left are particularly charming portraits). It includes exquisitely painted details such as the still life in the foreground showing two vases of flowers (all of them symbols of the Passion of Christ) and a sheaf of wheat referring to the name of Bethlehem.

Portinari was one of the best-known Italians in Bruges, the centre of commerce in northern Europe. Even after the Medici bank's most important branch closed down there in 1480, Portinari decided to remain. He finally returned to Florence in 1497, where he died four years later and was buried in the chapel beneath his altarpiece. When in the 17th century the triptych was dismantled, it was attributed to various Italian painters including Baldovinetti, and only recognised as Van der Goes' work in the 19th century.

Together with a polyptych by the earlier Flemish master Jan van Eyck, it is the largest-known 15th-century painting produced in the Low Countries (2.5m high and nearly 6m wide). Its arrival caused a sensation amongst the artists in Florence, who thereafter showed a new interest in accurately reproducing tiny naturalistic details, moving away from the pure, unornamented style of Masaccio. They had already absorbed the importance of the technique of oil painting from Van Eyck, who was well known in Italy in his lifetime. While in Bruges Portinari had both Memling and Van der Goes paint portraits of his wife, Maria Bandini Baroncelli (whom he had married in 1469 when she was just 14 years old), and he commissioned two other paintings from Memling during his time there (*see below, Room 22*). We now know that other Florentine merchants ordered paintings and tapestries from Flemish masters for their houses in Flanders and sometimes had them shipped home with them when they returned to Florence.

Van der Goes was clearly influenced by **Rogier van der Weyden**, whose important *Mourning over the Dead Christ* is exhibited beside the Portinari triptych. This used to hang in a chapel in the Medici villa of Careggi (probably surmounted by Verrocchio's relief now in the Bargello; *see p. 95*). We know that the artist, the best-known Flemish painter of his day, was in Rome for the Holy Year of 1450, and it seems that he must have come to Florence sometime during his journey since the composition is derived from a predella scene by Fra' Angelico which at that time was on the high altar of San Marco (it is now in Munich). Since Van der Goes' work is painted on oak, it must have been executed in Flanders, and its realism (note the Maries' tears) led many scholars in the past to attribute it to Memling or Dürer.

Also at this end of the room are three good works by Michelangelo's master **Domenico Ghirlandaio**: two beautiful altarpieces of the *Madonna Enthroned with Saints*, one with a lovely vase of flowers on a carpet, four delightful angels and orange trees behind the balustrade, and a tondo of the *Adoration of the Magi* with a pretty landscape (1487).

Room 15: Here are displayed the early Florentine works of **Leonardo da Vinci** and the paintings of his master, Verrocchio. Leonardo da Vinci's *Adoration of the Magi* (1481) is a huge, crowded composition, remarkable for its figure studies and unusual iconography. The painting was left unfinished when Leonardo left Florence for Milan; it remains in its preparatory stage of chiaroscuro drawn in a red earth pigment. His *Annunciation* was painted in Verrocchio's

studio. The extent of the master's intervention is unclear: it is thought that he was probably responsible for the design, for the figure of the Madonna and for the classical sarcophagus. The Virgin is seated with one foot just visible on the terracotta floor and her bed just suggested through the open door. Her face is beautifully illuminated and the leaves of her book and the veil over the lectern are very delicately painted. The angel kneels on a lawn covered with flowers, and the landscape beyond a row of cypresses stretches far into the background to a sea port beneath incredibly high mountains.

Verrocchio's *Baptism of Christ* was begun c. 1470. According to Vasari, the angel on the left was painted by the young Leonardo.

The Crucifix by **Luca Signorelli** is one of his most remarkable paintings: Mary Magdalene is shown at the foot of the Cross with a dramatic, strong, dark figure of Christ; while in the background scenes of the Crucifixion are set in a desolate landscape against a light ground. The botanical details are also exquisitely painted. There are also four works painted for Florentine churches by the Umbrian painter **Perugino**: the *Pietà*, *Prayer in the Garden*, and *Crucifix with Saints* come from a church outside Porta Pinti, destroyed in the Siege of Florence in 1529. The *Madonna with Sts Sebastian and John* (the figure of St Sebastian is particularly beautiful) was commissioned for an altar in the church of San Domenico di Fiesole and is signed and dated 1493 (it was acquired by the grand duke Peter Leopold in 1786).

Room 16: This room is known as the Sala delle Carte Geografiche and its walls were painted in 1589 for the Grand Duke Ferdinando I with maps of Tuscany by Stefano Bonsignori.

In the corridor, by the entrance to the Tribuna, is a male statue in Parian and rare black marble. Known as the *Borghese Ares*, it is a Roman copy of an Attic original, with restored arms and head).

Room 18: The beautiful octagonal **Tribuna**, inspired by Classical models, was designed by Bernardo Buontalenti for Francesco I (1584) to display the most valuable objects in the Medici collection. It has a mother-of-pearl dome and a fine pavement in *pietre dure*. (*It was closed at the time of writing and the arrangement described below will change when it reopens*). The octagonal table is a masterpiece of *pietre dure*, made in the Florence Opificio between 1633 and 1649 (to a design by Bernardino Poccetti and Jacopo Ligozzi). The magnificent cabinet in ebony and *pietre dure* belonged to Ferdinando II and dates from c. 1650.

Since the 17th century, the room has contained the most important Classical sculptures owned by the Medici, the most famous of which is the **Medici Venus** (*see box below*).

THE *MEDICI VENUS*

The Tribuna was for centuries the central attraction of the Uffizi, and most highly prized among all its treasures was the *Medici Venus*. It is one of six important ancient statues acquired by Cardinal Ferdinando de' Medici and brought from the Villa Medici in Rome in 1677–80 by Cosimo III. It is signed by 'Cleomenes, son of Apollodorus', and was probably made in Rome in the 1st century BC (perhaps a copy of a Greek original). Like the *Capitoline Venus* in Rome, the goddess is of the *Venus pudica* type, shown surprised while taking a bath and attempting to cover her nakedness with her hands. During the Grand Tour of Italy in the 18th century—when Classical works were much in vogue—the *Medici Venus* was renowned for her beauty and was possibly the most famous work of art in Florence. Numerous travellers left records of their admiration, including Goethe in 1740 and Edward Gibbon in 1764. Queen Charlotte, wife of George III, commissioned Johan Zoffany to paint a conversation piece of the room in 1772. From this time on, no more replicas were allowed to be made of the statue since there were fears that it would be damaged. It was one of the greatest trophies seized by Napoleon and taken to Paris, but was returned here in 1816 (in the interim it was 'replaced' by another statue of Venus, especially commissioned by Napoleon from Canova, and which is now in Palazzo Pitti; *see p. 242*). In the early 19th century, Hazlitt, Leigh Hunt, Byron and Shelley all left enthusiastic descriptions of the statue. Byron writes of it in ecstatic terms in *Childe Harold* ('the veil of heaven is half undrawn').

In the later 19th century, however, the *Medici Venus* found her admirers falling away, and she was eclipsed by her rival, the *Venus de Milo* (discovered in 1820).

The so-called *Arrotino* ('Knife-grinder') is now thought to represent a Scythian preparing to flay Marsyas, as part of a group of Apollo and Marsyas. It is the only surviving replica of an original by the school of Pergamon (3rd or 2nd century BC) and it was purchased by Cosimo I in 1558 on Vasari's advice. It is of extremely high quality (and has had very few restorations). The group of *Wrestlers* is a much-restored copy of a bronze original from the school of Pergamon, of which no other replicas are known (though only the two torsos are original). The moment of victory in the contest was signalled when the winner was able to place his knee on his opponent's back. The *Dancing Faun* is a beautifully restored work and the *Apollino* (*Young Apollo*) is derived from an *Apollo* by Praxiteles.

Around the walls are a remarkable series of distinguished **court portraits**, many of them of the family of Cosimo I commissioned from **Bronzino**. His masterpiece is the portrait of Cosimo's wife, Eleanor of Toledo, with their second son Giovanni, painted in 1545. It expresses Eleanor's powerful dynastic role as mother of Cosimo's children and the interest of the artist was clearly captured by the details of the gorgeous materials of her silk dress with its gold brocade and black velvet arabesques, and numerous pearls. Bronzino painted the other portrait hung here, of Giovanni as an infant, probably in the same year. With a much less formal air, he is shown grasping a bullfinch in one hand as he grins at us. We know that Cosimo had Giovanni nominated cardinal in 1560 in the hope that he would one day become pope but he died just two years later at the age of 19.

There is also a portrait here dating from 1551 of Cosimo's other son Francesco (who succeeded him as grand duke) as a boy, holding an open letter. Cosimo also had Bronzino paint the very beautiful portrait (against a lapis lazuli ground) of Bia, his illegitimate child born just before he married Eleanor, but who remained with him and was brought up with their children. Her father is recorded in the medallion at her neck. She died at the age of 5 or 6, the same year this was painted. The portrait of a young girl with a book is thought to represent Giulia, illegitimate daughter of Alessandro de' Medici, who also came to live with Cosimo's family after her father's death. Portraits by Bronzino of unknown sitters include the *Portrait of a Man*, an intellectual typical of his time. The pair of portraits of Cosimo's friends Bartolomeo Panciatichi (1541) and his wife Lucrezia di Gismondo Pucci (1545) are also famous works by Bronzino. Bartolomeo, born in Lyon in 1507, represented the Medici at the French court. He is shown with a forked red beard against a background of very strange architecture, while his beautiful wife is superbly portrayed bedecked with magnificent jewels but reverently holding a book of psalms.

The two well-known idealised portraits of Cosimo's famous ancestors Lorenzo the Magnificent and Cosimo il Vecchio are by Vasari and Pontormo. Although the arrangement of the room has changed over the centuries, the paintings of a *Girl with a Book of Petrarch* by Andrea del Sarto, the *Madonna and Child with the Young St John* by Pontormo, and the *Young St John the Baptist in the Desert* by Raphael (and his *bottega*) have all hung here since 1589.

Bronzino (1503–72)

Agnolo di Cosimo di Mariano was nicknamed Bronzino probably because of the colour of his fair hair. He began his artistic career around 1517 as a boy in the workshop of Pontormo, and he worked with this famous artist at the Certosa di Galluzzo in 1523–25 (*see p. 324*) and then on the tondi in the Capponi Chapel in Santa Felicita and in the choir of San Lorenzo (but these frescoes were later destroyed). The two artists remained close friends for many years, and art historians have sometimes found it hard to distinguish between their work so that attributions have changed over the centuries from one to the other. Bronzino was also a witty and learned poet, but is best remembered for his wonderful court portraits commissioned by the Medici family, the most important of which are hung here in the Tribuna. He also designed a series of magnificent tapestries for Palazzo Vecchio illustrating the story of Joseph, which were woven in Florence by Flemish masters. Towards the end of his life he painted a number of huge religious works which can be seen in the Museo dell'Opera di Santa Croce and Santissima Annunziata.

When his close friend and fellow painter Cristofano Allori died in 1541, Bronzino moved into his house to take care of his wife and children, one of whom, Alessandro (1535–1607), later became one of his most devoted students. It was he who delivered Bronzino's funeral oration. The (framed) fresco which hangs here of Bianca Cappello, the second wife of Francesco I, is by his hand.

Room 19: Rooms 19–23 have ceilings decorated with grotesques and views of Florence carried out in 1588. Room 19 contains four **portraits by Perugino**, among them those of a young boy and of Francesco delle Opere, a Florentine artisan who produced precious fabrics in Venice and was the brother of a friend of Perugino's. The influence of Memling is very evident in these portraits. There are also two beautiful tondi by Luca Signorelli of the *Madonna and Child*, one with allegorical figures in the background which clearly influenced Michelangelo. The portrait of Evangelista Scappi is by Francesco Francia and the half-length figure of *St Sebastian* by Lorenzo Costa. The *Crucifixion* by Marco Palmezzano shows the influence of Giovanni Bellini.

The *Annunciation*, with a lovely landscape beyond the loggia, and the remarkable female nude *Venus* are both interesting works by Lorenzo di Credi. *Perseus Liberating Andromeda* is Piero di Cosimo's most highly eccentric work. Dating from 1513, it shows the diminutive hero stepping neatly down from the heavens and then again improbably perched on the marine monster's back as it leers at the swooning Andromeda, whose fate seems very much compromised. But the crowd of very odd bystanders seem pleased nevertheless.

Room 20: Works by German artists. **Dürer** painted the *Adoration of the Magi* in 1504 after a visit to Italy. The *Portrait of the Artist's Father* is Dürer's first known work, painted when he was 19. The two bearded heads of the apostles St James and St Philip are also by him. **Lucas Cranach the Elder** is represented by two fine portraits of Martin Luther, whose Protestant cause he supported (the smaller one shows him with Filippo Melantone and the other with his wife Katherina Bore). Cranach also painted the tiny *St George* and the two much larger full-length figures of *Adam and Eve* (showing the influence of Dürer), as well as the *Madonna and Child*. The portrait of Cranach (formerly thought to be a self-portrait) was painted by his son, Lucas Cranach the Younger. There is also a fine *Portrait of a Boy* by the Netherlandish painter Joos van Cleve.

Room 21: The Venetian School. Paintings by **Giovanni Bellini** include a *Sacred Allegory* (with a lovely landscape), an exquisite painting of uncertain meaning, infused with an exalted humanist quality, and *Lamentation over the Dead Christ*, an unfinished painting left at the chiaroscuro stage. The other key painter of the Venetian Renaissance, **Giorgione**, is represented with the *Judgement of Solomon* and its companion piece the *Infant Moses Brought to Pharaoh*, showing the influence of Bel-lini. They are exhibited on either side of a splendid *Knight in Armour with his Page*, traditionally thought to be a portrait of the Venetian *condottiere* Gattamelata, by an unknown Venetian painter, but often attributed to Giorgione. The two large figures, usually identified as a prophet and sibyl, are attributed to Vittore Carpaccio.

Room 22: Fine portraits by Flemish and German artists. The five superb male portraits by **Hans Memling** are mostly of unidentified sitters, except for the one of Benedetto di Tommaso Portinari (Benedetto was the son of Pigello Portinari, director of the Milanese branch of the Medici bank and nephew of Tommaso Portinari, Memling's Italian patron; *see above, p. 119*). The portrait of a man holding a letter (probably an Italian living in Bruges), with a lovely tiny landscape in the background with a man on a grey horse riding through the countryside populated by swans and deer, was acquired by the Uffizi in 1989: in 1941 it was sold to Hitler by order of Mussolini. It was then returned in 1948 and kept in Palazzo Vecchio. Stolen in 1971, it was found again in Zurich in 1973.

FLEMISH INFLUENCES ON FLORENTINE PORTRAITURE

Memling was Van der Weyden's pupil and collaborator, and on his master's death he became the best-known Flemish painter of his day. He carried out numerous commissions for Italians in Flanders, especially portraits, since these were easy to transport. He was the first to adopt a three-quarter pose for his sitters (so that both eyes are visible), and to include the sitter's hands, and he introduced the idea of providing a landscape in the background. Florentine artists up to this time had painted portraits mostly in profile following the tradition of medals, but were quick to copy this innovation (see, for instance, Botticelli's *Portrait of a Man in a Red Hat* in Room 10–14, and later portraits by Perugino and Raphael).

Portraits by **Hans Holbein the Younger** include a self-portrait and a likeness of Sir Richard Southwell (1536), which was given by Thomas Howard, Earl of Arundel, to Cosimo II in 1620. The supposed portrait of Thomas More is now thought to be a work by the school of Holbein. The double *Portrait of a Man and his Wife* is by Joos van Cleve the Elder, and the *Adoration of the Magi* by Gerard David. In front of the window wall are two panels by **Antonello da Messina**, acquired by the state in 1996 as part of the Bardini bequest. They show the *Madonna and Child* and *St John the Evangelist*, and clearly reveal the influence of the Flemish school on this great Sicilian painter.

Room 23: Works by northern Italian artists, including three very fine works by **Mantegna**: a small triptych of the *Adoration of the Magi*, *Circumcision* and *Ascension*, exquisitely painted and preserving its beautiful frame; a remarkable portrait thought to show Cardinal Carlo de' Medici; and the tiny *Madonna delle Cave*. Another Leonardesque work is the small painting of *Narcissus* by Giovanni Antonio Boltraffio. The small *Portrait of a Gypsy Girl* is by Boccaccio Boccaccino. On the wall opposite are three good works by the Emilian artist **Correggio**: a tiny *Madonna in Glory*; the *Rest on the Flight* and *Madonna in Adoration of the Child*.

Room 24: The collection of miniatures (15th–18th century) is exhibited in this little oval room (only visible through the doorway) designed in 1781.

Third floor: South Corridor

The short South Corridor has a wonderful view. Across the river, on the extreme left, is San Miniato with its campanile on the skyline and the Forte di Belvedere. In the other direction, beyond the Uffizi building, is Palazzo Vecchio and the cupola of the Duomo. At the far end of the corridor you can see the tiled roof of the Corridoio Vasariano leading away to Ponte Vecchio. The Arno flows downstream beneath Ponte Santa Trínita and the bridges beyond. On the south bank the dome and campanile of Santo Spirito are prominent, and further downstream the dome of San Frediano in Cestello is visible.

Some fine pieces of ancient sculpture are arranged in the South Corridor. Outside Room 24, the *Sleeping Cupid* is a 16th-century copy in black basalt of a Hellenistic original. At the end of the East Corridor there is a Roman copy—made in the 1st century AD—of the famous original of an athlete carrying a spear (the *Doryphorus*) by the Greek master Polyclitus. On the window wall looking towards Palazzo Vecchio are Roman statues of *Demeter* (the copy of a Hellenistic original), *Leda* (restored by Giovanni Battista Foggini); *Eros and Psyche*; and *Apollo* (a copy of a Greek original by Praxiteles). In the centre is a fragment of a she-wolf in porphyry, a Roman copy of a 5th-century Greek original made at the time of the emperor Hadrian. In the corner (overlooking the Arno), the beautiful colossal head in Greek marble is probably a late Hellenistic original (one of the few in the whole gallery) of a triton. It was long thought to represent Alexander the Great dying; as the only portrait of the great conqueror known until 1780, it was considered extremely important and in the 16th and 17th centuries was one of the most frequently copied works in the whole gallery. It was restored in 1795 (including part of the hair and the nose).

Third floor: West Corridor

At the beginning of the West Corridor there are two gruesome statues of the satyr Marsyas, hung up and ready to be flayed by Apollo, both Roman copies of Hellenistic originals of the 3rd or 2nd century BC. The one in red marble was, according to Vasari, restored by Verrocchio, but the upper part of the torso is now thought to be the work of Mino da Fiesole. It is known that it belonged to Lorenzo the Magnificent, who kept it by the back entrance to Palazzo Medici in Via dei Ginori. The one opposite, which was formerly in the Capranica collection, entered the Uffizi in 1780.

The rooms off the West Corridor

Room 25: The famous *Doni Tondo* of the Holy Family by **Michelangelo** is his only finished tempera painting. It was painted for the marriage of Agnolo Doni with Maddalena Strozzi (1504–05), when the artist was 30 years old. Although owing much to Signorelli (*see Room 19*), it breaks with traditional representations of this familiar subject and signals a new moment in High Renaissance painting, pointing the way to the Sistine Chapel frescoes. The splendid contemporary frame is by Domenico del Tasso. The *Portrait of a Lady* is a beautiful work now thought to be by Ridolfo del Ghirlandaio (c. 1510). It is always known as 'La Monaca' ('The Nun'; she is holding a prayer book) and when purchased in 1819 by Ferdinando III it was thought to be by Leonardo da Vinci. Recently restored, it has a lovely view of Florence in the background. Also here are works by Fra' Bartolomeo, Mariotto Albertinelli (*Visitation*) and Francesco Granacci.

Room 26: Masterpieces by **Raphael**. *Leo X with Giulio de' Medici and Luigi de' Rossi* was painted shortly before the artist's death and is one of his most power-ful portrait groups; it was to have a great influence on Titian. The first Medici pope (son of Lorenzo the Magnificent) is shown with his two cousins whom he created cardinals: Giulio de' Medici later went on to become Pope Clement VII. The painting was commissioned by Leo X in Rome in 1518, so that it could be sent to Florence on the occasion of the wedding of Leo's brother Giuliano, Duke of Nemours, with Philiberte of Savoy, since Pope Leo was unable to attend. The various shades of red are extremely effective and all three prelates express their self-assurance through their at-titudes of proud independence. The por-trait of Julius II is usually thought to be a replica of a painting of the same subject in the National Gallery in London.

The *Madonna del Cardellino* ('Madon-na of the Goldfinch') is one of Raphael's most famous sacred works, probably painted around 1506 for the marriage of the artist's great friend, the rich merchant Lorenzo Nasi, to Sandra Canigiani. It was in the Nasi's house on Via de' Bardi in 1547 when it was ruined by a landslide caused by heavy autumn rain, and the panel was shattered. However, Lorenzo's son Giovanni Battista immediately gathered up the pieces and had it carefully repaired (perhaps by Ridolfo del Ghirlandaio). It remained in the Nasi family until 1639, when Cardinal Giovanni Carlo de' Medici purchased it from them. However, it remained in a very poor state, covered with an opaque yellow varnish, until restoration in 1999–2008. Its restoration has been recognised as one of the most successful operations of this kind ever made: it now probably looks very like it did when first painted.

Raphael's self-portrait, in a lovely frame, is painted with a remarkable freshness of touch. The *Portrait of a Young Man* (formerly thought to be Francesco Maria della Rovere) is also by Raphael, but other portraits here are now only attributed to him (including the man once thought to represent Perugino).

Other very fine works by three artists who were all friends include *Pietro Carnesecchi* (1527) by Domenico Puligo, *Young Man with Gloves* by Franciabigio, and the *Madonna of the Harpies* (named after the carvings on the throne) by Andrea del Sarto.

Room 27: Florentine Mannerism. **Rosso Fiorentino** is particularly well represented with a *Madonna and Saints* and two portraits, three of the few surviving Florentine works by the painter who went on to be court artist to Francis I at Fontainebleau. The geometrical forms of the nudes in the foreground of his *Moses Defending the Children of Jethro* (possibly a fragment) display a very original and modern tendency. There is a self-conscious denial of spatial depth and naturalistic proportions in order to emphasise the drama of the scene and

the virtuosity of the painter. There are also good works by **Pontormo**, including the portrait of Maria Salviati, widow of Giovanni delle Bande Nere (father of Cosimo I) and the *Martyrdom of St Maurice and the Eleven Thousand Martyrs*. His *Supper at Emmaus* (1525), painted for the Certosa del Galluzzo, is an uncharacteristic work (above the head of Christ is a surrealist symbol of God the Father). The portrait of the musician Francesco dell'Ajolle, formerly thought to be by Pontormo, is now attributed to the less well-known painter Pier Francesco di Jacopo Foschi. The *Holy Family with the Young St John*, with evident derivations from Classical sculpture, was painted by Bronzino for the Panciatichi, whose standard can be seen flying from the tower in the background.

Room 28: Some of the finest works by **Titian** include the **Venus of Urbino**, which was commissioned by Guidobaldo della Rovere, later Duke of Urbino, in 1538. It is one of the most beautiful nudes ever painted and has had a profound influence on subsequent European painting. **Flora** is another masterpiece, a seductive, exquisite portrait of a girl with beautiful hair, holding roses in her hand. The male portrait is known as the *Sick Man*. Other superb portraits by Titian here are Eleonora Gonzaga, Duchess of Urbino, in a splendid dress, and her husband Francesco Maria della Rovere, wearing armour; a Knight of Malta, charged with religious fervour; and Bishop Ludovico Beccadelli. The portrait of Pope Sixtus IV in profile, although full of character (and in bad condition), shows the intervention of Titian's *bottega*.

The *Death of Adonis* is a very fine work by the Venetian artist **Sebastiano del Piombo**. Beyond an autumnal landscape there are views of the Doge's Palace and the Piazzetta in Venice. Sebastiano also painted the beautiful *Portrait of a Lady* (formerly called *La Fornarina*). Works by another northern artist, Palma Vecchio, are also exhibited here, and include an unfinished portrait (thought to be a self-portrait) on the back of a portrait of a lady (c. 1515), acquired in 2001.

Rooms 29 and 30: The *Madonna dal collo lungo* ('Madonna with the long Neck') by **Parmigianino** (1534–36) is a work of extreme refinement and originality, typical of the Mannerist style. Also here are works by Dosso Dossi, another representative of the Emilian school. Room 30 has small works by his contemporary Garofalo.

Room 31: Works by the great Venetian painter **Paolo Veronese** include the *Annunciation*, designed around a perspective device in the centre of the picture. The work is delicately painted in simple colours, in contrast to the rich golden hues of the figure of St Barbara in the *Holy Family with St Barbara*, a work of the artist's maturity. When the curtains are open, the window offers a good view of Palazzo Vecchio, the Duomo and the top of Orsanmichele.

Room 32: *Leda and the Swan* is by the great Venetian painter **Tintoretto**, with the fine nude figure of Leda and her pretty serving girl; he also painted the portrait of his contemporary Jacopo Sansovino, the Tuscan architect and sculptor who built many fine buildings in Venice.

Room 33: 16th-century works by French artists. The tiny equestrian portrait of Francis I of France is by the court painter François Clouet. It was probably brought to Florence in 1589 by Christine of Lorraine, wife of Ferdinando I. The amusing painting of *Two Women in the Bath* is by the late 16th-century School of Fontainebleau. The *Christ Appearing to St Mary Magdalene* is by Lavinia Fontana, one of the few women painters represented in the gallery.

Room 34: Lorenzo Lotto and the 16th-century Lombard school. Small works by **Lorenzo Lotto** include the fine *Head of a Young Boy* and *Holy Family with Saints*. Another remarkable portrait (in poor condition) is that of an old man with long grey hair, thought to represent Teofilo Folengo, by an unknown 16th-century painter. Fine portraits by Giovanni Battista Moroni include Count Pietro Secco Suardi (1563), a full-length standing portrait and *Man with a Book*. The female nude is an extraordinary work, very unusual for its period since it lacks any mythological references, attributed to Bernardino Licino.

Room 35: Works by Federico Barocci include the *Madonna del Popolo*, a delightful crowded composition, a *Noli me Tangere*, and a portrait of Francesco Maria della Rovere.

Beyond the door on the left which leads to the stairs down to the exit, in the corridor (on the window wall), is a *Wounded Warrior*, kneeling, a Greek original of the 5th century BC (only the shield and arms have been restored). The head is antique but comes from another statue of a barbarian. The 'leather' armour is extremely delicately carved. Nearby are displayed a seated Apollo and, opposite, *Ganymede*, both of them Roman copies of Hellenistic originals.

Room 41 (*sometimes closed*): Fine works by **Rubens**. These include the *Triumphal Entry of Ferdinand of Austria into Antwerp*; portrait of Isabella Brant, the painter's first wife (c. 1625); and an equestrian portrait of Philip IV of Spain. Works by **Van Dyck** include portraits of Margaret of Lorraine, Suttermans's mother and John of Montfort and an equestrian portrait of the Emperor Charles V. There is also a portrait of Galileo by Suttermans.

Room 42: Called the **Niobe Room**, this was designed by Gaspare Maria Paoletti and Zanobi del Rosso in 1771–79 to house the statue group of *Niobe and her Children*, found in a vineyard near the Lateran in 1583, and bought to Florence in 1775 from the Villa Medici in Rome. These are Roman copies of Greek originals of the school of Skopas (early 4th century BC), but many of the figures are badly restored and others do not belong to the group (the lying figure of Niobe is in a different marble). On the end wall, to the right, is Niobe herself with one of

her children, and on the opposite wall is a statue of a pedagogue. The room was well restored after bomb damage in 1993 (*see p. 110*). On the end walls are two huge paintings by Rubens: *Henri IV Entering Paris*, and *Henri IV at the Battle of Ivry*, which were the first part of a cycle depicting the king's exploits.

Room 43: Venus, two satyrs and a cupid by Annibale Carracci.

Room 44: On the far wall are three splendid works by **Rembrandt**: *Self-portrait*, *Portrait of an Old Man* and *Self-portrait as an Old Man*. Also here are Dutch and Flemish works including Jan Steen's *Lunch-party* and a fine landscape by Jacob Ruysdael.

Room 45: 18th-century paintings. The Venetian school is represented by Piazzetta (*Susannah and the Elders*), Giovanni Battista Tiepolo, Francesco Guardi and Canaletto. Among the French and Spanish portraits are two of children by Chardin, two of Maria Theresa by Francisco Goya; *Vittorio Alfieri and The Countess of Albany* by François-Xavier Fabre, and *Marie-Adelaïde of France in Turkish Costume* by Jean-Etienne Liotard.

At the end of the West Corridor is a statuary group of Laocoön and his sons in the coils of the serpents by Baccio Bandinelli (restored in 2009), inspired by the famous Hellenistic work in the Vatican. In the corner is a sculpted boar (for long thought to be a copy, but which may be a Hellenistic original), the **model for the *Porcellino*** in the Mercato Nuovo. The Roman statue of a Nereid on a sea-horse is a copy of a Hellenistic original, and, opposite, the standing veiled female statue dates from the 2nd century AD.

From here you can go out onto the roof terrace of the Loggia della Signoria, from which there is a splendid close-up view of Palazzo Vecchio. There is a café here.

Leaving the West Corridor

At the top of the stairs signed to the exit are some Classical statues and inscriptions, and you can look into a small room beyond, where some of the most important Roman pieces are displayed: the *Spinario*, *Crouching Venus*, the *Sleeping Hermaphrodite*, a copy of a Greek original of the 2nd century BC, and two torsos.

A long flight of stairs descends to the *piano nobile* and the exit. In the West Corridor on the *piano nobile* is the huge marble **Medici Vase**, a neo-Attic work acquired by Lorenzo de' Medici. Beyond is a room with three works by Guido Reni, including *St Andrea Corsini* (a recent acquisition).

In the second room are **three masterpieces by Caravaggio**. Although the artist never visited Florence, all three works came to the city very soon after they were painted. The *Young Bacchus* is a very early work dating from around 1597 given to Ferdinando I by Carlo del Monte. The *Sacrifice of Isaac* is thought to have been painted for the Barberini family around 1601. The head of Medusa is on a canvas which was attached to a shield in the Medici collection of armour and was acquired by Ferdinando I in 1598. Other rooms have works by the so-called '*Caravaggeschi*' painters, a rather dismissive epithet which groups together some very skilled painters all of whom were promoted by Cosimo II, and are well represented here. The four who can be considered direct interpreters of Caravaggio's style are Bartolomeo Manfredi, Cecco del Caravaggio, Spadarino and Ribera. One of the works by Manfredi was acquired in 1994 after the Mafia bomb attack blew to pieces a painting entitled *The Concert* by the same artist. The fine works by Gherardo delle Notti, include a charming *Adoration of Christ*. Also here are works by Artemisia Gentileschi.

Palazzo della Zecca

Adjoining the side of the Loggia della Signoria, the ground floor of **Palazzo della Zecca**, with its well protected windows, is incorporated into the Uffizi building. The famous gold florins, first issued in 1252 by the government of the *Primo Popolo*, were minted here (the lily of Florence was on the obverse and St John the Baptist on the reverse). Florence and Genoa were the first Italian cities to mint their own coinage; the florin soon became the standard gold coin of Europe. The Sala delle Reali Poste here, built as a post office in 1866, is a fine hall with a huge skylight supported on a cast-iron framework. It is used for exhibitions. At the end of Via Lambertesca is the Porta delle Suppliche, added after 1574 by Buontalenti and surmounted by a bust of Francesco I, the masterpiece of Giovanni Bandini.

The Contini-Bonacossi Collection

The **Contini-Bonacossi Collection** is housed in a wing of the second floor of the Uffizi building (*entrance in Via Lambertesca; admission only by arrangement; see p. 109*). It is a choice collection made by Alessandro Contini-Bonacossi (with the advice of Roberto Longhi) and contains Italian and Spanish paintings as well as 15th–17th-century majolica and furniture. Works by artists not already represented in the Uffizi were favoured. Much of the collection was sold by the family after 1960 but they ceded this portion of it to the state in 1974. The paintings have frames typical of the 1920s. Some of the rooms have pretty 18th-century decorations.

Among the best works are a *Madonna and Child* by Duccio, a well-preserved altarpiece of St John the Baptist with stories from his life by Giovanni del Biondo, the *Madonna della Neve*, painted for the cathedral of Siena by Sassetta, two panels with scenes from the life of St Nicholas by Paolo Veneziano and a fresco from the castle of Trebbio showing the *Madonna and Child with Angels and Saints* and two children of the Pazzi Family by Andrea del Castagno. There are also fine Venetian and Spanish works.

THE CORRIDOIO VASARIANO

This was built by Vasari in five months to celebrate the marriage of Francesco de' Medici and Joanna of Austria in 1565 and provides unique views of the city. Nearly a kilometre long, its purpose was to connect Palazzo Vecchio via the Uffizi and Ponte Vecchio with the new residence of the Medici dukes at Palazzo Pitti, in the form of a private covered passageway. This was particularly convenient in wet weather, and it was sometimes used as a nursery for the children of the grand dukes. Since it has no steps, elderly or infirm members of the family were wheeled along it in basket chairs. Paintings were first hung here in the 19th century when the Savoy royalty put up their family portraits, and later in the century it was used as a deposit for the Uffizi. Since the early years of the 20th century, the Uffizi's celebrated collection of self-portraits has been hung here. It was started by Cardinal Leopoldo in the 17th century. Having acquired the self-portraits of Guercino and Pietro da Cortona, he went on to collect some 80 more artists' self-portraits in his lifetime. The collection continued to be augmented in the following centuries up to the present day. It is usually only open at certain periods of the year and only on guided visits by previous appointment; *see p 109*.

MUSEO GALILEO

Map 1, 8. Piazza dei Giudici. Open 9.30–6, Tues 9.30–1; T: 055 265311. Excellent research library open to students. Audio guides are available. www.museogalileo.it. The digital edition of the Complete Work of Galileo Galilei can be freely accessed at the following page of the museum's website: http://pinakes.imss.fi.it:8080/pinakestext/authors.seam
The Museo di Storia della Scienza was rearranged in 2010 and renamed Museo Galileo. It is housed in Palazzo Castellani, a fine medieval palace on the Arno named after its owners, an important Florentine family in the 14th century, whose wealth was based on the cloth trade. A monumental sundial, with a gnomon several metres high, was built in 2007 on the enlarged pavement outside the museum entrance.

Since the days of the first Medici grand duke, Cosimo I, Florence has held an extremely important place in the history of science, a fact which has often been obscured by the attention paid to its great collections of art. Many of the contents of this museum were owned by the Medici grand dukes and were displayed in the Uffizi. The museum also incorporates the Museum of Physics and Natural Sciences, opened in 1775 by Peter Leopold and moved here in 1929. Today the superbly displayed collection of scientific instruments from these grand-ducal collections provides a fascinating illustration of the history of science, with excellent multi-media supports, and labelling also in English.

First floor

Room I: An introductory display, with 16th-century instruments from the Medici collections. The polyhedric wooden sundial (by Stefano Bonsignori) has hexagonal and square faces each with its own gnomon. It was given its base when it was purchased by Ferdinando Meucci in 1876. The bronze planispheric astrolabe made by Egnazio Danti c. 1570 is known to have been lent to Galileo.

Room II: Astronomical instruments used for measuring time. Central case: precious celestial globe made by an Arab in Valencia around 1080 showing the constellations; an astrolabe dating from the 9th century; an armillary sphere made by Girolamo della Volpaia in 1564 (apparently as an instrument for teaching astronomy); and an astronomical clock from southern Germany (1575), an extraordinarily fine piece in gilded brass and silver which shows us all that was known about measuring time, the calendar, and the movement of the stars at the time it was made in 1575.

In the wall cases are 16th-century sundials and instruments for calculating the time at night by the position of the stars. Another case displays instruments designed (or used) by Galileo's last pupil Vincenzo Viviani, including astrolabes and a model of the solar orb. Works by the Schisslers, a family of instrument-makers from Germany, include quadrants and a mathematical compendium still with its tooled leather case. Dis-

played on its own is a wooden Aristotelian planetarium made in Italy c. 1600.

Room III contains a superb display of globes around a huge Ptolemaic armillary sphere built by Antonio Santucci in 1588 for Ferdinando I. It demonstrates the movements of celestial bodies: hidden in the centre is the coloured terrestrial globe; the numerous gilt rings which surround it represent the orbit of the planets. The adjoining **Room IV** has four globes made in Venice by Vincenzo Coronelli (1650–1718) for Louis XIV (with an illustration of how they were made). There is also a facsimile of Fra' Mauro's celebrated world map of 1459 (the original is in the Libreria Marciana in Venice).

Room V illustrates the science of navigation, symbolised by the marble bust of Amerigo Vespucci attributed to Giovanni Battista Foggini. The central case has displays illustrating how longitude was calculated. The largest case is devoted to the nautical instruments and gauges to measure tides, invented and used by Sir Robert Dudley (1574–1649), son of the first Sir Robert Dudley, Earl of Leicester, Queen Elizabeth I's favourite. He was a famous navigator and mapmaker who sailed to the West Indies before coming to live in Tuscany in 1605 (he died at the Villa Corsini on the outskirts of Florence). He became a naval engineer and administered the port of Livorno for

Ferdinando I and Ferdinando II. He also built warships and supervised the draining of the marshes between Livorno and Pisa.

Room VI: Instruments used as an aid in warfare. The central case displays some very fine surveying instruments made for Cosimo I. Another case has instruments invented for use in artillery operations. There is also a collection of 16th-century pieces brought back to Florence by Prince Mattias, brother of Ferdinando II, in 1635 when he returned from serving in the Thirty Years War, including an astrolabe made by Christoph Schissler. The largest wall case illustrates measurement and calculation with mathematical instruments, and compasses.

Room VII is entirely devoted to Galileo, and the science of motion.

Galileo Galilei (1564–1642)

Galileo was born in Pisa, and lived and died in Florence. He perfected the telescope, and discovered the four satellites of Jupiter in 1610. He was appointed Professor of Mathematics at Pisa University by Cardinal Ferdinando de' Medici (later grand duke), and then took up a chair at Padua University from 1592 to 1610, where he attracted pupils from all over Europe. He stayed in the Villa Medici (on the site of the Villa Demidoff at Pratolino) in 1605–06 as tutor to the future Cosimo II. In 1632, he published a defence of the Copernican theory of astronomy, and was condemned the following year by the Inquisition in Rome for his contention that the Earth was not at the centre of the Universe, but through the good offices of Grand Duke Ferdinando II he avoided imprisonment and spent the latter part of his life in Florence, where he died in 1642. He bought a house for his son Vincenzo on Costa San Giorgio and lived, practically as a prisoner, at Villa il Gioiello in Pian de' Giullari (*see p. 322*), under the protection of the grand duke. Although infirm and almost blind, he wrote some of his most important treatises here and was visited by Evangelista Torricelli, Vincenzo Viviani, Thomas Hobbes and possibly also Milton. His daughter Suor Maria Celeste lived at a convent nearby (although she predeceased her father by eight years): over a hundred letters from her to her father survive.

On his death Galileo was not allowed a Christian burial: it was not until 1737 that the Church authorities permitted his remains to be transferred from a room beneath the bell-tower in Santa Croce to the nave of the church and it was at that time that the Medici grand duke Gian Gastone had the monument there erected to him. He was later honoured by Grand Duke Leopold II when in 1841 he commissioned the tribuna in the Specola museum (*see p. 338*) in Galileo's memory. Eventually, in 1992, Pope John Paul II announced the rehabilitation of Galileo and cancelled the condemnation imposed on him in 1633. However, the 'Galileo case' still causes controversy and in 2008 a three-day international conference was held to discuss his relationship to the established Church.

The colossal marble bust of the great scientist holding his telescope and compasses was commissioned from Carlo Marcellini by Cosimo III in 1674. A case preserves the very instruments Galileo is thought to have used, including a pair of compasses, lodestones (of natural magnetic rock) and two thermoscopes (predecessors of the modern thermometer). Another wall case has even more precious works: the two telescopes actually made by Galileo in 1609–10 when the great scientist began the exploration of the skies (one of them was donated by him to Cosimo II), and the objective lens from the telescope which he used to discover the four largest moons of Jupiter (which he named the 'Medicean stars') but which was cracked before he presented it to Ferdinando II (the ivory and ebony frame was designed for it later, in 1677, by the Dutch engraver Vittorio Crosten). Also displayed here are facsimiles of Galileo's most important tracts, and models made for Grand Duke Peter Leopold in the late 18th century which illustrate some of Galileo's inventions. In a small central case are mementoes and relics of the famous scientist, proudly preserved by the Florentines: the 18th-century reliquary on an alabaster base preserves the bones of the middle finger of his right hand (which were removed from his tomb when his monument was erected in the church of Santa Croce) and the index finger bones and even a tooth that are also said to be his.

THE TELESCOPE

Although this fundamental scientific instrument is always associated primarily with Galileo, it seems that it already existed in a rudimentary form in the first years of the 17th century in various parts of Europe and that the great scientist probably came across some 'optical tubes' for sale as little more than popular toys on a visit to Venice. The British mathematician Thomas Harriot apparently had the idea of raising one of these to the heavens and he made drawings of the moon as seen, magnified, through them. In 1609 Galileo quickly perfected the telescope for use in his own astronomical observations so that he was able to study the surface of the moon 400 times larger than with the naked eye. He soon overcame his contemporaries' scepticism and was able to prove to them that his invention increased rather than distorted human vision. With his telescope he also identified the four satellites which orbit Jupiter, and the mass of stars which make up the Milky Way. By 1610 he had published the *Sidereus Nuncius*, dedicated to Cosimo II, in which he announced his discoveries with fascinating illustrations of what he had seen (still preserved in the Biblioteca Nazionale Centrale in Florence).

Room VIII is dedicated to the Accademia del Cimento, an experimental academy founded by Cardinal Leopoldo de' Medici in 1657 with his brother Ferdinando II, and the first scientific society in Europe. It has a superb display of blown glass thermometers and hydrometers. A wall case illustrates experiments to prove the possibility of creating a vacuum and the physics of fluids. An early calculator invented by the British diplomat Sir Samuel Morland in 1664 is also preserved here.

Room IX has instruments used in meteorology (including barometers, and hygrometers invented by Vincenzo Viviani). There are microscopes made by Francesco Redi and an early 18th-century compound microscope, as well as magnifying glasses. The splendid display of late 17th-century telescopes includes some very fine lenses made by Evangelista Torricelli and his contemporary Eustachio Divini, who were both particularly skilled in optics.

Second floor

The Lorraine Scientific Collections are displayed on this floor, including numerous exhibits related to Peter Leopold, grand duke in 1765–90.

In the centre of **Room X** is Peter Leopold's work desk, which he used for his chemical experiments. Around the walls are surgical instruments and wax and terracotta anatomical models made in Florence for use in obstetrics. Curiosities displayed here include a mechanical hand which writes a phrase by clockwork and a hydraulic pump made in 1794.

Room XI: This large hall has a magnificent display of models made in the 18th century illustrating experimental physics, including electrostatic machines. The Tellarium was a mechanical device for teaching astronomy, and the Orrery (invented in England) a type of planetarium—the one here was made in Florence in 1776 and demonstrates the heliocentric motion of Mercury, Venus and the Earth.

Room XII is devoted to instruments illustrating mechanics, while **Room XIII** has instruments illustrating optics, and the development of the electric current and electromagnetism with reference to Leopoldo Nobili (1784–1835) and, more famously, Alessandro Volta (1745–1827), inventor of the 'voltaic pile', ancestor of the modern battery, for which invention he was ennobled by Napoleon. The unit of electrical potential, the volt, is named after him.

Room XIV provides a history of the precision instrument industry in Europe in the 18th and 19th centuries, and displays microscopes and telescopes made in Italy by Giovanni Battista Amici.

Rooms XV and XVI have displays related to physics: measuring the atmosphere and light, and electricity and electromagnetism.

Room XVII is devoted to quantitative chemistry, including a large burning lens.

Room XVIII has instruments made specifically for domestic use, such as weighing machines, clocks, watches and barometers.

MEDICI FLORENCE, SAN LORENZO & SAN MARCO

Close together in a part of town just north of the centre are the palace built for Cosimo il Vecchio by Michelozzo, where the Medici lived until Cosimo I moved into Palazzo della Signoria, and the church of San Lorenzo, commissioned by the Medici from Brunelleschi and where the principal members of the family are buried. Nearby is the convent of San Marco, rebuilt by Michelozzo for Cosimo il Vecchio, who retained two cells for use as a retreat. It is famous for its frescoes and paintings by Fra' Angelico.

PALAZZO MEDICI-RICCARDI

Map 1, 2. Open 9–7 except Wed. T: 055 276 0340. Entrance at Via Cavour 3. Off the main courtyard is a room with an excellent multi-media display to help you identify the figures in Gozzoli's frescoes in the chapel. Only about 10 people can fit into the chapel at any one time. It is usually less crowded at lunchtime.

Palazzo Medici-Riccardi was built for Cosimo il Vecchio by Michelozzo after 1444 as his town mansion on Via Larga (renamed Via Cavour in the 19th century). Michelozzo was Cosimo's favourite architect: he also used him to design the convent of San Marco and his villas on the outskirts of Florence. Apart from the fine exterior, the main courtyard with classical reliefs in the tondi survives from this time, as well as Michelozzo's lovely little chapel on the first floor and the frescoes Cosimo commissioned for it from Benozzo Gozzoli. The palace remained the residence of the Medici family up until 1540. The Riccardi name comes from the wealthy banking family who purchased it from Ferdinando II in 1659. Part of their collection of ancient marble sculptures can be seen here, as well as the suite of rooms on the first floor decorated for them, culminating in a magnificent Baroque gallery with a ceiling painted by Luca Giordano. The palace is now the seat of the prefect, the provincial representative of central government, and of the Province of Florence, so only part of the ground and first floors can be visited.

THE MEDICI

The Medici first came to Florence from the fertile valley of the Mugello. They are recorded as money changers during the 13th century and as bankers in the 14th. The family emblem, the *palle*, red balls on a gold background, probably represents the coins of their earliest profession, although they have also been linked somewhat romantically in family legend to the dents on the shield received by a Medici knight in an encounter with a giant.

Giovanni di Bicci de' Medici (1360–1429), the founder of the family's great fortune and political respectability, started life humbly. He was in Florence by 1378, and worked his way up the family business until he was undisputed head of the bank. By 1401 he was well respected enough to be on the committee judging the competition for the Baptistery doors. But Giovanni never forgot that he was an outsider, and he carefully but quietly sided with popular feeling. It is said that he advised his son Cosimo (il Vecchio) never to go near the Piazza della Signoria unless summoned there, and never to make a show before the people or go against their will. Cosimo, already 40 when his father died in 1429, followed the advice.

It was Cosimo who set in hand the building of a family palace. Up to now the family had lived in a *palazzo* taken over from the Bardi family, but by the 1440s Cosimo felt secure enough in the city to build his own. However, he still needed to act prudently, and the story goes that the model produced by Brunelleschi was turned down by Cosimo as too ostentatious. Those attuned to Cosimo's ways have argued that the affair was set up to allow him to present the more modest palace built to the design of Michelozzo as a sign of his restraint. Visitors to the completed building would be greeted by Donatello's *David* and its Latin inscription exhorting the citizens to stand up against tyranny.

It seems clear that the palace was used for formal city business after 1458. It was also here that the bags which contained the names of citizens eligible for office were made up (the names were drawn out at random), and there is no doubt that Cosimo controlled the *accoppiatori*, the scrutineers of the appointments. Nevertheless, the Medici were never truly secure in their position. Even at the height of Lorenzo's power in the 1480s there were those who talked of Medici tyranny, and their rule collapsed quickly in 1494 with the inept behaviour of Lorenzo's son Piero. The Medici palace was sacked in an outburst of popular fury. Yet the family had an uncanny ability to reinvent itself. Few would have predicted that it would once again be a Medici, Cosimo I (1519–74), who would dominate the city after the siege of 1530, and this time to a greater extent than any of his predecessors. The glorification of the dynasty began with Cosimo's symbolic move out of the family residence into the seat of government, Palazzo della Signoria. The Medici palace was sold to the Riccardi family—though luckily its finest Medici treasure, the frescoes of the *Procession of the Magi*, remains intact.　　C.F.

The façade

The splendid façade, built in *pietra forte*, stands on a slight bend in the road which makes it clearly visible from the Duomo to the south and San Marco to the north. The bold rustication on the ground floor gives way to less pronounced blocks of stone on the storey above with its arched biforated windows. The row of windows is repeated on the top storey, which is built of compact smooth stones beneath a handsome classical cornice on the roofline. There is a pleasant stone bench at pavement level, for the use of the populace and visitors in the time of the Medici and for tired tourists today. The building was originally almost square, with one main portal flanked by two arched recesses and just ten windows on each of the upper floors, separated by string courses. The two pedimented windows on the ground floor were added later in 1517 when the ground-floor loggia was enclosed, but otherwise the façade remains as it was in the days of the Medici, and you can appreciate clearly how it served as a model for other Florentine palaces, in particular those built by the Strozzi and Pitti.

When the Riccardi took possession of the palace they extended the façade towards Piazza San Marco, adding another door and ground-floor window and seven more windows on each of the upper storeys. But they did this with great care, following exactly the style of the Medici façade, so that you would never know today that some two centuries separate the two ends. The large archway in the lower building on the extreme right, which once gave access to the stables and coach house, now opens into an arcaded gallery (used for exhibitions) through which you can walk from Via Cavour to Via de' Ginori at the back of the palace, emerging near the entrance to the Biblioteca Riccardiana (*see p. 141*).

Cortile d'Onore

The dignified main courtyard, which survives from Michelozzo's time, has composite colonnades and twelve tondi in relief (copies of ancient sculptures inspired by antique gems in the Medici collections) and the Medici arms. These were carried out c. 1460 by Donatello's circle (usually ascribed to Bertoldo di Giovanni) and are linked by graffiti festoons by Maso di Bartolomeo. When the Medici lived here, Donatello's *Judith and Holofernes* was in the garden, and his bronze *David* adorned the courtyard until 1495. The statue of *Orpheus and Cerberus*, under the arch towards the garden, was commissioned from Baccio Bandinelli by Leo X around 1515. After 1715 Francesco Riccardi arranged the walls of the courtyard as a museum of ancient sculpture, setting up numerous reliefs, inscriptions and busts inside decorative Baroque frames.

Museo dei Marmi

The museum is housed in vaulted underground rooms (the brick ramp, which survives from the original palace, would have been used by horses for access to their stables). The numerous ancient Roman marble busts on display here were owned by Riccardo Riccardi (1558–1612), an erudite collector and wealthy banker (who also founded the library next door; *see p. 141*). One of the best preserved, known as the *Riccardi Athlete*, is in the first room (on the end wall to the left). It probably dates from the time of Hadrian, like the lovely portrait of the empress Sabina also exhibited here. Beyond a room which displays finds made in 2003–04 when these rooms were being excavated (from shards of Roman ceramics to a 19th-century porcelain pipe), the last room has a fine bust of a child dating from the 3rd century AD. This is only a small part of the Riccardi's once famous collection of ancient marbles (in 1840 some 65 busts were moved to the Uffizi).

The chapel

The grand 17th-century staircase, designed for the Riccardi by Giovanni Battista Foggini, leads up from the Cortile d'Onore to the famous private chapel. Every grand palace and villa in Florence would have had a chapel for private devotion but this is one of the earliest to have survived. It is almost entirely as it was when designed by Michelozzo and frescoed by Benozzo Gozzoli for Cosimo il Vecchio, except that the entrance is now at one corner (where the frescoed wall had to be moved when the staircase was built) instead of through the little door in front of the altar (now used as an exit). Although your attention is immediately taken up with the delightful frescoes which entirely cover the walls, the architecture and furnishings are also of the greatest interest: it has a lovely carved and gilded wood ceiling and a splendid inlaid floor in red porphyry and green serpentine marble, and finely carved wooden choir stalls designed by Giuliano da Sangallo.

BENOZZO GOZZOLI'S FRESCO CYCLE

The Procession of the Magi to Bethlehem (begun in 1459 and finished before 1463) is one of the most pleasing fresco cycles of the Renaissance. It was probably commissioned from Benozzo Gozzoli by Cosimo il Vecchio, but it is known that his son Piero di Cosimo (il Gottoso; the Gouty) also took an active interest in the work, and the artist here produced his masterpiece. The procession was probably intended partly as an evocation of the festival held by the Compagnia dei Magi of San Marco at Epiphany, in which the Medici usually took part. The decorative cavalcade is shown in a charming landscape with hunting scenes, which seems to be inspired by Flemish tapestries. Some members of the Medici family are depicted wearing their emblem of the three ostrich feathers, but discussion continues about the identification of the various figures, a number of which are vivid portrait studies.

The frescoes were designed around an altarpiece (commissioned c. 1444–56) of the *Adoration of the Child* by Filippo Lippi, which was already in the palace. It remained here until 1494 when it was taken to Palazzo Vecchio, and after 1814 it found its way to Berlin. The present excellent copy, by an artist who worked in the *bottega* of Filippo Lippi, was put here in 1929. On the walls on either side of the altar, Gozzoli frescoed the beautiful landscapes with angels, recalling those of his master, Fra' Angelico. *(contd. overleaf)*

(*Contd. from previous page*) The procession is seen approaching along the distant hills on the right wall. The two men mounted on the extreme left at the head of the crowd are usually identified as Sigismondo Pandolfo Malatesta and Galeazzo Maria Sforza. In the crowd behind (just above their heads), the two boys in red hats may have been intended to portray Lorenzo and Giuliano, sons of Piero il Gottoso, then around ten and six years old. Above them, the man looking out of the fresco is a self-portrait of Benozzo with his signature in gold lettering on his (lighter) red hat. There are two other men shown mounted in the procession here: the man in a red beret on a mule is often taken as a portrait of Cosimo il Vecchio, while the man just in front of him, dressed in green and gold brocade on a grey horse with the Medici emblems on its bridle, may be his son, Piero il Gottoso. The man on foot beside the horses' heads could be Piero's brother Carlo or Giovanni. The young king who is looking out towards us on the right side of the scene on this wall, sitting on his splendid grey charger, is usually considered to be an idealised portrait of Lorenzo the Magnificent.

On the wall opposite the altar, the three girls on horseback with the Medici feathers in their hair may be references to Piero il Gottoso's daughters. The second king is dressed in splendid Oriental dress, with green and gold brocade. On the last wall, the older grey-bearded king on a grey mule was cut in two when the wall was moved to accommodate the staircase landing in the 17th century. In front of him the huntsman in blue with a cheetah sitting on his horse is sometimes taken to be an idealised portrait of Giuliano, son of Piero il Gottoso and later Duke of Nemours (*see p. 150*). The head of the man just in front of his horse, with a blue and white turban, may be a second self-portrait by Benozzo. The procession, with camels and horses, winds on uphill towards Bethlehem.

The Riccardi rooms

From the chapel there is access to the suite of grand state rooms decorated for the Riccardi after 1659, with coffered ceilings and hung with tapestries (those of the *Four Seasons* in the assembly room of the provincial government were made in Florence before 1643 from cartoons by Jacopo Vignali). In a display case outside the Galleria is a beautiful painting of the *Madonna and Child* by Filippo Lippi, a late work once owned by the Riccardi. The interesting sketch of a head, perhaps for a St Jerome, on the back, is also by Lippi.

The Baroque Galleria (1670–88) has a magnificent vault fresco by Luca Giordano (1683) symbolising the apotheosis of the second Medici dynasty. The white and gold stucco decoration of the walls, designed by Giovanni Battista Foggini, and the yellow marble doors also survive, together with four mirrors delightfully painted with animals, putti and floral motifs (some of which are the work of Antonio Domenico Gabbiani and Bartolomeo Bimbi). This is one of the very few grand interiors of this date to have survived intact in Florence.

Luca Giordano also frescoed the delightful reading room in the **Biblioteca Riccardi-ana** (*entrance at Via de' Ginori 10; open to scholars for consultation, weekdays 8–2*) in the palace's 17th-century wing. This private library, founded by Riccardo Riccardi and first opened to the public in 1718, still has its original bookshelves which contain illumi-nated manuscripts and precious incunabula.

SAN LORENZO

Map 1, 1. Open 10–5.30, Sun 1.30–5.30. Ticket office either in the cloister (left of the façade) or in the church. The ticket includes admission to the cloister and treasury in the crypt; sepa-rate ticket for the Biblioteca Laurenziana, entered from the cloister. Another ticket for the New Sacristy and Cappella dei Principi, entered from Piazza Madonna degli Aldobrandini (behind the east end of the church).

The church of San Lorenzo was intimately connected with the Medici after they com-missioned Brunelleschi to rebuild it in 1425 with their own family funds. It is the burial place of all the principal members of the family from Cosimo il Vecchio to Cosimo III. A basilica on this site, outside the old town walls, was consecrated by St Ambrose, Bishop of Milan, in 393, and is thought to have been the earliest church in Florence. St Zenobius, who was traditionally thought to have been present at the consecration, became bishop and was buried here when he died in 429. Unfortunately we know very little about the appearance of this church, which was reconsecrated by Nicholas II (who had been bishop of Florence) in the 11th century and remained the principal church of Florence up until the late 12th century, although the bishop's seat was probably transferred to the church of Santa Reparata (on the site of the present Duomo) in the late 7th century since it was in a more central position and inside the walls. San Lorenzo nevertheless continued to flourish as a wealthy parish church, with a hospital attached.

The exterior and project for the façade

The church, with the large dome of the Cappella dei Principi and the smaller cupola of the New Sacristy, rises above the market stalls of Piazza San Lorenzo. The church was restored by Ferdinando Ruggieri in 1740, at which time the campanile was added.

The west front remains in rough-hewn brick, as it has been since 1480. It had not been intended to remain thus. The Medici pope Leo X had held a competition for the façade design and the participants had included Raphael, Giuliano and Antonio da Sangallo, Jacopo Sansovino and Baccio d'Agnolo. However, in 1516 Michelangelo was given the commission. He designed a façade to rival the great monuments of antiq-uity, constructed entirely of marble (including twelve huge monolithic columns on the ground floor) and decorated with numerous marble and bronze sculptures. But after he had spent three years organising the quarrying of fine stone from quarries near Car-rara and transporting the stone to Florence, the pope suddenly cancelled the commis-sion. This may have been because he feared the ever-increasing expense and wished to

The bare brick front of San Lorenzo which never received the grand façade planned for it by Michelangelo, shown here in a drawing by him, preserved in the Casa Buonarroti.

have Michelangelo concentrate instead on providing a fitting mausoleum for his family inside the church. For Michelangelo it was the greatest disappointment of his professional career and he wrote a long letter to the pope expressing his distress and telling him that he considered his decision an insult. Michelangelo often felt constrained by the wishes and caprices of his patrons. It is tempting to wonder what would have happened if he had been freer to carry out the projects which most interested him. There is evidence that he believed the San Lorenzo façade would have been his finest work, and that he was still hoping some ten years later that he would be asked to return to the project: some 35 drawings he made for it survive. The wood model is preserved in Casa Buonarroti (*see p. 209*). When Michelangelo died, in 1564, it was San Lorenzo that was chosen as the place to hold the memorial service, on 14th July, organised by the Accademia del Disegno.

Interior of San Lorenzo

The majestic cruciform interior, designed by Brunelleschi, is one of the earliest and most harmonious architectural works of the Renaissance. The plan is derived from Roman basilicas. Making much use of grey *pietra serena* against the plain white walls, Brunelleschi here devised a totally new concept of architecture. The columns, pilasters, capitals and arches all have perfect mathematical proportions, and play on deliberate perspective devices particularly pleasing to the eye. The nave columns are heightened by pulvins above the capitals so the arcades are exceptionally high, and there are delicately carved cable-fluted Corinthian pilasters between the arches of the side chapels and in the transepts. Daylight floods the building through the large windows just below the ceiling and the oculi high up in the side aisles, and the lancet windows in the transepts and flat east wall. The dominant colours of grey and white are followed in the pavement, and the gilded coffered white ceiling enhances the light atmosphere. Very little other colour is at first apparent, as the side chapels are set back so that most of the painted altarpieces in them are invisible from the central nave (the frescoes in the dome over the crossing, carried out after Ruggieri's restoration by Vincenzo Meucci in 1742, disturb the harmony). Apparently Michelozzo carried out some work in the transepts, where the doors are surmounted by grey stone scallop shells, and at this time (the end of the 1420s) Brunelleschi unaccountably disappears from the church records. Building was completed to Brunelleschi's design by Antonio Ciacheri Manetti (1447–60) and Pagno di Lapo Portigiani (1463).

(A) Inner façade: Above the west door and supported by two grey stone columns, is a little **balcony built by Michelangelo** (1530) for Clement VII, for the exhibition of the Holy Relics (kept in a treasury behind the three doors). The great artist clearly did not wish to alter the classical effect of the interior created by his famous predecessor.

(B) Old Sacristy: Brunelleschi began the rebuilding of the church here, in the chapel commissioned by the founder of the Medici dynasty, Giovanni di Bicci de' Medici, as his burial place (it was completed by 1428, the year before Giovanni's death). It survives intact as one of the earliest and purest monuments of the Renaissance, centrally planned with a lovely umbrella vault. The decorative details are mainly by Donatello: above the frieze of cherubs' heads, the tondi in the pendentives and lunettes depict the four Evangelists seated at their desks (identified by their symbols) between very remarkable scenes from the life of St John the Evangelist. These are modelled in terracotta and plaster (so red, white and grey in colour), and are amongst Donatello's most original works. Over the two little doors are large reliefs of Sts Cosmas and Damian (patron saints of the Medici) and Sts Lawrence and Stephen (titular saint of the church and first Christian martyr). The former may have been designed by Michelozzo, who is known to have worked closely with both Donatello and Brunelleschi.

The dark blue fresco in the small dome over the altar depicts the night sky with the constellations as they appeared over Florence on 4th July 1442, probably painted (by Giuliano d'Arrigo, known as Il Pesello), under the direction of the astronomer Paolo dal Pozzo Toscanelli. It is thought to have marked the arrival in Florence of René of Anjou, after he had lost the throne of Naples.

The bronze doors have figures of the Apostles and martyrs in animated theological discussions (the iconography may come from Byzantine sources). They are usually considered the work of Donatello, but are now sometimes also attributed to Michelozzo. The raised seats and presses are decorated with exquisite inlay, and displayed on one of them is a terracotta portrait bust of a young man in an entirely natural pose representing St Lawrence (or St Leonard), a particularly charming work attributed to Donatello or Desiderio da Settignano.

The marble vesting table in the centre is 3m long, formed of two huge blocks of marble (the joint is carefully hidden with a bronze ivy leaf motif and the three inlaid bronze discs in the centre). Beneath it is the sarcophagus (decorated with

Entrance to Medici Chapels and New Sacristy

SAN LORENZO

A **Balcony by Michelangelo**
B **Old Sacristy**
C **Martelli Chapel (monument to Donatello)**
D **Pulpits by Donatello**
E **Tomb of Cosimo il Vecchio**
F **High Altar**
G **Tabernacle by Desiderio da Settignano**
H *Martyrdom of St Lawrence* **by Bronzino**
I **Cantoria**
J *Madonna and Child*
K *Christ in the Carpenter's Workshop*
L *Marriage of the Virgin* **by Rosso Fiorentino (and tomb slab of Landini)**
M **Cloister (entrance to Biblioteca Laurenziana)**
N **Cappella dei Principi**
O **New Sacristy (entrance from Medici Chapels)**

Entrance to Cloister, Crypt and Biblioteca Laurenziana

putti) of Giovanni di Bicci de' Medici, and his wife Piccarda Bueri, the parents of Cosimo il Vecchio, by Buggiano (c. 1433). Set into the wall is the much more elaborate (but rather less impressive) bronze sarcophagus of Giovanni and Piero de' Medici, the sons of Cosimo il Vecchio. This was commissioned from Verrocchio in 1472 by Lorenzo the Magnificent and his brother Giuliano.

(C) Martelli Chapel (*coin-operated light*): This chapel contains a monument to Donatello (d. 1466; buried in the vault below) erected in neo-Renaissance style in 1896. It was probably Donatello who designed the tomb opposite of Niccolò and Fioretta Martelli (c. 1464) in the delightful form of a marble 'wicker' basket. The painting of the *Annunciation*

is one of the most beautiful early works of Filippo Lippi, and the most important Renaissance altarpiece in the church, carefully designed to fit into Brunelleschi's architecture. Commissioned by the Martelli, it bears their arms. The figure of the Madonna, with her exquisitely painted hands, is particularly lovely, and Filippo decided to add two more angels behind Gabriel; they are evidently enjoying the scene.

(D) Donatello's pulpits: After his remarkable work in the Old Sacristy, and at the end of his long life, in around 1460, Donatello produced the panels of the bronze pulpits in the nave of the church. His very last works, they were finished by his pupils Bertoldo and Bartolomeo Bellano. It is now thought

Sleeping guard at the tomb. Detail from Donatello's *Pulpit of the Resurrection* (c. 1460).

that the panels may have been intended for the former high altar (there would have probably been a wooden pulpit): they only came to be fashioned into pulpits (probably for special orations rather than weekly sermons) in around 1560 when they were raised on the present marble Ionic columns. Exquisitely carved, many of the scenes describing the Passion are crowded and grim and present a unique iconography, but because of their elevation they are very difficult to see. Particularly fine, on the pulpit on the north side (Pulpit of the Passion), are the panels of the *Lamentation over the Dead Christ* and the *Entombment*, and on the south pulpit (Pulpit of the Resurrection) the *Maries at the Sepulchre* and *Christ in Limbo*. There is also a scene of the *Martyrdom of St Lawrence*, since he is the titular saint.

(E) Tomb of Cosimo il Vecchio: Protected by stanchions, three grilles in the pavement mark the burial place (Cosimo's simple tomb is in the crypt directly below). The slab is decorated with beautiful porphyry and green marble roundels and bronze shields with the Medici arms in porphyry. The simple inscription gives the date of his death (1464) and a reminder that the glorious epithet of 'Pater Patriae' was bestowed upon him by public decree. This stone was Verrocchio's first documented commission, in 1465, and the classical influence of Leon Battista Alberti is evident.

(F) High altar: The form of the original high altar of the church is unknown. This one, in *pietre dure*, to a design by Gaspare Maria Paoletti, one of Grand Duke Peter Leopold's most favoured architects, was consecrated in 1787. It incorporates a panel of the *Fall of Manna* designed by Bernardino Poccetti. Above is a Crucifix by Baccio da Montelupo, one of many made for churches in Tuscany by this local artist.

(G) Tabernacle by Desiderio da Settignano: Of extremely fine workmanship, dating from 1461, this was the first documented work made for the new church. Since it is so large it is thought that it may have been intended for the high altar. It has been moved several times and still looks somewhat out of place here.

(H) *Martyrdom of St Lawrence*: This huge rhetorical fresco dating from the late 1560s is the work of Bronzino, and it was to have been matched by another on the opposite side of the nave. It includes numerous references to works by Michelangelo, and the artificial poses reveal a decline in the artist's production. Bronzino and Pontormo decorated the choir, but their work was destroyed in the 18th century when Ruggieri restored the east end of the church.

(**I**) Over the door into the cloister is a cantoria, decorated in precious marbles, attributed to Donatello.

(**J**) In the first chapel in the north transept is a charming **statue of the Madonna and Child** in polychrome wood, attributed to a little-known sculptor called Giovanni di Francesco Fetti. The Madonna is smiling as the Child tickles her chin, and the popular devotional status of this image is attested by the number of ex-votos which fill the case behind it. It was made around 1380 and is one of the few Florentine statues from that period not made in marble or terracotta.

(**K**) *Christ in the Carpenter's Workshop*: This is a work by Pietro Annigoni, a Florentine painter who became well known in Britain when he painted a portrait of Queen Elizabeth II. This is one of the very few 20th-century works which hang in churches in the centre of Florence, although Annigoni painted other religious subjects for churches elsewhere in Italy, notably the basilica of St Anthony in Padua.

(**L**) *The Marriage of the Virgin* (1523) by Rosso Fiorentino. In this important Mannerist work, it is the female figures in the foreground which are the most striking, especially the one kneeling on the right, where the artist's interest in colour and light effects (as opposed to the facial features) is evident: her dress and matching turban are in bright green and the cloak is reduced to a splash of red. Above, and very much in the background, are the elongated figures of the subject of the painting: the Madonna is given rather less importance than Joseph, who is depicted (rather bizarrely) as a handsome young man in boots wearing a green and orange outfit.

On the wall is the Gothic **tomb-slab of Francesco Landini** (1398), showing him, evidently blind, holding an organ. Landini (also known as Landino) was born in 1325 and, having been blinded as a child, he found great solace in music. He worked as organist at San Lorenzo and was one of the most important composers of his time—his secular music is typical of the Florentine 'Ars Nova' style, and many of his beautiful madrigals survive (the term *madrigale* was coined at this period). The famous Squarcialupi Codex, dating from 1410/15, contains some 151 works by him.

The cloister and crypt

The canons' cloister was designed by Manetti (1457–62) and is entered from the north aisle or from the left of the façade. It has graceful arcades with Ionic capitals surrounding an orange tree. From here you can visit the crypt and treasury. Near the bottom of the steps is the pavement tomb of Donatello. In the vaults behind a locked grille you can see the simple classical tomb of Cosimo il Vecchio by Verrocchio, in a pilaster of the church. Nearby is the tomb of Ferdinand III, surrounded by commemorative inscriptions to the other Lorraine grand dukes, arranged here in 1874 by Emilio de Fabris.

At the entrance to the treasury there is a statue of the last descendant of the Medici family, the Electress Palatine, made in 1946 by Alfonso Boninsegni. A small part of the treasury (the rest is displayed in the Medici Chapels; *see overleaf*) is kept here, including goldsmiths' work and reliquaries dating from the 14th–19th centuries, a silver Crucifix by Michelozzo (c. 1444) and a reliquary bust of St Peter in gilded and painted wood (1522).

BIBLIOTECA LAURENZIANA

Open 9–1 except Sun and holidays and when exhibitions are being arranged; T: 055 210760. Exhibitions of the library's holdings are usually held about twice a year.

A staircase in the corner of the cloister, near a statue of the historian Paolo Giovio by Francesco da Sangallo (1560), ascends to the Biblioteca Laurenziana (Laurentian Library). It was begun by Michelangelo c. 1524 at the order of Clement VII (Giulio de' Medici) to house the collection of manuscripts made by Cosimo il Vecchio and Lorenzo the Magnificent, and it is known from letters how closely the Medici pope followed the work. It is a remarkable monument of Mannerist architecture, and Michelangelo also had to carry out major structural work in the pre-existing buildings on the ground floor of the cloister in order to support the weight of the new library: he built pilasters, supporting arches and barrel vaults under the pavement.

The solemn vestibule, filled with an elaborate free-standing staircase, was constructed by Vasari and Ammannati from Michelangelo's design in 1559–71. This highly idiosyncratic work (*see also p. 31*) has been interpreted by scholars in numerous ways, but whatever their conclusions, it clearly shows Michelangelo's sculptural conception of architecture. In the tall room there is a pronounced use of *pietra serena* in the blind windows and empty niches, columns and volutes, and to stand in this strange space cannot fail to affect you. All the elements combine to provide a vertical emphasis, and the columns and volutes are set into the wall, producing strange shadow effects. The decoration of the architectural elements is kept to a minimum, with subtle, Classically-inspired carvings. It seems that the very original idea of inserting the columns into the walls also contributed to the stability of the building. As Vasari observed, this room did much to encourage Michelangelo's successors to explore new designs, and the subversion of architectural rules meant that later architects no longer felt obliged to conform to established styles in their work.

The peaceful reading room, a long hall, provides an unexpected contrast. Here the angle at which the architectural decoration can be seen has been carefully calculated, and the carved desks, also by Michelangelo, form an intricate part of the design. It is interesting to note that the heavily decorated vestibule is invisible from the aisle (only a blank wall is framed in the doorway). The very fine wood ceiling and beautiful terracotta floor are by Santi Buglioni to a design by Tribolo, and the stained glass is original. Michelangelo had intended to add a triangular room at the end where the most precious books would have been kept.

Exhibitions from the precious works in the library are held every year in the adjoining rooms (the circular tribune was added in 1841). Most famous are the Greek and Latin manuscripts. The oldest codex is a 5th-century Virgil. The Codex Amiatinus, written in the monastery of Jarrow in England sometime before 716, ended up at the Abbey of San Salvatore on Monte Amiata in Tuscany and is the oldest complete text of the Vulgate version of the Bible (written on 1,030 sheets of vellum, it weighs about 50kg). There are 6th-century Syrian gospels and the oldest manuscript of Justinian's *Pandects* (6th–7th centuries). Choir books include one illuminated by Lorenzo Monaco and Attavante, and there is a Book of Hours which belonged to Lorenzo the Magnificent. Matteo Palmieri's *Città di Vita* has illuminations in the style of Pollaiolo and Botticelli. A treatise on architecture has manuscript notes by Leonardo da Vinci; and there is the manuscript of Cellini's *Autobiography*.

THE MEDICI CHAPELS

Map 1, 1 (Cappelle Medicee). Open 8.30–4.30; closed 2nd and 4th Sun and 1st, 3rd and 5th Mon of the month; T: 055 282984. Entrance in Piazza Madonna degli Aldobrandini, outside the east end of San Lorenzo. If you come before 9am you can sometimes enjoy Michelangelo's New Sacristy all to yourself.

The entrance to the Medici Chapels is through the crypt of the Cappella dei Principi, which was designed by Buontalenti and contains the tomb slabs of numerous members of the Medici family. The model of the chapel above was made in 1745 by Ferdinando Ruggieri. The elaborate reliquary (1687) is by Massimiliano Soldani Benzi. Since 1869 the chapels have been owned by the state and have been separated from their parish church, and so lost their important relationship to that building.

Cappella dei Principi

The Cappella dei Principi ('Chapel of the Princes') is the opulent mausoleum of the Medici grand dukes. It has been undergoing restoration since 1999. Ferdinando I decided to create the chapel, which he intended to have decorated with pilasters of costly jasper, and even thought of trying to move the Holy Sepulchre in Jerusalem here. Over 200 drawings survive of architectural projects for it, including some by Buontalenti and Giacomo della Porta, but in 1602 a competition was held and the duke's half-brother Don Giovanni de' Medici won, having presented an octagonal plan based on that of della Porta. Shortly afterwards Don Giovanni had to leave Florence for a battle in Flanders, leaving Matteo Nigetti in charge. The chapel was designed to be approached by a great arch from the choir at the east end of San Lorenzo and to provide a focal point for a magnificent altar of the sacrament.

Fewer than half the 50 windows planned by Don Giovanni were built, and some others have been covered with painted canvas, so that the dim lighting makes the atmosphere somewhat gloomy. Nevertheless, the dark-coloured marbles, beautiful red jasper and semi-precious stones which line the walls are still impressive and the frieze, made in the first years of the 17th century for the lowest part of the walls, is a *tour de force* of craftsmanship in *pietre dure*: the coats of arms of the 16 towns which were bishoprics of Tuscany alternate with 32 very beautiful inlaid funerary urns in red and green jasper. In the sarcophagi around the walls, from right to left, are buried Ferdinando II, Cosimo II, Ferdinando I, Cosimo I, Francesco I and Cosimo III. The tomb chests were all to have been surmounted by colossal statues in gilded bronze, but only those on the second and third sarcophagi, by Pietro and Ferdinando Tacca (1626–42), were ever made (commissioned by Christine of Lorraine). Behind and above the huge sarcophagi are panels of jasper against a grey marble background. Work continued after 1650, using cheaper materials, and it was not until 1836 that the decoration on the drum of the cupola was completed (but not to the original design, which had envisaged a covering in *pietre dure*). The vault frescoes of Old Testament subjects were also painted at this time by Pietro Benvenuti: even though he was elderly, he was chosen since he was director of the Accademia di Belle Arti.

The wooden altar, incorporating some 19th-century *pietre dure* panels, was hastily set up in 1938 and intended to be provisional. Ferdinando had planned a magnificent altar constructed almost entirely from rock crystal and including a temple some 12m high (a few columns and panels made for it are preserved in the Museo degli Argenti in Palazzo Pitti and Museo dell'Opera di Pietre Dure).

The treasury

Behind the altar, on the left, a corridor leads into a small strong room which displays the church treasury, chiefly reliquaries of the 14th–17th centuries. In the case in the centre is a processional banner with the Medici coat of arms presented to the basilica by Leo X, together with his pastoral staff (probably made before 1520) with St Lawrence holding his gridiron. The same pope's mitre, made in Rome in the 16th century and decorated with numerous baroque pearls, is kept in the end case.

New Sacristy

A back passage connects the Cappella dei Principi to the New Sacristy (Sagrestia Nuova), although both were originally approached directly from inside San Lorenzo. The New Sacristy was built in the south transept of the church to balance Brunelleschi's Old Sacristy. Inspired by Brunelleschi's beautiful architecture, it may have been begun by Giuliano da Sangallo c. 1491, though the structure we see today was commissioned in 1519 by the Medici pope Leo X from Michelangelo as a funerary chapel for the Medici family. Michelangelo worked on it up until 1524 and then again in 1530–33, but left it unfinished when he finally left Florence for Rome in 1534, in anger at the political climate in the city. It is built in dark *pietra serena* and white marble, in a severe style which produces a strange, cold atmosphere, in part due to the diffusion of light exclusively from above and the odd perspective devices on the upper parts of the walls. The lower part of the walls, with no fewer than eight doors (most of them false), is almost too crowded with architectural elements, while above the cornice the architecture is much more simple and evidently unfinished. Vasari is known to have worked on the chapel in 1550–56, but it has not been established just how much he intervened.

The Medici tombs

The tombs were commissioned by the Medici pope Clement VII in an attempt to re-establish the glory of the dynasty when the position of the Medici in Florence was at a particularly low ebb. Michelangelo executed only two of the three or more tombs originally projected.

To the left of the entrance is the **tomb of Lorenzo, Duke of Urbino** (1492–1519), grandson of Lorenzo the Magnificent. He was an unpopular ruler, who governed by force rather than by consensus. Machiavelli dedicated *The Prince* to him after he conquered Urbino in 1516–17. The statue of the duke shows nothing of this, portraying him seated, absorbed in meditation, and on the sarcophagus below are the reclining figures of *Dawn* (female) and *Dusk* (male). The elderly female figure, in an extraordinary headdress, is much more finished than the male.

Opposite is the **tomb of Giuliano, Duke of Nemours**, the third son of Lorenzo the Magnificent (1479–1516; he received his title from the king of France). Well-liked for the brief year that he ruled in Florence, he famously exonerated Machiavelli from charges of having taken part in a plot against him. But Giuliano was more interested in a life of ease than of politics. He counted Castiglione a personal friend (and is in fact one of the characters in *The Courtier*). On his sarcophagus are the figures of *Day* and *Night*. The muscular old woman representing Night, with her strange hairstyle, is accompanied by the symbols of darkness (the moon, the owl and a haunting mask with hollow eyes), and is considered to be among the finest of all Michelangelo's sculptures. The head of the male figure (*Day*) is hardly worked on at all and the marks of the sculptor's toothed chisel (or *gradina*) can clearly be seen (and they recall the 'hatching' made by Michelangelo's pen in his drawings). This massive nude seems to have been influenced by the ancient *Belvedere Torso* in the Vatican.

The entrance wall was intended to contain another architectural monument to Lorenzo the Magnificent and his brother Giuliano (murdered in the Pazzi Conspiracy); the only part carried out by Michelangelo is the ***Madonna and Child***. It is his last statue of a Madonna and one of his most beautiful. Her mystical expression of self-absorption in unforgettable. The fact that the sculptor hardly bothered to represent her right arm and that she appears to have only one leg, and that the large curly-haired Child has his face totally hidden from view, become unimportant details. As with the nude figures on the two sarcophagi, one is struck by the difficulties the sculptor created for himself in deciding on such a complicated pose. The much more prosaic figures on either side are St Cosmas and St Damian, the medical saints who were the patrons of the Medici, and are by Montorsoli and Raffaello da Montelupo. Lorenzo the Magnificent's coffin was transferred here from the Old Sacristy in 1559.

The austere altar bears two **candelabra designed by Michelangelo**: the delicate decorations both here and on the sides of the sarcophagi show how the great sculptor delighted in challenging the intricate carvings made by the ancient Romans. The candelabrum on the left was carved by his contemporary, Silvio Cosini; that on the right was made in 1741. On the walls behind the altar are **architectural graffiti**, some of them attributed to Michelangelo and others to his pupils, including Tribolo.

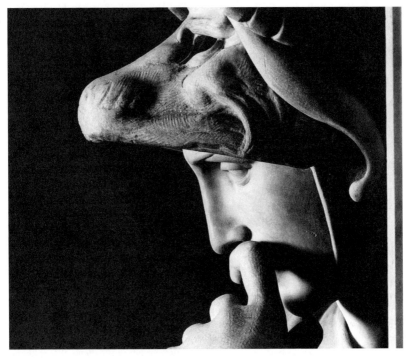

Detail from the tomb of Lorenzo de' Medici, Duke of Urbino, in the guise of a Roman general. Note the hatchmarks on the hand, made by Michelangelo's chisel.

The door to the left of the altar (*sadly kept locked*) gives access to a little room where charcoal drawings almost certainly by Michelangelo were discovered on the walls in 1975. It is thought that he hid here for a time under the protection of his friend, the prior of San Lorenzo, after the return of the Medici in 1530. Michelangelo had supported the Republican government (in fact his *David* had had its left arm broken in a pro-Republican revolt in 1527); when the Medici returned, the Florentine governors issued an order calling for his execution. Michelangelo went into hiding until later in the year when Pope Clement requested that he be treated with clemency.

THE MARKET AREA AROUND SAN LORENZO

The street market around **Piazza San Lorenzo** (*map 1, 2*) is very extensive, selling a great variety of clothes, leather bags and belts, costume jewellery, casual shoes, hats, gloves, scarves, and typical Florentine knicknacks. Despite its touristy feel, it is usually good value (*open throughout the day; closed Sun and Mon in winter*). The grandest palace on the piazza, with its open loggia on the top floor, belonged to the Della Stufa family in the 14th and 15th centuries. Just beyond the last market stall is a **monument by Baccio Bandinelli** to Giovanni de' Medici, always known as Giovanni delle Bande Nere ('of the black bands') from the black armour worn by his troops. The only important member of the Medici family to have a military career, his courage was famed and after his death in battle in 1526, aged only 28, he became a well-loved figure in Florence. He was the father of Cosimo I. The statue itself is much less successful than the large bas-relief on the base which shows Giovanni dispensing pardon to his enemies.

Via dell'Ariento is lined by two rows of market stalls. It passes the huge covered **Mercato Centrale**, or Mercato di San Lorenzo (*map 1, 1; open Mon–Sat 7–1; also 4.30–7.30 on Sat except in July and Aug*). This was once the principal food market in town but many of the stalls now cater for tourists. The magnificent cast-iron building (1874) by Giuseppe Mengoni—best known for the Galleria Vittorio Emanuele II in Milan—was provided with a mezzanine floor at the end of the 20th century for the sale of fruit and vegetables.

In the last few years many simple small Asian and Arab shops, selling food and clothing, have been opened in **Via Faenza**. A sign of the times in a town which up until a very few decades ago had a resident population almost exclusively of Italians.

THE CENACOLI OF FLORENCE

In the refectories of numerous monasteries in Florence and its environs there are frescoes depicting the Last Supper (*Cenacolo*), so that Christ and his disciples would keep the monks and nuns company as they dined and remind them of the divine meaning of the Eucharist. The earliest examples (such as that by Taddeo Gaddi at Santa Croce and another by Orcagna at Santo Spirito) formed the lower part of larger scenes including the Crucifixion, Tree of Life, and scenes of the Passion. It was Domenico Ghirlandaio who introduced the Last Supper as an autonomous scene, and he painted several lovely versions which can still be seen in Florence today. There are descriptions of the event in all four Gospels, thus the iconography often varies, although almost all of them from the 15th century onwards show the disciples seated at a long narrow table, in an interior, with Christ in the centre, usually flanked by Peter and John. Judas is often shown seated alone at the opposite side of the table. The moment depicted is usually that when Christ blesses the bread and wine and announces that He is to be betrayed.

Each artist varied the gesticulations of the disciples and the details of the interior. It is particularly interesting to study how the table was laid: before the 16th century each diner would share his board with his neighbour, but later, individual place settings were introduced. The carafes are shown filled with both water and wine since wine was always drunk diluted, as in ancient Roman times. Fruit such as cherries, oranges, lemons, apricots, pears, figs and melon are usually scattered on the tablecloths, which often have delightfully embroidered borders. Fruit was considered exotic as well as decorative, even if not usually eaten fresh since its nutritional value was for long unappreciated.

Although many monasteries were suppressed by Peter Leopold in 1785 and others in 1808, it is an extraordinary fact that no fewer than 33 *cenacoli* have survived in central Florence. Not all of them are open regularly, but amongst those that are, the most beautiful (apart from the three described in this chapter) include those by Domenico Ghirlandaio at Ognissanti (c. 1480; *see p. 285*) and that by Andrea del Sarto at San Salvi—indeed this last is perhaps the most beautiful of all (*see p. 333*). There are two lesser-known *cenacoli* worth seeking out in the Oltrarno: one by Sodoma in San Bartolomeo at Monteoliveto (c. 1515; *see p. 323*) and one by Franciabigio in the convent of the Calza, dating from the year before (*see p. 325*).

CENACOLO DI FULIGNO

Map 3, 5. Entrance at Via Faenza 40; open Tues, Thur, Sat 9–12.
This is a very peaceful spot in a busy part of the city. A Franciscan convent was founded here in the early 15th century, on the site of a hermitage of Sant'Onofrio, by a closed order of nuns from Foligno in Umbria. In 1800 the convent became an educational institute for orphans and poor girls. It was only in 1843 that the beautiful fresco of the *Last Supper* was discovered in the refectory (and it is still in very good condition). At first attributed to Raphael (whose bust by Emilio Santarelli was set up here at that time), it is now generally considered to be by the hand of Perugino (although some scholars believe it was executed by members of his *bottega*, including Giovan Maria di Bartolomeo, called Rocco Zoppo). Perugino probably designed the work while he was in Florence in the last decades of the 15th century. Painted in muted colours, the wistful disciples are delicately painted and the artist clearly enjoyed inventing the numerous different poses for their feet. The figure of St John, fast asleep next to Christ, is particularly memorable. In the background, seen through an unusual loggia with square pillars of different sizes, is a lovely landscape with clumps of delicate trees, typical of this great Umbrian painter: it provides the setting for a scene of the *Agony in the Garden*.

The painting of the *Crucifix between the Virgin and St Jerome*, from the church of the convent of San Girolamo in Fiesole, is also by Perugino. The other paintings exhibited here are by his contemporaries and followers, the best of which are those by Lorenzo di Credi (a tondo of the *Adoration of the Child*, a portrait of a young man, and four small paintings with lovely landscapes from the convent of San Gaggio).

The adjoining room exhibits a good fresco of the *Madonna and Saints* (late 15th or early 16th century) detached from a tabernacle on Via Vecchia Fiesolana, just below Fiesole, and very close to the convent of San Girolamo.

CENACOLO DI SANT'APOLLONIA

The approach along Via de' Ginori and Via San Gallo
Via de' Ginori (*map 3, 6*) is a good place to study the architecture of the palaces built by the well-off middle classes during the Renaissance. **Palazzo Neroni** (no. 7) has pronounced rustication with huge blocks of stone. This is where Diotisalvi di Neroni

lived before his exile as an enemy of the Medici in 1466. Neroni was a leading figure in Florentine politics in the turbulent period following Cosimo il Vecchio's death. Together with other noble Florentines, he tried to exclude Cosimo's son Piero from holding office but failed when a popular assembly called for his banishment. This was a significant moment in the consolidation of the (hereditary) power of the Medici. Next door is the larger **Palazzo Montauto** (no. 9), with two handsome ground-floor windows with herms of Artemis attributed to Ammannati. The graffiti decoration on the two upper floors survives from the 15th century. The adjoining **Palazzo Ginori** (no. 11) is the handsomest palace in the street. It is probably an early work by Baccio d'Agnolo (c. 1520). It has a pretty doorway and windows, and an open loggia on the top floor. Baccio d'Agnolo also built **Palazzo Taddei** (no. 15) for the merchant Taddeo Taddei, who commissioned the tondo from Michelangelo which now bears his name and is owned by the Royal Academy, London. Raphael, while staying here as a friend of the family in 1505, saw and copied the tondo (a plaque recording this event was put on the wrong house, at no. 17). On the ground floor is one of the best-known shops in Florence for musical instruments and scores (Ceccherini).

Across Via Guelfa is **Via San Gallo**. The University of Florence occupies a number of palaces and convents in this area, including Palazzo Castelli (Marucelli) at no. 10, which is one of the best works by Gherardo Silvani (1630), who built numerous palaces in the city in the 17th century. The elaborate doorway is flanked by two grotesque satyrs sculpted by Raffaello Curradi. The coat of arms above was set up by its later owner Emanuele Fenzi (1784–1875), a banker who financed the Florence–Livorno railway (which explains the presence of a steam engine in his emblem). Raphael designed Palazzo Pandolfini at no. 74 (*see p. 341*).

Cenacolo di Sant'Apollonia

Map 3, 4. Open 8.30–1.50; closed 1st, 3rd and 5th Sun and 2nd and 4th Mon of the month; T: 055 238 8607.

The former convent of Sant'Apollonia, founded in 1339 and enlarged in 1445, was opened to the public in 1891. This is usually a particularly peaceful place to visit. The vestibule contains works by Neri di Bicci and Paolo Schiavo, Andrea del Castagno's master. In the refectory is the *Last Supper*, the masterpiece of Andrea del Castagno, set in an unusual loggia, lined with huge, brightly-coloured marble panels, sphinxes at either end of the bench, and a great variety of abstract coloured patterns in playful perspective. This is the first of the great Renaissance frescoes of the *Last Supper* in Florence (and one of the most beautiful), thought to date from around 1447. It is extraordinarily innovative in the use of perspective to create the illusion of space, and a superb example of how Andrea, an unsentimental painter (his figures often appear more like sculptures placed against a severe, abstract backdrop), produces work of enormous power. This scene portrays the moment when Christ consecrates the bread and reveals the name of the person who will betray Him—the drama is expressed through the disciples' hands as well as their faces: John is shown resting on the left of Christ while Judas is on the viewer's side of the table. The work is undocumented and not mentioned by Vasari, but it must have been known to Andrea's contemporaries including Piero della Francesca. It was only discovered in 1808 since it had, up until then, been inside the convent of a closed order.

The equally fine but very damaged frescoes of the *Crucifixion*, *Deposition* and *Resurrection* above are also by Andrea. Also displayed are two very fine lunettes with the *Crucifixion between the Madonna and Saints* and a *Pietà with Two Angels*, both very powerful autograph works by Andrea, and two sinopie which provide a fascinating insight into the way he worked. The detached fresco fragments on the end wall with panels of painted marble are all that remains of important frescoes of stories from the life of the Virgin painted for Sant'Egidio by Domenico Veneziano, Piero della Francesca, Andrea del Castagno and Alesso Baldovinetti. But there is a curious sinopia displayed here by Domenico Veneziano showing a nude female figure and numerous lines apparently drawn to calculate perspective.

NB: From Piazza San Marco you can take bus no. 6 or no. 20 to see the most beautiful of all the Last Supper frescoes in Florence (by Andrea del Sarto) at the ex-convent of San Salvi, a beautifully-kept (and often deserted) museum. The journey takes about 10mins. For a full description, see p. 331.

THE CHURCH & CONVENT OF SAN MARCO

The church of San Marco

Founded in 1299 and rebuilt with the convent next door in 1442 (*map 4, 3*), the church assumed its present form in 1588 on a plan by Giambologna. The façade was added in 1778.

On the south side there is a devotional figure of the **seated Christ (1)** in wood dating from 1654. The first altarpiece **(2)** is by Santi di Tito. The ***Madonna and Six Saints*** **(3)** (1509) by Bartolomeo della Porta, who was a friar in the convent (also known as Fra' Bartolomeo), shows how strongly this painter was influenced by Raphael. The **Byzantine mosaic (4)** of the *Madonna in Prayer*, which, as can be seen, had to be cut into two pieces for its journey from Constantinople, is a remarkable work thought to date from the early 8th century and once to have adorned the old basilica of St Peter's in Rome. It is surrounded by frescoes of saints in imitation of mosaic, added in the 17th century. The **tribune (5)** at the east end was added in 1678 by Pier Francesco Silvani; and the dome was frescoed by Alessandro Gherardini in 1717.

The **sacristy (6)**, designed by Michelozzo, contains a black marble sarcophagus with the bronze figure of the prior of the convent, St Antoninus, attributed to Giambologna. The saint's body is buried in the **Chapel of St Antoninus (7)**, also designed by Giambologna, and it has paintings by his Florentine contemporaries Alessandro Allori (the *Risen Christ* on the altar) and Il Poppi (*Christ Healing the Leper*, and the *Calling of St Matthew* on the left and right walls). Outside the chapel are two large frescoes by Passignano illustrating the burial of St Antoninus.

On the north wall of the church, above a grim 19th-century statue of Savonarola, are the **tomb slabs of Pico della Mirandola and Poliziano (8)**. Pico (1463–94) was a great humanist scholar and Neoplatonic philosopher, and an extremely wealthy man. Poliziano (1454–94), a poet in the vernacular famous for his eloquence, was considered the most original genius among writers of his period. Both men were members of the Platonic Academy in Florence, a body which saw the birth of the humanist movement of the Renaissance. Their tombs were opened in 2007 and their death in the same year, from arsenic poisoning, was confirmed.

Above is a fragment of a fresco with angels and standards (part of a *Last Judgment* scene?) by Antonio Veneziano (1370). Beneath the second altar is the **tomb of Giorgio La Pira (9)** (1904–77), a Sicilian who served as mayor of Florence in the 1950s and '60s. Greatly respected for his profound Catholic faith and the work he did to help the under-privileged and promote peace throughout the world, he was beatified in 2005 and his tomb was moved here in 2007. In a niche at the west end of this wall is a charming little **crèche (10)**; the Christ Child in terracotta is a 15th-century work and all the figures are clothed in fabrics. On the west wall, there is a striking *Transfiguration* **(11)**, a painting of 1596 by the little-known painter Giovanni Battista Paggi.

MUSEO DI SAN MARCO (THE CONVENT)

Open 8.30–1.50, Sat–Sun 8.30–7; closed 1st, 3rd and 5th Sun and 2nd and 4th Mon of the month; T: 055 238 8608.

The Dominican convent of San Marco contains the Museo di San Marco, chiefly famed for its paintings and frescoes by Fra' Angelico, who was a monk here. Peaceful and beautifully maintained, this is one of the most delightful museums in Florence.

Originally a medieval house of the Benedictine community of Silvestrines, the monastery was transferred to the Observant Dominicans of San Domenico di Fiesole by Pope Eugenius IV in 1436 to please Cosimo il Vecchio. The following year Cosimo ordered Michelozzo to enlarge the buildings, and his surviving work includes the main cloisters, the pilgrims' hospice and the beautiful library on the first floor. The founding prior, the Dominican reformer Antonino Pierozzi (1389–1459), was made Archbishop of Florence in 1446. He was canonised as St Antoninus in 1523. The convent's most famous prior, however, was Savonarola (*see p. 34*), who dominated the religious and political scene in Florence in the last decade of the 15th century—terrorising his congregations through his fiery sermons. He remains one of the most interesting and controversial figures in Florentine history to this day. The museum was founded in 1869 and in 1921 nearly all Fra' Angelico's panel paintings were collected here from churches and convents in the environs of Florence and from other museums.

Ground floor

(A) Cloister of St Antoninus: With its broad arches and delicate Ionic capitals, this attractive cloister was built by Michelozzo. A venerable cedar of Leba-

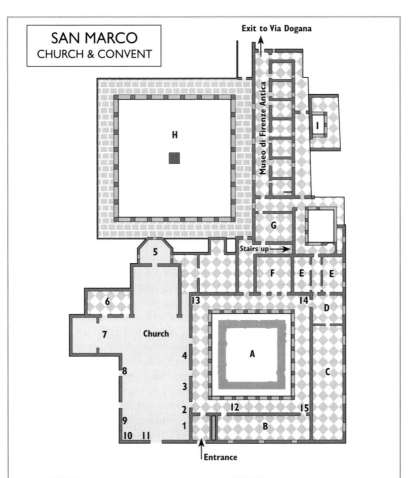

SAN MARCO
CHURCH & CONVENT

Exit to Via Dogana

Museo di Firenze Antica

I

H

G

Stairs up →

5

F E E

6 13 14 D

7 Church

4 A C

8

3

2 12 15

9 1 B

10 11

Entrance

CHURCH

1 *Seated Christ*
2 Altarpiece by Santi di Tito
3 *Madonna* by Bartolomeo della Porta
4 Byzantine mosaic
5 Tribune
6 Sacristy
7 Chapel of St Antoninus
8 Tombs of Pico and Poliziano
9 Tomb of Giorgio La Pira
10 Crèche
11 *Transfiguration*

CONVENT

A Cloister of St Antoninus
12 *St Thomas Aquinas*
13 *St Dominic, St Peter Martyr*
14 *Pietà*
15 *Christ as a Pilgrim*
B Pilgrims' Hospice
C Great Refectory
D Lavatorium
E Room with works by Fra' Bartolomeo
F Chapter House
G Small Refectory
H Cloister of St Dominic
I Chiostrino dei Silvestrini

non stands at its centre. The lunettes are decorated with early 17th-century frescoes showing scenes from the life of St Antoninus, begun by Bernardino Poccetti and finished by Matteo Rosselli, Michelangelo Cinganelli and others. In the corners are smaller **frescoes by Fra' Angelico**: *St Thomas Aquinas* **(12)** (very worn); *St Dominic at the Foot of the Cross* and *St Peter Martyr*, the first Dominican to die for his faith **(13)**; a restored *Pietà* **(14)**; and *Christ as a Pilgrim Welcomed by Two Dominicans* **(15)**.

(B) Pilgrims' Hospice: This lovely room, built by Michelozzo, is now hung with superb paintings by Fra' Angelico. Some are large altarpieces, while others are tiny works, exquisitely painted as if they were miniatures for illuminated manuscripts. All repay the closest examination and exude a joyous spirit, with superb colouring and decoration in gold leaf and numerous delightful botanical details. Most date from the 1430s and are very well preserved. The *Deposition*, one of Angelico's most beautiful paintings, was commissioned by Palla Strozzi for the church of Santa Trínita, c. 1435–40. The earlier cusps are the work of Lorenzo Monaco, a monk at the nearby convent of Santa Maria degli Angeli. The *Last Judgement* (1431; from Santa Maria degli Angeli) is painted with extraordinary skill and numerous charming details, including the dance of the blessed with angels in Paradise, which is separated from the vivid scenes of the damned in Hell by a stark representation of the empty tombs of the dead. The 35 beautifully painted small panels which served as cupboard doors in Santissima Annunziata illustrate scenes from the life

of Christ. The **Madonna della Stella** is a charming little reliquary tabernacle from Santa Maria Novella. Beyond is another *Deposition* painted for the Compagnia del Tempio (the lower part was damaged when the Arno flooded in 1966).

At the end of the room is the large **Tabernacle of the Linaioli**, with the Madonna enthroned against a brilliant background in gold leaf in designs of palmettes and rosettes inspired by Islamic silks and Oriental fabrics, which are known to have been in wide circulation amongst the wealthy in 15th-century Florence. The charming Madonna holding the standing Child is surrounded by a frame of twelve lovely angels and the predella survives intact: St Peter preaching with St Mark amongst his listeners; the *Adoration of the Magi*; and a scene of a miraculous hailstorm giving St Mark's executioners a thorough soaking just after his martyrdom. The shutters show St John the Baptist and St Mark (and St Mark appears again on the outer side, together with St Peter). This was Fra' Angelico's first public commission, from the flax-workers guild in 1433. It was returned here in 2011 after a spectacular ten-year restoration. The beautiful marble frame was designed by Lorenzo Ghiberti, whose work evidently influenced Fra' Angelico.

On the last wall are three more altarpieces of the *Madonna and Child*: one, a late work, painted for Bosco ai Frati (c. 1450) and another painted for the convent of the Annalena (which preserves most of its predella). Between them is the **Pala di San Marco**, commissioned by Cosimo for the high altar of the church around 1438–40. Its unusual, almost square shape is rare (although this was a format recommended by Brunelleschi). The subject is a *Sacra Conversazione* set in a lovely garden, but the unusual painting technique with which Angelico experimented, as well as poor restorations, have irreparably damaged the work. The predella illustrated the lives of the Medici patron saints Cosmas and Damian, but only two scenes have survived: one shows the two doctor saints carrying out a leg transplant and the other their burial along with other martyrs while a camel looks on (the setting is the convent of San Marco). When the altarpiece was removed from the church at the end of the 17th century the other panels were lost, but incredibly enough two tiny panels with two Dominican saints appeared on the English art market in 2006. They were purchased by the Italian state and are now also displayed here.

Also on this wall are two more exquisite small **reliquary tabernacles** from Santa Maria Novella, one with the *Coronation of the Virgin* and the other, even more beautiful, with a bright gold ground showing the *Annunciation* and *Adoration of the Magi*.

(C) Great Refectory: On the end wall is a fresco of *St Dominic and his Brethren fed by Angels* by Giovanni Antonio Sogliani (1536). Also displayed are 16th- and 17th-century paintings.

(D) Lavatorium: Here is a seated *Madonna and Child* in polychrome terracotta attributed to Luca della Robbia.

(E) Room with works by Fra' Bartolomeo: The works include a portrait of Savonarola in profile (Savonarola's preachings had convinced Bartolomeo to take the Dominican habit here in 1500). He also began the large *Madonna with St Anne and Other Saints* in monochrome, commissioned in 1510 by Piero Soderini, the last *gonfaloniere* of the Florentine Republic, for the Salone dei Cinquecento in Palazzo Vecchio, but never finished since the Medici returned in 1512. However, when the Republican government was restored in 1529, it was installed in the room for a few years.

(F) Chapter House: A large fresco of the *Crucifixion and Saints* by Fra' Angelico and assistants (1441–42) covers one wall. The figure of Mary Magdalene supporting the grieving Madonna is particularly striking. The convent bell, with a frieze of putti, was commissioned by Cosimo il Vecchio and is attributed to Donatello and Michelozzo. It was rung in defence of Savonarola before his arrest here, and after he was burnt at the stake it was seized and taken to San Miniato al Monte. In 1501 the friars of San Marco succeeded in having Pope Julius II order its return to them.

(G) Small Refectory: Here is a charming *Last Supper* frescoed by Domenico Ghirlandaio and his workshop. This is one of four similar frescoes of this subject painted by Ghirlandaio in Florence between 1476 and 1480.

First floor

The upstairs dormitory consists of 44 small cells beneath a huge wooden roof, each with its own vault and adorned with a fresco for each friar's private devotion by Fra'

Angelico and his assistants. It is still uncertain how many of the frescoes are by the hand of the master alone, and how many are by artists (whose names are unknown) employed in his studio. Others are attributed to Zanobi Strozzi and Benozzo Gozzoli. The old wooden shutters and doors have been preserved, and the cells retain their intimate atmosphere. At the head of the staircase is Fra' Angelico's **Annunciation (A)**, justly one of his most famous works, the scene set in a delightful loggia overlooking a garden.

Fra' Angelico (c. 1400–55)
Guido di Piero, born in the Mugello just north of Florence, became a Dominican monk around 1418 at the convent of San Domenico below Fiesole (where he took the name of Giovanni) and then moved to this convent. Because of the deeply religious sentiments in his paintings he came to be known as *angelico* and *beato* (blessed) since he seemed to be divinely inspired, and he was one of the most famous artists of his day. He painted numerous altarpieces for churches in and around Florence and also worked for Pope Eugenius IV in Rome and in the cathedral of Orvieto. His works have a universal appeal since they combine a deeply religious sentiment with a sense of serenity and joy, and seem to encourage meditation. At the same time they have a highly intellectual content, and carefully worked-out perspective and numerous complicated compositional elements. Angelico's use of colour is also remarkable and he was a master of the technique of fresco as well as that of panel painting and illumination.

Left corridor
Fra' Angelico's frescoes in the cells are as follows. Numbering follows that *in situ*:

(**1**) *Noli me tangere*.
(**3**) *Annunciation* (with a particularly beautiful angel).
(**5**) *Nativity* (perhaps with the help of an assistant).
(**6**) *Transfiguration*.
(**7**) *Mocking of Christ* in the presence of the Madonna and St Dominic (perhaps with the help of an assistant).
(**8**) *The Maries at the Sepulchre*.
(**9**) *Coronation of the Virgin*.

(**10**) *Presentation in the Temple*.
(**11**) *Madonna and Child with Saints* (probably by an assistant).
(**22**) A glass panel in the floor shows the remains of the old convent with two late 14th-century fresco fragments of a monk, a *Pietà* and geometric decoration.
(**23–29**) Frescoed by assistants. On the corridor wall outside is a *Madonna Enthroned with Saints*, attributed to the master himself.

Far corridor
The frescoes here, by followers of Fra' Angelico, all show Christ on the Cross. At first glance they look identical but each is slightly different.

(17) Important medieval fresco fragments (c. 1290–1310; among the earliest known in Florence), can be seen beneath the floor. They survive from the earlier Silvestrine convent and are thought to depict the founder, Silvestro Gozzolini, and St Anthony Abbot.

(16) The standard displayed here is traditionally supposed to be the one which Savonarola carried in processions and which he kept with him when preaching. Painted in tempera on linen and attributed to Francesco Botticini, it probably dates from the time when Savonarola first entered the convent.

(15) Here is displayed Savonarola's cloak, carefully preserved over the centuries by a series of (documented) proprietors. The pieces missing were cut out as relics. Also here is a small polychrome wooden Crucifix attributed to Baccio da Montelupo or Benedetto da Maiano, which used to be in Savonarola's cell.

(12–14) These three little rooms were occupied by Savonarola when he was prior in 1482–87 and 1490–98. Above the door is an oval detached fresco of the *Glory of St Catherine* by Alessandro Gherardini (1701). In the former chapel (12) is a monument to Savonarola, with a bronze bust and marble relief, by Giovanni Dupré (1873). Also here are detached frescoes by Fra' Bartolomeo, Savonarola's supporter and fellow friar, and a portrait of him (with the attributes of St Peter Martyr, c. 1497). A panel dating from c. 1498 shows the *Burning of Savonarola in Piazza della Signoria*, and there is also a book of his preachings and sermons. In the adjoining cell (13), arranged as a little study, is a 19th-century desk, and a chair traditionally supposed to have been used by the prelate. In the last cell (14) are some more Savonarola relics, fragments of Dominican habits, and another late 15th-century painting of the *Burning of Savonarola in Piazza della Signoria*.

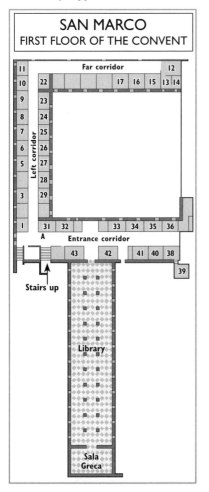

Entrance corridor
(31) The cell of St Antoninus, with

Christ in Limbo by an assistant of An-gelico, who probably also painted the scenes in the next four cells.

(32–35) Frescoes show the *Sermon on the Mount*, *Arrest of Christ*, *Agony in the Garden* and the *Institution of the Eucharist*.

(36) An unusual scene of Christ being nailed to the Cross.

(38–39) These cells were occupied as a retreat by Cosimo il Vecchio; the *Adoration of the Magi*, painted by Benozzo Gozzoli in collaboration with Fra' An-gelico, was restored in the 19th century.

(40–43) The worn frescoes of the *Crucifixion* are by Angelico's workshop.

The library

This light and delicate hall by Michelozzo (1441) is one of the most pleasing archi-tectural works of the Florentine Renaissance. The original emerald green colour of the frescoed *intonaco* on the walls and vaults was discovered recently under four layers of plaster (and this can now be seen in several places). It is known that the colour green was symbolic of contemplation and repose and was used on the walls of other Renais-sance libraries and studies. Before this discovery art historians had praised the clear lines of this hall, where the grey *pietra serena* stands out against the white walls and vaults, as representing a typical Renaissance interior.

The library of San Marco, the first of its kind in Europe, was famous for its collec-tion of works by ancient Greek and Roman authors and was augmented by donations from the Florentine humanists. However, dispersal of the books had already begun by the early 16th century, and in 1571 many of them went to the Biblioteca Laurenziana (and in the 19th century to the Biblioteca Nazionale). Some that remain are usually exhibited here, together with illuminated choirbooks and psalters (mostly 15th–16th century, including a missal illuminated by Fra' Angelico as a young man), and an ex-cellent small display illustrates the fascinating technique of manuscript illumination. Over the two doors are frescoes (1671) of the Blessed Albertus Magnus and his pupil St Thomas Aquinas. Above the two blocked doors on the left wall are small paintings of St Thomas and the Blessed Albertus Magnus teaching, by Zanobi Strozzi. At the end of the room is the Sala Greca, added in 1457, which preserves its painted ceiling from that time. The cupboards, dating from 1741, now contain vases made in Montelupo in 1570 for the pharmacy of San Marco.

Just outside the main entrance to the library is a plaque commemorating the arrest of Savonarola, which took place on this spot on the night of 8th April 1498.

Museo di Firenze Antica

The Museo di Firenze Antica, at the bottom of the stairs to the right, was founded in 1898 to house architectural fragments (many dating from the medieval and early Ren-aissance periods) salvaged during the demolition of part of the medieval city around the Mercato Vecchio and the Ghetto (*see p. 103*). The museum is arranged in the *foresteria*, the guest quarters of the convent. Some of the cells have a lunette over the door by Fra' Bartolomeo. One of the rooms displays the pavement tomb of Luigi Tornabuoni (1515), with its fine marble effigy in relief and another, with a 15th-century painted wooden ceiling, contains 14th–16th-century fragments of painted wall decoration and a wooden model of the church of San Giuseppe by Baccio d'Agnolo. From the windows can be seen the **Cloister of St Dominic (H)** (*not open to the public since it is still used by the Dominicans*), by Michelozzo (1437–43). The frescoes of the life of St Dominic were added in 1701 by Cosimo Ulivelli and others, when the statue of the saint was placed in the centre, surrounded by palm trees and box.

Material from the Sepolcreto di San Pancrazio has been arranged in the **Chiostrino dei Silvestrini (I)**, usually only open in summer.

The exit at the end of the corridor is through a little garden onto Via della Dogana.

GIARDINO DEI SEMPLICI (BOTANICAL GARDEN)

Map 4, 3. Open 1 April–15 Oct 10–7 every day; other months usually only at weekends; T: 055 234 6760 or 055 275 7402. Entrance at Via Micheli 3.

Semplici are 'simples', or medicinal herbs. In 1543 Cosimo I founded the botanical garden in Pisa (which contends with Padua the primacy of being the very first such garden in Europe) and just a few years later, in 1545–46, he commissioned Tribolo to lay out the garden on this site. The grand dukes of Florence took a great interest in the science of botany, especially in the Lorraine period from the end of the 18th to the beginning of the 19th centuries.

Today the garden, which has an area of some six acres, still contains medicinal plants, such as belladonna, mandrake, foxglove (digitalis) and periwinkle (vinca), as well as Tuscan flora including irises and lavender, and water plants. The azaleas grown in tubs are a special feature in early spring. The oldest tree in the garden is a yew planted in 1720, which grows close to a splendid cork oak dating from 1805. A magnificent cedar of Lebanon planted in 1795 also survives. In winter and autumn the greenhouses protect the tropical plants, palms, succulents, bromeliads, ferns, orchids and citrus fruits. The cycads constitute one of the largest collections in existence, with some 180 examples representing 38 different species. Two of the *Amorphophallus titanium* (otherwise known as the 'stinky plant') bloomed in June 2002.

The Botanical Museum (*entrance at Via Giorgio La Pira 4; admission by appointment only, T: 055 234 6760 or 055 275 7462*), founded in 1842, is the most important in Italy, with some four million specimens. It contains the Andrea Cesalpino Herbarium, compiled in 1563 and one of the oldest in the world. The Philip Barker Webb Herbarium (1854) contains plants collected by Charles Darwin on his first voyage in the *Beagle*. The museum is part of Florence University's study collections, which have been united under the title of Museo di Storia Naturale. An archive attached to the museum and library has the papers of Pier Antonio Micheli, founder of the first botanical society in Europe in Florence in 1716, and the correspondence of Giuseppe Raddi (1770–1829), who was sent to Brazil to collect flora by Ferdinando III.

PIAZZA SAN MARCO

This is one of the liveliest squares in the city (*map 4, 3–5*) but also one of the most traffic-ridden as numerous buses stop here. Its cafés are a meeting-place for students from the University and Academy of Art, both of which have their headquarters in the piazza. The statue in the centre is of General Manfredo Fanti, an important military and political figure in the movement for Italian Unity. He died in Florence in 1865.

On the west side of the square is the **Casina di Livia**, built by Grand Duke Peter Leopold in 1775 for his mistress Livia Raimondi (it is now used as an officers' club). A plaque on the garden wall beside five tall cypresses records the **site of the Giardino di San Marco**. We know from Vasari that this garden contained collections of antique sculpture put together by Cosimo il Vecchio and his grandson Lorenzo the Magnificent. Here it was that Lorenzo's great friend, the expert bronze caster Bertoldo di Giovanni, who had been a pupil of Donatello's, restored antique sculpture and instructed young sculptors. The painter Francesco Granacci took the 15-year-old Michelangelo to see the school and pointed him out to Lorenzo, who soon recognised his exceptional talents and obtained Michelangelo's father's permission for him to come and live in the Medici household.

On the east side of Piazza San Marco is the **Loggia dell'Ospedale di San Matteo**, one of the oldest porticoes in Florence (1384). The seven arches may have inspired Brunelleschi's Loggia degli Innocenti (*see p. 171*). This is now the seat of the Accademia di Belle Arti, an art school opened in 1784 by Grand Duke Peter Leopold. Over the doors are fine della Robbian lunettes: those showing the *Madonna della Cintola* and the *Resurrection* are by Andrea della Robbia. The Mannerist courtyard has unusual columns. A little chapel can sometimes be seen on request (*entrance at Via Cesare Battisti 11*). The charming scene of the *Rest on the Flight into Egypt*, one of Giovanni da San Giovanni's best frescoes, was moved here when the Academy was opened. It shows the Madonna stepping off a mule onto a stool while a woman with a child holding a cat look down from above.

GALLERIA DELL'ACCADEMIA

Map 4, 5. Entrance at Via Ricasoli 58. Open 8.30–6.50, closed Mon; in summer Thur, Fri and Sat also 8.30–11.30pm; T: 055 238 8609. The gallery can be very crowded with tour groups and there is often a long queue: it is therefore best to book a visit (T: 055 294883; see p. 109). The least crowded time is late afternoon. The works are all well labelled in English.

History of the Gallery
The gallery was founded for study purposes in 1784, with a group of paintings given to the Accademia di Belle Arti by Grand Duke Peter Leopold. After 1786 paintings from religious houses suppressed by Peter Leopold's brother, the Holy Roman Emperor Joseph II, as part of his reform of the Church, were transferred here. In 1873, a huge tribune was constructed to exhibit Michelangelo's *David*, when it was removed from its original location in Piazza della Signoria. The four *Slaves* and *St Matthew*, also by the great artist, were moved from the Boboli Gardens in 1909. Although the gallery is today famous above all for these sculptures, it also contains an important collection of Florentine paintings from all periods up to the 16th century, and a museum of musical instruments.

Sala del Colosso
This large room is named after Giambologna's huge plaster model (1582) for his *Rape of the Sabines* in the Loggia della Signoria (*see p. 35*), displayed in the centre. Numerous important **Florentine paintings from the 15th century and the first two decades of the 16th** now crowd the walls. These include (entrance wall) the panel (probably a bed-head or a wainscot) known as the *Cassone Adimari*, by Masaccio's younger brother, Lo Scheggia, which shows five couples dancing to music provided by musicians playing wind instruments. These are thought to represent wedding festivities: on the extreme left two servants bearing presents are entering a house which may be that of the bridal couple. The buildings in the background include the Baptistery. This work provides fascinating details about how the Florentines dressed in the mid-15th century and the appearance of the city at that time. Above hangs a *Madonna and Child with the Young St John and Two Angels*, a beautiful early work by Botticelli; Botticelli probably also painted the charming small Madonna with a seascape in the background, hung nearby. Also on this wall are *Scenes from Monastic Life* (or *The Thebaids*), thought to be by Paolo Uccello. On the next wall (above the door into the Museum of Musical Instruments) is an *Annunciation*, an early work by Filippino Lippi, a copy of a painting by his father, Fra' Filippo Lippi. Filippino also painted the *St John the Baptist and St Mary Magdalene*, and (on the wall opposite) the upper part of the *Descent from the Cross* (for the high altar of Santissima Annunziata; it was finished after Filippino's death in 1504 by Perugino). Also here is an *Assumption and Saints* signed by Perugino (and dated 1500). The beautiful altarpiece of *Sts Stephen, James and Peter* (the figure of St Stephen is particularly striking) is by Domenico Ghirlandaio.

Museum of Musical Instruments

Florence has held a special place in the history of music since the change of style between Jacopo Peri's musical drama *Dafne*, performed in Palazzo Corsi in 1597, and his *Euridice*, composed in 1600 to honour the marriage of Maria de' Medici (daughter of Francesco I) to Henri IV of France. First performed in Palazzo Pitti, it is generally held to mark the beginning of opera. The pianoforte was invented in Florence in 1711 by Bartolomeo Cristofori (1655–1731). The composer Jean-Baptiste Lully (1632–87) was born in the city.

The collection, begun by the last of the Medici and the Lorraine grand dukes, is one of the most interesting in Italy. There are 17th-century cellos including one by Nicolò Amati (c. 1650), a late 17th-century dulcimer, and the famous *Viola Medicea* built by Antonio Stradivari in 1690. A double bass is attributed to Bartolomeo Cristofori (1715). The violins include one by Antonio Stradivari (1716). In the second room are a harpsichord and an oval spinet by Bartolomeo Cristofori (1690) and an upright piano made in 1739 by his assistant Domenico del Mela.

MICHELANGELO'S *DAVID*

This is perhaps the most famous single work of art in Western civilisation and has become something of a cult image, all too familiar through endless reproductions, although it is not the work by which Michelangelo is best judged. It was commissioned by the city of Florence to stand outside Palazzo Vecchio, where its huge scale fits its setting. Here it seems out of place in its cold, heroic niche. The colossal block of marble, 5.17m high, quarried in 1464 for the Opera del Duomo, had been left abandoned in the cathedral workshop. The marble was offered to several other artists, including Andrea Sansovino and Leonardo da Vinci, before it was finally assigned to Michelangelo. The figure of David, uncharacteristic of Michelangelo's works, stands in a classical pose suited to the shallow marble block. The hero, a young colossus, is shown in the moment before his victory over Goliath. A celebration of the nude, the statue established Michelangelo as the foremost sculptor of his time, at the age of 29.

The Galleria

The tribune at the far end was specially built in 1882 by Emilio de Fabris to house **Michelangelo's *David*** when it was brought in under cover from Piazza della Signoria. On the walls are hung paintings by Michelangelo's Florentine contemporaries.

Five other great sculptures by Michelangelo are exhibited here. The four **Slaves** or *Prisoners* (variously dated 1521–23 or around 1530) were begun for the tomb of Pope Julius II, which was never finished. Other sculptures which were to form part of it are in San Pietro in Vincoli in Rome. The *Slaves* were presented to the Medici in 1564 by Michelangelo's nephew Leonardo. In the centre of the right side is **St Matthew**

Detail of Michelangelo's *David*, the work that established his reputation, sculpted as a symbol of the triumph over tyranny. Grand Duke Cosimo III preferred to cover its nudity under a tarpaulin.

(1504–08), one of the twelve Apostles commissioned from the sculptor by the Opera del Duomo for the cathedral, and the only one he ever began. It was left abandoned in the courtyard of the Opera del Duomo until 1831. These five sculptures are magnificent examples of Michelangelo's unfinished works, some of them barely blocked out, the famous *non-finito*, much discussed by scholars. They evoke Michelangelo's unique concept, expressed in his poetry, that the sculpture already exists within the block of stone and it is the sculptor's job merely to take away what is superfluous. The way in which Michelangelo confronted his task, as Cellini noted, was to begin from a frontal viewpoint, as if carving a high relief, and thus the statue gradually emerged from the marble. The marks made by his *gradina*, or tooth chisel, are very evident.

Ridolfo del Ghirlandaio painted the two very unusual scenes of St Zenobius, which include remarkable contemporary portraits among the crowds as well as views of Florence, and show the influence of northern painters as well as Raphael.

The Salone

At the end of the hall to the left of the *David* is a huge light room. This was formerly the ward of the hospital of San Matteo, which was founded in the 14th century; a small detached monochrome fresco by Pontormo of the interior of the hospital is displayed here. It is now filled with a delightful display of **plaster models by Lorenzo Bartolini** (1777–1850), considered the most important sculptor in Italy during his lifetime, arranged more or less as they were in his studio in Borgo San Frediano. They include the original models for his best-known works, including public monuments (the allegorical figures from the Demidoff monument on Lungarno Serristori are in the centre of the room), as well as numerous tombs and portrait busts. There are also some other 19th-century sculptures and paintings by members of the Accademia di Belle Arti.

Early Florentine paintings

Off the hall to the left of the *David* are three rooms which display the earliest Florentine paintings in the gallery. A room dedicated to works dating from the 13th and early 14th centuries contains a Crucifix by a Florentine painter close to Cimabue and a *Mary Magdalene*, with stories from her life, by an unknown artist named from this work. Another room displays paintings by Andrea Orcagna and his brothers Jacopo and Nardo di Cione, as well as a very fine *Man of Sorrows* (1365) by Giovanni da Milano, one of the most interesting painters to succeed Giotto. The last room contains works by other followers of Giotto, including Taddeo Gaddi and Bernardo Daddi, as well as a fresco fragment with a shepherd attributed to Giotto himself, detached from the Badia Fiorentina.

Florentine paintings from 1370–1430

These are exhibited on the first floor in an excellent new arrangement opened in 2011. The first room has works by Jacopo di Cione. The main hall, divided into sections, displays works by Niccolò di Pietro Gerini, a triptych signed and dated 1391 by Spinello Aretino, and a large polyptych by Giovanni del Biondo. In the second section is an exquisitely embroidered altar frontal which once adorned the high altar of Santa Maria

Novella, signed and dated 1336 by Jacopo di Cambio. In the centre is the *Coronation of the Virgin between Angels and Saints* and on the border are scenes from the life of the Virgin and numerous birds. This is one of the most spectacular artefacts made by Florentine craftsmen. Here are displayed some beautiful works by Lorenzo Monaco, including *Prayer in the Garden*, an early work painted around 1400 for the convent of Santa Maria degli Angeli, where Lorenzo was a monk. Other panels represent his highly refined Late Gothic period. At the end of the hall is a huge polyptych of the *Coronation of the Virgin* by Rossello di Jacopo Franchi and works by Starnina (who spent many years in Spain) and the Master of the Straus Madonna. In the last room there is a video demonstrating how these panel paintings were made. On the stairs down to the exit there is a display of 16th–18th-century Russian icons, which entered the Lorraine grand-ducal collections in 1771–78.

MUSEO DELL'OPIFICIO DELLE PIETRE DURE

Map 4, 5. Entrance at Via degli Alfani 78. Open daily 8.15–2 except Sun and holidays; T: 055 265111. Extremely well labelled.

The Opificio was founded in 1588 by the Medici grand duke Ferdinando I, to produce mosaics in hard or semi-precious stones. His brother Francesco I, who had died the previous year, invented the idea of making mosaics out of *pietre dure*, in imitation of Classical works in marble intarsia. This refined craft, perfected in Florence (also known as *mosaico fiorentino*), is remarkable for its durability. Exquisite pieces were made in the workshops (which moved here from the Uffizi in 1798) to decorate such objects as cabinets and tabletops. Many of the best examples are preserved in Palazzo Pitti. The grand dukes were fond of using them as gifts, often to foreign rulers. The most characteristic products are decorated with flowers, fruit and birds, against a black background. The small museum, founded here at the end of the 19th century, and beautifully arranged, provides a superb illustration of the workshop's history and production.

Highlights of the display are Francesco Ferrucci del Tadda's portrait of Cosimo I, as well as works made for the Cappella dei Principi in San Lorenzo. The mezzanine floor has 18th- and 19th-century work benches and instruments once used by the craftsmen. The 18th-century painted designs by Antonio Cioci, with shells and compositions with antique or porcelain vases, were used for the exquisite tabletops now in Palazzo Pitti.

There are 18th-century examples of scagliola work made from selenite and incised with a metal point in imitation of marble and *pietre dure*. Works in *pietre dure* continued to be produced here right up until the early years of the 20th century, as the pieces in Art Nouveau designs show.

Since 1975, the Opificio Institute has been the seat of a state-run restoration and conservation laboratory dedicated to the restoration of stone, marble, bronze, terracotta and *pietre dure*. Another branch of the restoration laboratory, largely concerned with paintings and frescoes, operates in the Fortezza da Basso.

Piazza Santissima Annunziata (*map 4, 5*) was designed by Brunelleschi. Surrounded on three sides by porticoes, it is the most beautiful square in Florence. The Spedale degli Innocenti has a portico by Brunelleschi with its famous della Robbia medallions, and the colonnade opposite, modelled on Brunelleschi's work, was designed over a century later by Antonio da Sangallo and Baccio d'Agnolo (1516–25). Sangallo was also responsible for the portico of the church itself (although this was finished in the 17th century).

Via dei Servi was used by Brunelleschi in his Renaissance design of the piazza to provide a magnificent view of the cupola of the Duomo. This street, on the line of an ancient thoroughfare leading north from the city, documented as early as the 12th century, is still lined by a number of handsome 16th-century palaces (*see Appendix*).

In the middle of the square is an **equestrian statue of Grand Duke Ferdinando I**, Giambologna's last work. It was cast in 1608 by his talented pupil Pietro Tacca, who also designed the base and the two small symmetrical bronze fountains with bizarre monsters and marine decorations, which are delightful Mannerist works. Fairs with market stalls are held in the piazza on certain days, including 25th March (the festival of the Annunciation), 7th Sept (and the weekend before) and 8th Dec.

Opposite the church is the red-brick **Palazzo Grifoni Budini Gattai**, home to the photo archives of the Kunsthistorisches Institut in Florence. The palace is thought to have been begun in 1557 by Ammannati for the Grifoni, probably to a design by Giuliano di Baccio d'Agnolo, then finished by Buontalenti and Giambologna. It has another ornate façade with decorative friezes on Via dei Servi, and a delightful garden. Browning's poem 'The Statue and the Bust' is set here:

> There's a palace in Florence, the world knows well,
> And a statue watches it from the square...

The story goes that as Ferdinando I rode by in the square below, he met the glance of a young bride at a window of this palace and they fell in love. Neither had the courage to consummate their love, and many years later, to perpetuate that moment, each decided to order their portraits to be put up here: Ferdinando's in the form of an equestrian statue (the first public monument to a Medici ruler in his own lifetime) and the lady's a della Robbia bust set on the window sill of a top-floor window (today pointed out as the one with one of its shutters always half-open).

SPEDALE DEGLI INNOCENTI

The Spedale degli Innocenti (correctly Ospedale degli Innocenti; *map 4, 5*) was opened in 1445 as a foundling hospital, the first institution of its kind in Europe. It is still dedicated to the education and care of children: up until 2000 it operated as an orphanage and it now has sheltered housing for children and families in need. Since 1988 it has also housed a research centre of the United Nations Children's Fund (UNICEF).

The Arte della Seta (silk weavers' guild) commissioned Brunelleschi (who, as a goldsmith, was a member of the guild) to begin work on the building in 1419. By the mid-16th century the hospice was already able to care for some 2,000 babies, a figure that had increased to 3,000 by the 19th century. The first school of obstetrics in Italy was founded here, and pioneering studies into nutrition and vaccination were carried out in the hospital (cows and goats were kept in the garden). Some of the 2,000 precious volumes dating from the 16th–19th centuries which formed part of the library of the Società Filoiatrica Fiorentina, a learned society of doctors founded by Giuseppe Bertini in 1812 for the study of medicine, are preserved here, including some rare medical tracts, as well as surgical instruments and models used for study purposes. The archives, housed in an 18th-century room with handsome 19th-century bookcases, are preserved intact, including the first register of 1445.

The exterior

The colonnade of nine arches (1419–26) is one of the first masterpieces of Renaissance architecture by Brunelleschi, inspired by Classical antiquity as well as local Romanesque buildings. The *pietra serena* columns are monolithic: these were much more costly to quarry and transport than composite columns but Brunelleschi was clearly inspired by the ancient Romans, who used columns such as these for their buildings. As in all his architectural works he gave great importance to refining the architectural details and ensuring that the joints, where necessary, were as inconspicuous as possible. It has recently been suggested that he studied the technical details used in the construction of the columns and pilasters in the atrium of the Pantheon in Rome, and copied them here and in many of his other Florentine works.

The last bays on the right and left were added in the 19th century. In the spandrels are delightful medallions, perhaps the best-known work of Andrea della Robbia (1487), each with a baby in swaddling-clothes against a bright blue background (the two end ones on each side are excellent copies made in 1842–43). Beneath the portico at the left end is the *rota* (turning-box or wheel), constructed in 1660 to receive abandoned babies (it was walled up in 1875). The church of the Innocenti (*open early mornings only*) was remodelled in Neoclassical style in 1786 by Bernardo Fallani.

Museo degli Innocenti

Part of the convent houses a museum (*open 10–7 every day; at the time of writing the museum was about to be expanded and other parts of the convent opened to the public*). At present the entrance (with the ticket office) leads into the main **Chiostro degli Uomini** (1422–45; reserved for the men who worked in the institute), which was decorated in 1596 with a clock-tower and graffiti (drawn with lime) showing the emblems of the Arte della Seta and the other two hospital foundations (San Gallo and Santa Maria alla

Scala), which were united here in the 15th century. Over the side door into the church is a pretty lunette of the *Annunciation* by Andrea della Robbia.

The oblong **Chiostro delle Donne** (1438) is another beautiful work by Brunelleschi, with 24 slender Ionic columns beneath a low loggia. The charming perspective of the colonnades is reminiscent of the background which appears in some Renaissance paintings. This part of the convent was reserved for the women who worked in the institute. There is now a collection of games and toys in rooms off the cloister, which is open to children (who can borrow them, as in a lending library).

At the end of the Chiostro delle Donne, a fine staircase (with a restored 14th-century statue of *St John the Evangelist* attributed to Simone Talenti) leads up to the UNICEF offices and the museum arranged in a long gallery (formerly the day nursery) overlooking Piazza Santissima Annunziata. Beside the entrance are two life-size crèche figures of Mary and Joseph in painted terracotta, attributed to a certain Marco della Robbia: before the *rota* was built in the 17th century, orphan babies used to be left between them. A small case displays a touching series of 19th-century identification tags left by destitute mothers with their babies, in the hope that one day they would be able to be reunited with them. The illuminated antiphonals used in the convent are also shown here. The most important paintings are on the wall opposite the windows: the *Madonnas Protecting the Innocents* are attributed to Domenico di Michelino and Jacopino del Conte; the triptychs are by the Master of the Griegg Crucifixion and Giovanni del Biondo; and the *Coronation of the Virgin* is considered the masterpiece of the unknown artist called the Master of the Straus Madonna (sometimes identified with Ambrogio di Baldese). On the left of the archway into the end room, the *Madonna and Child with an Angel* is an interesting early work by Botticelli, copied from his master Filippo Lippi.

The most precious work owned by the hospital is the splendid brightly-coloured *Adoration of the Magi* by Domenico Ghirlandaio, commissioned for the high altar of the convent church by the prior, Francesco Tesori (d. 1497), whose tomb slab has been placed in the floor here. Dated 1488, it includes a scene of the *Massacre of the Innocents* with two child saints in the foreground. There is a wonderful landscape with a river flowing into the sea with lots of ships. The predella, painted in the same year, is one of the few documented works by Bartolomeo di Giovanni. Also here is one of Luca della Robbia's most beautiful works: a *Madonna and Child* in white glazed terracotta (c. 1445–50). The painting of the *Madonna Enthroned* is by Piero di Cosimo, painted just a few years after Ghirlandaio's work. Against the window wall are two stout 17th-century chairs designed for the wet nurses. Steps lead down to a landing from which there is a view of Brunelleschi's original mighty beamed church ceiling, above the barrel vault inserted in 1785.

SANTISSIMA ANNUNZIATA

Map 4, 5. Open 7–12.30 & 4–6.30, holidays also 8.45–9.45pm.
The church of the Santissima Annunziata, the Most Holy Virgin Annunciate, was founded by the seven original Florentine members of the Servite Order in 1250 and re-

built, along with the cloister and atrium, by Michelozzo and others in 1444–81. Housing a famous painting of the *Annunciation*—held to be miraculous—it was one of the most important sanctuaries dedicated to the Madonna in Europe, and is still perhaps the church in the city which receives the greatest number of worshippers throughout the day. The feast-day of the Annunciation (25th March) began the new year in the Florentine calendar up until the 18th century. The central arch of the portico is ascribed to Antonio da Sangallo; the rest is by Giovanni Battista Caccini (1600), and the unusual paving beneath it has hexagonal stones of green yellow and grey *alberese*.

It was in this church, in 1817, that Leopold, last Grand Duke of Tuscany, married Maria Anna Carolina of Saxony. Leopold lost the Grand Duchy in 1859, leaving the city quietly in the early evening of 27th April, after an efficient—and bloodless—revolution.

Chiostrino dei Voti

The series of Mannerist frescoes on the walls (now sadly faded) is particularly interesting since most of them were painted in the second decade of the 16th century by the leading artists of the time. Right to left they are as follows:

(1) Rosso Fiorentino: *Assumption*, his first known work.

(2) Pontormo: *Visitation*, showing the influence of Andrea del Sarto.

(3) Franciabigio: *Marriage of the Virgin*—the head of the Virgin was damaged by the painter himself in a fit of anger. Beyond, the marble bas-relief of the *Madonna and Child* is by an unknown sculptor (sometimes attributed to Michelozzo).

(4) Andrea del Sarto: *Birth of the Virgin*.

(5) Andrea del Sarto: *Coming of the Magi*, containing Andrea's self-portrait in the right-hand corner. Two bronze stoups by Antonio Susini (1615) stand in front of the west door.

(6) Alesso Baldovinetti: *Nativity* (1460–62). The colours have faded because they were badly prepared by the artist. The landscape is particularly beautiful, stretching far away into the distance as the meandering river crosses the plain.

(7) Cosimo Rosselli: *Calling and Investiture of San Filippo Benizzi*, (1476).

(8–12) Andrea del Sarto: More scenes of San Filippo, interesting but damaged (1509–10).

Interior of Santissima Annunziata

The dark interior was heavily decorated in the late 17th century, with a rich ceiling to a design by Volterrano, who also frescoed the east end. There is a special atmosphere of devotion in this church.

(A) **Shrine of the Madonna:** Near the entrance to the church the pews are turned towards the west end since many services take place at this shrine, which is bedecked with ex-votos, hanging lamps and candles. The huge tabernacle (almost hidden by the devotional paraphernalia), commissioned by Piero il Gottoso, was designed by Michelozzo and executed by Pagno di Lapo Portigiani (1448–61) to protect the miraculous painting of the *Annuncia-*

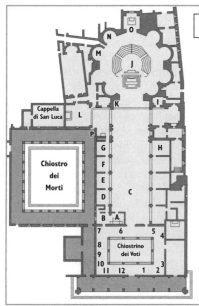

SANTISSIMA ANNUNZIATA

1-12 Mannerist frescoes
A Shrine of the Madonna
B Medici oratory
C Nave
D Cappella Feroni
E *Holy Trinity* by Andrea del Castagno
F *Last Judgement* by Allori
G *Assumption* by Perugino
H Monument to Orlando de' Medici
I *Dead Christ* by Bandinelli
J Tribune
K Tomb of Bishop Angelo Marzi Medici
L Chapel by Michelozzo
M *Madonna and Saints* by Perugino
N *Resurrection* by Bronzino
O Burial place of Giambologna
P *Madonna del Sacco*

tion, traditionally thought to have been painted by a friar who was miraculously assisted by an angel. The bronze grille provided by Maso di Bartolomeo to protect the original tabernacle survives.

(B) Former private oratory of the Medici: Still today this chapel is closed off from the rest of the church. Although it is covered with silver ex-votos, you can just see the exquisite small painting of the *Redeemer* (1515) by Andrea del Sarto, who is buried in the church. The five beautiful panels in *pietre dure* dating from 1671, with the symbols of the Virgin (the rose, lily, moon, sun and star), are less easy to make out from this distance.

(C) Nave: The stucco and painted decoration by Cosimo Ulivelli, Pier Francesco Silvani and Pier Dandini dates

from around 1703. The splendid organ (1509–21) by Domenico di Lorenzo da Lucca and Matteo da Prato is the oldest in the city and the second oldest in Italy. It is the only organ by Domenico di Lorenzo to have survived virtually intact. Its wonderful sound can be heard when concerts are given (usually around Christmas time).

(D) Cappella Feroni: A fine Baroque work by Giovanni Battista Foggini (1692). Behind the (hinged) altarpiece there is a fresco by Andrea del Castagno of *St Julian and the Saviour* (*it can sometimes be seen on request*).

(E) Over the altar is another fresco by Andrea del Castagno: the *Holy Trinity with St Jerome*. The chapel, including the vault, has good frescoes by Alessandro Allori (restored in 2010).

(F) The *Last Judgement* (left wall) by Allori is a copy of various figures in Michelangelo's fresco in the Sistine Chapel.

(G) *Assumption* by Perugino, painted in the first years of the 16th century for the high altar of the church.

(H) Monument to Orlando de' Medici, by Bernardo Rossellino (1456). Orlando, a cousin of Cosimo il Vecchio, was employed in his bank, and paid for some work in the church. His simple but lovely tomb is devoid of all religious references and has an exquisitely carved frieze and two little cherubs holding up the inscription.

(I) The sculpture of the ***Dead Christ supported by Nicodemus*** (harshly lit) is by Baccio Bandinelli. It marks the grand burial place of the artist and the head of Nicodemus is a self-portrait.

(J) Tribune (*the chapels can be visited from the north transept, described below*). Although begun by Michelozzo, this was completed by the great Renaissance architect Leon Battista Alberti in 1477 and paid for by his patron in Mantua, Ludovico Gonzaga. It has a very unusual design: a rotunda preceded by a triumphal arch, derived from ancient Roman architecture. It is one of Alberti's lesser-known works, difficult to appreciate beneath the later decorations, although the huge fresco of the *Coronation of the Virgin* by Volterrano is a fine work in itself.

The high altar, with a frontal by Giovanni Battista Foggini (1682), bears a silver ciborium. In the choir enclosure (*impossible to see*) the choir stalls and two lecterns are of English workmanship (15th century).

(K) On the left of the great arch is the tomb of Bishop Angelo Marzi Medici, signed by Francesco da Sangallo (1546) and with an expressive effigy of the relaxed-looking bishop.

(L) The chapel in the north transept is the work of Michelozzo (1445–47) and contains a terracotta statue of the *Baptist* by him, but the architecture is hard to appreciate since the walls were covered with *trompe l'œil* frescoes in the mid-18th-century. From here there is access to the radial chapels in the Tribune (*described above*).

(M) *Madonna and Saints* by Perugino, a delicate, serene painting.

(N) *Resurrection* by Bronzino, a very forceful and dramatic work dating from 1552. In the group of nine terrified soldiers, the one in the foreground shown lying on his back looking out of the painting is particularly memorable. The lovely angels above, surrounding the figure of Christ, provide a strong contrast in spirit.

(O) The very dark east chapel (*inconspicuous light on left*) was reconstructed by Giambologna as his own burial place and remains exactly as it was. It contains fine bronzes (the reliefs and the Crucifix; *at the time of writing removed for restoration*) all by his own hand, and statues in niches by his pupils. His closest follower, Pietro Tacca, is also buried here. The *Madonna and Child* is attributed to Bernardo Daddi.

Chiostro dei Morti

Not always open, but usually accessible from the church by the unlocked door behind a heavy red curtain in the left transept chapel, or from the door to the left under the portico.

The Chiostro dei Morti (Cloister of the Dead) is so named from its memorial slabs. Over the door into the church is a lunette fresco known as the **Madonna del Sacco** (**P**), one of Andrea del Sarto's most memorable and original works (*covered for restoration at the time of writing*). In a particularly tranquil atmosphere, the Holy Family are seen resting on the flight into Egypt on the step of a building. Joseph, his head in the shadows as he reads a book, is leaning on the white bundle (or sack, hence the name, 'del Sacco') containing their possessions tied with a blue ribbon, beautifully painted. The other colourful frescoed lunettes in the cloister are by Bernardino Poccetti, Matteo Rosselli and others: they are interesting documents of 17th-century Florence, illustrating the origins of the Servite Order. On the side towards the piazza can be seen traces of five Gothic windows which belonged to the Servite convent.

Cappella di San Luca

This chapel (*only open for services on special occasions*) has always belonged to the Accademia delle Arti del Disegno (*see p. 102*) and a special Mass for artists is held on St Luke's Day (18th Oct; Luke is the patron saint of artists, deriving from the tradition that he himself was a painter and made an icon of the Virgin). In the vault below are buried Cellini, Pontormo, Franciabigio, Montorsoli, Bartolini and many other artists. The chapel altarpiece of *St Luke Painting the Madonna* is an interesting self-portrait by Vasari, a founder-member of the Academy. The walls and ceiling were decorated by Pontormo, Alessandro Allori, Santi di Tito and Luca Giordano. The clay statues which lean dramatically out of their niches are the work of various Academicians, including Montorsoli (who was also a member of the Servite Order). The organ dates from 1702.

The **cloister of the former Compagnia della Santissima Annunziata** (or di San Pierino) is entered at Via Capponi 4, just out of Piazza Santissima Annunziata. Above the entrance is a lunette in glazed terracotta showing the *Annunciation* with two members of the confraternity in white hooded robes. It is the work of Santi Buglioni. The delightful little cloister has frescoes (c. 1585–90) by Bernardino Poccetti and others. The lunettes, representing the martyrdom of the Apostles, are separated by monochrome figures of the Theological Virtues, and, above the doors, the *Resurrection* and *Pietà*.

MUSEO ARCHEOLOGICO NAZIONALE

Map 4, 5. Open Tues–Fri 8.30–7, Sat and Sun 8.30–2; closed Mon. T: 055 23575. Entrance at Piazza Santissima Annunziata 9b. Ask here for the times when the upper floor is open.

Since 1879 the museum has been housed in Palazzo della Crocetta, originally used as a hunting lodge by Lorenzo the Magnificent, and in an extension which was built for Maria Maddalena, sister of Cosimo II, in 1619–20 by Giulio Parigi. It contains one of the most important collections of Etruscan antiquities in existence, though most of the section devoted to Etruscan sites in Tuscany was destroyed in the 1966 Arno flood and has never been reconstituted. The Egyptian collection is one of the best in Italy, and there is a wonderful collection of Attic vases and Roman bronze sculpture.

The museum has been undergoing rearrangement for decades, and the situation at the time of writing was disappointing. The entire museum has a very neglected feel. Many of the halls are kept empty unless in use for temporary exhibitions, and the upper floor with the Attic vases and masterpieces of Greek and Roman sculpture is only open at certain times of day. Only some of the most important pieces are described below.

Entrance halls and modern wing

An incongruous long exhibition hall on two levels was built some years ago right beside a covered passageway lit by small windows, which dates from 1620. This connected the monastery to the church of the Santissima Annunziata, and a balcony was built at the far end so that the invalid sister of Cosimo II could be present at Mass. At present the corridor is used to display the coin collection (*only open at certain times*) while the long hall is also used for temporary exhibitions.

First floor

Monumental bronze statues

The museum's three most famous monumental bronze statues were all acquired by Cosimo I soon after their discovery in the mid-16th century, and they have all been superbly restored. Displayed in a room on its own is the very beautiful **statue of Minerva**, slightly smaller than life-size and clearly modelled on the Greek Athena: she wears a Corinthian helmet and a mantle over a peplos. Thought to date from the early 3rd century BC, it may have been made in Magna Graecia (southern Italy), though it has also been taken to be a Greek original by Kephisodotos, father of Praxiteles, who was at work in Greece in the mid-4th century BC. Recent excavations in Arezzo near where it was found have suggested that it used to adorn the house of a wealthy private citizen in the 1st century AD.

The two other bronzes are exhibited in another small room. The ***Chimaera*** was found just outside a town gate of Arezzo in 1553. It represents the legendary monster, with the body and head of a lion, the head of a goat on its back, and a serpent's tail. The myth relates that the chimaera was killed by Bellerophon, mounted on his winged horse Pegasus, and this work is thought to have been part of a sculptural group which would have included the hero, since the chimaera is shown wounded and ferociously ready to attack its aggressor in a last attempt to save its life. The inscription on its foreleg records that it was an offering to the Etruscan god Tinia. When it was found it was without a tail, but this was provided in a restoration in the 18th century, and it was at that time that the clever idea was introduced of the snake biting the goat's horn. The sculpture was made with the lost wax technique, and is almost unanimously thought to be the work of an Etruscan craftsman from northern Etruria and to date from the 5th century BC, although some scholars have suggested it could be by a Greek sculptor at work a century later.

The ***Arringatore*** is an orator with a raised hand, a gesture of greeting to his listeners or perhaps a request for silence. It is a portrait of Aule Meteli (son of a certain Vel) and his simple dignity makes this perhaps the most moving of these three masterpieces. Found on the northern shore of Lake Trasimene, it is a votive statue made in seven parts, probably dating from around 90 BC, and the inscription is in Etruscan.

The charming Etruscan bronze head of a boy displayed here was found in Fiesole and dates from the last half of the 4th century.

Small Etruscan bronzes and cinerary urns
Small Etruscan bronzes are exhibited in a gallery still preserving the original 19th-century showcases. There are two rooms of cinerary urns, dating from the 4th century BC, in alabaster or volcanic tufa. One has a lifelike portrait of the deceased with the goddess Vanth. The most famous funerary work, the ***Mater Matuta***, a canopic statue of a woman (a portrait of the deceased) on a throne holding a baby, was not on view at the time of writing.

Egyptian Museum
The Egyptian Museum was founded by Leopold II after the expedition to Egypt in 1828–29 organised by Ippolito Rosellini (who published *The Monuments of Egypt and Nubia* in 1832–44) and François Champollion, the founder of modern Egyptology. The decoration of the rooms, in Egyptian style, was carried out in 1881–94. After the Egyptian Museum in Turin and the Vatican collection, this is considered the most important museum of its kind in Italy. Of the very earliest exhibits, two of the finest are the polychrome statuettes of maidservants, one preparing yeast for beer and the other kneading dough (c. 2480–2180 BC). The portrait of a young woman from the Fayyum necropolis dates from the Roman period (1st–2nd centuries AD). The very rare chariot made of wood and bone, found in a Theban tomb, dates from the 14th century BC (it was probably used by the man with whom it was buried). Other finds from Thebes (1552–1186 BC) include sarcophagi, vases and stelae. Around the walls are exhibited papyri of the Book of the Dead. Room VII contains finds from Saqqara (1552–1186 BC). Room VIII preserves its delightful old-fashioned showcases. It contains mummies and mummy cases, canopic vases, basketwork, furniture, objects of daily use and musical instruments.

Second floor: the Medici and Lorraine collections and later acquisitions

Etruscan antiquities (9th–1st centuries BC)
In the first room is displayed the Etruscan tomb of the noblewoman Larthia Seianti (wife of Sevnia), who reclines adorned with jewels on the sarcophagus (her name is incised on the border). It was found in Chiusi in 1877 and is dated 150 BC.

Rooms 2–5 display finds from Etruria from the Iron Age up to the Hellenistic period (9th–3rd centuries BC), including a carved ivory pyx and small gilded silver situla, both dating from the 7th century BC; canopic vases with human heads dating from the following century; and vases in the Orientalising style, some of the most interesting found in Pescia Romana; bucchero ware; incised bronze mirrors and plaques; and black- and red-figure vases from the Archaic and Classical periods.

Works by the indigenous Italic populations in the Greek colonies

Room 6 has bronzes found in Sardinia and Room 7 has bronze helmets and delicate ceramic vases (4th century BC) from Puglia. Room 8 is devoted to a large sarcophagus which preserves its 4th-century BC paintings of Amazons. This is a very rare survival and the inscriptions refer to the name of the woman who was buried inside.

The *Idolino* and small Roman bronzes

The collection of very fine Roman bronzes, many of them once owned by the Medici, is exhibited in the Gallery. At the other end of the room is the *Idolino*, a remarkable bronze statue of a young man and one of the most famous works in the collection. There used to be a long vine branch in his left hand (a fragment of which, recently identified in the Bargello, is now displayed here) and in the other hand there was a tray used for lights since the statue is thought to have served as a lampstand at banquets. There is still uncertainty about its date and attribution: the torso appears to date from the 1st century BC and the head is in the style of Polyclitus. It is now usually considered a Roman variation of a Greek type. It was found at Pesaro in 1530 and donated to Francesco Maria della Rovere, Duke of Urbino. In 1630 it passed to the Medici as part of the marriage settlement between Ferdinando II and Vittoria della Rovere. The pedestal dates from the mid-16th century.

The Roman bronze model of the branch of a tree with a serpent emerging from the trunk (1st century AD), found in the sea near the island of Gorgona in 1873, was used as a candelabrum for oil lamps.

Vases and sculptures from the Greek world

The chronological display begins off the other side of the Gallery in Room 10, where there are terracottas from the Cyclades (8th–6th centuries BC) and a statuette of a flautist, found in Cyprus (600–500 BC).

The wonderful collection of vases shows the development of the black- and red-figure styles from the 6th–4th centuries BC, with scenes from the Greek myths as well as from everyday life. The nucleus of the collection goes back to the time of the Medici, but it was considerably augmented by finds from excavations in later centuries. Room 11 has Corinthian ware and early Attic black-figure vases. In the centre is the famous **François Vase**. This huge and magnificent Attic krater, used for mixing wine and water at banquets, is beautifully proportioned despite its vast dimensions. It bears the signatures of the potter Ergotimos and the painter Cleitias. One of the earliest black-figure Attic vases known, it was made in Athens c. 570 BC and is a unique piece. It was discovered by Alessandro François in an Etruscan tomb at Fonte Rotella, Chiusi, in 1844 and was acquired by Leopold II in 1845. The decoration comprises six rows of more than 200 exquisite mythological scenes, identified by inscriptions. The largest and widest band shows the arrival of the gods after the wedding of Peleus and Thetis. In the band below, we can see the pursuit of Troilus by Achilles and the return of Hephaistos to Olympus. In the lowest band are six decorative groups of symbolic animals, while on the foot of the vase there is an exquisite little frieze showing the battle between the pygmies and cranes. Around the rim of the krater is the Calydonian boar-hunt and a dance of the youths and maidens liberated by the killing of the Minotaur by Theseus (who is shown playing the lyre, opposite Ariadne). In the band below, the chariot race at the funeral games of Patroclus is depicted, and the battle between Centaurs and Lapiths. On the handles are the winged figure of Artemis as queen of wild beasts, and Ajax carrying the dead body of Achilles (slain by Paris).

Room 12 has two Greek kouroi, the only examples to be seen on the Italian mainland. The larger one, known as *Apollo*, is usually dated around 530 BC. The *Apollino* is slightly later (520–510 BC). Room 13 has a magnificent display of Attic black-figure pottery (6th century BC).

Room 14 contains the bronze torso of an athlete, found in the sea off Livorno, and now thought to be a Greek original of c. 480–470 BC. Owned by Cosimo I, it is the earliest known example of a Greek bronze statue cast with the lost-wax technique. The horse's head here probably came from a Greek quadriga group of the 2nd–1st century BC. Owned by Lorenzo the Magnificent, it is thought that both Verrocchio and Donatello saw it in the garden of Palazzo Medici (where it was used as a fountain) before they began work on their own equestrian statues (Verrocchio's Colleoni Monument in Venice and Donatello's Gattamelata in Padua). Also here are numerous cases of red-figure Attic vases (530–450 BC), including some attributed to the Berlin Painter. There is a case of white-ground ceramics, including a delicately painted cup with Apollo, attributed to the Lyandros Painter (5th century BC). Another case displays two small Roman bronzes, one of which was integrated by Cellini in 1548 when he provided the horse.

Rooms 15–17 are often kept closed. The four bronze heads, known as the *Philosophers of Meloria*, found in the sea near Livorno in 1722, were long considered rare Roman replicas of Greek originals but they are now believed to be casts of marble Roman heads, made in the 17th century.

The fascinating Medici and Lorraine grand-ducal **collection of jewellery**, precious stones, gems and cameos, including goldsmiths' work from the 8th–3rd centuries BC, Hellenistic pieces and late antique jewellery (7th century AD), is not at present on view. Also locked away is the antique gold jewellery from the collection of Sir William Currie, donated to the museum in 1863 and which consists of Etruscan gold ornaments from southern Etruria.

The **garden** (*usually open on request; enquire at the ticket office*) was laid out in 1903 and the plants include pines and cedars of Lebanon, and tubs of azaleas in spring. Amongst the vegetation there are reconstructions (using the original stones) of Etruscan tombs in Tuscany. The Tomba Inghirami from Volterra is an exact replica, with the original urns inside.

SANTA MARIA NOVELLA
& ITS PIAZZA

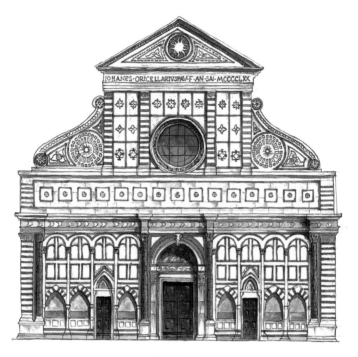

Map 3, 5. Open 9.30–5, Fri, Sun and holidays 1–5; T: 055 215918.

Santa Maria Novella is the most important Gothic church in Tuscany, built by the Dominicans after the grant of land in 1221, on the site of an earlier chapel. The design of the choir and transepts recalls the architecture of Cistercian churches in central Italy, but it was the Dominican friars Sisto and Ristoro who are thought to have been responsible for the magnificent vaulted nave, built in the 1290s. The church was completed under the direction of another friar, Jacopo Talenti, in the mid-14th century, when the great Dominican preacher Jacopo Passavanti was prior. A small group of Dominican friars still lives in part of the convent.

The façade

The lower part of the splendid marble façade above the Gothic arcaded recesses (the *avelli*, or family vaults of Florentine nobles) is typically Tuscan Romanesque in style and is also attributed to Fra' Jacopo Talenti. Its geometric design in white and dark green marble was inspired by the exteriors of the Baptistery and San Miniato al Monte. The upper part was completed together with the main doorway in 1456–70, and its classical lines are in perfect harmony with the earlier work. It was commissioned from the famous Renaissance architect Leon Battista Alberti by Giovanni Rucellai, and exquisite inlaid friezes bear the emblems of the Rucellai (a billowing ship's sail) and of the Medici (a ring with ostrich feathers), since in 1461 Giovanni's son Bernardo married Nannina, sister of his close friend Lorenzo the Magnificent. Below the tympanum, an inscription in handsome classical lettering records the name of the benefactor and the date 1470. Alberti also built Giovanni's town house, Palazzo Rucellai (*see p. 219*). The architect's ingenious use of scrolls to connect the nave roof with the lower aisle roofs was an innovation which was frequently copied in church façades of later centuries (Alberti only built the left scroll; that on the right, a perfect replica, was finally added in 1920). The simple tombstone of Bernardo Rucellai is placed as a marble and red porphyry 'doormat' at the main entrance (his name is inscribed on the riser of the step).

The campanile, attributed to Jacopo Talenti, was grafted onto an old watchtower. The Gothic arcades continue to the right of the façade, extending round the old cemetery.

Interior of Santa Maria Novella

The spacious nave has remarkably bold stone vaulting, so that the eye is immediately drawn upwards. The vaults and arches are given prominence by their decoration of striped or chequered dark grey *pietra serena*. The simple grey and white checked marble pavement echoes the ceiling. The composite pillars between nave and aisles have classical capitals and the bays decrease in width as they approach the three fine stained-glass lancet windows at the east end so that the perspective is particularly pleasing. The only colour on the ceiling are the rectangles of frescoed saints (dating from the 14th century) on the intrados of the nave arches. The interior was opened up by Vasari in 1565, when the rood screen (which formerly divided the church at the steps in the fourth bay) and the friars' choir were demolished. At this time the side altars were set up in the nave (replaced by the present neo-Gothic ones in the 19th century).

(A) Masaccio's *Trinity*: This famous fresco dates from 1427. It shows God the Father supporting the Cross, with the Virgin and St John the Evangelist and donors beneath it. On the sarcophagus at the bottom is a skeleton representing Adam's grave. The symbol of Death is thus shown beneath the symbol of the Resurrection. The fresco is one of the earliest works to use accurately the system of linear perspective developed by Brunelleschi; indeed, it may be that the architect himself intervened in the design of the shadowy niche and the pink architectural elements. The perfect composition gives it an almost metaphysical quality. The elderly Madonna, pointing out her Son to us, is unforgettable, as is the haunting figure of God the Father who seems, appropriately enough, to be in another world. The fresco was detached in the 16th century and was later moved several times to other places in the church.

(B) In the nave hangs a huge **Crucifix by Giotto**, an early work (c. 1290) which probably once adorned the rood screen. It is one of at least three monumental Crucifixes by Giotto to be seen in

Florentine churches (*see pp. 268 and 285*). Although painted well over a hundred years before Masaccio's fresco, it is interesting to confront these two great masters here at close range and see how both contributed in such a fundamental way to the development of Italian painting.

(C) **West wall:** The brilliantly coloured stained glass in the rose window dates from c. 1365 and is perhaps by Andrea di Bonaiuto. High up over the door is a little frescoed lunette of the *Nativity* attributed as an early work to Botticelli. The artist's famous *Adoration of the Magi*, now in the Uffizi (*see p. 117*), was commissioned for an altar here by a money-dealer called della Lama. On the west wall is a fresco of the *Annunciation* and a lovely painting of the same subject by Santi di Tito.

(D) **Monument to the Blessed Villana delle Botti** (1332–61) by Bernardo Rossellino (1451). Born into a wealthy merchant family, Villana renounced her riches and her husband and became a lay Dominican here.

(E) **Monument to Giovanni da Salerno:** Commemorating the founder of the friary, this is a very poor 16th-century imitation, by Vincenzo Danti, of the Botti monument. There are a number of altarpieces in this aisle by the 16th-century painter Giovanni Battista Naldini.

(F) **South transept:** There is a monument to Joseph, Patriarch of Constantinople, who attended the Council of Florence in 1439 (*see p. 187*).

(G) **Cappella Rucellai:** Preceded by the simple, classical sarcophagus of Paolo

Head of Christ, detail of the Crucifix painted by Giotto (c. 1290) in the nave of Santa Maria Novella (photograph taken before restoration).

Rucellai, this chapel housed Duccio's famous *Maestà* in the 18th century. When the work was removed to the Uffizi in 1948, it became known as the *Rucellai Madonna*. The chapel now contains a marble statue of the *Madonna and Child* signed by Nino Pisano, almost the only work in Florence by this Pisan sculptor, whose father Andrea produced wonderful sculptures for the Baptistery and Campanile. The bronze tomb slab of the Dominican general Lionardo Dati is by Lorenzo Ghiberti (1425). The walls have traces of 14th-century frescoes. The large *Martyrdom of St Catherine* (early 16th-century) is by Giuliano Bugiardini.

(H) **Cappella Bardi:** This chapel, recently restored, was formerly used by a *laudesi* brotherhood, who commissioned the *Maestà* from Duccio for this chapel (later moved to the Cappella Rucellai) in 1285. The damaged lunettes (very difficult to see just below the gilded stucco vault) were frescoed at the same time and have recently been attributed to Cimabue—if confirmed as such they would be the only frescoes known in Florence by this master, considered the founder of the Florentine school of painting (*see p. 24*). The bas-relief of Riccardo di Ricco Bardi kneeling before St Gregory dates from the year after his death, 1335, when his heirs took possession of the chapel. The altarpiece of the *Madonna of the Rosary* is by Giorgio Vasari.

(I) Cappella di Filippo Strozzi: This Gothic chapel, decorated with splendid exuberant **frescoes by Filippino Lippi**,

was acquired in 1486 by Filippo Strozzi a few years before he started work on his great palace (*see p. 217*). He commissioned the frescoes from Filippino as soon as the latter had finished work on the Brancacci Chapel in the church of the Carmine (*see p. 274*). The contract for the work survives, and makes copious mention of the necessity to add lapis lazuli to increase the brilliance of the colours: this was added to the surface *a secco*, that is, after the plaster had dried. The artist interrupted work when he was called to Rome to fresco the Carafa Chapel in Santa Maria sopra Minerva, and only finished the decoration after his return to Florence in 1502. Full of allusions to antiquity and including grotesques, the scenes are quite different from those in other Florentine fresco cycles of this period. Filippino was a su-

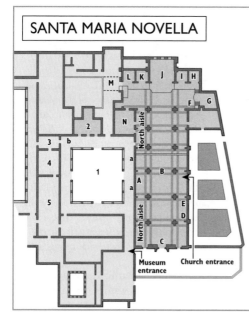

SANTA MARIA NOVELLA

CHURCH
A   Masaccio's *Trinity*
B   Crucifix by Giotto
C   West wall
D   Monument to Villana delle Botti
E   Mon. to Giovanni da Salerno
F   Mon. to Patriarch of Constantinople
G   Cappella Rucellai
H   Cappella Bardi
I   Cappella di Filippo Strozzi
J   Sanctuary (frescoes by Ghirlandaio)
K   Cappella Gondi
L   Cappella Gaddi
M   Cappella Strozzi
N   Sacristy

MUSEUM
1   Chiostro Verde
     a: Frescoes by Uccello
     b: *Madonna and Child*
2   Spanish Chapel
3   Passage
4   Cappella degli Ubriachi
5   Refectory

Head of a young woman, detail from Ghirlandaio's fresco cycle of the life of the Virgin in the sanctuary of Santa Maria Novella.

of young people determined to enjoy life during the plague year of 1348.

(J) Sanctuary: The main altar has a bronze Crucifix by Giambologna. The sanctuary is decorated with delightful **frescoes by Domenico Ghirlandaio**, who was buried in the church after his death (aged 45) from the plague. They were commissioned in 1485 by Giovanni Tornabuoni, whose sister Lucrezia married Piero il Gottoso. Giovanni was manager of the Rome branch of the Medici bank. The frescoes are Ghirlandaio's masterpiece, and he was assisted by his brother Davide, his brother-in-law Sebastiano Mainardi, and his pupils, including perhaps the young Michelangelo. They replaced a fresco cycle by Orcagna (fragments of which, with heads of prophets, have been detached from the vault). Many of the figures are portraits of the artist's contemporaries, including members of the Tornabuoni family, and the whole cycle mirrors Florentine life in the late 15th century.

On the right wall are scenes from the life of St John the Baptist, including (lower register) the *Angel Appearing to St Zacharias in the Temple* (with portraits of the Tornabuoni and famous humanist scholars), the *Visitation*, and (above) *Birth of St John the Baptist*.

On the left wall there are scenes from the life of the Virgin, including (lower register) the *Expulsion of Joachim from the Temple* (with members of the Tornabuoni family and, in the group on the right, the self-portraits of the artists) and the *Birth of the Virgin* (with portraits of the Tornabuoni ladies).

On the end wall, there are a *Coronation of the Virgin*, *Miracle of St Dominic*,

perb draughtsman, and the preparatory drawings survive in the Uffizi. On the right wall is the *Crucifixion of St Philip the Apostle* and his *Miracle Before the Temple of Mars* (on the extreme right is a portrait of Filippino's black servant). On the left wall is the *Martyrdom of St John the Evangelist* and the *Raising of Drusiana*. In the vault, the first part of the chapel to be painted, are *Adam*, *Noah*, *Abraham* and *Jacob*. Filippino also designed the beautiful stained-glass window and the splendid classical *trompe l'œil* frescoes in grisaille on the altar wall. Strozzi ordered that his black marble tomb, exquisitely carved by Benedetto da Maiano, should be given pride of place on the altar wall itself (although an altar was subsequently placed in front of it). In the *Decameron*, Boccaccio uses this part of the church as the meeting-place of a group

Death of St Peter Martyr, Annunciation, St John the Baptist in the Desert, and the two kneeling figures of the donors, Giovanni Tornabuoni and his wife Francesca Pitti. In the vault, the four Evangelists are shown. The stained-glass windows (c. 1491) were also designed by Ghirlandaio. The stalls are attributed to Baccio d'Agnolo.

(K) Cappella Gondi (restored in 2009): The handsome marble decoration, with six beautiful black marble columns of unknown origin, is by Giuliano da Sangallo. Here is kept a **Crucifix by Brunelleschi**, his only sculpture to survive in wood (obviously made to wear a loin cloth but this has since been removed). Vasari recounts the story that Brunelleschi carved this work after he had criticised Donatello for representing a mere 'peasant' on the Cross in his Crucifix (now in Santa Croce; *see p. 198*). When finished he invited Donatello to his house to show him how he thought the crucified Saviour was supposed to look. Donatello was so amazed by what he saw that he promptly dropped the food, including eggs, he had been carrying in his overalls for their lunch. When Brunelleschi remonstrated with him about the loss of their meal, Donatello declared that he had had his fill for that day, and that evidently Brunelleschi had been made to carve figures of Christ and Donatello figures of peasants. The damaged vault frescoes of the Evangelists may date from the late 13th century.

(L) Cappella Gaddi: Designed by Giovanni Antonio Dosio, this retains its 16th-century decorations by Alessandro Allori, Bronzino and Giovanni Bandini.

(M) Cappella Strozzi: A remarkably well-preserved example of a mid-14th-century Tuscan chapel. It contains celebrated frescoes (c. 1357) by Nardo di Cione; they are his most famous work and are carefully designed to cover the entire chapel. They represent (in the vault), *St Thomas Aquinas and the Virtues*; on the end wall, the *Last Judgement*; on the left wall, *Paradise*, a huge crowded composition; and on the right wall, *Hell*, a pictorial commentary on Dante's *Inferno*. The splendid frescoed decoration is completed on the intrados of the entrance arch with a frieze of saints. The stained-glass window was also designed by Nardo and his brother Andrea (better known as Orcagna), who painted the fine altarpiece of the *Redeemer Giving the Keys to St Peter and the Book of Wisdom to St Thomas Aquinas* (1357), remarkable for its unusual iconography.

(N) Sacristy (now the shop): The cross-vault is by Fra' Jacopo Talenti (c. 1350). The stained-glass windows date from 1386. On the left of the door is a lavabo in terracotta with a charming landscape—the first documented work by Giovanni della Robbia (1498); the upper part may be by his father Andrea. The huge cupboard on the opposite wall was designed by Buontalenti (1593). On the walls are 16th-century paintings, including a *Crucifixion* by Vasari.

North aisle: The pulpit was designed by Brunelleschi and executed by his adopted son Buggiano. The 16th-century altarpieces in this aisle are by Alessandro Allori, Vasari and Santi di Tito.

Museo di Santa Maria Novella

Open 9–5, weekday holidays 9–2; closed Fri and Sun; T: 055 282187. Entrance left of church.
The museum is arranged in part of the convent of Santa Maria Novella, which was one
of the richest and largest in Florence. It was here that the Council of Florence was held
in 1439 (*see box below*). Today the cloisters remain an oasis of calm in this busy part of
the city, but the museum has a rather shabby and abandoned feel to it.

THE COUNCIL OF FLORENCE

In 1434, after having been pelted with stones by opponents in Rome, the combative
Venetian-born pope, Eugenius IV, took refuge in Florence, where he lived for the
next nine years in apartments in Santa Maria Novella. In 1438, in an attempt
to heal the breach between the Roman and Byzantine churches, he convened
a council in Ferrara, which was moved south to Florence in the following year.

 The Medici were quick to take advantage of the prestige this would bring to the
city and immediately provided the funding. Joseph, the Patriarch of Constantinople,
and the Byzantine Emperor John VIII Palaeologus, both attended the council with
their magnificent retinues. The Peruzzi palaces near Santa Croce were requisitioned
for the emperor, while the papal court and some 700 churchmen, including 30
bishops and 500 horses, took up residence in Borgo Pinti. A public holiday was
declared when Pope Eugenius made his triumphal entry into the city on 27th
January, and in the following month Leonardo Bruni formally welcomed John VIII
with a ceremonial oration in Greek. Participants included numerous theologians
and some of the great humanists of the day, including Bruni and Poggio Bracciolini.

 All the sessions were held in Santa Maria Novella. Even though the patriarch
died suddenly during the proceedings, a letter was discovered in his room in which
he expressed his favour of union under the Roman Church. The monument to
him which can be seen today in the west transept of Santa Maria Novella includes
his frescoed portrait. The successful outcome of the council was solemnly
declared in the Duomo, beneath Brunelleschi's recently-completed dome (the
parchment which records the event is preserved in the Biblioteca Laurenziana).
As it turned out, no lasting union of the Greek and Roman churches followed,
for the agreement was rejected by both Catholic and Orthodox Christians. What
historians have identified as the true significance of this famous council is its role
in establishing the Medici as *de facto* rulers of Florence at a time when it was host
to some of the most powerful men in Europe.

Chiostro Verde

The Romanesque Chiostro Verde **(1)** (c. 1330–50), with roundels of Dominican saints
in the vaults, takes its name from the green colour of its famous decoration: the very
damaged frescoes by Paolo Uccello and assistants (including Dello Delli) are painted

in *terraverde*. They illustrate stories from Genesis (the biblical references are given), and the cycle begins at the far end of the east (entrance) walk beside the door into the church. The numerous frescoes with animals are particularly charming. The following scenes **(a)** are usually considered to be mostly by Paolo Uccello himself: the *Creation of Adam and the Animals*, the *Creation and Temptation of Eve* (c. 1425), the *Flood* and the *Recession of the Flood* (with Noah's Ark) and the *Sacrifice and Drunkenness of Noah* (c. 1446). Although much damaged, the frescoes are most remarkable for their figure studies and perspective effects; the Flood and Noah scenes are among the most mysterious and disturbing paintings of the Florentine Renaissance.

At the beginning of the north walk is a lunette of the *Madonna and Child* **(b)** dating from around 1330, possibly by the great Sienese painter Lippo Memmi.

Spanish Chapel

Off the cloister opens the Spanish Chapel, or Cappellone degli Spagnuoli **(2)**. It received its name in the 16th century when it was assigned by Eleanor of Toledo (wife of Cosimo I) to the Spanish members of her retinue. It was originally the chapter house, also built by Fra' Jacopo Talenti in the mid-14th century, with a splendid cross-vault and two fine Gothic windows. The walls and huge vault are entirely covered with colourful frescoes by Andrea di Bonaiuto (sometimes called Andrea da Firenze) and assistants (1366–69), the most important work by this otherwise little-known artist, who was influenced by the Sienese school of painting.

The pictorial decoration, on a monumental scale, is carefully designed to fit the wall space, and the frescoes are unusually large so every detail is very easy to see. They were clearly intended to provide inspiration and direction to the friars when they met here. In the vault are the *Resurrection*, *Ascension* and *Pentecost*. The *Navicella* is particularly beautiful and thought to have been painted before the other scenes by a master close to Giotto. On the altar wall are the *Via Dolorosa*, *Crucifixion* and *Descent into Limbo*. On the right wall are various scenes illustrating the mission, works and triumph of the Dominican Order. In front of the elaborate church, which seems to be the artist's vision of the completed Duomo (Andrea was one of a group of experts who was consulted about the design of the cathedral and its cupola at this time), is the Church Militant with the pope and emperor and Church dignitaries. In the foreground (right), behind a group of kneeling pilgrims, are the presumed portraits of Cimabue, Giotto, Boccaccio, Petrarch and Dante. The scene on the bottom right, *St Dominic Sending Forth the Hounds of the Lord* (a Latin pun on Dominicans, 'domini canes', 'dogs of the lord'), features St Peter Martyr and St Thomas Aquinas. Above, four seated figures symbolising the Vices are surrounded by representations of dancing Virtues. The *Dominican Friar Taking Confession* shows the way to salvation, and those absolved are sent on towards the Gate of Paradise guarded by St Peter. On the other side of the gate, the Blessed look up towards Christ in Judgement surrounded by angels.

The opposite wall shows the *Triumph of Catholic Doctrine*, personified by St Thomas Aquinas, shown enthroned beneath the winged Virtues. On his right and left are Doctors of the Church. In the Gothic choir-stalls below are 14 female figures symbolising the Arts and Sciences, with, at their feet, historical personages representing these disciplines. The complicated iconography provided by Dominican theologians was clearly meant to illustrate the strength of the doctrines put forward by Thomas Aquinas as opposed to heretical theories.

On the entrance wall is the *Life of St Peter Martyr* (damaged). The apse chapel was decorated in 1592 by Bernardino Poccetti and Alessandro Allori, and an early 17th-century marble Crucifix now hangs here.

The Chiostro Grande

At the end of a passage **(3)**, which displays the sinopie of Nardo di Cione's *Paradise* frescoes, can be seen (beyond a locked glass door) the imposing Chiostro Grande. The frescoes were carried out in the early 1580s by Bernardino Poccetti and others and are the first example in Florence of religious painting inspired by the Counter-Reformation. This part of the complex is now a police barracks and so only open on special occasions, but there is a remarkable vaulted dormitory, as well as the Cappella dei Papi built in 1515 for Leo X, with frescoes by Pontormo of the story of Veronica and putti on the barrel vault.

The Cappella degli Ubriachi and refectory

The 14th-century **Cappella degli Ubriachi (4)** was built by Fra' Jacopo Talenti and preserves the tomb slab of the Ubriachi family and traces of wall decoration showing their emblem. Here also are displayed frescoes of prophets by Orcagna and his school, detached from the vault of the church sanctuary, and the sinopie of the first frescoes by Uccello from the Chiostro Verde. In the showcases are charming reliquary busts (Sienese school, late 14th century), and a frontal made for the high altar of the church, beautifully embroidered with scenes from the life of the Virgin (Florentine, c. 1460–66).

The large **refectory (5)** has superb cross-vaulting by Talenti. On the entrance wall there is a large fresco of the *Manna in the Desert* by Alessandro Allori, which surrounds a good fresco attributed to a follower of Agnolo Gaddi, contemporary with the building and probably part of a larger composition which covered the entire wall. It shows the *Madonna Enthroned between Sts Thomas Aquinas, Dominic, John the Baptist and Peter Martyr* (the tiny figure of the prior of the convent, Fra' Jacopo Passavanti, is shown at the feet of St Dominic). On the left wall is a *Last Supper*, also by Allori (1583). The polyptych was signed and dated 1344 by Bernardo Daddi.

Other parts of the friary, including the oldest part, the Chiostrino dei Morti (c. 1270) and chapels adjoining it, with mid-14th-century frescoes, have been closed for restoration for many years.

PIAZZA SANTA MARIA NOVELLA

Piazza Santa Maria Novella (*map 3, 7*), with its irregular shape, was created by the Dominicans at the end of the 13th century. The two obelisks were set up in 1608 (resting on bronze tortoises by Giambologna) as turning posts in the course of the annual chariot race (*Palio dei Cocchi*), first held in 1563. It recalled the games in the stadia of ancient Rome (there may in fact have been Roman a stadium on this site). In 2010 the paving was renewed and the glass, wood and stainless steel 'benches' were installed in place of the central fountain. The changes have not been an unqualified success: the seats get too hot in summer and seem to have become favourite perches for pigeons.

Museo Nazionale Alinari della Fotografia

The museum (*map 3, 7; Piazza Santa Maria Novella 14; open 10–7.30 except Wed, but restoration work may cause changes; T: 055 216310, www.alinarifondazione.it*) is housed in the old Leopoldine building, a school which occupied the ex-convent opposite the church. It is preceded by the pretty Loggia di San Paolo (1489–96) with polychrome terracotta roundels of Franciscan saints by Andrea della Robbia, who also produced the beautiful lunette of the *Meeting of St Francis and St Dominic*, an event which traditionally took place here. Work is underway to restore the building to house a museum dedicated to the 20th-century Novecento art movement. Meanwhile part of the building can be visited to see the excellent Museum of Photography.

The museum was opened in 2006 by the distinguished Florentine firm of Fratelli Alinari, founded in 1852 and famous for its black and white photography, particularly for its documentation of Italy's art and architecture (the illustrations in this edition of *Blue Guide Florence* have been chosen exclusively from the Alinari Archive). The display is very well arranged in a labyrinth of little rooms on two floors (with images also projected on the ceiling and floor), and has excellent labels also in English. It documents the origins of photography worldwide (1839–60) and its various stages of development up to the present day. There are fascinating examples from the firm's collection of over three million black-and-white and colour negatives and some 900,000 vintage prints, as well as cameras from all epochs. This is one of the first museums to provide a specific area with tactile collages and captions in Braille.

The historic seat of the firm of Alinari, nearby at Largo Alinari 15 (at the station end of Via Nazionale), can be visited by appointment (*T: 055 23951 or 055 239 5232*).

Around Piazza Santa Maria Novella

The large **tabernacle on the corner of Via della Scala** contains an early 15th-century fresco by a little-known artist called Francesco d'Antonio. It marks the house where Henry James began writing his first novel, *Roderick Hudson*, in 1874. Earlier in the century both Longfellow and Emerson had also stayed in this piazza, at the Hotel Minerva (which still operates here). In Via della Scala itself (no. 16) are the shop and historic premises of the **Officina Profumo-Farmaceutica di Santa Maria Novella** (*map 3, 5; open every day 10.30–5.30; closed Sun in Aug*). The pharmacy, attached to the convent of Santa Maria Novella, had become important as a chemist's shop by the mid-16th century, and today it is still famous for the luxury perfumes, *eaux de cologne*, *pots pourris* and soaps produced in its laboratory. The shop occupies the 14th-century ex-chapel of San Niccolò, decorated in a delightful neo-Gothic style in 1848 and complete with

Exedra between the Functionalist Santa Maria Novella Station and the Palazzina Reale.
Photographed c. 1960 by the Florence-born photographer Vincenzo Balocchi (1892–1975).

all its furnishings. It has Art Nouveau lamps and ceiling frescoes representing the four continents. Overlooking the former physic garden is the herbalist's shop, which preserves its late 18th-century furnishings and pharmacy jars (including Montelupo ware). The museum has a gallery with numerous pharmacy jars, a little drawing room at the end, and the old distillery, still with its copper machinery. You can also visit the sacristy of San Niccolò, which has early 15th-century frescoes of the Passion, thought to be by Mariotto di Nardo. The charming old chemist's shop, which has a door on the Great Cloister of Santa Maria Novella, preserves its 18th-century decorations intact and has 17th-century vases including *albarelli* and mortars.

Just off the east side of Piazza Santa Maria Novella, along the winding Via delle Belle Donne, is the **Croce del Trebbio**, a granite column reconsecrated in 1338 with a Gothic capital bearing symbols of the Evangelists. Above this, protected by a quaint little wooden roof, is a Cross of the Pisan school. It is traditionally thought to commemorate a massacre of heretics which took place here in 1244. Its name comes from the Latin *trivium*, indicating the meeting point of three streets. At no. 14 in this street the painter Ingres had his studio from 1820–24.

Florence's main railway station, the **Stazione Centrale di Santa Maria Novella** (*map 3, 5*), is an excellent Functionalist building designed in 1935 by a group of Tuscan architects, including Giovanni Michelucci, Piero Berardi and Italo Gamberini. In the café inside there are two paintings by Florence-born Ottone Rosai. The handsome subsidiary pedestrian entrance (near the Fortezza da Basso) was designed in 1990 by Gae Aulenti.

THE DISTRICT OF SANTA CROCE

Piazza Santa Croce (*map 7, 1*) is in the centre of a distinctive district of the city, where the inhabitants in medieval times were occupied in the wool industry: Corso dei Tintori, which runs out of the piazza, is named after the dyers' workshops, documented here as early as 1313. Today there are still numerous narrow old streets of small houses nearby, but the artisans' workshops at street level which were a feature of this area up until the mid-20th century are now mostly replaced by small shops.

One of the most attractive and spacious squares in the city, the piazza has been used since the 14th century for tournaments, festivals and public spectacles, and the traditional football game celebrating St John's Day (24th June; *see p. 350*) has been held here for many centuries. One side of the piazza is lined with houses whose projecting upper storeys rest on brackets; these are known as *sporti* and were a familiar architectural feature of the medieval city (they were replaced in the 15th and 16th centuries by stone supports). One of the houses with *sporti* is **Palazzo dell'Antella**, built by Giulio Parigi, which has a polychrome facade, supposed to have been painted in just three weeks in 1619 by Giovanni da San Giovanni, Passignano, Matteo Rosselli, Ottavio Vannini and others. It includes a copy of Caravaggio's painting of the *Sleeping Cupid* (now in Palazzo Pitti; *see p. 238*), which had aroused much interest when it had arrived in Florence just ten years previously. Some of the simpler houses opposite have pretty loggias on the top floor. The handsome palace in the centre of the end of the square facing the church is **Palazzo Cocchi** (Serristori). It is thought to have been built above a 14th-century house around 1470–80 by Giuliano da Sangallo. The huge **statue of Dante**, beside the church, is by Enrico Pazzi (1865): it was erected with great pomp and ceremony in the centre of the piazza on the sixth centenary of the poet's birth, but after the Arno flood in 1966 it was moved to its present position (in 1972).

THE CHURCH OF SANTA CROCE

Open 9.30–5.30, Sun 1–5.30. Entrance fee includes the Pazzi Chapel and Museo dell'Opera di Santa Croce. Admission through the north door beneath a 14th-century arcade. Since it is easily reached by tour groups from their buses on the Viali, the church is usually unpleasantly crowded. The exterior of the Gothic apse can be seen at Via San Giuseppe 5. For information, and to book a visit to see the restored frescoes in the sanctuary, go to www.santacroceopera.it.

Santa Croce is the Franciscan church of Florence. It was rebuilt in 1294 and it is generally supposed that Arnolfo di Cambio was involved in the design, although there are no documents to prove this. The nave was still unfinished in 1375 and it was not consecrated until 1442. The church contains very fine sculptures, since for 500 years it has been the custom to erect monuments to notable citizens here; it is the burial place of the great artists Lorenzo Ghiberti and Michelangelo, the statesman Machiavelli and the scientist Galileo. But the church is above all famous for its frescoes by Giotto and his school in the chapels at the east end.

The campanile was added in 1842 by Gaetano Baccani. The bare stone front was covered with its neo-Gothic marble façade in 1857–63 by Niccolò Matas, and although its overall design is lacking in style, it is still a *tour de force* of local craftsmanship. The lunette of the *Triumph of the Cross* above the main door is by Giovanni Dupré. The cost of building the façade was paid for by an English benefactor, Francis Sloane.

Interior of Santa Croce

The huge wide interior has an open timber roof. The vista is closed by the polygonal sanctuary and the 14th-century stained glass in the east windows (the stained glass in the rose window at the top of the east wall was installed in 2009: it has the Franciscan symbol of the arm of Christ holding that of St Francis surrounded by a border of the red lilies of Florence). The Gothic church was rearranged by Vasari in 1560 when the choir and rood screen were demolished and the side altars added, designed by Francesco da Sangallo. The **pulpit** is usually considered the masterpiece of Benedetto da Maiano (1472–76). The beautifully composed work is decorated with delicately carved *Scenes from the Life of St Francis* and five *Virtues*.

GIOTTO'S FRESCOES IN SANTA CROCE

Giotto di Bondone (1266/7–1337) was born in the Mugello just north of Florence. A pupil of Cimabue and friend of Dante, his painting had a new monumentality and sense of volume which had never been achieved in medieval painting. His remarkable figures are given an intensely human significance, which the art historian Bernard Berenson defined as 'tactile values'. Giotto carried out his most famous frescoes in the Cappella degli Scrovegni in Padua in 1303–05 (the only cycle of his which survives intact). In Florence, he was appointed *capomaestro* of the Duomo works and was the architect of the Campanile (1334). Paintings by him which are still in Florence can be seen at the Uffizi and Museo Horne, and in the churches of Santa Maria Novella, Ognissanti and San Felice there are painted Crucifixes by his hand.

However, it is in the Peruzzi and Bardi chapels in Santa Croce (*described below*) that his greatest Florentine works survive. These frescoes were commissioned by the Peruzzi and Bardi, two of the richest merchant families in the city, and had a fundamental influence on Florentine painting. The Giottesque school continued to flourish in the city throughout the 14th century. Later Michelangelo came here to study the frescoes, and some of the drawings he made of them survive. When they were rediscovered in 1841–52, the lower scenes in the Bardi Chapel had been irreparably damaged by funerary monuments. They were restored by Gaetano Bianchi and others and the missing parts skilfully repainted, but in another restoration in 1957–61 the controversial decision was taken to remove the repainting so that the unsightly plasterwork now disturbs the overall effect of the scenes. (Bianchi's 'integrations' were preserved and can still be seen in a room, now used as a shop, near the sacristy).

The Peruzzi and Bardi chapels

(1) Peruzzi Chapel: The mural paintings (not true frescoes) by Giotto are damaged and in extremely poor condition. They were painted in the artist's maturity, probably after his return to Florence from Padua around 1334–37. The architectural settings contain references to Classical antiquity. In the archi- volt, there are eight heads of prophets; in the vault, symbols of the Evangelists; on the right wall, scenes from the life of St John the Evangelist (*Vision at Patmos, Raising of Drusiana, Ascent into Heaven*); and on the left wall, scenes from the life of St John the Baptist (*Zacharias and the Angel, Birth of St John, Herod's Feast*). A drawing by Michelangelo survives (now in the Louvre) of the two male figures on the left in the *Ascent*. The altarpiece of the *Madonna and Saints* is by Giotto's pupil Taddeo Gaddi.

(2) Bardi Chapel: The frescoes by Giotto were certainly designed by him, although it is possible that some parts were executed by his pupils. They are now usually dated between 1317 and 1319 and illustrate scenes from the life of St Francis. Giotto received commissions for other Franciscan fresco cycles in Rimini and Padua, both now lost, but his most famous works on this subject are in the upper church of San Francesco in Assisi. On the entrance arch is *St Francis Receiving the Stigmata*; in the vault, *Poverty*, *Chastity*, *Obedience* and the *Triumph of St Francis*. On the end wall are Franciscan saints, including St Catherine. Left wall: (lunette) *St Francis Stripping off his Garments*; (middle register) *St Francis Appearing to St Anthony at Arles*; and (lowest register) the *Death of St Francis*. Right wall: (lunette) *St Francis Giving the Rule of the Order*; (middle register) *St Francis Being Tried by Fire Before the Sultan* (a particularly fine work); and (lowest register) *St Francis Appearing to Brother Augustine and Bishop Guido of Assisi*. On the altar is a panel painting of the saint with 20 scenes from his life by a Florentine artist of the 13th century, now generally attributed to Coppo di Marcovaldo, the most important artist then at work in the city.

Other Giottesque works in Santa Croce

A group of Giotto's followers also carried out remarkable fresco cycles in Santa Croce, which is the best place in Florence to examine their work. Three examples appear below. The frescoes by Giovanni da Milano in the Rinuccini Chapel (30) are described on p. 201.

(3) Baroncelli Chapel: This chapel has frescoes of the life of the Virgin by **Taddeo Gaddi**, who worked with Giotto for many years and was his most faithful pupil. These are considered among his best works, executed in 1332–38, and reveal his talent as an innovator within the Giottesque school (they include one of the earliest known night scenes in fresco painting). On either side of the entrance arch are prophets and the tomb (right) of a member of the Baroncelli family (1327) with a *Madonna and Child* in the lunette, also by Gaddi. The altarpiece of the *Coronation of the Virgin* (restored) is by Giotto, perhaps with the intervention of his workshop (including possibly Taddeo). Taddeo also designed the stained glass in this chapel. His skill as a fresco painter can also be seen in the refectory (*see p. 204*). There are also important panel paintings by him in Santa Felicita and at San Martino a Mensola, and he may even have been responsible for the design of Ponte Vecchio.

On the back wall is a large 15th-century fresco of the *Madonna of the Girdle* by Bastiano Mainardi and a statue of the *Madonna and Child*, an austere work by Vincenzo Danti (c. 1568), showing the influence of Michelangelo.

(4) Castellani Chapel: Taddeo's son **Agnolo Gaddi** produced the frescoes

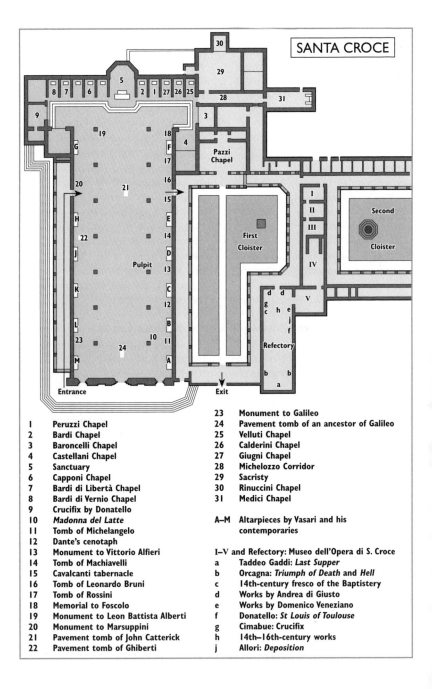

		23	Monument to Galileo
1	Peruzzi Chapel	24	Pavement tomb of an ancestor of Galileo
2	Bardi Chapel	25	Velluti Chapel
3	Baroncelli Chapel	26	Calderini Chapel
4	Castellani Chapel	27	Giugni Chapel
5	Sanctuary	28	Michelozzo Corridor
6	Capponi Chapel	29	Sacristy
7	Bardi di Libertà Chapel	30	Rinuccini Chapel
8	Bardi di Vernio Chapel	31	Medici Chapel
9	Crucifix by Donatello		
10	*Madonna del Latte*	A–M	Altarpieces by Vasari and his
11	Tomb of Michelangelo		contemporaries
12	Dante's cenotaph		
13	Monument to Vittorio Alfieri	I–V and Refectory: Museo dell'Opera di S. Croce
14	Tomb of Machiavelli	a	Taddeo Gaddi: *Last Supper*
15	Cavalcanti tabernacle	b	Orcagna: *Triumph of Death* and *Hell*
16	Tomb of Leonardo Bruni	c	14th-century fresco of the Baptistery
17	Tomb of Rossini	d	Works by Andrea di Giusto
18	Memorial to Foscolo	e	Works by Domenico Veneziano
19	Monument to Leon Battista Alberti	f	Donatello: *St Louis of Toulouse*
20	Monument to Marsuppini	g	Cimabue: Crucifix
21	Pavement tomb of John Catterick	h	14th–16th-century works
22	Pavement tomb of Ghiberti	j	Allori: *Deposition*

here. They depict (right) the stories of Sts Nicholas of Bari and John the Baptist, and (left) Sts Anthony Abbot and John the Evangelist. In around 1380, Agnolo received the more important commission to decorate the sanctuary. Like his father, Agnolo was also known as a designer of stained glass and he was responsible for the fine lancet windows at the east end (he also designed some of the stained glass for the Duomo). He was apparently also a sculptor, since some of the decoration on the Loggia della Signoria is attributed to him.

The painted gold-ground Crucifix is by Niccolò di Pietro Gerini. The 19th-century memorial, with two mourning 'angelic' children, to Louisa, Countess of Albany, who married Charles Stuart the Young Pretender (*see p. 342*) and later Vittorio Alfieri, is by Emilio Santarelli.

(5) Sanctuary and high altar: The polygonal vaulted space is entirely covered with **Agnolo Gaddi's frescoes** of Christ, the Evangelists, St Francis and the

Legend of the Cross. *NB: Their restoration was completed in 2011 but the scaffolding is expected to stay in place for some twelve months from the time of writing so that they can be viewed close up on guided visits (by previous appointment).*

Above the altar is a large polyptych, made up from panels by various hands in 1869 and given its neo-Gothic frame (probably designed by Niccolò Matas). Art historians now seem agreed that the most important (and original) sections, all from the late 14th century, are the central *Madonna and Saints* (by Niccolò di Pietro Gerini and Lorenzo di Niccolò), the four seated *Fathers of the Church* (by Giovanni del Biondo) and the central panel of the predella, which is a very fine work by Lorenzo Monaco. Above hangs a beautiful Crucifix by the Master of Figline (first half of the 14th century). The *Assumption of the Virgin*, frescoed above the chapel to the left of the sanctuary, is also attributed to this unknown master.

North transept chapels

The chapels in this part of the church are reserved for prayer and may thus not be visited by tourists. However, because many of them contain important works, including frescoes by followers of Giotto, they are described here.

(6) Capponi Chapel: Sculptures including a *Pietà* by the Florentine sculptor Libero Andreotti (1926) and two large reliefs by him, his most important completed public works.

(7) Bardi di Libertà Chapel: Another Giottesque painter was **Bernardo Daddi**, known for his charming panel paintings, many of which can be seen in the galleries and churches of Florence.

He decorated this chapel with frescoes of the lives of St Stephen and St Lawrence.

(8) Bardi di Vernio Chapel: Perhaps the most original of all the followers of Giotto was **Maso di Banco**, whose colourful frescoes of the life of St Sylvester and the emperor Constantine were carried out after 1367. It seems he also worked for the Opera del Duomo as a sculptor but he remains a rather mysterious figure and very few works are attributed to him with certainty. We know he worked in Giotto's studio and he clearly learnt from his master the way to imbue his figures with magisterial solemnity. His art had a great influence on painters working in the early 14th century in Florence.

(9) Donatello's Crucifix: This famous work is in is one of four chapels in the church patronised by the Bardi family.

It is a powerful early work by the great sculptor, dating from around 1412–15. Here perhaps for the first time Christ is represented with strong features and, as Donatello's friend Brunelleschi complained, a 'peasant's' body (*for the full story, as recounted by Vasari, see p. 186*). It is far removed from the spirit of earlier Tuscan Crucifixes with their stylised forms. Made of pear wood, it has moveable arms (so that it could be used in a Deposition scene).

The nave: tombs

(10) *Madonna del Latte*: A relief by Antonio Rossellino (1478) above the tomb of Francesco Nori, who was killed in the Pazzi Conspiracy (*see p. 203*).

(11) Tomb of Michelangelo: This rather disappointing monument was designed by Giorgio Vasari, who knew the great artist well and who described his life in his famous *Vite* (Michelangelo being the only living and fully active artist included in that book). The paintings and sculptures, none of them of particular distinction, are the work of artists of the Michelangelesque school (Battista Lorenzi, Valerio Cioli, Giovanni dell'Opera and Giovanni Battista Naldini). Michelangelo died in 1564 in Rome, where he had lived for the last 30 years of his life. Nevertheless, he always considered himself a Florentine, and his heir and nephew, Lionardo, saw to it that his body was returned to Florence for an elaborate funeral service in San Lorenzo before his burial here.

(12) Dante's cenotaph: A Neoclassical work by Stefano Ricci (1829). Dante,

exiled in 1302 as an opponent of the Guelph faction in the government, never returned to his native city (*see p. 77*). He died and was buried in Ravenna in 1321.

(13) Monument to Vittorio Alfieri: A very fine work by Canova. The central theme in the works of this tragic poet (1749–1803) is that of the liberty of the individual in opposition to tyranny, and in many ways he anticipated the spirit of Romanticism. After 1787 he lived in Florence with the Countess of Albany (*see p. 283*), and when he died here she commissioned Canova to erect this monument to him, in which the female figure of Italy is shown weeping at his tomb.

(14) Tomb of Machiavelli: The unusual monument to the great statesman, with a female figure representing an allegory of politics, is by Innocenzo Spinazzi (1787). It is the best work of this refined sculptor, showing a departure from Rococo forms in favour of Neoclassical elements.

Donatello's beautiful *Annunciation* on the Cavalcanti Tabernacle (c. 1440).

(15) Cavalcanti Tabernacle: This unusual monument has a beautiful high relief of the *Annunciation* in gilded limestone by Donatello. It was commissioned by Niccolò Cavalcanti for his chapel, which used to be beside the choir screen (its present unhappy position is not its original one). There is a remarkable spiritual bond between the figures of Mary and the Angel Gabriel, which makes this one of Donatello's most moving works. The architecture of the tabernacle and the background are intriguing and show the influence of Leon Battista Alberti. The six terracotta putti on top, who are playing with the garland, are delightful works, also by Donatello. As Vasari says, they look as if they are holding on tight to each other so that they don't tumble to the ground: their spirit is in deliberate contrast to the dramatic scene below.

(16) Tomb of Leonardo Bruni: By Bernardo Rossellino (c. 1446–47), this is one of the most harmonious and influential sepulchral monuments of the Renaissance. The architectural setting takes its inspiration from Brunelleschi. Bruni, who died in 1444, was an eminent Florentine humanist and a Greek scholar who translated Aristotle and Plato into Latin. Also an historian, he wrote an extremely important history 'in praise of the City of Florence', and he was the biographer of both Petrarch and Dante. He was papal secretary in 1405–15 and then Chancellor of the Republic in 1427, and was greatly admired by his contemporaries for his diplomatic ability and skill in public speaking. He was given an official public funeral in this church and on his tomb here he is shown crowned with a laurel wreath in a serene effigy. The touching epitaph was composed by Carlo Marsuppini, his successor as Chancellor, who is buried opposite (*see no. 20 overleaf*). In translation, the epitaph reads: 'Since Leonardo departed this life, history is in mourning and eloquence is dumb, and it is said that the Muses, Greek and Latin alike, cannot restrain their tears'.

(17) Tomb of Rossini: This memorial to the composer (1792–1868), by Giuseppe Cassioli, is a sad imitation of the Bruni tomb, and placed too close to it.

(18) Memorial to Foscolo: The sepulchral statue of Ugo Foscolo is by the Florentine sculptor Antonio Berti (1937). Foscolo (1778–1827), a well-known Italian poet, whose most famous poem is *I Sepolcri*, died in London in 1814; he was re-interred here in 1871.

(19) Monument to Leon Battista Alberti by Lorenzo Bartolini. Alberti died in Rome and was buried in Sant'Agostino but his tomb was lost during a restructuring of the church. This disappointing monument, set up on the nave pillar at the expense of a descendant in 1850, was left unfinished by Bartolini.

(20) Monument to Carlo Marsuppini: Marsuppini was a humanist scholar and Chancellor of the Republic (d. 1453). The monument is by Desiderio da Settignano, inspired by the Bruni monument opposite, and incorporates some exquisite carving. The fine classical sarcophagus may be the work of Verrocchio.

(21) Pavement tomb of John Catterick: Catterick was one of six English prelates present at the Council of Constance in 1417. He afterwards joined Pope Martin V's retinue as it travelled back towards Rome. When they arrived in Florence the pope appointed Catterick Bishop of Exeter, but he never took over his diocese as he died here just a month later. The worn tomb shows the bishop in a Gothic niche holding his crozier. There is a pretty border of stylised flowers in black, yellow and red marble inlay.

(22) Pavement tomb of Ghiberti: A handsome large tomb-slab with niello decoration and the emblem of an eagle within a wreath marks the burial place of the famous sculptor Lorenzo Ghiberti and his son Vittorio, also a sculptor.

(23) Monument to Galileo: The great scientist (1564–1642) spent the latter part of his life in Florence (*see p. 133*). The monument was set in up in 1737, to a design by Giovanni Battista Foggini (who carved the bust), when Galileo's remains were finally allowed a Christian burial inside the main church (his corpse was first interred in the little sacristy off the Medici Chapel; *see no. 31*). The statue of *Geometry* (on the right) is by Girolamo Ticciati, and that of *Astronomy* by Foggini's son Vincenzo. It is thought that Galileo's daughter Suor Maria Celeste, who died eight years before her father (*see p. 322*) is also buried here. Galileo's favourite pupil, the illustrious mathematician Vincenzo Viviani (1622–1703), left funds in his will towards this monument and is buried beside his master.

(24) Pavement tomb, with a relief of the scientist's ancestor and namesake Galileo Galilei, a well-known physician in 15th-century Florence.

The nave: painted altarpieces

The side altars were installed after 1560 and the altarpieces were painted by Vasari and his most important Florentine contemporaries.

South aisle: (A) Santi di Tito, *Crucifixion*; (B) Giorgio Vasari, *Way to Calvary*; (C) Jacopo Coppi del Meglio, *Ecce Homo*; (D) Alessandro Fei, *Flagellation*; (E) Andrea del Minga, *Agony in the Garden*;

(F) Cigoli and Giovanni Bilivert, *Entry of Christ into Jerusalem*.

North aisle: (G) Vasari, *Pentecost*; (H) Jan van der Straet, *Ascension*; (J) Vasari,

Incredulity of St Thomas; (K) Santi di Tito, *Supper at Emmaus*; (L) Santi di Tito, *Resurrection*; (M) Giovanni Battista Naldini, *Deposition*. Beside the fifth altar is a *Pietà* by Bronzino, painted for the tomb of Giovanni Battista della Fonte in 1569, one of the artist's last works.

South transept and sacristy

(25) Velluti Chapel: Here are some of the earliest frescoes in the church, damaged works by a follower of Cimabue (possibly Jacopo del Casentino, first half of the 14th century), illustrating the life of St Michael Archangel. The polyptych on the altar by Giovanni del Biondo dates from the latter part of the same century.

(26) Calderini Chapel: Designed by Gherardo Silvani, this preserves its decorations intact from the first decades of the 17th century, with a painted vault by Giovanni da San Giovanni and an altarpiece by Giovanni Bilivert. The Blessed Umiliana de' Cerchi (d. 1246) is buried here. Her remarkable silver reliquary bust, made in 1370–80, is displayed above her tomb.

(27) Giugni Chapel: Contains the tomb of Charlotte Bonaparte (d. 1839) by Lorenzo Bartolini. She was the daughter of Napoleon's brother Joseph, who became King of Naples in 1806 and King of Spain in 1808.

(28) Michelozzo Corridor: This passage, by Cosimo il Vecchio's favourite architect, contains a monument to Lorenzo Bartolini (d. 1850), the most important Italian sculptor of the early 19th century. He carved a number of sepulchral monuments in this church (*see 19 and 27*) and is commemorated here with a monument by his pupil Pasquale Romanelli.

(29) Sacristy: One wall has late 14th-century frescoes by Spinello Aretino and Niccolò di Pietro Gerini. Antiphonals are displayed in fine inlaid cupboards.

(30) Rinuccini Chapel: This little chapel, full of light, has survived intact from the late 14th century, protected by its Gothic grille bearing the name of the Rinuccini and the date 1371, and with the polyptych commissioned from Giovanni del Biondo still on the altar. It is entirely covered with scenes from the lives of the Virgin and St Mary Magdalene (1365) by Giovanni da Milano, a Lombard artist who worked for part of his life in Florence and was one of the best and most sophisticated followers of Giotto, although his output was limited (this is the only pictorial cycle known by him). Giovanni also frescoed the four busts of prophets on the vault and the remarkable tondo of the *Pantocrator* (painted on wood) in the key of the vault. His attention to detail is typical of artists who also produced illuminated manuscripts.

(31) Medici Chapel: This pleasant chapel by Michelozzo (1434), with contemporary paintings, contains an enamelled terracotta altarpiece of the *Madonna and Child with Angels* by Andrea della Robbia (c. 1480; the saints were probably added by an assistant). The door on the left of the altar gives access to the sacristy where Galileo was first buried.

The cloisters

Open at the same time and with the same ticket as the church. Entrance from inside the church (marked with an arrow on the plan on p. 196).

The **first cloister** dates from the 14th century. Beneath the arcade, along the bare Gothic flank of the church, is a gallery with a fine series of 19th-century monuments (including works by Aristodemo Costoli and Ulisse Cambi) from the Chiostro dei Morti (sadly demolished in 1969). On the lawn in a group of cypresses with acanthus plants is the seated *God the Father* by Baccio Bandinelli, made for the choir of the Duomo and now serving as a war memorial.

The **second cloister**, reached through a doorway by Michelozzo, is a beautiful work by Brunelleschi, finished in 1453 after his death. It is one of the most peaceful spots in the city, always full of birdsong.

The Pazzi Chapel

The Pazzi Chapel (Cappella dei Pazzi) is one of the most famous works by Brunelleschi. It was commissioned as a chapter house by Andrea de' Pazzi in 1429 or 1430. Most of the work was carried out by Brunelleschi from 1442 until his death in 1446, but it was not finished until the 1470s.

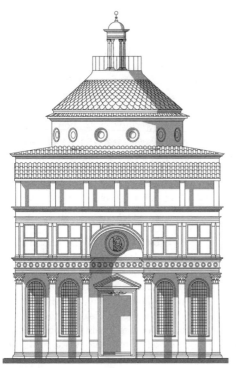

The portico may have been designed by Giuliano da Maiano. The terracotta frieze of cherubs' heads is attributed to the della Robbia workshop. In the centre of the barrel vault is a shallow cupola lined with delightful polychrome enamelled terracottas by Luca della Robbia, with a garland of fruit surrounding the Pazzi arms. Over the door is a medallion with *St Andrew*, also by Luca (c. 1461). The carved wooden door is by the Maiano brothers.

The serene interior is one of the masterpieces of the early Renaissance. Delicately carved *pietra serena* is used to articulate the architectural features against a plain white ground. The illumination in the chapel is increased by little oculi in the rib-vaulted dome. The twelve roundels in enamelled terracotta of the seated Apostles (c. 1442–52) are by Luca della Robbia. In the pendentives of the cupola are four polychrome roundels of the Evangelists, thought to have been added c. 1460. These may have been designed by Donatello and glazed by the della Robbia (although some scholars attribute them to Brunelleschi).

In the sanctuary are decorations by the school of Donatello and a stained-glass window attributed to Alesso Baldovinetti. The little dome here is painted with the constellations as they appeared over Florence on 4th July 1442 (the same cosmological position as depicted in the Old Sacristy of San Lorenzo; *see p. 143*). It was on this day that René of Anjou came to Florence from Naples, and while he was here he knighted Andrea de' Pazzi.

On the left of the chapel, nearly 6m above ground level, is a plaque marking the water level of the Arno in the flood of 1966.

THE PAZZI CONSPIRACY

In 1478 Francesco de' Pazzi came close to bringing Medici power in Florence to a bloody end. Though the Pazzi had little influence in Florentine affairs, they were an old-established banking family who had recently won business from the papacy under Sixtus IV, who distrusted Lorenzo the Magnificent and was suspicious of his alliance with Milan. Supported by Rome, Francesco and his fellow conspirators planned to assassinate Lorenzo and his brother Giuliano, at a moment when their attention was distracted by some kind of public spectacle. The event chosen was Mass in the Duomo. Giuliano's killers dealt him a mortal stab wound in the neck when he bowed his head in prayer. Lorenzo's assailants were less deft: Lorenzo parried the blow and vaulted to safety over the Communion rail, taking refuge in the north sacristy.

Soon the hue and cry was raised all over town. The conspirators were apprehended, and vengeance was terrible. All those complicit in the plot—and, in the ensuing confusion, many who were not—were hounded out and killed. The ringleaders had ropes fastened to their necks and were tossed from the high windows of Palazzo della Signoria (Palazzo Vecchio), to dangle to their deaths. At least 80 people lost their lives in the immediate aftermath and the Pazzi family was destroyed and their property seized.

The famous plot is considered the most dangerous moment the Medici faced during the whole of the 15th century. It came at a time when their banking fortunes were declining and Lorenzo was in open conflict with the papacy. But the failure to kill Lorenzo, and the lack of popular support for the Pazzi, resulted instead in a strengthening of the Medici position, and from then on the Florentines felt that Lorenzo's call for a personal armed guard to protect him was legitimate.

The most famous account of the conspiracy was written immediately after the event by Poliziano, who had been an eye-witness in the Duomo. An excellent recent book, *April Blood* by Lauro Martines, was published in 2003.

Museo dell'Opera di Santa Croce

Admission from the church and with the same ticket. The most interesting room is the refectory.

Rooms I–V: In Room I there is a painting of *St Louis of Toulouse with St Agatha* by Jacopo da Empoli and in Room II the reconstructed tomb of Gastone della Torre (1318/19) by Tino di Camaino. Room III has three very unusual large sketches which were detached from the walls of the Pazzi Chapel during restoration work in 1966: the colossal *Head of St John the Baptist* and an architectural study have been attributed by some scholars to Donatello; the other colossal head (with a halo) is attributed to Desiderio da Settignano. The striking *Assumption of the Virgin* was painted by Giuseppe Bezzuoli in 1849. In the corridor is a delightful fresco from the 15th-century tomb of a cardinal. Room IV, once a chapel, contains traces of late 13th-century painted decorations. Exhibited here are a painted 14th-century Crucifix by Lippo di Benivieni and enamelled terracottas by Andrea della Robbia and his workshop. Room V has stained-glass fragments (some of which are attributed to Giotto), a charming detached late 14th-century fresco showing St Anne teaching the young Madonna to sew, and a *Trinity and Saints* by Neri di Bicci.

Refectory: This splendid Gothic hall is decorated on the end wall with a huge fresco by Taddeo Gaddi of the *Last Supper* **(a)** below the Tree of the Cross and four scenes showing *St Louis of Toulouse*, *St Francis*, *St Benedict* and *Mary Magdalene Anointing the Feet of Christ in the House of Simon the Pharisee*.

On the side walls **(b)** there are fragments of a large fresco by Orcagna showing the *Triumph of Death* and *Hell*, which used to decorate the nave of the church before Vasari's side altars were set up. A fascinating 14th-century fresco **(c)**, attributed to Giovanni del Biondo, has one of the earliest views of the city (with the Baptistery and Duomo). Two beautiful works by Andrea di Giusto **(d)** depict *Christ Carrying the Cross* and the *Crucifixion*. The *St John the Baptist* and *St Francis* **(e)** are by Domenico Veneziano.

In a reconstructed tabernacle is Donatello's colossal gilded bronze **St Louis of Toulouse (f)**, commissioned by the Parte Guelfa for a niche in Orsanmichele (replaced there by the *Incredulity of St Thomas* by Verrocchio).

Cimabue's great **Crucifix (g)** was the most important work of art destroyed in the 1966 Arno flood: a skilled restoration has recuperated the little original paint that survived. Exhibited in the centre of the room **(h)** are 14th–15th-century works including a triptych by Nardo di Cione, *St John Gualbert and Stories from his Life* by Giovanni del Biondo, and *St James the Greater* by Lorenzo Monaco. The two huge 16th-century paintings hung here by Francesco Salviati (*Deposition*) and Bronzino (*Descent into Limbo*) have superb frames. Bronzino's work (over 4m by nearly 3m) includes his self-portrait and those of his contemporaries: the painter, dressed in blue with a gold sash, is in the upper left-hand part of the painting, and Bachiacca is looking over his shoulder. The head of Bronzino's master Pontormo appears in the background. At the top of the painting are numerous devilish monsters. The elaborate frame, probably designed by Bronzino himself and carved in Battista del Tasso's workshop, is decorated with cartouches and masks.

On the walls **(j)** there is a *Deposition* (1560) by Alessandro Allori and a *Trinity* by Cigoli.

Beneath the colonnade beside the exit (from the first cloister) is a very modest **memorial to Florence Nightingale**, named after the city where she was born in 1820. She is famous for her devotion to reform in medical care and the nursing profession. Florence became immediately popular as a girl's Christian name.

MUSEO HORNE

Map 7, 3. Entrance at Via de' Benci 6. open 9–1 except Sun and holidays; T: 055 244661. The works (unlabelled) are numbered to correspond to a catalogue lent to visitors. Excellent thematic tours for children can also be booked.

Palazzo Corsi is an attractive small palace (1495–1502), now generally attributed to Cronaca. The English art historian and architect Herbert Percy Horne (1864–1916) purchased it as his residence in 1911 and carefully restored every detail to its austere late 15th-century appearance. On his death he presented it to the Italian nation, along with his collection of 14th–16th-century paintings, sculpture and decorative arts (notably furniture and majolica). Horne's taste favoured severe, undecorated designs and the interior reflects his idea of the pure Renaissance style produced by Florentine artisans. Together with Roger Fry and Berenson he founded *The Burlington Magazine* in 1903 (Horne had a special interest in typography and in fact designed a typeface: Montallegro). His book on Botticelli is today recognised as a pioneering scholarly work: it was published in 1908 in just 240 copies but had an enormous influence.

Ground floor: The lovely courtyard has interesting capitals. Two rooms on the ground floor are used to display a selection of the 929 very fine drawings by Renaissance and 16th- and early 17th-century artists, which Horne collected from 1890. A ramp (originally for beasts of burden) leads down to the cellars where lectures are held.

First floor: Room I has works by Correggio, Dosso Dossi (*Allegory of Music*, c. 1530), Pietro Lorenzetti, Bernardo Daddi and Piero di Cosimo. In the wall case by the window is a fascinating tiny work by Masaccio: *Scenes from the Legend of St Julian*. On the left the saint is shown returning from the hunt with his dog (superbly drawn from behind) and being told by the devil (in the guise of a man) that his wife is in bed with a lover (in fact the bed is occupied by Julian's long-lost parents); the central scene shows the couple in bed; and the scene on the right shows Julian with his wife in despair after Julian has unwittingly killed his parents in rage. These two figures anticipate Masaccio's famous portrayal of Adam and Eve expelled from Paradise in the Brancacci Chapel (*illustrated on p.*

276). Unfortunately this exquisite work, which was once part of a triptych painted together with Masolino for the church of Santa Maria Maggiore, has been damaged by scratches (perhaps made by over-devout worshippers) and is in very poor condition. On the table are small *bozzetti* by Ammannati, Giambologna and Giovanfrancesco Rustici. The *Deposition* (on the wall opposite the windows) is a crowded composition by Benozzo Gozzoli: it was left unfinished at his death (the colours have darkened with time).

Room II contains the most precious piece in the collection, **Giotto's St Stephen**, one of the most important paintings known by the master. The gentle face is full of expression, as only Giotto was able to portray at this time, and the quality of the paint is exceptional, with the saint's robes exquisitely decorated. Stephen was one of the first seven deacons of the Church and here he is shown with his attribute of stones (on his head), recording his famous martyrdom when he was stoned to death (he was the first Christian martyr). Horne purchased the work in London in 1904 (for a tiny sum), having recognised it as the work of this great master. His attribution is now generally accepted by art historians, some of whom believe it to have been part of a polyptych (the central panel of which is in the National Gallery of Washington). It may have been painted around the same time as Giotto's frescoes in the Peruzzi

Chapel in Santa Croce. There are three painted *cassoni* here, including the most important chest in Horne's collection: the one with two putti painted in tempera by an artist working in Verrocchio's studio, perhaps Lorenzo di Credi.

Room III has a very fine tondo of the *Holy Family* by Beccafumi, in a beautiful contemporary frame, which came from the collection of Elia Volpi (acquired after Horne's death in 1934).

Second floor: Room I contains several fine pieces of 15th-century furniture. In the centre of the room is displayed a portable diptych attributed to Simone Martini. In the wall case on the far wall there is a tiny *Pietà* (a pax) by Filippo Lippi. The small panel from a marriage chest by Filippino Lippi (*Queen Vashti leaving the Palace of Susa*) is derived from a drawing by Botticelli. Beneath a contemporary copy of Leonardo's lost fresco of the *Battle of Anghiari* in Palazzo Vecchio is a *Madonna and Saints* attributed to the Master of the Horne Triptych, a 14th-century Florentine artist named from this panel.

On the window wall of Room II is a very small painting of the *Archangel Raphael, Tobias and St Jerome* by Neri di Bicci, and on the far wall, the *Drunkenness of Noah* (in a little tondo surrounded by putti), attributed to Beccafumi. The old kitchen, also on this floor, has a collection of interesting cutlery and utensils.

VIA DE' BENCI & DISTRICT

Via de' Benci (*map 7, 1–3*) is an old thoroughfare built along the line of the medieval city walls. From the 13th century onwards the **Alberti family**, influential merchants who had acquired their wealth as papal bankers and were patrons of the church of

Santa Croce, but who were exiled in 1387 for political reasons, owned numerous properties on this street, and their coat of arms of crossed chains can be seen on many of the houses here. Their shield is visible on the exterior of the Museo Horne, for example, and on their most important palace (Via de' Benci 8), trapezoidal in plan, which still has its old courtyard (*usually visible from the entrance portico*). The great architect Leon Battista (*see p. 220*) lived here for a time. On the east side of the street (no. 20) is **Palazzo Mellini-Fossi**, one of the first of many palaces in Florence to have its façade decorated with frescoes. The delightful mythological scenes of Perseus and Andromeda date from 1575. By the beginning of the 20th century only traces of them survived, but they were beautifully restored in 1996 by the Fossi family, who still live here.

The river end of the street was widened in the 15th century to accommodate its Renaissance palaces. The large **Palazzo Bardi alle Grazie** (no. 5), with a grey and white façade in imitation of brickwork, was built around 1430, probably by Brunelleschi, and it still has a fine courtyard (although the *portone* is almost always closed). Here the famous Camerata Fiorentina di Casa Bardi introduced operatic melodrama in 1598.

A little to the west, the bend in Via dei Neri at its junction with Via Mosca follows the shape of the Roman river port. Other traces of the Roman city can be seen in **Piazza Peruzzi**, a short way to the north (by an old-fashioned shop which sells fine ceramics, entered beneath an old arch; *map 7, 1*), where the houses on the right (no. 7 and no. 12 red) incorporate two arches of the Roman amphitheatre (2nd–3rd century AD) and you can also see other Roman fragments on the upper storeys. The (reconstructed) Peruzzi palace (with its façade on Borgo dei Greci) survives here amongst the other medieval buildings, many of which still have their *stemma* of six pears carved in *pietra forte*. Together with the Bardi, the Peruzzi had the most important banking company in Florence by the end of the 13th century but were declared insolvent by 1343. Via dei Bentaccordi, which leads out of Piazza Peruzzi, also quite clearly follows the shape of the amphitheatre, which is estimated to have held about 20,000 spectators.

The church of San Remigio

This is an ancient church (*map 7, 1; open 8.30–12 & 3–6.30*) founded in the 11th century, with an exterior built in *pietra forte*. The interior, a fine Gothic hall, contains fresco fragments by the school of Giotto and worn roundels of saints in the vaults (14th century). The beautiful panel painting of the *Madonna and Child* in the chapel to the right of the sanctuary (c. 1290) has in the past been attributed to both Duccio and Cimabue, but is now usually considered to be by a follower of Cimabue known from this work as the Master of San Remigio. The portrayal of the Christ Child, shown reaching up to hug his mother, is particularly delightful. In the chapel to the left of the sanctuary is a fine and unusual 16th-century painting of the *Immaculate Conception* by Empoli. At the beginning of the south aisle there is a 19th-century painting of the church's patron saint, Remigius, baptising Clovis, King of the Franks. In a room below the campanile (*admission on request*) there are monochrome frescoes with hunting scenes and in the refectory of the former convent upstairs are more very worn monochrome frescoes of scenes from the Last Supper and the Passion.

San Simone and Palazzo da Cintoia

The church of **San Simone** (*map 7, 1*; now used by the Ukrainian Uniate community) was founded in 1192–93. The fine doorway is in the style of Benedetto da Rovezzano. The sombre interior is by Gherardo Silvani (1630), with a 17th-century wooden ceiling. The lovely painting of *St Peter Enthroned* (first south altar) was painted by the Master of Santa Cecilia in 1307. *Christ Showing his Wounds to St Bernard* (1623) by Jacopo Vignali hangs over the last altar on the south side. On the altar opposite, the *Ecstasy of St Francis* is the only known work in Italy by Theodoor Rombouts (born in Antwerp in 1597). At the end of the north side, there is a charming Gothic tabernacle (1363) with a 15th-century bust of a lady surrounded by enamelled terracotta decoration by the della Robbia.

Opposite is **Vivoli**, which has for long been considered the best ice-cream shop in the city (*closed Mon, sometimes in Aug, and for a period in winter*). As the plaque records, this was once a 'humble room' where the sculptor Giovanni Dupré worked, whose 'name will last as long as the world exists'.

On Via delle Stinche, named after a prison on this site since the early 14th century, is **Palazzo da Cintoia** (Salviati), one of the most interesting medieval palaces to survive in the city. It dates from the 14th century and its façade in *pietra forte* has picturesque *sporti*.

Two interesting inscriptions

In **Via Giovanni da Verrazzano** (*map 7, 1*), one of the short streets which leads out of Piazza Santa Croce, on the wall between two garages (no. 8 red and no. 6 red), is one of the most fascinating and oldest inscriptions to have survived in Florence. The Latin text makes the wild claim that in the year 1300 the Tartars (or Mongols) captured Jerusalem from the Saracens and handed it over to the Christians. The last two lines, in Italian, record that in the same year a certain Ugolino made a pilgrimage to Rome, together with his wife. Scholars still discuss its significance. At the beginning of **Via del Fico**, which joins Via da Verrazzano to Via delle Pinzochere, there is another inscription set up by the 'Signori Otto di Guardia e Balia', a Florentine judicial body who oversaw law and order in the streets from the 14th–18th centuries. This is one of many inscriptions, mostly dating from the 17th century, exhorting citizens to good behaviour. This one in particular, which bans the presence of prostitutes, records a decree promulgated on 22nd Jan 1714. The peaceful Via del Fico is one of the last streets in the city to preserve its original 'crazy' paving and one of the very few entirely free of parked cars. If you follow it to its end, Via delle Pinzochere (the name comes from the Franciscan tertiary nuns whose job it was to keep the church of Santa Croce clean) leads directly (left) to the entrance to Casa Buonarroti.

CASA BUONARROTI

Map 7, 1. Open 9.30–1.30 except Tues; T. 055 241752. Free concerts in the courtyard in summer. Entrance at Via Ghibellina 70.

This property was purchased in 1508 by Michelangelo and is now a delightful museum dedicated to the great artist. It preserves three of his sculptures and some of his drawings and *bozzetti*. The intimate atmosphere provides a fascinating glimpse into the world of the private collector. On the second floor, there is an important library (*open to scholars*) with material relating to Michelangelo.

THE BUONARROTI FAMILY

The three houses on this site which belonged to Michelangelo were left by him to his only descendant, his nephew Lionardo, who joined the houses together following a plan already drawn up by Michelangelo. His son, Michelangelo Buonarroti the Younger (1568–1646), an art collector and man of letters, made part of the house into a gallery in 1612 as a memorial to his great-uncle. His small collection of Etruscan and Roman works was continued by the archaeologist Filippo Buonarroti (1661–1733). The last member of this branch of the Buonarroti family founded the present museum in 1858 (when the bust of Michelangelo was made for the façade), and it is still run by a foundation.

First floor

In the vestibule are 16th–19th-century portraits of Michelangelo based on a prototype (c. 1535) by Jacopino del Conte (also on view). The sword is thought to have belonged to the sculptor's ancestor Buonarroto Buonarroti, Captain of the Guelph party in 1392.

Works by Michelangelo

The room to the left of the vestibule contains two fascinating small sculptures: the **Madonna of the Steps**, a marble bas-relief, was carved when he was 15 or 16 (*pictured overleaf*). The low *schiacciato* technique shows the influence of Donatello, but here Michelangelo begins to reveal not only his extraordinary talent but also his astonishing originality. The Christ Child is turned away from the viewer (an innovative pose which was to be repeated in his *Madonna and Child* in the New Sacristy in San Lorenzo), while in the background he has added a charming scene of putti playing on the stairs (and calling to others just visible behind the Madonna). He successfully confers a great sense of dignity on the heavily robed Virgin (and has taken an obvious delight in the ana-tomical detail of her feet). A work intended for private devotion, possibly part of a trip-tych, we know that it was owned by the Medici in the 17th century and returned to the Buonarroti family. The **relief of a battle scene** is also one of his earliest works, carved just before the death of Lorenzo the Magnificent in 1492, and worked on a few years later but left unfinished. It is the only early work documented by his biographers Vasari and Condivi, and it also demonstrates Michelangelo's prodigious skill. Modelled on ancient sarcophagi, it represents a mythological battle between Greeks and Centaurs.

Another room (left) contains the original wooden **scale model for the façade of San Lorenzo**, designed by Michelangelo and sent for approval to Leo X in Rome in 1516, though the project was never carried out (*see p. 141*). The colossal torso by Michelangelo, a clay and wood model for a river god, was intended for the New Sacristy in San Lorenzo. It was presented by Ammannati to the Accademia del Disegno in 1583.

In the room in front of the stairs are displayed (in rotation) five or six of the museum's precious **drawings by Michelangelo**. The room to the right of the stairs has a fascinating display of small *bozzetti* in wax, terracotta, wood and plaster, attributed to Michelangelo and his circle. In the centre, the *Two Wrestlers* in terracotta is recognised as by the hand of Michelangelo (c. 1530). The wood Crucifix and the *River God* in wax are also attributed to him. The two terracottas of a female nude and a male torso may be by him, while the terracotta *Madonna and Child* (the head is missing) is attributed to Vincenzo Danti.

Madonna of the Steps (Madonna della Scala), Michelangelo's earliest known work (c. 1490).

The 17th-century rooms

Four rooms in an enfilade were designed by Michelangelo Buonarroti the Younger as a celebration of his famous great-uncle and his family. They have survived intact and offer an intriguing glimpse into the refined life of this connoisseur and collector. The rooms were decorated from 1613–37 with paintings on the ceilings and upper part of the walls, and still contain paintings and sculptures which belonged to the great sculptor's descendant. In the main room, the **Galleria**, Michelangelo Buonarroti the Younger commissioned paintings from some of the most important Florentine artists of his day to illustrate Michelangelo's life and apotheosis. On the wall opposite the statue of the sculptor by Antonio Novelli is a copy of the cartoon of the so-called *Epiphany* by Michelangelo's pupil Ascanio Condivi. In the niches on either side are statues representing the *Active and Contemplative Life* by Domenico Pieratti.

In the **Stanza della Notte e del Di'** there is a bronze head of Michelangelo, based on a death-mask and commissioned by his nephew Lionardo Buonarroti from Daniele da Volterra (1564–66). The portrait of Michelangelo in a turban is attributed to Giuliano Bugiardini. The exquisitely painted predella with colourful scenes from the life of St Nicholas of Bari is by Giovanni di Francesco. Michelangelo the Younger had his own portrait (also exhibited here) painted by Cristofano Allori.

The **Camera degli Angeli** served as a chapel. The splendid marble bust of Michelangelo the Younger has always been considered the masterpiece of Giuliano Finelli, Bernini's most important and most talented assistant. It dates from 1630 and the sitter's personal friendship with Pope Urban VIII is recorded through the inclusion of the Barberini emblem, the bee.

The **library** was decorated with a delightful frieze of illustrious Tuscans by Cecco Bravo, with the help of Domenico Pugliani and Matteo Rosselli. The collector's most precious pieces are displayed in the wall cupboards, including Roman fragments in marble and terracotta, and (in case 410), a beautiful terracotta head of a child attributed to the school of Verrocchio or Antonio Rossellino.

In the tiny **Stanzina dell'Apollo**, an alcove, there are Roman sculptures, including a statuette of Apollo and a fragment (the right arm and hand) from a good Roman copy of Myron's most famous work, his bronze *Discobolos* (*Discus Thrower*), which only survives in marble replicas made in ancient Rome.

Works illustrating the cult of Michelangelo

Reached from the room of the *bozzetti*, there is a room with two similar paintings of the *Noli me Tangere* derived from a lost cartoon by Michelangelo, one by Bronzino, and the other by Battista Franco, who was commissioned specifically by Cosimo I to incorporate drawings, paintings and sculptures by Michelangelo in his works. Beyond the Stanza dei Paesaggi decorated with early 18th-century frescoes, is a room dedicated to the cult of Michelangelo in the 19th century, which has a marble sculpture of the young Michelangelo at work by Cesare Zocchi. Beyond a narrow corridor, a few steps lead down to a little room with a wooden model for the 'carriage' built to transport the famous *David* from Piazza della Signoria to the Accademia in 1873.

Ground floor: the Buonarroti family collections

Here is displayed the archaeological collection of Etruscan and Roman works, including two 6th-century BC stelae from Fiesole in *pietra serena*, which are among the best-preserved Etruscan carvings of this period. The two Roman statues of magistrates (1st century AD), found in Florence in 1627, were restored for Michelangelo Buonarroti the Younger by Antonio Novelli.

The next room contains paintings and sculptures based on works by Michelangelo, many by unknown 16th-century artists. The small *Crucifixion* was copied by Marcello Venusti from a drawing made by Michelangelo for his close friend Vittoria Colonna (1490–1547), a remarkable Renaissance figure and poet. The unfinished statue of *Venus and Two Cupids* is attributed to Vincenzo Danti. The next room displays a charming portrait of three young men from the Buonarroti family by Gregorio Pagani. The love scene (perhaps Cornelia and Pompey) is a 16th-century Venetian copy of a lost work by Titian. In the courtyard, there is a statue made up from a Classical head and a medieval draped toga, a little Roman relief with two goats (1st century AD), and an ancient Ionic capital used as a model by Giuliano da Sangallo in the cloister of Santa Maria Maddalena dei Pazzi (see p. 228).

SANTA TRÍNITA
& VIA TORNABUONI

PIAZZA SANTA TRÍNITA

In the centre of this little space (*map 1, 5*), more a crossroads than a true piazza, stands the **Column of Justice**, a huge granite monolith set up in 1563 to commemorate Cosimo I's victory over his opponents (including the Strozzi; *see p. 217*) at Montemurlo in 1537. It was presented to the duke in 1560 by Pius IV, who took it from the Baths of Caracalla in Rome and had it transported all the way from there—on rollers as far as Civitavecchia, and then for the rest of the journey by sea and river. The porphyry figure of *Justice*, by Tadda (1581), has a bronze cloak added subsequently. The most impressive building here is the splendid battlemented **Palazzo Spini-Feroni**, one of the best-preserved and largest private medieval palaces in the city. It was built for Geri degli Spini in 1289, possibly by Lapo Tedesco, master of Arnolfo di Cambio, and was restored in the 19th century. The palace was bought by the *Comune* in 1846 and was the seat of the town council in 1860–70. In 1938 it was purchased by Salvatore Ferragamo, the famous shoe designer, who set up his shoe manufactory here. The shop is still on the ground floor and on the second floor is the **Museo Salvatore Ferragamo**, a private museum illustrating the history of the firm (*open Mon–Fri 9–1 & 2–6; closed Aug; prior appointment advisable; T: 055 336 0456*). It contains a collection of some 10,000 shoes made out of the most diverse materials; these are beautifully exhibited in rotation every two years, taking a particular theme or period. Ferragamo (1898–1960), born into a poor family in southern Italy, emigrated to America in 1914 and opened a shoe shop in Hollywood. He returned to Italy in 1927 and became world famous as a fashion shoe designer (his clients included Greta Garbo, Audrey Hepburn and Marilyn Monroe). After his death the firm remained in the hands of the family until 2006, when it became a public company. The elegant small **Palazzo Bartolini-Salimbeni** (on Via delle Terme, with a fine façade on Piazza Santa Trínita) dates from 1520–23 and is usually considered Baccio d'Agnolo's best work. The façade has very unusual windows and attractive niches. You can usually walk in to see the lovely little courtyard which has good graffiti decoration, and a delightful loggia on the first floor. The Hôtel du Nord was opened here in 1839, and Ralph Waldo Emerson, James Russell Lowell and Herman Melville all stayed here, although only Lowell is recorded on the plaque outside.

THE CHURCH OF SANTA TRÍNITA

Map 1, 5. Open 9–12 & 4–6. The church is unusually dark (the best light is in the morning), though each chapel has a light: the switches are inconspicuously placed to the left; coin-operated light for the Sassetti Chapel.

The pronunciation of the name of the church of Santa Trínita (the Latin pronunciation, as opposed to the Italian Santa Trinità) betrays its ancient foundation. A church of the

Vallombrosan Order existed on this site at least by 1077. Probably rebuilt in 1250–60, its present Gothic form dates from the end of the 14th century and is attributed to Neri di Fioravante. The façade was added by Buontalenti in 1593–94. The relief of the Trinity is by Giovanni Caccini, who also carved the statue of *St Alexius* in the niche. The campanile (1396–97) can just be seen behind to the left.

Interior of Santa Trínita

The fine interior has the austerity characteristic of all Cistercian churches. On the entrance wall, the interior façade of the Romanesque building survives. High up on the outside arches of many of the chapels are remains of 14th–15th-century frescoes; the most interesting are those by Giovanni dal Ponte outside the choir chapels.

South aisle: In the first chapel there is a highly venerated wooden Crucifix which may date from the 14th century. The third chapel has an altarpiece by Neri di Bicci (1481) and a very ruined detached fresco by Spinello Aretino. The fourth chapel has damaged but beautiful **frescoes of the life of the Virgin by Lorenzo Monaco** (1422). These are the most important frescoes by this elegant Late Gothic painter, who was an apprentice in the workshop of Agnolo Gaddi before becoming a monk in 1390 at the convent of Santa Maria degli Angeli. He carried out some exquisite illuminations for the choirbooks there and also maintained a painting studio outside the monastery. He exercised a great influence on Fra' Angelico and is today considered a fundamental protagonist of the Late Gothic style. The scene with the *Marriage of the Virgin* is especially beautiful, with a crowd of interested onlookers, including two little children, dressed in pink, deep in conversation on the extreme right. The young bride, dressed in white, has a typical Gothic elegance familiar from other works by Lorenzo. Opposite, the scene of the *Visitation* is remarkable especially for the extraordinary

townscape full of towers. The altarpiece is also by Lorenzo. The central scene with the *Annunciation* recalls Simone Martini's famous work in the Uffizi, but here the artist has inserted the view out through the room behind to a forest of tree trunks in front of a golden sky. The predella is exquisitely painted, and the scene of the *Flight into Egypt* particularly poignant.

Sacristy (*willingly opened on request*): Formerly a Strozzi chapel; the carved portal is ascribed to Lorenzo Ghiberti. It was begun by Onofrio Strozzi and completed by his son Palla, who was known for his learning as well as his wealth. He commissioned Onofrio's beautifully carved tomb here in 1421, in the unusual form of an open arched niche. It is also assigned to Lorenzo Ghiberti. The delicately painted flowers on the inside of the arch are by Gentile da Fabriano, the great painter from the Marche who had been called to Florence the previous year by Palla and who painted his famous *Adoration of the Magi* (now in the Uffizi) for this chapel in 1423. After the revolt against Cosimo il Vecchio led by Rinaldo degli Albizi in 1434, Palla was one of 500 Florentines who were banished from Florence. He died in exile in Padua. There are also some detached frescoes (note especially the *Noli me Tangere* and *Pietà*), and a grandfather clock in full working order.

Sassetti Chapel: This famous chapel, at the east end, is one of the best preserved Renaissance chapels in all Florence. Its delightful **frescoes of the life of St Francis by Domenico Ghirlandaio** were commissioned in 1483 by Francesco Sassetti, a merchant, manager of the Medici bank, and typical figure of Renaissance Florence. The scene in the lunette above the altar (*St Francis Receiving the Rule of the Order from Pope Honorius*) takes place in Piazza della Signoria and those present include (in the foreground, right) Lorenzo the Magnificent with Sassetti and his son, and, to his right, Antonio Pucci. On the stairs are Poliziano with Lorenzo's sons, Piero, Giovanni and Giuliano. In the *Miracle of the Boy Brought Back to Life* (beneath) is Piazza Santa Trínita (with the Romanesque façade of the church and the old Ponte Santa Trínita). The altarpiece of 1485, also by Ghirlandaio, shows the *Adoration of the Shepherds* and the group of shepherds is clearly derived from the huge Portinari altarpiece by Hugo van der Goes (*see p. 119*), which arrived in Florence just two years earlier. Ghirlandaio included his self-portrait in the shepherd on the left of the group, who seems to be pointing both to the Child and to the garland (*ghirlanda*) on the sarcophagus in allusion to his name. On the wall are frescoed the two kneeling figures of the donors, Francesco Sassetti and Nera Corsi, his wife. Their tombs here,

with black-veined marble sarcophagi, are attributed to Giuliano da Sangallo. The decoration of the chapel includes numerous references to Classical antiquity, illustrating the influence of the new spirit of the Renaissance (the sibyl announcing the coming of Christ to Augustus on the outside arch; the four sibyls on the vault; the Roman sarcophagus used as a manger in the *Adoration of the Shepherds*; and the carved details with bucrania on the tombs).

East end: In the sanctuary there is a 15th-century classical altar bearing the triple head symbolising the Trinity (this has survived even though similar iconographical images were considered blasphemous by Pope Urban VIII and in 1628 he ordered the destruction of all of them; *see illustration on p. 332*). The triptych above, painted by Mariotto di Nardo in 1424, represents the traditional image of the Trinity and Saints. The fine figures in the vault (*David*, *Abraham*, *Noah* and *Moses*) are almost all that remains of the fresco decoration by Alesso Baldovinetti (although the bishop-saint in a niche in the north aisle has also recently been attributed to him).

The first chapel left of the altar was redecorated in 1635 and the bronze altar frontal of the *Martyrdom of St Lawrence* is by Tiziano Aspetti. In the second chapel left of the altar is the tomb of Benozzo Federighi, Bishop of Fiesole (d. 1450), by Luca della Robbia (1454–57). This was moved here in 1896 from a deconsecrated church and is only part of the original monument, which was formerly in a raised position. The beautiful marble effigy is surrounded by an exquisite frame of enamelled terracotta mosaic on a gold ground.

North side: The little north transept chapel, decorated in 1574 by Domenico Cresti, called Passignano after his birthplace, contains a reliquary of St John Gualbert (*see below*).

In the fifth chapel of the north aisle is a fine wooden statue of *Mary Magdalene* by Desiderio da Settignano, finished by Benedetto da Maiano: both were better known for their reliefs and portrait busts, and this is one of the few life-size statues they made (and a rare instance of collaboration between the two artists). The next chapel has a large fresco by Neri di Bicci of St John Gualbert enthroned with saints and the blessed from the Vallombrosan Order he founded (detached from the cloister of the former monastery; *for the story of St John Gualbert, see p. 331*). Neri rarely worked in fresco so this is particularly interesting and the setting, a large circular chapel, is very unusual. High up on the outer arches are frescoes illustrating the life of St John Gualbert by Neri and his father Bicci di Lorenzo, and on the right wall of the chapel there is a charming painted *Annunciation* by Neri. This family of three generations of painters called Lorenzo, Bicci and Neri, are each confusingly known by their father's name—hence Lorenzo di Bicci (Lorenzo son of Bicci), Bicci di Lorenzo and Neri di Bicci. They were prolific artists, producing numerous altarpieces and frescoes for churches all over Tuscany from the late 14th century until the end of the 15th: their competent, engaging works seem little affected by

St Mary Magdalene, detail of the wood sculpture by Desiderio da Settignano, completed by Benedetto da Maiano (1455–65).

the major new developments that took place in art during the Renaissance. Neri di Bicci's account book and diary, which he kept between 1453 and 1475, survives at the Biblioteca Marucelliana: its 189 pages give us a fascinating glimpse of life in the city and the activity of a typical busy artist's *bottega*.

The next chapel has the tomb of Giuliano Davanzati (1444, attributed to Bernardo Rossellino), adapted from an early Christian sarcophagus with a relief of the *Good Shepherd*. The altarpiece of the *Coronation of the Virgin* with its predella is a lovely work by Bicci di Lorenzo. In the second chapel are good works by Ridolfo del Ghirlandaio, one of Domenico's nine children. The vault of the first chapel has early 17th-century works by Bernardino Poccetti, Giovanni Caccini and Empoli.

VIA TORNABUONI

Via Tornabuoni (*map 1, 5–3*), which runs from Piazza Santa Trínita away from the river, was once the most elegant street in Florence. It is still lined with shops and numerous palaces, including Palazzo Strozzi, a Renaissance masterpiece. The celebrated Palazzo Rucellai is close by.

The shops

In the 19th century and for much of the 20th, Via Tornabuoni was a stylish commercial thoroughfare. In the last few decades, however, its historic shops and cafés have been replaced by the boutiques of international fashion houses—but even some of these are now in financial straits and closing down. Here until 1986, for example, was the famous Café Doney, frequently mentioned in descriptions of the city and a meeting place for foreigners in Florence, including Edmond and Jules de Goncourt, 'Ouida', D.H. Lawrence, Norman Douglas and the Sitwells. Another café, Giacosa's, founded here in 1815, closed down in 2001. In the same year the 'English and American Chemists' which had opened in the street in 1843 (at no. 97) and had been replaced by a perfumery in 1974, also disappeared, although the international shoe shop which took over its premises was obliged to preserve its splendid old wooden showcases and furnishings (and its shop signs). The Florentine firm of Gucci, once renowned for its leather goods and shoes, also had its shop here for many years, but the family was bought out by a large fashion group in 1992, retaining only its name. The only old shop to survive today is Procacci, which has kept its Art Nouveau décor: it is a tiny luxury-quality grocer's once famous for its truffle sandwiches.

The palaces

The appearance of the medieval town, with its houses and towers clustered closely together, was radically changed when the wealthy Florentines of the Renaissance began to build their private residences in the early 15th century. Palazzo Medici (*see p. 136*) set an example for all later palaces, which were usually of three storeys, with imposing façades or portals marking their entrances, and a wide bench was often provided around the exterior. Handsome courtyards became a feature of the interiors, and there were sometimes gardens attached. The grand exteriors often had large blocks of roughhewn *pietra forte*, the size of which (and levels of finish) might vary from floor to floor, or, more simply, the surface would be covered with *intonaco* so that the stone decoration around the windows would appear more pronounced against the flat plasterwork. In the case of Alberti's famous Palazzo Rucellai, the building material used is disguised by patterns, in a unique design on a flat surface.

PALAZZO STROZZI

Map 1, 3. The courtyard, provided with benches, is open 9am–8pm (Thur 9am–11pm), and the piano nobile (when exhibitions are in progress) at the same times. www.palazzostrozzi.org.

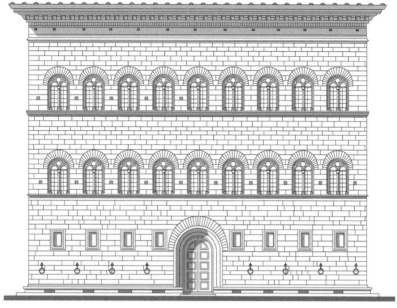

PALAZZO STROZZI

By far the most impressive palace on Via Tornabuoni is the huge Palazzo Strozzi, the last and grandest of the magnificent Renaissance palaces in Florence. It is a typical 15th-century town mansion—half-fortress, half-palace—with all three storeys of equal emphasis, constructed with large rough blocks of *pietra forte*, though it was never completely finished. It was begun in 1489 for the wealthy banker Filippo Strozzi, who spent the 1470s and 1480s buying up no fewer than 15 dwellings and shops in order to create enough room for it. Construction involved a workforce of some 100 men and the stone had to be brought from four quarries near Florence. The most complete side faces Piazza Strozzi. It is now generally thought that Benedetto da Maiano must have been mainly responsible for the design (although Strozzi himself probably took an active part) and Cronaca is known to have been involved at a certain stage: he designed the great projecting cornice, suggested by ancient Classical examples, which was left half-finished when Filippo Strozzi's heirs ran out of money. Cronaca also built the courtyard (completed in 1503). It seems that Baccio d'Agnolo was also involved in construction work after 1533. The very fine wrought-iron torch-holders and fantastic lanterns were designed by Benedetto da Maiano and executed by Caparra. The palace remained in the Strozzi family until 1937.

The palace today
The palace now houses the largest temporary exhibition space in Florence. Three ex-

hibitions a year are held on the *piano nobile* and concerts and other events are often arranged in the splendid courtyard, where there is a café and shop. All the exhibitions are geared to families, with labels also for children, and each show aims to provide incentives to visitors to seek out other places in Florence, especially those off the beaten track.

In a small room on the ground floor (next to the ticket office for exhibitions) is displayed a **wooden model of the palace**, made around 1489 by Giuliano da Sangallo. This is particularly precious as very few models of this kind, made when a private palace was being built, have survived. It is made in three pieces so that they can each be taken apart and studied on their own. The two finished sides are those which today face Via Strozzi and Piazza Strozzi.

The palace is also the seat of various institutes, including the **Gabinetto Scientifico Letterario G.P. Vieusseux**, which has an excellent lending library of works dating mostly from the 19th and 20th centuries, and covering literature, history, the arts and sciences, travel and biography (*open Mon–Fri 9–1 & 3–6; Sat 9–1*). The scientific and literary association from which the library takes its name was founded nearby in Palazzo Buondelmonti, on Via Tornabuoni, in 1819 by the Swiss scholar Gian Pietro Vieusseux. It ran a circulating library and was directed as a commercial enterprise with reading rooms and conversation rooms (where chess and other board games could be played) as well as a café. When Colville, the hero of W.D. Howells's *Indian Summer* (1886) visits it to try to find a short history of Florence he remarks that it is 'a place where sooner or later you meet everyone you know among the foreign residents at Florence'. It has been housed in Palazzo Strozzi since 1940, along with the Istituto Nazionale di Studi sul Rinascimento (National Institute of Renaissance Studies). In 2006 the Istituto Italiano di Scienze Umane (Human Sciences Institute, for post-doctoral students) was opened on the top floor, with Umbero Eco as one of its founders.

The crossroads in Via Tornabuoni

In Piazza Strozzi (*map 1, 3*), **Palazzo dello Strozzino**, also built for the Strozzi, has a façade by Michelozzo, completed by Giuliano da Maiano. The language school of the British Institute (*see p. 340*) has its headquarters here. Behind it and in its courtyard, Marcello Piacentini built the Odeon theatre and cinema in 1922. It retains its plush Art Nouveau decorations, including a stained-glass dome, and is one of the few cinemas in Florence which shows films in English.

The point where Via Tornabuoni is intersected by Via Strozzi, Via della Vigna Nuova and Via della Spada marks the centre of the Roman colony, where the decumanus maximus and cardo maximus crossed. The street plan in the centre still follows the Roman grid. The palace fitting the awkward site between Via della Vigna Nuova and Via della Spada was from 1614 the home of Sir Robert Dudley (1574–1649), Duke of Northumberland, son of the more famous Sir Robert Dudley, Earl of Leicester, who was Elizabeth I's favourite. Dudley was a navigator and mapmaker who in 1605, after failing to prove he was the Earl of Leicester's legitimate son, moved to Italy and embarked on a career as naval engineer, administering the port of Livorno for the Medici grand dukes

PALAZZO RUCELLAI

and supervising the draining of the marshes between Livorno and Pisa. The plaque was placed in Via della Vigna Nuova in the 19th century by his biographer John Temple Leader (*see p. 315*).

The corner house at Via Tornabuoni 13 (marked with a plaque) is the former Hôtel de la Pension Suisse, where George Eliot and her partner George Henry Lewes stayed on their first trip to Florence in 1860, when the idea came to them that she could take the city as the setting for an 'historical romance' (*Romola*).

PALAZZO RUCELLAI & BUILDINGS BY ALBERTI

On Via della Vigna Nuova, named the street of the 'new vineyard' since it was on the site of a huge orchard, is **Palazzo Rucellai** (*map 1, 3*), the town house of Giovanni Rucellai (1403–81), one of the most respected intellectual figures of Renaissance Florence (author of the *Zibaldone*, his memoirs) as well as one of the wealthiest businessmen in Europe (his bank was the second largest in Florence in the mid-15th century). Scholars now agree that the palace must have been designed by Leon Battista Alberti (*see box overleaf*), although it was actually built by Bernardo Rossellino (c. 1446–51). The dignified façade, with incised decoration, is in striking contrast to the heavy rustication of Palazzo Strozzi and the other Florentine palaces of the period. The three storeys, with classical pilasters and capitals of the three orders, are divided by delicately carved friezes bearing the Rucellai and Medici emblems. The five bays of the front were later increased on the right to seven bays. The design had a lasting influence on Italian architecture. The Rucellai family still live on the top floor while the *piano nobile* (which was decorated in the 18th century) has been occupied since 2001 by a United States university programme (The Institute at Palazzo Rucellai) and can be visited by appointment (*T: 055 264 5910; entrance at Via de' Palchetti 4*).

Leon Battista Alberti (1402–72)

The Alberti family are first mentioned in Florence at the end of the 12th century. They settled near Santa Croce, where their palaces can still be seen (*see pp. 306–07*). They became successful merchants and bankers and various members of the family served in the city government and as controllers of the Mint. However, from 1387 onwards they came into conflict with the political climate in the city and suffered periods of exile (during one of which, in Genoa in 1404, Leon Battista was born). The interdict was finally lifted in 1428.

Leon Battista is one of the most important figures of the Italian Renaissance, not only for the buildings he designed as architect but also for his treatises: *De Pictura*, *De Statua* and *De Re Aedificatoria*. In these he expounded new codes of aesthetics and ethics which greatly influenced the work produced by the humanist painters, sculptors and architects of his day. He examined the idea of beauty based on theories of *misura*, or proportion, and explored the mathematical intricacies of linear perspective. He was greatly influenced by ancient Roman architecture, with its barrel vaults, entablatures and polychrome marbles, and it is known that he accompanied Lorenzo the Magnificent, together with Giovanni Rucellai's son Bernardo, on a trip to Rome to study the ruins (Bernardo later married Lorenzo's sister).

Although Alberti worked on major buildings in other parts of Italy—in Rimini and Mantua—Florence was the place where he produced the most, under the generous patronage of Giovanni Rucellai, apparently also a close friend. Besides Palazzo Rucellai and the three other buildings near it, he also designed the upper façade of Santa Maria Novella (also for the Rucellai) and the choir of the church of Santissima Annunziata.

The **Loggia dei Rucellai**, also the work of Alberti, has three beautiful high arches and a graffiti frieze repeating the Rucellai emblems. This charming decorative piece of architecture, built to enhance the tiny piazza in front of the Rucellai palace, is now used by a fashion boutique and the arches of the loggia have been glassed in, so that many hurried visitors probably fail even to notice it.

The **former church of San Pancrazio** (*map 1, 3*) one of the oldest in the city, founded before 1000, was deconsecrated in 1809 and later used as a tobacco factory and then as a military store. The beautiful classical porch is by Alberti. Outside is a lion, carved in *pietra serena* which has weathered badly (this stone deteriorates quickly when exposed and for that reason is usually used only for interiors). Again, this is easy to miss, since the building has been entirely modernised and converted into the **Museo Marino Marini** (*open 10–5; closed Tues, Sun and holidays and the whole of Aug; T: 055 219432*), which displays works left to the city by the sculptor Marino Marini (1901–80). Exhibitions are held in the 15th-century crypt.

In Via della Spada (no. 18) is the entrance to the remarkable **Cappella del Santo Sepolcro** (or Cappella Rucellai; *usually open only on Sat at 5.30; closed July–Sept*), built by Alberti in 1467, also for Giovanni Rucellai. In the middle of the lovely barrel-vaulted oratory there is a perfectly preserved chapel by Alberti in inlaid marble with exquisite carving, the proportions of which recall the famous sanctuary of the Holy Sepulchre in Jerusalem.

OTHER PALACES ON VIA TORNABUONI

Palazzo del Circolo dell'Unione (no. 7), which may have been designed by Vasari, has a pretty doorway surmounted by a bust of Francesco I by Giambologna. On the corner of Via Strozzi is the huge **Palazzo Corsi Tornabuoni**, built in the mid-15th century for the Tornabuoni by Michelozzo (its courtyard is preserved although it was reconstructed in 1862). Radical restructuring inside to provide luxury apartments and shops was halted in 2010. The shoe shop opposite occupies the former premises of the Farmacia Inglese, founded in 1843, as the plaques on either side of the doorway record. The last palace on this side is the small **Palazzo Larderel** (no. 19), a model of High Renaissance architecture attributed to Giovanni Antonio Dosio, built in 1580 in a sandstone called *pietra bigia*. On the ground floor, in a pretty little room with a fireplace and the royal coat of arms, is the Erboristeria Inglese or Officina de' Tornabuoni, the successor to the English Pharmacy. This is now a herbalist which has its own laboratory producing natural cosmetics.

The last stretch of Via Tornabuoni, furthest from the river, is called Piazza Antinori after the palace which has been owned by the Antinori since 1506. **Palazzo Antinori** (no. 3) is one of the most beautiful smaller Renaissance palaces in Florence. Built in 1461–69, with a splendid courtyard, it is attributed to Giuliano da Maiano. It is a compact building sited between two narrow streets and decorated with flat rustication of blocks of stone of standard size. There is a delicate classical toothed frieze between each storey and another at the top of the façade beneath the overhanging roof. There are iron flagstaffs on two stories where banners or torches would be placed on festivals, and a seat on the pavement. The Antinori arms, in a different coloured stone, are prominent. The doorway is always open since the elegant Cantinetta Antinori wine bar, one of the oldest in the city, still operates here. The vaulted portico has pretty herring-bone paving and beyond you can look into the courtyard with its lovely columns on three sides and a well on the last side decorated with *peducci*. The Antinori are an old-established Florentine family, well-known for the wine they produce on their estates in Tuscany.

San Gaetano

This church (correctly Santi Michele e Gaetano; *map 1, 3; open 9–12 & 3–6.30 except Mon*) is preceded by a wide flight of steps. It is the most important 17th-century church in Florence. The fine façade (1648–83) was designed by Pier Francesco Silvani. There was a Romanesque church on this site, mentioned in 1055. The dark grey interior in *pietra serena* (best appreciated in the morning) was built in 1604–49 by Matteo Nigetti (possibly influenced by a design of Bernardo Buontalenti) and (after 1630) by Gherardo Silvani. The sombre decoration in various precious marbles and dark wood survives almost totally intact, and nearly all the frescoes and altarpieces were painted in the 1630s and 1640s by the most important artists of the day, including Ottavio Vannini, Jacopo Vignali, Angelo Michele Colonna, Matteo Rosselli, Fabrizio Boschi, Giovanni Bilivert, Lorenzo Lippi and Jacopo da Empoli. The colossal white marble statues (with bas-reliefs below) of the *Apostles* and *Evangelists* (1640–90) are by Giovanni Battista Foggini (*St Peter* and *St Paul* on the triumphal arch), Antonio Novelli and others. Splendid hangings in silk, gold thread and velvet from Lyon were made in Florence in 1728–50 to adorn the church on festivals; they still survive and are sometimes displayed.

In the first south chapel is a *Madonna* in glazed terracotta by Andrea della Robbia (1465–70). In the choir chapel the bronze Crucifix is by Giovanni Francesco Susini and is his most important work (1634–35). The third north chapel contains an altarpiece of the *Death of St Andrea Avellina*, signed and dated by the English painter Ignazio Enrico Hugford (1738), who was born in Pisa in 1703. He was a well-known collector and art dealer as well as an artist close to Anton Domenico Gabbiani. He painted some 280 portraits of illustrious painters, which were turned into engravings and published in 13 volumes between 1769 and 1775. In the next chapel there is a *Martyrdom of St Lawrence* by Pietro da Cortona (c. 1653).

MUSEO DI CASA MARTELLI

Map 1, 3. Open for guided visits (in English on request) on Thur afternoon and Sat morning by previous appointment, T: 055 294883. Entrance at Via Zannetti 8.

A house was acquired here by the Martelli family in 1520. Up until the mid-15th century they had been one of the richest merchant families in Florence and close friends of the Medici. Roberto Martelli (1408–64) was an important patron of Donatello. This palace was left to the bishop's curia by the last member of the Martelli family in 1986, on condition that it was preserved as a gallery. It has since been acquired by the state, which also purchased the Martelli coat of arms by Donatello, which was formerly here and is now in the Bargello. Apart from the family collections, the palace is particularly interesting for its lovely 18th- and early 19th-century ceiling paintings and its atmosphere of a patrician Florentine home. It contains one of the most important private collections left in Florence, formed by Marco di Francesco Martelli in the 1640s (and augmented by the Roman collection of Abbot Domenico Martelli, who died in 1735, and by later members of the family).

Tour of the house and collection

The handsome **staircase** (mid-17th century, retaining its original very fine wrought-iron balustrade) has a ceiling fresco of 1802 by Luigi Sabatelli (the coat of arms is a copy of the one by Donatello now in the Bargello). The two large paintings are by Ottavio Vannini.

In the first of the four rooms of the **Gallery**, with a lovely frescoed ceiling celebrating the Martelli family by Antonio Marini (1822), the paintings hung against the red walls include works by Salvatore Rosa, Luca Giordano, Francesco Francia (*Madonna and Child with Saints*), Santi di Tito (*Adam and Eve*) and Sebastiano Conca (*Mary Magdalene*). The next room has another lovely ceiling fresco dating from the early 19th century by Niccolò Contestabile. Here are hung two good works by Beccafumi and a portrait of Vittoria della Rovere as a child bride by Suttermans. The small room with green walls contains two works by Peter Brueghel the Younger (above the doors) and four works symbolising the four elements by Luca Giordano. The four small bronzes are by Massimiliano Soldani Benzi. The ceiling fresco is another delightful work by Antonio Marini. The last room, hung with wallpaper, has a late 18th-century ceiling fresco by Tommaso Gherardini illustrating a Tuscan Parnassus, with Ludovico Martelli included in the illustrious company alongside Dante. The wooden statuettes were made by a German artist in the early 18th century.

The **chapel** was created by the last member of the family, Francesco, in a room with secular ceiling frescoes by Vincenzo Meucci (1738–39). The yellow **drawing room** has late 18th-century silk wall hangings and another lovely ceiling by Meucci with allegories of the four continents. Here there is one of the best paintings in the collection, a tondo of the *Nativity* by Piero di Cosimo (dated 1510, acquired by the Martelli in 1648). The arrangement of the furniture recalls the room's purpose as a 'parlour'. The boudoir which opens off it was where the ladies would work at lace-making. The largest room, overlooking the courtyard, retains its lovely pavement and is the only room in the palace which has been restored. An adjoining room is entirely frescoed in Pompeian style by Gaetano Gucci (1780). The magnificent tall **ballroom**, provided with two balconies for the musicians, was decorated in the 18th and 19th centuries, when more doors and windows were added in *trompe l'oeil*.

On the ground floor the delightful **winter garden** was painted in the late 18th century by Gucci with a trellised vine, fountains and birds (the architectural elements such as the capitals date from the 15th-century building). From the courtyard, with another *trompe l'oeil* fresco, you can visit the extraordinary **Sala del Bagno**, or bath house, decorated in 1820 by Niccolò Contestabile, with lovely frescoed landscapes and ingenious false ruins in the niche with the marble bathtub. In an atrium is displayed the lovely bas-relief of the *Madonna and Child with St John*, attributed to Mino da Fiesole, removed from the tabernacle on the palace exterior.

SANT'AMBROGIO, BORGO DEGLI ALBIZI & BORGO PINTI

Mercato di Sant'Ambrogio

This is the busiest produce market in Florence (*map 4, 8; open Mon–Sat mornings and sometimes one or two afternoons, on a reduced scale*). The cast-iron building dates from 1873: butchers, grocers and fishmongers have their stalls inside, while fruit and vegetables, some grown locally, are sold from stalls outside. On the two short sides of the building there are stalls selling clothes, shoes, household linen, hardware and plants, all generally good value. It is especially crowded on Saturday mornings and its bustling character gives it an entirely genuine Florentine atmosphere. There is a large underground car park beneath the adjoining open space, called Largo Pietro Annigoni.

The church of Sant'Ambrogio

The church of Sant'Ambrogio (*map 4, 8; open 8–12 & 4–7*) was rebuilt in the late 13th century and it still has an open timber roof. The façade dates from the 19th century. The lively interior is cluttered with little temporary altars and shrines lit by candles since this is a place of worship where many Florentines like to stop by during their shopping expeditions. There are pretty Renaissance side altars. The east end, with its two handsome side chapels, was designed in 1716 by Giovanni Battista Foggini. Four important artists are buried here and their tomb slabs can be seen in the pavement: the sculptor Mino da Fiesole (1484); the painter and sculptor Verrocchio (1488); Cronaca, the architect of a number of fine palaces in the city (1508); and the painter Francesco Granacci (1541).

On the **south side** there are some beautiful frescoes and panel paintings, all dating from the 14th century. The grand fresco of the *Descent from the Cross* (with its sinopia) by Niccolò di Pietro Gerini; the *Madonna Enthroned with St John the Baptist and St Bartholomew* (second altar), attributed to the school of Orcagna; and the fragment of *St Onophrius* (fourth altar), attributed to the Master of Figline. At the end of this side, by the steps, there is a lovely painting of the *Madonna and Child*, with two saints and donors, attributed to Giovanni di Bartolomeo Cristiani, and in the chapel to the right of the sanctuary, an exquisite triptych of the *Madonna and Child with Saints* attributed to Lorenzo di Bicci. From here can be seen the two good 19th-century frescoes painted by Luigi Ademollo in Foggini's sanctuary.

In the chapel to the left of the sanctuary (the **Cappella del Miracolo**) is a delicately carved tabernacle by Mino da Fiesole (1481), which contains a miraculous chalice. Tradition relates how, in 1230, Uguccione, the parish priest, found blood instead of wine inside it while celebrating Mass. A large fresco here by Cosimo Rosselli shows a procession arriving at the door of the church where the priest is holding this very chalice. In the crowd are portraits of many of the artist's contemporaries as well as the artist's self-portrait (to the left). The sinopia is displayed on the wall nearby. Kneelers for worshippers are supplied at the foot of the balustrade since this has always been

Detail of the marble tabernacle containing a miraculous chalice, carved by Mino da Fiesole in 1481.

a place of great veneration (and the chalice was sometimes carried in processions to intercede for deliverance from the plague, or in other times of trouble), and Mino's tombstone can be seen here.

On the **north side**, the fourth altar has a painting of *St Anthony Abbot Enthroned* by Raffaellino del Garbo and the third altar has an altarpiece of the *Madonna in Glory with Saints* by Cosimo Rosselli, complete with its predella, both dating from the late 15th century. A wooden statuette of *St Sebastian* by Leonardo del Tasso stands in a graceful niche with a tiny painted roundel of the *Annunciation*, attributed to the workshop of Filippino Lippi (Tasso's tombstone is in the pavement here). The second altar has a 16th-century painting of the *Visitation* by Andrea Boscoli, and the first altar a fresco of the *Martyrdom of St Sebastian*—with the emaciated figure of the saint standing high up on a stake with his hands tied above his head—attributed to Agnolo Gaddi. The painting on the wall is by Alesso Baldovinetti (*Angels and Saints*) and his pupil Graffione (*Nativity*). The eight little angels are particularly charming.

The small space in front of the church, where six streets meet, was freed from traffic and provided with new paving and three benches in 2008 so that it has almost become a little piazza. It has a newspaper kiosk and usually a market stall (and there has been a popular tripe stall here, at the end of Via dei Macci, for many decades). The door next to the church leads into its former convent, now used by the restoration laboratory attached to the Biblioteca Nazionale (*see p. 335*). There is a charming little building in the angle between the peaceful Via di Mezzo (where a handsome palace portal on Borgo Pinti frames the view) and Via de' Pilastri; if you follow the latter street as far as the first road on the right you come to the entrance to the Synagogue.

The Synagogue and Jewish Museum

Map 4, 8. Open April–Oct 10–6, Nov–March 10–3; Fri always 10–2; closed Sat. Guided tours in English available. Entrance at Via Farini 6.

The tall green copper dome of the huge Synagogue is a conspicuous feature of the skyline of Florence. This elaborate building, in the Spanish-Moresco style, was erected in 1874–82 by Marco Treves, Mariano Falcini and Vincenzo Micheli. The striped decoration was carried out in travertine and red stone from Assisi. There is a small Jewish Museum on the upper floors (*well labelled also in English*). The display on the matroneum level includes silver, vestments and textiles dating from the 17th–18th centuries. The floor above has a collection of ceremonial objects donated by members of Jewish families in Florence. These include David Levi (whose portrait painted in 1853 by Antonio Ciseri is displayed here), who left money on his death in 1870 to acquire the property on which the synagogue was built. In the last room photographs document the late 19th- and 20th-century history of the Florentine Jewish community. In the garden, with memorials to those who were deported to concentration camps, are a Jewish school and a hospice for the elderly. There is also a library and small historic archive (the earliest surviving document is dated 1576).

THE JEWISH COMMUNITY IN FLORENCE

The Jews are first mentioned as a community in Florence in the 15th century when they were encouraged by the Republican government to operate in the city as money-lenders. Although in 1495 Savonarola saw to it that Jewish usury was outlawed, there is evidence that money-lenders from the Jewish community were sought out by Florentines for centuries (although many of them ended up in prison). In 1571 Cosimo I confined the Jews to a ghetto in the area north of the present Piazza della Repubblica (*see p. 103*), where they suffered terrible living conditions. It was only in 1779, under the Lorraine grand duke Peter Leopold, that the ghetto became the property of a number of wealthy Jewish families. Peter Leopold's successors relaxed the restrictions which had been imposed on the personal freedom of Jews in the community. However, the ghetto was not formally opened up until 1848, and it was demolished at the end of the 19th century. The Jewish cemetery in Florence is at Viale Ariosto 14 (*map 5, 2; open 1st Sun of the month 10–12*).

Piazza dei Ciompi

Piazza dei Ciompi (*map 4, 7*), west of the church of Sant'Ambrogio, is, at the time of writing, still the site of the junk and antiques market known as the 'Mercatino', though this is scheduled to be 'tidied up'. It used to be easy to find bargains here but in the last few years the prices have soared and business is much less good. A graceful loggia, designed in 1568 by Vasari and once used for the sale of fish in the Mercato Vecchio, was reconstructed here after the demolition of that area of the city: it looks somewhat incongruous in these humble surroundings.

A damaged inscription on a house in the piazza records the home of the sculptor Lorenzo Ghiberti, while Cimabue lived in Borgo Allegri, which—according to Vasari— was given this name after Cimabue's painting of the *Madonna in Maestà* (now in the Uffizi) left his studio in a joyous procession down the street. This story caught the imagination of the Pre-Raphaelite painter Frederic Leighton, and his painting showing the scene was greatly admired when exhibited at the Royal Academy in 1855 (it was purchased by Queen Victoria). There is a pleasant little public garden in this street, opened and maintained by old-age pensioners.

THE REVOLT OF THE CIOMPI

The *ciompi* were wool-carders, unskilled textile workers in the all-important cloth industry of Florence in the 13th and 14th centuries. A huge workforce was employed in cleaning and combing wool, which then went through the process of spinning and weaving, before bolts of cloth were washed, fulled and then dyed. In 1378 the *ciompi* led a revolt against harsh working conditions and pitiful pay. One of them, named Michele di Lando, accompanied by a huge crowd of workers and guildsmen, actually succeeded in entering Palazzo dei Priori and declaring himself 'Standard-bearer of Justice'. As a result the rebels won significant concessions, including (for a very short time) direct representation in the government of the city and the right to form a guild of some 9,000 workers (the total population at the time being around 55,000). But after only a few months the guild was outlawed by a *parlamento* of citizens and some of the *ciompi* were killed or exiled. The repercussions only led the powerful guilds to unite their political ambitions to those of the elite, so that the idea of guild republicanism was definitively abandoned in Florence, and fear of the poor and of workers' revolts was used to justify the use of arbitrary power by future regimes. Nevertheless, the protest and temporary victory of the *ciompi* remain a significant landmark in the long history of European labour relations.

BORGO DEGLI ALBIZI

Borgo degli Albizi (*map 4, 7*) is one of the handsomest streets in the city, following the line of the Roman Via Cassia, although it is rather narrow and dark so that it is difficult to step back and admire its palaces. Most of the ground floors are now occupied by shops and no cars are allowed. The Borgo is named after one of the wealthiest families in Florence in the 14th and 15th centuries, who owned numerous palaces in the street and who were rivals to the Medici for power. At no. 11, a 16th-century house bears a (rather unflattering) marble bust of Cosimo II. A medieval tower, which belonged to the Donati, rises from the top of this house. No. 10 has a bust of the poet Vincenzo Filicaia (1642–1707), who was born here. **Palazzo degli Alessandri** (no. 15) is the best-preserved of the palaces. A worn cornice divides the two storeys of its fine 14th-century façade in *pietra forte*, rusticated on the lower part. Canova had his studio here for a while.

The grandiose **Palazzo degli Albizi** (no. 12) was the principal residence of the Albizi. Their 14th-century tower (with its rough stone exterior) survives on the left (no. 14) but most of the palace was reconstructed by Silvani in the 17th century. The little *piazzetta* here is named after Piero Calamandrei (1889–1956), fondly remembered as one of the most eminent Florentines of the 20th century. Via delle Seggiole retains its 'crazy' paving. The huge **Palazzo Altoviti** (or dei Visacci; no. 18), which dates from the early 15th century, was enlarged in the late 16th century, when the amusing marble portraits of celebrated Florentine citizens by Caccini were placed on the façade. Those on the ground floor are carefully labelled. By Volta dei Ciechi there is a house (no. 22) with medieval fragments. Palazzo Matteucci Ramirez di Montalvo (no. 26) is by Ammannati (1568), and its worn graffiti decoration is attributed to Bernardino Poccetti. The owner set up the arms of his friend Cosimo I on the façade. On the corner of Via de' Giraldi is a 14th-century tabernacle with the *Madonna Enthroned*. Palazzo Vitali (no. 28) is another beautiful building attributed to Ammannati (late 16th century) and it also has a handsome coat of arms. The last palace on the right is the huge Palazzo Nonfinito, entered round the corner on Via del Proconsolo. It houses the Museo di Antropologia (*see p. 336*).

SANTA MARIA MADDALENA DEI PAZZI

Map 4, 5–7. Entrance near Borgo Pinti 58. Open 8–12 & 4–6; otherwise ring at no. 58.
The church is dedicated to Maria Maddalena (1566–1607), an invalid from a patrician Florentine family who became a Carmelite nun, had mystical visions and was known for her miraculous healing powers. Her cult became popular in Italy after her death in 1607 and she was canonised in 1669. She was a near contemporary of St Teresa of Avila, also a Carmelite mystic. The church was begun in 1257 and a Cistercian convent, founded here in 1321, was taken over by the Carmelites from 1628 until 1888. Fathers of the Assumption of the Augustinian Order (founded in Nîmes in 1850) have been here since 1926 (the church serves the French community of Florence). The cloister, really a quadriporticus, is memorable for its very beautiful large but compact Ionic capitals made by Giuliano da Sangallo in 1492 to support the low architrave.

Interior of the church
NB: The door of the church is kept closed but it is usually not locked. Although it is dark, there are inconspicuous light switches in each chapel.
The church is rather bare and seems neglected: it is certainly little visited. The side chapels were added in 1488–1526, with pretty carved arches in *pietra serena*. The *trompe l'œil* ceiling is by Jacopo Chiavistelli (1677), who also carried out decorations for Palazzo Pitti and a number of other Florentine palaces. His contemporary Cosimo Ulivelli added

the paintings high up above the nave arches. The works of art in the chapels range in date from the late 15th–early 19th centuries and many of them are unusual.

South side: The huge *Martyrdom of St Romulus* is signed and dated by Carlo Portelli (1557). The second chapel was delicately decorated in pretty gilded stucco in 1778. In the third chapel there is a *Coronation of the Virgin* by Matteo Rosselli in a fine frame of c. 1490. The fourth chapel has a *Madonna and Child with Saints*, the masterpiece of Domenico Puligo (1526; with a good frame by Baccio d'Agnolo). The fifth chapel has a stained-glass window of *St Francis* (c. 1500), and the sixth chapel early 19th-century frescoes by Luigi Catani and a small Crucifix attributed to Bernardo Buontalenti.

Main chapel: Well lit and with colourful marbles, this is one of the most important and complete examples of Florentine Baroque church decoration. It was designed in 1675 in honour of Santa Maria Maddalena by Ciro Ferri, who painted the high altarpiece, and by Pier Francesco Silvani. On the side walls are two paintings by Luca Giordano. The marble statues are by (left)

Antonio Montauti (c. 1690) and (right) Innocenzo Spinazzi (1781), including the remarkable female figure, her face enveloped in a veil, which is an allegory of Faith. The cupola was frescoed in 1701 by Pier Dandini.

North side: The Renaissance organ (restored in 1719) has a cantoria attributed to Giuliano da Sangallo. In the fourth chapel, in a pretty frame, is *St Ignatius and St Roch* by Raffaellino del Garbo, flanking a wood statue of St Sebastian. The third chapel has stained glass designed by Domenico del Ghirlandaio and on the altar is a wooden processional statue of the *Madonna and Child*. The painting of the *Agony in the Garden* by Santi di Tito is signed and dated 1591. The second chapel contains a *Coronation of the Virgin* (against a bright blue ground) by Cosimo Rosselli, in another fine frame. In the first chapel there is a *Nativity* by Cosimo Gamberucci, signed and dated 1618, and a painting of *St Lawrence* by Francesco Curradi (1610).

The former **chapter house** contains one of Perugino's masterpieces: a beautiful and well-preserved fresco of the *Crucifixion and Saints* (1493–96). (*Only open on Tues and Thur 2.30–5.30, except during school holidays. It is reached from the junction of Borgo Pinti with Via della Colonna in which (right) is the rather scruffy entrance to a large school: go up the steps and into a cloister and the chapter house is immediately on your left.*)

BORGO PINTI & THE PROTESTANT CEMETERY

At Borgo Pinti 68 is **Palazzo Panciatichi-Ximenes** (*map 4, 5*) purchased by Sebastiano di Tommaso Ximenes in 1603, when he employed Gherardo Silvani to restructure it (the façade dates from this time). Modifications c. 1720 include the atrium, a handsome double stair, and interior courtyard.

The huge **Palazzo Scala della Gherardesca** (no. 99; *map 4, 6*), now the Four Seasons Hotel (*see p. 358*), was enlarged and restructured in the early 18th century by Antonio Ferri, but the lovely courtyard, built in the 1470s by Giuliano da Sangallo, survives. The extremely interesting twelve rectangular bas-reliefs in stucco have recently been attributed to Bertoldo di Giovanni and dated 1482–85. Bartolomeo della Scala, who commissioned the building, was responsible for their iconography. He was Chancellor of the Republic in the late 15th century (vividly described by George Eliot in Chapter 7 of *Romola*). His descendants sold the property in 1585 to Cardinal Alessandro de' Medici and it passed to the Gherardesca family in 1605, though the façade still bears the emblem of the Della Scala (the *scala*, or ladder, and the motto 'step by step'). The palace is surrounded by a huge 19th-century garden in the English Romantic tradition, with a little Neoclassical temple designed by Giuseppe Cacialli in 1842. You can sometimes ask to see the courtyard, but the magnificent park is only accessible to the public once a year (*for information, see www.fourse asons.com or T: 055 26261; there are two other gates at Via Gino Capponi 54 and Piazza Donatello 12*). There are frescoes by Jan van der Straet in the courtyard off which a late 16th-century frescoed chapel survives (now used as a little drawing room) and some of the rooms on the *piano nobile* still have frescoes by Volterrano and Vincenzo Meucci, and Capodimonte tiled floors.

The Protestant Cemetery

Borgo Pinti ends in Piazzale Donatello (*map 4, 6*), very busy with traffic as it lies on the wide avenues (the Viali) which were laid out in 1865–69 by Giuseppe Poggi after he had demolished the last circle of medieval walls. The architect left some of the ancient gates as isolated monuments in the course of this ring-road. On an island in the centre of Piazzale Donatello is the Protestant Cemetery (*open Mon 9–12, Tues–Fri 2–5; ring at the main gate*), which has always been known as the Cimitero degli Inglesi, or 'English Cemetery'. It was opened in 1828 and many distinguished British, Swiss, North American, Italian and Russian non-Catholics are buried here. The cemetery was in use until 1878, when the new Cimitero degli Allori was opened on Via Senese, but in 1996 the Russian ballet dancer Evgenij Poljakov was allowed to be buried here. Since 2000 the cemetery has been well looked after by the custodian, who lives in the little gatehouse (dating from 1860) and runs a library here. Beneath the cypresses there are box hedges and iris, with daffodils in spring, and numerous pomegranate trees.

To the left of the central path Elizabeth Barrett Browning (1809–61) is buried. The tomb, raised on six little columns, was designed by Robert Browning and sculpted by Lord Leighton (finished by Luigi Giovannozzi). Behind it is the Pre-Raphaelite sarcophagus of Holman Hunt's wife Fanny, who died in childbirth in Fiesole at the age of 33. Also buried here are the poet Walter Savage Landor (1775–1864), the bibliophile Gian Pietro Vieusseux (1779–1863; *see p. 218*), the writer Fanny Trollope (1780–1863), the American sculptor Hiram Powers (1805–73), the Boston reformer Theodore Parker of Lexington (1810–60), Isa Blagden (1818–73; *see p. 323*) and Robert Davidsohn (1853–1937), the German historian of Florence.

PALAZZO PITTI & THE BOBOLI GARDENS

Map 6, 3. The ticket office is on the far right of the façade. One ticket for the Galleria Palatina, Appartamenti Reali and Galleria d'Arte Moderna, open 8.15–6.50 except Mon; another ticket for the Boboli Gardens (with the Museo delle Porcellane), Museo degli Argenti and Galleria del Costume (which also allows entrance to the Villa Bardini; see p. 292), open 8.15–dusk except 1st and last Mon of the month.

Free guided tours are provided every weekday of areas of the palace otherwise kept locked. Information desk in the Sala del Castagnoli (Room 3 on the plan on p. 235). Information and reservations, T: 055 294883 (Mon–Fri 8.30–6.30, Sat 8.30–12.30).

Off the courtyard are a museum shop, café, cloakroom, toilets (there are more toilets, usually much less busy, in the Galleria d'Arte Moderna), and lifts for the Galleria Palatina and the Museo d'Arte Moderna and Galleria del Costume. The Galleria del Costume has an additional entrance (and exit) in the Boboli Gardens. If you see there is a queue in Piazza Pitti, it is worth going to the Boboli ticket office at the Annalena Gate in Via Romana.

The majestic Palazzo Pitti was built by the merchant Luca Pitti as an effective demonstration of his wealth and power to his rivals the Medici. The *pietra forte* was quarried on this very site and the sloping hillside was chosen to make the palace even more imposing. Houses were demolished to create the wide piazza in front. The huge, rough-hewn blocks of golden stone vary in length. Since it is so hard, *pietra forte* was rarely used for sculpture, although the nine lions' heads beneath the windows are made from it.

In 1549, when the palace was bought by Eleanor of Toledo, wife of Cosimo I, its magnificence was increased and the beautiful Boboli Gardens were laid out behind it. It became the official seat of the Medici dynasty of grand dukes after Cosimo I moved here from Palazzo Vecchio (to which he connected the Pitti by means of the Corridoio Vasariano; *see p. 131*). The various ruling families of Florence continued to occupy the palace, or part of it, followed by the kings of united Italy, until in 1919 Vittorio Emanuele III presented it to the state.

History of the palace

The design is attributed to Brunelleschi, although building began c. 1457, after his death. Luca Fancelli is known to have worked on it, but it is generally considered that another architect, whose name is unknown, was also involved. The palace remained incomplete on the death of Luca Pitti in 1472; by then it consisted of the seven central bays with three doorways. Bartolomeo Ammannati took up work on the building c. 1560 and converted the two side doors of the façade into elaborate ground-floor windows. These were then copied after 1616 by Giulio and Alfonso Parigi the Younger, when they enlarged the façade to its present colossal dimensions (possibly following an original design). The two projecting wings were added later: the one on the right was built sometime after 1760, and the one on the left (known as the Rondò di Bacco) in the 19th century (it incorporates a small theatre, now used for lectures).

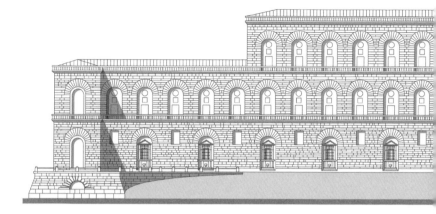

MUSEUMS & APARTMENTS IN PALAZZO PITTI

The huge palace contains the numerous apartments used in various seasons for over four centuries by the grand dukes and rulers of Florence and Tuscany, as well as the works of art acquired by them. The huge interior has decorations and furnishings made when the various suites of rooms were used by the different dynasties at different periods and this makes it a particularly fascinating, if confusing, place to visit. It houses a number of important museums, including the Galleria Palatina, with one of the finest collections of paintings in Italy; the Museo degli Argenti; and the Galleria d'Arte Moderna. In the Meridiana wing is the Galleria del Costume.

Some very interesting areas are only shown on guided tours, which you can usually join any day for no extra charge. These include the Appartamenti degli Arazzi and the Ritirata della Duchessa on the *piano nobile*, and the winter apartments on the top floor. At the time of writing the attic floor, known as the 'Mezzanino degli Occhi', was not open.

The courtyard

The central door in the façade leads through the atrium by Pasquale Poccianti (c. 1850) into the splendid courtyard (1560–70) by Bartolomeo Ammannati, which serves as a garden façade to the palace. It is a masterpiece of Florentine Mannerist architecture, with bold rustication in three orders. Nocturnal spectacles were held here from the 16th–18th centuries and it is still sometimes used for summer concerts. The lower fourth side is formed by a terrace with the Fontana del Carciofo (so named since it was once crowned by an artichoke), beyond which extend the Boboli Gardens.

The Grotto beneath the terrace was designed in 1635–42, with statues in the niches and in the water around a porphyry statue of *Moses* (the torso is an antique Roman work). At the end of the right and left colonnades are a restored Roman *Hercules* (c. AD 200) and (left) a charming bas-relief, set up in 1575, commemorating a mule who

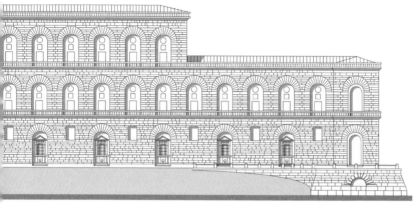

worked particularly hard during the construction of the courtyard. On the right side of the courtyard is the entrance to the Cappella Palatina (*only open on special occasions*), which dates from 1776. There are more Roman statues in the courtyard, including a gladiator and a colossal head of Pyrrhus, both with 16th-century additions.

Galleria Palatina

For opening times, see p. 231. The plan overleaf follows the room numbers on the plans in the gallery, but in situ the rooms are named rather than numbered. Only a selection of the paintings (all of which are labelled) is described. Particularly important works are given in bold.

NB: The masterpieces of the collection are in the six main rooms overlooking Piazza Pitti (numbers 27–32 on the plan). Unfortunately the present order of the visit means that these rooms have to be visited last: it is therefore important to save enough time and energy to do them justice (if pressed for time, proceed directly to the Sala dell'Iliade; p. 238).

Off the courtyard, Ammannati's Grand Staircase ascends past antique sculpture and late 17th-century busts to the gallery entrance. The celebrated Galleria Palatina is a splendid collection of paintings acquired by the Medici and Lorraine grand dukes, including numerous famous works by Raphael, Titian and Rubens. The collection owes its origins to the 17th-century Medici grand dukes and in particular to Cardinal Leopoldo, brother of Ferdinando II, and to Cosimo III and his eldest son the Crown Prince Ferdinando (d. 1713), who added Flemish paintings, works of the Bolognese and Veneto schools and altarpieces from Tuscan churches. Under the Lorraine grand dukes, in 1771, the paintings were installed in the present rooms, which had been decorated by Pietro da Cortona in the 1640s for Ferdinando II (*see p. 250*). The gallery was first opened regularly to the public in 1833, arranged more or less as it is today, and in 1911 it was acquired by the state.

The gallery maintains the character of a private, princely collection of the 17th–18th centuries. The aesthetic arrangement of the pictures produces a remarkable effect of magnificence. The elaborately carved and gilded frames, many of them original, and especially representative of the Mannerist, Baroque and Neoclassical styles, are particularly fine.

The entrance rooms

(1) Anticamera degli Staffieri: Decorated in the 18th century, it contains 16th-century sculptures by Pietro Francavilla (*Mercury*) and earlier works by Baccio Bandinelli (*Bacchus* and a bronze bust of Cosimo I). Bandinelli was the courtier artist *par excellence*, versatile to a degree which enabled him always to rise to the ducal command, be it architectural, sculptural or pictorial in nature. He was a virtuoso sculptor—a great performer, but not a true composer. His obsession with the colossal (see the huge bronze portrait head of Cosimo I by his workshop displayed in the next room, the Galleria delle Statue) masks a want of true sensitivity to subject or material.

(2) Galleria delle Statue: This was originally a loggia designed by Ammannati overlooking his courtyard: from the central window there is a splendid view of the Boboli Gardens (and the Forte di Belvedere on the skyline). The loggia was enclosed under the Lorraine grand dukes and decorated by Giuseppe Maria Terreni in 1790 as a sculpture gallery. The fine series of antique Roman statues and busts (all well labelled) were brought here from the Villa Medici in Rome.

(3) Sala del Castagnoli: The room takes its name from Giuseppe Castagnoli, the artist who decorated it in 1812. It contains a magnificent circular table in *pietre dure* (1837–50) with *Apollo and the Muses* (the bronze pedestal with the *Four Seasons* is by Giovanni Dupré). This was the last important work in *pietre dure* made in the grand-ducal workshop (*see p. 169*). Other very fine *pietre dure* tabletops and cabinets made in the workshop are also preserved in the palace. The colossal Roman statues of a Dacian prisoner and an emperor both came from the Villa Medici in Rome. There is an information desk here.

From Room 3 you can usually go right into the Volterrano Wing (Rooms 4–14) but if you have limited time, it is best to go straight ahead into Room 15. NB: If custodians are lacking, these rooms can be closed.

The Volterrano Wing

(4) Sala delle Allegorie: The allegories in question are Volterrano's frescoes on the richly-decorated stucco ceiling, which date from around 1658 and show the influence of Pietro da Cortona, who had been at work in Palazzo Pitti earlier in the century (*see p. 239*). The frescoes celebrate the grand duchess Vittoria della Rovere, with allegories of her virtues. Volterrano painted numerous other frescoes in Florence during the 17th century, including those in the dome of the

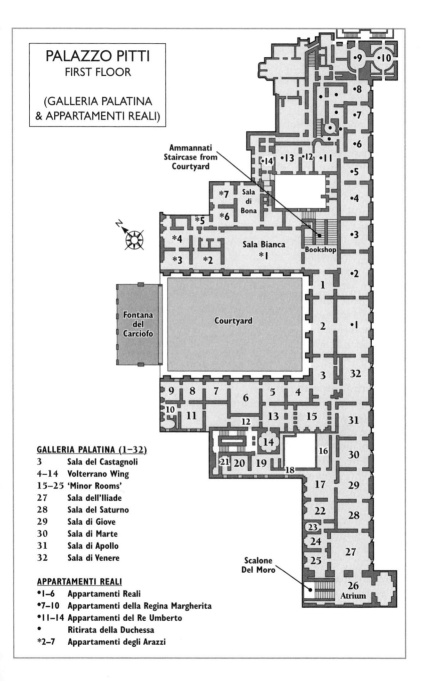

PALAZZO PITTI
FIRST FLOOR

(GALLERIA PALATINA
& APPARTAMENTI REALI)

Ammannati
Staircase from
Courtyard

*7 Sala
di
Bona
*5   *6
*4
*3   *2   Sala Bianca
*1   Bookshop

Fontana
del
Carciofo

Courtyard

GALLERIA PALATINA (1–32)
3   Sala del Castagnoli
4–14 Volterrano Wing
15–25 'Minor Rooms'
27   Sala dell'Iliade
28   Sala del Saturno
29   Sala di Giove
30   Sala di Marte
31   Sala di Apollo
32   Sala di Venere

APPARTAMENTI REALI
•1–6   Appartamenti Reali
•7–10 Appartamenti della Regina Margherita
•11–14 Appartamenti del Re Umberto
•   Ritirata della Duchessa
*2–7   Appartamenti degli Arazzi

Scalone
Del Moro

Atrium

tribune of Santissima Annunziata and in the Niccolini Chapel in Santa Croce. Other paintings by him include (on the entrance wall) *The Parson's Jest*, showing a jovial group enjoying the pranks of the Pievano Arlotto, a country chaplain who had a living near Fiesole and who was famous for his burlesques. After his death in 1484 his witticisms were recorded in print and Volterrano portrayed him in this well-known genre painting, which was owned by Crown Prince Ferdinando and provides an interesting glimpse into Florentine life of the time.

There are also works here by Giovanni da San Giovanni and his contemporaries Suttermans and Artemisia Gentileschi.

(5) Sala delle Belle Arti: Paintings by Carlo Dolci and Cigoli (d. 1613), one of the finest Florentine exponents of the transition from Mannerism to the Baroque.

(6) Salone d'Ercole: Frescoed in 1817–29 with Neoclassical scenes from the life of Hercules by Pietro Benvenuti, his most important work. He became director of the Accademia di Belle Arti in 1803 and received commissions from the court of Elisa Baciocchi. The huge Sèvres vase dates from the early 19th century.

The **Sala dell'Arca (13)** has a splendid frescoed frieze painted by Luigi Ademollo in 1816. Off it is the **Cappella delle Reliquie (14)**, an early 17th-century oval chapel built for Maria Maddalena of Austria, wife of Cosimo II. It is one of the earliest rooms in the palace to survive. The **Corridoio delle Miniature (12)** has tiny Dutch paintings acquired by Cosimo III in Holland in 1667 and a charming collection of paintings of fruit and vegetables by Giovanna Garzoni (1600–57), painted for Vittoria della Rovere. These were considered 'scientific illustrations' since very few women were 'artists' at this time.

The following rooms (7–11; *not open at the time of writing*), include the **Sala di Psiche (9)**, which has fine works by Salvatore Rosa, a Neapolitan artist with a character of great verve and self-confidence, best known for his landscape paintings of rugged and romantic scenery that did much to inform the notion of the Picturesque in England—and also coloured his reputation, adding greatly to his popularity. Rumours began to circulate that he himself was a brigand.

Rooms of the Napoleonic period

From the Sala del Castagnoli (Room 3) is the entrance to a series of rooms decorated in the Neoclassical style in the Napoleonic period, when Elisa Baciocchi was in residence. They contain the smaller works in the collection.

(15) Sala della Musica: Designed by Cacialli in 1811–21, with frescoes by Luigi Ademollo. The gilt-bronze and malachite table is by Pierre-Philippe Thomire, who at the height of his career was court engraver to Napoleon.

(16) Galleria del Poccetti: The beautiful table inlaid in *pietre dure* (1716) is attributed to Giovanni Battista Foggini (sculptor to the grand dukes from 1687). On either side of the door are a remarkable portrait in profile of Francesco da

Castiglione by Pontormo (also attributed to Rosso Fiorentino), and a **portrait of the Duke of Buckingham** by Rubens. It was Buckingham who negotiated the betrothal of Henrietta Maria, granddaughter of Francesco I, to the future Charles I of England. At the other end of the room is Rubens' **portrait of the Duchess of Buckingham**, and, above, a portrait of Cromwell by Peter Lely.

Hylas and the Nymphs is perhaps the masterpiece of Francesco Furini. He was a man of letters and ordained as a priest, as well as an artist who flourished at the Medici court from the time of Cosimo II to that of Ferdinando II. He rarely left Florence during his short life (except for visits to Rome, where he had contacts with Bernini). He stands out amongst his contemporaries for his personal style, in which he shows a particular interest in the female nude; many of his works are highly sensuous. It is known that he used lapis lazuli in his palette when painting his luminous flesh tones. His compositions tend to make much use of light effects and shade on dark backgrounds. Many of his superb drawings are preserved in the Uffizi.

(17) Sala di Prometeo: Here are the earliest paintings in the Pitti, including some good portraits and a number of fine tondi of the Madonna (by Signorelli and Beccafumi), the largest and most beautiful of which is the **tondo of the *Madonna and Child***, a charming composition with scenes from the life of the Virgin in the background. This is one of Filippo Lippi's best works and had an important influence on his contemporaries. His use of red is particularly effective. Above is a delightful *Young Bacchus* by Guido Reni

(the fine frame dates from the end of the 17th century). The damaged *Portrait of a Man*, in a typical Florentine headdress, is by Botticelli and the portrait of a lady in profile (called the *Bella Simonetta*) may be by him or his *bottega* (although some scholars think it could be a 19th-century work). The unusual portrait of a woman in profile in a white veil (once thought to be Caterina Sforza) is now attributed to Piero di Cosimo. Pontormo painted the complex scene of the *Ten Thousand Martyrs* in 1530, and the fine *Mary Magdalene* is by Il Bachiacca.

On the window wall: *Dance of Apollo with the Muses* by Baldassare Peruzzi (beneath is a table in scagliola with a copy of the painting).

(18) Corridoio delle Colonne: Hung with small Flemish paintings by Jan Brueghel (*Orpheus*), David Ryckaert (*Temptations of St Anthony*) and others.

(19) Sala della Giustizia: The superb *Portrait of a Man*, thought to be Vincenzo or Tommaso Mosti, is one of Titian's first portraits.

(21) Sala dei Putti: Exquisite still-lifes by Rachele Ruysch and a small monochrome *Three Graces* by Rubens.

(22) Sala di Ulisse: The beautiful small painting of the *Death of Lucrezia*, once part of a *cassone*, is by Filippino Lippi. Raphael's *Madonna dell'Impannata* (so named from the window covered with cloth instead of glass in the background) is a mature composition, perhaps with the collaboration of his workshop: the most beautiful part is the restless Child and serene Madonna.

(23) Empire bathroom by Giuseppe Cacialli (1813).

(24) Sala dell'Educazione di Giove: This contains one of the most famous Florentine works of the 17th century, *Judith with the Head of Holofernes* by Cristofano Allori (the artist is said to have portrayed himself as Holofernes, his mistress Mazzafirra as the haughty, insouciant Judith, and her mother as the anxious-looking maidservant). On the opposite wall is the well-known *Sleeping Cupid* (in its beautiful original frame) by Caravaggio, painted in Malta in 1608 and brought to Florence the following year. Beyond the door is a small portrait of Claude, Duc de Guise by Jean Clouet.

(25) Sala della Stufa: The beautiful frescoes by Pietro da Cortona, which recreate the effect of an open terrace, show the *Four Ages of the World*. This was Pietro's first work in Palazzo Pitti (1637) and the elaborate allegories include references to his patrons, Grand Duke Ferdinando II and his wife Vittoria della Rovere: the oak tree symbolises the name Rovere ('oak' in Italian) and the lion refers to the *Marzocco* (the heraldic lion) of Florence. This part of the palace was formerly a loggia and the vault fresco is by Matteo Rosselli (1622). The room was called *della stufa* (meaning 'of the stove') when heating was installed in this wing. The majolica pavement with the *Triumph of Bacchus* dates from 1640.

From here you can now go out to the **Atrium (26)** at the top of the Scalone Del Moro, a staircase in Renaissance style built by Luigi Del Moro in 1892–97. The Renaissance fountain is by Antonio Rossellino and Benedetto da Maiano. The bronze statue of a young boy, intended as an allegory of the Medici, is by Ammannati.

The main rooms

(27) Sala dell'Iliade: The ceiling (1819) is by Luigi Sabatelli, one of the most important Tuscan painters of the early 19th century, and illustrates Homer's *Iliad*. Two large paintings of the *Assumption* by Andrea del Sarto are hung here: that on the right wall is one of his most important late works. The other large painting on the third wall, the *Pala di San Marco*, is by Fra' Bartolomeo. Also on this wall are two full-length standing male portraits, both by Titian, one of them a portrait of Philip II of Spain. Above this is *Mary Magdalene* by Artemisia Gentileschi. Talented and independent, Gentileschi trained under her father, Orazio, who owed much to Caravaggio.

Dramatic Caraveggesque chiaroscuro certainly suited Artemisia's choice of subject matter. She had a particular affinity for the story of Judith and Holofernes (the *Judith* on the adjoining wall is hers, though her most famous treatment of the subject is in the Uffizi). Legend relates this to the fact that Artemisia was raped as a young woman and that her assailant was never brought to justice.

On the other side of the door, the small *Portrait of a Man* (thought to be a goldsmith) is by Ridolfo del Ghirlandaio and shows the influence of Raphael. He also painted the fine *Portrait of a Lady* on the next wall, hung beside Andrea del Sarto's altarpiece, on the other side of which is another beautiful portrait of a lady, known as **La Gravida** as it was thought the sitter was expecting a child when it was painted, attributed to Raphael or Ridolfo del Ghirlandaio. On the window wall hangs Rosso Fiorentino's **Pala Dei**, a typical Florentine Mannerist work painted in 1522 for Pietro Dei for the church of Santo Spirito; when Crown Prince Ferdinando acquired it in 1691, he had it enlarged to fit its new frame. On the last wall is an **equestrian portrait of Philip IV of Spain** by Velázquez. It manages to convey a sense of remarkable grandeur despite its very small size. On the other side of the door is a portrait of Count Valdemar Christian of Denmark by Justus Suttermans (who also painted Prince Mattias de' Medici on the opposite wall). This Flemish painter was appointed to the Medici court in 1619 and remained in its service until his death in 1681. It is through his numerous portraits that we know today what the most influential figures in 17th-century Florence looked like.

In the centre of the room is a fine early 19th-century marble group representing *Charity* by Lorenzo Bartolini.

THE BAROQUE CEILING DECORATIONS

The ceilings of the five reception rooms known as the Sala di Giove, Sala di Marte, Sala di Apollo, Sala di Venere and Sala di Saturno, named after the gods Jupiter (Jove), Mars, Apollo, Venus and Saturn, were beautifully decorated in the 1640s (probably in that order) for Ferdinando II by Pietro da Cortona, founder of the Roman Baroque school of painting. They illustrate the virtues of the young Medici prince and exalt the grand-ducal family by means of extravagant allegories (Ferdinando is represented by the figure of Hercules). The murals also celebrate Galileo and the discoveries he had made earlier in the century through numerous illustrations of the constellations and planets. The fine gilded and white stuccoes were carried out by both Roman and Florentine craftsmen. Even though this type of decoration was not copied in other Florentine palaces of the period, it was to have a great influence in the decoration of royal apartments all over Europe, including Versailles. Pietro left the ceilings unfinished when he departed from Florence in 1647, but they were completed by his able pupil Ciro Ferri some 20 years later (and they have recently been exquisitely restored).

---

(28) Sala di Saturno: Here are displayed some famous masterpieces by Raphael. His **Madonna della Seggiola**, a beautifully composed tondo (named after the chair, *seggiola*), is one of his most mature works (c. 1514–15), painted directly, without the help of an under-drawing. It has for long been one of the most popular paintings of the Madonna. We do not know who commissioned it, but it seems that it hung in Leo X's bedroom. By the end of the 16th century it was in Cardinal Ferdinando's collection in the Villa Medici in Rome, and when it came to Florence Cosimo I hung it in the Tribuna in the Uffizi. The splendid frame was designed for it by Giovanni Battista Foggini at the end of the 17th century. The Madonna is thought to be a portrait of Raphael's mistress known as 'La Fornarina'. The artist seems to have been influenced by Venetian painting here, and the colours are very unusual, including the apple-green cloak of the Madonna.

On the opposite wall is Raphael's *Madonna del Granduca*, probably an early work painted around 1505. It is named after Grand Duke Ferdinand III of Lorraine, who purchased it in 1800 while in exile in Vienna during the Napoleonic interlude in Florence, and when he brought it back here he kept it in his bedroom (it only entered the gallery in 1850). We know nothing about who it was painted for but since the preparatory drawing survives in Florence (now in the Gabinetto dei Disegni e Stampe in the Uffizi), this suggests it was a private commission from a Florentine. Scholars have for long discussed whether Raphael was responsible for the dark background (X-rays have revealed that the Madonna was formerly depicted in a loggia) but it is likely that the artist himself decided to change this (probably influenced by Leonardo da Vinci) and thus project the figures into the foreground, adding to their iconic significance.

Also on this wall is Raphael's **portrait of Tommaso Inghirami**. Inghirami was an intimate friend of Raphael's and secretary and librarian to Leo X, as well as an actor. This was painted around 1514 when Raphael was in Rome, and clearly shows that Tommaso became 'cross-eyed' after his right eye was damaged in an ac-

cident when he fell off a cart. His bright red cloak and hat and his hands are exquisitely painted (the book-rest was probably added in Raphael's workshop).

On the last wall are four more works by Raphael: the **portraits of Agnolo Doni and Maddalena Strozzi** were painted, probably as a diptych, about two years after their marriage in 1504. Agnolo, a rich merchant who was 34 when he married the 14-year-old Maddalena (member of one of the wealthiest families in Florence), also commissioned the tondo by Michelangelo now in the Uffizi (the *Doni Tondo*) and bought Donatello's bronze statue known as *Atys-Amorino*. There are echoes of Leonardo's *Mona Lisa* in Maddalena's pose, and the exquisite jewel at her neck reminds us of her wealth. The little unicorn symbolises her virginity. The tiny *Vision of Ezekiel*, a much later work, is hung between them. Ezekiel can just be seen at the bottom of the painting in a wonderful stormy landscape. This was purchased by Cosimo I and hung in the Tribuna of the Uffizi. It was painted in 1512 and shows the influence of Michelangelo's works in the Sistine Chapel.

The large altarpiece known as the *Madonna del Baldacchino*, commissioned from Raphael in 1507 by the Dei family for their chapel in Santo Spirito, was left unfinished when the artist was called away to Rome the following year. It is clearly only at a half-way stage, with none of the flesh-colour begun: these were always the last parts to be painted. The two angels in flight above are the most innovative elements in the painting but the entire composition set a new model for subsequent Florentine altarpieces. It was enlarged at the top by

Niccolò Cassana after Prince Ferdinando purchased it in 1697, in order to fit its present frame, a pair with that framing the painting by Fra' Bartolomeo on the same wall.

The portrait of Cardinal Dovizzi di Bibbiena lacks the force of the other portraits by Raphael here, and his workshop may have intervened in some areas. The cardinal had hoped that his niece Maria would marry Raphael, but she predeceased him. Also in this room is a very fine *Deposition* painted in 1495 by Raphael's master Perugino.

(29) Sala di Giove: This was the throne-room of the Medici and contains Pietro da Cortona's most refined decoration of the entire suite of rooms. The young prince Ferdinando is shown in glory, surrounded by the virtues. By the far door is Raphael's portrait of a lady known as **La Velata** ('Lady with a Veil'), one of his most beautiful paintings, probably dating from around 1516. The grace and dignity of the sitter pervade the work, rendered with a skill which anticipates the hand of Titian. The magnificent left sleeve receives all the attention, so that the painter could 'forget' the right one. It was purchased by Cosimo II de' Medici.

On the other side of the door is the beautiful Venetian painting known as the *Three Ages of Man* (though in fact it probably represents a concert); this has had various attributions, the most convincing of which seems to be Giorgione. On the wall opposite the window, the **Head of St Jerome**, an exquisite small work painted on paper, in an elaborate 19th-century frame, once attributed to Pollaiolo, is now thought to be by Verrocchio. On the next wall is Crown Prince Guidobaldo II

della Rovere in armour, with his dog (c. 1530), the first of many splendid official court portraits by Bronzino. The *Deposition* is Fra' Bartolomeo's last work and one of his best, although it is only a fragment. Next to the door, the *Young St John the Baptist* by Andrea del Sarto (1523) is one of the best-known representations of the Baptist. At the top of this wall, the *Madonna of the House-martin* is a delightful work by Guercino.

(30) Sala di Marte: The largest painting in the room is the **Consequences of War**, one of Rubens' most important works. It is an allegory showing Venus trying to prevent Mars going to war, while both figures are surrounded by its destructive and tragic results. It was painted in 1638 and sent by the artist to his friend and fellow countryman at the Medici court, Suttermans. Below are two beautiful small works by Andrea del Sarto, with scenes from the life of St Joseph. On the right hangs Titian's superb **portrait of Cardinal Ippolito de' Medici**, in Hungarian costume. The cardinal was the illegitimate son of the Duke of Nemours, Lorenzo the Magnificent's grandson. He was nominated cardinal against his wishes by Clement VII when he was twelve years old. He commissioned this portrait from Titian to celebrate his return from Hungary, where he had been successful in a battle against the Turks.

On the other side is a splendid *Portrait of a Man* in fur robes, by Veronese. On the next wall, two paintings of the *Madonna and Child* by the Spanish painter Murillo flank Rubens' delightful portrait group known as **The Four Philosophers** (from left to right: Rubens himself, his brother Philip, the Flemish humanist

Detail of Canova's famous *Venus Italica* (1812), inspired by ancient Greek and Roman nudes.

Justus Lipsius and Jan van Wouwer). Rubens' brother and Van Wouwer were both pupils of Lipsius, famous for his studies of Seneca (whose bust is shown in the painting). To the left of the door into the next room is an elegant official portrait of Cardinal Guido Bentivoglio by Van Dyck, dating from around 1623.

(31) Sala di Apollo: To the right of the entrance door is one of Titian's master-pieces, his *Portrait of a Gentleman*, pos-sibly the Genoese nobleman Gian Luigi Fieschi. On the other side of the door is Titian's *Mary Magdalene*, another beauti-fully painted work, which was frequently copied. Also on this wall is Andrea del Sarto's *Deposition* (1523). On the wall opposite the windows, the portrait of Vittoria della Rovere dressed as a Roman vestal is by Suttermans. On the next wall are hung a *Holy Family* by Andrea del Sarto, *Cleopatra* by Guido Reni and, beyond the door, a portrait of Isabella Clara Eugenia (governor of the Nether-lands), dressed in the habit of a nun, by Rubens, and a double portrait of Charles I and Henrietta Maria by Van Dyck.

(32) Sala di Venere: This room is named after the **Venus Italica**, sculpted by Canova and presented to Florence by Napoleon in 1812, in exchange for the *Medici Venus* which he had transported to Paris (*see p. 121*). It is one of the master-pieces of Neoclassical art in Florence. By the door is Titian's ***Portrait of a Lady (La Bella)***, commissioned by the Duke of Urbino in 1536, apparently an idealised portrait similar to the *Venus of Urbino* in the Uffizi. This superb work came to Florence as part of the dowry of Vittoria della Rovere in 1631, on her marriage to Ferdinando II. Also on this wall is Titian's exquisitely-painted **portrait of Pietro Aretino**, one of his most forceful works. Aretino was disappointed with the paint-ing, and after a quarrel with the artist he presented it to Cosimo I in 1545 (it was the first of the eleven portraits by Titian here to be hung in Palazzo Pitti). Above is a large seascape (one of a pair; the second is on the opposite wall), painted for Cardinal Gian Carlo de' Medici, one of Ferdinando II's brothers, by Salvatore Rosa. On the wall opposite the windows are two lovely landscapes by Rubens: ***Return from the Hayfields***, with a de-lightful joyful scene, and its companion, *Ulysses in the Phaeacian Isle*. The portrait of Pope Julius II is a copy by Titian of Raphael's painting which survives in two versions (one in the National Gallery, London, and one in the Uffizi).

The famous ***Concert*** (c. 1510–12) is a superb painting, the attribution of which has been much discussed. Some scholars believe it is by Titian, but it appears that more than one hand was involved, and Giorgione may have been responsible for the figure on the left. The portrait of Bac-cio Valori is by Sebastiano del Piombo.

Appartamenti Reali

Open as Galleria Palatina, but some of the rooms are usually closed for maintenance work in winter. Plan on p. 235.

These lavishly decorated rooms were used as state apartments from the 17th century onwards by the Medici and Lorraine grand dukes. They have been restored (as far as possible) to their appearance in 1880–1911, when they were first occupied by the royal House of Savoy, and the contents reflect their eclectic taste. The earlier neo-Baroque period of the 19th-century Lorraine grand dukes is recorded in the splendid silks and furnishings made in Florence and France, the sumptuous gilded chandeliers, Neoclassical mirrors and candelabra, well-preserved early 19th-century carpets from Tournai, huge Oriental vases and furniture decorated with *pietre dure*.

(•1) **Sala delle Nicchie:** This was first designed by Ammannati (1561–62) with black marble niches (*nicchie*) to house the Medici collection of antique statues and busts brought from Rome by Cosimo I. The Neoclassical decorations date from the late 18th century.

(•2) **Sala Verde:** On the wall opposite the window are delightful portraits of the daughters of Louis XV by Jean-Marc Nattier: Marie-Henriette is portrayed as Flora and Marie-Adelaïde as Diana. The portrait of a Knight of Malta (perhaps Antonio Martelli) is by Caravaggio. The very fine ebony cabinet was made for Vittoria della Rovere in 1677 and decorated with *pietre dure*.

(•3) **Sala del Trono:** The red damask curtains and wall hangings, made in France in 1853–54, are typical of the Napoleonic period. The Japanese vases date from the Edo period (c. 1700) and

the Chinese vases from the 19th century.

(•4) **Salotto Celeste:** The round table (1826) has a fine top in *pietre dure*, and the chandelier was made by the Dutch carver Vittorio Crosten in 1697. The room also contains a series of ten Medici portraits by Suttermans, in matching frames.

(•5) **Chapel:** Formerly the *alcova* (official bedroom) of Crown Prince Ferdinando (son of Cosimo III de' Medici). The *Madonna and Child* by Carlo Dolci is in a rich frame of ebony and *pietre dure* (1697), probably designed by Giovanni Battista Foggini.

(•6) **Sala dei Pappagalli:** The table, with a top in *pietre dure*, dates from 1790–1831 and the bronze clock-case is by Pierre-Philippe Thomire (c. 1812). The delightful scene of the Impruneta fair is by Filippo Napolitano.

From here it is usually possible to visit either the Appartamenti della Regina Margherita (*straight ahead*) or the Appartamenti del Re Umberto (*to the left*).

(•7–10) **Appartamenti della Regina Margherita:** These rooms form part of the suite of Queen Margherita of Savoy (1851–1926), wife of Umberto I. Her **Salotto** (•7) is decorated with yellow silk made in France c. 1805–10. The paintings include a delightful studio scene (based on Rubens' house in Antwerp) painted in the 17th century by Cornelis

de Baellieur. Beside it is an ebony cabinet decorated with ivory, alabaster and gilded bronze, which was produced in the grand-ducal workshop by Giovanni Battista Foggini and others in 1704. The **Camera della Regina** (•8) has a pretty bed decorated in 1885 and a *prie-dieu* in ebony and *pietre dure* made in 1687. From here you can usually look into the **Gabinetto Ovale** (•9), created by Gaspare Maria Paoletti soon after 1765 for Grand Duchess Maria Luisa, wife of Peter Leopold. The beautiful silk chinoiserie furnishings were made in Florence in 1780–83. Adjoining it is the **Gabinetto Rotondo** (•10), with 18th-century furniture and mirrors around the walls.

(•11–14) **Appartamenti del Re Umberto:** These were formerly the apartments of King Umberto I, King of Italy from 1878 until his assassination by an anarchist in 1900. The yellow **Camera del Re** (•11), decorated at the end of the 18th century, has a fine Empire-style table by Giuseppe Colzi (1822) in its centre. The small **Studio del Re** (•12), with yellow silk furnishings, dates from 1770.

(•) **Ritirata della Granduchessa:** *NB: Only shown on guided tours, usually as part of the visit to the Appartamenti degli Arazzi, see below. The entrance is in the corridor between the Sala dei Pappagalli (•6) and the Camera del Re (•11).* These five rooms, between the Appartamenti della Regina Margherita and those of Re Umberto, served as bathrooms and dressing rooms in the earlier Lorraine period. They preserve their delightful Neoclassical decorations intact. They were carried out for the Infanta of Spain, Maria Luisa of Bourbon, who married Peter Leopold in 1765. She bore him 16 children but we know little else about her life as grand duchess (and when in 1790 Peter Leopold became the Holy Roman Emperor Leopold II, she accompanied him back to Vienna).

The duke's bathroom has a sunken bathtub (with its original plumbing, extremely 'modern' for its time, carefully preserved) beneath a charmingly deco-rated skylight. The delightful little circular bathroom created for the duchess has a dome modelled on the Pantheon above a round bathing pool carved from Carrara marble. A boudoir has its walls and ceiling painted with figures inspired by Pompeian frescoes, bordered by delicate garlands of flowers, by Luigi Catani, and another has gilded stucco decoration. A little interior courtyard close by has lovely frescoes of a wood with magnificent trees and a niche for a classical statue of Calliope (always known as *Diana*) by Domenico Stagi (probably repainted by Giuseppe Castagnoli).

(*1–8) **Sala Bianca, Sala di Bona and Appartamenti degli Arazzi:** *NB: The Sala Bianca, Sala di Bona and adjoining two rooms are often used for exhibitions. At the time of writing the Appartamenti degli Arazzi could only be visited Tues–Fri on guided tours (ask at the ticket office; there is usually a notice on the table in the Sala del Castagnoli, Room 3, with the time of the next tour).* The **Sala Bianca** (*1) is a magnificent ballroom designed by Niccolò Gaspare Paoletti in the 1770s and named after its white walls. The adjoining **Sala di Bona** was entirely covered in 1607–09 with frescoes by Bernardino Poccetti, commissioned by Ferdinando I to celebrate his father Cosimo I. It is one of the few rooms in the palace which has survived with its original decorations carried out for the Medici. It is named after one of the frescoes on the two long walls showing the Medici victory over the Turks at Bona in north Africa (the other shows a victorious battle in Albania). On the barrel vault, Cosimo is shown nude in the guise of Jupiter, holding instruments symbolising his role in the building of the Tuscan state. Against a painted mosaic background are numerous allegorical figures, the *Triumph of David* and monochrome painted statues by this prolific painter who left numerous frescoes in churches and cloisters all over Florence. The two adjoining rooms (9 and 10) are also usually occupied during exhibitions.

(*2–7) Appartamenti degli Arazzi: These former guest rooms still have their ceiling decorations illustrating the Theological and Cardinal Virtues, commissioned by Ferdinando I (late 16th or early 17th century) from Cristofano Allori, Lodovico Cigoli, Passignano and Bernardino Poccetti. Many of the precious tapestries were made in the Gobelins factory (some to designs by Charles Le Brun and others by Jean-Baptiste Oudry); others were made in the Florentine workshops. The collection of Medici tapestries, many of which are still in store, is one of the largest in the world (together with those in Vienna and Spain). The furniture dates mostly from the early 18th and 19th centuries and there are also good clocks. In the **Sala della Carità (*3)** there is a marble sculpture representing an *Allegory of Music* by Vincenzo Consani. The **Loggetta (*5)**, enclosed in the 19th century, has charming vault frescoes (1588) of humorous domestic scenes by Alessandro Allori: women are depicted washing their hair, washing a dog and intent on other day-to-day duties, beneath a washing line where the laundry is blowing in the breeze. The **Sala di Prudenzia (*6)** has a very fine series of three tapestries showing children busy gardening in villas. The ceiling has grotesques inhabited by numerous lovely birds. The last room, the **Sala della Temperanza (*7)** has a series of tapestries illustrating the story of St John the Baptist, made in the Florentine tapestry workshops. The furniture includes an intriguing travelling desk made in 1807.

Galleria d'Arte Moderna

For opening times, see p. 231. Plan on p. 252.
On the floor above the Galleria Palatina is the Galleria d'Arte Moderna, opened in 1924. The collection was formed c. 1784 by Grand Duke Peter Leopold when it was part of the Accademia di Belle Arti. Later acquisitions were made by the Savoy rulers and by the *Comune* of Florence. Since 1914 it has been administered jointly by the *Comune* and the state, and the collection continues to be augmented. The works currently on show, arranged chronologically and by schools, cover the period from the mid-18th century up to the First World War. Tuscan art of the 19th century is particularly well represented, notably the Macchiaioli School, which was active before 1864. These artists took their inspiration directly from nature and their paintings are characterised by *macchie*, or spots of colour. The most important Macchiaioli painters, who could be termed Tuscan Impressionists, are Giovanni Fattori, Silvestro Lega and Telemaco Signorini.

(1) Neoclassicism: On the entrance wall hangs *Hercules at the Crossroads* by Pompeo Batoni (1742), which was purchased for Palazzo Pitti by Ferdinand

III in 1818. The charming seated statue of *Psyche*, by the window, is by Pietro Tenerani (1816–17).

(2) The French occupation: The most famous artist who worked for the French court was Canova, whose signed bust of the muse Calliope (1812) is displayed here. It is a very fine work which retains its original patina (numerous other Neoclassical marble works were later polished). It is probably an idealised portrait of Elisa Baciocchi, Napoleon's sister, whom Napoleon appointed Grand Duchess of Tuscany in 1809; she is also shown here with her daughter in the Boboli Gardens, in a painting by Giuseppe Bezzuoli.

(3) Florence before Italian Unification: The portrait of Maria Luisa of Bourbon-Parma (with two red roses in her hair) is by François-Xavier Fabre. Maria Luisa was 'Queen of Etruria' until she was widowed in 1803, when she became regent for her son, but in 1807 left for Portugal with the 11-year-old boy and her place was taken by Napoleon's sister, Elisa Baciocchi. The sumptuous lapis lazuli centrepiece, decorated with mosaics and pearls, was made for Napoleon.

(4) Demidoff Room: This room records the wealthy Russian family who lived in Florence from 1820 onwards.

(5) Romantic historical paintings, including a huge scene by Giuseppe Bezzuoli (1829).

(6–7) Later 19th-century painters including Giuseppe Abbati, and 19th-century portraits.

Ballroom: Begun c. 1825 by Pasquale Poccianti, this displays early 19th-century statues, including two of the *Young Bacchus* by Giovanni Dupré.

Poccianti Staircase: The grand staircase installed by Poccianti between 1815 and 1847, to provide a splendid approach to the ballroom directly from Ammannati's courtyard, now serves as an alternative exit. It makes copious use of *pietra serena*, with its carved Doric, Ionic and Corinthian capitals and decorative garlands and insignia. The stucco vault reflects the light from the windows and a gilded iron balustrade follows the steps.

(8) Portraits, including a self-portrait by Giovanni Fattori dating from 1854, who also painted the *Portrait of a Man* (c. 1865) and the oval portrait of Signora Biliotti (1870).

(9) 19th-century landscapes showing the influence of the Barbizon school of French painters, including a pastoral scene by Serafino de Tivoli.

(10) The Cristiano Banti Collection: Banti (1824–1904) was a Tuscan painter, collector and friend of the artist Giovanni Boldini. It contains works by Banti himself and a portrait of him by Boldini, as well as numerous charming portraits of Banti's daughter Alaide as a child (many of them by Boldini, who fell in love with her) and (by Michele Gordigiani) as a grown woman.

(11) The Diego Martelli Collection: Martelli (1839–96) gave hospitality to some of the best-known Macchiaioli painters including Fattori and Lega at his home in Castiglioncello on the Tuscan coast. On the window wall are two portraits of Martelli by Federico Zandomeneghi, who lived in Paris and was clearly influenced by contemporary French painters: he also painted the works entitled *In Bed* and *Honeymoon*. Martelli acquired the two landscapes by Camille Pissarro before the Impressionists came into fashion. The protagonists of the Macchiaioli School well represented here by small works include Giovanni Fattori, Silvestro Lega (the charming *Walk in the Garden* and *Portrait of a Peasant Girl*) and Giuseppe Abbati.

(12): Above the fireplace is *Singing a Stornello* (a traditional Tuscan folk song) by Silvestro Lega, a conversation piece showing a scene in a villa in the environs of Florence, pervaded with a delightfully evocative atmosphere.

(13) Military scenes: The large historical canvas by Giovanni Fattori shows the desolate Italian camp after the Battle of Magenta in 1859, when the French and Italians (the Piedmontese) beat the Austrian troops in the Second War of Independence.

(14–15) Historical works by Antonio Ciseri, Gabriele Castagnola and Stefano Ussi.

(16): This room contains a bust of Giuseppe Verdi, commissioned by him from the Neapolitan sculptor Vincenzo Gemito. Here are more battle scenes by Giovanni Fattori and Carlo Ademollo and a 19th-century stand for the Crown of Italy.

(17) Portraits of the bourgeoisie from the 1870s and 1880s, including several by Vittorio Corcos (*Lady with a Dog and Umbrella* in particular shows the influence of elegant Parisian life).

(18) Masterpieces of the Macchiaioli School: On the wall opposite the windows are three fine works by Giovanni Fattori: *Ritratto della figliastra*, a portrait of his step-daughter; and two late works, the dramatic *Staffato*, showing a horse bolting and dragging its rider to death (his foot having been caught in the stirrup) and a solitary white horse (*Cavallo Bianco*), both of which express Fattori's sad last years when he was unjustly ostracised by his contemporaries. Next to them is displayed Telemaco Signorini's *Bagno penale di Portoferraio*, showing a prison scene. On the wall opposite the entrance are landscapes of the Maremma (in southwest Tuscany) by Fattori, and another famous work (in two versions) by him: the *Libecciata*, representing a windy day at the coast with a stormy sea behind a windblown tamarisk tree—an allegory of life, devoid of human figures. In the table case is Fattori's well-known *Rotonda di Palmieri*, a charming beach scene at Livorno (1866), and other delightful small works by Signorini.

(19) Ambron Collection of Macchiaioli and post-Macchiaioli works: On the wall opposite the entrance, Giovanni Fattori's small early portrait of *La cugina Argia* is displayed next to Telemaco Signorini's *Leith*, a grey street scene painted during a visit to Scotland in 1881.

(20): On the far wall are two charming paintings by Telemaco Signorini (*Sep-*

tember in Settignano and *Hot August Day in Pietramala*) flanked by two Maremma scenes by Fattori. On the opposite wall are idyllic country scenes by Egisto Ferroni, typical of the paintings favoured by Florentine bourgeois society in the 1880s.

(**22**): Hanging on the wall opposite the entrance are a *Cemetery Scene in Constantinople* by the important Neapolitan painter Domenico Morelli and a fine landscape (*On the Banks of the Olfanto*) by Giuseppe de Nittis.

(**23**) **Late 19th-century Tuscan works** influenced by contemporary European painting, including a portrait of the frivolous Bruna Pagliano, dressed in black, by Edoardo Gelli.

(**24**) **Divisionism and Symbolism:** This illustrates the beginning of these two art movements in the first years of the 20th century. There are some early works by Plinio Nomellini and sculptures by Medardo Rosso.

(**25**) **Macchiaioli paintings** including works by Giovanni Fattori, Telemaco Signorini, Silvestro Lega and Giuseppe Abbati.

(**26**) **Portraits by Elisabeth Chaplin** (1890–1982), who lived in Florence and donated most of her works to the gallery in 1974.

(**27**) **Early 20th-century works:** Armando Spadini (1883–1925) and Oscar Ghiglia (1876–1945).

(**30**): Works acquired at an exhibition in Florence in 1922 by Galileo Chini, Francesco Franchetti and others.

Quartiere d'Inverno (or Quartiere della Duchessa d'Aosta)

This group of rooms (I–XV; *plan on p. 252*), decorated in the late 18th and early 19th centuries, can only be seen by appointment (*T: 055 294883*). They were used by the Medici grand dukes in winter, but are now named after their last occupants, the Duchess of Aosta and Prince Luigi of the royal house of Savoy. Luigi, eldest son of Umberto I, became King Vittorio Emanuele III on Umberto's assassination, though for most of his reign he was overshadowed by Mussolini. These rooms were his home until his abdication in 1946, when Italy voted to become a republic. He died in exile the following year. The rooms are interesting for their 18th- and 19th-century decorations and furniture.

Mezzanino degli Occhi

These 13 rooms at the very top of the palace, beneath the eaves, are named after their large round windows (recalling eyes, or *occhi*). Closed at the time of writing, there are plans to use them to exhibit the Galleria d'Arte Moderna's holdings dating from 1922–45. These are by the best-known artists of the period including Arturo Tosi, Mario Sironi, Giovanni Colacicchi, Felice Casorati, Ardengo Soffici, Filippo de Pisis, Carlo Carrà, Gino Severini and Giorgio de Chirico.

THE MEDICI AT PALAZZO PITTI

Ferdinando I (grand duke 1587–1609)

When Ferdinando became a cardinal he bought the Villa Medici in Rome (in 1576) and turned it into one of the grandest residences in the city, with a famous collection of ancient Roman sculpture. But just ten years later, on the death of his brother (Francesco I), he had to renounce his cardinal's hat and move back to Florence to succeed him, taking Christine of Lorraine as his wife. It was Ferdinando who transferred the grand-ducal residence permanently to the Pitti (up until now used by the Medici only for ceremonial occasions). He arranged two other important marriages in the family which were also public spectacles: that of his niece Maria to Henri IV in 1600, and his heir Cosimo to Maria Maddalena of Austria. He was Tuscany's most impressive ruler in the modern era, and carried out important agricultural reforms and land reclamation schemes throughout the region, and proclaimed Livorno a free port with religious liberty. He had Buontalenti build the villas of the Petraia and Artimino close to Florence, where he would enjoy the country air.

Cosimo II (grand duke 1609–21)

Although Cosimo suffered from ill health and died of tuberculosis at the age of 30, he oversaw the work to enlarge Palazzo Pitti by adding the two side wings, and he arranged a small gallery on the *piano nobile* where he hung Raphael's painting known as *La Velata*.

Ferdinando II (grand duke 1621–70)

Ferdinando was only eleven when his father (Cosimo II) died and so his mother Maria Maddalena and his grandmother Christine acted as regents. His two cardinal brothers also had an important influence on him. Cardinal Leopoldo, who acted as his minister of foreign affairs in Tuscany, had a great interest in science and was a passionate collector with a particular interest in Venetian paintings, in drawings, and in self-portraits. In 1654 he purchased *The Concert*, attributed at the time to Giorgione but now thought to be an early work by Titian and still one of the masterpieces of the Galleria Palatina. Ferdinando's other Cardinal brother, Gian Carlo, had a special interest in music and theatre, and kept Ferdinando informed on the artistic activities in Rome under Pope Urban VIII. Another brother, Mattias, who commanded the Tuscan army, put together the remarkable collection of ivories still to be seen in the Museo degli Argenti (*see p. 256*).

According to Harold Acton in *The Last Medici* (1932, revised 1958), 'Ferdinando had only to steer a lukewarm, unambitious course between France, Austria, and Spain, and this he did with skill and equanimity. Because of his neutrality he had a reputation for profound wisdom and knowledge of statecraft. Enjoying this prestige under peaceful conditions, Ferdinando decided to encourage the sciences and arts in the bountiful tradition of his ancestors.'

During Ferdinando's long reign, the Pitti reached its maximum splendour: as well as his family and brothers, some 160 members of his court lived here. The grand duke spent the winter on the *piano nobile* of the palace and the summer in the cooler ground-floor apartments. He married Vittoria della Rovere, daughter of the Duke of Urbino, and inherited as part of her dowry some masterpieces by Raphael and Titian. Ferdinando commissioned the frescoes by Pietro da Cortona for the palace, marking the transition from the late Renaissance to the splendours of the Baroque period.

Cosimo III (grand duke 1670–1723)
Cosimo III held the office of grand duke for longer than all the other Medici but he proved a totally inept ruler, ignoring the interests of Tuscany. In addition, his marriage to Marguerite-Louise d'Orléans was a disaster. An atmosphere of decadence took hold, although recent research has revealed that Cosimo, venerating the memory of his uncle Cardinal Leopoldo, did take special care of the works of art in Palazzo Pitti and began collecting together the paintings which in the following centuries formed the Galleria Palatina. Indeed the most popular of all the pictures in the gallery, Raphael's *Madonna della Seggiola*, was moved here by him from the Tribuna of the Uffizi, and given its sumptuous frame.

Crown Prince Ferdinando (died 1713)
Destined to succeed his father Cosimo III, Ferdinando predeceased him in 1713. Nevertheless, he is remembered for his passionate interest in art and music, and he made some important acquisitions for the Medici collections, including Parmigianino's *Madonna dal collo lungo*, Andrea del Sarto's *Madonna of the Harpies*, and Titian's *Portrait of a Gentleman*. He was also interested in little-known contemporary painters such as Livio Mehus and Magnasco. Though he had a habit of removing paintings he particularly liked from churches in Florence and Tuscany, he did replace them with copies.

Gian Gastone (grand duke 1723–37)
The second son of Cosimo III, Gian Gastone succeeded his father since his elder brother had died without heirs. He was an introvert interested in scientific studies and his rule was marked, like that of his father, by an increasing air of decadence. He became an alcoholic and led a dissipated life in his bedroom, refusing to appear in public for the last eight years of his reign. His vulgarity and his more repulsive personal habits have tended to obscure the positive aspects of his rule, which included the revoking of anti-Semitic legislation.

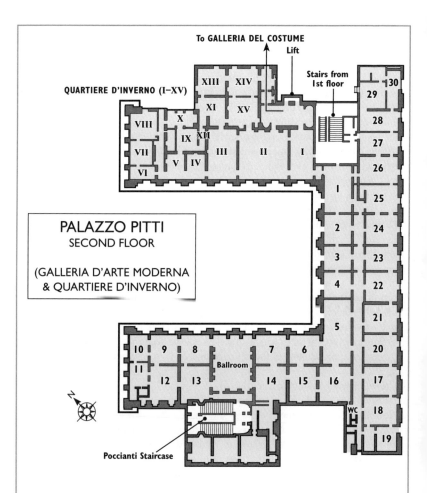

To GALLERIA DEL COSTUME
Lift

QUARTIERE D'INVERNO (I–XV)

Stairs from
1st floor

PALAZZO PITTI
SECOND FLOOR

(GALLERIA D'ARTE MODERNA
& QUARTIERE D'INVERNO)

Ballroom

WC

Poccianti Staircase

HIGHLIGHTS OF THE GALLERIA D'ARTE MODERNA

1	Neoclassicism	11	Diego Martelli Collection
2	The French occupation	12	Silvestro Lega
3	Before Italian Unification	13	Giovanni Fattori
4	Demidoff Room	18–20	The Macchiaioli (Fattori and Signorini)
5	Romantic Historicism	24	Divisionism and Symbolism
6	Later 19th century	25	The Macchiaioli
7–8	Giovanni Fattori		
10	Cristiano Banti Collection		

Galleria del Costume

For opening times, see above p. 231. Entrance on the second floor from near the Galleria d'Arte Moderna, or from the Boboli Gardens.

The Meridiana Wing of Palazzo Pitti, which faces the Boboli Gardens, was begun for the Lorraine grand dukes in 1776 by Gaspare Maria Paoletti and was finished in 1832 by Pasquale Poccianti. The decoration of the rooms dates mostly from the 1860s. Founded in 1983, the Galleria del Costume is the only museum of the history of fashion in Italy. The collection is made up largely from private donations—which continue all the time—and illustrates the history of costume from the 18th to the mid-20th centuries. The beautiful displays of clothes are changed about every two years and frequent exhibitions are held. There are also some clothes dating from the 16th century, including those worn by Eleanor of Toledo, wife of Cosimo I de' Medici, and her son Don Garzia. The precious 18th-century collection includes some rare men's apparel. The Umberto Tirelli (1928–90) collection of costumes used in theatre and film productions has been donated to the museum. Other donations include those of the Sicilian noblewoman Donna Franca Florio, and (in 2000) the fashion designer Gianfranco Ferrè. Decorating the rooms are contemporary paintings and sculpture from the Galleria d'Arte Moderna.

Museo degli Argenti

For opening times, see above p. 231. Entrance from the left side of the courtyard.

The Museo degli Argenti is arranged in the summer apartments of the grand dukes, some of which were used as state rooms. The eclectic collection, formed by the Medici and Lorraine grand dukes, includes precious objects in silver, ivory, amber and *pietre dure*, including antique pieces, jewellery, and some exotic curiosities. The silver (after which the museum takes its name) was first exhibited in the middle of the 19th century and in the 20th century all that remained of the grand-ducal treasury (formerly kept in the Uffizi) was transferred here and opened to the public. The main rooms on the ground floor are often used for exhibitions.

Ground floor

Sala di Luca Pitti: Named after the first owner of the palace, who is commemorated here in a delightful polychrome terracotta bust (15th century). The series of later terracotta busts portray the seven Medici grand dukes from Alessandro to Gian Gastone. In the small room to the right is displayed 18th-century Chinese and Japanese porcelain.

Sala di Giovanni da San Giovanni: Exuberant and colourful frescoes by Giovanni da San Giovanni completely cover the walls and ceiling. They were begun in 1634 after the marriage of Ferdinando II and Vittoria della Rovere (an allegory of which is represented on the ceiling). The apotheosis of the Medici family is illustrated on the walls, through the life of Lorenzo the Magnificent. The sequence begins at the far end of the entrance wall, which has two scenes symbolising the destruction of Culture, including the Muses fleeing from Mount Parnassus. The particularly successful third scene (around the entrance door) shows the Muses and poets finding refuge in Tuscany (represented by an allegorical female figure). The two scenes on the adjacent short wall, by San Giovanni's pupil Cecco Bravo, show Lorenzo the Magnificent receiving the Muses, and Prudence instructing Lorenzo (as a consequence, Peace, represented by a woman on the lower part of the wall, takes off her armour, while high above, War, in the form of the chariot of Mars, gallops away). The scenes on the window wall are by Ottavio Vannini: the central one shows Lorenzo seated in the sculpture garden of San Marco while the young Michelangelo presents him with his sculpture of the head of a faun. On the last wall, two scenes by Francesco Furini show Lorenzo at the Villa Careggi surrounded by members of the Platonic Academy and an elaborate allegory of his death. On the painted pilasters are *trompe l'œil* bas-reliefs of Classical myths and the seasons.

Sala Buia: The central case displays 16 magnificent *pietre dure* vases which belonged to Lorenzo the Magnificent and which bear his monogram: 'LA V.R.MED'. Although it is very difficult to date many of them and their provenance is usually unknown, they include late Imperial Roman works, as well as Byzantine and medieval Venetian pieces. Others come from Persia and Egypt. The collection was begun by Piero il Gottoso and enlarged by Lorenzo. Many of the vases were formerly used as reliquaries and were mounted in silver-gilt in the 15th century or later in the grand-ducal workshops. Four more cases display ex-

quisite smaller works, including Roman cups and dishes in *pietre dure*, and some Byzantine works (most of them with later mounts).

Lorenzo the Magnificent's death-mask is displayed next to his portrait by Luigi Fiammingo: the smile on his notably wide mouth is unforgettable.

The rock crystal and agate columns by Buontalenti and *pietre dure* statuettes by Orazio Mochi were made for the ciborium for the Cappella dei Principi (*see p. 149*), commissioned by Don Giovanni de' Medici but never finished.

Sala delle Cornice: In the Grotticina, with its small fountain and frescoed ceiling with birds (1623–34) and its lovely pavement in *pietre dure* and soft stone, there is a display of 17th- and 18th-century frames, including four by the Dutch craftsman Vittorio Crosten (who also carved the base of the *pietre dure* table made in Prague in the early 17th century). The exquisitely carved limewood relief by Grinling Gibbons was presented to Cosimo III in 1682 by Charles II of England.

Cappella: Decorated by local craftsmen in 1623–34. The ebony *prie-dieu* is exquisitely decorated in *pietre dure*.

Reception rooms: The three rooms beyond the Cappella are decorated with delightful *trompe l'œil* frescoes by the Bolognese painters Angelo Michele Colonna and Agostino Mitelli (1635–41), who worked as partners for over 20 years. The frescoes—which are in exceptionally good condition—cover the wall surfaces with architectural perspectives, animated by the occasional human figure. There are a number of very fine tables in antique porphyry, agate and *pietre dure*. The exquisite cabinet was commissioned from Giovanni Battista Foggini in 1709 by Cosimo III as a wedding present for his favourite child, Anna Maria Luisa. It is the most famous of the many cabinets and tabletops designed in *pietre dure* by Foggini for the Medici. Foggini was a particularly versatile artist who also worked as a painter and architect as well as producing small bronzes and reliquaries, and even perhaps the frame commissioned by Cosimo III for Raphael's *Madonna della Seggiola*.

Anna Maria Luisa de' Medici, the Electress Palatine (1667–1743)
In 1691 Anna Maria Luisa married the Elector Palatine, Johann Wilhelm von Pfalz-Neuburg, by proxy in the Duomo of Florence (her brother, Crown Prince Ferdinando, stood in for him). Contemporary accounts record the 24-year-old bride bedecked with magnificent jewels and the grand celebrations which lasted many days. She immediately left for Düsseldorf, where she spent the next 25 years living in royal style with her cultivated husband. Together they formed a superb collection of works of art from paintings to jewels, but had no children. When Johann died in 1716 she returned to Florence, bringing with her her jewellery (and also Foggini's cabinet described above).

She is fondly remembered in Florence for the 'Family Pact' which she drew up just a few months after the death of her brother Gian Gastone in 1737. This left the Medici artistic heritage (including paintings, sculpture, scientific instruments and libraries) to the Lorraine grand dukes for 'the ornament of the state, the utility of the public, and in order to attract the attention of foreigners'—and only on the condition that not a single work would ever leave Florence or Tuscany. Only her jewels were seized at her death (*for their subsequent history, see overleaf*).

The rooms towards the Boboli Gardens were the living quarters of the grand dukes. It is here and on the mezzanine floor that their eclectic collection of personal keepsakes is displayed—these include gifts presented by other ruling families and *objets d'art* made specially for them.

Ivories Collection: The two rooms to the left contain one of the most important collections in the world of 17th-century ivories, many of them made for Cardinal Leopoldo by the German artists Balthasar Permoser, Balthasar Stockamer and Christoph Daniel Schenck (who made the *Madonna*, signed and dated 1680). Stockamer came to Italy in the service of Cardinal Leopoldo, and Pietro da Cortona made some wax models for him to produce in ivory. Permoser worked in Dresden but is known to have been in Italy from 1686–90. Particularly remarkable from a technical point of view are the elaborate composition of Curtius riding his horse into the abyss; and the seated long-haired dog, given to

Maria Maddalena of Austria by her husband Cosimo II. The fantastic collection of turned ivory vases in winding, spiralling shapes made by Marcus Heiden and his pupil Johann Eisenberg in 1618–31 was seized at the Siege of Coburg during the Thirty Years War by the young prince Mattias de' Medici. The artist, the greatest master of the technique of turning using a lathe, who was trapped inside the town during the siege, saw them disappear and presumed they had been destroyed; instead the prince was busy bartering for them outside the walls. The mystery remains how these incredibly delicate works survived both the war and the journey to Florence.

Mezzanine floor

A pretty little staircase leads up to the mezzanine floor where the grand-ducal collection of jewellery has always been kept.

The Medici jewellery collections:
The magnificent collection of ancient Roman and Renaissance jewels, gems and cameos is one of the most important in existence. Cosimo il Vecchio began collecting these precious objects and we know that he possessed 24 by the time of his death. All the subsequent members of his family continued to augment the collection and the last member of the ruling dynasty, Anna Maria Luisa, the

Electress Palatine, owned some 1,800 pieces. At her death in 1743, the new Grand Duke, Franz Stephan of Lorraine (in great need of money), ordered that her jewels be seized, arguing that they were her personal possessions and thus not part of the family inheritance tied to Florence through her 'Family Pact'. Those that were not sold or melted down ended up in Vienna, where they remained until 1923, when some of them were returned.

A central display case contains a relief of Cosimo I and his family in *pietre dure* by Giovanni Antonio de' Rossi (1557–62; it used to contain a medallion with the personification of Florence); an oval in *pietre dure* by Bernardo Gaffurri of the equestrian statue of Cosimo I in Piazza della Signoria (1598); a Roman head of Hercules; and seven bas-reliefs in gold set on precious stones made by Giambologna for the Studiolo of Francesco I (in Palazzo Vecchio). Around the walls are cases of cameos arranged by subject matter: these were the most valuable part of the Medici collection and were an im-

Ivory cameo of the portly Pope Leo X
(Giovanni de' Medici).

portant iconographical source for the art of the Renaissance. They include ancient Roman pieces as well as Renaissance works, and casts of some of the most important were taken in order to produce small bronze reliefs or plaquettes in the 15th century. In the cases above is an exquisite series of miniature busts in rock crystal and turquoise, some of them dating from the ancient Roman period, and tiny vases in precious stones made in the 16th century. The chessboard in *pietre dure* was designed by Jacopo Ligozzi.

The adjoining room has numerous charming pieces in the form of animals made with huge baroque pearls, rings with cameos and intaglio, and an ex-voto in precious stones of Cosimo II at prayer, made in the grand-ducal workshops in 1617–24.

Exotic treasures: The rooms at the top of the stairs on the left contain gold and silversmiths' work from the Treasury of Ferdinand III, brought to Florence in 1814 (mainly from Salzburg), including elaborate nautilus shells, a double chalice made from an ostrich egg mounted in silver-gilt (c. 1370–80) and two ornamental cups made from buffalo horns with silver-gilt mounts (14th century). The series of silver-gilt dishes from Salzburg was made by Paul Hübner, c. 1590.

In the Loggetta (enclosed in the 19th century) there are delightful painted decorations by Poccetti's pupil Michelangelo Cinganelli and his workshop (1622). Here are four 17th-century Mexican vases and two small Persian (Isfahan) carpets made in the same century. Cinganelli also painted the next room, which overlooks the courtyard and contains exotic and rare objects from all over the world. These include an Islamic powder horn, nautilus shells, 17th-century shell figurines, and a mitre with scenes of the Passion depicted in gold thread and birds' feathers (Mexican, c. 1545).

The last three rooms have 18th- and 19th-century jewellery and a collection of portrait miniatures (16th–19th century), all of them recent donations.

Return down the stairs to visit the last two rooms on the ground floor on the way to the exit.

Camera da letto del Granduca Gian Gastone: This was the bedchamber of the last Medici grand duke (*see p. 251*) and was the room in which he spent most of his time. It now contains three splendid gilded wood display cabinets with 16th–17th-century amber and ivories. On an 18th-century table there is an amber centrepiece in the form of a fountain (c. 1610). The framed terracotta models of the *Four Seasons* are by Soldani Benzi. The portrait of Maria Maddalena of Austria is by Suttermans.

In the last room are exquisite vessels in rock crystal and *pietre dure* including, to the left of the entrance, a lapis lazuli vase (1583) designed by Buontalenti, a rock crystal vase in the form of a bird (c. 1589), a lapis lazuli shell with a snake handle in enamelled gold, and a reliquary casket in rock crystal and gilded silver by Valerio Belli (1532). The next case contains a rock crystal goblet with an intricately decorated enamelled gold lid, thought to have been made for Henri II of France.

BOBOLI GARDENS

Map 6, 5. Open 8.30–dusk, closed on first and last Mon of the month; T: 055 265 1838. There are at present four entrances (with ticket offices): one from the courtyard of Palazzo Pitti, one at the Annalena Gate on Via Romana (see plan), one at the gate at Porta Romana and one at the gate at the top of the hill which leads into Forte di Belvedere. The Grotta Grande is open on the hour at 11, 1, 3 and 4 (also at 5 in March, and also at 5 and 6 from June–Oct). Combined ticket with the Museo degli Argenti, Museo del Costume, and including entrance to the Museo delle Porcellane. The ticket also allows entrance to the Villa Bardini (see p. 292).

On the hillside behind Palazzo Pitti lie the magnificent Boboli Gardens, among the most beautiful and best-preserved gardens in Italy, laid out for Cosimo I on the slope of the hill stretching up from behind Palazzo Pitti to Forte di Belvedere. They were designed by Tribolo, the 'father of the Italian formal garden' and a talented hydraulic engineer: he made creative use of fountains and cascades and provided an irrigation system. The gardens were continued after his death in 1550 by his son-in-law Davide Fortini, as well as by Vasari and Ammannati. After 1574, Francesco I employed Bernardo Buontalenti to direct the works. The gardens were extended downhill to the west in the early 17th century by Giulio Parigi and his son Alfonso. The Parigi were especially known for their talents as set designers and architects. Alfonso the Elder (c. 1535–90) was called in by Ammannati to help with work at the Pitti, but his son Giulio (1571–1635) became more famous for his work for the grand dukes as a stage designer and civil engineer (it was he who produced some of the most spectacular celebrations for the wedding of Cosimo II and Maria Maddalena of Austria; *see box on p. 261*).

The gardens were opened to the public in 1766. The origin of the name Boboli is unknown, but it may derive from the name of the former proprietors of the hillside (Borbolini). The plants are predominantly evergreen, and a special feature of the gardens has always been the tall double hedges (5m–8m high) formed by a variety of shrubs and bushes in different shades of green—laurel, laurustinus, viburnum, box, myrtle and prunus—below a higher hedge of ilex. About half the area of the gardens is covered with ilex woods: these thickets were used up to 1772 for netting small birds. The first deciduous trees were planted in 1812. The botanical sections of the gardens introduced by the Medici, where mulberries, potatoes and pineapples were once grown, no longer survive.

The Medici boasted that they had a collection of some 100 varieties of citrus fruits, although these were probably mostly of the same species with only tiny differences. Apart from their decorative value, they were also used for perfumes. The most famous variety, known as the *bizzerie*, was the result of a mistaken graft in 1630, which combined an orange and a lemon plant. About 550 plants are still cultivated in pots (and some 10 or 20 plants are renewed each year with a graft from the bitter orange). They are housed during the winter in glasshouses and put outside in late April (a job which takes some four days now with the help of a tractor).

There are plans to restore the 17th-century waterworks created by Buontalenti and the Parigi to irrigate the gardens and feed the fountains: at present only two fountains

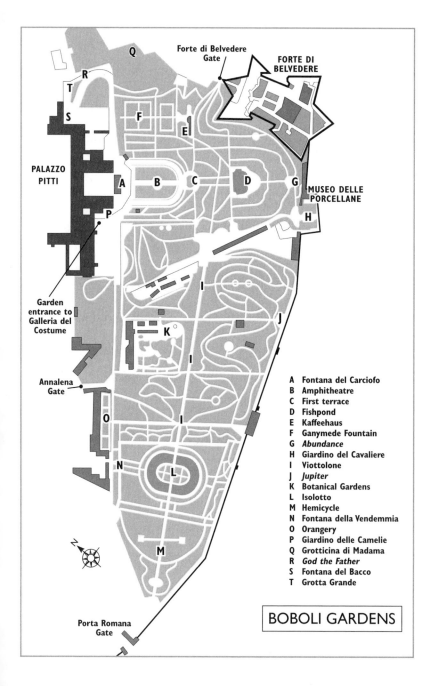

BOBOLI GARDENS

A Fontana del Carciofo
B Amphitheatre
C First terrace
D Fishpond
E Kaffeehaus
F Ganymede Fountain
G *Abundance*
H Giardino del Cavaliere
I Viottolone
J *Jupiter*
K Botanical Gardens
L Isolotto
M Hemicycle
N Fontana della Vendemmia
O Orangery
P Giardino delle Camelie
Q Grotticina di Madama
R *God the Father*
S Fontana del Bacco
T Grotta Grande

work of the hundreds that once played here, and there were also hidden water jets to take visitors unawares.

About 170 statues decorate the walks, a typical feature of Renaissance gardens, derived from ancient Roman villas. Many of them are restored Roman works, while others remain unidentified; some came to Florence in the 18th century from the Medici collection in Rome and others in the 18th and early 19th centuries from the Villa di Pratolino outside Florence. Two worn statues recognised as works by Cellini just before the Second World War are now in the Bargello. Some of the statues have been restored *in situ*; others have been removed for restoration and may not be returned. Casts of some of the marble statues have replaced the originals.

A WALK THROUGH THE GARDENS

The entrance at the back of the courtyard of Palazzo Pitti emerges onto the terrace behind the palace, overlooking the magnificent garden façade and courtyard with the lovely Baroque **Fontana del Carciofo (A)**, by Francesco Susini (1641), named after a bronze artichoke on top, which has been lost. It has twelve little statues of cupids on the basin. It replaced a fine 16th-century fountain by Ammannati (now reassembled in the Bargello). There is a wonderful view of the Duomo and Campanile from the terrace.

The **Amphitheatre (B)** was laid out as a garden (probably with hedges, ilexes and olive trees) by Ammannati in 1599, in imitation of a Roman circus. The open-air theatre was constructed in 1630–35 by Giulio and Alfonso Parigi for the spectacles held here by the Medici. The obelisk of Rameses II, taken from Heliopolis by the Romans in 30 BC, found its way to the Villa Medici in Rome in the 17th century. It was set up here in 1789. The huge granite basin, from the Baths of Caracalla, was installed in 1840. Some of the restored statues in the niches (which alternate with vases) are Roman and others were made in the 16th and 17th centuries. The Amphitheatre was often used for elaborate theatrical performances designed to exalt the prestige of the Medici and offer the public entertainment on a grand scale—sometimes there were elephants or horses combined with fantastic scenery and dramatic lighting.

A series of terraces rises above the Amphitheatre. On the **first terrace (C)** are three Roman statues, including a fine *Ceres*, and there are hedged walks with pretty vistas on either side. On the upper level is a large **fishpond (D)** with a copy by the skilled Mannerist sculptor Stoldo Lorenzi (1571) of a fine statue of *Neptune*, an allegory of Cosimo I as Prince of the Seas. The pond was surrounded by terraces in the 17th century and planted with plane trees in the Napoleonic era.

Romantic winding alleys overshadowed by ilexes and a cypress grove (where a grassy bank is covered with wild anemones in February) lead to the green Rococo **Kaffeehaus (E)** (*closed*). It was built in 1775 by Zanobi del Rosso as a pavilion for Peter Leopold to while away lazy afternoons. In the garden in front of it, there is a cast of the **Ganymede Fountain (F)**. The 16th-century original is attributed to Stoldo Lorenzi.

Behind the Kaffeehaus a gravel path leads up past (left) another secluded area of the gardens at its eastern limit with a little tumble-down terrace and another fine view, to the Forte di Belvedere gate. From here a broad path skirts the mighty walls of the Forte di Belvedere to the colossal **statue of *Abundance* (G)**, in a niche of bay and ilex, at the top of the garden. Begun by Giambologna as a portrait of Joanna of Austria, first wife of Francesco I, it was originally intended for a column in Piazza San Marco. Instead it was finished—and transformed into an allegory of Abundance—by Pietro Tacca, pupil of Giambologna and successor to him as sculptor to the Medici grand dukes. It was placed here in 1636 by order of Joanna's daughter, Maria de' Medici.

GRAND-DUCAL WEDDINGS

Lorenzo the Magnificent was the first Medici to marry into a noble family, the Orsini of Rome. He set a trend that was to continue. From the time of Cosimo I, the grand dukes arranged marriages in order to strengthen alliances even outside Italy, with other European rulers. The ablest grand duke in this sense was perhaps Ferdinando I, who gave his niece Maria's hand to Henri IV of France in 1600 and then allied himself to the Imperial and Spanish royal houses by choosing Maria Maddalena, daughter of the Archduke Charles of Austria and sister of the queen of Philip III of Spain, as the bride for his heir Cosimo, thus ensuring a balance of power in the interests of Tuscany. Cosimo's wedding in 1608 was celebrated in such style that it was remembered long afterwards as the grandest celebration of its kind ever produced. It was clear that the sumptuous festivities were intended to impress both Ferdinando's own subjects as well as to transmit political messages to the royal houses of all Europe. For several days after the triumphant entry of the bride into the city, accompanied by a magnificent procession all the way to Palazzo Pitti, there were masked balls, banquets, jousts, equestrian ballet performances, concerts with choirs, and mock naval battles on the Arno, all with their own particular allegorical significance. Giulio Parigi made elaborate floats for the musical processions down the river, the designs for which survive. The best musicians of the day were brought specially to Florence and music was commissioned from the court composers, among them Girolamo Frescobaldi and Jacopo Peri. Michelangelo's great-nephew and namesake, Michelangelo Buonarroti the Younger, produced a play for the occasion entitled *The Judgement of Paris*. The *Notte d'Amore*, which consisted of a series of dance tableaux set to music by Lorenzo Allegri, lasted throughout all of one night. After such great pomp it is sad to think that Cosimo, who became Grand Duke Cosimo II at his father's death only a year after his marriage, died of tuberculosis at the age of just 30. He was clearly interested in works of art of all kinds, and we know that he chose an exquisitely carved little ivory dog, still in the Museo degli Argenti (*see p. 255*), as a present for his bride.

A short double flight of steps to the right, designed in 1792, continues to the **Giardino del Cavaliere (H)**, a delightful secluded garden laid out at the time of Cosimo III on a bastion constructed by Michelangelo in 1529 in front of a garden pavilion. Today it has miniature box hedges and a wall covered with climbing roses, but it is the wonderful view over the two low parapets which makes this one of the most charming spots in the entire garden. It embraces the rural outskirts of the city, with fields and olive groves dotted with beautiful old villas. The fountain has a putto attributed to Pierino da Vinci or Stoldo Lorenzi, and bronze monkeys attributed to the little known sculptor Camillo Mariani.

Museo delle Porcellane

Open as the gardens; closed on the 2nd and 4th Sun and the 1st, 3rd and 5th Mon of the month; T: 055 238 8605.

The museum is housed in the 17th-century Casino del Cavaliere. The building may have been used by Cardinal Leopoldo for meetings of the Accademia del Cimento (*see p. 134*). It was rebuilt in the 18th century for the Lorraine grand dukes by Zanobi del Rosso. The museum contains a well-displayed collection of 18th–19th-century Italian, German and French porcelain from the Medici and Lorraine grand-ducal collections. The last Medici grand duke, Gian Gastone, whose wife was from Saxony, had a special interest in porcelain, which was much in vogue in the early 18th century. Room 1 displays 18th-century French porcelain (Tournai, Chantilly, Vincennes, Sèvres, including the delicate *alzata da ostriche*, used for serving oysters). In the centre, beneath a Venetian chandelier, are two Sèvres dinner services which belonged to Elisa Baciocchi (Grand Duchess of Tuscany) and a plaque with a portrait of her brother Napoleon in Sèvres porcelain, after François Gérard (1809–10). Examples from the Doccia Ginori factory include works made in 1736 for the Lorraine family and a 19th-century service with views of Florence. In the second room are works in biscuit ware made in Vienna, and in the last room chinoiserie ware from Meissen as well as examples of Worcester porcelain (1770).

The lower gardens

The magnificent long **Viottolone (I)** descends steeply through the lower part of the gardens. This majestic cypress avenue was planted in 1612 by Giulio Parigi (some of the trees are now suffering from disease). It is lined with statues, many of them restored Roman works from the Villa Medici in Rome and others carved in the 16th and 17th centuries. The 17th-century arboured walks beneath ilex trellises, and the little gardens to the right and left with delightful vistas, are amongst the most beautiful spots in the gardens.

There are casts of the two fine Roman statues now displayed in the courtyard of Palazzo Pitti. On the right is a garden where citrus fruit trees are cultivated. On either side of the avenue are two more Roman statues, one of a divinity (restored c. 1610–20) and one of a matron with a veil. They were given to Cosimo I on a visit to Rome in 1560. At the first crossing are four statues of the Four Seasons—*Spring* and *Winter* by Giovanni Battista Caccini (c. 1608; replaced by copies), and *Summer* and *Autumn* by Pietro Francavilla. A path to the left ends at a copy of a colossal **bust of Jupiter (J)** by Giambologna or his school. An unusual path, lined with a water 'staircase' composed of late 16th-century fountains with grotesque heads, follows a stretch of the 13th-century city walls.

On the other side of the Viottolone, an ilex tunnel dating from the 17th century leads to remains of the **Botanical Gardens (K)**. The Sicilian botanist Filippo Parlatore (director between 1842 and 1872) designed the circular pools for aquatic plants. At the next crossing, lower down the Viottolone and beyond two more restored Roman statues, are three more statues (again restored Roman works). The main avenue continues downhill past a 16th-century statue to end at a short 19th-century avenue of plane trees which runs across it at right angles (the orangery described below can be seen at the right end). Of the four statues here, two are restored Roman works: *Aesculapius* has an antique torso and a head restored by Gian Simone Cioli in the early 17th century. The statue of *Venus*, usually considered an allegory of Secrecy, also has an antique torso (it was restored by Giovanni Francesco Susini). The statue of *Andromeda* dates from the 17th century. Beyond, in niches in the hedges, are two groups of statues depicting folk games; the one on the left is by Orazio Mochi and Romolo Ferrucci del Tadda (17th century) and the one on the right was added c. 1770 by Giovanni Battista Capezzuoli.

The **Isolotto (L)**, or Vasca dell'Isola, was laid out by Giulio Parigi in 1612, when it had some 200 fountains. The island recalls the design of the so-called Naval Theatre, Hadrian's retreat at his villa near Tivoli. A circular moat with fine sculptural decorations surrounds an island and the huge **Fountain of Oceanus**, designed by Tribolo for Cosimo II. Three statues of the rivers Nile, Ganges and Euphrates surround the central figure of Neptune, which is a copy (c. 1910) by Raffaello Romanelli of the original by Giambologna, which is now in the Bargello. These stand above a huge granite basin quarried by Tribolo in Elba—the design included another large basin, but it cracked during transportation. There used to be several hundred fountains playing here. Some 200 terracotta pots, some still with the Medici crest, filled with citrus trees, are put out here from the end of April and the island is usually open at this time.

Four marble statues of cupids (one of which has been removed) by Domenico Pieratti, Cosimo Salvestrini and Giovanni Francesco Susini (with Giovanni Battista Pieratti) were placed to the north and south of the island in 1623–24. On the other two sides, by the gates with capricorns (the emblems of Cosimo II) on the gateposts, are grotesque harpies by the school of Giambologna to a design by Giulio Parigi (these are copies of the originals, made in marble by Innocenzo Spinazzi in 1776). In the water are *Perseus on Horseback*, restored by Giovanni Battista Pieratti, and *Andromeda*, also attributed to Pieratti. Surrounding the water is a high ilex hedge with niches cut into it, which contain delightful restored 17th-century statues in *pietra serena* (some of them in very poor condition and propped up by scaffolding) of peasants and hunters by Giovanni Battista and Domenico Pieratti. Other statues include *Two Men Fighting*, a *Hunter with Two Dogs* and a *Moorish Hunter* (removed and restored) by Gian Simone and Valerio Cioli, Bartolomeo Rossi and Francesco Generini. The dogs are by Romolo Ferrucci del Tadda.

Beyond two small 17th-century obelisks made in Carrara marble is the **Hemicycle (M)**, an English-style green surrounded by plane trees, which provides a cool playground for children in summer. The two Roman columns in Egyptian granite surmounted by Neoclassical vases were purchased from Lord Cowper by Grand Duke Peter Leopold. On the central path are a statue of *Vulcan* by Chiarissimo Fancelli, and a 16th-century seated female statue. Some of the colossal busts in the laurel hedge which surrounds the lawn are Roman (including the fine *Head of Zeus*, although the bust is modern). At the Porta Romana gate is a statue of *Perseus* by Vincenzo Danti.

A path leads back through the gardens following the left wall along Via Romana. Beyond a statue of a peasant at work by Valerio and Simone Cioli is the **Fontana della Vendemmia (N)** (1599–1608), also by the Cioli (showing a grape harvest), beside two terracotta dogs by Romolo Ferrucci del Tadda.

Entered through a fine gate dating from 1818 is the handsome **Orangery (O)**, built by Zanobi del Rosso (1777–78) and painted in its original green and white colour. The pots of citrus trees are kept here in winter. The 18th-century gardens in front are planted with antique roses and camellias, and four Roman statues adorn the walls. This was on the site of a small zoo for exotic animals. Near the Annalena Gate is a small grotto with statues of *Adam* and *Eve*.

Giardino delle Camelie

Below the Fontana del Carciofo, on the extreme left, is a secret hanging garden; this is the Giardino delle Camelie, which is open for three weeks in late March and early April when the camellias are in flower (*usually on Tues, Thur and Sat, 10–12*). In the 17th century, this was a small private water garden with two grottoes, one in the form of an arch, beside an exit from the apartment of Prince Mattias, brother of Grand Duke Ferdinando II. Camellias, first introduced into Italy around 1780, were planted here in the early 19th century, and all 42 different species were replanted in the 1990s, although the taller ones survive from the first garden.

The route to the exit

Beyond the Fontana del Carciofo, a wide gravel carriageway descends past two pine trees (right) at the entrance to a narrow path lined with box hedges, which leads through a pretty little garden of parterres with peonies and roses to the **Grotticina di Madama (Q)** (*you can look into it through the gate*). This was the first grotto to be built in the gardens, which later became famous for them. It was commissioned by Eleanor of Toledo in 1553–55 and is the work of Davide Fortini and Marco del Tasso. The sculptures are by Baccio Bandinelli and Giovanni Fancelli. It contains stalactites and bizarre goats. The frescoes in the vault, with putti and grotesques and rustic decorations, are the last documented work commissioned from Bachiacca by the Medici (but have been much repainted), and the fine terracotta pavement was designed by Santi Buglioni.

The gravel road continues to wind down past a rose garden and a colossal **seated figure of *God the Father* (R)** by Baccio Bandinelli. It was made for the high altar of the Duomo, but was moved here in 1824 and has been known ever since as *Jupiter*. The beginning of the carriageway is flanked by two colossal porphyry and marble Roman statues of Dacian prisoners (2nd century AD; brought here from the Villa Medici in Rome), with bas-reliefs of the late 3rd century on their pedestals.

On the right is a cast of the so-called **Fontana del Bacco (S)**, really an amusing statue of Pietro Barbino, the pot-bellied dwarf of Cosimo I, seated on a turtle, by Valerio Cioli (1560).

Steps descend to the **Grotta Grande (T)** (*opened on the hour; see p. 258*). The original 16th-century paving with pebble mosaic in the forecourt was discovered during recent restoration work. The grotto was begun in 1557 by Vasari, and was finished by Ammannati and Buontalenti (1583–93). On the façade the two statues of *Apollo* (or *David*) and *Ceres* (or *Cleopatra*) in the niches are by Baccio Bandinelli, and the lovely decoration above was added by Giovanni del Tadda. Here are two female figures in relief on either side of the Medici arms, and lovely reliefs of goats and tortoises beneath garlands of seashells. Above, the spongework forms huge drips, seemingly about to fall to the ground. The interior completely preserves its intimate 16th-century atmosphere, although unfortunately the effect has been altered by the fact that there is no longer running water. The walls of the first chamber are covered with fantastic limestone figures and animals carved by Piero di Tommaso Mati (on a design by Buontalenti). There are two extraordinary red reclining females drowning in mud, and the landscape and trees are also submerged by dripping mud clots. Francesco I installed Michelangelo's unfinished *Slaves* here in 1585 (replaced by casts when the originals were removed to the Accademia in 1908). The charming painted

Venus Emerging from her Bath (c. 1570) by Giambologna, in the Grotta Grande.

vault, with a central tondo once open to the sky, populated with more animals and birds, is by Bernardino Poccetti. Beyond is a sculptural group of *Paris Abducting Helen* by Vincenzo de' Rossi (a gift from the sculptor to Cosimo I). The innermost grotto contains a very beautiful statue of *Venus Emerging from her Bath* by Giambologna, designed to be seen from every point of view.

The exit from the Boboli Gardens takes you out into **Piazza Pitti** (*map 6, 3*), where, in the pretty row of houses facing the palace, no. 16 was the home of Paolo dal Pozzo Toscanelli (1397–1482), mathematician and cosmographer, and one of the most celebrated scientists of his day. It is said that before setting out on his journey to the Americas, Columbus sought Toscanelli's advice. Toscanelli's most famous memorial in Florence is the gnomon in the Duomo (*see pp. 57–58*). Dostoyevsky wrote *The Idiot* while staying at no. 21 in 1868.

THE OLTRARNO

The south bank of the Arno is known as the Oltrarno (meaning 'beyond the Arno'). It is a district away from the heart of the city and so generally more peaceful. When Cosimo I moved his household to Palazzo Pitti in 1549, Florence gained what was in effect a royal residence, and noble families built *palazzi* for themselves nearby. A number of the streets in the area, notably Via Maggio and Via di Santo Spirito, still preserve some of this courtly flavour. But the Oltrarno has also traditionally been the district of Florence where artisans lived and worked, and the area around Borgo San Frediano retains a genuine local atmosphere and some skilled cabinet-makers, gilders and picture-framers still have their workshops here. The two most important churches in the Oltrarno are Santo Spirito and Santa Maria del Carmine. Santa Felicita and the eastern Oltrarno are described on p. 287.

Via Maggio

Via Maggio (*map 6, 1–3*) begins at the foot of Ponte Santa Trínita. Its name (from *Maggiore*, or 'greatest') is a reminder of its origin as the principal and widest street of the Oltrarno (it is still busy with traffic). It was opened soon after Ponte Santa Trínita was first built in 1252, and it became a fashionable residential street after the grand dukes moved to Palazzo Pitti. It was the first street in Florence to be illuminated by gas (in 1845; the rest of the town was provided with gas lamps the following year). Fine palaces still line the street, many of them with their family coats of arms, and during the daytime you can walk in through the atria of some of them to see their handsome courtyards. Many elegant antique shops occupy their ground floors: this is the most important street in Florence for those wishing to buy important works of art. It is also worth exploring the series of narrow old streets which lead off to the east.

Palazzo Ricasoli, on the east side of Via Maggio (no. 7), is the tallest palace in the street: it dates from around 1520 and was formerly owned by the Ridolfi, who built several other palaces nearby. The wrought-iron work on the façade would have been used for torches and banners on special occasions. The *portone* is usually open so that you can visit the beautiful courtyard with columns on three sides (and *peducci* on the fourth) and you can see the remains of a grotto in the second court beyond. Just to the left (at no. 15r) is the lovely shop of Petra Casini, which has been on this street for some 30 years. It is still run by a family of gem-cutters who for generations have worked hard and semi-precious stones, and they also make customised jewellery.

Opposite, flying the Union Jack, is **Palazzo Machiavelli** (nos 16–18), which once belonged to a branch of the great statesman's family. It was divided in two in the 19th century (as the façade shows) but the interior is well preserved, having been bought by the Anglicans in 1877–1905. On part of the ground floor is **St Mark's Anglican church** (*the Anglican liturgy is still celebrated here, with traditional Tractarian pomp and splendour, every Sun morning at 10.30; times of other services are posted up outside. The* *church and palace, the vicar's residence, can sometimes be visited on request in the mornings*). Founded in 1870 by Anglo-Catholic zealots led by the Rev. Charles Tooth, St Mark's is traditionally High Church. The interior is a Tractarian–Byzantine–Renaissance fantasy created by the Florentine resident John Roddam Spencer-Stanhope in 1877–79. The pre-Raphaelite decoration, designed in detail by Spencer-Stanhope, survives virtually intact, including the bronze lamps, stencilled walls and fittings. A chalice incorporates the engagement ring of Holman Hunt's wife, donated to the church following her death in childbirth in 1866 (Spencer-Stanhope was a disciple of Holman Hunt), and the treasury and vestments have been carefully preserved.

Further up the street on the same side is the **Palazzo di Bianca Cappello** (no. 26), covered with good graffiti decoration attributed to Bernardino Poccetti (c. 1579). The house was built by Grand Duke Francesco I for the beautiful Venetian girl Bianca Cappello, who was first his mistress and then his wife. Opposite (at no. 13), Palazzo Ridolfi was built in the late 16th century and is attributed to Santi di Tito. You can usually walk in through the atrium to admire its beautiful and very well-preserved courtyard.

Palazzo Corsini Suarez (or Commenda di Firenze; no. 42) is named after Baldassare Suarez of Portugal, who acquired the palace in 1590. It was built in the late 14th century and reconstructed in the 16th, partly by Gherardo Silvani, and has unusually large windows. It is now the seat of the Archivio Contemporaneo Alessandro Bonsanti, a branch of the Vieusseux Library (*see p. 218*), and preserves the papers (and in some cases even the possessions) of some important 20th-century writers, artists, musicians and playwrights. Opposite, at no 61r, there is a nice little shop which specialises in chocolate (Pasticceria Dolcissima).

Via Maggio ends in **Piazza San Felice**. A column, 12m high and without a capital, made from breccia marble from Seravezza, was returned here in 1992: it had first been set up in 1572 by Cosimo I.

Casa Guidi

Map 6, 3. Open April–Nov Mon, Wed, Fri 3–6; T: 055 354457. Since 1993 the apartment has been owned by Eton College and is leased to The Landmark Trust. It can be rented for short lets; see p. 360. Entrance at Piazza San Felice 8.

The 15th-century Palazzo Guidi was acquired in 1619 by Count Camillo Guidi, secretary of state for the Medici. The apartment on the first floor is known as Casa Guidi since it was always called thus by Elizabeth Barrett Browning; it is here that she wrote her famous poem *Casa Guidi Windows*. After their secret marriage in England in 1846, Robert Browning and Elizabeth Barrett escaped to the continent and settled in Florence the following year. Their son Robert, always known as 'Pen', was born here in 1849. Because of Elizabeth's delicate health she rarely went out, but they had many visitors and an 'at home' atmosphere is recorded by many friends who frequented Elizabeth's 'salon', where poetry would be circulated and many high-brow expatriate women congregated. Elizabeth took an active interest in the cause of Italian independence from Austrian rule (see her *Aurora Leigh*). When she died here from TB in 1861 she was buried in the English Cemetery (*see p. 230*). Robert took Pen back to England and never returned to Florence.

The four rooms which can be visited have as far as possible been given the appearance they had in the Brownings' day, combined with an atmosphere which vividly recalls the two great poets. In 1995 The Landmark Trust also helped restore and refurnish the rooms and today they are responsible for the costly maintenance of the apartment. The dining room has paintings of Elizabeth as a young girl, and photos of her when she lived here. In Robert's small study, a bronze sculpture of the two poets' clasped hands, made in 1853 by their friend Harriet Hosmer, is preserved. In the living room, with its green walls, the portrait busts of the two poets are by their intimate friend William Wetmore Story. The small oil painting of the room was commissioned by Robert just after Elizabeth's death. Visitors are free to consult the library of works by and relating to the Brownings. The bedroom has a portrait of Elizabeth's father, from whom she was estranged after her marriage.

San Felice

The simple 14th-century church (*map 6, 3; open Mon–Fri 9–11.30 & 4–7, Sat 9–11.30*) was altered in the mid-16th century when it was taken over by the Dominicans. The Renaissance façade and the sanctuary are almost certainly by Michelozzo (1457). In the very cluttered interior, above the first half of the nave, there is a closed gallery supported by eight columns and a pretty vault, added as a nuns' choir in the mid-16th century. On the west wall are early 18th-century funerary monuments, and on the first north altar is a lovely triptych by a follower of Botticelli (known as the Master of Apollo and Daphne). Over the altar opposite are remains of a fresco of the *Pietà* attributed to Niccolò di Pietro Gerini (interesting for its unusual iconography).

In the open nave (south side) there is a terracotta group of the *Pietà* dating from the early 17th century, an altarpiece by Ridolfo Ghirlandaio, and a lunette fresco of the *Virgin of the Sacred Girdle* (late 14th-century Florentine). Over the high altar hangs a large Crucifix, which has recently been restored and its attribution to Giotto confirmed. On the north side there is a delightful fresco of the titular saint (c. 1636; recently restored) by Giovanni da San Giovanni (the angels are by Volterrano) and a triptych with four saints by Neri di Bicci (painted for the church) beneath a frescoed lunette of the 14th century.

In the adjoining convent (*ring for admission at the school at no. 6 to the left of the church façade*) there is a *Last Supper* painted by Matteo Rosselli in 1614.

Via Romana

This is a street of simple houses which winds its way out of the centre of Florence to the gate in the old walls. On its way it passes numerous small shops and some artisans' workshops, including framers and bookbinders. Its side streets are particularly attractive—and much more peaceful—since Via Romana itself is unfortunately disturbed by fast traffic. The road ends at **Porta Romana** (*map 5, 6*), a well-preserved gate built in 1328 to a design by Andrea Orcagna. In 1331 Giovanni Pisano sculpted the lily of Florence in marble for the keystone of the arch. In the lunette is an early 14th-century fresco of the *Madonna and Child Enthroned with Saints*. Outside the gate is an incongruous colossal statue called *Dietro-fronte* ('Back to Front'; 1981–84), apparently a woman weighed down by a stone block on her head, by Michelangelo Pistoletto. He gave it to the *Comune* and it was set up here in the 1980s, where it has remained, despite the protests of local residents. From the car park in the lane between the old city walls and the wall of Giardino Torrigiani (*see p. 334*), you can go through a small gate in the walls and up the steps to the walkway along the top and into the Porta Romana guard-house over Via Romana.

SANTO SPIRITO

The delightful **Piazza Santo Spirito** (*map 6, 3*) has a fountain and a few trees, a little daily market and some pleasant cafés. The square is surrounded with modest houses except for **Palazzo Guadagni** (no. 10), probably built by Cronaca c. 1505. Its pleasing, well-proportioned façade with a top-floor loggia became the model for many 16th-century Florentine mansions (it is now part of a hotel; *see p. 362*). Borgo Tegolaio, which leads out of one corner of the piazza, is a medieval street which takes its name from the *tegola* kilns (a *tegola* is a roof tile) which were once here. In Via delle Caldaie the wool-dyers had their workshops. Numerous artisans' workshops—cabinet-makers, restorers, gilders, frame-makers—are still to be found in the vicinity, and give this area a character all of its own.

THE CHURCH OF SANTO SPIRITO

The modest but very appealing 18th-century façade of the church of Santo Spirito fronts the square (*map 6, 3; open 9.30–12.30 & 4–5.30 except Wed*). On the left is the rough stone wall of the convent's refectory and behind rises a familiar feature of the Florence skyline, Baccio d'Agnolo's slender campanile (1503). Santo Spirito is an early Augustinian foundation, dating from 1250, just six years after Pope Innocent IV had commanded Tuscan hermits to adopt the rule of St Augustine, a rule which the Dominicans also accepted. The first church was begun in 1292, and by the end of the 14th century, the convent had become a centre of intellectual life in the city, with an extremely important library. In 1428 Brunelleschi was commissioned to design a new church, the project for which he had completed by 1434–35. However, building was not begun until 1444, just two years before the great architect's death. Construction continued for most of the 15th century, first under the direction of his collaborator Antonio Manetti. It is surprising that the names of the other artists involved are unknown considering that this is such a beautiful and important building.

Interior of Santo Spirito

The interior is a superb creation of the Renaissance, remarkable for its harmonious proportions, its solemn colour, and the perspective of the colonnades and vaulted aisles, but it also points the way forward to the more elaborate and less delicate 16th-century style of architecture. The plan is a Latin cross with a dome over the crossing. The colonnade has 35 columns in *pietra forte* (including the four piers of the dome) with fine Corinthian capitals and imposts above. It continues around the transepts and east end to form an unbroken arcade.

The elaborate high altar (1599–1607) has a *pietre dure* ciborium inspired by the altar designed (but never completed) for the Cappella dei Principi of San Lorenzo, and statues by Giovanni Battista Caccini beneath a high baldacchino. It replaces a simpler altar designed by Brunelleschi, and despite being a fine Baroque work in itself, it disturbs the overall harmony of the interior. The cupola was completed by Salvi d'Andrea, who also designed the handsome interior façade in the 1480s. The stained glass oculus is from a cartoon by Perugino. Only some of the loveliest painted altarpieces, commissioned by various Florentine families for their chapels in the semicircular niches around the walls, are described below, since all of them are labelled *in situ*.

(**A**) The *Martyrdom of St Stephen* is one of Passignano's best works (early 17th century). The artist left many altarpieces and frescoes all over the region.

(**B**) The *Madonna del Soccorso* is a 15th-century painting whose author has recently been rescued from anonymity and recognised as Domenico di Zanobi (formerly called the Master of the Johnson Nativity). The story told is that of a mother threatening her miscreant child with the devil at which, to her consternation, the devil actually appears. The child is shown being succoured (hence '*soccorso*') by the Madonna, who is depicted towering above the mother, child and devil wielding a stick, but she is still a beautifully composed, elegantly-dressed figure. The scene takes place in a court with a colourful pavement and marble walls, above which can be seen a row of stylised trees (typical of the backgrounds of numerous Florentine paintings and frescoes).

(**C**) The polychrome marble niche (1601) is by Bernardo Buontalenti, one of the most skilled of the Florentine Mannerist artists. It encloses a 14th-century wooden Crucifix from the earlier church.

(**D**) The altarpiece of the **Madonna and Child with the Young St John, Saints and Donors**—the donors are Tanai and Nanna (Capponi) dei Nerli—is one of the best and most mature works of Filippino Lippi, executed sometime after 1494. In the background is an interesting early view of Florence, showing Tanai in a red cloak, taking leave of his family in front of Palazzo dei Nerli near Porta San Frediano (*map 5, 2*) before setting out on a journey. There are numerous classical elements in the altarpiece, and the 'dialogue' between the Young St John and the Christ Child is an interesting detail which was to be developed by

later painters such as Leonardo da Vinci. The splendid original frame was also designed by Filippino.

(**E**) The original painting of the *Vision of St Bernard* by Perugino (now in Munich) was replaced in 1656 by a beautiful (and almost indistinguishable) copy by Felice Ficherelli. In past centuries this was often an accepted practice when a family wished to enjoy for themselves an important painting they had commissioned, and Ficherelli was known above all as a copyist.

(**F**) The *Marriage of the Virgin* is the best work by the early 18th-century Florentine artist Giovanni Camillo Sagrestani. The sarcophagus of Neri Capponi, who was one of the early benefactors of the church and who died in 1457, is by the *bottega* of Bernardo Rossellino and it was the only tomb that was allowed inside the church.

(**G**) The *Madonna and Saints*, in a beautiful contemporary frame, is a good painting in the style of Lorenzo di Credi by an unknown artist, named after this work as the Master of the Santo Spirito Conversazione.

(**H**) The polyptych of the *Madonna and Child with Saints*, the earliest painting in the church (c. 1340), is by Maso di Banco, one of the most interesting followers of Giotto, but unfortunately it is poorly preserved.

(**I**) The Pitti family chapel, which belonged to Luca Pitti from 1458, still contains the altarpiece of the *Eleven Thousand Martyrs*, commissioned by

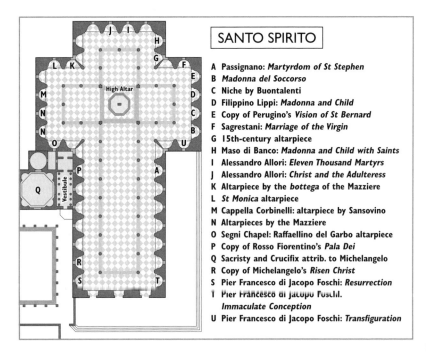

SANTO SPIRITO

A Passignano: *Martyrdom of St Stephen*
B *Madonna del Soccorso*
C Niche by Buontalenti
D Filippino Lippi: *Madonna and Child*
E Copy of Perugino's *Vision of St Bernard*
F Sagrestani: *Marriage of the Virgin*
G 15th-century altarpiece
H Maso di Banco: *Madonna and Child with Saints*
I Alessandro Allori: *Eleven Thousand Martyrs*
J Alessandro Allori: *Christ and the Adulteress*
K Altarpiece by the *bottega* of the Mazziere
L *St Monica* altarpiece
M Cappella Corbinelli: altarpiece by Sansovino
N Altarpieces by the Mazziere
O Segni Chapel: Raffaellino del Garbo altarpiece
P Copy of Rosso Fiorentino's *Pala Dei*
Q Sacristy and Crucifix attrib. to Michelangelo
R Copy of Michelangelo's *Risen Christ*
S Pier Francesco di Jacopo Foschi: *Resurrection*
T Pier Francesco di Jacopo Foschi: *Immaculate Conception*
U Pier Francesco di Jacopo Foschi: *Transfiguration*

the family from the best-known artist of the day, Alessandro Allori (1574). It is remarkable for its figure studies of the male nude and incorporates a portrait of Allori's patron, Cosimo I, in the centre (with a beard). The predella is especially interesting for the view of Palazzo Pitti before it was enlarged, with its owner Luca Pitti standing outside (in a red hat). The original 15th-century altar frontal with a painting of *St Luke* by Neri di Bicci survives, one of a number still *in situ* in the church.

(**J**) This chapel preserves its original little 15th-century stained glass tondo and altar frontal, but the splendid altarpiece of ***Christ and the Adulteress*** is another very fine work. Signed and dated 1577 by Alessandro Allori, it foreshadows the

17th century. The beautiful figure of the adulteress is particularly striking.

(**K**) The *Madonna Enthroned Between Sts John the Evangelist and Bartholomew* is attributed to the *bottega* of the Mazziere brothers (Antonio di Donnino del Mazziere was born in 1497 and died in 1547). Formerly known as the Master of Santo Spirito, these artists are at present only known for their work in this church.

(**L**) **Altarpiece of St Monica**, the mother of St Augustine, with Augustinian nuns. Traditionally attributed to the minor artist Francesco Botticini, this is now thought by many scholars to be the work of his famous contemporary Verrocchio, whose *bottega* included the young Leonardo da Vinci. It is a very unusual and beautifully composed painting in muted tones with the striking dark habits of the nuns exquisitely painted. The two circles of nuns include intense character studies.

(**M**) The **Cappella Corbinelli** has a beautiful altarpiece sculpted by Andrea Sansovino, with statues in two niches of *St Matthew* and *St James* above a carved predella with reliefs of scenes from their lives and a *Last Supper*. The two tondi illustrate the *Annunciation*, and in the lunette above is the *Coronation of the Virgin*. The classical pilasters bear reliefs of the symbols of the Passion. The altar frontal has a beautifully carved *Pietà*. After 1502, Sansovino completed the decoration of the chapel by adding the side panels in marble. This was the only chapel in the church in which a sculptured rather than a painted altarpiece was allowed, since it was used for the Holy Sacrament. The balustrade dates from the 17th century.

(**N**) The particularly fine *Trinity with Sts Mary Magdalene and Catherine* is attributed to the Mazziere brothers, as is the *Madonna and Child with Saints* in the next chapel.

(**O**) The **Segni Chapel** has a beautiful *Madonna Enthroned with Saints* by Raffaellino del Garbo (1505), the only one of four altarpieces commissioned from him for this church which has remained here. The altar frontal is attributed to the *bottega* of the Mazziere brothers.

(**P**) The copy by Francesco Petrucci of Rosso Fiorentino's *Pala Dei* was commissioned by Crown Prince Ferdinando in 1691 when he removed the original to Palazzo Pitti. The copy is particularly interesting since it shows the original dimensions of the altarpiece (it was enlarged when it was hung in the Pitti).

(**Q**) A door (*opened on request*) beneath the organ leads into a grandiose **vestibule** with twelve Corinthian columns supporting an elaborately coffered barrel vault, built in *pietra serena* by Cronaca in 1491 to a design by Giuliano da Sangallo. The decoration includes the Medici coat of arms and doves, and tondi with mythological scenes which are copies of the antique gems owned by Lorenzo the Magnificent. A cloister of the convent can be seen through the glass door here.

The adjoining **sacristy** is an octagonal chamber inspired by the architectural works of Brunelleschi; it has Corinthian pilasters with delicately carved capitals also designed by Sangallo (1489), beneath a lantern and dome. After its restoration in 2000, a **Crucifix attributed to Michelangelo** in painted poplar wood, found in Santo Spirito in 1963, has been displayed here. It is known that the prior of the convent allowed Michelangelo to study anatomy here in the early 1490s. Documents also confirm that Michelangelo made a Crucifix for the Augustinians for the high altar of this church, which was thought to have been lost. Many scholars believe this is that Crucifix. Exquisitely carved, it shows the slight figure of Christ in an unusual *contrapposto* position, a design subsequently much copied.

(**R**) In this chapel there is a 1579 copy of the *Risen Christ* by Michelangelo in the church of Santa Maria sopra Minerva in Rome (in the opposite chapel can be seen a free copy made in 1549 of the artist's more famous *Pietà* in St Peter's).

(**S**) The *Resurrection* is one of three works in the church by Pier Francesco

di Jacopo Foschi, a little-known 16th-century painter whose work deserves greater study. His *Immaculate Conception* (**T**) is in the chapel immediately opposite and his *Transfiguration* (**U**) is in the south transept.

The **second cloister** is a beautiful work by Bartolomeo Ammannati (c. 1565): its unusual design incorporates a portico of three arches in the centre of each side. It is now part of a military barracks but the cloister and chapel are usually open to the public on a few days every year. Off the cloister is the Cappella Corsini with tombs—dating from the Gothic to the Baroque period—of various members of this famous Florentine family, many of whom held high ecclesiastical office, including Lorenzo, who became Pope Clement XII: his tomb bears his bust by Gherardo Silvani (1731).

The refectory

Open only on Sat; in summer 9–5, in winter 10.30–1.30; T: 055 287043. Entrance to the left of the church, at no. 29.

The refectory is the only part of the 14th-century convent to survive. Above a fresco of the *Last Supper* (almost totally ruined) is a huge **Crucifixion** (also damaged), both of them painted c. 1360–65. They are attributed to Andrea Orcagna and his *bottega*, which probably included his brother Nardo di Cione. A partial restoration, after years of neglect, revealed one of the most dramatic scenes of the Crucifixion in 14th-century Florentine painting.

The **Fondazione Salvatore Romano** is also displayed here. This collection of sculpture from many different periods (hand-list available), left to the city by the Neapolitan antiquarian Salvatore Romano in 1946, includes in the centre of the room an *Angel* (no. 44) and *Virtue* (or a caryatid; no. 38), both fine statuettes by Tino di Camaino.

SANTA MARIA DEL CARMINE & THE BRANCACCI CHAPEL

Map 5, 2–4. Open 10–4.30; Sun and holidays 1–4.30; closed Tues. Entrance through the cloisters. Combined ticket with Palazzo Vecchio. Visitors should book in advance (T: 055 276 8558) but if you are on your own you can often go straight in. Only 30 people may enter at a time.

The church of Santa Maria del Carmine (which was never given a façade) is famous for its frescoes by Masaccio in the Brancacci Chapel. A Carmelite convent was founded here in 1250 and the first church begun in 1268.

The cloisters

The attractive cloisters have four trees around a well and frescoes in the lunettes. In one refectory here (where a video is shown to visitors about the Brancacci Chapel) there is a *Last Supper* by Alessandro Allori and detached 14th-century frescoes.

In a second refectory, known as the Sala Vanni (*only open for concerts*), is the *Supper in the House of the Pharisee* by Francesco Vanni. Another wing of this huge convent can be seen in Via della Chiesa (off Via de' Serragli), formerly used by the Albergo Popolare (no. 68), built in 1930 as a hospice for the poor (and, with 125 beds, still used to house those in need).

MASACCIO & THE BRANCACCI CHAPEL

In his will of 1367 Piero Brancacci left money for a chapel to be decorated in his memory in this church. Little was accomplished until around 1424, when a distant relative, Felice Brancacci, a rich silk merchant and statesman, took over the ownership of the chapel and commissioned the frescoes of the life of St Peter (the subject was evidently a tribute to the founder's name).

The design of the whole cycle may be Masolino's, and he worked on the frescoes together with his pupil Masaccio. Masaccio seems to have assumed full responsibility after Masolino departed for Rome in 1428. Later that year Masaccio himself broke off work abruptly for an unknown reason, and also left for Rome, where by the end of the year he was dead, aged only 27. Brancacci drew up a will in 1432 in which he instructed his heirs to complete the decoration of the chapel after his death. In fact he was exiled from Florence in 1436 as an enemy of the Medici and never returned. The cycle was only completed some 50 years later by Filippino Lippi (c. 1480–85), who carefully integrated his style with that of Masaccio, possibly following an earlier design. This is a moving example of how subtly Renaissance artists were able to 'complete' earlier works of art. In 1690, the chapel was saved from demolition through the efforts of the Accademia del Disegno and Vittoria della Rovere, mother of Cosimo III. In the 18th century the church was devastated by fire, and the lunettes and vault of the chapel, probably frescoed by Masolino, were destroyed.

Masaccio's frescoes were at once recognised as a masterpiece and profoundly influenced the Florentine Renaissance: all the major artists of the 15th century came here to study them. They combine a perfect application of the new rules of perspective with a remarkable use of chiaroscuro. 'Masaccio,' said Bernard Berenson, 'like Giotto a century earlier…(was) a great master of the significant… endowed to the highest degree with a sense of tactile values, and with a skill in rendering them. In a career of but a few years he gave to Florentine painting the direction it pursued to the end.' The frescoes were restored in 1983–89, when it was found that an egg-based substance had been applied to the surface in the late 18th century, causing mould to form and obscuring the colour. Today the superb colouring and details of the landscapes can once again be appreciated.

The frescoes

Upper row

Entrance arch: Masolino, *Temptation of Adam and Eve.*

Right wall: Masolino, *St Peter, Accompanied by St John, Brings Tabitha to Life* and *St Peter Heals a Lame Man* (with a charming view of Florence in the background). The figures on the left and some details in the background may be by the hand of Masaccio.

Right of the altar: Masaccio, *St Peter Baptising.*

Left of the altar: Masolino, *St Peter Preaching.*

Left wall: Masaccio, *The Tribute Money*, perhaps the painter's masterpiece. Three episodes are depicted in the same scene: in the centre, Christ, surrounded by the Apostles, outside the gates of the city is asked by an official (with his back to us) to pay the tribute money owing to the city. Christ indicates a lake to St Peter, and (on the left) Peter is shown extracting the money from the mouth of a fish at the side of a lake. The scene on the right shows Peter handing over the tribute money to the official. The head of Christ has been attributed by some scholars to Masolino.

Entrance arch: Masaccio, *Expulsion of Adam and Eve from Paradise*, one of the most moving works of the Renaissance: it is known to have been painted in just four days, and shows the artist's remark-

Faces of desolation: Adam and Eve expelled from the Garden of Eden, by Masaccio (before 1428).

able skill in depicting the human figure (recalling also Classical sculpture). The poignant figures are charged with great emotion.

Lower row

Entrance arch: Filippino Lippi, *Release of St Peter from Prison*.

Right wall: Filippino Lippi, *Sts Peter and Paul Before the Proconsul* and the *Crucifixion of St Peter*.

Right of the altar: Masaccio, *St Peter and St John Distributing Alms*.

Left of the altar: Masaccio, *St Peter, Followed by St John, Healing the Sick with his Shadow*.

Left wall: Masaccio, *St Peter Enthroned* with portraits of friars, his last work. The three Carmelites standing on the left of the throne and the head of the kneeling one are by the hand of Masaccio, while the two other kneeling figures are by Filippino. The four figures to the right include Masaccio's self-portrait (the man in red looking directly at us), and the man behind him in a hood is thought to portray Brunelleschi. The smallest head in the group may be Masolino, and the man in profile in front in a light grey cloak has recently been identified with Leon Battista Alberti (who would have been aged just 24 at the time). The next half of this panel was begun by Masaccio and finished by Filippino. It shows *St Peter Bringing the Emperor's Nephew to Life* (the faces executed by Masaccio are more strongly illuminated; Filippino's figures are, in contrast, flatter and stand as if in shadow).

Entrance arch: Filippino Lippi, *St Peter in Prison Visited by St Paul* (to a design by Masaccio).

During restoration work, fragments of frescoes attributed to Masaccio—including two heads and part of the scene with *St Peter Healing the Sick with His Shadow*—were found behind the 18th-century altar (since removed). The lovely altarpiece, the **Madonna del Carmine**, known as the 'Madonna del Popolo', is the earliest of the huge *Maestà* painted for churches in the city (*see p. 113*) and one of the very few works of this date not removed to a museum. It was probably made around 1270 for the high altar of the first church, but was already in this chapel by 1460. Once attributed to Coppo di Marcovaldo, it is now thought to be by the anonymous Master of Sant'Agata.

The church

The huge wide interior of the church (*open 9–12 & 4.30–6*) was rebuilt in an undistinguished late Baroque style in 1782. The best thing in it is the sumptuous Chapel of Sant'Andrea Corsini, commissioned in 1675–83 by Bartolomeo and Neri Corsini from Pier Francesco Silvani in honour of their ancestor Andrea Corsini, who died in 1374 and was canonised in 1629. It is one of the most important Baroque works in Florence, with a ceiling by Luca Giordano (1682) and marble and silver reliefs by Giovanni Battista Foggini.

Around the Carmine

The chapel in the little piazza to the left of the church façade has been turned into a wine bar for Roberto Cavalli, the fashion designer. Via dell'Ardiglione, the little street to the left of the church, is worth exploring to see the simple house, just beyond the archway, which was the birthplace of Filippo Lippi (it bears a plaque).

Fra' Filippo Lippi (c. 1406–69)

Filippo started out life as a friar at the Carmine. From a poor family and orphaned as a child, when still only a boy of around 15, he took his vows just a few years before Masaccio began work on his famous frescoes, so he would have watched the great artist at work: his earliest paintings clearly show Masaccio's influence. In 1456, when chaplain to a convent in Prato, he abducted a nun named Lucrezia Buti and they had a child, Filippino. The scandal was resolved through the good offices of Cosimo il Vecchio when Pope Pius II agreed that they could both be released from their vows and live together as man and wife.

We know comparatively little else about Filippo's life, although he came into contact with Fra' Angelico (and they even painted a panel together, now in the National Gallery of Washington). The influence of Donatello was also extremely important, and Filippo's depictions of the Christ Child owe much to the sculptor. He was singled out by Cosimo il Vecchio and became one of the first official artists to work for the Medici. He is above all notable for his skill in depicting human gestures and expressions, revealing his interest in human relationships rather than in more abstracted forms of perception. The most important group of paintings by him is in the Uffizi (*see p. 115*).

He is immortalised in a dramatic monologue by Browning in which the jovial friar admits his lack of vocation but explains how monastic life gave him the opportunity to observe human nature and human physiognomy, which served him so well as a painter. His patter evidently wins the favour of the night watchmen who catch him revelling late at night in the streets (which since the early 14th century had been illuminated by lanterns). Filippo's influence on later artists was considerable. It has been pointed out that Leonardo da Vinci must have been influenced by the wild rocky landscapes in the background of some of his paintings. He is now considered one of the greatest artists of the Renaissance, and his son Filippino also excelled as one of the major artists of his day.

SAN FREDIANO

Borgo San Frediano (*map 5, 2*) gives its name to a district typical of this part of the city, with numerous artisans' houses and workshops, once the heart of the Oltrarno. The street passes the bare stone exterior of the large church of **San Frediano in Cestello** (*usually open 9.30–11.30 & 5–6*), which has a rough-hewn façade facing the river. It was rebuilt in 1680–89 by Antonio Maria Ferri and its fine dome is a conspicuous feature. Inside, all six side chapels have good frescoed decoration in the domes, spandrels and lunettes, carried out at the end of the 17th and the beginning of the 18th centuries by Florentine painters (including Giovanni Camillo Sagrestani, Matteo Bonechi, Alessandro Gherardini, Antonio Domenico Gabbiani, Pier Dandini and Antonio Franchi) who also executed the altarpieces. Gabbiani, who was considered the most important artist of his time in Florence, carried out the very fine frescoes on the main dome. In the last chapel on the north side there is a polychrome wooden statue of the *Madonna and Child* by the 14th-century Pisan or Florentine school.

At Via Lorenzo Bartolini 4 (with a row of artisans' workshops opposite) is the entrance to the driveway and little garden around the **Antico Setificio Fiorentino** (*map 5, 2*), a silk-weaving factory which was moved here in 1786. Twelve artisans still use the 17th- and 18th-century hand looms and late 19th-century machinery to produce exquisite silk fabrics, which are hand-dyed and woven to traditional designs. There is also a showroom (*open Mon–Fri 9–1 & 2–5*).

The road ends at a stretch of wall with crenellations, the best-preserved part of the last circle of **medieval walls** built by the *Comune* in 1284–1333. It runs from the Torrino di Santa Rosa on the banks of the Arno to the **Porta San Frediano**. This gate, with its high tower, built in 1324 (perhaps by Andrea Pisano), protected the road to Pisa. It preserves interesting ironwork as well as its huge wooden doors, decorated with nail heads, with their old locks. The city's emblem, an iris (*see box below*) is carved high up on the tower. Just outside the gate there is a little public garden which extends to the river, and tucked away in the corner here is the Sabatino *trattoria*, a local favourite.

At Borgo San Frediano 70 is the extraordinary **Galleria Romanelli** (*open Mon–Sat 9–1 & 3–7*), opened in 1860 on the Lungarno degli Acciaioli but now occupying the huge former courtyard and studio of the famous 19th-century sculptor Lorenzo Bartolini (it was taken over by Pasquale Romanelli in 1851). Ever since then it has been used by sculptors in the Romanelli family and today you can visit the historic *gipsoteca* with thousands of plaster casts, as well as the showroom where reproductions in marble and bronze of the great Italian masterpieces of sculpture can be seen, and the sculpture studio, still active, where sculpture classes are also held.

THE SYMBOL OF FLORENCE: LILY OR IRIS?

Although always known as the Lily of Florence, the city's true emblem was an iris (in Italian also called *giaggiolo*). This was at first a white flower on a red ground, but the Guelphs later changed the colours to a red flower on a white ground. It should not be confused with the fleur-de-lys of the French house of Anjou, to be seen all over Europe (and also in Florence). A red iris is unknown in nature, but beautiful white and purple irises grow in profusion in spring all over the countryside near Florence. The emblem usually includes two stylised symmetrical roses, perhaps because they were symbols of the Virgin since the month of May, when they bloom, is dedicated to her.

THE BANKS OF THE ARNO

The River Arno is a great feature of the Florence townscape, even though nowadays it is only occasionally used for skulling. Once navigable all the way from the coast, it was of great importance to the livelihood of the city: during the Middle Ages mills on the Arno were used in the wool industry, on which Florence's economy was based from the 13th century onwards. By this time all four bridges in the centre of the city had been built: the other bridges up and down stream were only added after 1836. As much as it brought prosperity, however, the Arno also brought devastation. Since the first recorded flood in 1177, the river has overflowed its banks no fewer than 57 times (small plaques throughout the city show the level the water reached during some of these inundations). The last great flood was in 1966, when buildings, works of art and hundreds of artisans' workshops were severely damaged. The roads along the embankment, known as the Lungarni (singular, Lungarno), lined with handsome palaces and some elegant shops, are lovely places to walk and enjoy the magnificent open views. A number of small churches close to the river are also described here.

View upstream of the Arno in around 1900, with Ponte Santa Trínita, Ponte Vecchio beyond it and the tower of Palazzo Vecchio on the skyline on the left. In the foreground, washerwomen are at work on the embankment.

PONTE VECCHIO

Standing near the site of the Roman river crossing (which was a little farther upstream), Ponte Vecchio (*map 1, 5*) was the only bridge over the Arno until 1218. The present bridge of three arches was reconstructed after a flood in 1345, probably by Taddeo Gaddi, better known as a painter of the Giottesque school (but the bridge is also attributed to the architect Neri di Fioravante). It is known that this bridge already had the little rectangular 'piazza' in the centre, as it does today. The bridge on this site has been lined by shops since the 13th century, but it was only after an edict issued by Grand Duke Ferdinando I in 1593 that the butchers' shops and grocery stalls were replaced by those of goldsmiths and silversmiths, and they remain here to this day. These excellent jewellers, whose shops with pretty fronts with wooden shutters and awnings overhang the river supported on brackets, maintain the skilled tradition of Florentine goldsmiths, whose work first became famous in the 15th century. Many of the greatest Renaissance artists trained as goldsmiths (including Ghiberti, Brunelleschi and Donatello). The most famous Florentine goldsmith was the 16th-century sculptor Benvenuto Cellini, who was aptly recorded in 1900 when his bust was set up in the middle of the bridge. The goldsmiths of present-day Florence can be seen at work in the Casa dell'Orafo, a rambling edifice in an alley beside the dark Volta dei Girolami close to the north end of the bridge. Above the shops on one side of the bridge are the round windows of the Corridoio Vasariano, the covered way built by Vasari (*see p. 131*) to link Palazzo Vecchio with Palazzo Pitti on the other side of the river. It leaves the bridge on the south side, supported on elegant brackets in order not to disturb the (restored) Torre dei Mannelli, the medieval angle tower which served as a defence on the Arno. The fame of Ponte Vecchio saved it from war damage in 1944 (although numerous ancient buildings at either end were blown up instead, in order to render it impassable). From the centre of the bridge, where there is a sundial which survives from 1345 on the corner of a house, there is a superb view of Ponte Santa Trínita, the finest of all the bridges across the Arno (*see overleaf*).

LUNGARNO ACCIAIOLI & SANTI APOSTOLI

From the north end of Ponte Vecchio, Lungarno Acciaioli follows the Arno with a good view of the bridge and its shops built out above the river. Some of the smartest small shops in Florence are in the area of the Lungarno here. At no. 14 William Holman Hunt, co-founder of the Pre-Raphaelite Brotherhood in 1848, stayed in 1867.

Narrow alleyways connect the Lungarno with Borgo Santi Apostoli, a Roman road which led from outside the south gate of the city to the Via Cassia, the ancient road for Rome. One of these alleys leads to the attractive little Piazza del Limbo, so named because of a cemetery here for unbaptised infants, with the church of Santi Apostoli (*described overleaf*). In a group of old houses overhanging the opposite bank of the river, the little tower and river gate belonging to the church of San Jacopo sopr'Arno can be seen.

Santi Apostoli

Santi Apostoli (*map 1, 5; open 10–12 & 3–5*), with its Romanesque stone façade, is one of the oldest parish churches in the city. Mentioned in the sources as early as 1075, it probably dates from the previous century. The façade bears a 16th-century inscription which proudly states that the church was founded by Charlemagne and consecrated in 805 in the presence of his paladins Roland and Oliver. Although this is a legend, we do know that the emperor stayed in Florence at least once, on his way south to Rome at Christmas time in 786. The east end and campanile, the upper part of which is attributed to Baccio d'Agnolo, can be seen from the piazza behind.

The basilican interior has fine green marble-coursed monolithic columns and capitals which are Roman spolia. It contains 16th-century funerary monuments to members of the Altoviti family, who lived in the parish and were benefactors of the church. At the end of the north aisle is the tomb of Prior Oddo Altoviti, by Benedetto da Rovezzano (with a Classical sarcophagus); Benedetto probably also built the prior's palace for him, which survives in the piazza outside (at no. 1), as well as the stoup in the nave and the handsome doorway of the church itself. In the apse Antonio Altoviti, Archbishop of Florence, is commemorated in a monument by Giovanni Antonio Dosio, and two busts above the side doors by Giovanni Battista Caccini show Antonio in pride of place beside Charlemagne.

On the left of the apse is the beautiful enamelled terracotta Tabernacle of the Sacrament (1512) by Andrea della Robbia (and assistants). Below are two beautiful sculpted panels from the tomb of Donato Acciaioli (1333), member of another well-known family who resided in this area and were also patrons of the church. The high altarpiece is a beautiful late 14th-century Gothic polyptych of the *Madonna Enthroned with Saints and Angels*, complete with its predella. It is probably by Jacopo di Cione with the help of Niccolò di Pietro Gerini. In the north aisle there are 16th-century altarpieces by Maso di San Friano (*Nativity*) and Giorgio Vasari (*Immaculate Conception*).

In the piazza, where an old lane leads out to the Arno, Palazzo Rosselli del Turco has a relief of the *Madonna* by Benedetto da Maiano. The main façade in the Borgo is by Baccio d'Agnolo (1517). The 14th-century Palazzi Acciaioli at no. 8 preserves its tower, bearing the emblem of the Certosa del Galluzzo, founded by Niccolò Acciaioli (1340–65).

Part of the building at no. 27 (red) Borgo Santi Apostoli dates from the 13th century, as does Palazzo Usimbardi (Acciaioli) at no. 19 (red). In the 19th century, when it was the Grand Hotel Royal, Ruskin, Dickens, Swinburne, Longfellow and Henry James all stayed here.

PONTE SANTA TRÍNITA

A bridge has spanned the Arno on this site since 1252, though the present Ponte Sante Trínita (*map 1, 5*) dates only from 1957. It is an exact replica of the graceful bridge commissioned in 1567 by Cosimo I from Bartolomeo Ammannati and which is his masterpiece. It is probable that Ammannati submitted his project to Michelangelo for approval: the great artist had toyed with the idea of accepting an invitation in 1506 from Sultan Beyazit II to build a bridge across the Bosphorus in Constantinople.

Its high flat arches, known as catenaries (from the Latin *catena*, chain) recreate the unique curve of a chain suspended between two terminal points. The statues of the Four Seasons were set up on the parapet for the marriage of Cosimo II; *Spring* (on the corner of Lungarno Acciaioli) is the best work of Pietro Francavilla (1593).

The bridge was destroyed in 1944 when it was mined by the retreating German army. The replacement was financed by public subscription from a committee presided over by Bernard Berenson, and built under the careful direction of the architect Riccardo Gizdulich and the engineer Emilio Brizzi. Most of the original decorative details and the four statues from the parapet were salvaged from the bed of the river (although the head of *Spring*, for long thought to have been lost in the war, was dredged up from the Arno only in 1961).

LUNGARNO CORSINI & PONTE ALLA CARRAIA

Palazzo Masetti (Castelbarco; *map 6, 1*) is where Louisa, Countess of Albany, widow of Prince Charles Edward Stuart, the Young Pretender (*see p. 342*), lived from 1793 until her death in 1824. Her famous salon was frequented by Chateaubriand, Shelley, Byron, Foscolo and Von Platen. The dramatist Alfieri, her second husband, died here in 1803. The Countess was later joined here by François-Xavier Fabre, the French painter. She is buried in Santa Croce. The British Consulate occupied this palace up until 2011 when it was closed down (so that Florence is left with only an Honorary Consul, to the consternation of many British residents, as well as Florentines: the British diplomatic presence in Florence goes back half a millennium).

The Lungarno here is dominated by the huge **Palazzo Corsini**, in grandiose Roman Baroque style, and very different from other Florentine town houses of this period. It was begun in 1656 by Alfonso Parigi the Younger and Ferdinando Tacca, and continued (after 1685) by Antonio Ferri (perhaps to a design by Pier Francesco Silvani). It was not completed until around 1737. The façade is crowned by statues and has a terrace overlooking the river. It is host to a biennial autumn antiques fair (odd years: 2013, 2015, 2017), one of the best-known and oldest such events in Italy, and at present that is unfortunately the only time part of the interior, with its late 17th-century frescoes, can be seen. The Galleria Corsini, the most important private art collection in Florence, has been dismantled and put into store (*for information, T: 055 218994*).

Ponte alla Carraia

Ponte alla Carraia (*map 6, 1*) was the second bridge to be built over the Arno after Ponte Vecchio. Constructed in wood on stone piles in 1218–20, it was first called Ponte Nuovo. It was reconstructed after floods in 1269 and 1333; the 14th-century bridge may have been designed by Giotto. In 1559 it was repaired by Ammannati and then enlarged in 1867; it was replaced by a new bridge (a copy of the original) after it was blown up in 1944.

OGNISSANTI

Map 3, 7. Open 7–12.30 & 4–7.30, Sun and holidays 8.45–1 & 5–7.30.

The church of Ognissanti (All Saints) was founded in 1256 by the Umiliati, a Benedictine Order particularly skilled in manufacturing wool. This area of the city became one of the main centres of the woollen cloth industry, on which medieval Florence based her economy. The diagonal stone dyke in the Arno here was built to serve the watermills on the river.

In 1561 the church was taken over by the Franciscans (and friars and nuns of the Franciscan Order of the Immaculate Conception now live here) and it was rebuilt in the 17th century. The original *pietra serena* façade by Matteo Nigetti (1637) was replaced in 1872 by a very handsome one in white travertine (a stone typical of Rome but hardly ever used in Florence). Above the portal is a lunette of the *Coronation of the Virgin* ascribed to Benedetto Buglioni, virtually the only artist who still knew how to produce fine works in glazed terracotta after the della Robbia workshop halted production in the early 16th century. The campanile dates from 1258.

Interior of Ognissanti

The *trompe l'œil* ceiling frescoes date from 1770. The fine large pavement tomb of Antonio di Vitale de' Medici, a philosopher and doctor who paid for the original façade and died in 1656, bears the Medici arms in marble intarsia (his brother, Alessandro de' Medici, is recorded in the fine polychrome terracotta della Robbian coat of arms outside).

South side: The frescoes of the *Pietà* and the *Madonna della Misericordia*, early works by Domenico Ghirlandaio, are interesting as the Madonna is shown protecting members of the Vespucci family (Amerigo is supposed to be the young boy whose head appears between the Madonna and the man in the dark cloak). The family tombstone (1471) is in the pavement left of the altar. The Vespucci, who lived in Borgo Ognissanti, were merchants involved in the manufacture of silk. As supporters of the Medici, they held political office in the 15th century. Amerigo (1454–1512), a Medici agent in Seville, gave his name to the continent of America, having made two voyages in 1499 and 1501–02 following the route charted by his Italian contemporary Columbus. Their

neighbours in Borgo Ognissanti were the Filipepi, the most famous of whom was Sandro who became known as Botticelli, probably because he was apprenticed to a jeweller as a boy (*battigello* means silversmith), and who is also buried in the church.

The Vespucci, who are known to have commissioned some works from Botticelli (the scholarly Giorgio Antonio di Ser Amerigo was a friend of the humanist Marsilio Ficino), also apparently paid for his **fresco of St Augustine**, the philosopher and Father of the Church (between the third and fourth altars), which is the artist's most important work in Florence to survive in a church for which it was made (1480). It is also one of the few frescoes in the city by Botticelli, and shows his skill also in this technique. St Augustine is portrayed deep in thought in his study with a mechanical clock behind him and an armillary sphere in front, probably at the moment in which he has a vision of the death of St Jerome.

Together with the pendant of the erudite *St Jerome* opposite (by Domenico Ghirlandaio), it used to be on the choir screen of the church, but it was moved when the church was altered in 1564 and carefully (and successfully) detached in 1966. Ghirlandaio's work is dated 1480 (on the desk), and the exquisite detail of the objects in his study, including the saint's spectacles, two ink pots, and books in Greek, Latin and Hebrew, recall contemporary Flemish works. It is rare to see such carefully painted details in a fresco.

Transepts and east end: The frescoes and stuccoes in the Baroque chapels in the south transept date from the early 18th century. In the chapel to the right, with pretty stuccoes, the dome is frescoed by Matteo Bonechi, and there are two frescoes on the side walls by Vincenzo Meucci. The small portable organ here was built by Giovanni Francesco Cacioli of Lucca and Tronci of Pistoia (1741). The simple round tombstone in the pavement marks the **burial place of Sandro Filipepi** (**Botticelli**). In the chapel at the end of this transept, the two late 16th-century paintings on the side walls are interesting as they show the dress of Florentines of that time. In the chapel to the left, the *Martyrdom of St Andrew* is a good painting by Matteo Rosselli. Here the handsome **pavement tomb of Lorenzo Lenzi** (d. 1442), with a coat of arms bearing a bronze relief of the head of a bull, is a little-studied work which has sometimes been attributed to the great bronze sculptor Lorenzo Ghiberti.

The choir chapel is decorated with precious marbles and has delightful frescoes in the dome (1616–17) by Giovanni da San Giovanni, with numerous angels. The beautiful **high altar** (1593–1605), probably by Jacopo Ligozzi, has a frontal of exquisite workmanship, in polychrome marble intarsia and mother-of-pearl, and three mosaic panels in *commesso fiorentino*, with a tabernacle above in *pietre dure*. In the chapel at the end of the north transept a magnificent large painted **Crucifix** was installed in 2010 after a ten-year restoration, and its attribution to the hand of Giotto was confirmed. It is dated around 1310–15, so later than his great Crucifix in Santa Maria Novella. In a niche below the steps up to the chapel there is a dramatic sculpture of the *Dead Christ* (17th century).

Cenacolo di Ognissanti

On the left of the church is the entrance to the convent (no. 42; *open Mon, Tues and Sat 9–12*). In the vestibule are early 17th-century frescoes of the life of the Virgin. The 15th-century cloister, with reused Ionic capitals, in the style of Michelozzo, was altered in the 16th century. It incorporates octagonal pilasters which support part of the Gothic church. The 13th-century campanile can also be seen here. In the centre is an olive tree and there are little beds of irises and rosemary on the lawn. The frescoes of the life of St Francis were executed in the first decades of the 17th century under the direction of Jacopo Ligozzi. We know that in 1752 Sir Joshua Reynolds came here to copy them.

The pretty vaulted refectory, with its lavabos and pulpit in *pietra serena*, contains a **Last Supper** by **Domenico Ghirlandaio** (dated 1480), the most beautiful of his several frescoes of this subject in Florence. The details of the plants in the background, the birds, the pewter ewers, and brass tray, the vase of flowers, as well as the apricots and cherries on the table with its embroidered tablecloth, claim our attention and the figures of Christ and the disciples seem to take second place (although only they appear in the sinopia displayed on the wall nearby). The plants, fruit and birds all represent Christian symbols. The fresco of the *Annunciation* dates from 1369. There are plans to exhibit here a charming 15th-century *Madonna and Child* in polychrome terracotta by Nanni di Bartolo, which belongs to the church.

THE CASCINE

Lungarno Vespucci was opened in the 19th century: it leads downstream from Ponte alla Carraia, past the American Consulate (Florence has had an American Consul since 1825). Beyond the end of the Lungarno begins the huge park of the Cascine (*map 2, 5*), which lines the right bank of the river for over three kilometres. It is the largest public park in Florence, although only a few hundred metres wide, with fine woods. During the day it is used as a recreation ground by Florentines, old and young, and huge public concerts and festivals are held here in summer. The best time to come here is on Tuesday morning, when a very big general market (excellent value) is held at the foot of the new bridge (for the tram and pedestrians) over the Arno. Here you can buy anything from a pair of jeans to a budgerigar, as well as a good sandwich which you can enjoy sitting on a bench on the banks of the river. It is very conveniently reached by tram (*every 3mins: the stop is in Viale degli Olmi, just short of the bridge; terminus at Santa Maria Novella station*).

The park's name comes from a dairy-farm (*cascina*) that was acquired by Duke Alessandro de' Medici, and it was later used as a ducal chase for the hunting of deer. In the 18th century public spectacles and festivals were held here but it was first opened regularly to the public in the first years of the 19th century by Elisa Baciocchi. Shelley wrote his famous *Ode to the West Wind* here. On the broad walk along the Arno, magnolia trees and laurel hedges with bays of ilex have been replanted. At the extreme far end of the park, a very well-preserved little pavilion, known as the Monumento dell'Indiano, commemorates Rajaram Chuttraputti, the Maharajah of Kolhapur, who died in Florence in 1870 at the age of 20 on his return from England to India and was cremated here by the British, at the confluence of the Arno and Mugnone rivers, according to the Brahmin rites. The fine bust is signed by Charles Fuller, a British sculptor resident at the time in Florence. At this point the view is dominated by a suspension bridge built over the Arno in 1978.

An 8-kilometre cycling path runs from here along the Arno as far as the Renai park at Signa, which is open in summer and where boats and canoes can be hired, and there are swimming facilities (*see www.parcorenai.it*).

SANTA FELICITA & THE SOUTH BANK OF THE ARNO

The **church of Santa Felicita** (*map 6, 3–4; open 9.30–12.30 & 3.30–6 except Sun, when there is a service in the morning; sacristy only open Fri 3.30–5.30*) disputes with San Lorenzo the primacy of being the very first church in Florence, since an inscription was found here dated 405. Its position on the south side of the river where the Cassia Nova (AD 123), a busy consular road from Rome, reached the city, makes it a likely place for the Syrian Greek merchants to have settled when they brought with them the message of Christianity at the end of the 4th or beginning of the 5th century. In the little piazza in front of the church stands a granite column of 1381, erected by the nuns of the Benedictine monastery here, apparently to mark the site of an ancient monument in the form of a pyramid. It was the Benedictines who built the first church on this site. Many tombstones and inscriptions from the early Christian cemetery have been found here. It seems that a larger basilica was soon erected, and then another church in the 10th century. The present church was built in 1736–39 by Ferdinando Ruggieri, and his design for the interior takes its inspiration from late 16th-century Florentine architecture.

Interior of Santa Felicita

The church is chiefly visited for its superb **works by Pontormo in the Cappella Capponi**, considered among the masterpieces of 16th-century Florentine painting (*coin-operated light essential*). They were commissioned by Ludovico Capponi in 1525, after he purchased the chapel from the Barbadori. The remarkable altarpiece of the *Deposition* (correctly, *The Transportation of the Dead Body of Christ; see box overleaf*) is in a magnificent contemporary frame attributed to Baccio d'Agnolo. The head of Nicodemus on the right may be Pontormo's self-portrait. The fresco of the *Annunciation* was detached when it was restored. The tondi of the Evangelists in the cupola are by Pontormo (*St John the Evangelist*) and Bronzino (the other three, although their attribution between these two masters is still under discussion). The chapel was originally designed for the Barbadori by Brunelleschi (1419–23), but the cupola was rebuilt when Pontormo painted it, and this was replaced by yet another, lower, dome in 1739 when some of its frescoes were destroyed. The stained-glass window is by Guillaume de Marcillat (1526), a French artist who lived in Arezzo, famous as a designer of stained glass.

Over the fourth south altar is a striking painting, the *Martyrdom of the Maccabee Brothers*, by Antonio Ciseri (1863). The choir chapel was designed by Lodovico Cigoli in 1610–22. The signature of a little-known painter called Lorenzo della Sciorina was found on the high altarpiece of the *Adoration of the Shepherds* during restoration (it had traditionally been attributed to Santi di Tito). The second chapel has a painted altarpiece showing a miracle of the archangel Raphael and Tobias by Ignazio Hugford.

The pretty **sacristy** off the right transept (*for opening times, see above*) was built in 1473, by a pupil of Brunelleschi, and modified in the 19th century when the attractive lavabo and altar were added. It was well restored in 2006 and contains some precious works of art. The lovely polychrome terracotta half-figure of the *Madonna and Child* is attributed to Luca della Robbia or his *bottega*. The polyptych (c. 1354) of the *Madonna and Child with Saints* is by Taddeo Gaddi. The *Pietà* is by Domenico di Zanobi. The splendid panel (1464) by Neri di Bicci shows St Felicity with her seven children. The predella mistakenly illustrates the story of the mother of the Seven Maccabees. Since St Felicity was martyred together with her seven children, in the 2nd century AD, she has often been confused with the mother of the biblical Maccabees. There are a number of other illustrations of her story in this church: in a painting by Giorgio Berti (1810) in the first south chapel and in the cupola above the sanctuary, where she and her children are shown in glory (Michelangelo Cinganelli; 1617–19).

The **chapter house** (*sometimes unlocked on request*) has a fresco of the *Crucifixion* signed and dated 1387 by Niccolò di Pietro Gerini, and another of *St Felicity* by Cosimo Ulivelli. Some 75 remarkable ancient inscriptions have survived from the Early Christian cemetery attached to the church. The earliest of these is a memorial to a certain Theoteknos, dated 1st July 405. Another records Maria, the daughter of John of Nicerta (present-day Syria), who died here 'in the faith' at only three years old on 10th April 417.

MANNERISM & PONTORMO'S 'DEPOSITION'

The term 'Mannerism' denotes the deliberate and cultivated stylisation of human and architectural forms which characterises much of the art produced in Italy in the 16th century, and most especially in Florence. That stylisation consisted in a variety of effects: the elongation of figures, a tendency to kaleidoscopic colour in drapery, the use of architectural elements to perform functions often contrary to their traditional purpose, and the construction of expressive, but often wholly artificial, poses for groups of figures. In this way Mannerism is a rejection of the restraint and naturalism of classical style: the emphasis is more on virtuosity, both formal and technical, with the artist holding our attention as performer and entertainer. The great Mannerist artists in Florence—Pontormo and Rosso Fiorentino—turned their backs on the desire to give the illusion of reality which had so dominated early and high Renaissance art, in order to create images and effects of formalised elegance, capable nonetheless of conveying intense feeling.

Pontormo's *Deposition* in the Capponi Chapel of Santa Felicita is a superb example of Mannerist painting. The colour is no longer achieved through careful naturalism and unifying tones, but by an unreal and startling brilliance of contrasts; the mutilation and the heaviness of the dead body—so central to the pathos evoked by earlier representations of this scene—is here transformed into an airy weightlessness of great beauty but almost total unphysicality; and the figures do not seem to inhabit the three-dimensional space which would have been so painstakingly created around them by a Filippo Lippi or a Piero della Francesca, but to float instead on the surface with no immediately logical relation one to another. The breach with naturalism intensifies the scene's spirituality and the picture's theatrical effect.   N.McG.

THE EASTERN OLTRARNO: VIA DE' BARDI

The winding **Via de' Bardi** (*map 6, 4*) is named after the palaces of the Bardi, one of the richest banking families in medieval Florence, bankrupted by loans to King Edward III of England to fund his war with France. At the foot of Ponte Vecchio, the street passes beneath the Corridoio Vasariano and then, beyond the archway where the old Costa dei Magnoli runs uphill to Costa San Giorgio, it becomes a well-preserved narrow medieval street of noble town houses. On the raised pavement towards the Arno, the statue of *St John the Baptist* is by Giuliano Vangi.

The Capponi family (whose chapel is in Santa Felicita) own three palaces in a row (with their gardens across the street). The splendid **Palazzo Capponi delle Rovinate** (no. 36; the name recalls the ruins of the house across the street, which collapsed in a landslide in 1547, destroying Raphael's *Madonna del Cardellino*; *see p. 126*) was built for the banker and ambassador Niccolò da Uzzano in the early 15th century, and on his death it went to his daughter's husband's family, the Capponi, who have lived here ever since. It has rough blocks of stone on the exterior of the lower floor and two handsome windows and stone seats on either side of its entrance, which still has its original studded wooden doors and the black-and-white Capponi coat of arms above. At the near end, by the two huge doors which gave access to the family storerooms and wine cellars (the Cantina Capponi), there is a little niche with its original wooden door just big enough for a flask of wine to be passed through: many of the more important Florentine families used to sell the wine directly from their country estates in this way, and a number of similar niches survive low down on the façades of Florence's old town houses. The Capponi family archives and art collection survive here in rooms splendidly decorated in the 18th and 19th centuries (*admission by appointment*). The paintings include works by Suttermans and Pontormo (*St Jerome*), as well as five seascapes and landscapes by Salvatore Rosa.

Next door is **Palazzo Larioni dei Bardi** (no. 30), which has a courtyard begun by Michelozzo and perhaps completed by Benedetto da Maiano. The third palace, **Palazzo Canigiani** (no. 28–30), has a Neoclassical façade. The English scholar of Florentine Renaissance sculpture John Pope Hennessy (1913–94) lived here at the end of his life. He was made an honorary citizen of Florence.

At no. 24 is the little church of **Santa Lucia dei Magnoli** (*open for services on Sat at 5.30 and Sun at 11; on weekdays only if you hear the bell ring*). The lunette over the door is by Benedetto Buglioni. Inside is a beautiful painting of *St Lucy*, one of the few works in Florence by the great Sienese artist Pietro Lorenzetti (and the only one still in a Florentine church).

Piazza dei Mozzi

The fine old **Palazzi dei Mozzi** were built in the 13th–14th centuries and are among the most noble private houses of medieval Florence. The severe façades in *pietra forte* have ground-floor arches and follow the slight bend in the road. The Mozzi were one of the richest Florentine families in the 13th century but, like the Bardi, they lost most of their wealth in the 14th century. Gregory X was their guest in 1273, when he stopped in Florence on his way to the Council of Lyons. While here he negotiated a peace between the Guelphs and Ghibellines, and a church dedicated to him as San Gregorio 'alla Pace' was founded here. It is now incorporated in the Museo Stefano Bardini building (*see below*). The Mozzi palaces contain the vast collection inherited by Stefano Bardini's son Ugo (1892–1965), with numerous marble architectural fragments recuperated from the demolitions in the old centre of Florence as well as decorative arts, paintings and sculpture. They are still being catalogued but there are long-term plans to open a museum, perhaps to be combined with the Museo Stefano Bardini (*described below*).

MUSEO STEFANO BARDINI

Map 6, 4. Entrance just round the corner from Piazza dei Mozzi at Via dei Renai 37. Open Sat, Sun and Mon 11–5. The labelling is very poor, especially on the ground floor.

This is an eclectic museum, containing medieval and Renaissance sculpture, paintings, carpets, arms and armour, small bronzes, architectural fragments, woodwork, drawings, furniture, tombs, coats of arms, doorways, wooden ceilings and decorative arts of all kinds. It is arranged as a 'show-room', with bright blue walls, as it probably looked in Bardini's day. Stefano Bardini (1836–1922) began life as an artist but made his name as an art dealer in the 1870s and '80s, quick to take advantage of the opportunities provided when some important Florentine families, such as the Strozzi and Capponi, decided to sell off their precious possessions. It was partly through him that Renaissance fine and applied art became greatly sought-after by foreign buyers, and he organised auctions and supplied numerous museums all over the world with masterpieces, including the Isabella Stewart Gardner Museum in Boston, the Louvre, the National Gallery of Washington, the Hermitage and the Berlin museum (through the collaboration of Wilhelm Bode), at a time when there were no restrictions on exporting artworks. He was also on hand to recuperate numerous architectural elements from palaces during the demolitions in the old centre of Florence. He bought and restored the Castello di Marignolle and Torre del Gallo in the hills above Florence, as well as this building (purchased from the Mozzi in 1881). After a last sale in 1918 in New York, he created this museum which he left to the city of Florence on his death.

Ground floor

The main hall was formerly a courtyard, which Bardini covered with a 16th-century coffered ceiling, substituting the panels with glass. The large Gothic arch is a pastiche, created with various Sienese statuettes and reliefs. It frames a niche with a beautiful statue of *Charity* by Tino di Camaino (1311–23), showing a woman suckling two babies. Also here are two pulpits, one dating from the late 15th century and the other made up by Bardini from Cosmatesque fragments. A small console on the right wall displays a female head which may be by Nicola Pisano.

In the room towards the street there is more sculpture. A small room is decorated with a large fresco dating from the early 15th century showing a female figure pulling back a curtain with a delightful geometric design. This was carefully detached by Bardini from a building in Lombardy and is still very well preserved. The very fine small marble sarcophagus with a tondo bearing the three faces of the Trinity is a Renaissance work carved by Pagno di Lapo Portigiani (1449–52) for an altar in the Santissima Annunziata (*for a note on the iconography, see p. 214*). The other two pieces are acquisitions made after Bardini's time. The original bronze boar known as the *Porcellino* (formerly in the Mercato Nuovo; *see p. 103*) was moved here in 2004 when it was replaced *in situ* by a copy. It was cast by Pietro Tacca in 1633, based on a marble Hellenistic original (now in the Uffizi). The other bronze is by Tacca's master Giambologna: it is an exquisitely carved satyr or '*diavolino*', an amusing bizarre figure commissioned by Bernardo Vecchietti for the exterior of his palace in Via Strozzi (it was the support for a flagstaff).

The room at the foot of the main stairs has two chimneypieces recomposed by Bardini and a fragment of a huge ancient Roman porphyry basin. The vaulted room off the stair landing was once the church of San Gregorio alla Pace (*see opposite*). It contains Bardini's important collection of arms and armour. Displayed on its own opposite the entrance is a very rare late 14th-century painted crest in the form of a dragon's head, made from leather and pastiglia. The small showcase on the right wall contains two bronze helmets, one of which dates from the 6th century BC.

Staircase

The staircase has a magnificent display of **Persian and Turkish carpets**, rehung as they were in Bardini's day. Although he had a particular interest in carpets (it is estimated that some 120 must have passed through his hands), only 21 were left in the collection on his death. However, there are about the same number in his son Ugo's collection across the road, and if these were brought together they would make up perhaps the most important collection in Europe, both for quantity and quality. When carpets began to be brought to Europe in the 15th century, Italy became an important centre from which they were distributed to other countries. It is known that one of the most famous and valuable carpets in the world, the Boston Hunting Carpet from Persia, was acquired (for a song!) by Bardini in 1879 from the Torrigiani in Florence. He was instrumental in encouraging an interest in carpets as works of art, and had a number of them carefully restored.

Upper floor

The rooms on the upper floor all have very fine painted wood ceilings from other palaces, installed here by Bardini.

The small room at the top of the stairs displays a dramatic painting of *Atlas* by Guercino (commissioned by Don Lorenzo de' Medici in 1646). The room towards the street displays (between the windows) the most precious painting in the collection: a processional standard of St Michael by Antonio Pollaiolo (possibly with the help of his brother Piero and dated sometime before 1465). The *St John the Baptist* by Michele Giambono is one of a number of gold-ground paintings displayed here. On the end wall (unfortunately just too high up to allow close examination) is the most precious carpet in Bardini's collection: an exquisite fragment of a Kashan carpet made in the 16th century in northern Persia, with numerous birds and animals in pairs amidst vegetation which includes cypress trees, with Kufic lettering in the border. Although woven in wool, it also has some metallic and silk threads.

The next room has two cases of small bronzes. The last room is named after the numerous frames charmingly displayed here (they date from the 15th century onwards). The finest piece of sculpture here is the lovely Umbrian *Madonna and Child* in painted wood (late 13th or early 14th century). It has been beautifully restored and the original colours refound, including the red clothes of the Child and the decorative 'carpet' behind (the Madonna's crown seems to have been added by Bardini, probably to hide woodworm damage). Also here are painted leather panels, shoes and fabrics.

Stairs lead down to a room with a huge Crucifix and numerous 15th- and 16th-century *cassoni*. The two most precious pieces of sculpture in the museum are displayed here side by side, now both thought to be by Donatello: the *Madonna dei Cordai*, a very unusual polychrome work on a wood base in stucco, glass, leather and mosaic. Although recently restored, it is still very damaged. It is thought to date from sometime before 1443. The beautiful high relief of the Madonna with the standing Child in polychrome terracotta is in a very different style. It, too, has recently been restored and the colours are now magnificent.

THE PARK & VILLA BARDINI

Map 6, 4. Entrances to the park at Via de' Bardi 1 (red) and Costa San Giorgio 4. Open 8.15–dusk (closed first and last Mon of the month). Ticket includes admission to the Boboli Gardens (which can be entered from a gate 5mins from the exit from the Bardini park on Costa San Giorgio), as well as the Museo degli Argenti and Museo del Costume, both in Palazzo Pitti. Separate ticket at the Costa San Giorgio entrance for admission to the two museums and temporary exhibitions in Villa Bardini (open 10–4, Sat and Sun 10–6; closed Mon and Tues).

The park

This huge garden, acquired by the Mozzi in the 16th century, stretches right up to the walls at the top of the hill. It has been restored and is now well kept, and is a lovely place to wander and enjoy the magnificent views over all Florence. In the centre there is a long staircase which leads up to a delightful loggia, reconstructed by Stefano Bardini. The beds on either side are planted (and labelled) according to the seasons. There are hedged walks on either side, as well as some streams, grottoes and statuary. Tubs of azaleas flower here in spring.

Villa Bardini and its museums

It is thought that Gherardo Silvani built this villa in its wonderful position overlooking Florence around 1641. It was acquired by the Mozzi family in 1839, and in 1913 by Stefano Bardini, who took up residence here. It was restored a few years ago as a temporary exhibition space as well as home to the **Museo della Fondazione**

Roberto Capucci, where the fascinating creations of the 'artist-tailor' Roberto Capucci are shown in changing exhibitions and his entire archive, including his drawings, is preserved along with some 400 gowns. Born in 1930, he worked in Paris in the 1960s and then spent time in India in the 1970s, and is a stylist who has always operated outside the normal world of fashion design. Also here is the **Museo Pietro Annigoni**, with representative works by the Florentine painter.

OUTSIDE PORTA SAN GIORGIO

This pretty lane called Costa San Giorgio leads uphill from the Villa Bardini entrance between the high walls of rural villas to **Porta San Giorgio** (*map 6, 6*), which has a fresco by Bicci di Lorenzo. Dating from 1260, the gate forms part of the walls built to protect the Oltrarno in 1258, and is the oldest to have survived in the city. On the outer face is a copy of a stone relief of *St George* (the original is in Palazzo Vecchio), thought to have been made in the same year as the gate. Just outside is the **Forte di Belvedere** (*no access at the time of writing*), a huge fortress designed by Buontalenti (probably using plans drawn up by Don Giovanni de' Medici) in the shape of a six-pointed star. It was built by order of Ferdinando I in 1590, ostensibly for the defence of the city, but in reality to dominate it. The handsome Palazzetto at its centre has a loggia and two façades, one facing the city and the other facing south. The best of all views of Florence is to be had from the ramparts.

Via di San Leonardo

Via di San Leonardo, one of the most beautiful and best-preserved roads on the outskirts of Florence (but beware of cars), leads out of the city beyond the Forte di Belvedere. It passes through countryside, lined with villas and their gardens and between olive groves behind high walls. Some of the pretty incised decoration on the plaster of the walls survives. Preceded by a charming little garden with four cypresses, is the church of **San Leonardo in Arcetri** (*map 6, 6; open for services at 5 or 6pm on Sat, and 8–11am on Sun and holidays; at other times ring at no. 25*), founded in the 11th century. It contains a pulpit of the early 13th century, with beautiful bas-reliefs removed from the church of San Pier Scheraggio. The paintings date from the 15th century: the high altarpiece of the *Madonna and Child with Saints* by Lorenzo di Niccolò; the *Madonna of the Sacred Girdle with Saints* and an *Annunciation with Angels and Saints* (decorating a tabernacle), both by Neri di Bicci; and a damaged *Tobias and the Angel* by the Master of San Miniato.

The lovely road continues past a house on the right (no. 64) where a plaque records Tchaikovsky's stay in 1878, to Viale Galileo, across which you continue a beautiful walk to Pian de' Giullari (*see p. 321*).

VIA SAN NICCOLÒ & LUNGARNO SERRISTORI

Via di San Niccolò (*map 7, 3*) is a narrow street of medieval houses. Palazzo Alemanni (no. 68) is decorated with a row of little demons, copies from Giambologna. At 89a is the entrance to Palazzo Vegni, which has an historic garden reaching up to the walls (*open weekends in summer and in July–Aug also on Thur*).

San Niccolò Oltrarno

Map 7, 3. Open 8–10.30 & 5.30–6.30 (winter), 6–7 (summer). Sacristy opened on request if a custodian is available, but you can almost always visit it between 10.30 and 11.30 on Sun. Founded in the 11th century, the church (also known as San Niccolò sopr'Arno) was rebuilt at the end of the 14th century. The painted altarpieces are by artists born in the mid-16th century (Empoli, Il Poppi, Alessandro Fei, Alessandro Allori and Giovanni Battista Naldini). There is also a wooden Crucifix by Michelozzo. The precious organ by Dionisio Romani dates from 1581. Several interesting frescoes were found beneath the 16th-century altars during restoration work after the 1966 flood. In the chapel at the end of the south side there is a delightful fresco of St Ansanus, attributed to the little-known painter Francesco d'Antonio, together with its sinopia.

Also at the end of the south aisle is the entrance to the **sacristy** in the 15th-century Quaratesi Chapel (*for admission, see above*), which contains a very interesting collection of paintings. Behind a *pietra serena* tabernacle, carved by the *bottega* of Michelozzo, the beautiful fresco of the *Madonna della Cintola*, a work of the Florentine school, bears the date 1450. It is very probably by the hand of Alesso Baldovinetti (although it also has affinities with works by his contemporary Giovanni di Francesco, and even Andrea del Castagno). It includes beautiful details such as the red and white roses heaped up in the classical sarcophagus, a river flowing towards the wonderful landscape in the background dotted with villas and country churches (reminiscent of Monte Morello just outside Florence), and the seated deer in the grass overgrown with wildflowers, which recalls medieval tapestries. During its recent restoration it was discovered that many details of the fresco had been gilded. Beneath it is a 14th-century triptych attributed to an unknown artist named the Master of San Niccolò from this work. The two paintings on panel on either side are by Bicci di Lorenzo (*Madonna and Saints*; 1440) and his son Neri di Bicci (*Trinity with Four Saints*; 1463). On the window wall are five panels from a polyptych by Gentile da Fabriano which were restored in 2007: although still very damaged (they suffered in a fire in the church in 1897), they are remarkable for their very unusual iconography: *St Louis of Toulouse*; the *Resurrection of Lazarus* (with his sisters Mary and Martha); (central panel) the Virgin and Jesus interceding before the throne of God the Father, represented as a king (below are the seven heavens recognised in medieval cosmology); three saints including Cosmas and Damian; and St Bernard of Clairvaux. Gentile also painted the Quaratesi polyptych (four panels of which are preserved in the Uffizi) for the high altar of this church. Also here are two small paintings of *St Michael* and *St Gabriel Archangel* by Il Poppi (*removed for restoration at the time of writing*) and a curious small painting of the *Mysteries of the Rosary* by his contemporary Giovanni Battista Naldini. On the opposite wall are 17th-century Florentine paintings. On the entrance wall is a *Madonna Enthroned with Saints* by Bicci di Lorenzo.

Lungarno Serristori

Behind the church towards the Arno rises the large rust-coloured **Palazzo Serristori** (*map 7, 3*; 1515; river front 1873). It is now privately owned and may become a hotel. The Russian Nicola Demidoff (1773–1828) took up residence here when he moved to Florence from Paris in 1820, having made his fortune in mining in Siberia. He was a great benefactor and founded a school. In the little public garden here there is a monument to him, commissioned from Lorenzo Bartolini by his sons Paolo and Anatolio in 1830. It includes four allegorical figures of *Art*, *Charity*, *Truth* and *Siberia*.

At Lungarno Serristori 25, the Austrian lyric poet Rainer Maria Rilke stayed in 1898: 'At the Lungarno Serristori,' he wrote, 'not far from the Ponte alle Grazie, stands the house whose flat roof—both its closed-in part and its part wide-open to the sky—is mine.' (*The Florence Diary*)

In Piazza Poggi stands the massive **Porta San Niccolò**, with a high tower, built around 1340. There are plans to open it to the public. A monument to Galileo was set up here in 1997, donated to the city by the sculptor Giò Pomodoro—its size (9m high) caused consternation to many.

Casa Rodolfo Siviero

Map 7, 3. Entrance at Lungarno Serristori 1. Open Sat 10–6 (in summer 10–2 & 3–7) and throughout the year also Sun and Mon 10–1. The works are unlabelled but a hand-list, also in English, is lent to visitors. T: 055 234 5219.

This 19th-century neo-Renaissance house attributed to Giuseppe Poggi, on the corner of the Lungarno and Piazza Poggi, was bought in 1944 by Rodolfo Siviero, who made a name for himself recovering works of art stolen from Italy during and after the last war. The house is filled with a miscellany of objects from Siviero's private collection: there are Roman works (note the restored fragment of 4th-century Roman mosaic in opus sectile); 15th-century paintings including a *Nativity* attributed to Domenico di Zanobi; 14th- and 15th-century sculptures; 17th-century paintings including landscapes by Jan Frans van Bloemen; and 20th-century paintings by Giorgio de Chirico. But it is perhaps above all interesting as it provides a glimpse into a private residence of the 20th century, still with its furnishings. The dining room ceiling was painted by Stefano Ussi in the 19th century.

From Piazza Poggi, a ramp leads uphill to San Miniato, but the approach described in the next chapter is much prettier.

THE HILL & CHURCH OF
SAN MINIATO

Map 7. Accessible directly by bus 12 from Stazione Santa Maria Novella and Porta Romana to a request stop at the foot of the steps (just before Piazzale Michelangelo). It can also be reached by the steps from Porta San Niccolò, but if you have time, the following route on foot is highly recommended (bus 13 can then be taken back to Porta Romana and Stazione Santa Maria Novella).

THE APPROACH TO SAN MINIATO

The incomparably beautiful church of San Miniato al Monte is memorably approached on foot along a route which begins at Porta San Miniato (*map 7, 3*), a simple 14th-century arch in the walls. Outside the gate Via di Belvedere, a picturesque country lane with olive trees, climbs westwards up the hillside to Forte di Belvedere, following the straight line of the city walls. Via Monte alle Croci leads straight uphill: this is the way to San Miniato. On the corner with Via dei Bastioni there is a lovely tabernacle with a carved but worn frieze enclosing a fresco of the *Madonna and Child Enthroned*, by a 16th-century painter (restored in 2008). The road now begins to climb more steeply and it crosses the Erta Canina, a lovely old road (*which provides an alternative but less direct approach to San Miniato, well worth following if you have the time. The road seems to have taken its name from the dogs (cane) who would enjoy the steep run uphill here. It soon becomes a pebbled path between walls (with wonderful views back of Florence) and it is very well kept with new cast-iron street lamps. Further up it retains its original paving as it passes between interesting old houses*). The stepped ramp called Via di San Salvatore al Monte diverges from Via Monte alle Croci. The plaque records Dante's recollection of this climb up the steps to San Miniato. Today it is lined on one side by ancient cypresses between the Stations of the Cross, and on the other by the wall of the little municipal rose garden (*open May and June 8–8*), with 370 cultivars. Nine delightful sculptures by the Belgian artist Jean-Michel Folon (d. 2005) were donated to the rose garden by his widow in 2009. At the top a flight of steps emerges on the busy Viale Galileo. Cross over and continue directly up the steps opposite, to the church of San Salvatore al Monte.

San Salvatore al Monte

In a grove of cypresses on the side of the hill, just below San Miniato al Monte, this is a Franciscan church (*map 7, 6*) of gracious simplicity by Cronaca, which Michelangelo called his *bella villanella* (his 'pretty country maid'). The interior, which now has a rather gloomy abandoned feel about it, has an open timber roof. On the west wall is a bust by Andrea Ferrucci of Marcello Adriani, a chancellor of the Florentine Republic, who died in 1521. On the north side are small 16th-century stained-glass windows: the one over the south side door is attributed to Perugino. There are two terracotta groups of the *Deposition*, one attributed to Santi Buglioni, and the other (over the north door) attributed to Giovanni della Robbia.

At the end of the north side is an early 15th-century painting of the *Pietà* attributed to Neri di Bicci, and at the end of the south side panels of saints by Rossello di Jacopo Franchi. In the sanctuary (left wall) the *Madonna Enthroned* is by Giovanni dal Ponte. The Crucifix here is by Andrea Ferrucci (c. 1506).

The hill of San Miniato al Monte and the Porte Sante cemetery

From the side door of San Salvatore, follow the winding road uphill to the massive gate (with the Medici arms above it) through the fortifications around the church of San Miniato al Monte. This *fortezza* originated in a hastily improvised defence-work designed by Michelangelo when Florence's last Republican government put him in charge of the city's fortifications, at a time when it had become apparent that the Imperial troops allied with the pope were preparing a siege. Michelangelo had no hesitation in dedicating his services to his native city, even though the Medici pope Clement VII had been his friend and patron in Rome (in the complicated aftermath, and after Florence's capitulation in 1530, the pope in fact forgave the artist for his rebellion). In 1553, Cosimo I converted San Miniato into a real fortress with the help of Francesco da Sangallo, Tribolo and others. The walls now enclose a large monumental cemetery, called the **Porte Sante**, laid out in 1854 by Niccolò Matas and finished by Mariano Falcini in 1864. Surrounded by cypresses, it has numerous neo-Gothic chapels and well-carved tombs. Collodi (Carlo Lorenzini), author of *Pinocchio*, is buried here, as well as the writer Vasco Pratolini (1913–91) and the painter Pietro Annigoni. Near the entrance is the tomb of the sculptor Libero Andreotti (1875–1933), with a striking bronze of the *Resurrection*. Another bronze *Resurrection of Christ* marks the tomb of John Temple Leader (*see p. 315*), with busts of him and his wife by his friend Dante Sodini.

There is a good view here of the massive stone campanile which replaced the bell-tower of San Miniato which collapsed in 1499; it was begun after 1523 from a design by Baccio d'Agnolo, but was never finished. During the siege Michelangelo mounted two cannon here, and protected the bell-tower from hostile artillery by a screen of mattresses.

You emerge on a wide terrace in front of the church, where there is a stunning view across the city. In the distance, the Villa della Petraia with its tower is prominent at the foot of Monte Morello. Directly below the terrace is a monumental flight of steps built in white travertine in the 19th century and a cemetery created in 1839.

SAN MINIATO AL MONTE

Map 7, 8. Open 8–12 & 2.30–6 (winter); 8–12 & 2–7 (summer).
The finest of all Tuscan Romanesque basilicas, with a famous façade, San Miniato is also one of the most beautiful churches in Italy. Together with the Baptistery and San Lorenzo, it was the most important church in 11th-century Florence. Its position

on a green hill above the city is incomparable. The interior, beautifully kept and uncluttered, has an atmosphere of deep spirituality now rare to find in other churches of this importance.

HISTORY OF SAN MINIATO AL MONTE

The deacon Minias was a member of the early Christian community from the East who settled in Florence. A legend even suggested he was an Oriental prince, the son of the King of Armenia. He is thought to have been martyred c. 250 during the persecutions of the emperor Decius, and buried on this hillside. The present church, built in 1013 by Bishop Hildebrand, is on the site of a shrine protecting the tomb of St Minias. The Benedictine Cluniac monastery, founded here at the same time by the Holy Roman Emperor Henry II, was one of the first important religious houses in Tuscany. In the 17th century it was used as a hospital, and later as a poorhouse. In 1924, the Olivetan Benedictine monks returned here: they still live in the monastery and look after the church, which has been extremely well restored over the years.

Exterior of San Miniato

The façade, begun c. 1090, is built of white and dark greenish marble in a geometric design reminiscent of the Baptistery. Above the exquisite little window in the form of an aedicule is a 13th-century mosaic (remade in 1861) of *Christ between the Virgin and St Minias*, the warrior-martyr. In the tympanum, supported by two small figures in relief, the middle band of marble inlay repeats the motifs of the pavement inside. It is crowned by an eagle with outstretched wings standing on a bale of cloth, emblem of the Arte di Calimala (the cloth-importers guild), who looked after the fabric of the building.

Interior of San Miniato

The superb interior, built in 1018–63, survives practically in its original state. Its design is unique in Florentine church architecture, with a raised choir above a large hall crypt. Many of the column capitals came from Roman temples in the city. The pavement is composed of tomb slabs, except for the centre of the nave which has seven exquisite marble intarsia panels (1207), designed like a carpet, with signs of the Zodiac and animal motifs. The decoration on the inside of the upper part of the nave walls, in imitation of the façade, was carried out at the end of the 19th century, when the open timber roof, with polychrome decoration, was also restored.

Cappella del Crocifisso: This exquisite tabernacle at the end of the nave was commissioned by Piero il Gottoso from Michelozzo in 1448. It is superbly carved and ingeniously designed to fit a setting that was built some 400 years earlier. It was made to house the venerated Crucifix which is said to have bowed approvingly to St John Gualbert (*see p. 331*); the painted panels of the doors of the cupboard which protected the miraculous Crucifix are by Agnolo Gaddi (1394–96). The enamelled terracotta roof and ceiling are the work of Luca della Robbia. The inlaid coloured marble frieze bears the emblem of Piero de' Medici (whose arms also appear on the back of the tabernacle). The copper eagles on the roof are by Maso di Bartolomeo.

Aisles: On the outer stone walls of the aisles are a number of frescoes: the earliest date from the late 13th century and are by the steps up to the choir on the north side (*Virgin Annunciate* and a fragment of a *Nativity*). The *Madonna Enthroned with Six Saints* in the southwest corner of the nave is by Paolo Schiavo (1436) and the huge *St Christopher* next to it dates from the 14th century or earlier. In the north aisle are two detached frescoes (a *Madonna and Child with Saints* and a *Crucifixion with Seven Saints*) by Mariotto di Nardo. The fine painted Crucifix, thought to date from c. 1285, shows *Christ Triumphant*, and although the face of Christ has been severely damaged, the rest of the decoration survives, with Christ blessing in the disc of the cimasa and two angels below and on the two terminals. On either side of the figure of Christ are the mourning figures of the Madonna and St John, and at the bottom of the Cross the *Denial of St Peter*. While recognising that this work is one of the most important of its time, art historians have not so far identified with certainty the name of the painter.

Chapel of the Cardinal of Portugal: Built onto the north wall of the church, this is the funerary chapel of Cardinal Jacopo di Lusitania, who died in Florence at the age of 25. It was begun in 1460 by Antonio Manetti, Brunelleschi's pupil (who also worked on the church of Santo Spirito), and finished, after his death in the same year, probably under the direction of Antonio Rossellino. It incorporates some of the best workmanship of the Florentine Renaissance. The exquisitely-carved tomb of the cardinal is by Antonio Rossellino (1461–66). The ceiling has five medallions (1461) by Luca della Robbia. These represent the Cardinal Virtues and the Holy Ghost against a background of tiles decorated with classical cubes in yellow, green and purple, and are among the masterpieces of Luca's enamelled terracotta work. The altarpiece of *Three Saints* by Antonio and Piero del Pollaiolo (1466–67) was replaced by a copy when the original was moved to the Uffizi. The frescoed decoration of this wall, including two angels, is by the same artists. Above the marble bishop's throne on the west wall is a painting of the *Annunciation* by Alesso Baldovinetti (1466–73), who also frescoed the Evangelists and Fathers of the Church in the lunettes beside the windows and in the spandrels.

Choir: Steps lead up to the raised choir which has a beautiful marble transenna (dating from 1207), and pulpit, also faced with marble. The lectern is supported by an eagle above a carved figure standing on a lion's head, a rare example in Florence of figure sculpture of this date used to decorate an architectural feature. The low columns have huge antique capitals.

Apse (*light at the top of the stairs on right*): The beautiful inlaid blind arcade has six small Roman columns between opaque windows. The mosaic representing *Christ between the Virgin and St Minias*, with symbols of the Evangelists (1297), was first restored in 1491 by Alesso Baldovinetti. Behind the simple Renaissance altar, in keeping with the style of the Romanesque church, is a Crucifix attributed to the della Robbia. The carved and inlaid stalls date from 1466–70. The altarpiece to the right of the apse, by Jacopo del Casentino, shows St Minias and scenes from his life.

Sacristy: Situated to the south of the apse (*and not always open*), the sacristy (1387) is covered with frescoes by Spinello Aretino; in the vault are the Evangelists and in the lunettes the *Life of St Benedict*, one of Spinello's best works (restored in 1840). There is also a polychrome bust of St Minias (wearing a crown) attributed to Nanni di Bartolo, two della Robbia statuettes, and stalls like those in the choir. In the lunette above the little door is a *Pietà* recently attributed to Giovanni da Piamonte (1470–72). Just outside the sacristy, on the walls of the choir, there are some very early frescoes of saints (13th century).

Crypt: The 11th-century crypt (beneath the choir) has beautiful slender columns, many of them with antique capitals. The original 11th-century altar contains the relics of St Minias. The small vaults are decorated with frescoes of saints and prophets against a blue ground by Taddeo Gaddi.

West wall: Here is the simple tomb of the poet Giuseppe Giusti (1800–50) and a monument by Emilio Santarelli to the Tuscan artist Giuseppe Bezzuoli (1784–1855) .

The cloister

The fine cloister of the Benedictine monastery (*admission only by special permission*), on the right side of the church, was begun c. 1425. On the upper loggia, damaged fragments of frescoes in *terraverde* are recognised as some of the most interesting works known by Paolo Uccello, illustrating scenes from monastic legends with remarkable perspectives and a beautiful figure of a woman. The sinopie are preserved in a room off the cloister. One of the frescoes dates from the 16th century and is signed by Bernardo Buontalenti. On the lower walk is a fragment of a sinopia attributed to Andrea del Castagno.

The bishop's palace

On the right of the church façade is the crenellated bishop's palace, with attractive twin windows. This dates from 1295 and it was used as a summer residence by the bishops of Florence from the 14th–16th centuries. In later centuries it was used as a barracks and hospital and was restored in the 20th century.

PIAZZALE MICHELANGELO

Viale dei Colli is the name given to the sequence of three avenues lined with fine trees and public gardens—Viale Michelangelo, Viale Galileo and Viale Machiavelli—which form a spectacular roadway 6km long, laid out by Giuseppe Poggi in 1865–70. It is one of the most panoramic drives near Florence, following a winding course from Piazza Ferrucci via Piazzale Michelangelo and the steps below San Miniato, to Porta Romana. The Viale is followed by bus nos. 12 and 13.

As a central feature, Poggi created **Piazzale Michelangelo** (*map 7, 5–6*), a contrived viewpoint with a balustrade surrounding a huge terrace from which there is a remarkable panorama of the city. He also designed the monument to Michelangelo, which consists of bronze reproductions of some of his famous marble statues in the city, including the *David*; and the Palazzina del Caffè (now a restaurant). Today the terrace is little more than a coach park, always crowded with tourists. The view takes in the entire city as well as its surrounding hills, and beyond—on a clear day—you can see as far as the plain of Pistoia and the peaks of the Apennines. The view down the Arno centres on Ponte Vecchio. Straight ahead is the hill of Fiesole.

Below the terrace is a delightful iris garden (Giardino dell'Iris; *open in May, 10–12.30 & 3–7.30; entrance on the right of the balustrade*) with some 2,500 varieties; a red iris on a white ground is the symbol of Florence (*see p. 279*). An international competition has been held here annually since 1957.

NB: For a fuller description, see Blue Guide Tuscany.

FIESOLE

The little town of Fiesole (pop. 15,000) sits on a hill overlooking the valleys of the Arno and the Mugnone, with splendid views of Florence. The principal sights are the Roman theatre, Etruscan walls, cathedral, and small museums, all sited close together off the main piazza. There are lovely walks in the vicinity. Fiesole has always been a fashionable residential district, much favoured by foreigners in the 19th century, when its beautiful hillside was enhanced by fine villas surrounded by romantic gardens and stately cypress groves. It is crowded with Florentines and visitors in summer, when its position (295m) makes it one of the coolest places in the neighbourhood. Indeed, Fiesole has always been known for its salubrious air. It is here that the story-tellers in Boccaccio's *Decameron* come to escape the plague raging in the city below.

How to get there
Bus no 7, which leaves every 15mins from Piazza San Marco (map 4, 5) goes to Fiesole via the hamlet of San Domenico; journey time about 20mins. Fiesole is also a lovely place to approach on foot: there are five old roads from the bottom of the hill to San Domenico: Via di Barbacane from Piazza Edison; Via della Piazzola, Via delle Forbici, or Via Boccaccio from near Piazza delle Cure; or Via di Camerata from Via Lungo Affrico. These are all extremely beautiful country roads and from the bottom of the hill the walk only takes around 1hr.

HISTORY OF FIESOLE

The foundation of Fiesole predates that of Florence by many centuries. Excavations have proved that the hill was inhabited before the Bronze Age. The site of *Faesulae*, on a hilltop above a river valley, was typical of Etruscan settlements. Probably founded in the 6th or 5th century BC, it became one of the chief cities of the Etruscan confederacy. It is first mentioned in 283 BC, when its inhabitants, in alliance with other Etruscans, were defeated by the Romans at Lake Vadimone. With the Roman occupation it became the most important town in Etruria, but the barbarian invasions led to its decline. In 854, the county of Fiesole was merged with that of Florence. After a decisive battle in 1125, in which only the cathedral and the bishop's palace escaped destruction, Florence finally gained control of Fiesole.

Piazza Mino da Fiesole, where the bus terminates, is the spacious main square of the town, named after the Renaissance sculptor (1429–84) of the same name. Born at Poppi in the Casentino, Mino made Fiesole his home and left some of his best works in its cathedral. At the top end of the piazza, the old Palazzo Pretorio, now the town hall, which has a loggia decorated with the coats of arms of many *podestà*, stands next to the quaint porch of **Santa Maria Primerana**. This little church, rebuilt in the 16th–17th centuries, contains a painted Crucifix of c. 1350 (restored in 2008), a bas-relief with a self-portrait in profile of Francesco da Sangallo, and a Crucifix with the *Madonna and Saints* by Andrea della Robbia. In a Gothic tabernacle in the sanctuary there is a highly venerated painting of the Madonna dating from around 1255 (although much repainted over the centuries). The damaged frescoes here are by Niccolò di Pietro Gerini.

In the piazza, the equestrian monument (1906) records the meeting between Vittorio Emanuele II and Garibaldi at Teano in southern Italy in 1860, when the handshake between the king and popular hero symbolised the unification of Italy.

The cathedral of San Romolo

The cathedral (*open 7.30–12 & 3–5 or 6*) was founded in 1028 and enlarged in the 13th and 14th centuries, but heavily restored in 1878–83. The tall bell-tower of 1213 (the crenellations were added later) is visible from Florence and the surrounding hills.

The bare stone interior, with a raised choir above a hall crypt, is similar in plan to San Miniato al Monte. The massive columns have fine capitals (some of them Roman). Above the west door there is a garlanded niche containing a statue of St Romulus (San Romolo), Bishop of Fiesole, by Giovanni della Robbia (1521). On brackets here and in the aisles is a series of 16th-century terracotta busts of apostles, all of them looking towards the altar. The handsome high altar in grey-green and white marble dates from 1273.

Stairs lead up to the choir. On the right is the little **Cappella Salutati**, which has vault frescoes of the Evangelists by Cosimo Rosselli and two of Mino da Fiesole's best sculptures: the tomb of Bishop Leonardo Salutati (1465) with a fine portrait bust, and an altarpiece. Over the high altar stands a splendid large altarpiece by Bicci di Lorenzo (c. 1440), with the *Madonna and Child and Sts Alexander, Peter, Romulus and Donatus*. The apse is frescoed by Nicodemo Ferrucci (late 16th century). In a chapel on the left is a marble altarpiece by Andrea Ferrucci (1493).

The **crypt** (*coin-operated light*) has four little columns with interesting primitive capitals. Behind the screen, surrounding the altar of St Romulus, are four marble columns with charming antique Ionic capitals. The vault was painted in the 15th century in lapis lazuli with stars. In the apse is a marble reliquary urn. The lunettes (late 15th century) are frescoed with stories of St Romulus. **Roman remains** can be seen below the pavement. The granite font is the work of Francesco del Tadda (1569). A small chapel contains an early 13th-century painting of the *Madonna and Child Enthroned* (the *Madonna del Soccorso*), showing the influence of Byzantine icons. Recent excavations here have revealed traces of Roman buildings of the 1st–2nd centuries AD, including a temple (visible near the font) and foundations of the first cathedral.

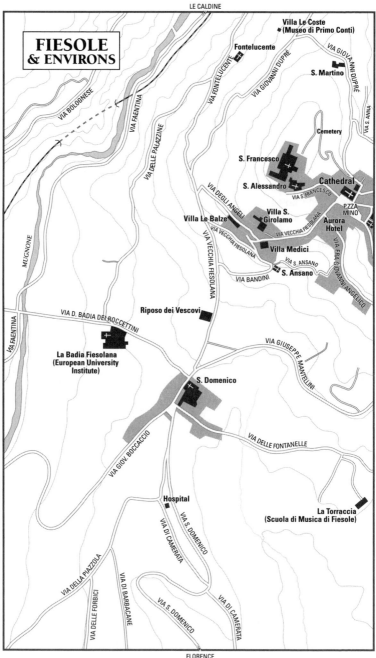

LE CALDINE

FIESOLE & ENVIRONS

Villa Le Coste
(Museo di Primo Conti)

VIA GIOVANNI DUPRÉ

Fontelucente

S. Martino

VIA FONTELUCENTE

VIA GIOVANNI DUPRÉ

VIA BOLOGNESE

VIA FAENTINA

VIA S. ANNA

VIA DELLE PALAZZINE

Cemetery

S. Francesco

S. Alessandro

Cathedral

VIA DEGLI ANGELI

VIA S. FRANCESCO

P.ZZA MINO

Villa S. Girolamo

Villa Le Balze

Aurora Hotel

VIA VECCHIA FIESOLANA

Villa Medici

VIA VECCHIA FIESOLANA

VIA FRA GIOVANNI ANGELICO

MUGNONE

VIA S. ANSANO

S. Ansano

VIA BANDINI

Riposo dei Vescovi

VIA FAENTINA

VIA D. BADIA DEI ROCCETTINI

VIA GIUSEPPE MANTELLINI

La Badia Fiesolana
(European University
Institute)

S. Domenico

VIA DELLE FONTANELLE

VIA GIOV. BOCCACCIO

Hospital

La Torraccia
(Scuola di Musica di Fiesole)

VIA S. DOMENICO

VIA DI CAMERATA

VIA DELLA PIAZZOLA

VIA DI BARBACANE

VIA S. DOMENICO

VIA DI CAMERATA

VIA DELLE FORBICI

FLORENCE

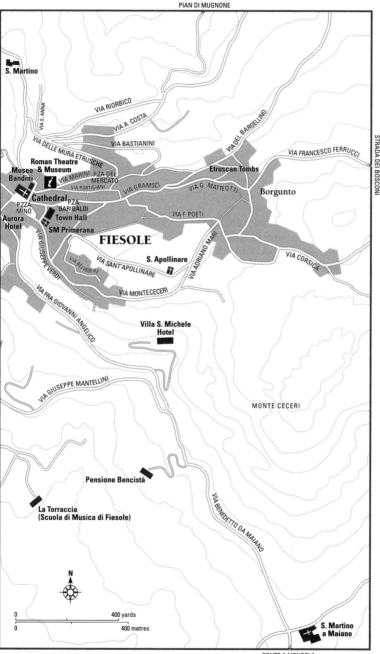

PIAN DI MUGNONE

STRADA DEI BOSCONI

S. Martino

VIA RIORBICO

VIA S. ANNA

VIA A. COSTA

VIA BASTIANINI

VIA DELLE MURA ETRUSCHE

VIA DEL BARGELLINO

VIA FRANCESCO FERRUCCI

Roman Theatre
Museo & Museum
Bandini

Etruscan Tombs

VIA MARINI PZA DEL MERCATO

VIA PORTIGIANI

VIA GRAMSCI

VIA G. MATTEOTTI

Borgunto

Cathedral

PZA MINO

PZA GARIBALDI

Town Hall

VIA F. POETI

Aurora Hotel

SM Primerana

FIESOLE

S. Apollinare

VIA GIUSEPPE VERDI

VIA BELVEDERE

VIA SANT'APOLLINARE

VIA ADRIANO MARI

VIA CORSICA

VIA MONTECECERI

VIA FRA GIOVANNI ANGELICO

Villa S. Michele
Hotel

VIA GIUSEPPE MANTELLINI

MONTE CECERI

Pensione Bencistà

La Torraccia
(Scuola di Musica di Fiesole)

VIA BENEDETTO DA MAIANO

N

0   400 yards
0   400 metres

S. Martino
a Maiano

PONTE A MENSOLA,
VILLA I TATTI & SETTIGNANO

The hill of San Francesco

Via San Francesco, a very steep paved lane, climbs the hill (with magnificent views over Florence) past the church of **Sant' Alessandro** (*open only for exhibitions*), traditionally thought to stand on the site of an Etruscan and Roman temple. It was probably founded in the 6th century and so is the oldest church in Fiesole. The bare basilican interior is remarkable for its very beautiful green-grey veined cipollino marble columns with Ionic capitals and bases from a Roman building.

At the top of the hill, on the site of the Etruscan and later Roman acropolis, are the conventual buildings of **San Francesco**, now also an infirmary. The church (*open 9–12 & 3–6 or 7*) dates from c. 1330 and was restored in neo-Gothic style in 1905–07, with an attractive little rose window. The choir arch is attributed to Benedetto da Maiano. Over the high altar there is a *Crucifixion and Saints* by Neri di Bicci. On the south side (first altar), the *Marriage of St Catherine* by Cenni di Francesco is surrounded by paintings of the early 19th century. On the second altar there is an *Immaculate Conception* by Piero di Cosimo. On the north side (first altar) is an *Adoration of the Magi* by the school of Cosimo Rosselli and (second altar) and *Annunciation* by Raffaellino del Garbo.

In the friary there are several charming little cloisters, some remains of the Etruscan walls and a **missionary museum** (*open weekdays except Mon 9.30–12 & 3–5 or 7, Sun and holidays 9–11 & 3–5 or 7*) of Eastern *objets d'art* (mostly unlabelled) and a particularly interesting Egyptian collection (including a statuette thought to represent a wife of Rameses II) and works from China (including bronzes and Ming and Qing vases). However, the provenance and date of many of these are unknown. From the piazza outside, a gate leads into a public park with an ilex wood, through which shady paths lead back downhill to the main square.

The Roman theatre

Open April–Sept 10–7 except Tues; rest of the year 10–6 except Tues and Wed. Ticket also valid for the Museo Civico and Museo Bandini. There is a café in the grounds.

From Piazza Mino, the street behind the apse of the cathedral leads to the entrance to the Roman theatre and archaeological excavations, and the Museo Civico. From the terrace there is a view of the excavations in a plantation of olive trees and a superb view of the beautiful countryside beyond.

The **theatre**, built at the end of the 1st century BC, was enlarged by Claudius and Septimius Severus. The cavea, which was partly dug out from the hillside (the sides are supported on vaults), is 34m across and held 3,000 spectators. The seats on the right side are intact; the others have been restored with smaller blocks of stone. Plays and concerts are performed here every summer.

To the right of the theatre are the **Roman baths** (reconstructed in 1892), probably built in the 1st century AD and enlarged by Hadrian. In front are three rectangular swimming baths. The chambers near the three arches (arbitrarily reconstructed) consist of the hypocausis, with circular ovens where the water was heated, the caldarium with its hypocaust, and the tepidarium. In front of the arches is the palaestra, and behind them the frigidarium. A small terrace here provides a fine view of a long stretch of the

Etruscan walls which once enclosed the city (4th–3rd century BC; reinforced in the Roman and medieval periods), with a gateway.

W.D. Howells on the Roman theatre

…visited the ruins of the Roman theatre and stretch of Etruscan wall beyond it. The former seems older than the latter, whose huge blocks of stone lie as firmly and evenly in their courses as if placed there a year ago: the turf creeps to the edge at top, and some small trees nod along the crest of the wall, whose ancient face, clean, and bare, looks sternly out over a vast prospect, now young, and smiling in the first delight of spring.

from *Indian Summer*, 1886

On the other side of the theatre (to the northwest) is a **Roman temple** (1st century BC), with its basement intact, and, on a lower level, remains of an **Etruscan temple** (4th or early 3rd century BC), both of them approached by steps. Nearby are copies of the two original altars (the larger one is Roman). In this area a Lombard necropolis (6th–7th century AD) has also been excavated. There is a stretch of Roman road near the theatre.

Museo Civico

The museum was purpose-built for the collection in 1912–14 and its exterior is an idealised reconstruction of the Roman temple. The decoration of the portico, with its rosettes, clearly takes its inspiration from the fragment of the original frieze which is displayed here. Its contents include not only the numerous donations made to the town by private collectors at the end of the 19th century and the bequest of a spectacular collection of Greek vases made by Alfiero Costantini in 1985, but also material from excavations in the area of the Roman theatre and in other parts of town.

Highlights on the **ground floor** include the Stele Fiesolana (early 5th century BC), showing a funerary banquet (note the cockerel beneath the table) and dancing and hunting scenes, surrounded by decorative friezes (also at the sides). Above there are two seated lions beneath a palmette decoration. A small cippus found in Piazza Mino bears an inscription referring to the Capitoline Triad (Jupiter, Juno and Minerva), so proving that there was a capitolium here (remains of which have been found and identified in the cathedral crypt). Room 3 contains interesting finds from the area of the Roman theatre and temples. The so-called 'She-wolf' in bronze (in fact the torso of a lioness), found on the probable site of the Capitol, is a Hellenistic Etruscan work, not Roman. It is very fine, and one of the largest antique bronzes to have survived anywhere of this date (apart from equestrian statues).

The **upper floor** has some of the most precious works, including Corinthian, Attic and Puglian vases. The exquisite red-figure vases (late 6th century BC) include a pelike with Theseus and the Minotaur, a stamnos signed by Hermonax (460–450 BC) and a fine lekythos with the figure of Eros attributed to the Pan Painter (480 BC).

Museo Bandini

Opening times (and combined ticket) as for the Roman theatre and Museo Civico. Entrance opposite.

This collection of 13th–15th-century paintings and sculpture formerly belonged to Angelo Maria Bandini (1726–1803), a Fiesole-born scholar and cleric. It illustrates his particular interest in the Italian primitives at a time when this period of painting was given little consideration, but the provenance of nearly all of the works is tantalisingly unrecorded. Since 1913 the collection has been housed in this attractive little building, designed especially for it by Giuseppe Castellucci. Bandini seems to have particularly favoured works with a strong narrative content. The arrangement is chronological.

First floor

Room 1: The first room provides an excellent illustration of Florentine gold-ground painting, particularly early 14th-century works. The Giottesque painter Bernardo Daddi is represented by a very fine panel showing St John the Evangelist writing his gospel. The *Annunciation* by Taddeo Gaddi was part of a polyptych commissioned for Santa Maria della Croce al Tempio in Florence (the emblems of the confraternity were found in the upper corners during restoration in 1980). It is a very beautiful work showing a great spiritual bond between the angel and the Madonna, who is seated on a Cosmatesque throne. The iconography was to be copied numerous times by Taddeo's successors, including Lorenzo Monaco. The gold ground and the haloes have beautifully decorated borders which enabled scholars to identify two other panels (of saints) which must have belonged to the same work (one now in private hands and the other in the Metropolitan Museum in New York). Taddeo's son Agnolo painted the charming *Madonna of Humility*.

The panel showing the *Madonna del Parto* with a donor by Nardo di Cione is extremely interesting for its exceptional iconography since it depicts not only the pregnant Madonna, but also the 'Queen of the Heavens', as described in *Revelation* 12:1–2: 'And there appeared a great wonder in heaven; a woman clothed with the sun, and the moon under her feet, and upon her head a crown of twelve stars: And she being with child cried, travailing in birth, and pained to be delivered.'

The tiny, very refined work painted on glass with gold graffito showing Christ as the Man of Sorrows with symbols of the Passion and mourning figures is a very rare piece attributed to a Florentine artist in the workshop of Giotto.

Room 2: The four panels decorated with scenes of triumphs (*Love*, *Chastity*, *Time* and *Eternity*) are thought to be the work of Jacopo del Sellaio, who received his nickname from his father's profession as a saddler. He was a pupil of Filippo Lippi and influenced by Botticelli and Ghirlandaio. The *Triumph of Chastity* shows a young woman on a pedestal, while Lucretia and Penelope, famous for their virtue, bind Love and deprive him of his wings. The chariot is drawn by two unicorns, symbols of female purity.

At the head of the procession is Chastity, carrying a huge red flag fluttering in the wind and bearing a symbolic ermine. The *Triumph of Time* shows the bent figure of an old man with an hourglass, on a chariot drawn by two graceful deer. The *Triumph of Eternity* shows allegorical figures of the three Theological Virtues on a chariot drawn by the symbols of the Evangelists. Christ, above an armillary sphere and surrounded by angels, scatters blue cornflowers which charmingly decorate the entire scene. These panels were probably used as furnishings in a private house, and the presence of the three crescent moons, symbol of the Strozzi, suggest that they were commissioned by that family.

Ground floor

Here are displayed some very early sculptural fragments (1320) from the altar of the Baptistery of Florence, and a very beautiful painted terracotta relief of the *Madonna and Child* formerly in the Bishop's Palace which, since its recent restoration, has been attributed to Brunelleschi. The bust of the Saviour in polychrome terracotta is attributed to a follower of Benedetto da Maiano and dated c. 1490–1500. The small marble relief attributed to Giovanni Bandini is exquisitely carved. It is thought to portray his master Baccio Bandinelli in the guise of St John the Evangelist.

There is also a delightful display of colourful enamelled terracottas by the Della Robbia (the magnificent tondo of the *Adoration of the Child* is by Andrea). Also well represented are the Buglioni family, the only artists able to emulate the Della Robbia after their workshop closed down. In the lunette of *Christ and St John the Baptist in the Wilderness*, the landscape of rocks seems reminiscent of the hillside of Fiesole.

WALKS IN FIESOLE

NB: The gardens of a number of private villas are usually opened on Thur afternoons from April–June and in Sept and Oct, with a specialist guide. Information and booking from the Comune of Fiesole; T. 055 596 1293 or 055 596 1284. Otherwise you can sometimes contact the villas themselves (details in the text below).

Montececeri

From Piazza Mino, Via Giuseppe Verdi climbs steeply uphill to Via Montececeri, which has magnificent views over Florence. At the top, in Via Mari, can be seen a stretch of the **Etruscan walls**. Via Montececeri leads across to the extensive **woods of Montececeri**, which up to 1929 were used as a quarry for *pietra serena*, worked for centuries by the local stonemasons. The bare slopes and disused quarries were planted with oak, conifers, cypresses and pines. There are some lovely (signposted) paths here with views extending to Settignano and beyond. At the highest point (410m) a memorial stone records the flying experiments which Leonardo da Vinci carried out here.

Via Dupré and Fontelucente

Behind the cathedral, Via Dupré descends past the Roman theatre to circle the hillside of San Francesco. It passes the 16th-century **Villa Le Coste** (no. 18) where the painter Primo Conti (1900–88) lived. A museum (*open weekdays 9–1*) contains a representative collection of his work and is also well worth visiting to see the pretty garden with its wonderful views of the hillside of Fiesole. The peaceful byroad descends past **Villa Dupré** (no. 19), the former home of Giovanni Dupré, one of the most famous Italian sculptors of the 19th century.

Further on, the steep and narrow Via Fontelucente (beware of cars) descends to the church of **Fontelucente** (*only open for services at 10 on Sun and feast days*), built in 1692 over a spring in a beautiful isolated spot above the Mugnone valley (Via delle Palazzine here is another pretty road which skirts the hillside to the Badia Fiesolana), while this road soon meets Via Vecchia Fiesolana (*see below*).

Villa Medici

Via Vecchia Fiesolana, perhaps Fiesole's most beautiful road and once the only road up from Florence, descends steeply from the lower end of Piazza Mino to San Domenico. At the beginning there is a wonderful view of the duomo of Florence far below, framed between the walls. Opposite the former convent of San Girolamo is Villa Medici (*entrance at Via Fra' Giovanni di Fiesole 2, reached by Via Sant'Ansano; privately owned but the garden is willingly shown, usually on weekdays 9–1 but only by appointment via fax, 055 239 8994, or com.toscana@airc.it*). It was begun around 1453 for Giovanni de' Medici, the cultivated son of Cosimo il Vecchio who predeceased his father. Its design, the core of which survives to this day, was innovative in that it opened onto a panorama and was intimately connected to its garden by a series of terraces. It later became the favourite retreat of Giovanni's nephew Lorenzo the Magnificent, and Agnolo Poliziano and Pico della Mirandola, together with members of the Platonic Academy, frequently met here. The villa, enlarged in the 17th and 18th centuries, was bought in 1862 by the painter and collector William Blundell Spence, and in 1911 by Lady Sibyl Cutting (wife of the architect Geoffrey Scott), whose daughter Iris Origo (1902–88), the historian and biographer, made additions to the garden, which is one of the earliest of the Renaissance, built on several terraces on the steep hillside with a superb view of Florence. It is at its best after Easter. Cecil Pinsent worked on the box-edged geometric garden on the lower terrace in 1915.

Villa Le Balze

Entrance at Via Vecchia Fiesolana 26; garden open by appointment weekdays 9–4; T: 055 59208, info@villalebalze.org.

Beyond the garden entrance can be glimpsed one of the garden 'rooms' created by Cecil Pinsent for the American philosopher Charles Augustus Strong. The villa was built for him by Geoffrey Scott in Renaissance style in 1913. It was left by his daughter to Georgetown University in 1979. Just below there is a superb view of all Florence beyond a row of venerable cypresses lining the road.

Riposo dei Vescovi

The 'Bishops' Rest' (*Via Vecchia Fiesolana 62; garden open by Comune of Fiesole, see p. 309*) was the halting place in the 16th century for the bishops of Fiesole on their way up the hill from their residence in Florence. Dutch and Swiss owners in the late 19th century carried out alterations in an eclectic Jugendstil and neo-Gothic style, and these were continued by the Dutch painter W.O.J. Nieuwenkamp (1874–1950) when he bought the house in 1926. The splendid Romantic park, with numerous cypresses, covers the steep hillside all the way down to Via delle Palazzine. The box hedges are beautifully tended.

SAN DOMENICO DI FIESOLE

The **church of San Domenico** (*open 8.30–12 & 4.30–6*) dates from 1406–35; the portico (1635) and campanile (1611–13) were added by Matteo Nigetti. In this convent Fra' Angelico first entered the religious order (after 1437 he moved down to the convent of San Marco). The painting he made for the high altar of the church is preserved here, although it is now in a side chapel (*there is a light on the right*): the *Madonna Enthroned* is surrounded with angels and three Dominican saints in their black and white robes (Dominic, Thomas Aquinas and Peter Martyr) with St Barnabas (included to honour a wealthy patron of the convent called Barnaba degli Agli). Formerly a late-Gothic triptych with a gold ground, it was altered in 1501 when it was enlarged at the top and the architectural background and landscapes were added by Lorenzo di Credi, and the frame was redesigned (the paintings of saints are by a follower of Lorenzo Monaco). The panels of the predella are copies; the originals are in the National Gallery, London.

The side chapels have Renaissance arches in *pietra serena* and some of the altarpieces have handsome Mannerist frames. The fine chancel designed by Giovanni Caccini and the gilded wooden tabernacle by Andrea Balatri both date from the first years of the 17th century. On the south side there is a wooden Crucifix dating from the mid-14th century, a painting of the *Crucifixion* attributed to Jacopo del Sellaio and a *Baptism of Christ* by Lorenzo di Credi.

On the north side there is an *Annunciation* by Jacopo da Empoli (1615) and an *Epiphany* by Giovanni Antonio Sogliani (completed by Santi di Tito).

Only a few monks remain today (much of the convent is occupied by a department of the European University Institute) and it is not always easy to gain access to the little chapter house (*ring at no. 4, right of the church*). This contains a beautiful fresco of the *Crucifixion* by Fra' Angelico (c. 1430) and a detached fresco (with its sinopia) of the *Madonna and Child*, also attributed to him. In the orchard is the Cappella delle Beatitudine (1588), with frescoes by Lodovico Buti.

Badia Fiesolana

This was the cathedral of Fiesole until 1025. Its lovely position is traditionally associated with the spot where St Romulus was martyred in the reign of the emperor Domitian. A certain Donatus, thought to have been an Irishman, was elected to the bishop's see when he stopped here on his return from a pilgrimage to Rome, and was canonised after his death in 876. The church was rebuilt in the 15th century under the direction of Cosimo il Vecchio, who founded a library here with the help of Vespasiano da Bisticci. The European University Institute set itself up in the conventual buildings in 1976. The rough stone front of the church (*open 9–5.30; Sat 9–12*) incorporates the beautiful façade of the smaller Romanesque church with inlaid marble decoration. The interior, entered through the 15th-century cloister, has an interesting plan derived from Brunelleschi (begun in 1456). The side chapels have handsome round arches in *pietra serena* by Francesco di Simone Ferrucci. The east end, also decorated with *pietra serena*, has an elegant inscription to Piero de' Medici (Il Gottoso, father of Lorenzo the Magnificent) and the date of 1466. The high altar in *pietre dure* (1612) was designed by Pietro Tacca.

SETTIGNANO

Bus no. 10 leaves every 20mins from Stazione Santa Maria Novella and Piazza San Marco to Settignano via Ponte a Mensola; journey time 30mins.

Settignano (178m), a peaceful village on a pleasant hill, is little visited by tourists. It has narrow, picturesque lanes and many fine villas surrounded by luxurious gardens. Delightful country walks can be taken in the vicinity. The name is thought to come from Septimius, a Roman soldier to whom land here was allocated during the colonisation of the countryside around Florence. It is known for its school of sculptors, the most famous of whom were Desiderio (1428–64) and the Gamberelli brothers (known as Antonio and Bernardo Rossellino; 1427–79 and 1409–64).

The **church of Santa Maria** stands in the piazza where the bus terminates. It contains a charming group of the *Madonna and Child with Two Angels* in white enamelled terracotta, attributed to the workshop of Andrea della Robbia. The pulpit was designed by Bernardo Buontalenti. In the dome above the high altar is an *Assumption of the Virgin* by Pier Dandini. On the north side, the second altar has a painted terracotta statuette of *St Lucy* attributed to Michelozzo, surrounded by frescoes of 1593.

Via dei Buonarroti-Simoni

From the right of the church in Settignano, the raised lane called Via Capponcina leads downhill to Via dei Buonarroti-Simoni and Villa Michelangelo (no. 65; *no admission*), the ancestral home of the Buonarroti family, where Michelangelo spent his youth (a charcoal drawing of a triton or satyr, attributed to him, was found on the kitchen wall, and was detached and restored in 1979). Numerous letters addressed to this house survive from the great architect to his father and brothers who lived here while Michelangelo was carrying out his papal commissions in Rome. Farther downhill, surrounded by a garden with cypresses and pine trees, is Villa La Capponcina (no. 32), where Gabriele d'Annunzio lived in 1898–1910 and where he wrote most of his best works. From here you can continue on foot downhill to Via Madonna delle Grazie, which becomes a footpath before crossing a little footbridge over the Mensola to the hamlet of Ponte a Mensola.

Villa Gamberaia

Privately owned; garden open 9–6 or 7; Sun and holidays 9–5; ring the bell; T: 055 697205.
Entrance at Via del Rossellino 72. Reached on foot from the piazza by a lovely walk of about
15mins. Take the narrow Via de' Fancelli downhill to the quiet little Via de' Pianerottolo, which
joins Via Rossellino.

The famous garden is considered one of the most representative of Tuscany, in an extraordinarily peaceful and unspoilt spot, with wonderful views. Immaculately maintained, it was laid out in 1717 by Andrea Capponi and restored in 1905–13 by Catherine Jeanne Keshko, the Romanian wife of Prince Eugenio Ghyka. She replaced the formal beds of the parterres overlooking the Arno valley by pools designed around a fountain. The vegetation here is predominantly cypress and topiary of Irish yew, with box hedges around roses and topiary spheres of phillyrea. An exedra of cypresses clipped into blind arches encloses the far end of the parterre, outside which is a bay hedge: only one arch is open to the wonderful view. From the terrace there is another view, beyond olive groves, of Settignano on its ridge and the Duomo of Florence beyond. The topiary, for which the garden is also famous, was restored after 1924. There is also a little ilex wood (or *bosco*) with periwinkles and ivy in the undergrowth, as well as ancient cypresses and pine trees (the huge tree at the end of the garden is a Corsican pine). There is an elaborate grotto, a garden 'room', with numerous statues, off the long bowling green (with a fine collection of azaleas), which ends at a nymphaeum.

PONTE A MENSOLA

Bus 10 leaves every 20mins from Stazione Santa Maria Novella and Piazza San Marco to
Settignano via Ponte a Mensola; journey time 25mins.

The village of Ponte a Mensola lies at the foot of the hill of Settignano. In Via Poggio Gherardo is the park of the **Villa di Poggio Gherardo** (*no admission*), traditionally thought to be the setting for the earliest episodes in Boccaccio's *Decameron*. In 1888, it was purchased by Janet and Henry Ross: Janet, an expert on Tuscan villas and Tuscan food, died here in 1927. Downhill towards Florence is the sports centre of Coverciano with a football museum. The town's stadium, in the district of Campo di Marte, was built by Pier Luigi Nervi in 1932.

San Martino a Mensola

Open in the morning on Mon; other days except Sun 4–6; services on Sat at 6 and Sun at
10.30; at other times ring at the parish office at no. 4 under the portico on the right.

This 9th-century Benedictine church is in a beautiful position above the village of Ponte a Mensola. It was founded by St Andrew, thought to have been a Scotsman and archdeacon to the bishop of Fiesole, Donatus, who in turn was probably from Ireland. It is preceded by a 17th-century loggia. The 15th-century campanile was damaged by lightning in 1867.

The graceful 15th-century interior replaced the Romanesque church (remains of which have been found beneath the nave). It was restored in 1857 by Giuseppe

Fancelli and again in 1999. The sanctuary is preceded by a beautifully carved arch in *pietra serena* with two pretty little tabernacles. On the high altar is a triptych of the *Madonna and Child* with the donor and saints (the donor is Amerigo Zati) by a follower of Orcagna (1391), known, from this painting, as the Master of San Martino a Mensola. Beneath it is the wooden casket which formerly contained St Andrew's body, decorated with fine paintings of 1389 illustrating his life. The other painted altarpieces are particularly fine and include a triptych by Taddeo Gaddi, an *Annunciation* by a follower of Fra' Angelico, and a *Madonna and Four Saints* by Neri di Bicci.

In the pavement, a stone marks the burial place of St Andrew. The church also preserves his wooden reliquary bust, which dates from the end of the 14th century. After its restoration it will be placed in the crypt.

Corbignano

In Via di Corbignano, a peaceful old country lane, is **Villa Boccaccio** (no. 4; rebuilt), once owned by the father of Giovanni Boccaccio, who probably spent his youth here.

Above the charming little hamlet of Corbignano itself is the **Oratorio della Madonna del Vannella** (1719–21; *open for a service on the last Sun of the month, otherwise T: 055 604418*). The fresco of the *Madonna and Child*, believed by Berenson to be an early work by Botticelli, was for centuries venerated by the stonemasons and sculptors of Settignano. The road ends at the cemetery of Settignano.

Giovanni Boccaccio (1312–75)
The birthplace of the celebrated author Giovanni Boccaccio is uncertain: perhaps Certaldo, a small Tuscan town, or even Paris, where his Florentine father had mercantile interests, but he lived most of his life in Florence. His *Decameron* (1348–58) is a brilliant secular work which established him as the father of Italian prose and which had a great influence on European literature (including Chaucer). The book is a collection of tales told by seven ladies and three gentlemen who decide to leave the centre of Florence in order to escape the plague of 1348; they spend ten days in the garden of a villa in the surrounding hills recounting stories to each other. The Villa di Poggio Gherardo and the villa now known as Villa Palmieri are both thought to have been settings for some of the earliest episodes, and other places in the environs of Florence near Fiesole are associated with the book. Boccaccio acted as ambassador for Florence after 1350 and was a close friend of the poet and the first great humanist Petrarch (1304–74) as well as of Dante.

Villa I Tatti

House and garden not open to the public but shown to scholars with a letter of presentation, by previous appointment (in small groups usually on Tues and Wed afternoons); T: 055 603251. Main entrance Via Vincigliata 26.

The little by-road leads from the church of San Martino across a bridge over the Mensola to a group of houses by the garden entrance to Villa I Tatti. The locality was known as 'Tatti' at least as early as the 15th century. The house was acquired by John Temple Leader in 1854, and by Bernard Berenson, the pioneer scholar of the Italian Renaissance, in 1905.

The villa contains Berenson's library and photographic library as well as his exquisite collection of Italian paintings (including works by Domenico Veneziano, Sassetta, Michele Giambono, Cima da Conegliano, Luca Signorelli, Bergognone and Lorenzo Lotto) and a small but choice selection of Oriental works of art. The lovely Italianate garden was laid out by Cecil Pinsent in 1911–15, in imitation of an early Renaissance garden. The terraces are planted with symmetrical parterres and descend the steep hillside surrounded by high hedges of cypress. Beyond the garden, which is beautifully kept, is a small ilex wood.

WALKS BEYOND PONTE A MENSOLA

Castello di Vincigliata

From Villa I Tatti, the very long Via di Vincigliata continues uphill through cypress woods to the **Castello di Vincigliata** (*privately owned and used for receptions, www. castellodivincigliata.it*), which was purchased in 1855 by John Temple Leader, a wealthy entrepreneur who had come to live in Florence in 1850 and remained here until his death in 1903. The castle was a complete ruin when he purchased it. Originally built in 1031, it had been destroyed, together with much of Fiesole, by Sir John Hawkwood in 1364, early in his career when he was captain of the Pisan army. The famous English mercenary (*see p. 56*) is said to have found Florence too strongly defended and so had turned his sword on properties in the surrounding hills instead. Temple Leader appointed a local architect, Giuseppe Fancelli, to rebuild the castle in neo-Gothic style, with the help of skilled stonemasons from Settignano and the painter Gaetano Bianchi. He also acquired many farms and villas between Settignano and Fiesole, and numerous stone quarries which he closed down and planted with woods. He wrote biographies of Sir Robert Dudley and Sir John Hawkwood, and contributed generously to the funds spent on the new façade of the Duomo. During his lifetime the castle, which he used as a museum of medieval and Renaissance works of art, was one of the most important 'sites' of Florence, and he was visited by numerous distinguished travellers.

The road now ascends past **Castel di Poggio** (*no. 4; park and interior sometimes shown by appointment; T: 055 59174; www.casteldipoggio.it*) and **Villa Peyron al Bosco di Fontelucente** (*no. 2; the lovely garden opened by Comune of Fiesole, see p. 309*). It meets Via di Bosconi just east of Fiesole.

Maiano

Reached by the pretty Via Poggio Gherardo, the **Villa di Maiano** (now Corsini) was restored in 1850–63 by Felice Francolini for John Temple Leader (*see above*). Privately owned, it is used for receptions but is sometimes shown by appointment (*T: 055*

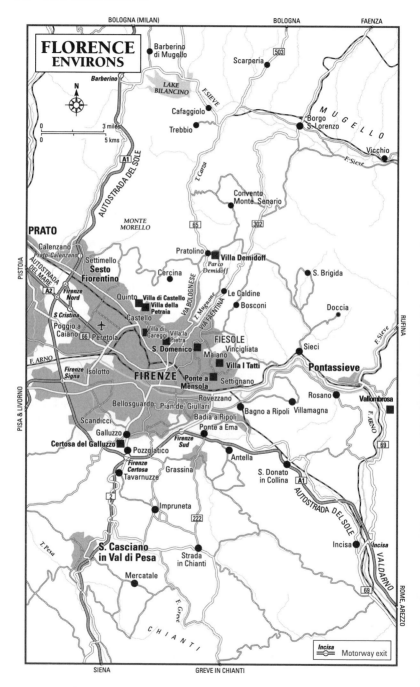

599600). The little hamlet of Maiano was the home of the brothers Benedetto and Giuliano da Maiano (1442–92 and 1432–90), who were well known sculptors and architects. The church of **San Martino a Maiano** (*open Wed 4.30–7, or ring at no. 6*) is of ancient foundation and was restored by Temple Leader. The choir is decorated with *pietra serena*. Above the west door, in its original frame, is a *Madonna and Child with St John and Two Saints* by Giovanni Battista Naldini. A farm (produce for sale) now occupies the Benedictine monastery. A road continues uphill to end near a disused quarry of *pietra serena*. Beyond, a broad path continues up through woods to the Via di Bosconi, east of Fiesole.

THE MEDICI VILLAS OF LA PETRAIA & CASTELLO

Three villas on the northwestern outskirts of Florence were all Medici residences. The **Villa di Careggi**, although historically the most important, was closed for restoration at the time of writing. A 14th-century farmhouse enlarged by Michelozzo, it became the literary and artistic centre of the Medici court and is traditionally taken as the meeting place of the famous Platonic Academy, founded in the late 1450s, which saw the birth of the humanist movement of the Renaissance. Cosimo il Vecchio, Piero il Gottoso, and Lorenzo the Magnificent all died in the villa. In 1844–45 George Frederic Watts painted a fresco in its garden loggia. The subject is the murder of Pietro Leoni, Lorenzo the Magnificent's doctor—who, legend says, was thrown into the well in the courtyard, accused of failing to save Lorenzo's life. He had attempted to cure his patient's uricaemia with a philtre of powdered emeralds.

The two other villas, described below, are very close to each other (*10mins' walk*) and both have large, well-kept gardens of great interest. Although you should definitely take a bus to cross the uninteresting northern suburbs of Florence, there are pretty country walks in the hills behind the villas themselves.

How to get there
Bus 28 from Stazione Santa Maria Novella for Sesto Fiorentino (every 10mins; journey time about 30mins): the second 'Castello' request stop is the one for La Petraia, and the last 'Castello' request stop is the one for Villa di Castello.

VILLA DELLA PETRAIA

Garden open 8.15–dusk except 2nd and 3rd Mon of the month. The interior is shown by a custodian about every 45mins (ring the bell). You are asked to telephone before your visit; T: 055 452691. Combined ticket with the Villa di Castello gardens.

Standing on the site of a 14th-century castle of the Strozzi, the villa was rebuilt in 1575 (preserving the castle tower) for Grand Duke Ferdinando I by Buontalenti. In 1864–70 Vittorio Emanuele II lived here. In 1919 Vittorio Emanuele III presented it to the state.

The garden

The beautiful lower garden was designed for Ferdinando, with symmetrical parterres on terraces descending from the moat in front of the villa which served as a fishpond as well as a cistern for irrigation (it is now full of goldfish and carp). It was altered in the 19th century under the influence of Victorian taste, but dwarf pear trees and persimmons have recently been replanted and the meadows of wild flowers (particularly beautiful in early spring) are left uncut as they were in the days of the Medici grand dukes.

On the upper terrace, on either side of the villa, pots of orange and lemon trees are put out around Easter time. The beautiful fountain by Tribolo and Pierino da Vinci, with a bronze statue of *Fiorenza* (Florence wringing the water of the Arno and Mugnone from her hair) by Giambologna, has been replaced by a fine copy and the original has been moved inside. The beautiful female nude, probably cast in the 1570s, represents the new State of Tuscany under Cosimo I as an allegory of Venus, goddess of fertility. On the other side of the villa is a charming symmetrical *giardino segreto*, a modern recreation of the way it would have looked at the turn of the 16th and 17th centuries. This had rare plants such as asparagus, artichokes and tulips. It is at its best from late Feb–April. A magnificent park, with ancient cypresses, extends behind the villa to the east. The park and gardens are beautifully maintained.

The villa

The 16th-century **courtyard** was covered with a glass roof and given a Venetian floor and chandelier so that it could be used as a ballroom by Vittorio Emanuele II. The very fine frescoes beneath the two side loggias, illustrating the history of the Medici family, are by Volterrano (1636–46); those on the other two walls have late 16th-century *grottesche* by Cosimo Daddi. In two rooms off the courtyard are displayed the bronze *Antaeus and Hercules* by Ammannati (1558–59) and four bronze putti (by Tribolo and Pierino da Vinci), all from a fountain in the garden of Villa di Castello (*see opposite*).

The splendid **Sala Rossa** is hung with tapestries: four of them are 18th-century Flemish works from Parma and the other was made in Florence in the 17th century. The huge 19th-century carpet was restored *in situ*. There is a collection of clocks here and in the following rooms. In the **chapel** (1682–95), with frescoes attributed to Pier Dandini, is a painting of the *Madonna and Child* by Pier Francesco Fiorentino and an altarpiece of the *Holy Family* by the school of Andrea del Sarto.

The **private apartments on the first floor** are decorated in Neoclassical style. In a room off the loggia is the original bronze statue of *Fiorenza*. The bedroom of the 'Bella Rosina', wife of Vittorio Emanuele II, decorated in blue damask, has fine early 19th-century Piedmontese furniture. The Salotto Giallo, with yellow walls in the style known as 'retour d'Egypte', has French chairs and a travelling desk in the Empire style. In another chapel are frescoes by Cosimo Daddi and a copy of Raphael's *Madonna dell'Impannata* (original in Palazzo Pitti; *see p. 237*). The billiard room is a remarkable period piece, hung with 17th-century paintings by Francesco Curradi, Passignano, and two by Matteo Rosselli. There is a collection of late 19th- or early 20th-century parlour games and mid-19th-century alabasters.

VILLA DI CASTELLO

Admission to the gardens only, 8.15–dusk; closed 2nd and 3rd Mon of the month; telephone before your visit, T: 055 454791. Combined ticket with Villa della Petraia.

In front of Villa Corsini, Via di Castello leads in 5mins to Villa di Castello. Although the fountains have been altered and some of the statues removed over the centuries, this is the Medici garden which perhaps best preserves its 16th-century appearance, and it was the model for all subsequent Italianate gardens. It is still of the greatest botanical interest, especially for its magnificent tubs of citrus trees.

The villa was acquired by Giovanni and Lorenzo di Pierfrancesco de' Medici, Lorenzo the Magnificent's younger cousins, in 1476. Here they hung Botticelli's famous *Birth of Venus*. His *Primavera* and *Pallas and the Centaur* were also later brought here (and all remained in the house until 1761). The villa, inherited by Giovanni delle Bande Nere, was sacked during the siege of 1530 (*see p. 15*) but restored for Giovanni's son, Cosimo I, by Bronzino and Pontormo. It was bought by the state in 1919.

The gardens

Cosimo I employed Tribolo to design the gardens in 1541. The fountains were laid out on a central axis and were intended as symbolic celebrations of the establishment of the Medici family as absolute monarchs in Tuscany. The design was altered in the 18th century when the great marble fountain by Tribolo (assisted by Pierino da Vinci) was moved to its central position: formerly it was the fountain closest to the villa: the crowning bronze figures of *Hercules and Antaeus* by Ammannati (1559–60) represented the triumph of Hercules (or Cosimo) over Vice. Since its restoration it has been exhibited in the Villa della Petraia (*see above*). A copy of the exquisitely carved base, some 6m high, has been installed *in situ* here. The fountain which was originally in the centre, representing Florence as chief city of the Grand Duchy, no longer exists, although the crowning figure of *Fiorenza* survives in the Villa della Petraia.

The elaborate, well-preserved grotto beneath the terrace was probably designed by Tribolo. It is full of exotic animals, is encrusted with shell mosaics and stalactites and lined with natural stone taken from real grottoes. The huge basin on the left has beautifully-carved decorations also thought to be by Tribolo. Giambologna's bronze birds, now in the Bargello, were removed from here. In the floor and around the walls are water spouts: visitors (who were 'locked in' by a gate) were regularly surprised by a thorough drenching from their hosts. On the upper terrace is a colossus by Ammannati representing *Appennino* rising out of a pool and feeling the cold.

In the charming little *giardino segreto* (*opened on request*), created in the late 17th century by Cosimo III, is an unusual variety of cream-coloured Indian jasmine (in flower from July–Oct). The lower area of this little garden has about 400 varieties of aromatic and medicinal herbs which were known to have been cultivated here in the 16th century (including some 20 varieties each of thyme and of sage).

The garden is at its best from April–June and when the magnificent collection of citrus trees, in some 1,000 terracotta tubs, are put out for the summer. There are over a hundred varieties, including some that are ancient and unique. The garden is beautifully maintained and the gardeners use no chemical fertilisers.

MUSEO STIBBERT, VILLA LA PIETRA & VILLA DEMIDOFF

Museo Stibbert

Beyond map 4, 1. Entrance at no. 4 Via Montughi. Open Mon, Tues, Wed 10–2; Fri, Sat, Sun 10–6; closed Thur. Tours begin every hour on the hour. Tours given in English by appointment: T: 055 475520. The Japanese collection, considered the best in Europe, is open by appointment on Fri and Sun at 3 and on Sat at 11. There is a little café on the ground floor with a few tables in the garden. Bus 4 from Piazza Unità Italiana (map 3, 5) to Via Vittorio Emanuele II (request stop for Via Stibbert). Park, landscaped in Victorian style, open 9–dusk except Thur.

The museum was created by the Englishman Frederick Stibbert (1838–1906) in his home here. Born in Florence to an Italian mother and English father, Stibbert inherited a great fortune (his grandfather had been part of the East India Company) and became a collector, traveller, artist—and, in 1866, a Garibaldian hero.

The period rooms were designed for Stibbert's eclectic collection: heavily decorated and bizarre in atmosphere, they are crammed with an extraordinary variety of objects. His particular interest and field of study was armour and costume: the huge neo-Gothic hall (decorated by Gaetano Bianchi) is an extraordinary sight. It is filled with a cavalcade of fully armed horses and knights of the 16th century, with six soldiers wearing 16th-century Asiatic armour. The armour found in the tomb of Giovanni delle Bande Nere is also exhibited here in a niche. The Sala del Condottiere displays a 15th-century mercenary mounted on his steed. There is tournament and battle armour dating back to Etruscan and Roman times, and one of the finest collections of spurs in existence. The Sala Moresca has a superb display of Asiatic armour, much of it Turkish. At the time of writing, only about 20 rooms could be visited, since the first floor was being restored.

Villa La Pietra

Tours of the garden and villa by appointment on Fri afternoon; garden only on Tues morning. There are also two (free) open weeks a year in April and Oct—for information T: 055 500 7210; villa.lapietra@nyu.edu. Bus 25 from Piazza San Marco (map 4, 5) to the request stop on Via Bolognese at La Pietra.

From the Museo Stibbert the lovely old Via di Montughi leads uphill to emerge on the Via Bolognese, the old Roman road to Bologna, in front of the gate of Villa La Pietra (no. 120), surrounded by fields of olives and preceded by a splendid long avenue of cypresses above pink China rose-bushes.

The villa was built in the 1460s for the Sassetti (Francesco Sassetti was manager of the Medici bank under Lorenzo the Magnificent) and sold to the Capponi in 1545. In the first years of the 20th century Arthur Acton's wealthy American wife Hortense

Mitchell purchased the property. It was the birthplace and residence of their son, the aesthete and historian Sir Harold Acton (1904–94), one of the most famous Anglo-Florentines of the last century, who was made an honorary citizen of Florence in 1986. He bequeathed the villa to New York University and it is now used as a branch campus for undergraduate students. The villa contains one of the most interesting private collections of works of art in Florence, including a notable group of early Tuscan paintings, and the rooms are still fully furnished as they were in the Actons' day.

The beautiful garden, a successful imitation of a 16th-century Tuscan garden, was created by the Actons: it is now being restored. It is a green garden, on a very large scale, in which some 200 17th-century allegorical statues, some by Orazio Marinali (who produced much of statuary for the Palladian villas around Vicenza), are a special feature. Designed to be viewed from the upper terrace and the house, it is laid out in 'rooms' on different levels. The planting is predominantly box, yew, cypress and ilex. There is a green theatre and good topiary, and a *boschetto* of laurels. The very high terrace attached to the house has cascades of banksia rose and wisteria. The charming walled kitchen garden is decorated with shell mosaic. This was part of the original Renaissance garden and its pear trees and box and myrtle hedges have been replanted. The beds along the walls have viola and iris and yellow roses. Here orange and lemon trees are kept in pots, and two huge Portugal laurels grow in front of the orangery built in the 1650s. The 57-acre estate includes four boundary villas.

Villa Demidoff at Pratolino

Open March–Oct Sun and holidays 10–7; April–Sept Thur, Fri, Sat, Sun 10–8; T: 055 409427. No dogs. Bus 25 from Piazza San Marco (map 4, 5). Journey time about 40mins.
Farther out of Florence, the Via Bolognese follows the long ruined walls of the huge park of Villa Demidoff, the main entrance of which is at Pratolino. Some 17–18 hectares of the splendid, well-kept park belong to the province and are open to the public. This is one of the most beautiful open spaces near the city and its fields and woods make it a lovely place to picnic. There is a café-restaurant in one of the farm buildings. The most remarkable sight is Giambologna's colossal *Appennino* (1580): the giant is pressing down the head of a monster (water used to gush out of its mouth). This is almost the only survival from the famous garden created by Buontalenti for Francesco I, the villa of which was demolished in 1824. Paolo Demidoff, son of Nicola, a Russian emigré from St Petersburg, built his residence in 1872 in the service wing of the Medici villa, and his descendants lived here until 1955.

PIAN DE' GIULLARI

Best reached on foot from Ponte Vecchio via Costa San Giorgio and Via di San Leonardo (map 6). Bus 38B from Porta Romana (map 5, 6); only by booking, T: 199500794 or 800019794.
For Pian de' Giullari, at the junction with Via di San Leonardo keep left uphill along Via Viviani, which skirts the garden wall of Villa Capponi, bought in 1928 by Henry

and Esther Clifford, who entertained numerous well-known Americans here. The beautiful garden (*which can sometimes be seen by previous appointment; T: 055 223465*) preserves its 16th-century character. After this Via Pian de' Giullari soon meets Via Torre del Gallo, named after the conspicuous tower rebuilt in medieval style by the antiquarian Stefano Bardini in 1902. In the picturesque little village of Pian de' Giullari (also known as Arcetri) stands **Villa di Gioiello** (no. 42), the house where the aged Galileo lived from 1631 until his death in 1642. The 16th-century house and farm, with a loggia overlooking its lovely gardens, are not open regularly (*ask at the Museo della Specola for information about admission times; T: 055 275 7456*). Beyond are several more lovely country roads, which provide beautiful, peaceful walks. Via San Matteo in Arcetri passes the rebuilt convent where Galileo's daughter Suor Maria Celeste lived as a nun, before her death in 1634 at the age of 33. A hundred and twenty-four remarkable letters from her to Galileo survive. In the other direction from Pian de' Giullari (signposted for Santa Margherita a Montici) the old road continues past **Villa Ravà** (no. 71), purchased by Francesco Guicciardini in 1527, who wrote his famous *History of Italy* here. Guicciardini shared Machiavelli's view that only strong and ruthless government would lead to political survival. He was employed by two Medici popes, Leo X (1513–21) and Clement VII (1523–34). His *History* gives a merciless analysis of many rulers, including those whom he had served.

Beyond several more villas, the road continues through open countryside and climbs up to the church of Santa Margherita a Montici (*open Sun 10–12.30*). This has a distinctive crenellated campanile and occupies a splendid position, with views of the two valleys of the Arno and Ema. The church contains two paintings by the Master of Santa Cecilia, one of which, *St Margaret and Scenes from her Life*, is thought to date from before 1300. Also in the sanctuary is a ciborium by Andrea Sansovino.

MONTEOLIVETO & BELLOSGUARDO

Bus 12 from Piazza Santa Maria Novella to Viale Raffaello Sanzio (for Monteoliveto) and Piazza Torquato Tasso (for Bellosguardo). Also bus 42 (only by booking; T: 199500794, or 800019794) for Bellosguardo (going on to Marignolle) from Porta Romana. Both can also be approached on foot from the Oltrarno.

Monteoliveto and Bellosguardo are lovely residential districts with some large villas where a number of writers stayed in the 19th century. There are superb views of Florence from the road up to Bellosguardo and delightful walks nearby.

Monteoliveto

On the south bank of the Arno, near Ponte della Vittoria, is the thickly wooded hill of Monteoliveto (*map 5, 1*). It is reached via Viale Raffaello Sanzio and (right) Via di Monteoliveto. The church of **San Bartolomeo** (*open 9–1; for admission, ring at no. 72a*), was founded in 1334 by monks from the convent of Monteoliveto Maggiore in Tuscany, and rebuilt in the 15th century; it has been restored several times since. The west wall and triumphal arch have good frescoes by Bernardino Poccetti. On the second altar on the south side there is an *Assumption of the Virgin* signed and dated 1592 by Domenico Passignano, below which is a little reliquary case with a charming 18th-century figure of the Virgin as a baby. On the high altar, the *Entry of Christ into Jerusalem* is a copy by Il Poppi of an altarpiece by Santi di Tito. The domed sanctuary and triumphal arch are interesting works which show the influence of Leon Battista Alberti and Francesco da Sangallo. On the left wall there is a fresco fragment (with its sinopia opposite) of the *Last Supper* by Sodoma. The first altarpiece on the north side is by Domenico Passignano and his follower Fabrizio Boschi, and the second altarpiece is by Simone Pignone. There are also six 18th-century scagliola altar-frontals.

The road ends in front of an entrance to the **Villa Strozzi** (*open daily 9–dusk*). This has a beautiful wooded park with fine views of Bellosguardo. It is now used by a school of design. There are two other entrances, one on Via Pisana and one on Via Soffiano.

Bellosguardo

Bellosguardo, approached from Piazza San Francesco di Paola, is appropriately named for its lovely view. In the piazza stands the church of **San Francesco di Paola** (*map 5, 3; open for services only*), built in 1593. It has early 18th-century decorations and a detached fresco of the *Madonna del Parto* by Taddeo Gaddi.

Via di Bellosguardo climbs uphill to a little walled public garden behind a hedge, with a few pines and cypresses. Here is the **Villa dello Strozzino**, a fine Renaissance villa with a pretty loggia at one corner. On the right, the extremely narrow (and picturesque) Via Monteoliveto leads to the ancient little **church of San Vito** (*open for a service on Sun mornings*) with a pretty porch. Via di Bellosguardo continues uphill with a superb view back of Florence. On the right beside a group of pine trees is **Villa Brichieri-Colombi** (no. 20). When Isa Blagden was a tenant here from 1856–61 she saw a great deal of her close friends the Brownings. Later in the same century the villa was rented by Constance Fenimore Woolson who sublet it to her friend Henry James for a few months and it was here in 1887 that he wrote *The Aspern Papers*.

The old road narrows and a sharp turn left (Via Roti Michelozzi) ends at **Torre di Bellosguardo** (*map 5, 5*), now a hotel, with a delightful garden and magnificent views of Florence. Adjoining it (*entrance from Piazza di Bellosguardo*) is the **Villa dell'Ombrellino**, rented by Galileo in 1617–31 before he moved to Arcetri (Pian de' Giullari; *see opposite*). In 1924 it was bought by Colonel George Keppel and his wife Alice, a glamorous hostess best known as the mistress of King Edward VII. Their daughter, the writer Violet Trefusis, an intimate friend of Virginia Woolf and Vita Sackville-West, lived here in the 1950s and '60s.

Piazza di Bellosguardo has a few trees and at no. 6 stands the **Villa Mercedes**, also known as Villa Belvedere al Saraceno, by Baccio d'Agnolo with a charming courtyard. It is thought that Henry James took this villa as a model for the Villa Pandolfini in *Roderick Hudson* (1875) and also as the residence of Gilbert Osmond in *The Portrait of a Lady*. Via San Carlo leads downhill out of the piazza towards the conspicuous tower of **Villa di Montauto**, where Nathaniel Hawthorne stayed in the 1850s. It provided the setting for the castle of Monte Beni, home to the Tuscan count named Donatello, in *The Marble Faun* (1860).

Villa La Colombaia (*map 5, 7*) with a closed-in loggia, now a convent school, is where Florence Nightingale was born in 1820. She was the first person ever to be called Florence, from the city of her birth. From here the lovely old Via delle Campora can be followed back down to Porta Romana.

CERTOSA DEL GALLUZZO

Bus 37 from Piazza Santa Maria Novella (every 20mins); request stop below the hill of the Certosa. Journey time about 30mins. Certosa open 9–11.30 & 3–5.30 (winter 3–5); closed Mon; T: 055 204 9226. Tours are conducted by the monks about every half-hour.

Via Senese begins at Porta Romana (*map 5, 6*), from where it climbs and then descends through Gelsomino to Galluzzo, passing (right) the thick cypresses of the **Cimitero Evangelico degli Allori**. Formerly, this was a cemetery for Orthodox Greeks, but since 1878 it has been used for all non-Catholics.

Beyond the village of **Galluzzo**, immediately to the right of the road on the Colle di Montaguto, stands the Certosa, a historic monastery remarkable for its peaceful atmosphere and interesting for its architecture as well as its frescoes by Pontormo. It was founded in 1342 by Niccolò Acciaioli. Today only six monks remain.

On the upper floor of the Palazzo degli Studi, begun by Niccolò Acciaioli as a meeting place for young Florentines to study the liberal arts, five **frescoed lunettes of the Passion cycle** (severely damaged) by Pontormo (1522–25) are exhibited—they are among Pontormo's most important works and were detached from the Great Cloister. They were painted when he came here to escape the plague in Florence in 1522. Behind the Crucifix, which dates from 1350–60, are five oil paintings by Jacopo Chimenti, known as Empoli, which are excellent copies of Pontormo's lunettes showing their original appearance. Also here is a fresco by Empoli of the *Sermon on the Mount*, detached from the top of the stairs, and another copy by him of a work by Pontormo, this time his *Supper at Emmaus*, now in the Uffizi.

The spacious courtyard dates from 1545. The 16th-century façade of the church is by Cosimo Fancelli. The interior is divided into two parts: the monk's choir has fine vaulting and good 16th-century stalls. On the east wall is a fresco by Bernardino Poccetti (1591–92). The visit continues through the extensive conventual buildings. The colloquio, reserved for conversation with visitors, has interesting 16th-century stained glass, and beyond is a charming little cloister reconstructed in the late 16th century by Giovanni Fancelli. The secluded Great Cloister is decorated with 66 tondi containing white majolica busts of saints and prophets, by Andrea and Giovanni della Robbia. In the centre is a well of 1521 and the monks' cemetery, still in use. One of the monks' cells, at the beginning of the right walk, may be visited; they each have three rooms, a loggia and a little garden. Most of the cells have a fresco over the door, and a little window through which food was passed.

APPENDIX

The buildings and monuments here are described in brief since many of them are not open regularly to the public and are either of less importance than those described in the main body of the guide or are outside the historic centre of the city.

CHURCHES, ORATORIES & CONVENTS

Convitto della Calza

Map 5, 6. Piazza della Calza.
With an attractive asymmetrical loggia, this was first built as a hospital (in 1362) and later became a convent. It was restored in 2000 as a home for retired prelates, a hostel for visiting churchmen and pilgrim groups, a conference centre and a hotel. In the refectory (*admission on request at no. 6*) there is a *Last Supper* by Franciabigio and on the walls pretty frames with frescoes by 18th-century Florentine artists including Tommaso Gherardini and Giuseppe Zocchi.

Gesù Pellegrino

Map 3, 4. Via San Gallo
Small church rebuilt in 1588 by Giovanni Antonio Dosio with a fresco cycle (1590) and three altarpieces by Giovanni Balducci (Il Cosci). In the nave is the tomb slab of the Pievano Arlotto (1400–84), rector of the church and subject of a famous painting by Volterrano (*see p. 236*). The inscription reads: 'This tomb was ordered by the Pievano Arlotto for himself and for whoever wishes to enter it'.

Holy Trinity

Map 4, 3. Via Micheli 26.
Owned by the Waldensian Community since 1967. The Waldensians, who originated in the south of France c. 1170, were condemned by the Lateran Council in 1184 and fled to northern Italy where they settled, especially in the district around Turin. An Anglican church, built by Domenico Giraldi, was founded here in 1846. The present neo-Gothic building, with stained-glass windows, was designed in 1892 by the English architect George Frederick Bodley. The choir screen and wooden stalls, also by Bodley, were made in Florence in 1902 by the workshop of Mariano Coppedè.

Montedomini (ex-convent of)

Map 7, 4. Via dei Malcontenti.
This huge hospice for the elderly (now partly used by the University) is on the site of a 15th-century hospital, later used by two Franciscan convents of closed orders (Montedomini and Monticelli). The buildings were redesigned as a hospice in the early 19th century by Giuseppe del Rosso, and it became a workhouse in 1860. It incorporates a church, consecrated in 1573, with a vault painted by Agostino Veracini in the 18th century. A wing of the hospice, used from 1894–1938 as a military hospital, has painted decorations by Galileo Chini.

Russian Church

Map 3, 2. Via Leone X. Open for services (sung Mass) on the 3rd Sun of the month and on major Church festivals.
Built with funds raised from the large Russian colony in Florence (which included the wealthy Demidoff family) and consecrated in

1904. Throughout most of the 19th century, Florence was a fashionable place to spend the winter for aristocratic Russian families. The architects were Russian, and the pretty majolica decoration on the exterior was carried out by the Ulisse Cantagalli workshop. It is now a national monument owned by the Russian Orthodox community of Florence.

Sant'Agata

Map 4, 3–1. Via San Gallo 110.
The façade (1592) is by Allori, as is the high altarpiece of the *Marriage at Cana*. Other paintings are attributed to Lorenzo di Credi, Lorenzo Lippi and Neri di Bicci.

Sant'Agnese

Map 3, 4. Via Guelfa 79.
A pretty little Baroque chapel (early 18th century) with frescoes by the school of Sagrestani. It is now incorporated in an old people's home.

San Barnaba

Map 3, 6. Via Guelfa.
Used by the Filipino community. The 14th-century portal bears a della Robbian lunette. The pretty interior was remodelled in 1700 and there is a Baroque organ above the nuns' choir. The painting of the *Flagellation* is attributed to Giovanni Maria Butteri, a pupil of Bronzino.

San Carlo dei Lombardi

Map 1, 6. Via Calzaioli.
Dating from 1349–1404, with a severe (much ruined) façade. Inside, on the left wall, is a carved polychrome wood Crucifix by Orcagna (c. 1360), clearly showing the influence of Giotto. At its foot has been placed a bronze statue of Padre Pio, since 2002 St Pius of Pietrelcina. Images of this immensely popular figure can be seen today in almost every church in Italy, though the story of his stigmata and special sanctity have been questioned by scholars.

Sant'Egidio

Map 4, 7. Via Bufalini.
The church of the hospital of Santa Maria Nuova, founded in 1286 by Folco Portinari (believed to be the father of Dante's Beatrice) and still one of the main hospitals of Florence. The entrance is beneath an unusual portico (1574–1612) by Bernardo Buontalenti. In the interior are remains of Portinari's tomb and a splendid high altar with a ciborium in *pietre dure* (1666). A door to the right of the church (*usually kept closed; admission through the hospital buildings*) leads into a cloister, the oldest part of the hospital, with a *Pietà* by Giovanni della Robbia. To the left of the church, in another old courtyard, is the tomb slab of Monna Tessa, the servant of Portinari, who persuaded him to found the hospital. In the offices of the Presidenza, above (*opened on certain days of the year or by appointment*) are a *Madonna and Child* by Andrea della Robbia and detached frescoes of *Martin V Consecrating the Church*, by Bicci di Lorenzo (with its sinopia) and the same pope confirming its privileges, by Andrea di Giusto (repainted). Folco's descendant Tommaso Portinari had Hugo van der Goes paint a huge triptych for the high altar when in Bruges in the 15th century (now in the Uffizi; *see p. 119*).

Santa Elisabetta delle Convertite

Map 5, 4. Via del Campuccio.
Deconsecrated, now used as a hall for concerts and lectures. The interior preserves a beautiful triumphal arch (1494) which shows the influence of Brunelleschi, and a frescoed ceiling with the *Glory of St Mary Magdalene* by Alessandro Gherardini (1703). Frescoes with stories of martyrs, almost certainly by

Bernardino Poccetti, have been discovered in the nuns' choir.

San Filippo Neri
Map 6, 2. Piazza San Firenze.
San Firenze, a huge Baroque building at present occupied by the law courts, designed by Francesco Zanobi del Rosso (1772–75), is flanked by two church façades designed by Ferdinando Ruggieri (1715). The church of San Filippo Neri (left), by Gherardo and Pier Francesco Silvani (1633–48), has an unusually tall interior, decorated in 1712–14 (the ceiling was painted by Giovanni Camillo Sagrestani). In the Chapel of the Sacrament the painting of the *Ten Thousand Martyrs* is the largest altarpiece produced by Bachiacca. The law courts are scheduled to move out of the centre of Florence to the vast new Palazzo di Giustizia, designed by Leonardo Ricci: although completed some years ago it has remained empty as it is apparently proving difficult to furnish and maintain. Much bigger than any other building in the vicinity of the city, it has irreparably altered the skyline of Florence and its townscape.

San Francesco dei Vanchetoni (oratory of)
Map 3, 7. Via Palazzuolo 17. The custodian lives next door and sometimes shows it on request.
Often used for concerts, the oratory was built in 1602 by Giovanni Nigetti, with a vestibule and façade by Matteo Nigetti (1620). The ceiling frescoes are by Pietro Liberi, Volterrano, Cecco Bravo and others. The chapel behind the altar contains a 16th-century Crucifix and the charming sacristy has inlaid cupboards.

San Giorgio sulla Costa (or Spirito Santo)
Map 6, 4. Costa San Giorgio. Open only for a service at 10.30 on Sun.
Used by the Romanian Orthodox community.

It has one of the best Baroque interiors in Florence (by Giovanni Battista Foggini; 1705). The altarpieces are by Tommaso Redi, Jacopo Vignali and Passignano, and on the ceiling is the *Glory of St George* by Alessandro Gherardini. The high altar is also by Foggini. The church contains a rare mechanical organ of c. 1570 by Onofrio Zeffirini.

San Giovanni di Dio
Map 3, 7. Borgo Ognissanti.
Built by Carlo Marcellini (1702–13) next to the ex-hospital of San Giovanni di Dio, founded in 1380 by the Vespucci family (closed down in 1982). It was enlarged in 1702–13 to incorporate the Vespucci house on this site, including the birthplace of Amerigo (*see p. 284*). In the fine atrium (1735) are sculptures by Girolamo Ticciati.

San Giovannino dei Cavalieri
Map 3, 4. Via San Gallo 66.
The unusual vestibule has original cupboards. In the tribune, surrounded by worn frescoes by Alessandro Gherardini (1703), is a large *Crucifixion* by Lorenzo Monaco. At the end of the right aisle is an *Annunciation*, a painting by the Master of the Castello Nativity. On the right wall is a worn fresco of *St Michael Archangel* by Francesco Granacci. In the left aisle is a *Nativity* by Bicci di Lorenzo and a *Coronation of the Virgin* by his son, Neri di Bicci. On the west wall is the *Birth of the Baptist* by Santi di Tito and the *Beheading of the Baptist* by Pier Dandini.

San Giovannino degli Scolopi
Map 1, 2. Via de' Martelli.
This little church was begun in 1579 by Ammannati, who designed the second north chapel as his burial place (1592). The fourth south chapel was built in 1692–1712 for Grand Duke Cosimo III. The altarpiece of

the *Preaching of St Francis Xavier* is the best work of Francesco Curradi. The vault fresco is by Pier Dandini and the stucco angels are by Girolamo Ticciati. The first chapel on the left has angels, *Jacob's Dream* and the *Fall of Lucifer* by Jacopo Ligozzi. The altarpiece is by Alessandro Allori. The confessionals date from the late 17th century.

San Giuseppe
Map 7, 2. Via di San Giuseppe. Open 5–7; Wed also 9.30–12.
Built in 1519 to a design by Baccio d'Agnolo. The portal dates from 1852 (thought to be based on a design by Michelangelo). The oratory, with pretty graffiti decoration, and the elegant campanile (designed by Baccio d'Agnolo) both date from 1934.

The handsome interior has pretty frescoes by Sigismondo Betti in the centre of the vault and in the choir (1754), with architectural perspectives by Pietro Anderlini. The organ, with its original mechanism, is by the workshop of the Agati of Pistoia (1764). The first south chapel has a 16th-century lunette (left side) and an unusual funerary monument by Odoardo Fantacchiotti (1854). The second chapel was decorated in 1705. The damaged triptych attributed to Taddeo Gaddi and the 14th-century carved wooden Crucifix both belonged to the Compagnia di Santa Maria della Croce al Tempio. The third chapel has frescoes by Luigi Ademollo (1840), and on the altar is a *Nativity*, an early work by Santi di Tito. Above the high altar, inlaid with a floral decoration in *pietre dure* in 1930, is a painted Crucifix by the early 15th-century Florentine school. The 17th-century stalls and 16th-century paintings in octagonal frames complete the decoration of the choir. On the north side, the third chapel (left wall) contains an *Annunciation* attributed to the Master of Serumido; the second chapel

has an early 16th-century copy of the fresco of the *Madonna del Giglio* (formerly in the tabernacle outside the church) and a painted Crucifix attributed to Lorenzo Monaco. The first chapel (left wall) has *San Francesco di Paola Healing a Sick Man* by Santi di Tito and, on the altar, a polychrome wooden Crucifix of the 17th century and two later figures.

San Jacopo sopr'Arno
Map 1, 5. Borgo San Jacopo.
Now the Greek Orthodox church. Preceded by a portico of three arches, possibly dating from the 11th century, transported here in 1529 from a demolished church. In the interior, now used for concerts and exhibitions, the Baroque design of 1709 and the 18th-century painted decoration have survived.

San Jacopo tra i Fossi
Map 7, 1. Via de' Benci.
Evangelical church with a fine 18th-century ceiling incorporating a painting by Alessandro Gherardini.

St James's
Map 2, 6. Via Bernardo Rucellai 9. Open for services, admission on request in the morning.
The neo-Gothic American Episcopal church (1908–11). It has good stained glass by Italian craftsmen, including a rose window by Ezio Giovannozzi. A fine new pipe organ, particularly adapted for congregational singing, was installed in 2009, built in Liverpool, UK, by the firm of Willis.

Santa Maria degli Angeli
Map 4, 5. Via degli Alfani 39.
Remodelled in 1676, the **church** is now used for lectures. The unusual interior has a barrel vault with frescoes by Alessandro Gherardini and stuccoes by Vittorio Barbieri and Alessandro Lombardi. In the former refectory

is a *Last Supper* (1543) by Ridolfo del Ghirlandaio, restored in 2000. The cloister on the right of the church has graffiti decoration and lunettes by Bernardino Poccetti and busts attributed to Caccini and Francavilla. Off the cloister is a little chapel (1599) with a fresco in the dome by Poccetti, who probably also painted the altarpiece. There are also sculptured medallions attributed to Caccini and Francavilla.

Also part of the same former monastic complex is the **Rotonda**, an octagonal building begun by Brunelleschi in 1434 as a memorial to Filippo degli Scolari (d. 1424), who served the King of Hungary in a number of battles against the Turks and was nicknamed 'Pippo Spano'—probably after he was made the king's chief officer (*ispán* in Hungarian). Filippo was a cultivated man and a patron of the arts (it is thought that he himself commissioned the project for the Rotonda just before his death), and apparently it was he who called the painter Masolino to Hungary in 1426, where he worked for an Italian patron. The Rotonda was left unfinished in 1437. Modelled on the Temple of Minerva Medica in Rome, it was one of the first centralised buildings of the Renaissance. After a period of use as a church, it was completed as a lecture hall in 1959 and is now used as a language laboratory for Florence University (perhaps not altogether inappropriate for a building built to honour a Florentine who spoke German, Hungarian, Wallachian, Bohemian and Polish).

Santa Maria dei Candeli

Map 4, 7. Corner of Via dei Pilastri. Deconsecrated. Redesigned by Giovanni Battista Foggini in 1704, with a ceiling fresco by Niccolò Lapi.

Santa Maria della Croce al Tempio

Map 7, 2. Via di San Giuseppe.

Deconsecrated church which has frescoes attributed to Bicci di Lorenzo.

Santa Maria Maggiore

Map 1, 3. Via Cerretani. Open 7–12 & 3.30–5.30. The rough exterior in *pietra forte* has (high up on the street corner, left of the two windows) a half-bust of a woman in marble embedded in the masonry, fondly known as 'Berta'. It is almost certainly an ancient Roman carving. The church is of ancient foundation (first mentioned in 1021), and was rebuilt in its present Gothic Cistercian form at the end of the 13th century. The most precious work is in the chapel to the left of the choir: a very unusual painted wood relief of the **Madonna Enthroned**, the date of which has been much discussed. Some scholars considered it a Byzantine work of the 12th century but since restoration it is thought to be a late work by the first great Florentine painter, Coppo di Marcovaldo. Against a bright gold background, and decorated with small, very colourful painted scenes, the Madonna is holding the Child in front of her, in the Byzantine manner.

A single column survives here from the tomb of Brunetto Latini (1220–95), who was Chancellor of the first popular government of 1250–60. Although Dante condemns him to Hell, he also remembers him with great affection (and devotes Canto XV of the *Inferno* to him). The tomb of Bruno Beccuti bears a very worn effigy attributed to Tino di Camaino, but the earlier sarcophagus, which belonged to the Lupicini family and is decorated with their coat of arms and two pelicans, is dated 1272. On the west wall and in the sanctuary are 14th-century frescoes. St Francis is recorded in two painted altarpieces: on the first north altar (by Matteo Rosselli) and on the third south altar (by Pier Dandini). Later works include neo-Gothic stained glass at the east end (1901) and an altarpiece of

Santa Rita, painted in the mid-20th century by the local painter Primo Conti.

Santa Maria a Ricorboli
Beyond map 7, 6. Via Fortini.
In a chapel in the north aisle is a very late, damaged *Madonna and Child* by Giotto.

San Michele Visdomini
Map 1, 4. Via dei Servi.
Also known as San Michelino, this church was demolished in 1363 to make way for the east end of the Duomo, and, incredibly enough, reconstructed on this site a few years later. It is of ancient foundation and is known to have been enlarged by the Visdomini family in the 11th century. Inside, on the right side, is a *Holy Family* by Pontormo (commissioned in 1518 by Francesco Pucci). The other altarpieces are by late 16th-century painters (Empoli, Il Poppi and Passignano). The 18th-century vault fresco in the crossing showing the *Fall of Satan* is by Niccolò Lapi. In a chapel at the east end are fragmentary 14th-century frescoes and sinopie attributed to Spinello Aretino, and a 14th-century wood Crucifix. A plaque on the façade records the burial here of the great painter Filippino Lippi.

San Niccolò al Ceppo (oratory of)
Map 7, 1. Via Pandolfini 5.
Built in 1561 for a confraternity founded in the 14th century (now used for concerts). In the vestibule are two oval paintings of saints by Onorio Marinari (1695) and a *trompe l'œil* ceiling by Giovanni Domenico Ferretti (c. 1735). The stucco statue of the *Madonna and Child* is by Camillo Camillani (1572). The oratory has 17th-century wooden benches and a frescoed ceiling by Ferretti, Pietro Anderlini and Domenico and Francesco Papi. The altarpiece of the *Crucifixion* is by Francesco Curradi, and on the walls are a

Visitation and *St Nicholas with Two Members of the Confraternity* by Giovanni Antonio Sogliani (1517–21). The *Crucifixion with St Nicholas of Bari and St Francis* is by Fra' Angelico. Outside on the corner of the street (Canto alla Badessa) is a tabernacle with a 16th-century fresco of the *Annunciation* by Giovanni Balducci.

San Paolino
Map 3, 7. Via Palazzuolo.
Founded in the 10th century, it has a bare façade. The interior was rebuilt in 1669 by Giovanni Battista Balatri and is interesting for its 17th–18th-century paintings. The first south chapel contains two Albizi funerary monuments attributed to the *bottega* of Giovanni Battista Foggini. In the second chapel there is an *Annunciation* by a follower of Giovanni Antonio Sogliani and two paintings by (left) Francesco di Antonio Ciseri (1891) and (right) Volterrano. The south transept has a polychrome marble altar and an altarpiece of the *Death of St Joseph* by Giovanni Domenico Ferretti. On either side of this are the *Marriage of the Virgin* by Vincenzo Meucci and the *Rest on the Flight* by Ignazio Hugford. In the sanctuary is the *Ecstasy of St Paul* by Francesco Curradi. The north transept has a marble altar by Girolamo Ticciati and another altarpiece by Francesco Curradi. In the first north chapel is *Christ in the Garden* by Tommaso Gherardini and (right wall), the *Adoration of the Magi* by Giovanni Domenico Ferretti. The pretty 18th-century confessionals have tondi painted by Ottaviano Dandini.

San Piero in Gattolino
Map 5, 6. Via Romana.
Known to have existed by the 9th century, it was rebuilt in the late 16th or early 17th century largely financed by a parishioner called Ser Umido. In the sanctuary there

is a *Madonna and Child* attributed to an anonymous master named 'Serumido' from the alternative name of the church (also attributed to Alessandro Gherardini). On the north side is a small 15th-century wood Crucifix. The oratory off the south side has pretty decorations with quadratura of 1770.

San Salvatore al Vescovo

Map 1, 3. Piazza dell'Olio.
Incorporated in the huge Palazzo Arcivescovile, partially reconstructed by Giovanni Antonio Dosio in 1584 (the façade was rebuilt in 1895 when the piazza was enlarged). The church interior was entirely frescoed in 1737–38 with quadratura by Pietro Anderlini and an *Ascension* in the vault by Vincenzo Meucci. The frescoes in the apse and dome, and the monochrome figures of the Apostles, are all by Giovanni Domenico Ferretti. The little Romanesque façade of the earlier church can be seen in Piazza dell'Olio.

San Salvi (ex-convent of)

Map p. 408. Via San Salvi 16. Open 8.30–1.50; closed Mon; T: 055 238 8603. Bus no. 6 from Stazione Santa Maria Novella via Piazza San Marco or no. 20 from Piazza San Marco to the request stop on Via Lungo L'Affrico. Walk back 10m or so and take Via Tito Speri to the church of San Michele. The entrance to the convent is just round the corner in Via San Salvi.
The refectory of the former abbey of San Salvi contains a celebrated fresco of the *Last Supper* by Andrea del Sarto—known as the *Cenacolo di San Salvi*—and the conventual buildings house an excellent small museum of mainly 16th-century works, many of them from deconsecrated churches or museum deposits. Although a short way outside the historic centre of the city, this is an extremely pleasant place to visit since it is usually very peaceful, and the *Last Supper* is the most famous fresco

of the subject (*see p. 152*) in Italy after that by Leonardo da Vinci in Milan.

St Salvius was a monk and hermit who was appointed bishop of Albi in France before his death c. 615. The abbey on this site, dedicated to him, was of the Vallombrosan Order of Benedictines, founded by St John Gualbert (*see below*). It was restored in the 16th century when the monks commissioned the *Last Supper* from Andrea del Sarto. From 1534 a closed order of Vallombrosan nuns took over the convent and they remained here until it was suppressed in 1817.

John Gualbert was a Florentine nobleman who changed his way of life after he saw a Crucifix in the church of San Miniato al Monte bow approvingly to him when he pardoned his brother's assassin. He founded a Benedictine monastery in the hills of Vallombrosa in 1040, which is still one of the most famous monasteries near Florence. The new order flourished and another monastery was created nine years later at Badia a Passignano, a short way south of Florence. It was there that Gualbert died (in 1073) and is buried. One of the first churches to be founded after his death was Santa Trínita in Florence, which preserves a reliquary and 15th-century frescoes of his life. He was canonised in 1193.

The **long gallery**, with fine vaulting, is hung with large 16th-century altarpieces, all of them labelled. The earliest works include a detached fresco attributed to Davide Ghirlandaio, a *Madonna and Child with Saints* by Cosimo Rosselli and a *Trinity* by Giovanni Antonio Sogliani. The two lunettes are by Suor Plautilla Nelli, interesting as one of the very first women painters recorded by Vasari. She was a Dominican nun and a prolific painter, although only very few of her works have yet been identified. The *Crucifix with St Francis and St Mary Magdalene* is a fine

The three heads symbolising the Holy Trinity of God the Father, Son and Holy Ghost, painted by Andrea del Sarto as the central tondo on the arch above his *Last Supper*.

painting with a lovely landscape by Antonio del Ceraiolo. This painting is one of two Vasari mentions in his *Lives of the Artists* by this painter who started out his career in the workshop of Lorenzo di Credi and later worked with Ridolfo del Ghirlandaio. He was clearly influenced by the painters who belonged to the school of San Marco and inspired by Savonarola's teachings. He is little-known today but art historians have identified a corpus of some 30 attributed works to him. Other 16th-century painters represented here include Francesco Brina, Giovanni Balducci and Il Poppi. In the room at the end, there are some very beautifully carved reliefs made by Benedetto da Rovezzano, commissioned from him in 1505 for a funerary monument which was to have been erected in the abbey of Badia a Passignano to commemorate St John Gualbert. The pieces were wilfully damaged during the Imperial siege of 1530 (when the

Holy Roman Emperor Charles V sent an army to Florence to reinstate the Medici).

Two more rooms, one with a lavabo by Benedetto da Rovezzano and the other with a huge fireplace which served the convent kitchen, contain paintings by contemporaries or followers of Andrea del Sarto. Beneath the fireplace has been hung a detached fresco of the *Noli me Tangere* by Franciabigio (with a particularly lovely figure of the Magdalene). On the right is a lovely portrait of a lady in a turban, a copy by the little-known artist Tommaso di Stefano Lunetti of a work by Domenico Puligo. Other 16th-century works in this room include a *Madonna* with the two most famous Vallombrosan saints, John Gualbert and Bernardo degli Uberti, by Maso di San Friano, a tondo of the *Madonna and Child and Young St John* by Gerolamo della Pacchia and an *Annunciation* by Giovanni Antonio Sogliani. The *Madonna and Child* with Saints attributed to a painter active in Fiesole is dated 1493. In the adjoining room there is another good work by Sogliani, an interesting Madonna and Child by Giuliano Bugiardini and a Madonna Enthroned between Sts Francis and Zenobius by Raffaellino del Garbo. The painting of St Jerome in the Desert by Bartolomeo di Giovanni includes some lovely details (note the barn owl).

The **refectory** contains Andrea del Sarto's celebrated Cenacolo (1511–27), a masterpiece of Florentine fresco which is remarkable for its colouring and dramatic movement. Each disciple is beautifully painted; Judas is shown seated on Christ's right (suggesting with his hand that he is the traitor) and St John on His left. The bare feet and hand gestures of all those present are fascinating. The austerity of the setting (even the table is bare except for a few plates and pieces of bread) is relieved by the charming detail of two servants observing the scene from a balcony above. It is extremely well preserved, as the convent was a closed order and remained inaccessible until the early 19th century. The tondi of saints and the Trinity (illustrated opposite) on the intrados of the arch were the first part of the fresco to be painted (the grottesche are by del Sarto's little-known collaborator Andrea di Cosimo Feltrini). Some of the studies made by Andrea for this work are shown in the drawings displayed in two cases (facsimiles of the originals in the Uffizi).

Around the walls are displayed works connected to Andrea del Sarto, including two autograph works: a very ruined fresco of the Annunciation detached from the Sdrucciolo di Orsanmichele, and a Noli me Tangere from the convent of San Gallo, with a lovely landscape. The small Crucifixion with Tobias and the Archangel Raphael (with Tobias' dog in the foreground), which once hung in the Tribuna of the Uffizi, is attributed to him, and the four

paintings depicting the story of St John the Baptist are fine copies from works by him. The detached fresco of the Adoration of the Shepherds is by Franciabigio. Above the door is a worn fresco by Pontormo with a pontifical emblem and allegorical figures detached from the portico of the Santissima Annunziata, and there are two panel paintings here by Pontormo: the Madonna and Child with the Young St John and St Catherine of Alexandria.

San Michele a San Salvi is a 14th–16th-century church (open 8.30–12 & 4–7) preceded by a worn portico. At the west end are detached frescoes including a Madonna and Child by Lorenzo di Bicci from a street tabernacle. In the sanctuary are ceiling frescoes by Vincenzo Meucci. In a chapel off the south transept there are interesting remains of early 15th-century frescoes in terraverde and in another chapel close by is a very unusual marble high relief of Beata Umiltà (Rosanese Negusanti, 1226–1310), attributed to Orcagna. She is holding an open book and a bunch of twigs, and the lamb's skin over her head is a symbol of humility. Her wrinkled face shows her age. From here you can visit the charming late 14th-century **cloister** (the small upper loggia was added in the 15th century), where, over the entrance to the chapter house, there is a lunette relief of St John Gualbert and Two Vallombrosan Monks by Benedetto da Rovezzano.

San Sebastiano 'dei Bini' (oratory of) Map 6, 3. Via Romana. Open Fri, Sat, Sun, 3–6. Has some interesting works by Giovanni Bilivert, Baccio d'Agnolo, Pier Francesco Foschi and others.

Santo Stefano al Ponte Map 1, 5. Via Por Santa Maria. In a secluded little piazza, this is a very old church, first built in 969, but severely damaged in the Uffizi bomb explosion in 1993 (*see p. 110*). The handsome Romanesque decoration of the façade dates from 1233. The interior (now used as a concert hall) was altered by Ferdinando Tacca in 1649. It contains altarpieces by Santi di Tito and Matteo Rosselli, a painting by Jacopo di Cione, and a bronze altar frontal of the *Stoning of St Stephen* by Ferdinando Tacca. At the elaborate east end, the altar steps (removed from Santa Trínita) are a remarkable Mannerist work by Buontalenti (1574). Beneath is a large crypt.

San Tommaso d'Aquino (oratory of)
Map 4, 7. Via della Pergola 8.
Built in 1567 to a design by Santi di Tito, who also painted the high altarpiece with the *Crucifix and St Thomas*.

Scalzo, Chiostro dello
Map 4, 3. Via Cavour 69. Open Mon, Thur and Sat 8.15–1.50; T: 055 238 8604.
This charming cloister has fine monochrome frescoes by Andrea del Sarto (1510–26). They depict the life of St John the Baptist (two of the scenes are by Franciabigio).

GARDENS

Giardino Corsi
Map 5, 4. Via Romana.
A delightful little raised garden laid out in 1801–10 by Giuseppe Manetti, with fine trees. The house (now the Pensione Annalena) at Via Romana 34, with a plant nursery, was the principal residence of Luigi Dallapiccola, a composer (1904–75) who lived most of his life in Florence and is known for his opera *Ulisse*, completed in 1968.

Giardino Torrigiani
Map 5, 4. Open a few days each year.

The biggest private garden in Florence, with fine trees. It was created by Pietro Torrigiani (1773–1848) and encloses a stretch of town walls built by Cosimo I. The fantastic neo-Gothic tower was built by Gaetano Baccani in 1821 as an astronomical observatory. The gardens are decorated with 19th-century sculptures by Pio Fedi, a pupil of Lorenzo Bartolini, whose former studio at Via de' Serragli 99 still has sculptures by him on its façade (a tondo held up by two angels, his bust, and lions).

LIBRARIES

Archivio di Stato
Map 7, 2. Viale della Giovine Italia.
The Florence National Archives, housed in a building designed by Italo Gamberini. Founded in 1582, the archives date back to the 8th century and provide scholars with a wealth of information on the political and economic history of the city.

Archivio Storico del Comune di Firenze
Map 4, 7. Via dell'Oriuolo 33.

The 18th-century Palazzo Bastogi houses the archives of the Comune of Florence, established by Peter Leopold in 1781 (the documents cover the period up until 1960). The main hall has Neoclassical stuccoes and painted decoration.

Biblioteca del Consiglio Regionale (Identità Toscana)
Map 3, 6. Palazzo Panciatichi, Via Cavour 2.
Excellent small lending library specialising

in the political, social, cultural and environmental history of Tuscany. It is especially interesting for its 20th-century material on the smaller municipalities.

Biblioteca Magliabechiana
Map 1, 6. Galleria degli Uffizi.
Named after Angelo Magliabechi, librarian of the Palatina and Laurenziana libraries under Cosimo III. At his death in 1714 he left funds for a library building as well as his own library of 30,000 books, and it was built in a former theatre in the Uffizi building under the direction of Giovanni Battista Foggini, and first opened to the public in 1747. As its holdings grew, space ran out and in 1935 it was moved to a new building and renamed the Biblioteca Nazionale (*see below*). The magnificent main reading room, flooded with light, has been carefully restored. The specialised library connected to the Galleria degli Uffizi is now housed here.

Biblioteca Marucelliana
Map 3, 6. Via Cavour 43–47.
Founded by Francesco di Alessandro Marucelli (1625–1703) and opened to the public in 1752 in the present building, built (in the garden of the Marucelli property) by Alessandro Dori (the reading room retains its 18th-century bookcases and the holdings now number over 300,000 volumes). It is particularly rich in works on Florence and also has a very fine collection of prints and drawings (particularly important for its 17th-century works). The original wood model of the library can be seen through a window from Via Cavour.

Biblioteca Nazionale
Map 7, 3. Piazza Cavalleggeri.
The most important library in Florence: its origins go back to a bequest from the great librarian Angelo Magliabechi. The Libreria Magliabechiana (*see above*) was moved here in 1935, to a new building begun especially for it in 1911 by Cesare Bazzani. It incorporates the Biblioteca Palatina-Medicea (1711) and the library of Ferdinand III (1861), together with several monastic collections. It includes an important collection of material relating to Dante and Galileo. It became a copyright library for books published in Italy in 1870. In 1966, nearly a third of the library's holdings was damaged when the Arno flooded, and an inscription beneath the portico recalls the numerous Italians and foreigners who came to help salvage the precious volumes from the water and mud. A restoration centre next to the church of Sant'Ambrogio is still at work conserving them.

Biblioteca delle Oblate
Map 4, 7. Via dell'Oriuolo.
Housed in the ex-convent of the Oblate, this is Florence's newest library (opened in 2006), with a café, WiFi and places where you can listen to music or watch films.

Istituto Geografico Militare
Map 4, 5. Via Battisti. Open Mon–Fri 9–12.
This institute has a remarkable cartographic library with works up to 1862 and an archive (maps from 1863–1963). The later material, principally maps made after 1963, is kept in a splendid building on Viale Strozzi (*map 3, 4*), where maps are also on sale.

MUSEUMS

Collezione Della Ragione
At the time of writing none of the collections were *on display but there are long-term plans to make space for them at the Leopoldine in Piazza Santa*

Maria Novella (see p. 190).

The Alberto della Ragione collection of 20th-century Italian art includes mostly representational works by Arturo Tosi, Carlo Carrà, Giorgio Morandi, Ottone Rosai, Gino Severini, Mario Sironi, Felice Casorati, Giorgio de Chirico, Arturo Martini, Virgilio Guidi, Massimo Campigli, Filippo de Pisis, Lucio Fontana, Marino Marini, Carlo Levi, Mario Mafai, Scipione, Giacomo Manzù, Corrado Cagli and Renato Guttuso. Other collections of 20th-century Italian art owned by the municipality include 58 paintings by Ottone Rosai and twelve by Filippo de Pisis.

Museo di Antropologia ed Etnologia
Map 1, 4. Via del Proconsolo 12. Open 9–1 except Wed, Sat 9–5; T: 055 239 6449.
Housed in the huge Palazzo Nonfinito, begun in 1593 by Buontalenti but left unfinished, hence its name. The great courtyard is attributed to Cigoli. The collection was founded in 1869 by Paolo Mantegazza and it was the first museum of its kind in Europe. It is still the most important ethnological and anthropological museum in Italy. The collection, still displayed in its charming old-fashioned showcases (although not very well labelled), covers Africa (notably Ethiopia, Eritrea, Somalia and Libya); north Pakistan (a rare collection of material relating to the Kalash people); South America (including mummies from Peru, collected in 1883) and Mexico; Asia (Melanesia, Sumatra, Tibet and Japan, with the Fosco Maraini collection of Ainu material); and artefacts from the Pacific Ocean, probably acquired by Captain Cook on his last voyage in 1776–79.

Museo Diocesano di Santo Stefano al Ponte
Map 1, 5. Santo Stefano al Ponte. Not open regularly. For information, T: 055 225843.
Displays works of art removed for safe-keeping from churches, some of them now deconsecrated. There are some interesting Tuscan works from the 14th–15th centuries. The most important works are in the sacristy. The *Madonna and Child* by Giotto (from the church of San Giorgio alla Costa, dated 1295–1300) has been heavily restored after damage in 1993. Also here are two Madonnas by Domenico di Michelino; a bust of the Blessed Davanzati by Pietro Tacca; an *Annunciation*, a *Madonna* and a triptych by the Master of the Straus Madonna; an *Annunciation* by Bicci di Lorenzo; *St Julian* by Masolino (c. 1420); and an exquisite predella with the *Adoration of the Magi* by Paolo Uccello (c. 1437). The carved wooden *Lamentation* group is by the *bottega* of Orcagna (1360–65) and the reliquary bust of San Cresci is by Bernardo Holzmann (to a design by Giovanni Battista Foggini).

Museo di Firenze com'era
Closed at the time of writing. Formerly in the ex-convent of the Oblate (map 4, 7). There were plans at the time of writing to move it to Palazzo Vecchio, where it will be renamed the Museo della Città.
The most interesting items in the museum collection are as follows: a 19th-century copy in tempera of the *Pianta della Catena*, a famous woodcut of Florence attributed to Lucantonio degli Uberti and made around 1482, which is named after the chain (*catena*) which frames it. It is a copy of an engraving by the print-maker and cartographer Francesco Rosselli (half-brother of the painter Cosimo Rosselli). It shows a bird's eye view in oblique perspective of the city from the hill of Monteoliveto to the southwest, and it includes a portrayal of the artist himself sitting in the foreground as he draws the scene.

The first topographical plan of Florence, a magnificent work drawn by Stefano Bonsignori in 1584 for Grand Duke Francesco

I. It makes use of an ideal perspective from an elevated viewpoint, and the city is represented using extremely accurate planimetric measurements. This copy is the only coloured version which survives.

The three sets of huge keys used to lock three gates in the city walls (San Frediano, San Gallo and Porta Romana). Those of San Gallo were lost in 1865 but turned up at a Sotheby's sale in 1936. The charming series of lunettes of the Medici villas and their gardens are by the Flemish painter Justus Utens (1599) and are extremely interesting as a record of these properties. There are maps of Florence from the 17th–19th centuries and views of the city by Thomas Patch and Giuseppe Maria Terreni, and engravings by Telemaco Signorini of the Mercato Vecchio in 1874 before its demolition. The fine series of engravings (1754), with views of the city and villas in the environs, are by Giuseppe Zocchi. The elevations and sections of the Duomo, Baptistery and Campanile published by Sgrilli in 1755, were drawn by Giovanni Battista Nelli, who made the first measured survey of these buildings for the Opera del Duomo. The famous *Fiera of Impruneta* was engraved by Jacques Callot in 1620. There are also prehistoric and Roman finds and a model of the Roman town.

Museo Fiorentino di Preistoria
Map 4, 7. Via Sant'Egidio 21 (also entered from the ex-convent of the Oblate in Via dell'Oriuolo). Open Mon 2–5, Tues and Thur 9.30–4.30, Wed, Fri and Sat 9.30–12.30; closed Sun; T: 055 295159.
Museum of prehistory with well-labelled material arranged chronologically and geographically. The lower hall is dedicated to Italy, and includes a human skull of the Palaeolithic era found at Olmo near Arezzo in 1865; the upper hall displays material

from Europe, Africa and Asia, including an interesting collection from the Graziosi expedition to the Sahara.

Museo di Geologia e Paleontologia and Museo di Mineralogia e Litologia
Map 4, 3. Via La Pira 4. Open Mon, Tues, Thur, Fri, Sun 9–1, Sat 9–5; closed Wed; T: 055 275 7536 and 055 275 7537.
The geological and palaeontological collection, the most important of its kind in Italy, includes material from the grand-ducal collections: vertebrates, skeletons of mammals from the Lower Pleistocene period, a gallery of invertebrates and plants, and a research section. The mineral and lithological collection includes samples of minerals and rocks from Elba, the Medici collection of worked stones, and a huge Brazilian topaz weighing 151kg (the second largest in the world).

Gipsoteca (Istituto d'Arte)
Map 6, 5. Porta Romana. Admission by appointment at the art school.
This art school just outside Porta Romana, in the former royal stables, owns a remarkable museum of plaster casts of antique and Renaissance sculptures, including many by Donatello and Michelangelo. They were mostly made at the end of the 19th and the beginning of the 20th centuries by Giuseppe Lelli; his son left them to the Institute in 1922. The collection is arranged in a splendid hall. Nearby is a building known as Le Pagliere, which serves as a deposit for restored sculptures from the Boboli Gardens.

Museo della Porcellana di Doccia
Viale Pratese 31, Sesto Fiorentino. Bus 28 from Stazione Santa Maria Novella. Open Wed–Sat 10–1 & 2–6; T: 055 420 7767.
Next to the Ginori porcelain factory in the northern suburb of Sesto Fiorentino, in a fine

modern building by Piero Berardi (1965). Contains a large, well-displayed collection of porcelain made in the Doccia factory founded by Marchese Carlo Ginori in 1735. The exhibit includes early pieces painted by Carl Wendelin Anreiter von Zirnfeld of Vienna, and the first models by Gaspero Bruschi and Massimiliano Soldani. The firm, known as Richard-Ginori since 1896, continues to flourish. Ginori seconds can be purchased from the warehouse across the road.

La Specola
Map 6, 3. Via Romana.
Housed in Palazzo Torrigiani, built in 1775 by Gaspare Maria Paoletti as a natural history museum, this is the largest collection of its kind in Italy, known as La Specola from the astronomical observatory in a small tower, built here by Grand Duke Peter Leopold. It was here, in 1814, that Sir Humphrey Davy and Michael Faraday used Galileo's 'great burning glass' to explode the diamond. The

Neoclassical Tribuna di Galileo on the first floor, with elaborate marble and mosaic decorations, was commissioned by Leopold II in 1841 to celebrate the great scientist. It was built by Giuseppe Martelli and the statue of Galileo is by Aristodemo Costoli. On the third floor is the Zoological Collection (*open 9.30–4.30; closed Mon*). The exhibits, most of them collected during expeditions in the late 19th and early 20th centuries, are still charmingly arranged in old-fashioned showcases. There is also a remarkable display of anatomical models in wax (around 1,400 of them), made in 1775–1814 by Clemente Susini and others, which illustrate all the parts of the human body and include a lifesize figure of a man, known as '*lo scorticato*' since the skin is entirely absent. At a time when corpses were not used to study anatomy these were of particular interest, and although they were never actually used by the medical profession, they were one of the great 'sights' for visitors to Florence throughout the 19th century.

PALACES, VILLAS & FORTS

Art Nouveau Houses
Beyond map 7, 2. Via Scipione Ammirato.
The two best examples of this style are Villino Broggi-Caraceni (no. 99, built in 1911) and Villino Ravazzini (no. 101, dating from 1907–08). Both are by Giovanni Michelazzi with ceramic decoration by Galileo Chini. There is another house of the same date by Michelazzi at Borgo Ognissanti 26 (*map 2, 8*). In the southern part of the town, at Via Giano della Bella 9 and 13 (*map 5, 4*), there are two more well-preserved Art Nouveau villas.

Palazzo Antinori-Corsini
Map 7, 1. Borgo Santa Croce 6.
The beautiful courtyard dates from the end of the 15th century.

Palazzo Borghese
Map 1, 6. Via Ghibellina 110.
This grandiose pile, with its Neoclassical façade by Gaetano Baccani (1822), was built in less than a year by Camillo Borghese, husband of Pauline Bonaparte (sister of Napoleon), for a party to celebrate the second marriage of Ferdinand III. The elaborate period rooms (now used by a club; *admission sometimes granted*) are heavily decorated with chandeliers and gilded mirrors.

Palazzo Capponi
Map 4, 3–5. Via Gino Capponi 26.
Built in 1698–1713 by Carlo Fontana, with a fine garden. The poet Giuseppe Giusti died here in 1850.

Palazzo dei Congressi

Map 3, 3. Via Valfonda 3.
International conference centre opened in 1964 on the site of a Contini-Bonacossi villa. Its park was created in 1871 by the French poet Alphonse Lamartine.

Palazzo Corsini sul Prato

Map 2, 6. Via Il Prato 58.
The present residence of the Corsini family. Begun in 1591 by Buontalenti, it was acquired in 1621 by Filippo di Lorenzo Corsini, who employed Gherardo Silvani to complete it. The fine garden has interesting statuary and parterres (*viewing on request, Mon–Sat 9–1 & 2–5*).

Fortezza da Basso

Map 3, 3. Open for exhibitions.
This huge pentagonal fortress, designed by Antonio da Sangallo the Younger, is of the first importance in the history of military architecture. The exterior wall in brick and *pietra forte* is still intact. Sangallo's keep on Viale Strozzi incorporates the medieval tower of Porta Faenza. The fortress was erected by order of Alessandro de' Medici in 1534 to strengthen his position as Duke of Florence (he had been brought to power by the armies of the Holy Roman Emperor in 1530) and as a refuge in times of trouble. It became a symbol of Medici tyranny and Alessandro was assassinated here by his cousin Lorenzaccio in 1537. It was very soon obsolete as the grand dukes had little need to defend themselves. Ever since, it has been something of a white elephant—used at various times as a prison, an arsenal and a barracks. It became an exhibition centre in 1967. The area within the walls was brutally transformed when a huge prefabricated steel building covered with aluminium was built in 1978, and another (circular) one in 1987. A long 19th-century building has been used since 1966 as a restoration centre. Public gardens have been laid out on the glacis. The Fortezza is used as a venue for the Mostra dell'Artigianato (an old-established international exhibition of artisans' work) and the prestigious 'Pitti' fashion shows, both held annually.

Palazzo Frescobaldi

Map 6, 1. Via Santo Spirito 9–13.
Still the residence of this well-known Florentine family, this consists of two adjoining palaces: above the door of the larger one, at no. 11, is a copy of a little bronze satyr by Giambologna. You can usually see the garden from here, and nobody seems to mind if you venture into it through the passageway which gives access to several interior courtyards (where the expert carpet dealer Boralevi has his showroom). The garden was replanted at the end of the 19th century, and has circular bay hedges, pots of azaleas and a Baroque grotto, as well as a magnificent old wisteria.

Palazzo Giugni

Map 4, 5. Via degli Alfani 48.
A beautiful Florentine palace, the courtyard of which can usually be seen through the open door. It is a characteristic work by Ammannati (1571) with a small garden (with orange trees and a grotto). The interesting garden façade, with a loggia, bears a copy of the family coat of arms (the original can be seen in the courtyard). The international Lyceum Club for ladies has occupied rooms on the first floor since 1953 and it maintains a tradition of high-quality concerts, exhibitions and lectures. Founded in 1908 by Constance Smedley (who had founded the first such club in London in 1904), the first exhibition of the Impressionists in Italy was held here in 1910. The well-kept rooms are delightfully furnished and include a library

and a 17th-century *galleria* which preserves
its decorations intact, including paintings by
Alessandro Gherardini.

Palazzo Gondi

Map 1, 6. Piazza San Firenze 2.
A very fine palace built c. 1489 by Giuliano
da Sangallo with a pretty little courtyard (now
occupied by a florist). It was completed (and
the façade on Via de' Gondi added) with great
care by Giuseppe Poggi in 1872–84.

Palazzo Guicciardini

Map 6, 3. Via Guicciardini 15.
This palace was reconstructed by Gherardo
Silvani in 1620, on the site of the residence
of Luigi di Piero Guicciardini, *Gonfaloniere di
Giustizia*, which was burnt down during the
Ciompi revolt in 1378 (*see p. 227*). The great
commentator on Florentine affairs Francesco
Guicciardini was born here in 1483. On his
retirement from political life in 1530, he wrote
his famous *History of Italy*. Part of the façade
has remains of graffiti decoration. In the
courtyard is a large stucco relief of *Hercules
and Cacus* attributed to Antonio Pollaiolo.
Beyond can be seen the little garden, created
in the 17th century but replanted in 1922. On
the wall are numerous ancient reliefs.

Palazzo Lanfredini (British Institute)

Map 6, 1. Lungarno Guicciardini 9.
By Baccio d'Agnolo, with bright graffiti
decoration (restored). On part of the ground
floor and first floor are the library and the
office of the director of the British Institute,
a non-profit independent institution whose
role is to maintain a library of English books
in the city, and to promote British culture in
Italy and Italian culture to English-speaking
visitors. It was founded in 1917 by a group
of Anglo-Florentines and received a Royal
Charter in 1923. The Lending Library (with

about 50,000 volumes, the largest collection
of English books in Italy) was named after
its benefactor, Harold Acton, in 1989 (and,
on his death in 1994, he bequeathed the
premises to the Institute). Augmented over
the years by the donations of Anglo-American
residents, it can be used for a small fee and
retains the atmosphere of a 19th-century
general browsing library. The reading room
has comfortable armchairs and English
newspapers. Public lectures are held here
on most Wednesdays (usually at 6pm). The
Institute is also known for its language school
and courses in art history.

In the late 18th century there were two inns
on this Lungarno which were favourite places
for the English to stay. 'Charles's' was run by
an Irishman called Hatfield, and amongst his
guests was Edward Gibbon when he came
through Florence on his way to Rome. 'Widow
Vannini's', at the foot of Ponte alla Carraia, was
where Tobias Smollett often stayed.

Palazzo Manelli-Riccardi

Map 1, 1. Via Faenza.
Dates from the mid-16th century. Its painted
façade is now very ruined but the fine bust of
Ferdinando I, made for it at the same time by
Giovanni Bandini, still survives.

Palazzo Manetti

Map 6, 1. Via di Santo Spirito 23.
With a plain stone façade and just eight
windows, dating from the 15th century.
This was the home of Sir Horace Mann, who
lived in Florence in 1740–86 and served as
English resident and later envoy to the Tuscan
court. He invited Horace Walpole and the
poet Thomas Gray to stay in his guest-house
nearby (Casa Ambrogi, one of the houses at
the south end of Ponte Vecchio which were
destroyed in 1944) during their tour of the
Continent. Although Mann and Walpole

never met again, they corresponded regularly over the next 40 years. Mann's letters provide a remarkable picture of 18th-century Florence even though Walpole's missives have far greater literary worth. Mann, although perhaps rather a dreary character, was recorded by many English visitors to Florence in the late 18th century for his kindness, and at the end of his life he was promoted to the office of Minister Plenipotentiary. It was perhaps partly through him that Florence became so attractive to English visitors, many of whom chose to stay here for a while on their Grand Tour rather than hurrying on to Rome as those before them had done.

Casino Mediceo
Map 4, 3. Via Cavour 57.
Now occupied by law courts, this was built for Francesco I by Bernardo Buontalenti (1568–74) and used by the duke as a studio for his scientific studies.

Casa Morra
Map 7, 1. Borgo Santa Croce 8.
This house belonged to Giorgio Vasari and still contains frescoes by him.

Palazzo Niccolini
Map 3, 6. Via dei Servi 15.
Designed in 1548–50 by Baccio d'Agnolo, who built a number of fine palaces in Florence in the 16th century, some of the best of which are on Via Tornabuoni. Its beautiful façade is typical of Florentine palaces of this period. The small courtyard has graffiti decoration, and in the garden beyond is an elaborate double loggia, probably by Giovanni Antonio Dosio.

Palazzo degli Orti Oricellari
Map 2, 6. Via degli Orti Oricellari. Open on certain days of the year.

Now owned by a bank, this palace contains a fresco by Pietro da Cortona. The Orti Oricellari were famous as a Renaissance *selva*, or forest: all that survives today is the colossal 17th-century statue of *Polyphemus* by Antonio Novelli (an extraordinary sight which can also be seen in winter, when the trees are no longer in leaf, from outside the garden in Via Bernardo Rucellai).

Palazzo Pandolfini
Map 4, 3. Via San Gallo 74.
Built in 1516–20 as a villa (then on the outskirts of the town) for Giannozzo Pandolfini, Bishop of Troia, who is recorded in the handsome inscription. The rustication and pedimented windows are more typical of Roman buildings of this time, and it is known that the palace was designed by Raphael, even though it was executed after he had left for Rome, by the two brothers Giovanni Francesco and Aristotile da Sangallo (members of a large family of architects at work between Florence and Rome in the 15th–16th centuries). The main door into the portico is almost always open so you can also see the pretty garden façade. The symbol of the Pandolfini (the dolphin), who still own the palace, is present on the pilasters and capitals and even on the old iron lantern hanging in the portico.

Palazzo Pazzi-Quaratesi
Map 1, 4. Via del Proconsolo 10.
Handsome palace attributed to Giuliano da Maiano (1458–69). The Pazzi coat of arms (removed from the exterior) is displayed in the vestibule which leads to a pretty courtyard (with good capitals).

Palazzo dei Pucci
Map 3, 6. Via dei Servi.
One of the largest palaces in the city, named

after the old-established Florentine family who still live here. Emilio Pucci was a famous fashion designer. The central part of the long façade dates from the 16th century and is in part attributed to Ammannati; the wings on either side are 17th-century extensions. On the corner is the worn Pucci coat of arms by Baccio da Montelupo.

Palazzo di San Clemente
Map 4, 3. Corner of Via Micheli and Via Gino Capponi.
This is an interesting building by Gherardo Silvani, one of the most prolific Florentine architects of the 17th century. In the entrance hall is the British royal coat of arms. In 1777 the palace was bought by Charles Stuart, the Young Pretender (Bonnie Prince Charlie), who was born in Rome in 1720. After his defeat by the English at Culloden in 1746, he spent some years in France, where he assumed the title Charles III of Great Britain, but where his habitual drunkenness cost him many of his supporters. He retired to Florence, where he also stayed at the Palazzo Corsini and Palazzo Guadagni. In 1772 he married Louisa, Countess of Albany, though the marriage was a disaster and she fled from here to the nearby Convento delle Bianchette in 1780, before beginning a liaison with the dramatist Vittorio Alfieri. The Young Pretender died in Rome in 1788. He is buried in the Vatican grottoes.

Palazzo Spinelli
Map 7, 1. Borgo Santa Croce 10.
Built in 1460–70, this has good graffiti decoration on the façade and in the courtyard. Numerous other 15th-century palaces were once decorated in this way.

Palazzo Strozzi-Niccolini
Map 1, 4. Piazza del Duomo.
This bears a 19th-century plaque and bust

of Donatello since it stands on the site of a house where the sculptor had his studio. The nearby Palazzo Strozzi-Sacrati, also in Piazza del Duomo, is now the seat of the president of the region of Tuscany.

Villa il Tasso
Beyond map 7, 6. Via Benedetto Fortini 30. Open to scholars by prior arrangement.
The art historian Roberto Longhi lived here from 1930 until his death in 1970. His collection of paintings includes works by Caravaggio and Guido Reni. The oldest part of the house dates from the late 15th century, but Longhi added a library wing in 1939.

Palazzo Torrigiani (*see La Specola; p. 338*).

Villino Trollope
Map 3, 4. Piazza dell'Indipendenza.
The piazza was laid out in 1869 as the first of the 19th-century squares in Florence. At the north corner stands the Villino Trollope, where Fanny Trollope lived from 1849 until her death in 1863. Her son Anthony wrote *Doctor Thorne* here in 1857. In 1887 Thomas Hardy stayed in a *pensione* in the building.

Palazzo Vivarelli-Colonna
Map 7, 1. Via Ghibellina 30.
Seat of the Assessorato alla Cultura (the city's cultural department). The interior is interesting for its early 19th-century frescoes by Angiolo Angiolini and Francesco Nenci. The little walled garden, which is open to the public on some days, was laid out in the early 18th century, with an elaborate Baroque wall-fountain in the form of a grotto with shells added in the 19th century, and a painted background. The central fountain, decorated with an eagle and a serpent, is surrounded by Renaissance parterres, with beds marked out in *pietra serena*.

Walter Savage Landor house

Map 5, 4. Via della Chiesa 93.

Walter Savage Landor died here in 1864. He was a famous poet in his day and had lived from 1829–35 in the Villa Gherardesca at San Domenico below Fiesole: his extravagant, opinionated personality made him one of the best-known foreign residents in Florence. He was befriended by Robert Browning, who lived nearby at Casa Guidi (*see p. 267*).

Casa Zuccari

Map 4, 5. Via Giuseppe Giusti 43.

This little two-storey house with rustication and red brick (opposite the excellent German Institute library at no. 44) was built by the painter Federico Zuccari as his studio when he was called to Florence in 1574, the year of Vasari's death, in order to complete the frescoes on the cupola of the Duomo. The bizarre façade (which bears the date 1568 and Zuccari's signature above the two upper windows) has three unfinished reliefs, or trophies, of artists' materials and tools (the originals are now kept inside) and ironwork which incorporates the symbol of a cone used in confectionery (a play on the artist's name, *zucchero*, or sugar). Across the garden, the larger house on the corner of Via Capponi was built by the painter Andrea del Sarto in 1520 on his return from France (and this was where he died ten years later). This was also purchased by Zuccari and the vaulted room he frescoed on the ground floor in 1579 with an allegory of Time (including very interesting landscapes and a scene of the painter himself with his family in the interior) survives, as well as the garden loggia he added. He also set up his emblem on the corner of the building with its two cornucopia and including the coat of arms of the Medici, his patrons. Zuccari, who was born in the Marche, travelled a great deal throughout his life and he worked in Flanders and Spain. In Italy many of his works can still be seen in Rome. However, he had a stormy relationship with Florence (his cupola frescoes were not appreciated) and he had sold the house by 1601. Since 1988 the building has been owned by the German Institute of Art History (Kunsthistorisches Institut).

STREET TABERNACLES

There are numerous street tabernacles all over the city, each with a painted or sculpted image, and many are still honoured daily with flowers and candles. Some are described in the guide; others are listed below.

14th-century tabernacles: These include the *Madonna and Child* on the corner of Via Faenza and Via Nazionale (in an 18th-century tabernacle; *map 1, 1*); the fresco of the *Madonna and Child with Saints* in a stone tabernacle on the corner between Via del Porcellana and Via Palazzuolo (*map 3, 7*); the fresco in the tabernacle on the corner of Borgo Pinti and Via Alfani (*map 4, 7–5*); and the fresco of the *Madonna* in a fine tabernacle in Piazza Piattellina, just out of Piazza del Carmine (*map 5, 2*). On the corner between Via del Leone and Via della Chiesa (*map 5, 4*), a modern glass tabernacle protects a fresco of the *Madonna Enthroned with Angels*, a 1958 copy of a painting by Giottino (c. 1356), detached and removed in 1943.

15th-century tabernacles: The large Tabernacolo delle Cinque Lampade ('of the five lamps') on the corner of Via de' Pucci and Via Ricasoli (*map 1, 2*) has a fresco by

Cosimo Rosselli. At Via Panicale 39 (*map 3, 6*) there is a fresco in a niche by the circle of Botticelli. A tabernacle in Via Sant'Antonino (on the corner of Piazza Unità Italiana; *map 3, 5*) contains an enamelled terracotta *Madonna and Child* by Andrea della Robbia, and in Via Pietrapiana (corner of Via de' Pepi; *map 7, 1*) there is a tabernacle with a fine relief of the *Madonna and Child* attributed to Donatello. On the corner of Via San Giovanni and Borgo San Frediano (*map 5, 2*) is a tabernacle with a 15th-century *Madonna and Child with Angels*.

16th-century tabernacles: The tabernacle at Via Porta Rossa 77 (*map 1, 5*) has a *Crucifix between Saints* attributed to Giovanni Battista Naldini. In Via Taddea (*map 1, 2*), the *Crucifixion* is by Giovanni Antonio Sogliani. The large tabernacle at Via Giusti 27 (*map 4, 5*) contains a *Resurrection of Christ* by Alessandro Fei. In the 1520s Giovanni della Robbia executed the huge enamelled terracotta tabernacle above a fountain in Via

Nazionale (*map 3, 6*) as well as the statuette of *St Ambrose* high up on the corner of Via de' Macci and Borgo La Croce (*map 7, 2*).

In Via delle Conce, named after the old tanneries, a tabernacle in *pietra serena* (1704) on the corner of Via dei Conciatori (*map 7, 2*) contains a copy made c. 1920 of an early 16th-century painting of the *Madonna and Child* from the church of San Giuseppe.

17th-century tabernacles: There are two frescoed early 17th-century tabernacles by Giovanni da San Giovanni: one of the *Madonna* in Via Faenza (*map 3, 5*) and another showing Senator Girolamo Novelli displaying acts of charity to prisoners in Via Ghibellina (*map 4, 7*). On a corner of Via dei Cimatori (*map 1, 6*), at the Canto alla Quarconia, lit by a wrought-iron lamp, there is a fresco of the *Madonna and Child Appearing to St Filippo Neri* by Alessandro Gherardini, one of the last tabernacles to be erected in the centre of the city.

THEATRES

Teatro Comunale
Map 2, 5–6. Corso Italia.
The most important concert hall in the city, with a seating capacity of 2,100. The disappointing interior was rebuilt in 1961. The music festival known as Maggio Musicale is held here from May–July. At the time of writing, a huge new auditorium designed by Paolo Desideri was being built close by on the edge of the Parco delle Cascine.

Teatro Goldoni
Map 5, 4. Via Sant Maria.
Nineteenth-century theatre (just 420 seats) with a charming interior with a circular vestibule and horseshoe auditorium, decorated by Giuseppe del Rosso.

Teatro della Pergola
Map 4, 7. Via della Pergola 18.
On the site of a wooden theatre erected in 1656 by Ferdinando Tacca (famous for the comedies performed there), the present theatre dates from the 19th century. Gordon Craig, actor and stage designer and son of Ellen Terry, was director here in 1906.

Teatro Verdi
Map 7, 1. Via Ghibellina.
Founded by Girolamo Pagliano and built by Telemaco Bonaiuti, this huge theatre was opened in 1854. The largest cinema screen in Italy was installed here after 1966. It is also used for drama and concerts, and is the seat of the Orchestra Regionale Toscana.

PRACTICAL INFORMATION

When to go

The most pleasant time to visit is May, or October and November when the temperature is often still quite high. Spring can be wet and cold until well after Easter. The most crowded periods of the year are from Easter to June and in September. The winter is cold, though it is the least crowded season for the major museums. It is usually extremely hot and oppressive in July and August. In August the city is empty of Florentines, and numerous shops, bars and restaurants close down for the whole month.

Disabled travellers

The tourist agency website (www.firenzeturismo.it) has a section on special needs, and they publish a guide indicating the best routes for wheelchairs. In the agency's list of hotels, those which cater to the disabled are indicated. For information on facilities on trains and assistance with getting on and off them at the Stazione Santa Maria Novella, T: 1993 03060. The disabled are entitled to a *carta blu*, which gives a discount on the fare. Trains equipped to carry wheelchairs are indicated on the website of the Italian State Railways (*www.trenitalia.it*). The city bus service provides facilities for wheelchairs on certain lines (*T: 800 424500; www.ataf.net*). There are free parking spaces for disabled drivers. Many pavements have been redesigned to facilitate wheelchair use but some are too narrow, making the historic centre a difficult place to move around.

Tourist offices (APT offices)

The main information office of the Agenzia per il Turismo di Firenze (APT) is at 1 (red) Via Cavour (*map 1, 2; T: 055 290832 or 055 290833, www.firenzeturismo.it; open Mon–Sat 8.30–6.30, Sun 8.30–1.30*). They offer a (free) list of hotels, a map, and up-to-date information on opening times and exhibitions. There is a subsidiary office at the airport. The municipality (*Comune*) of Florence runs information offices near Santa Croce at Borgo Santa Croce 29 (red) (*map 7, 1; T: 055 234 0444*) and at Piazza Stazione 4 (*map 3, 5; T: 055 212245*).

The Firenze Card

Valid for 72hrs, this allows free access to some 30 museums and monuments (and priority visits without the need to queue) and free bus travel. Available from tourist information offices and some museums. For more information, see www.firenzecard.it.

GETTING AROUND

Airports

The small airport of Florence (Amerigo Vespucci at Peretola), a few kilometres north of

Florence, has flights from Europe as well as internal domestic flights. Its short runway means that it is sometimes closed in strong winds or bad weather. SITA shuttle bus (Volainbus) every 30mins (at the time of writing from 6am–8pm) from the arrivals terminus to the SITA bus station next to Stazione Santa Maria Novella in about 20mins. Tickets can be bought on board. Taxis are also usually available (*otherwise T: 055 4242, 055 4390*).

Pisa airport, 85km west of Florence, is larger. There is a railway station in the airport (best to buy tickets from machines on the platform as there is often a queue in the arrivals hall). Trains to Florence take just under 1hr but only run every 2hrs or so and you often have to change at Pisa Central, 5mins down the line). There are town buses (no. 7; every 15mins) from the airport to Pisa Central, from where the trains to Florence are much more frequent. There are also coach services from the airport to Florence, run by Terravision (*T: 050 26080, www.terravision.eu*).

Bologna airport, over 100km north of Florence, has numerous flights from Europe and is in many ways the most useful airport for Florence. There is an excellent bus service (Aerobus) every 20mins to Bologna station in about 15mins. This runs from the station 5.55am–11.30pm and from the airport 8.30am–11.45pm. There are frequent fast trains (Freccia Rossa) from Bologna to Florence which take only 30mins (but are much more expensive than the Intercity trains which take around 1hr).

Driving in Florence

The centre of Florence is closed to all non-residents' cars from Mon–Fri 7.30am–7.30pm; Sat 7.30am–6pm (and also usually at night in summer), except on holidays. The limited traffic zone (ZTL) includes virtually all the area within the Viali (the radial avenues around the old centre) and the Oltrarno and is electronically controlled. Fines are stiff and cars are sometimes towed away. Having a hotel reservation does not mean you qualify as a resident: access is allowed to hotels and garages if you book ahead and give them your license plate number, but cars can only be parked outside hotels for a maximum of 1hr (and must display a card supplied by the hotel). Access is allowed for disabled drivers (and parking places are reserved for them). On certain days of the year, the whole of Florence is closed to traffic (10am–6.30pm) in an attempt to combat pollution. However, visitors arriving on those days are sometimes allowed access. For information, contact the municipality (*T: 055 055*).

There are underground **car parks** beneath Piazza Stazione (*map 3, 5*) and the Parterre (north of Piazza della Libertà; *map 4, 1*), both open 24rs. There is a large car park along the inside of the walls between Porta Romana and Piazza Tasso (entered from Piazza della Calza; *map 5, 6*). The car park beneath the Mercato Centrale (San Lorenzo; *map 3, 6*) is open 24hrs, but is used by shoppers and is expensive after the first 90mins from 7–2. The underground car park near the market of Sant'Ambrogio (*map 7, 2*), open 24hrs, is used by shoppers in the morning (cheap rate limited to 2hrs). There is another underground car park nearby in Piazza Beccaria.

A number of streets and *piazze*, and some of the Viali, also now have pay parking (blue lines), operational from 8am–8pm or later (tickets from automatic machines).

Other parking areas (white lines) are usually reserved for residents (check the signs at the beginning and on the same side of the street). Florence also has a number of garages (Via Nazionale, Via Ghibellina, Borgo Ognissanti, and in some hotels).

In the event of an **accident**, the traffic police can be called (T: 055 3283333 or, in emergencies, 055 3285). For emergency breakdown service, dial 116 (in Florence, T: 055 524861). If your car is towed away, it will probably be taken to Via Allende (Area Novoli; T: 055 4224142), where it can be retrieved after the payment of a heavy fine. The municipal police (Vigili Urbani; T: 055 212290), who wear blue uniform in winter and light blue in the summer, are usually helpful.

By train

Stazione di Santa Maria Novella (*map 3, 5*) is the main station and is very close to the centre of the city. It is well served by buses and taxis and there is an underground car park. Some trains now stop only at Firenze Campo di Marte or Firenze Rifredi, both less central but with bus services to the centre (nos. 13 and, at night, 70 from Campo di Marte, and nos. 28 and 20 from Rifredi).

By bus

Buses tend to be crowded and it is usually more pleasant to walk, especially as the centre is so small. The town bus service is run by ATAF (*www.ataf.net; T: 800 424500 or 1991 04245 from mobile phones*).

Small **electric buses** (C1, C2, C3 and D) follow interesting routes through the historic centre and are well worth taking for the ride, especially if you are on your first visit to Florence. They run Mon–Sat every 10 or 15mins from 7 or 8am to 7 or 8pm (line D also runs on Sun) and their routes are indicated at each bus stop.

Bus tickets can be bought at tobacconists, newspaper kiosks and some bars. One ticket provides unlimited travel on any bus for 90mins. There are numerous types of cumulative tickets which vary in price: valid for 24hrs, three or seven days, or for a calendar month. The *Carta Agile*, an electronic ticket, is the cheapest solution. Holders of the Firenze Card (*see p. 345*) are entitled to free bus transport. For a small extra charge you can also purchase a ticket from the driver as soon as you board the bus. You have to stamp your ticket (or validate the *Carta Agile*) at automatic machines when you board the bus: if you are found travelling without a valid ticket you are liable to a heavy fine.

As in other large cities, you should always beware of pickpockets on buses, and it is advisable to avoid very crowded buses by waiting for the next one.

By taxi

Taxis (painted white) have meters. The fare includes service, so tipping is not necessary. They are hired from ranks or by telephone: there are no cruising taxis. There are ranks at Stazione Santa Maria Novella, Piazza San Marco, Piazza Santa Trínita, Piazza del Duomo, Piazza della Repubblica, Porta Romana and elsewhere. For radio taxis, T: 055 4390, 055 4242 or 055 200 1326. A supplement is charged for night service and luggage.

Twelve horse-drawn cabs survive (in 1869 there were 518). From Easter to early Oct they can be hired in Piazza Duomo or Piazza della Signoria, and you should agree the fare before starting the journey.

By bicycle

Bicycles can be rented by the hour or for the day (*7.30–6 or 7pm except Sun and holidays*) from Stazione Santa Maria Novella, Piazza Annigoni (market of Sant'Ambrogio), Piazza Santa Croce and Stazione Campo di Marte (*contact Cooperative Ulisse, www.cooperativaulisse.it; T: 055 650 5295*). There are also private bike-hire firms which also have mountain bikes, including Alinari (*Via San Zanobi 38r, T: 055 280500*) and Florence by Bike (*Via San Zanobi 120, T: 055 488992; map 3, 4*).

MUSEUMS, GALLERIES & MONUMENTS

There is an excellent telephone booking service for the state-owned museums of Florence (*T: 055 294883; Mon–Fri 8.30–6.30, Sat 8.30–12.30; or online: www.firenzemusei.it*) which, for a small extra charge, allows you to enter at a specific time without having to queue (you collect and pay for the ticket at the museum just before the booked time). You can also buy tickets for any of the state museums at the box office of Firenze Musei in Via Calzaioli (church of Orsanmichele; *map 1, 6; open Mon–Sat 10–5.30, T: 055 239 6051*).

Hours of admission are given with individual entries. Opening times vary and often change without warning, so those given in the text may not be completely accurate. An up-to-date list of opening times is always available at the APT offices (*see p. 345*), but even this can be inaccurate. To make certain the times are correct, it is worth telephoning first. Ticket offices close 30mins (45mins at the Uffizi) before closing time.

Sometimes state museums are closed on the main public holidays: 1 Jan, Easter Day, 25 April, 1 May, 15 Aug and Christmas Day, but at Easter and Christmas they now usually have special opening times; for up-to-date information, ask at the APT.

Museum Week (*La Settimana dei Musei Italiani*) is an annual event (usually in March or April). Entrance to most state-owned museums is free and some have longer opening hours, while private collections may be specially opened. For information, toll free, T: 800 991199; www.beniculturali.it.

For a week, usually in late spring (*Settimana della Cultura Scientifica*), the scientific institutes in the city are opened to the public and special exhibitions, lectures and tours held.

On 18th Feb there are celebrations in honour of Anna Maria Luisa de' Medici (on the anniversary of her death), who left the Medici art treasures to the people of Florence in 1737, and there is free entry to all state and municipal museums in the city on that day.

There is free admission to all state-owned galleries and monuments for EU citizens under the age of 18 and over 65, and for EU students between the ages of 18 and 26 there is usually a 50 percent discount (take your passport for proof of age and nationality). There is free admission to some 30 museums owned by the state and the *Comune* for holders of the Firenze Card (*see p. 345*).

CHURCH SERVICES & FESTIVALS

The opening times of churches vary a great deal; those of the major churches have been given in the text. Some of the most important churches (Santa Croce, Santa Maria Novella, San Lorenzo) charge an entrance fee and stay open 9.30–5 and are well illuminated. Others usually close at midday and do not reopen until 4 or 5, and a few are open only for services. Sometimes there are coin-operated lights for altarpieces and frescoes. A pair of binoculars can be especially useful to study details. You may not be allowed into some churches if you are wearing shorts or have bare shoulders; in the Duomo you will be given a paper tabard to cover yourself. In the text the terms north and south refer to the liturgical north (left) and south (right), taking the high altar as the east end.

Roman Catholic services

On Sunday and, in the principal churches, often on weekdays, Mass is celebrated up to midday and from 6 until 7 in the evening. Confessions are heard in English on Sunday at the Duomo, San Lorenzo, San Marco, Santa Trínita, Santa Croce, Orsanmichele and San Miniato al Monte.

Non-Catholic churches and places of worship

Anglican: St Mark's, Via Maggio 16 (*map 6, 3*).
American Episcopalian: St James, Via Bernardo Rucellai 9 (*map 2, 6*).
Lutheran: Lungarno Torrigiani 11 (*map 6, 4*).
Waldensian: Via Micheli 26 (*map 4, 3*).
Russian Orthodox: Via Leone X 8 (*map 3, 2*).
Jewish Synagogue: Via Farini 4 (*map 4, 8*).

FESTIVALS

On saints' days, Mass and vespers with music are celebrated in the churches dedicated to the saints concerned. The feast of the patron saint of Florence, St John the Baptist (24th June), is a local holiday and special services are held. Other major festivals are described below.

Scoppio del Carro: This is the most famous traditional religious festival in Florence, held in and around the Duomo on Easter Day. Its origin appears to go back to the Florentine capture of a war carriage from Fiesole in 1152.

Around 9 o'clock on Easter morning, a tall wooden carriage known as the *brindellone* (which dates from 1764), covered with fireworks, leaves its huge garage on Il Prato drawn by two pairs of white oxen (dressed for the occasion). It is preceded by a procession of Florentines in historical costume and a band of drummers and buglers. The *brindellone* trundles down Borgo Ognissanti, Via della Vigna Nuova and through Piazza della Repubblica, where the procession is joined by another parade from the church of Santi Apostoli carrying with them the sacred flint. This is supposed to have been brought back from the Holy Sepulchre in Jerusalem by a member of the Pazzi family during the First Crusade. As the two groups join, there is a display of flag-throwing. Once at its destination, outside the main door of the Duomo, the *brindellone* is laden with more flags and fireworks.

Soon after 10 o'clock the clergy, with a large copper basin containing holy water, process out of the main door of the Duomo into the Baptistery, where a short service is held. On his way back to the Duomo, the bishop blesses the *brindellone* with the holy water. A magnificent procession now forms at the west door preceded by the huge flag with a red cross on a white field, the emblem of the *popolo* of Florence, and followed by all the clergy as well as members of the confraternities. All the doors of the Duomo are open and you can either watch the spectacle from the crowded piazza or, better still, join the congregation inside, where, during the *Gloria*, at a sign from the archbishop, a 'dove' (activated by a rocket and placed at the top of a column which is set up beneath the dome) is lit and sent along a taut wire all the way down the central aisle to ignite the fireworks on the *brindellone* outside (after which the dove rockets back to the column, where it disintegrates). The great dramatic explosion, which lasts several minutes, activates catherine wheels and flags which open and hurtle round the summit of the cart. The sound, accompanied by the ringing of all the church bells, reverberates magnificently inside the Duomo, while the piazza outside is filled with dense smoke. Formerly, the mechanism of the 'dove' was less sophisticated and was sometimes not successful; if it failed to ignite the *brindellone* and return safely into the cathedral it augured a poor harvest.

St John's Day: St John the Baptist (San Giovanni) is the patron saint of Florence. His feast, 24th June, is a local holiday celebrated with fireworks at Piazzale Michelangelo at 10pm.

Calcio Storico Fiorentino: This is a 'football' game in 16th-century costume held in three heats during the latter part of June (the final game always takes place on 24th June in the afternoon or early evening), usually in Piazza Santa Croce. The teams represent the four *quartiere* of the city: Santa Croce (*azzurri*; blue); Santa Maria Novella (*rossi*; red); Santo Spirito (*bianchi*; white); and San Giovanni (*verdi*; green). Tickets are sold at Box Office (*see p. 354*) or at Teatro Verdi in Via Ghibellina (you can also book online and pick up your ticket at the Teatro Verdi; *map 7, 1*). The more expensive tickets are for numbered places: the most comfortable seats (and those with the most shade) are on the south side of the piazza. The game is preceded by a splendid procession in period costume, with flag-throwers and bands, which takes some 40mins to enter the arena. After *la grida*, the presentation of arms, a cannon shot signals the start of the game (which is played with few rules and considerable violence). A *caccia* or goal (when the ball is sent into the low net along one of the short sides) is announced by two cannon shots fired from the steps of Santa Croce. In recent years some of the games have had to be suspended and teams disqualified because of excessive violence. But new rules were introduced in 2008 and there is hope that the game will return to being a more pleasant event.

Festa della Rificolona: On 7th Sept, the eve of the Birth of the Virgin, the *Festa della Rificolona* is celebrated by children carrying colourful paper lanterns through the streets (especially in Piazza Santissima Annunziata). Some children now carry pea-shooters with which they try to destroy the lanterns. The name is a corruption of *fierucolone*, the name given to the peasant women from the surrounding countryside who came to Florence carrying lanterns for the ancient traditional festival to honour the Virgin at Santissima Annunziata.

Festival of the Annunziata: *see p. 353.*

Festa del Grillo: On Ascension Day there is a large fair in the Cascine where crickets were traditionally sold in little cages: since 1999 this has no longer been allowed but the fair still takes place and is a lively event for children.

SHOPS & MARKETS

Street numbers refer to the red numbering system, rather than the numbers in black or blue (*see note on p. 357*).

Antique shops: In Via Maggio (*map 6, 3*) and the small streets leading to Piazza Pitti, as well as in Via dei Fossi (*map 3, 7*) and Borgo San Jacopo (*map 6, 1–3*).

Books and music: Shops specialising in English books include Paperback Exchange (Via delle Oche 4; *map 1, 4*); BM Bookshop (Borgo Ognissanti 4; *map 2, 8*). The largest bookshops in Florence (which also stock English books) include Feltrinelli (Via de' Cerretani 30; *map 1, 3*); Feltrinelli International (Via Cavour 12; *map 1, 2*; Edison (Piazza della Repubblica; *map 1, 3*) and Libreria Martelli (Via Martelli; *map 1, 2–4*). Bookshops specialising in art history include Salimbeni (Via Palmieri 14; *map 7, 1*) and Art & Libri

(Via dei Fossi 32; *map 3, 7*). The bookshop on the ground floor of the Uffizi has a specialised section of art history books (it can be visited without having to purchase a ticket; entrance through the door and metal detector for pre-booked tickets). The Libreria de' Servi, or FirenzeLibri (Via dei Servi 52; *map 4, 5*) also specialises in second-hand books (they have two smaller bookshops at Borgo Allegri 16 and on Piazza Salvemini). An excellent small shop with a vast range of CDs of classical music and an extremely knowledgeable owner is Fenice, Via Santa Reparata 8b (*map 3, 4*).

Ceramics: Italian pottery is sold at Sbigoli (Via Sant'Egidio 4; *map 4, 7*). Ceramica Artistica Migliori (Via de' Benci 39; *map 7, 1*) makes good copies of classic Italian majolica. Andreini (Borgo degli Albizi 63; *map 4, 7*) also sells majolica. Richard-Ginori ceramics are sold at Via dei Rondinelli 17 (*map 1, 3*).

Clothes: The smartest fashion shops are in Via Tornabuoni (where Gucci and Ferragamo are famous for their shoes and handbags) and Via della Vigna Nuova (*map 1, 3*). Many of the best-known clothes shops are on or near Via Roma and Via dei Calzaioli (*map 1, 4*). Loretta Capponi (*Piazza Antinori 4; map 1, 3*), sells exquisite hand-made lace and embroidery. A well-known hat shop is Borsalino (*Via Porta Rossa 40; map 1, 5*), and delightful ladies' hats are sold at Grevi (*Via della Spada 11; map 1, 3*). Straw hats can still be found on some stalls at San Lorenzo market. An old-established shop specialising in smart childrens' clothes is Anichini (*Via del Parione 59; map 1, 5*).

Fabrics: Exquisite hand-woven silk is made and sold at the Antico Setificio Fiorentino (Via Lorenzo Bartolini 4; *map 5, 2*), owned by Cristina Pucci. Lisa Corti Home Textile Emporium (Piazza Ghiberti 33; market of Sant'Ambrogio) sells lovely and unusual fabrics (including velvet, organza and muslin) for home furnishings as well as clothes and accessories.

Jewellery: This is a speciality of Florentine craftsmen: the shops on Ponte Vecchio and its immediate vicinity have superb displays. Some of these specialise in pearls, silver, gold or semi-precious stones. Artisans who repair jewellery (or make it to order) have their workshops in the Casa dell'Orafo close by. In the Ol-

trarno district Petra Casini (Via Maggio 15; *map 6, 3*) is a shop run by a family of gem-cutters who also make customised jewellery. At Via Santo Spirito 58 (*map 6, 1*) Angela Caputi has earned a reputation as a designer of modern jewellery (she has another shop on the other side of the Arno at Borgo Santi Apostoli 44).

Leather: Florence is well known for its leather goods (handbags, purses, belts and jackets), which are sold in the open-air markets of San Lorenzo and the Porcellino (Mercato Nuovo; *map 1, 5*), and from the stalls in Piazza San Firenze and Borgo dei Greci. There are also numerous shops specialising in leather, including Bojola (Via Rondinelli 25; *map 1, 3*). The large leather 'factories' in the district of Santa Croce cater mostly for tour groups and their guides.

Markets: The main food market in Florence is the Mercato Centrale, also known as the Mercato di San Lorenzo, in a covered market building near the church (*map 3, 6; open Mon–Sat 7–1; also 4.30–7.30 on Sat except in July and Aug*). Near the church of Sant'Ambrogio (*map 4, 8; open weekday mornings, and also sometimes on Wed and Fri afternoons*), butchers and grocers have their shops in a market building, and fruit and vegetables are sold from stalls outside.

The biggest general market in Florence is in the streets near San Lorenzo where stalls sell clothing, leatherwork, cheap jewellery and shoes, generally of good quality (*open throughout the day every day except Sun and Mon from mid-Nov to mid-Dec, and in Jan and Feb*). Another similar general market is the Porcellino (Mercato Nuovo; *map 1, 5*) open at the same times.

There are also stalls in Piazza San Firenze and Borgo dei Greci (*map 1, 6*) which sell similar goods. At Sant'Ambrogio there is also an excellent general market (new and second-hand clothing, hardware, household linens, shoes) open in the mornings (except Sun). A very large general market is held every Tues morning at Le Cascine (*map 2, 5*).

The Mercatino delle Pulci (flea market) is open weekdays in Piazza dei Ciompi (*map 4, 7*).

An organic food market is held every third Sun in Piazza Santo Spirito (*map 6, 3*), and around 7th Sept, 8th Dec and 25th March (feasts of the Nativity of the Virgin, Immaculate Conception and Annunciation) in Piazza Santissima Annunziata. On the second Sun of the month, a market of artisans' work is held in Piazza Santo Spirito. There is a market of organic products every first Sat of the month in Piazza della Repubblica (*map 1, 3*). Artigianato e Palazzo is a festival of handmade artisans' wares held for three days in late May or early June in the garden of Palazzo Corsini sul Prato (entrance at Via della Scala 115; *map 2, 6*).

The Mostra Mercato di Piante e Fiori is a splendid flower show which takes place for about a week around the end of April or beginning of May and again in the autumn at the Giardino dell'Orticoltura (just above Via XX Settembre (*map 4, 1*), entrances on Via Vittorio Emanuele II and on Via Bolognese 17).

Soap and perfume: Very fine soap and perfumes are made by the Officina Profumo-Farmaceutica di Santa Maria Novella (Via della Scala 16; *map 3, 5; see p. 190*). At Via Tornabuoni 19 is the Erboristeria Inglese or Officina de' Tornabuoni (*see p. 221*). Ortigia (Borgo San Jacopo 12; *map 6, 1–3*) sells its own products which are based on the scents from plants native to Sicily, exquisitely packaged. Simpler products produced in various monasteries are sold at Monastica, a charming little shop in the convent of the Badia Fiorentina (*see p. 79*).

Stationery: A speciality of Florence is its fine marbled paper. The best known shop is Giulio Giannini (Piazza Pitti 37; *map 6, 3*), and nearby Il Torchio (Via de' Bardi 17; *map 6, 4*) is a book-binder which also sells beautiful stationery. Il Papiro has several branches, including Piazza Duomo 24. Vannucchi (Via Condotta 26; *map 1, 6*) also sells fine stationery. A less well-known shop with excellent hand-made products made on the spot by a family of artisans (also to order) is Lo Scrittoio (Via Nazionale 126; *map 3, 6*). Simple Florentine paper products are also sold in stationers' shops and in the open-air markets. An elegant shop which has been in business for many decades, favoured by Florentines for personalised stationery, is Pineider (Piazza della Signoria 13).

ENTERTAINMENT

Listings information

Concerts, theatre performances and exhibitions are advertised in the local press and on posters. *Eventi/Events* is an up-to-date free list of these printed every month by the

APT. There is another similar monthly leaflet called *Florence and Tuscany News* (www. informacitta.net). *The Florentine* (www.theflorentine.net) is a small free newspaper in English which comes out every two weeks, and has useful listings of upcoming events. More old-fashioned is the free publication issued every two months in English by Chiavi d'oro. More detailed information is supplied in *Firenze Spettacolo* (www.firenzespettacolo.it), published every month and sold at newsagents—a few pages of the main events are in English. The large-format *Visit Art Firenze* comes out twice a year in English and Italian with news on exhibitions and cultural events.

Tickets for many events are sold at Box Office (Via delle Vecchie Carceri 1, Le Murate, a short street which runs between Via dell'Agnolo and Via Ghibellina; *map 7, 2; T: 055 210804; tickets on line at www.boxol.it*). It has a branch ticket office in Palazzo Strozzi open 9am–7pm. Otherwise it is often possible to buy tickets at the venue on the evening of the performance.

Music

Maggio Musicale, an annual music festival (May–July) is held at the Teatro Comunale (Corso Italia 16; *map 2, 5–6*). Chamber music concerts are organised by the Amici della Musica Jan–April and Oct–Dec at La Pergola Theatre (Via della Pergola 18; *map 4, 7*). The Orchestra Regionale Toscana holds concerts regularly at the Teatro Verdi (*map 7, 1*) and the Orchestra da Camera Fiorentina holds chamber music concerts (usually at Orsanmichele; *map 1, 6*). Concerts are often held in the courtyard of Palazzo Pitti and in the Boboli Gardens in summer.

Florence has a number of historic organs, including those in the churches of Santissima Annunziata, San Niccolò sopr'Arno, the Badia Fiorentina and San Giorgio alla Costa. Organ concerts are often held in winter.

Estate Fiesolana is an annual festival of music, drama and films held from the end of June to the end of August in the Roman theatre in Fiesole.

ADDITIONAL INFORMATION

Banking services

Banks are usually open from 8.30–1.30 & 2.30 or 2.45–3.30 or 3.45 or later every day except Sat, Sun and holidays. Some banks now open also on Sat mornings. They close early (about 11) on days preceding national holidays. Money can also be changed at exchange offices (*cambio*) and at travel agencies (but usually at a less advantageous rate), as well as at some post offices and main railway stations. Some hotels, restaurants and shops exchange money, but usually at a lower rate.

Consulates and embassies

The British, American, Canadian, Australian, Irish and New Zealand embassies are in Rome. There is an American Consulate in Florence at Lungarno Vespucci 38 (*map 2, 8; T: 055 239 8276*). The British Consulate was closed down in 2011.

Crime and personal security

There are three categories of policemen in Italy: **Vigili Urbani**, municipal police, who wear blue uniforms in winter and light blue during the summer; their headquarters are at Piazzale di Porta al Prato 6, T: 055 328 3333; **Carabinieri**, military police, who wear a black uniform with a red stripe down the side of the trousers; their headquarters are at Borgo Ognissanti 48, T: 112; **Polizia di Stato**, state police, who wear dark blue jackets and light blue trousers; the Central Police Station (Questura) is at Via Zara 2, T: 055 49771, map 4, 3; they also have an office (the Commissariato Firenze San Giovanni) at Via Pietrapiana 50 (red); T: 055 203911, map 4, 7.

Crime should be reported at once. If it is theft, it should be reported to either the Polizia di Stato or the Carabinieri. A detailed statement has to be given in order to get an official document confirming loss or damage (*denunzia di smarrimento*), which is essential for insurance claims. Interpreters are usually provided. If you have legal problems, contact the APT office at Via Cavour 1 (red).

As in cities all over the world, pick-pocketing is a widespread problem. Don't carry valuables in handbags and take extra care on buses. You should also be careful when using a credit card to withdraw money from ATMs. Cash, documents and valuables should be left in hotel safes and it is a good idea to make photocopies of all important documents in case of loss. Italian law requires everyone to carry some form of identification with a photograph: it is therefore best to keep your passport with you.

Emergencies

For all emergencies, T: 113 (Polizia di Stato) or 112 (Carbinieri): the switchboard will coordinate the help you need.

First aid services (*Pronto Soccorso*) are available at hospitals, railway stations and airports. The most central hospital is Santa Maria Nuova (Piazza Santa Maria Nuova 1; T: 055 27581; map 4, 7). A volunteer service (AVO) helps translate for non-Italian patients in hospitals (T: 055 425 0126).

First-aid and ambulance emergency 24hr service, T: 118.

Ambulance services (run by volunteers of the Misericordia), Piazza del Duomo; T: 055 212222; (run by volunteers of the Fratellanza Militare); T: 055 215555.

Mobile coronary unit, T: 055 283394.

Fire brigade, T: 115.

Road assistance, T: 116.

Health and insurance

EU citizens have the right to claim health care in Italy if they have the E111 form, available from post offices. There are also a number of private holiday health insurance policies, certainly advisable for visitors from outside the EU. Keep the receipt (*ricevuta*) and medical report (*cartella clinica*) to present to your insurer if you have to make a claim.

Lost property

The central office of the Comune is at Via Veracini 5 (*map 2, 1; T: 055 334802; open*

Mon–Fri 9.30–12.30 on Tues and Thur also 2.30–4.30). To report the loss or theft of a credit card, call: Visa, T: 800 819014; Mastercard, T: 800 870866; American Express: T: 06 729 00347.

Opening hours

Large shops and department stores and shops in the centre of Florence are open all day (9.30 or 10–7.30), and are sometimes also open on Sun, but many others close for three or four hours in the middle of the day and are closed on Sun. As a general rule smaller shops and local stores are open Mon–Sat except between 1 and 4, and on Mon morning for most of the year (in summer they usually close on Sat afternoon and open on Mon morning). Hardware shops are usually closed on Sat afternoon and open Mon morning. Local food shops usually open Mon–Sat 7.30 or 8–1 & 5–7.30 or 8, but are closed on Wed afternoon for most of the year. The Billa supermarket in Via Pietrapiana (*map 4, 7*) is usually open on Sun and holidays.

From mid-June to mid-Sept all shops close on Sat afternoon. Government offices usually work weekdays 8–1.30 or 2.

Pharmacies

Pharmacies (*farmacie*) are usually open Mon–Fri 9–1 & 4–7.30 or 8. Some are open 24hrs a day, including those at the Stazione Santa Maria Novella, at Via Calzaioli 7 (*map 1, 4*), and at Piazza San Giovanni 20 (*map 1, 4*). A few are open on Sat, Sun (and holidays) and at night: these are listed on the door of every pharmacy.

Photography

Rules about photography vary in museums and churches, so it is always best to ask first for permission (the use of a flash is often prohibited).

Postal services

The main post offices are in Via Pietrapiana 53 (*map 4, 7*) and Via Pellicceria (*map 1, 5*) and they are open 8.15am–7pm (except on the last day of the month when they are open 8.15–midday); on Sat they are open 8.30–1.30. Branch post offices are usually open Mon–Fri 8.15–1.30 (Sat 8.30–1.30). There is a small post office in the Uffizi. Stamps are also usually sold at tobacconists (displaying a blue 'T' sign).

Public holidays

The main holidays in Italy, when offices, shops and schools are closed, are as follows:

1 January	New Year's Day
25 April	Liberation Day
Easter Monday	
1 May	Labour Day
15 August	Assumption
1 November	All Saints' Day
8 December	Immaculate Conception

25 December   Christmas Day
26 December   St Stephen

In addition, the festival of the patron saint of Florence, St John the Baptist, is celebrated on 24th June as a local holiday in the city.

Some museums are closed on 24th June, Easter Sunday and 15th Aug, although sometimes some of the state museums remain open on these days. There is usually no public transport on 1st May and the afternoon of Christmas Day.

Street numbering

In Florence, the numbers of all private residences are written in blue or black, and those of all shops (and restaurants) in red, so the same number often occurs in blue or black and in red in the same street. In the main text red numbers are denoted with the letter 'r' or 'red'.

Telephones

Telephone numbers in Italy can have from seven to eleven numbers. All require the area code, whether you are making a local call or a call from outside Florence. Directory assistance (in Italian) is available by dialling 12. For international calls, dial 170, and for directory assistance, 4176. International telephone cards, which offer considerable savings, are widely available from tobacconists displaying a blue 'T' sign.

Italy country code: 39
Florence area code: 055
Dialling UK from Italy: 0044 + number
Dialling US from Italy: 001 + number
Dialling Florence from Europe: 0039 055 + number
Dialling Florence from the US: 011 39 055 + number

Tipping

Most prices in hotels and restaurants include a service charge, and so tipping is far less widespread in Italy than it is in North America. Even taxi-drivers rarely expect more than a euro or two added to the charge (which officially includes service). In restaurants, prices are almost always inclusive of service. In hotels, porters who show you to your room and help with your luggage, or find you a taxi, usually expect a few euro.

Toilets

There are modern public toilets (you will need small change) run by the municipality in the subway of the Stazione Santa Maria Novella, in Via della Stufa (near the church of San Lorenzo), in Via Filippina on the corner of Via Borgognone (near Palazzo Vecchio), in Borgo Santa Croce (near the church of Santa Croce), inside the market of Sant'Ambrogio, inside the market of San Lorenzo (Via dell'Ariento), in Via dello Sprone (near Palazzo Pitti) and at Piazzale Michelangelo. The Opera del Duomo (OPA) has smart new toilets in Piazza San Giovanni 7 (by the Baptistery). All museums also have toilets.

ACCOMMODATION

The APT of Florence produces an annual free listing of all the hotels and other types of accommodation available in Florence, with their prices. There are five official categories of hotel in Italy from luxury 5-star to the most simple 1-star establishments. Some hotels are classified separately as *Residenze d'Epoca* (Historic Residences): these must be in buildings of special historic or architectural interest and able to offer hospitality to no more than 25 people at a time. Hotels called *Affittacamere* have a maximum of six rooms and are often in the owner's home, so similar to B&B-type accommodation. *Ostelli* (hostels) provide the cheapest and simplest accommodation, while *case per ferie* are hostels (for all ages) usually run by religious organisations, with or without en-suite bathrooms, and often as cheap as youth hostels. They sometimes have rather spartan accommodation and often have restricted hours and early curfews, but are generally well run.

It is essential to book well in advance in summer, at Easter and in Sept and Oct; you are usually asked to send a deposit or leave a credit card number to confirm the booking. You may claim the deposit back if you cancel at least 72hrs in advance.

The listing below is a selection of some of the best places to stay arranged according to price. Prices per double room per night:

€€€€ €500–900 and above
€€€   €300–400
€€   around €200
€   around €100

BLUE GUIDES RECOMMENDED

Hotels, restaurants and *osterie* that are particularly good choices in their category—in terms of excellence, location, charm, value for money or the quality of the experience they provide—carry the Blue Guides Recommended sign:■. All these establishments have been visited and selected by our authors, editors or contributors as places they have particularly enjoyed and would be happy to recommend to others. To keep our entries up-to-date, reader feedback is essential: please do not hesitate to contact us (www.blueguides.com) with any views, corrections or suggestions, or join our online discussion forum.

€€€€

Four Seasons Hotel Firenze. ■ *Borgo Pinti 99, T: 055 26261, www.fourseasons.com/florence.*

117 rooms. Map 4, 6. Opened in 2008 by the well-known Canadian luxury hotel chain which owns some 85 hotels all over the world. It occupies the splendid Palazzo della

Gherardesca (*see p. 230*), surrounded by the largest private garden in Florence. The entire property, including a former 16th-century convent in the garden (with an entrance on Via Gino Capponi), has been spectacularly restored and the lovely 11-acre garden still has the aspect of romantic 19th-century parkland, supplied with a swimming pool and spa building. Restaurant Il Pelagio (*see p. 365*) also has tables outside; in summer you can have a light meal by the pool. Nicely central; under 10mins walk from Piazza San Marco. A night in the Royal Suite may cost you some €15,000, but if that does not surprise you then this is the place for you.

Helvetia e Bristol. ▬ *Via de' Pescioni 2, T: 055 26651, www.royaldemeure.com. 52 rooms. Map 1, 3.* Elegant but small enough to be cosy with it. Beautifully furnished, with superbly-appointed rooms and marble bathrooms. The small restaurant serves good snacks and full meals.

JK Place. *Piazza Santa Maria Novella 7, T: 055 264 5181, www.jkplace.com. 20 rooms. Map 3, 7.* Stylish boutique hotel on Piazza Santa Maria Novella. The bedrooms could be a little larger but they are beautifully furnished.

Lungarno. *Borgo San Jacopo 14, T: 055 27261, www.lungarnohotels.com. 73 rooms. Map 1, 5.* Old-established hotel near Ponte Vecchio which was built following the destruction of this area in the Second World War. The rooms have balconies directly on the Arno so are very quiet. There are numerous comfortable public rooms on the ground floor. It is now one of four hotels in this central area owned by the Ferragamo. Convenient for those with a car as it has its own garage.

Palazzo Magnani Feroni. ▬ *Borgo San Frediano 5, T: 055 239 9544, www.*

florencepalace.it. 12 suites. Map 5, 2. A sumptuous 16th-century *palazzo* opened as a *Residenza d'Epoca* in 2001. The deluxe suites on the upper floors are well worth the additional expense for their size and extra light. Drinks and dinner are served on a wonderful rooftop terrace.

Riva Lofts Florence. *Via Baccio Bandinelli, 94f, T: 055 713 0272, www.rivalofts.com. 8 rooms. Beyond map 2, 5.* An extremely elegant place recently voted one of the finest hotels in the world. In a 19th-century building restored by the architect Claudio Nardi, it is in an unusual position on the edge of the unremarkable suburb of Isolotto, beyond Ponte della Vittoria. The independent suites supplied with every modern comfort, including kitchens and minimalist furnishings, look across the river to the huge park of the Cascine. Swimming pool in the garden.

Villa Medici. *Via Il Prato 42, T: 055 277171, www.sinahotels.com. 103 rooms. Map 2, 6.* Typical of the 1960s but more pleasantly and simply furnished than the other 5-star hotels in the centre. The small swimming pool is in a little garden at the back.

€€€

Antica Torre di Via Tornabuoni. ▬ *Via Tornabuoni 1, T: 055 265 8161, www. tornabuoni1.com. 19 rooms. Map 1, 5.* Opened in 2001 and recently expanded into the adjoining Palazzo Gianfigliazzi, this is an excellent *Residenza d'Epoca* with one of the most magnificent roof terraces in all Florence, where breakfast is served and where there is ample room to sit and enjoy the lovely views. The twelve rooms on the fourth and fifth floor of the medieval tower are small but delightful, some with medieval features, and with their windows overlooking the rooftops. The seven on the top floor of Palazzo Gianfigliazzi are larger and overlook the Arno, and include a suite with its own terrace. There are also self-catering apartments for rent on the third floor of the palace. Delightful staff. No groups.

Casa Guidi. *Piazza San Felice 8. Map 6, 3.* The Brownings' former apartment which remains much as it was in their day (*see p. 267*) can be rented for short lets by the week from The Landmark Trust (*T: +44 1628 825925; bookings@landmarktrust.org.uk; in Italy T: 041 522 2481, landmarktrust@fastwebnet.it*).

Inpiazzadellasignoria. ■ *Via dei Magazzini 2, T: 055 239 9546, www.inpiazzadellasignoria. com 10 rooms. Map 1, 6.* A *Residenza d'Epoca* opened in a 15th-century palace in 2001 by Alessandro and Sonia Pini and, as the name suggests, it is entered from Piazza della Signoria (although only two of the rooms have windows on the piazza). The others are quiet, and all of them are simply but attractively furnished. There are three self-catering apartments to rent by the week on the top floor. Extremely cordial and helpful management.

J & J. ■ *Via di Mezzo 20, T: 055 26312, www.jandjhotel.com. 20 rooms. Map 4, 7.* A 16th-century convent sensitively converted into a delightful hotel. The large rooms are particularly attractive, spacious and tastefully furnished—although there is no lift. It is tucked away on a very quiet road in a pleasant district with lots of good restaurants. Family run, with friendly staff.

Tornabuoni Beacci. *Via Tornabuoni 3, T: 055 212645, www.tornabuonihotels.com. 50 rooms. Map 1, 5.* Set on Florence's smartest street, an old-established hotel where many well-known

Anglo-Americans have stayed (the earliest guestbook dates from 1918), and which was enlarged in 2010. On the top floor of two adjoining palaces, it still has an old-fashioned, slightly shabby atmosphere. There is a large sitting room and some of the bedrooms have 18th-century frescoes. On the charming roof terrace, which is usually a bower of flowers, breakfast and dinner are served.

Torre di Bellosguardo. *Via Roti Michelozzi 2, T: 055 229 8145, www.torrebellosguardo.com. Map 5, 5.* On the famous hill of Bellosguardo, with, as the name promises, a wonderful view.

€€

Annalena. *Via Romana 34, T: 055 222402, www.hotelannalena.it. 9 rooms. Map 6, 3.* Opened as a *pensione* in 1919 and much frequented in the 20th century by the British for its old-world charm. Under new management since 2007, it now has a slightly eccentric air. Six rooms overlooking a pretty garden where plants are sold have french windows out onto a long terrace, and three others share another quiet roof terrace. The rooms are all very small. No lift.

Antica Dimora Johlea. ■ *Via San Gallo 80, T: 055 463 3292, www.johanna.it. 6 rooms. Map 4, 3.* On the top floor of a 19th-century palace in a peaceful residential street close to Piazza San Marco, this is the most charming and comfortable of no fewer than five small hotels in Florence (officially classed as 'Bed and Breakfast') under the same excellent management. All the rooms have four-poster beds, and there is a lovely rooftop terrace. Close by, on either side of the beautiful Palazzo Pandolfini, are the Antica Dimora Firenze (*Via San Gallo 72, T: 055 462 7296, www.anticadimorafirenze.it, 6 rooms*) and the

Residenze Johlea (*Via San Gallo 76, T: 055 4633292, www.johanna.it, 6 rooms*).

Bretagna. *Lungarno Corsini 6, T: 055 289618, www.bretagna.it. 30 rooms. Map 6, 1.* In a very fine central position, the charmingly old-fashioned living room and dining room with large windows and high ceilings overlooking the Arno have echoes of E.M. Forster. Recently upgraded into a *Residenza d'Epoca*, the rooms vary a great deal: approached off a balcony from the dining room (and facing an inner courtyard) are the four most interesting rooms, extremely spacious with their 19th-century decorations intact, but which some might find gloomy. On the third floor two of the rooms have fine views, but those on the fourth floor, just restored, have the best outlook: some on the front looking over the Arno and others on the back looking across the roofs to the campanile of Santa Trínita. The bathrooms are new but rather small.

La Scaletta. *Via Guicciardini 13, T: 055 283028, www.hotellascaletta.it. 16 rooms. Map 6, 3.* An old-established family-run hotel which has recently been upgraded. The delightful roof terrace has views of Palazzo Pitti and the Boboli Gardens. The quietest rooms (including numbers 33, 20, 21 and 22) are all on the back overlooking the Boboli, others are on an inner courtyard, and those on Via Guicciardini have double glazing. Most of them are spacious with terracotta floors and old-fashioned furniture. Well run. Restaurant open from May–Oct.

Loggiato dei Serviti. *Piazza Santissima Annunziata 3, T: 055 289592, www. loggiatodeiservitihotel.it. 34 rooms. Map 4, 5.* In a lovely palace with vaulted rooms in the most beautiful square in Florence, converted with great taste into a small hotel. The simple furnishings and stone floors make it cool and pleasant, and the rooms have lovely city views.

Porta Rossa. *Via Porta Rossa 19, T: 055 271 0911, www.nh-hotels.it. 72 rooms. Map 1, 5.* Historic hotel in the heart of the city. It is now owned by a Spanish hotel chain, and reopened in 2010 after renovations which brightened up the décor while carefully retaining the Art Nouveau stained glass and decorations. With grey and white marble floors and spacious bedrooms with high ceilings, it still has much of its old furniture. No restaurant. Friendly, efficient staff.

Relais Uffizi. *Via Chiasso del Buco 16 (Chiasso de' Baroncelli), T: 055 267 6239, www. relaisuffizi.it. 15 rooms. Map 1, 5.* Tucked away in an ancient, very picturesque passageway approached from Chiasso de' Baroncelli, which leads out of Piazza della Signoria. You take a lift from the handsome entranceway up to a winding corridor and the sitting room and breakfast room have a superb view over Piazza della Signoria. The rooms, with their beamed ceilings, are simply furnished with four-poster beds and the staff are very friendly.

Residenza Casanuova. ■ *Via della Mattonaia 21, T: 055 234 3413, www.residenzacasanuova. it. 5 rooms. Map 4, 8.* On the top floor of a 19th-century house just a few metres from the busy market of Sant'Ambrogio. The owner's grandmother, Signora Casanuova, lived here and it has been kept the way she furnished it, with the addition of some of her possessions (including her jaunty hats!). Officially a 'bed and breakfast', there are four delightful double rooms (and one single), all of them with shiny parquet floors and immaculately kept. They are cheerful and bright with large windows. A charming little roof terrace has a few tables where you can sit and read in peace.

Torre Guelfa. *Borgo Santi Apostoli 8, T: 055 239 6338, www.hoteltorreguelfa.com. 12 rooms. Map 1, 5.* This efficiently-run hotel is set in a beautiful old 13th-century palace which has been well renovated. All rooms have bathrooms, most have air conditioning. Pleasant single rooms also. A lovely loggia is used for breakfast and there is a delightful living room. A 19th-century wooden stair leads up to the exceptionally high tower which has breathtaking views.

€

Boboli. *Via Romana 63, T: 055 229 8645, www.hotelboboli.com. 18 rooms. Map 5, 6.* A simple but pleasant hotel. The rooms, with small bathrooms, are on three floors (no lift). Only a few are on the back, but those on Via Romana have double glazing. Good views from the rooms on the upper floors.

Palazzo Guadagni. ■ *Piazza Santo Spirito 9, T: 055 265 8376, www.palazzoguadagni.com. 12 rooms. Map 6, 3.* On the two upper floors of one of the most beautiful palaces in the Oltrarno. Opened in 2009 and furnished with great taste. The lovely gallery which opens onto the magnificent loggia (with comfortable cane chairs) is a very special feature. The seven airy rooms on this floor have frescoed ceilings and old painted floors, and the five on the top floor (reached by stairs) are a little simpler but have even better views towards Palazzo Pitti. All the bathrooms are new and particularly spacious, with pretty tiles from Vietri. The breakfast room at the back looks across the roofs towards

Palazzo Pitti. The three rooms on the first floor (two of them very spacious with huge windows overlooking the piazza, with 18th-century frescoed ceilings and old-fashioned furnishings) are run as a bed and breakfast by the same excellent management (*www.residenzasspirito.com*).

Scoti. ■ *Via Tornabuoni 7, T: 055 292128, www.hotelscoti.com. 11 rooms. Map 1, 5.* In a palace on Florence's smartest street, this is still named after its late 19th-century owners and it has a devoted clientèle (especially favoured by English academics). Since 1996 it has been very well run by an Australian who lives here with her family and provides the exceptionally friendly atmosphere. Rooms are large, all with their own bathrooms, and very quiet on an inner courtyard or overlooking the rooftops. The atmosphere is old-fashioned with simple marble floors. The charming main room has frescoes attributed to Tommaso Gherardini (1770).

The **Residence Angeli** in the same building (and under the same management) has five rooms overlooking Via Tornabuoni so these are noisier (but the prices are therefore lower). Prices do not include breakfast, but this can be ordered on request.

Soggiorno Battistero. ■ *Piazza San Giovanni 1, T: 055 295143, www.soggiornobattistero.it 7 rooms. Map 1, 4.* This has a prime location. On the third floor, five of the rooms look out directly onto the roof of the Baptistery. Rooms are spacious and breakfast is served in your room. An excellent choice and extremely reasonable. No lift.

Hostels

Reliable hostels include the following: Santa Monaca (*Via Santa Monaca 6, T: 055 268338, www.ostello.it; map 5, 2*); Archi Rossi (*Via Faenza 94r, T: 055 290804, www.hostelarchirossi.com; map 3, 3*); Sette Santi (*Viale dei Mille 11, T: 055 504 8452, www.7santi.com; beyond map 4, 4*).

Monastery accommodation

Casa SS. Nome di Gesù, Francescane Missionarie di Maria (*Piazza del Carmine 21, T: 055 213856, www.fmmfirenze.it*); C.S.D. Istituto Gould (*Via de' Serragli 49, T: 055 212576, www.istitutogould. it*); Suore Oblate dell'Assunzione (*Borgo Pinti 15, T: 055 2480582*); Convitto della Calza (*Piazza della Calza 6, T: 055 222287, www.calza.it*); Villa La Stella (*Via Jacopone da Todi 12; off Via di San Domenico, T: 055 508 8018, www.villalastella.it, map p. 304*); Villa Maria SS. Assunta (*Via delle Forbici 38, T: 055 577690*), on a lovely country road but rather far from the bus stop.

ACCOMMODATION IN THE ENVIRONS

Fiesole

€€€€ **Villa San Michele**. *Via Doccia 4, T: 055 567 8200, www.villasanmichele.orient-express.com. Map p. 305.* Grand hotel on the hillside overlooking Florence below Fiesole, with a renowned cocktail bar and restaurant. This has been one of the most famous hotels in the environs of Florence for many years. Open Easter–end Nov. Surrounded by a garden and with swimming pool.

€€€ **Villa Aurora**. *Piazza Mino 39, T: 055 59363, www.villaurora.net. Map p. 304.* The best hotel in the centre of Fiesole. Family-owned and courteously run, it first opened at the end of the 19th century and retains its spacious, rather grand atmosphere of former days, when members of the Italian royal family stayed here as well as the poets Carducci and d'Annunzio. All the rooms are very different and prices vary. Most have recently been tastefully redecorated and the bathrooms modernised. Room 31 has a small balcony with a panoramic view of Florence, and room 11, although smaller, has its own private terrace. Restaurant (*closed Mon in winter*) and bar. Sometimes used for weddings.

€€ **Bencistà**. ■ *Via Benedetto da Maiano 4, T: 055 59163, www.bencista.com 40 rooms. Closed from around 15 Nov–15 March. Map p. 305.* On the hillside below Fiesole in a splendid quiet position, approached by a drive which winds downhill from the road between Fiesole and Maiano. This is a charming old rambling villa owned by the very cordial Simoni family, who live here and have run the hotel since 1927. You are welcomed into its memorable old-fashioned atmosphere with numerous living rooms, a library and dining room which all retain their furnishings from the beginning of the 20th century. Beneath an ancient wisteria there is a lovely terrace on various levels which leads down past banksia roses into the garden and olive groves beyond, with stunning views of Florence. Half-board terms are very reasonable. Light lunches are also available to order and afternoon tea is always served between 3.30 and 6. Ideal also for families as it has spacious grounds with a swing and an old ping-pong table. You can leave your car here as it is a walk of less than 10mins to the nearest no. 7 bus stop (reached also by a charming narrow path up the hill) for Florence and Fiesole. An ideal place to avoid the heat and bustle of Florence in spring, summer and autumn, and yet within 30mins of the centre by bus, and it provides you with a very rare glimpse into the delightful life of a Florentine country villa.

Bagno a Ripoli and Candeli (*map p. 316*)

€€€€ **Villa La Massa**. *Via La Massa 6, Candeli, T: 055 62611, www.villamassa.it.* A grand hotel which was opened some years ago. Restaurant and swimming pool.

€€ **Le Civette**. *Via del Carota 3 (La Fonte), T:*
055 698335, www.lecivetteresort.it. Delightful
agriturismo just southeast of Bagno a Ripoli,
immersed in beautiful peaceful countryside.
Run by Giuseppina Chiari Alifani and her
son who carefully restored this simple 19th-
century farmhouse in 2004, in an olive grove
full of roses and lavender. Half-board can be
arranged with neighbouring *trattorie* or meals
ordered to be brought in. Excellent brunch
on Sun. Swimming pool. Minimum stay of
two nights.

Le Caldine *(map p. 316)*
€ **Fattoria il Leccio**. ■ *Via Caldine 4, T: 055*
540329, 3936126150 or 3488108950, www.
olioleccio.it. In spectacular countryside just
beyond Fiesole (about 1km above the hamlet
of Le Caldine, served by train and bus to
Florence) this very peaceful *agriturismo* has
a lovely one-bedroom apartment with two
living rooms and an outside patio as well as
a two-bedroom apartment on two floors with
two bathrooms, both beautifully furnished
and equipped. The English-speaking owners,
who live next door and produce excellent

olive oil from their extensive groves, are
extremely welcoming. Secluded swimming
pool. Ideal if you have your own transport.
Available for short lets (preferably by the
week) at very reasonable prices.

€ **Montereggi**. *Via Santa Maria Maddalena 8,*
T: 055 540014, www.montereggi.it. Agriturismo
in a lovely position beyond the locality of Le
Caldine, about 8km beyond Fiesole, reached
along Via Faentina. Only really suitable if you
have a car (although there are infrequent bus
services to Florence as well as a station quite
nearby on a branch railway line). Apartments
with small kitchens. Swimming pool.

Villamagna *(map p. 316)*
€ **Turrita**. *Via San Romolo 102, T: 055*
631506, www.turrita.it. An *agriturismo* with
four apartments, with a wonderful view
of Florence. Near the no. 48 bus stop for
Florence and about 1km from the village of
Villamagna. Surrounded by cultivated fields of
vineyards and orchards. Beautifully restored
and well furnished, with modern bathrooms.
Swimming pool. Minimum stay two nights.

FOOD & DRINK

There are numerous restaurants of all categories all over the city and a good inexpensive meal
can be found with little difficulty. The selection below takes the quality of the food as the main
consideration, and places in the centre of the city have been preferred. Prices almost always
include service, so ask the waiter if the service charge has been added before leaving a tip, though
is customary to leave a few euro on the table as a sign of appreciation.

A selection of a few restaurants is given below. Price categories are per person for dinner (wine
excluded):

€€€€ over €125
€€€ €80–€125
€€ €30–€80
€ under €30

For Blue Guides Recommended ■, see p. 358.

€€€€

Enoteca Pinchiorri. *Via Ghibellina 87, T: 055 242777. Closed all day Sun and Mon, and Tues and Wed lunchtime. Map 7, 1.* One of the most famous and expensive restaurants in Italy, which has managed to retain its reputation (and three Michelin stars) since it opened in 1974. Run by Giorgio Pinchiorri and Annie Feolde, it has an exceptional selection of wines, arguably the best in Italy, and a remarkably creative cuisine. On the ground floor of a palace, it can seat about 80 people in two comfortable rooms, one with a balcony. In good weather there are tables in the interior courtyard and in a loggia off it. There is a set menu for €225, but the minimum you can spend *à la carte* is around €250 a head (all prices exclusive of wine).

Il Pelagio del Four Seasons. Opened just a few years ago in Florence's most luxurious hotel (*see p. 358*), this has earned a good reputation. The chef, Vito Mollica, is internationally known.

€€€€–€€€

Ora d'Aria. *Via dei Georgofili 11, T: 055 200 1699. Map 1, 6.* Opened a few years ago by an imaginative young chef, Marco Stabile, this has become one of the best-known restaurants in Florence in this price bracket. Admired by food critics for its innovative quality. Discreet atmosphere. Closed Sun and Mon at lunch.

€€€

Alle Murate. *Via del Proconsolo 16, T: 055 240618. Evenings only. Closed Mon. Map 1, 4.* The remarkable feature of this restaurant is its 14th-century frescoes on the vault and

upper walls of the main dining room, which were uncovered and cleaned by the owner in 2005 (*see p. 83*). Ask for a table here rather than in the basement, where it can be rather chilly. With an attractive modern décor, this restaurant specialises in fish and Tuscan food (you can choose one of two menus, or *à la carte*). Very efficiently run by pleasant staff.

Il Cibreo. *Via Andrea del Verrocchio 8, T: 055 234 1100. Map 7, 2.* Run by Fabio Picchi, this is one of the best-known restaurants in Florence, recommended in all the restaurant guides. It is best to book well in advance. With informal service and without a menu, it somehow resembles an Italian restaurant in North America. Not cheap and the wine can be disappointing. Bear in mind that on the menu outside service is included, but this is not specified on your bill.

The *trattoria* next door in Via dei Macci has the same chef but a reduced menu, and costs half. You can also eat the same food across the street at the Caffè del Cibreo (*closed Sun and Mon*). This has tables outside, but even here the prices are in the higher category. At the theatre opposite, the Circolo Teatro del Sale (*Via dei Macci 111; closed Sun and Mon*), Fabio Picchi and his staff serve good food before performances. It is self-service and you can eat all you wish (but you must first take out annual membership of the theatre club!). Once a member, you can also come here for a pleasant quiet breakfast or lunch.

€€

Acqua al Due. *Via Vigna Vecchia 40, T: 055 284170. Evenings only. Map 7, 1.* One of the very few restaurants in the city that stays open until late (1am). Frequented by actors and theatre-goers, it has good pasta dishes, and the steak is served in an original way.

Alla Vecchia Bettola. ■ *Viale Ariosto 32,*
T: 055 224158. Closed Sun and Mon. Map 5,
2. Typical Florentine *trattoria* on the edge
of the Oltrarno. Excellent food and service.
It is almost always crowded and noisy, but
well worth the experience. You can also eat
outside.

Cammillo. *Borgo San Jacopo 57r, T: 055*
212427. Map 1, 5. Old-established restaurant
with a high standard. Good sound Tuscan
food. Don't be put off by the very long menu,
seek advice from the helpful waiters. Well
worth a visit.

Il Cavolo Nero. *Via dell'Ardiglione 22, T:*
055 294744. Closed Sun. Map 5, 4. Set in a
delightful little side street, this is a pleasant
restaurant, with creative and well-presented
international cuisine. It has the atmosphere of
an English or French restaurant rather than a
traditional Tuscan establishment. You can eat
outside in summer in an interior courtyard.

Domani. *Via Romana 80, T: 055 221166.*
Closed Sun and Mon. Map 5, 6. An excellent
fish restaurant which serves a superb variety
of Japanese and Italian cuisine. It is one of the
best places to eat in Florence and is very good
value, despite the fact that the setting is rather
anonymous and without much character.
Popular with Japanese visitors.

Fusion Bar and Restaurant. *Vicolo dell'Oro 3.*
T: 055 27263 or 055 272 66987. Map 1, 5.
Well known for its chic atmosphere and
Japanese food. Run by the Ferragamo inside
their Gallery Hotel Art. Popular for brunch
on Sat and Sun when you can eat all you wish
for little over 20 euro.

Latini. *Via Palchetti 6 (behind Palazzo Rucellai),*
T: 055 210916. Closed Mon. Map 3, 7. Long

famous as a typical Florentine *trattoria* with
long, crowded tables and Tuscan cuisine, and
a bustling atmosphere. However, its fame has
meant that there are usually queues on the
street outside (and the food is no better than
many other restaurants in the price range).

Le Mossacce. *Via Proconsolo 55, T: 055*
294361. Closed Sat and Sun. Map 1, 4. Close
to the Bargello, this has been open for many
years and serves good-quality food of a
consistently high standard at very reasonable
prices. Very crowded and reservations are
usually not accepted, but the service is
extremely fast. No credit cards.

Oliviero. *Via delle Terme 51, T: 055 212421.*
Closed Sun. Map 1, 5. A comfortable restaurant
with great charm and excellent service. It has
a well-known chef and is a little cheaper than
the other restaurants in this category.

Osteria dei Benci. *Via dei Benci 13, T: 055*
234 4923. Map 7, 1. Opened by a law student
at Florence university, this is modelled on a
typical Florentine *trattoria* and has a youthful
following. It serves good Tuscan food,
specialising in meat (excellent raw ham and
Florentine steaks). Very good desserts.

Osteria di Santo Spirito. *Piazza Santo Spirito*
16, T: 055 238 2383. Map 6, 3. Once a typical
Florentine *osteria*, now transformed and given
a trendier atmosphere. However, the food is
good and there are tables outside in one of
the loveliest squares in Florence.

Osteria Tornabuoni. *Palazzo Tornabuoni, Via*
dei Corsi 5r and Via Tornabuoni, T: 055 277
3520. Closed Sun. Map 1, 3. Recently opened
in this grand palace with a modern touch.
It specialises in Tuscan food. Obikà in the
courtyard is less formal, and cheaper: it is

part of a Neapolitan chain of restaurants with good-quality ingredients from southern Italy.

La Pentola dell'Oro. ■ *Via di Mezzo 24, T: 055 241808. Map 4, 7.* Run by Giuseppe Alessi, a scholar of Renaissance cuisine who produces excellent traditional Tuscan dishes with local wine. This is a place in a category all of its own, with an imaginative menu and a consistently high standard. The main dining area is in a cool cellar. Family run, with Alessi's wife in control in the kitchen and his son sharing the management. In the room upstairs the food is also excellent but with a much less elaborate menu, reflected in the lower prices.

Il Santo Bevitore. *Via di Santo Spirito 64r, T: 055 211264. Closed Sun. Map 6, 1.* Good, rather unusual food served in a large, sometimes noisy room (there are two smaller, quieter rooms at the side). Lunch is simple and reasonably priced; dinner more elaborate and the prices are higher. There is a little shop next door where you can have a glass of wine and quick snack.

Il Troia (Trattoria Sostanza). ■ *Via Porcellana 29, T: 055 212691. Closed Sat and Sun in winter; Sun only in summer. No credit cards. Map 3, 7.* Founded in 1869, this has maintained the character of a genuine Florentine *trattoria*. It can sit only about 40 people in one long, narrow room with marble tables (some of which you share). Some elderly locals come here for lunch every day (and their napkins are kept for them). It has a restrained, distinguished atmosphere, with professional service. It serves traditional Tuscan fare and is particularly famous for its T-bone steaks (*bistecca alla fiorentina*). You are expected to eat a full meal, so if you are looking for a swift snack between sightseeing trips, this is not the place. There are two

sittings for dinner: one at 7.30, and the other at 9 (when locals tend to come). It is always advisable to book in the evenings.

€

Antico Ristoro di' Cambi. *Via Sant'Onofrio 1, T: 055 217134. Closed Sun. Map 5, 2.* This began as a *vinaio* in the heart of the district of San Frediano and it retains the atmosphere of a traditional Florentine *osteria*, always busy and with a fast turnover. It serves excellent classic Tuscan dishes, including good steak and tripe. Even though large, it can be difficult to find a place and is not somewhere you can linger over your meal; the tables can also be crowded. There are lots of tables outside in the charming little Piazza del Tiratoio.

Benvenuto. *Via della Mosca 16, T: 055 214833. Closed Sun. Map 1, 6.* An established and reliable *trattoria*, with standard Tuscan cuisine.

Borgo Antico. *Piazza Santo Spirito 6, T: 055 210437. Map 6, 3.* Typical *trattoria* in one of the most attractive squares in Florence. Tables outside in summer. Also a pizzeria.

La Casalinga. ■ *Via dei Michelozzi 9, T: 055 218624. Closed Sun. Map 6, 3.* One of the best simple, cheap places to eat in Florence, just out of Piazza Santo Spirito. Run by a very friendly family, and often quite hectic at lunchtime when it is full of builders, foreign students and tourists. Good house wine.

I Fratellini. *Via Ghibellina 27r. Closed Sat and Sun. Map 7, 1.* This grocery shop serves good meals at lunchtime. It has no name outside (only 'Salumeria, Vini, Trattoria'). Chickens are roasted in an open fire and traditional Florentine dishes are served. Popular with locals who live or work in the area.

Mario. *Via Rosina 2 (Via Sant'Orsola), T: 055 218550. Lunchtime only. Closed Sun. Map 3, 6.* In a side street close to the market of San Lorenzo. Always crowded with stall-holders and locals, a few tiny wooden tables and stools, efficient service and traditional Tuscan food for very reasonable prices. A favourite cheap eating place in Florence, and just the answer if you need a quick, substantial meal.

Da Nerbone. *Mercato Centrale di San Lorenzo. Closed Sun. Map 3, 6.* A good cheap place to eat inside the busy market. Stall-holders eat here as well as discerning Florentines.

I Raddi. ■ *Via dell'Ardiglione 47 (off Via de' Serragli), T: 055 211072. Closed Sun. Map 5, 4.* Tucked away in a very quiet street in the Oltrarno. At lunchtime you can choose a dish for just €2 (with the addition of a cover charge and wine) and in the evenings (but not on Fri or weekends) there is a dinner menu for just €16, all included. Typical good Tuscan fare as well as unusual dishes invented by the chef. Delicious desserts. The wine is served directly from the vat by the door. It has just one well-designed room (on two levels and with annexes) which is comfortable and has a very pleasant, spacious feel to it. It can be very busy so it is advisable to book. This is a place much frequented by Florentines and is an excellent choice if you want a very reasonable quick simple meal, or wish to take your time over a more elaborate one.

Sabatino. ■ *Via Pisana 2, T: 055 225955. Closed Sat and Sun. Map 5, 1.* Established many years ago in Borgo San Frediano as one of the most typical cheap places to eat in Florence. It is now just outside Porta San Frediano, but retains the same atmosphere and is run by an extremely friendly family. It is frequented by elderly Florentines who live nearby and go there most days for lunch, as well as artisans who work in the area. Well worth a visit.

Da Sergio (Gozzi). *Piazza San Lorenzo 8, T: 055 281941. Lunch only. Closed Sun. Map 1, 2.* Family-run *trattoria* behind the market stalls outside the church of San Lorenzo. This has been a good, simple place to eat for many years, although perhaps a little more expensive than other restaurants in this category. But a good solution if you are in the area.

Il Sipario. *Via de' Serragli 104. T: 055 228 0924. Open for lunch Mon–Fri 12.15–2.30. Map p. 5, 4.* Run by a charity for the disabled. Excellent simple food in an airy, spacious locale off an inner courtyard, with a happy atmosphere. You choose one of three three-course menus which include wine and coffee. Extremely good value.

Al Tranvai. *Piazza Tasso 14, T: 055 225197. Closed Sat and Sun. Map 5, 4.* Good cheap food. The atmosphere is friendly and there are tables outside. At lunch, the clientèle is mostly local, while in the evening it is favoured more by young people and by visitors to the city.

Vegetarian and specialist restaurants

Il Vegetariano di Ambrosini (*Via delle Ruote 30, T: 055 475030; map 3, 4*) is perhaps the best vegetarian restaurant in Florence. Other options include **Gauguin** (*Via degli Alfani 24, T: 055 234 0616; map 4, 5*) and **Brac** (*Via dei Vagellai 18; map 1, 8*). **Ruth's** (*Via Farini 2a, T: 055 248 0888, next to the synagogue; map 4, 8*) is lacking totally in atmosphere but has good fresh Kosher food, very reasonably priced.

Restaurants in the environs

These are mostly reasonably priced, and many have tables outside.

Arcetri (Pian de' Giullari): Omero (*Via Pian de' Giullari 11; T: 055 220053*).

Galluzzo: Da Bibe (*Via delle Bagnese 1, Ponte all'Asse; T: 055 204 9085*).

Maiano: La Graziella (*T: 055 599963; closed Tues*); Le Cave di Maiano (*T: 055 59133*).

Pratolino: Villa Vecchia, Vaglia (*T: 055 409476*).

Ponte a Mensola: Osvaldo (*T: 055 603972*); La Capponcina (*Via San Romano 17; T: 055 697037*).

Wine bars (*enoteche*)

Le Volpi e l'Uva (*Piazza de' Rossi 1/Piazza Santa Felicita, T: 055 239 8132, closed Sun; map 6, 3–4*) is a pleasant little wine bar (closes at 9pm) where you sit at the counter or at one of the tables outside, with a very fine selection of wines and interesting food (including a very wide range of cheeses), and sometimes there are also good sweets. **Fuori Porta** (*Via Monte alle Croci 10, T: 055 234 2483, closed Sun; map 7, 5*) is outside Porta San Miniato, with outdoor tables in a particularly pleasant and peaceful area of the city. A delightful wine bar with very fine wines which you can also order by the glass, and good simple snacks.

Vinai

These are traditional Florentine wine bars which sell wine by the glass and good simple food. Many of them have closed down in the last few decades, but the few that are left are well worth seeking out, as they have a very special atmosphere and are much loved by Florentines. The *vinaio* at Via degli Alfani 70 (*map 4, 5*) and the one in Via della Chiesa (corner of Via delle Caldaie; *map 6, 3*) both have seating; others are no more than 'holes in the wall' but have excellent snacks (as well as a good selection of wines) which you eat standing on the pavement. Examples are Cantina Ristori (Antico Noè; *Volta di San Piero 6; map 4, 7*); Donatello (*Via de' Neri, corner of Via de' Benci; map 7, 3*); Fratellini (*Via dei Cimatori 38; map 1, 6*); and the *vinaio* at Piazza Castellani 25 (*map 1, 6*).

Snacks

Mariano (*Via Parione 19; open 8–3.30 & 5–8; map 1, 5*), on a side street off Piazza Santa Trínita, is entered down a few steps. The two small rooms with brick vaults were probably once the stables attached to the convent of the church. The present owner (helped by his wife and son) used to run a grocery shop here (inherited from his father) and since the 1970s this has been a place where you can have a very good sandwich made to order, with especially good cheeses, and wine by the glass, in a very friendly atmosphere. There are a few stools and tables. It has a very loyal elegant local Florentine clientèle. At **'Ino** (*Via dei Georgofili 3, corner of Via de' Girolami, just behind the Uffizi*) you can order a sandwich or cold snack and sit and enjoy it in a rather smart modern atmosphere. Not a place to come if you are in a hurry. Excellent salads and cheeses, and if you find it hard to make a choice, follow the owner's suggestion. You can also order a grand picnic to take away. Other good sources of snacks are **Caffè Italiano** (*Via della Condotta 56; map 1, 6*) and **Boccadama** (*Piazza Santa Croce 25; map 7, 1*). **Procacci** in Via Tornabuoni (*map 1, 3; T: 055 211656*), once famous for its truffle sandwiches, has an unusual selection of cheeses.

Snack bars that open late include **Du Monde** (*Via San Niccolò 103; map 7, 3*) and **Eskimo** (*Via dei Canacci 12; map 3, 5–7*).

Friggitorie are small shops which fry snacks (sweet and savoury) and sell them over the counter. Though popular, many have closed down in the last few years. Snacks include doughnuts (*ciambelle* and *bomboloni*), rice fritters (*frittelle di riso*), and *coccoli* (simple fritters made with water, flour, yeast and salt), as well as pizza and *schiacciato* (flat bread topped with oil and salt).

Trippai sell tripe, a Florentine speciality, in sandwiches from barrows on street corners in Via dell'Ariento (*map 3, 6*), Piazza de' Cimatori (Via Dante Alighieri; *map 1, 6*), Via dei Macci (corner of Borgo La Croce; *map 7, 2*), Piazza del Porcellino (Mercato Nuovo; *map 1, 5*) and outside Porta Romana (*map 5, 6*).

Leonardo (*Via Pecori 5; closed Sat; map 1, 3*) is a very cheap self-service restaurant. On the first floor of a modern building it has absolutely no atmosphere, and, indeed is almost shabby, but it has very sound food at give-away prices.

Cafés and cake shops (*pasticcerie*)

Cafés (bars) are open all day and *pasticcerie* also almost always function as cafés. Most customers choose to eat and drink standing up—you pay the cashier first, and show the receipt to the barman in order to get served. In almost all bars, if you sit at a table you are charged considerably more—at least double—and are given waiter service (you should not pay first).

The most famous café in the city, and the most elegant, is **Rivoire** in Piazza Signoria (famous for its chocolate), with numerous tables outside. Old-established cafés in Piazza della Repubblica include **Le Giubbe Rosse** and **Gilli**. Less famous but also very popular with Florentines is **Patrizio Cosi** (*Borgo degli Albizi 11; map 1, 4*), a good cake shop which also has the great advantage that you can sit down for no extra charge. **Caffetteria La Loggia** (*Via Pietrapiana 12r; map 4, 7*) is a place where the locals like to come for a coffee and bun in the middle of the morning and it can be very crowded but well worth a visit. It is still old-fashioned, with wall sconces and just one or two tables, but the cakes are delicious (with a Neapolitan flavour) and it is still one of the cheapest places in Florence to have a coffee.

The best cake shop is **Dolci e Dolcezze** (*Piazza Beccaria 8; map 4, 8*), but it has no seating. The **Pasticceria Alcedo Falli** in Fiesole (*Via Gramsci 29*) also makes particularly good cakes and pastries. In Settignano, try **Caffè Desiderio** in Piazza Tommaseo.

A café specialising in tea is **La Via del Tè** (*Piazza Ghiberti 22; map 7, 2*). **Caffèlatte** (*Via degli Alfani 39; open 8–midnight except Sun; map 4, 5*) is a delightful little café in an old dairy with its original furniture and counter. **O Cafè** (*Via de' Bardi 54–64r, very close to Ponte Vecchio; open until 1.30am; map 1, 7*) is an ultramodern cocktail bar with honest prices (you can sit on a stool for no extra charge, or be served at a table overlooking the Arno). Very good cakes and sandwiches freshly made. **Caffè delle Oblate** (*Via dell'Oriuolo 26; closed Mon; map 4, 7*), on the roof terrace of a former convent (with a fine view), is much frequented by young students who sit here in the cloisters where they can use their computers. The lively atmosphere increases in the evenings when there are often musical performances.

Chocolate shops

The following are just some of the pretty little shops which serve and sell their own chocolate in various forms (in exquisite packaging):

Arte del Cioccolato (*Chiasso de' Soldanieri, a tiny cul-de-sac leading off Via Porta Rossa just off Via Tornabuoni, T: 055 217136, www.artedelcioccolato.it; open 10–8, Mon 2–8; map 1, 5*). This has the famous chocolate produced by Roberto Catinari at Agliana (south of Pistoia); **Coccole cioccolato** (*Via Ginori 55; map 3, 6*); **Dolcissima Firenze** (*Via Maggio 61r, T: 055 239 6268, closed Mon; map 6, 3*); **La Bottega del Cioccolato** (*Via de' Macci 50, T 055 200 1609; map 7, 2*); **Vestri** (*Borgo degli Albizi 11; map 4, 7*), also for ice creams; **Florian** (*Via del Parione 28r, T: 055 284291; map 1, 5*), a modest branch of Venice's famous Caffè Florian; **Café Rivoire** (*Piazza della Signoria*).

Ice cream

Vivoli (*Via Isola delle Stinche 7; map 7, 1*) is widely considered the best ice cream shop in Florence, and you can also sit at a table (inside) for no extra charge. Another old-established place which makes its own ice creams is the delightfully named **Perchè no?** ('Why not?'; *Via dei Tavolini 19; map 1, 4–6*). Amongst the many new ice cream shops, the best and most sophisticated is probably **Carapina** (*Via Lambertesca 18; map 1, 6*), with its 'minimal chic' décor. Its fruit ices are made exclusively of fresh fruit in season, with the addition of only water and sugar, and it has a wide range of particularly good and interesting flavours produced with organic products.

Other good places are **Bar Latteria I Cugini** (*Borgo Pinti 69r; closed Sat; map 4, 6*), **Carabei** (*Via Ricasoli 60r, near the corner of Via Alfani; map 3, 6*), an excellent place to savour Sicilian ice creams and sorbets (no seating) and **Il Gelato di Filo** (*Via San Miniato 5; map 7, 3*), another very traditional ice cream shop, no more than a hole in the wall near the church of San Niccolò.

Food for picnics

Excellent food for picnics can be bought at delicatessens (*pizzicherie*), grocery shops (*alimentari*) and bakeries (*fornai*). Sandwiches (*panini*) are made up on request, and bakeries often sell good individual pizzas, rolls and cakes. In the autumn, many bakeries sell *schiacciata all'uva*, a delicious bready dough topped with fresh black grapes and cooked in the oven. *Pan di Ramerino* is a bun with rosemary and raisins (traditionally made for Easter but now usually available all year round). *Fritelle di San Giuseppe* are fritters made with rice, eggs, milk and lemon rind; *cenci* are simpler fritters.

A classic place to sample Florentine nightlife is **Il Jazz Club** (*Borgo Pinti 18; map 4, 7*).

GLOSSARY

Aedicule, small opening framed by two columns and a pediment, originally used in classical architecture

Albarello (pl. *albarelli*), cylindrical shaped pharmacy jar, usually slightly waisted and produced by numerous potteries in Italy from the 15th–18th centuries

Alberese, white Tuscan building stone

Amorino (pl. *amorini*), in art and architecture, a chubby, winged male child (*cf putto*)

Amphora, antique vase, usually of large dimensions, for oil and other liquids

Antefix, an ornament at the eaves of the roof to hide the join between tiles

Antiphonal, choir-book containing a collection of antiphons—verses sung in response by two choirs

Apostles, those who spread the Christian word, traditionally twelve in number, being the eleven disciples (without Judas) plus St Paul

Apse, vaulted semicircular end wall of the chancel of a church or of a chapel

Archaic, period in Greek civilisation preceding the Classical era: from about 750 BC–480 BC

Architrave, the horizontal beam running above the columns in ancient architecture

Archivolt, a moulded architrave carried around an arch

Arte (pl. *arti*), guild or corporation

Assumption, the ascension of the Virgin to Heaven, 'assumed' by the power of God

Attic, topmost storey of a classical building, hiding the spring of the roof; in art it refers to a style from Attica in Greece

Avello (pl. *avelli*), family burial vault

Badia, from *abbazia*, an abbey

Baldacchino, canopy supported by columns, usually over an altar

Basilica, originally a Roman hall used for public administration; in Christian architecture an aisled church with a clerestory and apse and no transepts

Bas-relief, sculpture in low relief

Biforated, of an aperture, divided into two lights or openings

Biscuit (or bisque), fired but unglazed earthenware or pottery

Black-figure ware, ancient Greek pottery style of the 7th–5th centuries BC where the figures appear black against a clay-coloured ground

Borgo, a suburb; a street leading away from the centre of a town

Bottega, the studio of an artist; the pupils who worked under his direction

Bozzetto (pl. *bozzetti*), sketch, often used to describe a small model for a piece of sculpture

Bucchero, Etruscan black terracotta ware

Bucrania, decorative motif of ox's skulls, often surrounded by garlands, derived from Classical sculpture

Calimala, the cloth-importers guild

Campanile, bell-tower

Canopic jar (or vase), ancient Egyptian urn used to preserve the internal organs

Cantoria (pl. *cantorie*), singing-gallery in a church

Capitolium, ancient Roman temple dedicated to the trio of gods worshipped on the Capitoline Hill at Rome: Jupiter, Juno and Minerva

Cappella, chapel

Capomaestro, director of works or master-builder

Cardo, the main street of a Roman town, at

right-angles to the decumanus

Cartoon, from *cartone*, meaning a large sheet of paper—a full-size preparatory drawing for a painting or fresco

Cassone, a marriage chest, typically decorated with appropriate scenes such as the Story of Esther or depictions of courtly life. It would be filled with household linen to start the bride out in her married life

Cavea, the part of a theatre or amphitheatre occupied by the rows of seats

Cenacolo (pl. *cenacoli*), a scene of the Last Supper (in the refectory of a convent)

Chiaroscuro, distribution of light and shade in a painting

Ciborium, casket or tabernacle containing the Host (Communion bread)

Cimasa, the topmost section of an altarpiece

Cinquecento, Italian term for the 'fifteen-hundreds' i.e. the 16th century

Cipollino, onion marble; greyish marble with streaks of white or green

Cippus (pl. *cippae*), sepulchral monument in the form of an altar

Classical, pertaining to the art of the ancient world, properly to that of Greece from 480–323 BC. When spelled with a lower-case 'c', it denotes classicising art inspired by ancient models

Colloquio, Parlour in an ecclesiastic building for conversation or visitors

Commesso fiorentino, Florentine mosaic, the art of working *pietre dure*, hard or semi-precious stones

Contrapposto, a pose in which the body is twisted. First used in classical statuary, it is characteristic of Michelangelo's sculpture and works by the Mannerist school

Corbel, a projecting block, usually of stone

Cornice, topmost part of a temple entablature; any projecting ornamental moulding at the top of a building beneath the roof

Cosmatesque, inlaid marble work using

mosaic and coloured glass and stone laid in geometric of figurative patterns

Crenellations, battlements, specifically the indented parts (*cf merlon*)

Cupola, dome

Diptych, painting or ivory tablet in two wings or sections

Dossal, a cloth hung behind the altar or at the sides of the chancel

Duomo, cathedral

Evangelists, the authors of the four Gospels, Matthew, Mark, Luke and John, often denoted in art by their symbols (man/angel, lion, bull and eagle)

Exedra, semicircular recess

Ex-voto, tablet or small painting expressing gratitude to a saint

Foresteria, guest-wing of a monastery

Fresco (in Italian, *affresco*), painting executed on wet plaster (*intonaco*). On the rough plaster (*arriccio*) beneath, the artist made a sketch (or sinopia, *qv*) which was covered little by little as work on the fresco proceeded. Since the *intonaco* had to be wet during this work, it was applied each day only to that part of the wall on which the artist was sure that he could complete the fresco (these areas, which can now often be detected by restorers, are known as *giornate*). From the 16th century onwards cartoons (*cartoni*) were used to help the artist with the over-all design: the *cartone* was transferred on to the *intonaco* either by pricking the outline with small holes over which a powder was dusted, or by means of a stylus which left an incised line on the wet plaster. In the 1960s and 1970s, many frescoes were detached from the walls on which they were executed and so the sinopie beneath were discovered (and sometimes also detached)

Gonfalone, banner of a medieval guild or commune

Gonfaloniere, chief magistrate or official of a medieval Italian Republic, the bearer of the Republic's *gonfalone* (*qv*)

Graffiti, design on a wall made with an iron tool on a prepared surface, the design showing in white. Also used loosely to describe scratched designs or words on walls

Greek cross, church plan based on a cross with arms of equal length

Grisaille, painting in various tones of grey

Grottesche (or grotesques), a style of painting or stucco decoration used by the ancient Romans and discovered in the 1490s in the Domus Aurea in Rome (then underground, hence its name, from 'grotto'). The delicate ornamental decoration, normally on a light background, is characterized by fantastical motifs with intricate patterns of volutes, festoons, garlands, and borders of twisted vegetation and flowers interspersed with small winged human or animal figures, birds, masques, griffins, and sphinxes. This type of decoration became very fashionable and was widely copied by late Renaissance artists

Hemicycle, a semicircular structure, room, arena or wall

Hypocaust, ancient Roman heating system in which hot air circulated under the floor and between double walls

Incunabula, any book printed before 1500

Intarsia, a decorative inlay made from wood, marble or metal

Intonaco, plaster

Intrados, underside or soffit of an arch

Kouroi, from the Greek word for young man (*kouros*), used to describe standing, nude male statues in the Greek Archaic style

Krater, a large, open bowl used for mixing wines, especially in ancient Greece

Lantern, a small circular or polygonal turret with windows all round, crowning a roof or a dome

Latin cross, a cross with a long vertical arm, usually used to described the plan of a church

Lavabo (pl. *lavabi*), hand-basin usually outside a refectory or in a sacristy

Lavatorium, the Latin name for a room with large hand-basins (*lavabi*) in stone or marble outside a convent refectory where the rites of purification were carried out before a meal

Lekythos, an ancient Greek vase, tall and narrow-necked with one handle, used as a vessel for oil

Loggia, covered gallery or balcony, usually preceding a larger building

Lunette, semicircular space in a vault or ceiling, or above a door or window, often decorated with a painting or relief

Lungarno (pl. *Lungarni*), a road which follows the banks of the Arno

Maestà, representation of the Madonna and Child enthroned in majesty

Majolica (or Maiolica), a type of earthenware glazed with bright metallic oxides that was originally imported to Italy from Majorca and was extensively made in Italy during the Renaissance

Mandorla, tapered, almond-shaped aura around a holy figure (usually Christ or the Virgin)

Medallion, large medal; loosely, a circular ornament

Merlon, the rising part of a parapet, alternating with indented crenellations to form a battlement

Monochrome, painting or drawing in one colour only

Monolith, single stone (usually a column)

Navicella, in art, a symbolic representation of the Christian Church as a ship, buffeted by storms but never sinking

Niello, black substance (usually a compound

of sulphur and silver) used in an engraved design, or an object so decorated

Oculus, round window

Opera (e.g. del Duomo), the office in charge of the fabric of a building (in this case the Cathedral)

Opus sectile, mosaic or paving of thin slabs of coloured marble cut in thin geometrical shapes

Orientalising, ancient decorative style originating in the Near East, characterised by great exuberance, in contrast to the austere native Greek style

Pala, large altarpiece

Palazzo (pl. *palazzi*), palace, any dignified and important building

Palaestra, a public place devoted to training athletes in ancient Greece or Rome

Passion, the Crucifixion, suffering and death of Christ

Pastiglia, plaster applied to wood or leather in layers and then carved and gilded in bas-relief

Pax, sacred object used by a priest for the blessing of peace and offered for the kiss of the faithful; usually circular, engraved, enamelled, or painted in a rich gold or silver frame

Peducci (sing. *peduccio*), a hanging capital, from which springs an arch or vault; a corbel

Pelike, ancient type of large vase with a wide lip from where two lateral handles descend vertically to join the belly

Pendentive, concave spandrel beneath a dome

Piano nobile, main floor of a palace

Pietà, representation of the Virgin mourning the dead Christ (sometimes with other figures)

Pietre dure, hard or semi-precious stones, often used in the form of mosaics to decorate furniture such as cabinets and table-tops

Pietra forte, fine-grained, highly resistant limey sandstone used as a building material in Florence, and often for the rustication of palace façades

Pietra serena, fine-grained dark grey sandstone, easy to carve. Although generally not sufficiently resistant for the exterior of buildings, it was used to decorate many Renaissance interiors in Florence

Pilaster, a shallow pier or rectangular column projecting only slightly from the wall

Pinnacle, a small turret-like termination crowning spires, buttresses and roofs

Pluteus (pl. *plutei*), marble panel, usually decorated; a series of them used to form a parapet to precede the altar of a church

Podestà, chief magistrate who ruled a medieval city with the help of a council and representatives from the corporations. He had to be someone who was not a Florentine, and was also a military leader

Polyptych, painting or panel in more than three sections

Portone main entrance (large enough for carriages) to a *palazzo* or villa

Predella, small painting or panel, usually in sections, attached below a large altarpiece, illustrating scenes of a story such as the life of a saint, or of the Virgin

Presepio, literally crib or manger. A group of statuary of which the central subject is the Infant Jesus in the manger

Pulvin, cushion stone between the capital and the impost block

Putto (pl. *putti*), figure sculpted or painted, usually nude, of a chubby male child without wings (*cf amorino*)

Pyx, small container for Communion bread

Quadratura, painted architectural perspectives (see also *trompe l'oeil*)

Quadriga, a two-wheeled chariot drawn by four horses abreast

Quadriporticus, rectangular court or atrium arcaded on all four sides, derived from the atria in front of palaeochristian basilicas

Quatrefoil, four-lobed design

Quattrocento, Italian term for the 'fourteen hundreds' i.e. the 15th century

Rood screen, a screen below the Rood or Crucifix dividing the nave from the chancel of a church

Scagliola, imitation marble or *pietre dure* (*qv*) made from selenite

Scarsella, the rectangular recess of the tribune of the Florence Baptistery, first called by this name by the early 14th-century chronicler Giovanni Villani. Now also sometimes used for the rectangular sanctuary in a church

Schiacciato, term used to describe very low relief in sculpture, where there is an emphasis on the delicate line rather than the depth of the panel (a technique perfected by Donatello)

Sinopia (pl. *sinopie*), large sketch for a fresco made on the rough wall in a red earth pigment called sinopia (because it originally came from Sinope, a town on the Black Sea). When a fresco is detached for restoration, it is possible to see the sinopia beneath, which can also be separated from the wall

Situla, water bucket for ritual use

Spandrel, surface between two arches in an arcade or the triangular space on either side of an arch

Spolia, architectural elements from an earlier building recycled in a newer one

Sporti, overhang, or projecting upper storey of a building, characteristic of medieval houses in Florence

Stamnos, type of ancient vase, big-bellied with two small handles and a lid

Stele (pl. *stelae*), upright stone bearing a monumental inscription

Stemma (pl. *stemme*), coat of arms or heraldic device

Stoup, vessel for Holy Water, usually near the west door of a church

Stucco (pl. *stucchi*), plaster-work

Tempera, a painting medium of powdered pigment bound together, in its simplest form, by a mixture of egg yolk and water

Tepidarium, room for warm baths in a Roman bath

Term, pedestal or terminal figure in human form, tapering towards the base

Terraverde, green earth pigment, sometimes used in frescoes

Tessera, small cube of marble, stone or glass used in mosaic work

Thermae, originally simply Roman baths, later elaborate buildings fitted with libraries, assembly rooms, gymnasia and circuses

Tondo, (pl. *tondi*) round painting or relief

Transenna, open grille or screen, usually of marble, in an early Christian church

Tribune, the apse of a Christian basilica that contains the bishop's throne or the throne itself

Triptych, painting or tablet in three sections

Triton, river god

Trompe l'œil, literally, a 'deception of the eye'; used to describe illusionist decoration and painted architectural perspectives

Tympanum, the area between the top of a doorway and the arch above it; also the triangular space enclosed by the mouldings of a pediment

Viale (pl. *viali*), wide avenue

Villa, country house with its garden

Virtues, the Theological Virtues are Faith, Hope and Charity; the Cardinal Virtues are Prudence, Fortitude, Temperance and Justice

INDEX

Explanatory or more detailed references (where there are many), or references to places where an artist's work is best represented, are given in bold. Numbers in italics are picture references. Dates are given for all artists, architects and sculptors. 'Attrib' after an artist's name indicates a work attributed to him or her (not always securely).

continued from p. 4

Editor-in-chief: Annabel Barber

Maps © Blue Guides Ltd

Architectural elevations: Michael Mansell RIBA & Gabriella Juhász
Floor plans and watercolours: Imre Bába

Photo editing and pre-press: Hadley Kincade

Cover image: Detail from *Pallas and the Centaur* by Sandro Botticelli, in the Uffizi Gallery,
© TheArtArchive/Corbis/Red Dot. Spine photo © istockphoto.com/tulla.
Frontispiece: Idealised likeness of Lorenzo the Magnificent, from Benozzo Gozzoli's *Procession of the Magi* frescoes in Palazzo Medici-Riccardi, courtesy of Seat Archive/Alinari Archives.

All other interior photographs courtesy of Alinari Archives:
Alinari Archives, Florence: pp. 37, 63, 80, 91, 100, 103, 113 (left), 118, 142, 183, 185, 191, 199, 215, 276, 280, 332; Seat Archive/Alinari Archives: p. 225; Reproduced with the permission of the Opera di Santa Maria del Fiore: pp. 69, 70; Reproduced with the permission of the Ministero per i Beni e le Attività Culturali: p. 113 (centre and right); Raffaello Bencini/ Alinari Archives: p. 45; Raffaello Bencini/Alinari Archives–Reproduced with the permission of the Ministero per i Beni e le Attività Culturali: p. 265; Finsiel/Alinari Archives–Reproduced with the permission of permission of the Ministero per i Beni e le Attività Culturali: p. 96; Aurelio Amendola/Alinari Archives: pp. 145, 151, 210; Aurelio Amendola/Alinari Archives–Reproduced with the permission of the Ministero per i Beni e le Attività Culturali: pp. 167, 242; Nicolò Orsi Battaglini/Alinari Archives–Reproduced with the permission of the Ministero per i Beni e le Attività Culturali: p. 256.

The extract on p. 108 from *Renaissance Florence on Five Florins a Day* (Thames & Hudson, 2010) is reproduced with kind permission of the author. Charles FitzRoy is a director of Fine Art Travel, which leads cultural tours to Italy (including Florence) and other destinations in Europe (www.finearttravel.co.uk).

For this edition the author is particularly grateful to the following for their invaluable help:
Graham Avery, John Treacy Beyer, Donato Bramanti, Françoise Chiarini, Peggy Haines, Mario Iozzo, Cristina Francois Lombardi, Serena Pini, Roberta Romoli, Roberto Torzini.

The editor would like to thank Joanna Lace.

Material prepared for press by Anikó Kuzmich
Printed in Hungary by Dürer Nyomda Kft, Gyula.

ISBN 978–1–905131–52–5

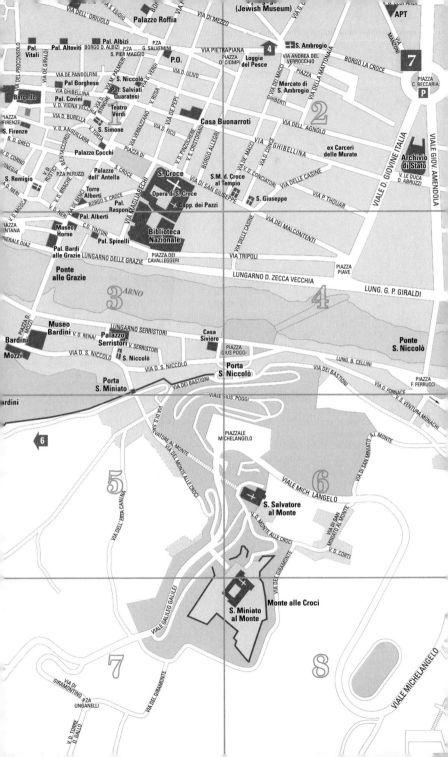

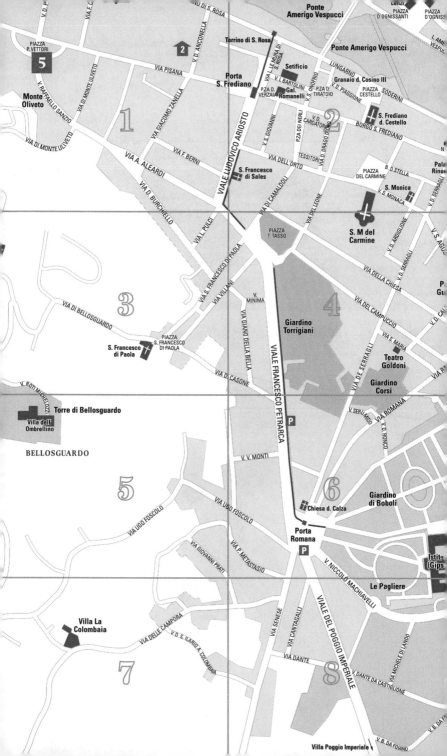

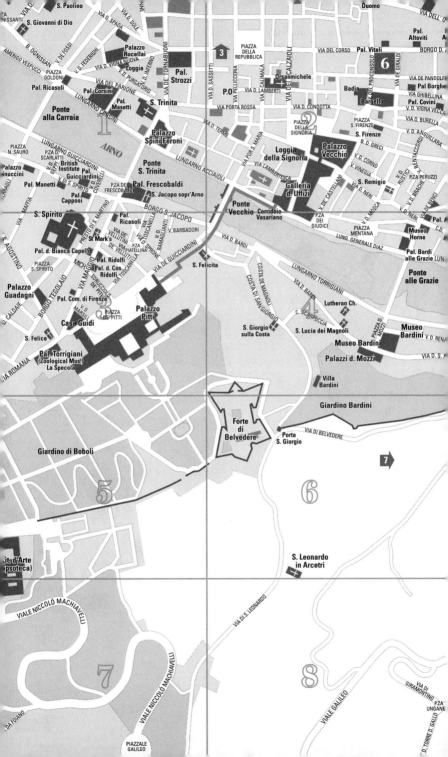

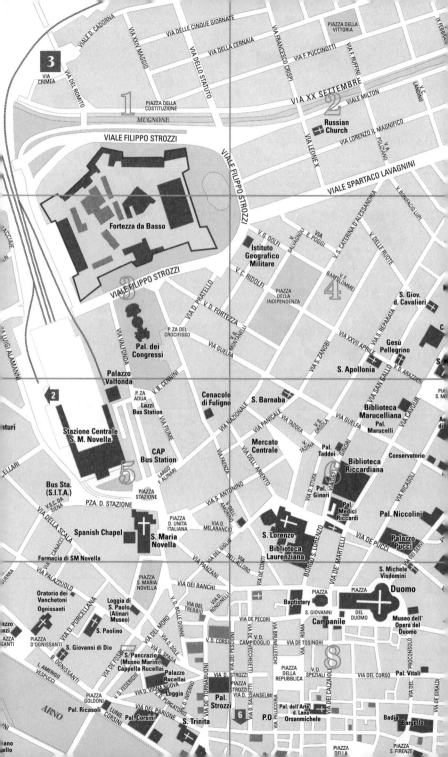

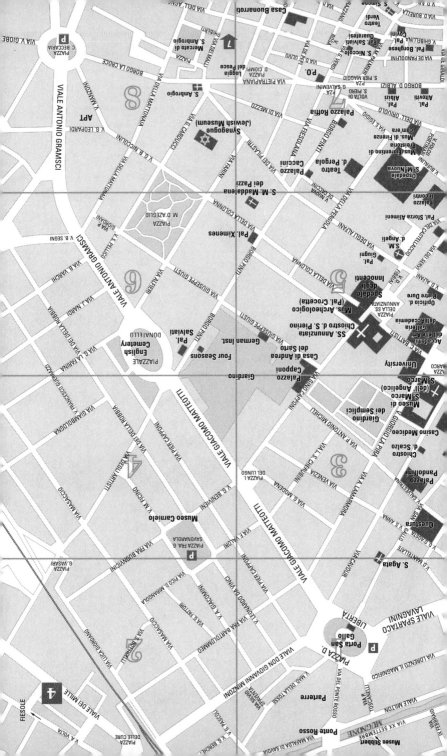

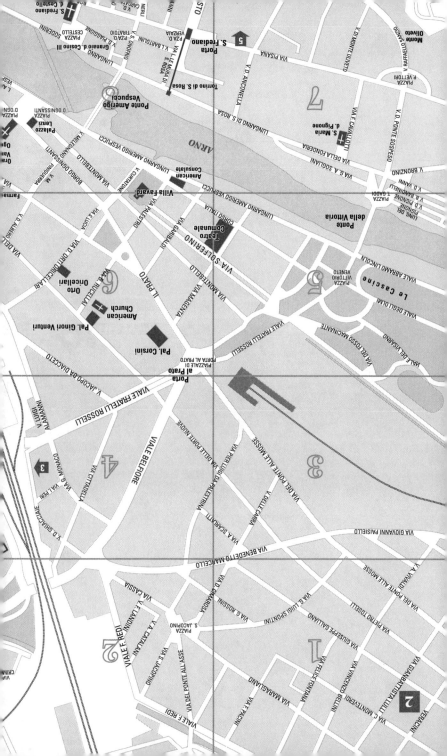

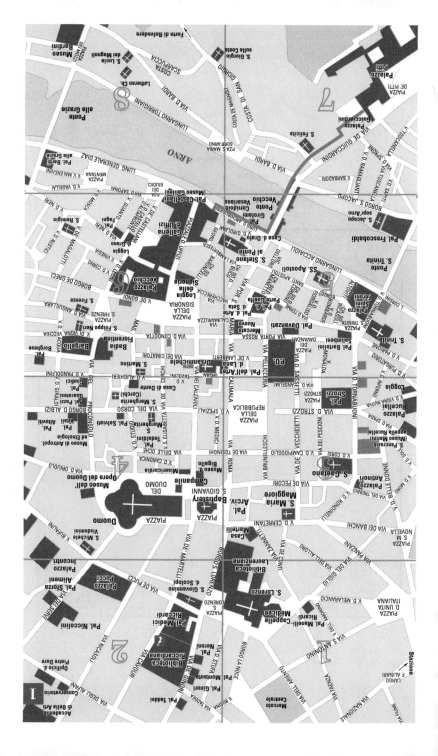

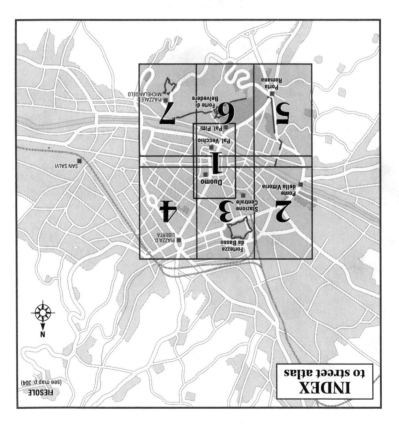

INDEX to street atlas

FIESOLE
(see map p. 304)

N

SAN SALVI

PIAZZA D. LIBERTA

Fortezza da Basso

Stazione Centrale

Duomo

Pal. Vecchio

Pal. Pitti

Forte di Belvedere

PIAZZALE MICHELANGELO

Porta Romana

Ponte della Vittoria

1

2

3

4

5

6

7

Scale of Maps 2 – 7

0   200 yards
0   200 metres

Scale of Florence Centre map 1

0   100 yards
0   100 metres